THE ELEMENT
ENCYCLOPEDIA
OF
BIRTHDAYS

THE ELEMENT
ENCYCLOPEDIA
OF
BIRTHDAYS

Know your birthday
Discover your true personality
Reveal your destiny

Theresa Cheung

HarperCollins*Publishers*
77–85 Fulham Palace Road,
Hammersmith, London W6 8JB
www.harpercollins.co.uk

First published by HarperCollins*Publishers* 2007

10 9 8 7 6 5 4 3

Text illustrations by Andy Paciorek

A catalogue record of this book is
available from the British Library

ISBN 978-0-00-785048-8

Printed in China

Contents

Acknowledgments

This enormous project would not have been completed without the help of some unique and amazing people. Thank you to Katy Carrington for her extraordinary vision, insight, and encouragement; to Mark Bolland for his excellent editing and valued input; to Andy Paciorek for the wonderful illustrations; to Colin Hall for the fantastic page design; to Graham Holmes for his accomplished typesetting; and to Simon Gerratt for his skill, patience, and brilliance in making sure everything came together in one piece and on time. Last, but by no means least, special thanks to Ray, Robert, and Ruth for the love, inspiration, and support they give me every single day of each and every year.

Introduction

'As above, so below'

The Element Encyclopedia of Birthdays is a complete guide to personality and destiny for people born on each of the 366 days of the year. Simply by knowing the date of your birth you can gain insightful and astonishingly accurate luck-making information about yourself—your strengths, weaknesses, health, relationships, destiny, career, and life goals—as well as your friends, family, lovers, colleagues, and even people you have just met.

The power of your birthday is determined not just by your ruling planet but by a number of other invisible influences and patterns in place the day you were born. This book reaches far beyond basic Sun sign horoscopes, looking at these influences and patterns through the lens of psychological astrology, numerology, Tarot, and color theory or chromatherapy.

To help you understand how your birthday profile has been compiled you'll find the basic principles of these ancient arts and how they have put their stamp on you explained below; but if you want to dive straight into a specific birth date, yours or one of somebody you know, you can always return here another time. However you decide to read this book, never forget that every person is born unique and full of potential.

The birthday profile

What exactly is a birthday profile? In short, it's the rebirth of four ancient arts—astrology, numerology, Tarot, and color theory or chromatherapy—joined together by a modern psychological interpretation. This combination results in a blend of cosmic and earthly influences that can significantly affect your personality and destiny, providing you with invaluable insight into yourself as well as the lives, feelings, hopes, and fears of family, friends and colleagues.

A brief introduction to astrology

Astrology sees humankind as being influenced not only by hereditary factors and the environment, but also by the state of our solar system at the moment of birth. The Sun, Moon and planets are regarded as basic life-forces, the tools we live by as well as the basis of our very substance. These planetary forces take on different forms, depending on their zodiacal position and on the way they relate to one another.

Astrology is one of the most ancient of the surviving occult sciences, and evidence of highly sophisticated systems in Babylonian, Egyptian and Aztec cultures has survived. For centuries in the West, astrology was a revered method of divination (fortune telling) supported by royal courts. With the development of science in the seventeenth century, astrology was relegated to the realm of superstition, but it never fell completely out of favor and today it is hugely popular, followed by people from all walks of life.

Popular astrology is concerned with the reading of a horoscope, a chart of the positions of the planets, Sun, Moon, and stars at the moment of one's birth and interpreting the influence of the planets on human affairs. The Sun travels through the twelve signs of the zodiac through the course of the year and so when someone is said to have been born under Pisces, they were born when the Sun was passing through the portion of the zodiac named after the constellation of Pisces.

Each of the 12 signs has its own personality traits (see pages x–xi), with the daily position of the planets, and the element associated with the planet — fire, water, earth, and air—also affecting each Sun sign. In addition, for serious astrologers, as the Sun passes through the zodiac sign over the course of a month, it passes through three decanates, making each decanate approximately ten days long. Each of the decanates adds its own associated planet and sign influences to the basic influences of the Sun sign. Therefore by considering the decanate as well as the Sun sign, the reading for an individual's birthday is fine-tuned. For example, an Aries born sometime in the third decanate (April 10 to 21) will also be under the influence of the third decanate sign of Sagittarius and the planet associated with Sagittarius, which is Jupiter. The ancient Egyptians considered the decanates as important as the Sun signs themselves.

Progressions are another widely used technique in the system of prediction. With this method the Sun takes about thirty years to journey (or progress) through each sign of the zodiac and in a person's life-time it will typically progress through three to four zodiac signs, depending on the lifespan of the individual and their date of birth. Each time the Sun progresses from one sign to another, this indicates a significant birthday or time in your life when there is likely to be a dramatic change in either your circumstances or outlook. For example, the progressed Sun of a Scorpio born on November 9 will move into Sagittarius at the age of thirteen, into Capricorn at the age of forty-three and then Aquarius at the age of seventy-three.

Fixed stars associated with a particular day of the year also exert additional influences, but if decanates and progressions sound confusing, don't worry; to use this book you don't need to do any math or look anything up in complicated tables as the calculations and relevant interpretations have been taken into account when each birthday profile was compiled. All you need to do is read and enjoy.

Skeptics argue that astrology's suggested link between planetary position and human destiny is unproven, but recent scientific research about the seasons and even the month in which a person is born appears to suggest otherwise.

In the early 1970s, Professor Alan Smithers of Manchester University compiled data from the British population census showing clearly that architects tended to be born in the spring, secretaries in the summer, miners in the fall and electricians in the winter. He also asked members of the British Astrological Association (BAA) to indicate which signs were associated with the professions of nurse and labor union official. Without knowing what the BAA predicted, Smithers conducted a large survey of nurses and labor officials and discovered that, just as the astrologers had indicated, there was a statistical bias toward nurses being born under the signs of Taurus, Cancer, Virgo, Scorpio and Pisces, and labor union officials being born under one or other of the other signs.

Other research has focused on the influence of one star in particular, the Sun. This is because a type of radiation emitted by the Sun, ultraviolet (UVR), is believed to cause genetic changes in the developing baby that may have a shaping effect on their life and personality. This could explain why many of us believe that common characteristics and fates are shared by those born at the same time of the year. For example, researchers at the University of Rostock in Germany have analyzed data to see if the month in which you are born affects how long you will live. It does. Their research found that your chances of living beyond 100 were up to 16 percent higher than average if you were born in December, but if you were born in June, your chances were 23 per cent lower. Another study carried out by researchers at the University of Chicago and published in the *Journal of Anti-Aging Medicine* backed this up, finding that those born in December lived longer by about three years.

Experts believe that the reason people born in December might live longer could be that they were conceived in March, possibly avoiding the most harmful effects of radiation early on. They argue that solar radiation peaks at conception affect personality and health later in life and therefore where you are born is perhaps more important that the month you were born.

Here's a roundup of some findings by different researchers to date.

Happiness: Happy people are more likely to have been born in June, July and August, according to a University of Vienna study. Meanwhile a study at the University of Tokyo found that people born in December, January and February were likely to be more pessimistic than those born at other times of the year.

Personality: Psychiatrists at the University of Umea, in Sweden, looked at personality differences in 2,000 people and found that women born between February and April were more likely to be novelty seekers than those born in October and February. Men born in spring were more likely to be impulsive, while those born in winter were prone to introspection.

Intelligence: Winter-born children may end up being bigger and more academically inclined than those born in summer. Psychiatrists and anthropologists from Harvard and Queensland universities tracked the development of 21,000 boys and girls over seven years, finding seasonal variations in intelligence, weight, height, and head size. Another study from the University of Vienna, however, indicated that female students born in spring and summer achieved better exam marks than those born in fall and winter.

Health: Research from the University Hospital Clinic of Modena, Italy, showed that women born in the fall have the fewest symptoms at menopause and those born in spring have the most. Work at Bristol University has shown that those born in winter have a greater risk of developing heart disease, while another study from the University of Southampton indicated that being born in the winter months may increase the risk of obesity.

True to your sign?

Aries
(March 21 to April 19)

The first sign of the zodiac is a fire sign ruled by Mars. The symbol of Aries is the ram. Aries-born people are typically dynamic, energetic and motivated toward action. Assertive is a good way to describe people born under this sign. They tend to be enterprising, impulsive, warm-hearted, and confident free spirits who say what they mean and mean what they say, although they can also be impatient, rash, tactless, excitable and bossy.

Taurus
(April 20 to May 20)

The second sign of the zodiac is an earth sign ruled by Venus. The symbol of Taurus is the bull. Taureans are typically reliable, loyal and patient individuals with a discriminating taste for quality and the good things in life. A good word to describe them would be determined. These people like to improve their knowledge so that they can make the best out of their intelligence and practicality, but they can also be lazy, materialistic and moody at times.

Gemini
(May 21 to June 20)

The third sign of the zodiac is an air sign ruled by Mercury. The symbol of Gemini is the twins. Geminis are often intellectual and natural communicators who are driven to forward thinking and analyzing, their minds capable of going anywhere. A good word to describe them would be inquisitive, but at times they can be inconsistent and changeable. Their endearing zest for ideas and something new can make committing to anyone and anything problematic.

Cancer
(June 21 to July 22)

The fourth sign of the zodiac is a water sign ruled by the Moon. The symbol of cancer is the crab. Being ruled by the Moon, these people are often highly creative and intuitive. A good word to describe them would be sensitive, but at times they can be oversensitive and insecure. Their empathy and good sense of humor win them many admirers but their moodiness can also be confusing.

Leo
(July 23 to August 22)

The fifth sign of the zodiac is a fire sign ruled by the Sun. The symbol of Leo is the lion. Like the Sun, these people are magnetic and bright, attracting the attention of everything they influence; charismatic would be a good word to describe them. Their lives are typically full of activity and they are often courageous, natural leaders but they are also prone to arrogance and attention seeking.

Virgo
(August 23 to September 23)

The sixth sign of the zodiac is an earth sign ruled by Mercury. The symbol of Virgo is the virgin. They are logical, analytical and practical, and their minds are intellectually oriented and capable of maintaining strong focus. A good word to describe them would be methodical; however, due to their perfectionist natures, these people can be self-critical, which may in turn make them critical of others.

Libra
(September 23 to October 22)

The seventh sign of the zodiac is an earth sign ruled by Venus. The symbol of Libra is the scales. Those born under Libra tend to be peace loving and agreeable, harmonious people, and balanced would be a good word to describe them. They are also naturally empathetic but their natural ability to understand the viewpoint of everyone can be interpreted as insecurity and indecisiveness.

Scorpio
(October 23 to November 21)

The eighth sign of the Zodiac is a water sign ruled by Mars and Pluto. The symbol for Scorpio is the scorpion. Scorpios are passionate, focused and sensual, and intense would be a good word to describe them. They can be highly sensitive and intuitive but they can also be secretive and destructive.

Sagittarius
(November 22 to December 21)

The ninth sign of the Zodiac is a fire sign ruled by Jupiter. The symbol for Sagittarius is the archer. Those born under Sagittarius tend to be unconventional and idealistic, and open minded would be a good word to describe them. They can be visionary and spiritually minded but they can also be reckless and ruthless.

Capricorn
(December 22 to January 19)

The tenth sign of the Zodiac is an earth sign ruled by Saturn. The symbol for Capricorn is the goat. Capricorn natives are often persistent and cautious, and steady would be a good word to describe them. They can be self-disciplined, stable and warm hearted but they can also be inflexible and mean at times.

Aquarius
(January 20 to February 18)

The eleventh sign of the Zodiac is an air sign ruled by Saturn and Uranus. The symbol of Aquarius is the water carrier. Aquarians are often idealistic, intellectual and unconventional, and a good word to describe them would be independent. They can be generous and altruistic but can also be unpredictable and emotionally detached.

Pisces
(February 19 to March 20)

The twelfth sign of the Zodiac is a water sign ruled by the planets Jupiter and Neptune. The symbol for Pisces is two fish. Pisceans can be intuitive and creative, and imaginative would be a good word to describe them. They can also be highly spiritual but they can also be dreamy, impractical and impressionable at times.

A brief introduction to numerology

Numerology assigns characteristics to the cosmic combinations of the digits 1 to 9, suggesting traits and weaknesses for every day of the year. It is based on the concept that the universe is mathematically constructed and the vibrational energy of people, places and things can be expressed through numbers. By reducing birth dates and names to numbers a person's personality and destiny can, allegedly, be determined.

Although numerology probably has its origins in ancient Babylonia and among the early Hebrews, and many different numerology systems have been used in different parts of the world, numerology is most often associated with the fifth-century BC Greek mathematician and philosopher, Pythagoras. Pythagoras believed that there were mathematical connections between the gods, men and numbers that could be codified and if certain number patterns appeared they could be used to predict the fate of a person. According to Pythagoras, numbers were the source of energy in the world and the numbers 1 to 9 represent the nine stages of life. He is quoted as having said, "The world is built upon the power of numbers."

In numerology all numbers are reduced to a number between 1 and 9 and each number is also associated with a letter of the alphabet. Any larger number than 9 can be reduced to a single digit by adding all the digits together; for example, the number 123 becomes 1 + 2 + 3 = 6. The qualities of 123 are therefore equivalent to the symbolic number 6. Using the single digits as a guide, the patterns of different dates and a person's name can be analyzed to define character and predict the future. Briefly, the numbers 1 to 9 represent:

1 Independent, creative, ambitious, extrovert
Downside: can be selfish with tunnel vision

2 Sensitive, domestic, imaginative, musical
Downside: can be timid and gullible

3 Scientific, powerful, knowledgeable, multi-talented
Downside: can be superficial and hedonistic

4 Practical, stable, honest, trustworthy
Downside: can be stubborn and overly serious

5 Energetic, sensual, daring, flirtatious
Downside: can find it hard to commit

6 Perfectionist, creative, artistic, compassionate
Downside: can be supersensitive and overemotional

7 Intellectual, philosophical, imaginative, intuitive
Downside: can be impractical and secretive

8 Practical, just, trustworthy, powerful
Downside: can be opinionated, impatient and intolerant

9 Spiritual, humanitarian, visionary and healer
Downside: can be self-serving, possessive and volatile

What astrology does through stars and Sun signs, numerology does through numbers. Like astrology, numerology is a symbolic system and one of the many tools we can use to understand ourselves and our life purpose better. Just as astrologers believe no one sign is better than another, numerologists believe no number is better or worse than any other. All the numbers have potential as well as a downside. The downside simply suggests challenges associated with this number; if these challenges can be faced and overcome, they can be a source of incredible strength.

In this book we will focus particularly on the qualitative interpretations of numbers in relation to a person's date of birth. In numerology, your date of birth is thought to have a permanent influence on your life. Although you grow older and may change your name, your birth date number (for example, if you were born April 17 your birth date number is 1 + 7 = 8) always remains constant.

A brief introduction to Tarot

Your birth sign and your birth date number are also associated with specific Tarot cards.

Although the true origins of Tarot cards are unknown and may date back to ancient Egypt, the Tarot cards that we know today were created in Italy during the fifteenth century. The Tarot deck consists of seventy-eight cards in total, comprising the twenty-two major arcana cards which the nineteenth-century French occultist Eliphas Levi saw as having symbolic links to the twenty-two letters of the Hebrew alphabet, and the fifty-six minor arcana cards which are divided into four suits: wands, representing the element of fire; swords, the element of air; cups, the element of water; and pentacles, the element of earth. Many versions of the Tarot deck are in use today but most are based on the Rider–Waite deck designed by Arthur Edward Waite and Pamela Colman Smith in 1910.

Although each minor arcana card has a divinatory meaning, the major arcana cards are of greater significance in this book because they represent both archetypal symbols and the quest for self-knowledge. Their meanings are briefly summarized below:

The Fool: represents the divine child, one who is completely trusting of God. The Fool is beginning a journey and has no idea where it will lead, but is peaceful and content, and is living from his heart.

The Magician: represents creative power and having many options. Called the Magus in other Tarot decks, the Magician has access to all four elements of the Tarot to manifest the divine work he has come to earth to achieve.

The High Priestess: represents the psychic self, intuition, dreams and developing one's inner spiritual intuition.

The Empress: represents the ability to adapt and flow according to the needs of the moment.

The Emperor: is the balance to the Empress and represents work, money, grounding, and the ability to fully manifest on the material plane.

The Hierophant: a symbol of one's own inner spiritual authority, also known as your Higher Self. It's also a compilation of the previous four cards, synthesizing these initial stages of spiritual growth on a new level.

The Lovers: represent the awareness of opposites, the relationship between opposites, and the ability to balance what appear to be different aspects of the self.

The Chariot: represents an alignment of your personal will with the divine will, and the transformation of the personal self toward a more planetary consciousness.

Justice: represents a karmic rebalancing process, so what has been out of harmony within your consciousness will be brought into a proper relationship with God's love.

The Hermit: represents a time when the soul must learn to walk alone through darkness, guided by God and the inner light of spirit.

The Wheel of Fortune: represents a time of awakening to the awareness of one's own destiny and soul purpose.

Strength: represents the integration between the higher and lower self. This card is sometimes interpreted as the learning process of seeing yourself as capable of having what you want.

The Hanged Man: this card represents a deep spiritual surrender where all is given to God. The process of surrender turns the soul "upside down," so that life and God can be experienced from a new perspective.

Death: represents a letting-go process related to old emotional patterns, especially in relationships.

Temperance: a card of integration, transformation and alchemy, representing the transformation of opposites into a new element.

The Devil: represents the awareness of one's own negativity and darkness, and can also represent an encounter with negative energies.

The Tower: represents the shattering of illusion and the shattering of an old structure, which can be either a personality structure or a physical one.

The Star: represents divine spiritual healing and an opening to the higher dimension of light. This was made possible through the previous lessons which released the soul from illusion.

The Moon: symbolizes creativity, nurturing, family, and the emergence of subconscious negativity that has come to the surface to be healed and transformed.

The Sun: represents confidence and the emergence of one's true self, stepping out into visibility in its full spiritual and physical embodiment.

Judgment: represents resurrection and rebirth, and is a symbol of this time we are living in, the time of total transformation.

The World: represents a celebration of dance of life, and a time of completion of a major cycle. The World card includes all the previous cards, just as we are all a total of all the steps we have taken on our path. It is a time of fulfillment and joy.

Many astrologers and numerologists believe that the major arcana cards are related to astrological and numerological personality tendencies; for example, the Emperor card is ruled by the planet Mars, the astrological sign of Aries and the symbolic power of the number 5. As such these arcana cards present a powerful means of promoting self-awareness, especially when their implications are considered in conjunction with those indicated by astrology and numerology.

A brief introduction to color healing

According to color analysts or chromatherapists, every color is believed to vibrate with its own energy and to have specific effects on individuals. Seven colors in particular—red, orange, yellow, green, blue, indigo and violet, the colors of the rainbow—have carried religious, occult and mystical significance since ancient times (see box on page xvi). In the late nineteenth century color theory began to receive attention in the West; in 1878 Edwin Babbitt published *The Principles of Light and Colour*, highlighting ancient Pythagorean correspondences between music, color, numbers, and sound.

Today modern science is able to provide evidence for some of the ancient claims about color. In the 1980s it was shown that colored light can trigger biochemical reactions in the body. Later research confirmed that blues and greens have a soothing effect, helping to lower stress, brain-wave activity and blood pressure. Warm colors such as orange and red have been shown to have a stimulating effect. Given the research, it is small wonder then that many psychologists use color to produce beneficial effects in the home, workplace and hospitals.

Putting it all together!

There was a star danced,
and under that was I born

William Shakespeare, *Much Ado About Nothing*

As you can see, the basic principles of astrology, numerology, Tarot, and color analysis are interrelated, and this book uses a combination of them all to highlight the old axiom, "As above, so below." There is a world of possibility contained in each date of birth. You were born during a particular season, under a particular Sun sign, fixed star, and decanate. You have a ruling planet and belong to a particular element—air, earth, water, or fire. Each day also has a numerical vibration and color vibration that has a specific meaning and significance, and these vibrations can suggest numbers, dates and colors that are likely to be more beneficial than others. All these factors shape your personality and life experience; when combined with a modern psychological perspective, they can create a unique and in-depth personality profile for each day of the year.

The psychological approach used in this book involves you in becoming an expert on yourself and others. Think of your birthday profile as a modern tool to assist you on your voyage of self-discovery by translating and fine tuning the symbolic wisdom of your Sun sign, birth number, Tarot card, and personal colors into user-friendly advice. Use that advice to help you develop a deeper understanding of what makes you and other people tick. Use it to help you discover what your strengths are and to find ways to compensate for your weaknesses. Use it to work towards positive growth and change in all aspects of your life. Use it to help you attract luck and success into your life.

Ultimately this book is a celebration of growth and change—the process of growth and change that can be seen each year as the seasons melt into one another; the process of growth and change that can be seen in all human development and transformation.

Only by finding ways to change and work towards your true potential today can you transform your tomorrows and start discovering all the wonderful gifts the universe has bestowed upon you. Your birthday profile is a defining factor that distinguishes you from other people. But never forget that your profile

Healing benefits of color

Each of the seven colors of the spectrum is associated with specific healing properties.

Violet

Violet promotes enlightenment, revelation, and spiritual awakening. Holistic healthcare providers use violet to soothe organs, relax muscles, and calm the nervous system.

Indigo

Indigo is also sedative and calming. It is said to promote intuition. Indigo may be useful in controlling bleeding and abscesses.

Blue

Blue promotes communication and knowledge. It eliminates toxins, and is used to treat liver disorders and jaundice.

Green

Because it is located in the middle of the color spectrum, green is associated with balance. Green is calming and is used by Ayurvedic practitioners to promote the healing of ulcers. It is said to have antiseptic, germicidal and anti-bacterial properties.

Yellow

Yellow is a sensory stimulant associated with wisdom and clarity. Yellow is thought to have decongestant and anti-bacterial properties, and is useful in stimulating both the digestive system and the lymphatic system.

Orange

Orange promotes pleasure, enthusiasm, and sexual stimulation. Ayurvedic practitioners believe it has anti-bacterial properties and may be useful in easing digestive system discomforts, such as flatulence or cramps.

Red

Red promotes energy, empowerment and stimulation. Physically, it is thought to improve circulation and stimulate red blood cell production.

In astrology and numerology, each astrological sign and number has an associated color or colors and, according to color therapists, these colors have a special significance in the birthday profile because our lives can be enhanced by surrounding ourselves with the colors that are most harmonious with our own personal vibrations for that day.

merely highlights *potential* strengths and weaknesses, and that you always have a choice. You can refuse to budge or you can seize the day. You can wait for luck or you can make your own luck. You can sleep or you can dance under the stars!

Birthday quotes

And in the end, it's not the years in your life that count. It's the life in your years.
  Abraham Lincoln

The more you praise and celebrate your life, the more there is in life to celebrate.
  Oprah Winfrey

The best birthdays of all are those that haven't arrived yet.
  Robert Orben

The bad news is time flies. The good news is you're the pilot.
  Michael Althsuler

Our birthdays are feathers in the broad wing of time.
  Jean Paul Richter

Let us celebrate the occasion with wine and sweet words.
  Plautus

Birthdays? Yes, in a general way;
For the most if not for the best of men:
You were born (I suppose) on a certain day:
So was I: or perhaps in the night: what then?
  James Kenneth Stephen

All the world is birthday cake, so take a piece, but not too much.
  George Harrison

Mere color, unspoiled by meaning, and unallied with definite form, can speak to the soul in a thousand different ways.
  Oscar Wilde

Astrology is assured of recognition from psychology, without further restrictions, because astrology represents the summation of all the psychological knowledge of antiquity.
  C. G. Jung

Numbers rule the universe.
  Pythagoras

From our birthday, until we die,
Is but the winking of an eye.
  William Butler Yeats

There are three hundred and sixty-four days when you might get un-birthday presents ... and only one for birthday presents, you know.
  Lewis Carroll

Old age: a great sense of calm and freedom. When the passions have relaxed their hold, you may have escaped, not from one master but from many.
  Plato

No wise man ever wished to be younger.
  Jonathan Swift

One of the signs of passing youth is the birth of a sense of fellowship with other human beings as we take our place among them.
Virginia Woolf

The greatest comfort of my old age, and that which gives me the highest satisfaction, is the pleasing remembrance of the many benefits and friendly offices I have done to others.
Marcus Cato

If I'd known I was going to live this long [100 years], I'd have taken better care of myself.
Ubie Blake

May you live all the days of your life.
Jonathan Swift

Old age isn't so bad when you consider the alternative.
Maurice Chevalier

Birthdays are good for you. The more you have, the longer you live.
Anonymous

THE ELEMENT
ENCYCLOPEDIA
OF
BIRTHDAYS

1 January

the birthday of self-improvement

Full of energy and enthusiasm, those born on January 1 like to show others the way forward. Once they settle on a goal, their drive, integrity and originality attract good fortune and assure success. However, the very qualities that draw success to them can also hold them back.

It is extremely important for people born on January 1 to realize that "mistakes" are going to happen in life. If they go through life expecting that things will always turn out the way they wanted and that people will always do what they said they would do, they will feel perpetually frustrated when life does not go according to plan. They need to deviate from the familiar, learn from mistakes and accept the unexpected. And when they are finally able to turn rejection into resolve they will discover an emotional resilience that will drive them forward and break through their fear.

Above all, January 1 people value dedication, discipline and anything to do with education, psychology and study. They truly are born to lead and inspire, both at home and at work. There is always a voice inside them urging them to work harder, faster and longer. This quality can make them charismatic achievers who set an example to others. They are the bosses who burn the midnight oil, the teachers who give up their spare time to help struggling pupils or the politicians who take a pay cut. The only disadvantage is that they can get so caught up in the process of self-improvement that they forget their goal, their sense of humor and the bigger picture.

January 1 people, especially those under the age of thirty, do run the risk of becoming too focused on work and responsibility, and pushing themselves and others hard in the process. But once they figure out that optimism, resilience and listening to the opinions of others are just as important ingredients for success and happiness as hard work and dedication they possess tremendous potential for creativity, insight and inspired leadership.

On the **dark** side
Oversensitive, impatient, manipulative

At your **best**
Drive, dedication, honesty

Love *Overpowering and seductive*

The seductive power and drive of those born on January 1 can be so strong that unchallenged it can overpower others. They like variety and constant challenge and if their relationships don't hold their interest they can get bored quickly and become controlling. However, once they get involved with someone creative who can keep them on their toes, and who can give them a sense of peace and security when things aren't going to plan, they tend to stay involved.

Health *Danger of burnout*

Emotional and physical burnout is the biggest health worry for people born on this day; because they can be so self-critical they can suffer from bouts of depression. It is extremely important for them to have people in their lives with whom they can talk about their insecurities. This could be family, friends or counselors. Stress-related illnesses, such as headaches and high blood pressure, as well as comfort eating and digestive problems, are also areas of concern. They need to make sure they avoid alcohol, smoking and reliance on caffeine and sugar, and that they get plenty of fresh air, exercise and relaxation. Three drops of lavender essential oil on a handkerchief to breathe in when life is moving too fast will give them a much-needed pick-me-up.

Career *Born specialist*

These people like to be in charge so they are often attracted to careers that offer them this possibility. In business they like to work as a planner, producer, CEO or account manager and, if these are not possible options, to be self-employed. They can also be attracted to politics, education, engineering, astronomy, geology and medicine but any career that allows them to specialize in and rise to the top of a particular rather than a general field will appeal.

Destiny *To be a voice of the people*

The life task for people born on January 1 is to recognize that weaknesses in themselves and others are not necessarily insurmountable obstacles and that with a change of perspective weaknesses can become strengths. This insight, along with the realization that everyone has something to offer, will help give them the emotional strength to fulfill their destiny as a voice of the people.

Power Thought
" When one door closes, another always opens for me "

Signs & symbols

Sun sign: Capricorn

Ruling planet: Saturn, the teacher

Symbol: The Horned Goat

Birth date ruler: Sun; the individual

Tarot card: The Devil (instinct)

Favorable numbers: 1, 2

Lucky days: Saturday and Sunday, especially when these days fall on 1 and 2 of the month

Lucky colors: Dark blue, orange and baked clay brown

Birthstone: Garnet

2 January

the birthday of the intuitive leader

Your greatest challenge is ...

overcoming feelings of isolation and loneliness

The way forward is ...

to go beyond your dark moods, recreate yourself and achieve a goal that involves the help and healing of others.

You're drawn to people born on ...

June 22 to July 22

You share the same desire to live love or friendship to its limits and together your energies can flourish, flow and grow.

Luck maker

Expect luck

Luck follows expectation. Once you expect luck, then you lose your hesitancy and commit to taking actions that will draw it to you.

Those born on January 2 have a remarkable ability to tune into their surroundings, and this sensitivity toward others, combined with their unusual insight into what makes other people tick, can put them head and shoulders above less observant people.

The intuitive power of these people can, however, work against them, making them at times feel alone and different, rather than unique and natural. But once they are able to recognize and celebrate their uniqueness, January 2 people can unlock incredible energy, creativity, endurance, flexibility and commitment. And when their confidence is high, their intuition works at its best with an extremely powerful shift toward this inner life around the age of forty-nine. Unfortunately their acute sensitivity also makes them prone to unpredictability and extreme mood swings. These can create problems for them and for those who care about them. However, once they become aware that they are masters of their own thoughts, a more stable self-confidence will emerge.

Although by nature reserved, January 2 people possess an uncanny knack of being in the right place at the right time; this gives them excellent opportunities for success. If they believe in themselves they can go all the way to the top. If they cannot believe in themselves they may find that they are working in positions beneath their abilities. The same applies to their relationships; if they lower their expectations and don't set clear boundaries they could find that their gentle nature is taken advantage of by others.

Extremely hard working and committed, those born on this day make highly dependable team leaders and negotiators. The danger is that they can overburden themselves with huge responsibilities and this, coupled with their belief that they are different in some way, can set them up to experience frustration and alienation from others. Even though they are often more than capable of fulfilling their responsibilities it is extremely important for them to keep both their feet on the ground with hobbies, social activities and time spent relaxing with family and friends.

On the dark side

Moody, antisocial, indecisive

At your best

Sensitive, spiritual, intuitive

Power Thought

"I deserve the best in life"

Love *Intoxicating passion*

January 2 people know that love holds mystery and magic. They want to be carried away by passion but it also scares them, meaning that they can come across as indecisive and uncommitted. Once in a relationship they can be passionate lovers but their generous and loyal nature can mean that they stay for too long in relationships that are not going anywhere. What they need is someone who shares their sensitivity, their goals and their strong sense of purpose.

Health *Find your inner child*

People born on this day tend to suffer from problems, such as stress, anxiety and fatigue, that are created either by an unhealthy, hectic lifestyle that allows little time for fun and relaxation or by chronic worrying and indecisiveness. Leisure activities that bring out the child in them such as roller skating, finger painting, rock climbing or dancing can help those born on this day escape from their introspection. They also need to take special care of their teeth, gums, hair, skin and bones, especially in the legs, by eating a healthy diet rich in nutritious fruits and vegetables. If stress is a constant part of their life, they should try to burn a chamomile-, lavender- or sandalwood-scented candle. These produce a calming effect.

Career *Born teachers and healers*

The highly intuitive nature of these people makes them natural teachers, social workers and healers, but they can also do well in public relations or as managers of others. Their desire for reflection and love of people watching mean that, especially later in life, they have a talent for writing or journalism. On the other hand, they may choose careers such as photography, music, comedy or the theater to express their uniqueness.

Destiny *To educate others*

When those born on this day conquer their shyness and fear of expressing their individuality, they often encourage others to do the same. They have a tremendous capacity to connect with others and their destiny is to inspire by example, to heal and to educate.

Signs & symbols

Sun sign: Capricorn

Ruling planet: Saturn, the teacher

Symbol: The Horned Goat

Birth date ruler: Moon, the intuitive

Tarot card: The High Priestess (intuition)

Favorable numbers: 2, 3

Lucky days: Saturday and Monday, especially when these days fall on 2 and 3 of the month

Lucky colors: Dark blue, silver and light brown

Birthstone: Garnet

3 January

the birthday of determination

Failure is never an option for people born on January 3. They often have a wild, impulsive energy but they are not quitters. It is not in their nature to pass along responsibilities, and their persistence and sense of duty mean that they can overcome incredible odds. Sometimes, however, their stubbornness to see things through to the bitter end, combined with their inability to admit defeat, can make them appear inflexible and intolerant.

Stubborn by nature, January 3 people can impose unbearable pressure not just on themselves but also on others, and when pushed into a corner they can resort to using their charm to help them get what they want. This isn't to say they are dishonest—dishonesty isn't in their nature—but they are capable of using their seductive powers if they think it will help them achieve their goals.

The rock-solid determination of people born on January 3 can stretch the patience of those around them; in fact opposition and barriers just tend to strengthen their resolve even further and they are at their most inventive when challenged or confronted. It really is hard to throw them off course, and even if it looks like they have lost or need to reconsider they will secretly be planning their comeback or, in some cases, their revenge. The only chink in their armor is that appearance matters a bit too much too them. Nothing pleases them more than a compliment. They have a strong eye for beauty and style but their intolerance for imperfection can, if left unchecked, exasperate and occasionally alienate others.

With their survival instinct and natural understanding that determination is power, people born on January 3 possess the potential for outstanding success, and they can and do overcome impossible odds. Typically, in their forties, sometimes sooner, they tend to realize that they are at their happiest and best when they connect with their intuition; this enables them to find ways to develop their unique talents and leave their personal stamp on the world.

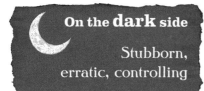
At your best

Charming, controlled, determined

Love *Protective of loved ones*

People born on January 3 are capable of unconditional love and are drawn to the security, comfort and happiness that family life can bring. Their determination applies to their relationships as well, and they want these to work. They love the routine of family life and are extremely protective of loved ones, sometimes overly protective. The only danger is that they are vulnerable to flattery; if they aren't getting admiration and respect from their loved ones, they may well try to seek it elsewhere.

Health *Set a goal of eating one new fruit and vegetable a week!*

An early-to-bed and early-to-rise routine, combined with a healthy, balanced diet rich in a wide variety of fruit and vegetables, and forms of competitive exercise such as swimming or athletics, will keep people born on this day running smoothly. Concerns and anxieties about appearance and/or aging should be managed not by quick fixes such as cosmetic surgery but by regular health check-ups, attention to diet and lifestyle, and a multi-vitamin and mineral supplement. A few drops of the following essential oils on a handkerchief to breathe in will help produce inner security and self-acceptance when anxiety about aging threatens to overwhelm: frankincense, jasmine, sandalwood, and bergamot.

Career *Born self-starters*

These people have good financial know-how and tend to be able to accumulate plenty of money. They often function better in small rather than large businesses, or when they are self-employed. Music, drama, comedy and media hold their appeal but they are also very good at fighting for humanitarian issues or pushing forward social reforms, so they can also excel in politics, charity work, career counseling and education; perhaps even running for office one day.

Destiny *To show others that the impossible can be possible*

Once people born on this day have discovered that they can be committed to a cause without losing their identity, their personality is so powerful that they have no trouble influencing others and winning against all the odds. Their destiny is to show others that the impossible is possible and that determination can yield remarkable results.

Power Thought

❝ The darkest hour is before the dawn and I will come shining through ❞

Signs & symbols

Sun sign: Capricorn

Ruling planet: Saturn, the teacher

Symbol: The Horned Goat

Birth date ruler: Jupiter, the philosopher

Tarot card: The Empress (creativity)

Favorable numbers: 3, 4

Lucky days: Saturday and Thursday, especially when these days fall on 3 and 4 of the month

Lucky colors: Dark gray, purple and pale brown

Birthstone: Garnet

January 3

4 January

the birthday of the eclectic

Those born on January 4 like everything eclectic. In other words, they like to collect, sort and then select only the best, and they use this quick-witted, creative approach in all aspects of their lives. A list of their friends looks like a media mogul's address book, and their work résumé—with numerous stints in different lines of work—reflects their curious personality and unlimited powers of imagination. To others this may look like an undisciplined and erratic approach, but there is always method in the madness of those born on this day. By learning all that can be learned from a variety of sources, they eventually emerge triumphant with an encyclopedic knowledge of life that appears to serve them well in almost any situation.

Because of their eclectic nature and interest in so many aspects of life, January 4 people tend to be the catalyst that stirs up issues in others and makes them face things that they might rather not face. They are very direct people and any interaction with them has to have meaning and purpose, otherwise they quickly lose interest. Their directness and inability to indulge in chit-chat can work against them—as idle conversation is often a means of establishing rapport and common ground with others—but more often than not their ability to sum up a situation and to come straight to the point is welcomed as a breath of fresh air.

Although these people do know how to have fun—especially when they are young—they don't tend to be diverted by the trivial for long. In their thirties and beyond they prefer to exert their considerable energies and talents on a variety of projects to give them fulfillment; these are the years when their potential for professional success comes to the fore. Those born on this day really do need to concentrate their energies on finding a line of work that indulges their need for change but also allows them to be the creative, spontaneous and innovative person they were born to be.

On the dark side
Cold, controlling, intolerant

At your best
Independent, imaginative, methodical

Love *Effortlessly attract admirers*

With their quick wit and encyclopedic knowledge, January 4 people naturally attract friends and admirers. Their changeable nature can sometimes make it hard for loved ones to keep up or know where they are coming from, and—until they find someone who is equally vibrant and experimental—their relationships can be a bit hit and miss. Their directness can be off-putting but underneath there lies a sensitive and caring person.

Health *The mind–body link*

The need of those born on this day for experimentation means that getting into a healthy lifestyle routine is not always easy to achieve. Over-reliance on caffeine and/or mood-changing drugs to feed their over-active mind is also a danger. It is extremely important for them to understand that a healthy body equals a healthy mind and for their minds to work at an optimum level they need to take care of themselves by eating sensibly, getting enough sleep and taking regular exercise. Meditation will be particularly beneficial. Ginger essential oils are known to clear the head and improve memory, so if they have a load of work or study in front of them, a ginger-scented aromatic candle is a good choice.

Career *Born motivators*

It is vital for these people to choose a career that gives them plenty of variety, such as those within the media or travel industries. Their love of knowledge and great communication skills suggests that they can also make great motivators and teachers, as well as scientists, lawyers, researchers, writers, statesmen or stateswomen, journalists and inventors. Whatever career they choose, their ability to inform and inspire others has the potential to bring them great success and respect from their colleagues.

Destiny *To inform and inspire others*

The life path of people born on this day is to gather knowledge and to put all that knowledge to positive use. They can do this by showing the world ways to reconcile the practical with the idealistic. Through their help and creativity, visions of a better world can be realized. Their destiny is to inform and inspire.

Power Thought
" Today, I will stick to my guns "

Signs & symbols

Sun sign: Capricorn

Ruling planet: Saturn, the teacher

Symbol: The Horned Goat

Birth date ruler: Uranus, the visionary

Tarot card: The Emperor (authority)

Favorable numbers: 4, 5

Lucky days: Saturday and Sunday, especially when these days fall on 4 and 5 of the month

Lucky colors: Gray, blue, silver, cognac brown

Birthstone: Garnet

January 4

5 January

the birthday of resilience

Your greatest challenge is ...

understanding what you want from life

The way forward is ...

to try new things to find out what gets you really excited.

You're drawn to people born on ...

August 24 to September 23

You share a love of communication and your mutual understanding can create an unbreakable bond of trust and loyalty.

Luck maker

Set the right level of positivity

For enthusiasm to be effective, sometimes it has to be low key; people need to feel motivated by you, not cornered or smothered.

Those born on January 5 have a great deal of emotional resilience, possessing the ability to recover quickly from setbacks and difficult situations. They can do this because, unlike other less resilient souls, they have the remarkable ability to leave the past where it belongs—in the past. They also have an understanding that loss and disappointment are part of life's journey, and this understanding means they are often wise beyond their years.

Their leadership qualities are strong and they are capable of great dedication and personal sacrifice. They are the resourceful, centered person to whom people turn in a crisis and they thrive on this kind of dynamic. The only danger is that January 5 people can get easily bored when there is no crisis.

Although people born on this day can bounce back from disaster, this doesn't mean to say they are thick skinned. They can appear emotionally aloof at times but more often than not this hides a deeply sensitive and empathetic nature that is simply afraid to reveal or give of itself unconditionally. If they do open up it is only to the most trusted and valued of friends and loved ones.

Their resilient approach to life wins people born on this day many admirers but taken to extremes it can also make them unrealistically optimistic. They need to avoid becoming so upbeat in their approach that they ignore the motives and minimize the concerns of people around them.

Although they should keep their options open and stay flexible, people born on this day are at their best when they have a plan of action. They have a tendency to avoid responsibility and commitment in their teens and twenties but, until they choose a path, they will never feel truly fulfilled. By their early forties, often somewhat sooner, they have usually learned to rein in their curiosity and their love of adventure and travel, choosing a path or a purpose that allows them to concentrate on and express their extraordinary potential for bringing out the best in other people.

At your best

Powerful, expressive, spiritual

Love *Head first*

People born on January 5 are attracted by intelligence and they find verbal banter extremely seductive. Understanding and communication in a relationship are of crucial importance to them. If they feel they can't be completely open or understood they are unlikely to commit to a relationship. This isn't to say, however, that they don't appreciate the physical side of relationships as they have a healthy sexual appetite; it is simply that for them love, like sex, starts in the head.

Health *Athletes should take good care of themselves.*

Because of their emotional resilience, people born on this day recover well from injuries, illnesses and accidents. They should not, however, take their physical and emotional strength for granted; like everyone else, they need to make sure they eat well and get plenty of exercise. They need to pay particular attention to their health in midlife and beyond, when they are most likely to run the risk of neglecting their personal needs for a relationship, work or cause. To help themselves stay vibrant, and full of life, burning grapefruit, lemon-, orange- and rose-scented candles may well do the trick.

Career *Born mediators*

These people need to work in a harmonious environment and they thrive in positions in which they can be a mediator or communicator or where they are needed to put a positive spin on things. Advertising, politics and law could appeal but they may also find great satisfaction in careers that involve service or sharing feelings and experiences with others such as teaching, medicine, entertainment, counseling and psychology.

Destiny *To be the rock when others are floundering*

Once they have learned balance and the ability to listen sensitively to others, the life path of those born on this day is to inspire and motivate others with their resilient approach to life. Their destiny is to be the person to whom people turn in a crisis, the rock when others are floundering.

Signs & symbols

Sun sign: Capricorn

Ruling planet: Saturn, the teacher

Symbol: The Horned Goat

Birth date ruler: Mercury, the communicator

Tarot card: The Hierophant (guidance)

Favorable numbers: 5, 6

Lucky days: Saturday and Wednesday, especially when these days fall on 5 and 6 of the month

Lucky colors: Gray, blue, green, pale rose

Birthstone: Garnet

January 5

6 January

the birthday of the philosopher

People born on January 6 are forever looking beneath the surface for meaning and significance in events. They always try to see the spark of goodness in others but this spiritual, philosophical approach to life can mean that other people often dismiss them as childlike or naïve, in the process underestimating their tremendous energy and intelligence.

Although philosophical in their thinking, January 6 people are extremely ambitious and goal orientated, tending eventually to get what they want in life. Willing to work hard and dedicate themselves to their goals, those born on this day can overcome their natural shyness, introspection and gentleness when they are called to defend their convictions and their ideals. However, because they trust their instincts so much and believe that everything that happens to them has significance, there is a danger of them always rejecting alternative viewpoints and being labeled unrealistic, unreasonable and stubborn at times. The tendency to expect others to think like them can prove too challenging for those who are not as philosophically minded.

Despite their stubborn streak and outspokenness, January 6 people also have a tender side to them that can be easily hurt when their input isn't valued or people don't take them seriously. They may deal with their hurt by rebelling against authority or indulging in irresponsible behavior, but later in life, around the age of forty-five, they learn that, although cathartic, constant rebellion can never be the whole answer. It is important for them to find a place to express their wild side, but sport or work or study is often their savior because it provides the boundaries and calls upon the discipline they need to help them handle their emotions and channel their energies.

At the end of the day, even when criticized or rejected, the idealism and honesty of people born on January 6 never fails to shine through. Once they find what they should devote their life to, their determination and ability to impart their ideals in an inspirational way will attract both admirers and considerable success their way.

On the dark side

Naïve, unrealistic, unreasonable

At your best

Idealistic, philosophical, understanding

Power Thought

❝ I help others by listening to them ❞

Love *In love with love*

Relationships have a powerful, overwhelming effect on people born on January 6 and they run the risk of getting lost in them. Sometimes they can give the impression that they are more in love with the idea of love than with the person themselves; it is important for them to learn to take in a relationship as well as give. Having a wide circle of intelligent friends can stop them becoming overly dependent on a partner.

Health *Ease up on yourself*

Those born on this day need to make sure that their passion for ideals and for others does not make them neglect their own health and well-being. They need to eat healthily and get plenty of sleep so that they can tackle life's challenges with their irresistible energy. At some point in their life they might suffer from some kind of skin problem, but this usually clears up when attention is paid to diet and lifestyle. There is a danger that they can get caught up by overly strict or demanding diet or lifestyle changes recommended by charismatic gurus, such as diets that eliminate food groups or overdose on protein. They need to remember that the key to a healthy diet, as well as to a healthy life, is balance. Sociable forms of exercise such as dancing and aerobics are recommended, and a few drops of lemon essential oil on their pillow or bedclothes at night will help them go to sleep and wake up refreshed.

Career *Born visionaries*

In work, as in life, these people have a vision; if they can't communicate it effectively in their profession, they may decide to go it alone, either by setting up their own business or by becoming self-employed. They make ideal therapists, doctors, counselors, engineers, architects, property developers, computer programmers, psychologists or alternative health practitioners. They may also be drawn toward religion or spirituality.

Destiny *Help others learn about themselves*

The life task of people born on this day is to spread the message that it is possible to unite opposites, the positive and the negative, the idealistic with the practical, the spiritual and the mundane. Their destiny is to help others deal with their fears and uncertainties, and discover their own truth.

Signs & symbols

Sun sign: Capricorn

Ruling planet: Saturn, the teacher

Symbol: The Horned Goat

Birth date ruler: Venus, the lover

Tarot card: The Lovers (choices)

Favorable numbers: 6, 7

Lucky days: Saturday and Friday, especially when these days fall on 6 and 7 of the month

Lucky colors: Black, blue, green, pink

Birthstone: Garnet

January 6

7 January

the birthday of the practical dreamer

Although those born on January 7 give the impression of being serious and intense, they are irresistibly drawn to anything different, strange and unfamiliar. They have a strong sense of duty and responsibility but secretly dream of living an unconventional life in which they can follow their own rules.

Mentally those born on this day are both logical and intuitive, which makes them unique. They are artists with a scientific mind or scientists with an intuitive flair. They have the instinctive gift of being able to sense the moods of other people and, despite their apparent distance from a situation, they can often understand more about what is going on around them than anyone else. Their nature is also highly sensitive. They find it hard to switch off from the suffering and injustices of the world; as a result, they may frequently become involved in charity work or generously give their time for the benefit of others. Because they can tune in so quickly to what is going on around them, they are always in danger of absorbing negativity from others. Seeking out situations and people that are positive and steady, and avoiding the negative, are therefore important.

January 7 people are dreamers but they rarely let themselves get carried away. As a result, their occasional tendency to drift off into a world of their own can make them feel lonely and cut off from everything and everyone around them. They often have a real sense of connection with the natural world and an extraordinary imagination. Fascination with the mystical, with unexplained phenomena and the afterlife is common, especially after the age of forty-four, sometimes sooner, although fear of being criticized or thought "weird" may prevent them from pursuing their interests.

It is extremely important for those born on this day to develop their self-confidence and to accept that the opinions of others, although valuable, are not final. In this way they will be able to let their frustration go and find the freedom of expression that is so crucial for their happiness and fulfillment.

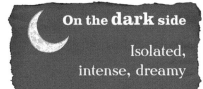

Love *Hot and intense*

Relationships with people born on January 7 tend to be very intense; they are attracted to people who are broad minded, unusual or different in some way. Until they develop their self-confidence, they are not always good at asking for what they want, or letting their guard down and showing their true feelings. However, when they feel secure in themselves and in a relationship, they are loyal and passionate partners.

Health *Sleep matters*

People born on this day tend to be highly sensitive, and as a result fatigue and stress can be a problem. They are particularly susceptible to digestive disorders and need to make sure they eat a fiber-rich diet and take plenty of exercise. Unusual forms of exercise like Tai Chi may appeal. Because fatigue is a common problem, they may need to make sure they eat plenty of foods rich in iron, such as tofu, turkey and legumes, to protect against anemia—a common cause of fatigue—and get more sleep. They should aim for between six and eight hours a night because a good night's sleep is extremely important for them. A glass of chamomile tea can help them unwind before sleep.

Career *Born planners*

These people thrive in careers that require them to use their mind and their imaginative powers. They make great teachers, writers, career counselors and artists, but their humanitarian focus may also lead them toward charitable or social work. They are willing to work behind the scenes as a producer, programmer or agent and their superb organizational skills could also point them to roles in administration, research or management.

Destiny *To unite opposites*

The life path of those born on this day is to learn to have faith in themselves. Once they can do that, their destiny is to share their talent with the world by crossing boundaries, healing differences and uniting opposites.

Power Thought

66 I am good enough just the way I am 99

January 7

Signs & symbols

Sun sign: Capricorn

Ruling planet: Saturn, the teacher

Symbol: The Horned Goat

Birth date ruler: Neptune, the speculator

Tarot card: The Chariot (resilience)

Favorable numbers: 7, 8

Lucky days: Saturday and Monday, especially when these days fall on 7 and 8 of the month

Lucky colors: Black, gray, rouge, sky blue

Birthstone: Garnet

8 January

the birthday of dynamic strength

Your greatest challenge is …

handling the feeling that others aren't giving you enough respect

The way forward is …

to understand that respect is a two-way street; if you want respect, treat others with respect first.

You're drawn to people born on …

December 22 to January 20

You share a mutual respect and admiration for each other and this creates a powerful and exciting dynamic.

Luck maker

Give and receive in equal measure

When you help or give to someone else, without expecting anything in return, you double your chances of both luck and happiness.

People born on January 8 always make their presence felt. They are born with stunning potential to rise and shine above all obstacles and make an impact on the world around them.

Those born on this day expect to be acknowledged by others; as a result, others always come away impressed. Single-minded, hard-working, courageous and forceful, they have the potential within them to achieve almost everything they want. Because of their determined nature there can sometimes be a tendency to overdo things, so they need to make sure they do not become too obsessive by spending time with friends and loved ones, and having plenty of interests.

The belief, enthusiasm and dedication that people born on this day have for projects they love is not the only thing that makes them stand out from the crowd. They also possess great charm and sensitivity, and the ability to put people at ease. Although naturally intuitive, it is important that they do not let practicality and worldly ambition obscure this talent as it will serve them well in all areas of life, in particular their close personal relationships. After the age of forty-three their intuition and emotional sensitivity often increase.

The irony is that despite their almost superhuman confidence and self-possessed exterior, underneath they do from time to time feel anxious and insecure, with a tendency to wallow in dark moods and become despondent and demanding. Their hidden insecurities can also manifest in an impatience and intolerance of others or an egotistical desire to put others down. Every now and again they need to step off the pedestal they have made for themselves so that they can devote both their time and their considerable energy to nurturing friendships based on mutual love, understanding and respect.

If they can stay positive and develop tolerance and humility in their relationships with others, there is nothing to hold back people born on this day. They are meant to shine and, with their inspired awareness, inner strength and self-discipline, shine they well.

Love *Intense and passionate*

Those born on January 8 can have the tendency to be controlling; in some circumstances they may become obsessive and jealous. They need to check this tendency as it can destroy relationships. Having said that, they can be extremely warm and generous in a relationship when they feel secure enough to let down their guard and trust someone else.

Health *Time to play*

Competitive sports appeal to people born on this day but they might benefit more from playing games like charades, because such games give them a chance to laugh both at themselves and with others. Because they possess a tendency to push themselves too hard, they need to watch out for stress-related illnesses such as headaches, insomnia and depression. They also need to watch their posture, especially if they spend much of their day hunched in front of work or a computer. They should avoid rich food and steer clear of drugs altogether. If stress is a constant part of their daily routine, burning a chamomile-, lavender- or sandalwood-scented candle can produce a calming effect.

Career *Born achievers*

Whatever career these people choose, they tend to rise to the top, be it in the arts (where they can employ their imagination), the sciences (where they can employ their analytical skills), business (where they can employ their explosive impact on others) or humanitarian work (where they can employ their understanding and sympathetic nature). They can also make great designers and property developers, and their ability to communicate, teach and inspire others may lead them to education, politics, spirituality, medicine and philosophy.

Destiny *To rise above the odds*

The life path of people born on this day is to rise above the odds. Once they have developed their communication skills and the ability to put others at their ease, their destiny is to show others that the possibilities are always there and that if they keep positive and put in the necessary hard work they will be victorious.

Power Thought

66 Recognizing the positive in others, I recognize the positive in myself 99

Signs & symbols

Sun sign: Capricorn

Ruling planet: Saturn, the teacher

Symbol: The Horned Goat

Birth date ruler: Saturn, the teacher

Tarot card: Strength (passion)

Favorable numbers: 8, 9

Lucky day: Saturday, especially when it falls on 8 and 9 of the month

Lucky colors: Black, gray, rose red and white

Birthstone: Garnet

January 8

9 January

the birthday of the striver

People born on January 9 tend to be fast-acting, thinking and feeling. They want to rise to the top and will do what it takes to get them there. In both their work and their home life they strive for nothing but the best. They demand high standards from both themselves and others, and they detest mediocrity with a passion. Yet because January 9 people place a high value on initiative and their personal freedom, they often prefer to work or forge ahead alone rather than in a group.

So focused are January 9 people on striving that they rarely take time to savor their achievements or even the present moment; they find it particularly hard to relax or switch off. It is of great importance for them to have a partner, friend or even a pet to help them unwind and take themselves and their goals a little less seriously. Typically around the age of forty-two, sometimes sooner, their sensitivity toward others and their inner life becomes more prominent.

January 9 people are amazingly good at overcoming obstacles and difficulties, and can bounce back from almost anything. However in the process of recovery they can also manifest a ruthless side. If knocked down they will claw their way back by whatever means are available, even if that means upsetting trusted friends along the way and making enemies. They need to learn that one of the secrets of success is not to have enemies. Anger, sometimes violent anger, is often their first response, but if they can remain a little more detached and learn some objectivity they will discover that there are always other ways of dealing with a frustrating situation.

Totally fearless, those born on this day have an abundance of admirable qualities. If they can learn to listen to their conscience and strive to maintain balance as hard as they strive to attain success, there is nothing to stop them enjoying the liberating benefits of a purposeful life that sparkles with happiness and excitement.

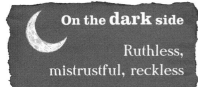

At your best
Ambitious, forceful, resilient

Love *Ardent lovers*

People born on January 9 are passionate and ardent lovers. They are forceful and energetic, and need a partner who can understand and keep up with their physical energy. They are also extremely idealistic about relationships and believe in having a soul mate. Family is also extremely important for people born on this day and they are capable of making enormous sacrifice for those they love.

Health *Take more time out*

Because they tend to drive themselves so hard, those born on this day are prone to stress, fatigue and a lowered immune system. In other words, if they don't take care of themselves they can lose a lot of time to poor health and infection. It is essential that they take regular time out and eat a healthy and balanced diet to ensure they are getting all the nutrients they need to stay strong and healthy. As far as exercise is concerned, gentle exercise is recommended as they can be fatally attracted to extreme and dangerous sports. They may be reluctant to take a gentle daily workout or even go on holiday, but both are essential for them to help restore balance in their lives. A cup of lemon balm herbal tea will help promote digestion and induce calm.

Career *Born experimenters*

The need to progress means that these people need jobs that promise advancement, variety or excitement. If they are drawn to business, they may be interested in marketing or advertising. Other careers that can attract them include politics, the media, the arts or any job that involves plenty of travel and challenge. Astronomy and computer programming may hold particular appeal. They may well experiment with a variety of careers until they settle in and excel in their chosen vocation.

Destiny *To break through barriers*

Ambitious and driven, people born on this day lead by example, showing others that going that extra mile really can make a difference. Once they have learned to focus more on the present moment than the future reward, their destiny is to break through outmoded ways of behavior and in the process strive to make the world a better place.

Signs & symbols

Sun sign: Capricorn

Ruling planet: Saturn, the teacher

Symbol: The Horned Goat

Birth date ruler: Mars, the warrior

Tarot card: The Hermit (inner strength)

Favorable numbers: 1, 9

Lucky days: Saturday and Tuesday, especially when these days fall on 1 and 9 of the month

Lucky colors: Black, gray, bright red

Birthstone: Garnet

January 9

10 January

the birthday of the realist

Your greatest challenge is …

showing your true feelings

The way forward is …

to tell yourself that vulnerability is not a sign of weakness but a sign of strength.

You're drawn to people born on …

July 24 to August 23

You share a passion for directness and a love of the unconventional; this can create a stimulating and intense bond.

Luck maker

Pay others compliments more often

The more you can make others feel good about themselves, the more impressed they are likely to be by you.

People born on January 10 are a force to be reckoned with. They feel an irresistible urge to speak their mind at all times. As a result they are highly valued by others for their honesty and for their realistic assessment of a situation. They are never afraid to support an unconventional viewpoint and to champion the underdog.

Those born on this day tell it like it is, and this quality can bring them success and admiration, taking them to the very top. On the downside, their inability to sugarcoat or dress up the truth can on occasion upset people around them, stopping them advancing as fast in life as their more diplomatic peers. The trouble with the straight-shooting approach is that it doesn't take into account the possibility of hope, and so January 10 people can sometimes come across as grumpy. This isn't, however, a fair reflection of their personality. They are neither negative people nor are they unhappy; they just see things the way they are, warts and all. Typically around the age of forty-one, often sooner, they become more emotionally sensitive to the needs of others.

Although the no-nonsense approach of people born on this day can shock others on first contact, in the long term people often find their clear-sighted approach very refreshing; in times of crisis or uncertainty people will seek advice from people born on this day. Although more than happy to take on this role—as the respect of others is important for them—the very same qualities that earned them respect from others can also create distance as they may find it hard to empathize with people less able to cope with change and the ups and downs of life. Once they begin to understand that not everyone is as clear-sighted as they are, and that a gentle approach can help them achieve their objectives more effectively, people born on this day discover that not only can they earn the lasting loyalty of others, they also have the ability to make a powerful impact on the world around them.

On the **dark** side

Tactless, jealous, distant

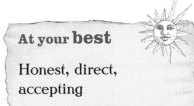

At your **best**

Honest, direct, accepting

Love *Not a closed book*

There is a tendency for those born on January 10 to come across as a bit of a closed book. Lack of trust in others can make them act in a controlling, jealous and sometimes unfaithful manner. Material considerations can also become too important a factor in close relationships. However, when they find a lover who sees the generosity and vulnerability behind their pride and their rough and ready exterior, they can be sensual and passionate lovers.

Health *Stay flexible*

The tough, hardy exterior of people born on this day can manifest in health problems associated with rigidity, such as backache, arthritis, poor circulation and so on. They need to find an energetic physical outlet such as squash, aerobics or rock climbing; yoga or stretching for flexibility can help temper their strength with calmness. A healthy diet and plenty of fresh air and sunshine are also recommended, as these will help keep them feeling physically and emotionally light. If they find themselves feeling sad for no apparent reason, a bergamot-scented candle can help lift their mood. Wearing, meditating on and surrounding themselves with the color orange will encourage them to be more spontaneous.

Career *Born troubleshooters*

Careers in which they can solve problems for others or troubleshoot have great appeal for these people; for example, building, construction or computer programming. If attracted to the arts, financial rewards will be important; they will go for big-business ideas rather than specialist niches and they are also likely to excel in careers that offer good financial return, such as management, advertising and promotion. Their unconventional flair may lead them to explore the unknown; space tourist travel may have particular appeal.

Destiny *To bring others closer to the truth*

The life path of people born on this day is to bring others closer to the truth with their honest and realistic assessment of situations. Their destiny is to make an impact on others and the world they live in with their spirited determination and no-fuss approach to problem solving.

Signs & symbols

Sun sign: Capricorn

Ruling planet: Saturn, the teacher

Symbol: The Horned Goat

Birth date ruler: Sun, the individual

Tarot card: The Wheel of Fortune (change)

Favorable numbers: 1, 2

Lucky days: Saturday and Sunday, especially when these days fall on 1 and 2 of the month

Lucky colors: Black, Bombay brown, orange

Birthstone: Garnet

January 10

11 January

the birthday of the expert assessor

Those born on January 11 have a natural talent for assessing every situation and measuring everyone they meet. They find little difficulty in discarding what isn't needed and see to the heart of people and situations, judging them according to their own very high standards. When the formidable powers of perception of people born on this day are combined with their great intelligence, this results in individuals who are outstanding decision makers.

Underlying this talent for assessment is a strong sense of justice that always strives to be fair. They feel compelled to do the right thing in life and to pass judgment but sometimes they can have problems distinguishing what the right thing or judgment is for them and what the right thing is for others. As a result they can easily convince themselves into thinking that they need to take responsibility for everyone and everything; this is when problems can start, as it can lead to domineering or controlling behavior and the belief that their word really is the law.

It is important for people born on this day to learn to pronounce their opinions less forcibly so that they do not offend those who do not share their point of view. This won't always be easy, but alongside their inflexibility there is also a very caring and compassionate nature. If they can tap more into that, they will begin to understand that it is not just their right, but everybody's right, to have a difference of opinion. Typically around the age of forty, often sooner, their emotional sensitivity becomes stronger and they develop a more powerful inner life.

Those born on this day place high standards on others but they place even higher standards upon themselves. Because they have the courage and determination to live up to these standards, they often do find themselves in the very position they crave: that of the judgment maker. Others will seek them out for advice, judgment and, when they learn to be a little less inflexible, inspiration.

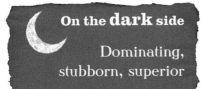
Love *Loyal and devoted*

Once people born on January 11 find a partner who can stimulate their mind or inspire them creatively, they are extremely loyal and devoted. Although relating comes naturally to them, they can at times be reluctant to open up emotionally. There is also a danger that they can take on too much responsibility for the relationship; they need to learn sometimes to stand back, open their heart and let their partner take the lead.

Health *Take care of their own needs*

These people need to be extremely careful that they don't suffer from compassion overload, by wearing themselves out caring for others or fighting for their rights. They need to learn to let go every now and again and to care for their own needs, both physical and emotional. When it comes to diet, they need to avoid anything restrictive or excessive and enjoy a balanced and varied diet; perhaps with a multi-vitamin and mineral to guard against nutritional deficiencies. They should also make sure they get regular, gentle exercise. Burning candles scented with cypress, clary sage, jasmine, coriander, cloves or sandalwood and wearing, meditating or surrounding themselves with the color silver should help them feel more secure and at peace.

Career *Born helpers*

People born on this day are drawn toward careers where they can help others. Their compassion means that they excel in education, teaching or careers working with children or students, counseling or psychology. They may also be drawn to careers in research in which they can use their sharp, incisive mind, or careers in which they can fight injustice, such as politics, social work, law or even the clergy. They also make fine alternative therapists and astrologers, and their skill in communication suggests a knack for writing, music and the arts.

Destiny *To help others turn dreams into reality*

Once they have learned to develop compassion and sensitivity toward the weaknesses of others, the life path of people born on this day is to fight injustice in the world and right wrongs. By so doing they will discover their destiny, which is to help others turn hopes and dreams into practical reality.

Signs & symbols

Sun sign: Capricorn

Ruling planet: Saturn, the teacher

Symbol: The Horned Goat

Birth date ruler: Moon, the intuitive

Tarot card: Justice (discernment)

Favorable numbers: 2, 3

Lucky days: Saturday and Monday, especially when these days fall on 2 and 3 of the month

Lucky colors: Black, doe brown, silvery white

Birthstone: Garnet

January 11

12 January

the birthday of
single-mindedness

People born on January 12 don't do things by half measures and once they have settled on a goal they pursue it with intense and single-minded dedication. Whatever their calling in life, whether it be raising a family, teaching a class or running for president, it becomes their single purpose in life. They are forever on the look-out for opportunities, ideas and people that can help them achieve their goals. Because work is so important to them and they run the risk of sacrificing their personal identity to it, it is vital that they choose their careers wisely.

The need to be the center of attention that characterizes people born on this day is more often than not a result of putting their emotional life on hold in pursuit of their goals in life. Sometimes they can be so driven that they lose touch not only with their friends and family but also with themselves. It is extremely important therefore for people born on this day to remember to respect not only their own feelings but also the feelings of others. They need to carve out a personal life separate from work and a spiritual life that gives them regular time out. Typically around the age of thirty-nine, hopefully sooner, they place more emphasis on their emotional life; this is reflected in their dreams and their visions, as well as the way in which they interact with others.

The single-minded approach of people born on this day, combined with their sharp wit and strong level of commitment, can promise great potential for success. And if all that wasn't enough, they also appear to be blessed with uncanny good fortune. Just as they can swing between high and low moods, their lives can also swing between disaster and sudden good fortune. Out of the blue they may receive a gift, a promotion or the break that they need. Finding balance by placing more emphasis on emotional and spiritual ideals is the key to their survival and their ability to attract all that they need to rise to the very top.

On the **dark** side
Restricted, extreme, arrogant

At your **best**
Tolerant, dedicated, insightful

Love *Learn to relax*

Those born on January 12 are attracted to people who share their single-minded approach to life. They are, however, actually happier with people who are less driven and single-minded and who have a more casual, relaxed approach. Such people can give them the perspective and the fun they need to unwind. Although they may appear confident when it comes to affairs of the heart, they can be reserved and may find it hard to commit or make the first move.

Health *Don't take your health for granted*

Those born on this day tend to take their health for granted as they pursue their goals. More often than not they have a strong constitution and remarkable energy but if they neglect their health or burn the midnight oil for too long they are at risk of becoming overweight, unfit or malnourished. It is important for them to have a routine of regular exercise, and to eat regular meals and snacks to keep their energy and their metabolism on the go. Meditation will encourage their self-awareness and to stop themselves from overeating sweet foods to keep their energy levels up, the sweet smell of vanilla will help stop that sweet tooth.

Career *Born winners*

The sky really is the limit for these people. They are likely to succeed in whatever career they choose because they are so single-minded in their approach. The biggest struggle for them is not likely to be progressing in their career but deciding what career to pursue in the first place. If they decide to become self-employed they can do well as a trader, an agent or a negotiator. Although independent-minded, they can work well in cooperative situations, often excelling in diplomacy, politics, coaching and team sports. They may also wish to explore their considerable artistic and musical talents.

Destiny *To dedicate themselves to a cause or purpose*

The life path of people born on this day is to dedicate themselves to a purpose or cause. Once they are able to find a sense of balance, their destiny is to live through glory as well as defeat and in the process achieve true greatness.

Signs & symbols

Sun sign: Capricorn

Ruling planet: Saturn, the teacher

Symbol: The Horned Goat

Birth date ruler: Jupiter, the philosopher

Tarot card: The Hanged Man (reflection)

Favorable numbers: 3, 4

Lucky days: Saturday and Thursday, especially when these days fall on 3 and 4 of the month

Lucky colors: Black, gingerbread brown, purple

Birthstone: Garnet

January 12

13 January

the birthday of progression

Your greatest challenge is ...

knowing how to cope with anger or disappointment

The way forward is ...

to understand that painful feelings are only released when they are faced. Remember the only way out is through.

You're drawn to people born on ...

October 24 to November 22

You share a broad outlook and a passion for accomplishment and this can create an imaginative and exciting union.

Luck maker

Have faith

Unwavering self-belief when the going gets tough generates the ability and enthusiasm you need to succeed.

Progression is the key word for those born on January 13. They never stand still, always moving forward in their lives, whatever their circumstances or start in life. Their ability to overcome obstacles and make even the most difficult of transitions or tasks seem easy gives them a natural charisma.

Those who make life seem easy are universally favored, and people born on this day not only have the ability to succeed; they also have the ability to keep their cool when all around are losing theirs. When setbacks occur they pick themselves up, learn from their mistakes and do all it takes to reach their goals; and reach them they will.

People born on this day have no problems leaving their past behind them. They understand the importance of letting go in order to progress and move beyond limitations. They particularly enjoy initiating new projects and ideas, and they work steadily and in a disciplined way until they have attained what they desire. Although their imagination and intelligence give them the potential to succeed in many areas, the arena of social and humanitarian reform has particular appeal for them. Of course they feel disappointment and disillusion at times—they are human like everyone else—but typically after the age of thirty-eight, more often than not sooner, they discover the importance of making their mind work for rather than against themselves.

It's impossible for people born on January 13 to hold back in any way and they cannot see the point of doing anything unless one hundred per cent of one's attention and energy is given. If others are not committed or are lazy or not paying attention, they will let them know. They will progress faster if they can understand that not everyone has the same drive or need for achievement as they have, and that sometimes the price for having high ideals means that they have to stand alone. By taking time out to relax they can discover whether they have being pushing themselves too hard or have become too detached from the world they are so committed to improving.

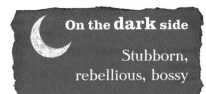

On the dark side

Stubborn, rebellious, bossy

At your best

High achiever, expert, revolutionary

Love *Charismatic flirts*

People born on January 13 tend to be attracted to a partner from whom they can learn or who are a step higher than them on the social ladder. They need to respect and admire their partner rather than the other way round and take great pride in his or her success or accomplishment. Until they find someone to whom they feel ready to commit, their charismatic personality naturally attracts admirers and can mean they will have an erratic love life, sometimes with numerous partners in succession.

Health *Healthy is better than perfect*

Those born on this day are likely to look after their health as they learn early in life that a healthy body leads to a healthy mind. They need to take care that they do not become too obsessive, however, and worry about their health to the extent that every ache and pain has meaning. Exercise is important to keep them flexible and toned but again they need to take care that they do not overwork themselves in a quest for physical perfection. Spending more time in nature or reading, meditating or surrounding themselves with shades of green should help keep them grounded and disciplined but also flexible enough to change course if it becomes necessary.

Career *Born advisors*

The ability of these people to stay calm in a crisis ideally suits them to careers in medicine, the armed forces, personal relations and the emergency services. They may also be attracted to education, where the fields of philosophy and psychology may be of particular interest. Their obligation to society and making the world a better place may draw them toward humanitarian causes. Imaginative and creative enough to work alone, these individuals are also happy working for others in advisory or specialist roles.

Destiny *To make the world a more harmonious place*

The life path of people born on this day is to rise above adversity and help others do the same. Once they have found the courage to stand alone and have learned to respect differences as well as similarities in others, their destiny is to make the world a more harmonious place by bringing people together and settling disputes.

Signs & symbols

Sun sign: Capricorn

Ruling planet: Saturn, the teacher

Symbol: The Horned Goat

Birth date ruler: Uranus, the visionary

Tarot card: Death (change)

Favorable numbers: 4, 5

Lucky days: Saturday and Sunday, especially when these days fall on 4 and 5 of the month

Lucky colors: Black, fir green, sky blue

Birthstone: Garnet

January 13

14 January

the birthday of conviction

One of the greatest strengths of those born on January 14 is their ability to take in vast amounts of information and still see the bigger picture. They are shrewd judges of people and situations, and their inquisitive mind is forever hungry for new ideas, new information and new challenges. Because they have this panoramic view, they are particularly good at decision making. Their strong sense of right and wrong, combined with their highly developed sense of conviction and certainty, makes them excellent and much-sought-after peacemakers, both at home and at work.

Unfortunately the conviction and certainty possessed by those born on this day also have their attendant dangers. Once they have settled on a course of action, it is almost impossible for them to change course and they may go to extreme lengths to see things through to the bitter end. Ironically for people who are so uncompromising and committed in their work life, they aren't always able to make that same level of commitment to their personal life. In fact their personal life definitely takes second place. This may be because they believe that emotions and connections with other people are a distraction from their primary purpose in life, but it may also be the result of a fear of being disappointed. The way forward for them is to apply the same level of commitment to potential friends and partners, and to learn to respect and appreciate the emotional support of others.

Although they appear to be extremely confident and have the ability to implement radical change, they are inwardly far more complex than they appear. Behind the solid, strong image and the apparent love of risk-taking and innovation lies a person who often feels misunderstood; these feelings are heightened if they haven't found a direction in life to which to devote their considerable energies. Once they understand that it is not leadership, material wealth or high rank that they crave but personal freedom and the ability to bring about positive change in the world, they can leave their insecurities behind and achieve miracles.

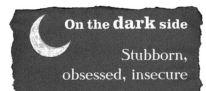
Love *Passions run deep*

The passions of those born on January 14 run deep and they are typically uncomplicated by jealousy. Family, friends and loved ones need to be extremely faithful, patient and understanding but it is well worth the effort as they make adventurous and exciting lovers. Their ideal partner is somebody with a like mind who does not get jealous or possessive and supports them in their convictions.

Health *Accident prone*

Fortunately, people born on this day are unlikely to be tempted by drugs, drink or smoking and this has a protective effect on their health, both physical and emotional. Unfortunately, despite their common-sense approach to health, they are often guilty of driving themselves too hard or living on the edge. Their body inevitably pays the price with accidents and stress-related headaches and insomnia. They are attracted to extreme sports but their health would be better served by gentle to moderate exercise, such as cycling or swimming. A cup of lemon balm or passion-flower herbal tea before bed time will help them sleep well and relieve any aches and pains.

Career *Born people watchers*

It is important for these people to find an outlet for their powers of observation, their ability to see the whole picture and their untapped well of creativity. Writing and photography may be of particular interest, as might property development and design, but because of their unusual ambition and determination they can master almost any skill or career. The media, public relations and advertising may appeal, and as might careers in business, banking and the stock exchange.

Destiny *To introduce positive reforms*

The life path of people born on this day is to find a cause to which they can devote their considerable energy. Once they have learned the importance of connections with others they will discover their destiny, which is to introduce reforms or groundbreaking ways of doing or looking at things.

Signs & symbols

Sun sign: Capricorn

Ruling planet: Saturn, the teacher

Symbol: The Horned Goat

Birth date ruler: Mercury, the communicator

Tarot card: Temperance (moderation)

Favorable numbers: 5, 6

Lucky days: Saturday and Wednesday, especially when these days fall on 5 and 6 of the month

Lucky colors: Black, Arctic green, azure

Birthstone: Garnet

January 14

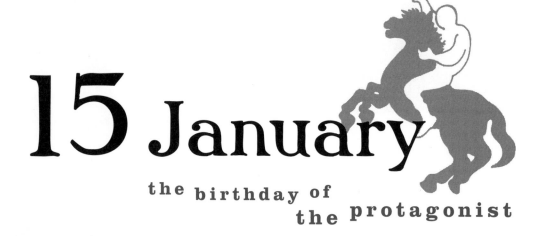

15 January

the birthday of the protagonist

Idealistic, ambitious and determined, those born on January 15 have a strong desire to lead and inspire. For them, nothing occurs which does not have some deep ethical significance, and this, coupled with their uncanny sense of the motivations of others, gives them a talent for seeing life as an exciting drama, pregnant with possibilities for both good and evil.

Motivated perhaps by inspirational role models in their childhood or student years, those born on this day are full of innovative ideas and dynamic energy, combined with a passionate desire to make the world a better place. They are especially sensitive to the feelings of others, giving them great interpersonal skills. They have the ability to win others over to their position, and although others may find them uncompromising at times, they will also admire their seductive and fascinating power and are more than happy to follow their lead.

The Achilles heel for people born on this day is their desire for recognition or credit. They are unlikely to feel fulfilled toiling anonymously for their cause as they feel it is their purpose to lead and raise awareness. Since they are most likely to devote themselves to idealistic and ethical concerns, this is not generally a problem; but if they are drawn toward matters less worthy of them, there is a danger that this need for praise and recognition can become obsessive and ego-driven.

People born on this day do like the world to see them as the invincible conqueror and, with their dramatic flair, people tend to see them in exactly that way. This can create problems for them, however, because they possess a sensitive, generous and vulnerable side that needs to be allowed to express itself. Typically at around the age of thirty-six, sometimes sooner, their emotional sensitivity becomes more enhanced. This shift toward the inner life is an extremely positive thing for people born on this day, because when they are able to manage rather than suppress their hidden vulnerabilities they will discover what it really is like to be the protagonist and wear a hero's crown.

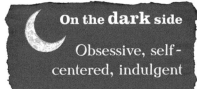

On the dark side

Obsessive, self-centered, indulgent

At your best

Idealistic, dedicated, inspirational

Love *Passionate by nature*

People born on January 15 have a powerful sex drive and a passionate nature. They are attracted to partners who can match their emotional and physical energy and who give them lots of attention and admiration. When they fall in love they give all of their body and mind but before they reach that point in their emotional life they will almost certainly have experimented a great deal sexually.

Health *Moderation is key*

The pleasure-seeking side of people born on this day can lead to excess. They need to watch that their love of rich food and pleasure does not lead to weight gain and excess. They also need to be careful that they don't swing the other way and become excessively strict in their diet and exercise regime. Moderation in diet and exercise is extremely important. Joining a sports team or gym would be particularly beneficial as it would help them get fit while others admire their progress. They may suffer from poor circulation and feel the cold more than most. Sensitive skin also suffers in strong sunlight. Wearing, meditating on or surrounding themselves with shades of blue and green will help keep them balanced and uplifted.

Career *Born campaigners*

These people often find themselves speaking or arguing on behalf of others, fighting for human rights or leading a campaign to raise awareness. They may actively seek out this role or find that at some point in their life it is thrust upon them, finding that the challenge suits them. Whatever career they choose—be it social reform, architecture, management, fine art, civil rights campaigning, health care or science—they are likely to be dramatic, innovative and just a cut above the rest.

Destiny *To be a voice of the people*

The life path of people born on this day is to find a vocation in which they truly believe. Once they find a goal or a direction that is worthy of them and understand that in the drama of their life other people have their parts to play, the destiny of people born on this day is to be the voice of the people.

Signs & symbols

Sun sign: Capricorn

Ruling planet: Saturn, the teacher

Symbol: The Horned Goat

Birth date ruler: Venus, the lover

Tarot card: The Devil (instinct)

Favorable numbers: 6, 7

Lucky days: Saturday and Friday, especially when these days fall on 6 and 7 of the month

Lucky colors: Black, dark blue, pink, woody brown

Birthstone: Garnet

January 15

16 January

the birthday of satisfaction

Those born on January 16 love the idea of successfully completing projects to the best of their ability. They have great organizational skills and it gives them enormous satisfaction and fulfillment to see a job well done. Although satisfactory completion is their goal, it is important for them not to become overly critical or negative about themselves or others when results are not as good as expected.

January 16 people prefer structure, routine and certainty to variation and uncertainty, as they believe it will increase their chances of accomplishing tasks or projects. Paradoxically, though, when their lives become too structured they can become restless and prone to risk-taking or attempting impossible challenges or goals.

Even though they are often highly valued and admired, when things don't go according to plan they can become over-anxious about their future direction, or prone to the belief that they can never live up to their own expectations. It's possible that in childhood great things were expected of them by their parents and this created a tendency toward introspection and living in the future; if allowed to develop to its extreme, this can lead to feelings of inferiority and despair. They need to understand that they are destined for success, but driving themselves and others into the ground in the process is not necessarily the right approach. Once they have learned to value what they do have, they will discover that the satisfaction they crave comes not just from a job well done but from within and from close personal relationships.

Typically around the age of thirty-five, often sooner, they reach a turning-point that emphasizes the importance of being more in touch with their emotions and the present moment. Above all, they must not settle for fear and uncertainty about what may happen in the future because within them is the strength they need to deal with setbacks; once they can view their mistakes not as failures but as opportunities to learn and grow, they have the potential for an extraordinary life.

Love *Actions speak louder than words*

Those born on January 16 can have trouble admitting to their feelings. They prefer to show their love to partners, family and friends by doing things, helping out, encouraging or buying small gifts every so often. There is also a side to them which longs for freedom and is prone to irresponsible behavior. They need to find a partner to whom they feel comfortable opening up and who can give them both the security and the freedom they need to be the caring, loyal and generous lover they can be.

Health *Kick-start*

People born on this day can become lazy or complacent about their health, and their energy levels may slump as a result. They need to eat regular meals and snacks to keep them going at full speed ahead. Energetic forms of exercise are recommended, as is a diet low in sugar, processed and refined food, and full of energy-boosting nutrient-rich vegetables and whole grains. They also need to make sure they have around eight hours' sleep a night; any more than this will have the opposite effect and make them feel lethargic. Drinking green tea (instead of black tea, tea with milk, or coffee) will give them an instant energy boost.

Career *Born managers*

In the world of business, these people make excellent managers or troubleshooters and their systematic approach to life also makes them great organizers, accountants and administrators. Publishing and law are also careers that appeal to them, as well as careers that involve dealing with the public, such as sales, personal relations or teaching. They may also find outlets for their emotional expression in music or the arts.

Destiny *To help others do things the right way*

The life path of people born on this day is to communicate to others the importance of doing things the right way and the satisfaction that can be gained from seeing tasks through to the end. Their destiny is to leave the world not just a tidier but a happier place.

Signs & symbols

Sun sign: Capricorn

Ruling planet: Saturn, the teacher

Symbol: The Horned Goat

Birth date ruler: Neptune, the speculator

Tarot card: The Tower (breakthrough)

Favorable numbers: 7, 8

Lucky days: Saturday and Monday, especially when these days fall on 7 and 8 of the month

Lucky colors: Brown, blue

Birthstone: Garnet

January 16

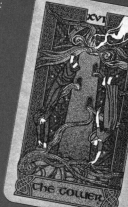

17 January

the birthday of the leader

People born on January 17 prefer to take the lead, not because they are highly ambitious, egotistical or driven to succeed, but because having assessed the situation and weighed up the pros and cons, it is clear to them that they really are the best person for the job. Despite being cautious and respectful of tradition, people born on this day can also hold some progressive ideas with respect to social reform. They like not only to lead but also to help others.

A defining characteristic of people born on this day is their firm self-belief and strong will. Often their tough-minded approach to life has developed as a result of early hardships, and these difficulties may have taught them that the only person upon whom they can really rely at the end of the day is themselves. This gives them an almost superhuman degree of self-control that is simultaneously inspirational and alarming to others. They really do know the meaning of the word "struggle," and are a model of success achieved through one's own efforts.

Leading and defending their position as leader come naturally to people born on this day. Their uncompromising attitude to life and to work can alienate others, and they would do well to learn that there are alternative ways to get people on their side, such as cooperation and good will. Perhaps because of the struggles they have been through, or the past hurts they have experienced, they can find it hard to trust others.

Although those born on this day realize how important it is to feel in control of their lives, there is a danger for some of them in focusing their energy on changing their outside circumstances instead of the way they think and feel about themselves. Fortunately, in their early thirties, often earlier, there is a shift toward this inner life. Once they begin to understand that self-control starts from within not without—and that negative thoughts and feelings can be challenged—their originality and directness aren't just admired by others, they are considered inspirational.

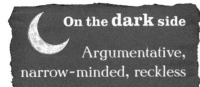
Power Thought

"It is my attitude that counts "

Love *The freedom to love*

Just as people born on January 17 like to take the lead in their working and social life, the same applies to their intimate relationships. Although loyal, loving and generous, they can also be extremely domineering and controlling; as they are attracted to equally powerful, independent people, such tendencies can create tension. They need to learn that freedom and independence are as valid and important in a relationship as intimacy and trust.

Health *Work it out*

People born on this day must be careful that they don't rely too much on stimulants such as caffeine and nicotine to keep their energy levels high. They need to realize that a healthy, balanced diet with plenty of sleep and exercise is the best way to prevent fatigue and boost concentration. Because they have a tendency to repress their emotions, especially their anger, they need to find activities such as competitive or extreme sports in which they can safely express this side of their nature before it erupts in their daily lives. Volunteer work will also help boost their morale. They will benefit from regular reflexology massages and from wearing, meditating on or surrounding themselves with shades of brown, as this color will encourage them to relax.

Career *Born disciplinarians*

These people value careers in which self-control, organization and discipline are important, such as the armed forces, the police force or the clergy. They are also extremely good at delegating and supervising others, so management roles, politics and the civil service may appeal. They may also have an interest in food, fashion or catering, as well as careers in which they can inspire others, such as teaching and charity work.

Destiny *To lead others by their fine example*

The life path of people born on this day is to use their self-discipline and self-control to overcome adversity. Once they have learned to get others on their side with cooperation and mutual understanding, and to lead by example, their destiny is to encourage others to work harmoniously together.

Signs & symbols

Sun sign: Capricorn

Ruling planet: Saturn, the teacher

Symbol: The Horned Goat

Birth date ruler: Saturn, the teacher

Tarot card: The Star (hope)

Favorable numbers: 8, 9

Lucky day: Saturday, especially when it falls on 8 and 9 of the month

Lucky colors: All shades of black, brown and green

Birthstone: Garnet

January 17

18 January

the birthday of fantasy

Your greatest challenge is ...

learning to concentrate for long periods of time

The way forward is ...

to never stop day-dreaming, as this is the secret to your creativity; but if you persistently notice that your mind wanders away from what you are supposed to be focusing on right now, simply say to yourself: Be here now.

You're drawn to people born on ...

March 21 to April 20

You share a mutual passion for togetherness and rebellion, and this creates a powerful and intense bond.

Luck maker

Finish what you start

Lucky people have discipline and are willing to do things they don't like doing because they know it will help them reach their goal.

The imaginative and creative powers of people born on January 18 can lead them to extraordinary heights. They have a quick wit that can delight others, and their company and irreverent opinions are always in demand. In fact they often attract other people like a magnet.

Optimistic, trusting and childlike in nature, the only things that can bring down these friendly souls are rules, regulations and authority. Although they have boundless energy and drive, and love interacting with people, they don't tend to thrive in a team or in a mundane job, unless they are one hundred per cent committed. They place an extremely high value on independence of thought and action; this can lead to reckless behavior and a stubborn refusal to conform. This trait is evident in both childhood and adulthood, and all the normal procedures for dealing with their rebellion don't tend to work; they will simply withdraw even more as a result. They need to find an environment in which their need for freedom is respected, and once they do find that their gratitude, loyalty and devotion to it will be immense. They also need to make sure that they find ways to express their playful and friendly side, and their original sense of humor, as this will help them keep bitterness at bay.

People born on this day can become bored quickly, losing their concentration and retreating into a world of fantasy or fits of temper if their needs aren't being met or becoming restless and impatient if they feel too confined by responsibilities. They need to learn to find ways to deal more appropriately with a situation; this kind of emotional maturity tends to emerge in their early thirties, sometimes sooner, sometimes later. Asking them to be more realistic simply isn't an option—the way forward is for them not to deny their fantasies but to find ways to positively integrate their innovative ideas and extraordinary insights into their lives. By so doing they will be able to make not just their own lives—but those of all they touch—truly magical.

On the dark side

Childish, impractical, undisciplined

At your best

Visionary, creative, stimulating

Love *Head over heels*

Those with this birthday tend to throw themselves deeply into relationships and adore spending all their time with their loved ones. Some partners may find this too suffocating and this can deeply hurt those January 18 people to the extent that they hold back too much in future relationships. They often possess the fear that they will not find a soul mate who also wants to throw themselves into a relationship, but in the majority of cases they are successful.

Health *Stay cool*

Those born on this day need to be careful that they don't disappear into a dreamland by experimenting with mood-altering substances. They can keep their energy levels and their mood constant by getting plenty of sleep and engaging in regular exercise. Because they live so much in their heads, they also need to be careful that they don't forget to eat regular meals and snacks. They need to keep their feet firmly on the ground with plenty of outside hobbies and interests; wearing and meditating on earthy colors such as brown and green will help them feel more grounded.

Career *Born creators*

These people have vast creative potential and if a field interests them they are likely to be successful in it. Once they learn how to combine their creativity with practical ability, the fields of advertising or fashion may appeal, as might the world of business, property development and banking. Their idealism may also draw them toward teaching, medicine and charity work; the dramatic side of their nature that enjoys entertaining others may draw them toward the arts, film, media and theater.

Destiny *To help others find their courage*

The life path of people born on this day is to help others see the magic in almost any situation. Their destiny is not just to delight with their flights of fantasy but also to encourage others to take a bold, original and creative perspective on life.

Signs & symbols

Sun sign: Capricorn

Ruling planet: Saturn, the teacher

Symbol: The Horned Goat

Birth date ruler: Mars, the warrior

Tarot card: The Moon (imagination)

Favorable numbers: 1, 9

Lucky days: Saturday and Tuesday, especially when these days fall on 1 and 9 of the month

Lucky colors: Black, bright red and reddish brown

Birthstone: Garnet

January 18

19 January

the birthday of originality

Those born on January 19 are honest and direct people with a great sense of the beauty in life. They have the ability to look at the world as if through the eyes of a child, seeing everything in a joyous light. Above all they are people of energy and wonder. This is the birthday of true originality.

The originality that defines people born on this day goes hand in hand with a personality that is independent and free-spirited. They really don't care too much what people think and can from time to time indulge in flamboyant or outrageous behavior. Even if they appear respectable on the outside, anyone who gets to know them will soon appreciate what a truly unique individual they are.

January 19 people often surprise others with their reactions because they are able to sense what others miss. Occasionally they will fight against their intuitive side but it is important for them to find ways to balance and incorporate it into their lives. Typically around the age of thirty-two, frequently sooner, there is an emphasis toward their inner life. They learn the importance of working with, not against, their intuition.

These people are destined to shine brightly and to attract others to them like magnets; those born on this day who try to fit in or repress their creativity and originality are on the road to unhappiness. It may take a while before others understand their undoubted gifts but the power of these people is so great that they have the ability to win almost anyone over to their side. The only danger is that the dynamism and unconventionality of these people can lead to attention-seeking and sometimes immature behavior in an attempt to impress. They may also find it hard to lead to stable lives, constantly changing focus and unable to balance their imaginative powers with normal working life.

Blessed with natural drive, curiosity and originality of thought, when they have finally learned to be true to themselves and others, not only can they lead and inspire others, there is the potential for real greatness.

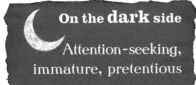
At your **best**

Curious, free-spirited, independent

Love *Highs and lows*

People born on this day are energetic, intense and flamboyant lovers. They can also go from extremes of happiness to extremes of despondency so it is important for them to find an understanding, stable partner who can help them achieve a kind of balance and keep them on the straight and narrow. They need someone who enjoys their ardor but can also give them the occasional reality check.

Health *Pace yourself*

January 19 people don't just use a lot of energy, they burn it, so it is important for them to learn to conserve energy to pace themselves, otherwise they are in danger of collapse from extreme fatigue. A balanced diet and regular exercise will help give them a foundation and a structure. Sports should be energetic but not too competitive, and as far as diet goes they need to cut down on alcohol and sugar. Meditation and other mind–body exercises from yoga and tai chi that encourage balance and harmony will be particularly beneficial. Wearing, meditating on or surrounding themselves with shades of light brown or orange will help balance their energy so they feel alert without feeling anxious or overwhelmed.

Career *Born movers and shakers*

These people tend to do better in solitary professions, but they can also work well in a group as long as they are allowed to use their imagination. They are drawn toward artistic or scientific fields where they can receive acclaim for their efforts. They are also drawn toward sports and other professions such as rock climbing, archeology or exploring that require them to be physical as well as careers where they can be experts, advisors or consultants.

Destiny *To make an impact on the world*

The life path of people born on this day is to achieve a balance between their imaginative and their daily lives. Once they can do that their destiny is to inspire others with their original ideas and to make an unforgettable impact on the world.

Signs & symbols

Sun sign: Capricorn

Ruling planet: Saturn, the teacher

Symbol: The Horned Goat

Birth date ruler: Sun, the individual

Tarot card: The Sun (enthusiasm)

Favorable numbers: 1, 2

Lucky days: Saturday and Sunday, especially when these days fall on 1 and 2 of the month

Lucky colors: Black, orange and lion brown

Birthstone: Garnet

January 19

20 January

the birthday of the ad-libber

People born on January 20 are life's ad-libbers. They may not always be sure where they are going but they also have no doubt that they will get somewhere. They are liberal, sensitive and charming individuals with a remarkable skill for cooperation and improvisation. They are constantly learning, adapting and perfecting their skills, and these qualities helps them climb the ladder of success, sometimes to the very top.

Others may sometimes mistake people born on this day as dreamy, disorganized and scatter-brained. Although they give the appearance of confusion, every detail is stored in their methodical and analytical mind and they simply have an original way of approaching life. They are capable of remarkable endurance, their flexible style ensuring that they overcome the toughest of setbacks with their sense of humor intact.

People born on this day have a genuine compassion and love for people, and will go to extraordinary lengths to help them. They are typically supportive of the underdog but when they are thrown into the role of leader they can come across as dictatorial. It is important for them to carefully consider their approach to leadership, given that their attitude toward the authority of others tends to be light-hearted rather than respectful.

Although they appear tough, the respect of others is extremely important, sometimes too important to them. They need to learn to trust their own judgments more as they are usually right. Fortunately, around the age of thirty there is often a turning point which heightens their sense of self-worth and emphasizes the need for working with their gut instinct.

The considerable personal charm and flexibility that characterizes people born on this day suggests that they have the potential to become well-rounded personalities. Once they can build a sense of self-worth and find a direction and sense of balance, people born on January 20 can display surprisingly intense powers of concentration and commitment that not only assure success but also win them the lasting admiration and respect of others.

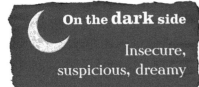
At your **best**

Agreeable, intuitive, focused

Love *Charming and intense*

In love, people born on January 20 have a great sense of fun and spontaneity, and they make charming, optimistic and supportive lovers. There is a tendency for them to become insecure when they are deeply involved and to obsess too much about a partner's opinion. They need to learn to apply their same relaxed and go-with-the-flow approach to life to their relationships.

Health *Heed the warning signs*

People born on this day may go through periods of recurring poor health. On the whole their optimistic, flexible approach always helps them through but if they can learn to pay attention to warning signs they can ensure that they don't succumb to poor health in the first place. Regular health checks are important, as is an immune-boosting diet rich in fiber, whole grains and vegetables, and a regular exercise routine. They may also find that alternative therapies such as aromatherapy, hypnotherapy and homeopathy offer them a sense of well-being and calm. Wearing amethyst jewelry or placing an amethyst crystal under their pillow will also help calm their emotions and reduce stress.

Career *Born healers*

Any career that involves dealing with the public will attract these people, as they genuinely care for the well-being of others. They can also achieve much in medical and scientific fields, and their ability to communicate well means that they make great teachers, counselors and advisors and entrepreneurs. On the other hand, they also have latent creative abilities, and careers that put these to good use, such as writing (in particular science fiction), music and the media, may also appeal.

Destiny *To show others the way forward*

The life path of people born on this day is to build up a sense of self-worth essential to their growth. Once they feel confident enough to progress, their destiny is to create harmony in the world by showing everyone a way forward.

Signs & symbols

Sun sign:
Capricorn/Aquarius

Ruling planet: Saturn, the teacher/Uranus, the visionary

Symbol: The Horned Goat/The Water Carrier

Birth date ruler: Moon, the intuitive

Tarot card: Judgment (responsibility)

Favorable numbers: 2, 3

Lucky days: Saturday and Monday, especially when these days fall on 2 and 3 of the month

Lucky colors: Sky blue, silvery white, light mahogany

Birthstone: Amethyst

January 20

21 January

the birthday of the trendsetter

Your greatest challenge is ...

learning to distinguish between your fear and your intuition

The way forward is ...

to understand that intuition is a lot quieter than fear; you just know something without a lot of words to explain it.

You're drawn to people born on ...

November 23 to December 21

You are both adventurous spirits and this creates an intensely rewarding union.

Luck maker

Connect with your feelings

The next time you have a decision to make, check in with your feelings and your intuition *before* you proceed.

Those born on January 21 are life's trendsetters. It doesn't matter what they are doing or what they are saying, people tend to want to follow them and listen to their opinions. They also have tremendous charm and the ability to get along with just about anyone; when all this is combined with their soaring ambition, they have all they need to get to the top.

Freedom of expression is particularly important for people born on this day. They will never find happiness if they are forced to follow the rules or expectations of others, needing to be allowed to follow their own instincts. If they make mistakes it will still be beneficial as they have the ability to learn from their mistakes.

Leadership is something that those born on this day would seem ideally suited to and they often find it thrust upon them, but in the long term they are not natural leaders. This is because they simply aren't ruthless enough to impose discipline and routine. They are the people with the ideas and the energy to start something new, but it is up to others to see it through to the end.

Alongside their undoubted star quality, people born on this day have a tendency to speak quickly, sometimes spilling out their ideas in a confused way. They also have a tremendous need to be liked, and this can lead to debilitating nervousness and indecision. It is important for them to acknowledge the importance of thinking before they speak and to be less swayed by others' criticism. Fortunately, a turning point occurs around their thirtieth birthday, sometimes sooner, when their sense of self matures and they begin to rely more on their own instincts.

Their unusual charm and personality enable them to forge ahead in life and to go places very few people are able to go. They don't like to be tied down but if they can learn that a little staying power sometimes goes a long way, these boldly original people really can break boundaries and set new limits for others to aspire to.

On the **dark** side

Needy, chaotic, nervous

At your **best**

Inventive, optimistic, likable

Love *Adventurous*

The warmth and charm of people born January 21 can be very appealing to others. They do not like to be tied down and they like to experiment and explore within relationships. This does not mean they are incapable of settling down; it just means they need a partner who reassures them and understands their need for adventure and variety.

Health *Play a round of golf*

People born on this day like to experiment with diets and exercise regimes, and could even create a lifestyle plan of their own to pass on to others. Because of their open-minded and knowledgeable approach to health they tend to understand the connection between diet, lifestyle and good health, and so are likely to take care of themselves. Having said that, they need to careful that they don't take things to extremes; activities that are both healthy and social, like golf or rambling, are extremely positive for them. If stress threatens their sense of well-being, burning a chamomile-, lavender- or sandalwood-scented candle can help produce a calming effect.

Career *Born artists*

The combination of innovation and sensitivity that marks these people gives them great potential to succeed in the arts, in particular novel writing. Their charming personality also gives them the ability to generate ideas; they will excel in any career which values this skill, such as academia, technology, sales or business. On the other hand their natural empathy with the underdog may also lead them into the arenas of charity work, politics, law and social reform.

Destiny *To inspire and improve the lives of others*

The life path of people born on this day is to understand that they need to trust and act upon their instincts. Once they have learned that lesson, their destiny is to inspire and improve the lives of others.

Signs & symbols

Sun sign: Aquarius

Ruling planet: Uranus, the visionary

Symbol: The Water Carrier

Birth date ruler: Jupiter, the philosopher

Tarot card: The World (fulfillment)

Favorable numbers: 3, 4

Lucky days: Saturday and Thursday, especially when these days fall on 3 and 4 of the month

Lucky colors: Sky blue and purple or mauve

Birthstone: Amethyst

January 21

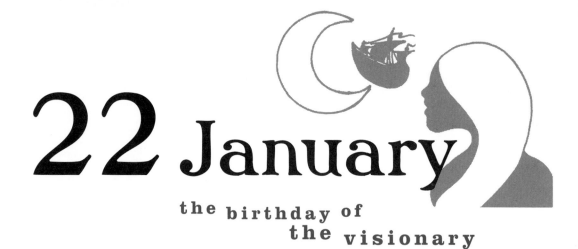

22 January

the birthday of the visionary

Your greatest challenge is …

avoiding feeling unable to commit to a person or a project

The way forward is …

to find out what's holding you back. If it is fear, be the bold, adventurous person you really are and take a risk.

You're drawn to people born on …

October 24 to November 22

You share a passion for adventure and revolution, and this creates a dynamic and like-minded bond.

Luck maker

Learn to handle impatience

When you are impatient, angry or bored, you can't attract good things into your life.

People born on January 22 have an electrifying energy about them. Their imaginative powers are often so advanced that the world isn't always ready for them. This can create a sense of frustration, but if they believe in themselves, hold onto their vision and direct their energy constructively, the world will eventually sit up and notice. Their greatest enemy is not responsibility or even authority but tedium and bureaucracy.

The restless, explosive energy of people born on this day gives them the ability to be extraordinarily successful in whatever goal they choose but they do need to learn the importance of patience and discipline if they are to find stability and satisfaction in their lives. If people born on this day don't understand or they can't see their way ahead they are also likely to lose their temper, with explosive results. They would make their lives considerably easier if they learned to appreciate the opinions of others more, even if they differ from their own. This will fuel their creativity further and encourage others to work cooperatively with them instead of against them. Fortunately, by the age of twenty-nine they typically begin to develop a sense of self-restraint and discipline, and this will mark an important turning point in their life.

Above all, people born on this day have the ability to reach out to the world and to explain or present it with something totally unique. Being an unconventional visionary is their special gift. They don't just break the rules, they destroy them and make new ones.

Not surprisingly their uncompromising approach to life will earn them a number of critics along the way, but opposition neither surprises nor disturbs them. Honor and being true to themselves are important, and they will always do what they know to be right, regardless of what others think. This is a high-risk approach to life that has its dangers, but they should never be scared to be themselves—others will respect, admire and ultimately benefit from them for it.

On the dark side

Headstrong, hasty, explosive

At your best

Passionate, imaginative, ground-breaking

Love *Catch me if you can*

People born on January 22 are never short of admirers but they may find relationships challenging as their head is always off in a new direction. They are prone to mood swings and are drawn toward intelligent and progressive thinkers who share their love of adventure and constant change. However, once they find a partner who is able to keep up and cope, they really do enjoy and benefit from the peace and stability a close relationship can bring.

Health *Life in the fast line*

People born on this day tend to live life in the fast lane so they need to watch their blood pressure and susceptibility to stress-related illnesses. As far as diet is concerned regular meals and snacks are essential to keep their energy levels high, and they should never go on fasts or extreme diets. Vigorous exercise is recommended to help them work off some of that energy, as are mind–body therapies, such as meditation, that can help them get in touch with their inner self. Wearing, meditating and surrounding themselves with light green and blue will encourage them to take action and to enjoy moderation.

Career *Born travelers*

These people don't just need variety; it is their life force, so they thrive in careers that offer them fast change and plenty of travel and do not involve routine. They make great travel guides, pilots, astronauts, airline personnel and navigators, as well as accomplished journalists, actors, musicians, artists, poets and even chefs. Whatever career they choose, these multi-talented individuals need action and constant challenge, otherwise they quickly lose interest.

Destiny *To amaze those around them*

The life path of people born on this day is to learn to control their tendency to flit from one project to another, one relationship to the next, without exploring fully or really getting to know another person. Once they have learned the importance of patience and introspection, they have the potential to amaze those around them, whatever they choose to do.

Power Thought

" I choose balance, harmony and peace, and I express it in my life "

Signs & symbols

Sun sign: Aquarius

Ruling planet: Uranus, the visionary

Symbol: The Water Carrier

Birth date ruler: Uranus, the visionary

Tarot card: The Fool (freedom)

Favorable numbers: 4, 5

Lucky days: Saturday and Sunday, especially when these days fall on 4 and 5 of the month

Lucky colors: Sky blue, silver, turquoise

Birthstone: Amethyst

January 22

23 January

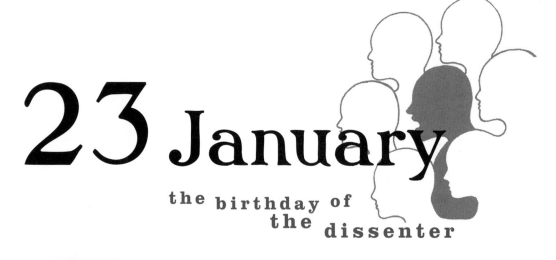

the birthday of the dissenter

People born on January 23 are dissenters. They dislike and often refuse to take orders or even advice from other people and prefer to live according to their own rules, devoting themselves to their own ideals. Although this approach has its risks, more often than not their courageous and buoyant character sees them making, rather than obeying, the rules.

Rarely motivated by financial reward alone, January 23 people are idealistic and desire to live a richly rewarding life. This quality, along with their original thinking and natural sense of style, makes them stand out from the crowd in a positive way. They truly are inspirational figures.

Despite their can-do attitude and charisma, people born on this day never feel quite worthy of the admiration they attract. Although this adds further to their charm, it can sometimes hold them back. However, once they are able to believe in themselves, there is nothing to stop them achieving their own dreams.

With their splendid disregard for convention and highly intellectual and original approach to life, January 23 people find that they can get along with almost everyone they meet, although people with more materialistic motivations present a challenge; people who throw their money about, or who are trying to impress others and climb socially, particularly repulse them. This is because integrity and moral strength are the ideals by which they live their lives.

Understanding the limitations of the human body, those born on this day prefer to live an intellectual life. This can make those close to them occasionally feel excluded and it is important for them to understand that they need a fully integrated personality able to offer others a sensitive depth of understanding. Typically around the age of twenty-eight they become more emotionally receptive and sensitive toward the needs of others.

If those born on this day can make sure that their fascination with the abstract does not take precedence over their personal relationships, they have the potential to become rebels not just with a cause but with ideals that will have an influence on the world around them.

Love *Marriage of minds*

Those born on January 23 definitely need a partner who can challenge them intellectually, as they love to talk about almost anything. They need the freedom to be themselves but also the stability of a secure and loyal partner. They need to be careful that their independent and self-reliant attitude doesn't make partners think they don't need anyone but themselves. These people need a close relationship far more than they would ever admit to.

Health *Headstrong*

Those born on this day are distrustful of doctors and only seek medical advice as a last resort. They like to feel that they are the expert on their health and they will have strong beliefs about the food they eat and the kind of exercise routines they undertake. Because of this, they can either be extremely fanatical about their health or completely disinterested; it is important for them to learn to seek the advice of experts when it is appropriate, because although most of the time they are the best judge of what works for them, sometimes they aren't. Reading, meditating or surrounding themselves with the color purple will encourage them to be more open-minded and to accept change with trust and optimism.

Career *Born academics*

These people are naturally drawn to intellectual pursuits, thriving in student or academic environments. Their analytical mind also marks them out as potential scientists, although any career which can keep their mind constantly stimulated will appeal. Their more practical side may be drawn to business or market research, their idealistic side may attract them toward charity work, their rebellious side may draw them toward working on their own as an entrepreneur; but whatever career they choose, their originality will find ways to express itself in a unique and creative way.

Destiny *To bring fresh new insights into the world*

The life path of people born on this day is to learn to keep their feet firmly on the ground without losing their rebellious streak and individuality in the process. Their destiny is to bring fresh and new insights into the world and to encourage others to see things they normally take for granted in a wholly new light.

Signs & symbols

Sun sign: Aquarius

Ruling planet: Uranus, the visionary

Symbol: The Water Carrier

Birth date ruler: Mercury, the communicator

Tarot card: The Hierophant (guidance)

Favorable numbers: 5, 6

Lucky days: Saturday and Wednesday, especially when these days fall on 5 and 6 of the month

Lucky colors: Aquamarine blue, green, purple

Birthstone: Amethyst

January 23

47

24 January

the birthday of the idol

Your greatest challenge is ...

learning not to fear criticism

The way forward is ...

to use criticism as a powerful incentive to learn and improve. As flattering as praise is, it teaches us nothing, so instead of seeking praise seek criticism.

You're drawn to people born on ...

April 21 to May 21

You are both restrained on the outside but fiercely passionate on the inside and this creates a deep, mutual understanding.

Luck maker

Stop waiting for things to be perfect

Don't wait for the perfect opportunity to come along; make the one you have in hand the best you possibly can.

People born on January 24 are blessed with the ability to stun all those who come into contact with them with their larger-than-life glamor. Everybody wants a piece of them and they are never short of admirers.

Although people are drawn to them sometimes to the point of infatuation, those born on this day have an aloof quality about them. Few know them really well and even fewer get close enough to know their hearts. This may be because behind their natural ability to excite others there is a deep-seated fear of experiencing a negative reaction. To protect themselves from this they prefer to keep everyone at arm's length and to keep quiet about what really excites them. In the short term this approach seems to only increase their popularity, but in the long run this suppression of their true feelings can lead to emotional damage. It is important for them to move away from suspicion of others to the belief that true friends will appreciate them just as they are. Typically around the age of twenty-seven there is a turning point, which suggests a movement away from total independence to greater emotional sensitivity.

Despite feeling insecure at times and misunderstood most of the time, the unique qualities and spark of genius people born on this day possess mean that they are never short of original ideas. They are capable of making great breakthroughs in their careers while at the same time being a delight to have around. They do enjoy being in this position but the danger is that it can lead to vanity. It really is better for their psychological growth to come down to earth with everybody else from time to time.

If those born on this day can find the courage to break down the barriers they have put up and become the person they really are, they may lose some of their idol status but they will gain something far greater in return: self-knowledge. And when they are finally able to understand themselves better, the potential for true greatness lies within them.

On the **dark** side

Vain, insecure, aloof

At your **best**

Energetic, exciting, stunning

Love *Never short of admirers*

People born on January 24 are rarely without a partner; their destiny is to attract others to them. Having said that, they do have problems letting themselves go fully in a relationship, and although they have a loving, generous heart, intense emotions frighten them. They need a partner who is willing to give them the time and space they need to open up fully.

Health *Don't get obsessed*

Those born on this day tend to be extremely careful with their health and appearance; it is important that they don't become obsessed with their diet, or an exercise or beauty regime. When it comes to their health, balance in all things is crucial. They would particularly benefit from group sporting activities that take the focus away from them and onto a team, as well as time spent relaxing with family and friends. Wearing, meditating on and surrounding themselves with warm down-to-earth colors such as brown and green will help stimulate their creativity and interaction with others.

Career *Born nature lovers*

Fear of the disapproval and non-acceptance of others often means that these people are at their happiest among children, or working with animals or with nature, as here they feel they can experience a level of trust and understanding that is perhaps lacking in their relationships with people. With their keen intelligence they are likely to succeed in almost any career, but they may find themselves drawn toward philosophy, religion, law, education, sociology, psychology, astrology, writing or the entertainment world.

Destiny *To inspire others with their desire to improve the world*

The life path of people born on this day is to learn to feel comfortable with the person they are and not to create false images of themselves. Once they are able to open up, their destiny is to inspire others with their honesty, integrity and genuine desire to make the world a better place.

Power Thought

" I joyously give to life and life joyously gives to me "

Signs & symbols

Sun sign: Aquarius

Ruling planet: Uranus, the visionary

Symbol: The Water Carrier

Birth date ruler: Venus, the lover

Tarot card: The Hierophant (guidance)

Favorable numbers: 6, 7

Lucky days: Saturday and Friday, especially when these days fall on 6 and 7 of the month

Lucky colors: Electric blue, cerise, lilac

Birthstone: Amethyst

25 January

the birthday of purpose

Your greatest challenge is …

finding direction or a purpose in life

The way forward is …

to let feelings of envy point you in the direction of what you need.

You're drawn to people born on …

February 20 to March 20

You share a passion for debate and generosity, and this creates a loving and supportive bond.

Luck maker

Be realistic

Lucky people value what they know they can achieve. Stay with reality and try to make things better, not perfect.

People born on January 25 come into this world with a powerful sense of destiny or purpose. They feel as if they have been sent with a mission, and until they are able to find and then achieve that mission they will feel unfulfilled.

If those born on this day are able to find a sense of purpose, their hardworking and disciplined approach to life will assure their success. They have the ability to focus their energies on their goals; these goals tend to be for the good of others rather than for themselves alone. They are at their happiest when they are totally immersed in a project, but their over-involvement is never at the expense of their individuality. People born on this day refuse to conform, and personal freedom is extremely important to them. Friendship is also important for them, and with their sharp wit they are never boring.

People born on this day are trendsetters, and you will often see them working one step ahead of the rest, using their intuition to push forward in a new direction. Occasionally they run the risk of pushing themselves too far forward and their off-the-wall experimentation with their appearance and their ideas can leave others feeling bewildered. This willingness to experiment is all part of the powerful sense of destiny that marks the out. Although they do see themselves as uniquely talented, they can also see themselves as uniquely flawed, and when there is tendency to dwell too much on their supposed deficiencies this can result in self-defeating behavior. It is important for them to come to terms with who they are and to feel comfortable with their personality. Typically around the age of twenty-six, sometimes later, they develop a greater sense of emotional identity and honesty.

Once people born on this day recognize that there really is nothing wrong with them and that emotions are not fixed but constantly changing, they have the potential to become bold and effective leaders in their work and dynamic and fascinating people in their personal life.

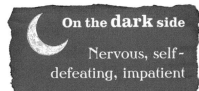
At your best

Profound, altruistic, individual

Love *The soul mate*

People born on January 25 believe strongly in the idea of a soul mate—that person out there who completes them. Although this means that they can be extremely romantic, generous and passionate lovers, their need for total involvement from their partner can at times be too intense. They are drawn toward people who appreciate their need for life and love to be extraordinary.

Health *Stay positive*

Those born on this day need to be careful that they do not fall into a state of depression when they feel they are not fulfilling their life purpose. It is crucial for them to keep a positive attitude toward themselves; the best way to achieve this is not just through positive thinking but through a healthy diet, a regular exercise routine and an active social life. They also need to make sure they do not smoke or eat a diet too high in protein or saturated fat, as these could lead to poor mental, physical and emotional health. If they are feeling negative and uncertain, burning bergamot-, lavender- and sandalwood-scented candles may help change their perspective. They may also benefit from thought-changing therapies such as cognitive development or hypnotherapy.

Career *Born achievers*

The danger for these people is to be without direction, drifting from job to job, project to project, and scattering their energy and focus. In fact the choice of a career is perhaps more important than anything else for these determined individuals, as once they have settled on a course they tend to do very well in any profession. Writing, sociology and counseling, as well as music and the arts, might suit their curious personality; sales, marketing or financial negotiation might utilize their fine organizational talents. They also make accomplished electricians, inventors and technologists.

Destiny *To share their sense of purpose with the world*

The life path of people born on this day is to learn to like and trust themselves, and to accept both their limitations and their strengths. Once they are able to do this, they will be able to find their sense of purpose and to share their magnificent gifts with the world.

Power Thought

" My goal is to love myself more today than yesterday "

Signs & symbols

Sun sign: Aquarius

Ruling planet: Uranus, the visionary

Symbol: The Water Carrier

Birth date ruler: Neptune, the speculator

Tarot card: The Chariot (resilience)

Favorable numbers: 7, 8

Lucky days: Saturday and Monday, especially when these days fall on 7 and 8 of the month

Lucky colors: Bright blue, sea green, mellow mauve

Birthstone: Amethyst

January 25

26 January

the birthday of the last word

People born on January 26 are strong-willed, enterprising individuals with a commanding presence. They like to be spearheading new trends and ideas, and their determination and success-orientated approach to life give them the potential to turn their dreams into reality.

The commanding air of authority, and insistence on having the last word, that people born on this day are blessed with make them excellent leaders and they excel at motivating and organizing other people. They firmly believe that for things to move forward the only way is for somebody—preferably themselves—to take control. They are pioneers of new ventures who generally earn the respect of others, in particular those who are subordinate to them.

While they have an honest approach and an air of authority, people born on this day are not known for their patience. They are prone to making snap decisions about people and to taking decisions without consulting others. This can lead to trouble and antagonism from others; the one thing people born on this day don't like is having their authority questioned. It is important for them to keep an open mind about others and to carefully weigh up the pros and cons before making decisions. Once they are able to recognize the importance of compromise, their down-to-earth approach and dynamic energy will guarantee their success and the loyalty of others.

Those born on this day are usually to be found where the action is. They are extremely success orientated, but to lead a fully balanced life and to achieve greater happiness they do need to pay more attention to their inner life and their relationships with others. Fortunately, after the age of approximately twenty-five, sometimes later, they begin to become more sensitive and inner-focused and less externally orientated.

Part of the secret of the success that people born on this day attract is their ability to recover from setbacks. During troubled times in childhood and adolescence they learned that they have the ability to surprise all who doubt them and, once they know what they want, nothing can stand in their way.

At your **best**

Dynamic, enterprising, determined

Love *Born flirts*

People born on January 26 are born flirts and run the risk of getting involved with someone else for the wrong reasons; perhaps because they feel that person will help them climb the ladder of success. This is a dangerous approach to love and one they should avoid at all costs because they are capable of giving a relationship their all.

Health *Early to rise*

People born on this day need to avoid extremes, and an early-to-bed, early-to-rise routine benefits their health. They need to watch out for sudden bursts of anger and frustration which can make them accident prone, particularly around the legs, knees and ankles. Competition sports are not advised but moderate exercise—such as walking, swimming and cycling—is. As far as diet is concerned, they should cut down their intake of meat and dairy products, and focus more on whole grains, vegetables, legumes, nuts, and seeds, with omega-3 fish oils if their skin gets dry or sensitive. Placing an amethyst crystal under their pillow or wearing amethyst jewelry will help induce feelings of calm and contentment.

Career *Natural leader*

Without a doubt, these people possess natural qualities for leadership, and this will take them far if they avoid power struggles. Their ability to spot opportunities makes them great sales leaders, agents, negotiators, CEOs, managers, and advisors. Alternatively, their individual approach may express itself in the world of media and entertainment or they may find fulfillment as a consultant or natural therapist.

Destiny *Trendsetter*

The life path of people born on this day is to learn to motivate people with the spirit of cooperation rather than the spirit of dictatorship. Once they have learned the importance of compromise, their destiny is to be at the forefront of new trends and ideas.

Power Thought

66 Today I will be prepared to see life differently 99

Signs & symbols

Sun sign: Aquarius

Ruling planet: Uranus, the visionary

Symbol: The Water Carrier

Birth date ruler: Saturn, the teacher

Tarot card: Strength (passion)

Favorable numbers: 8, 9

Lucky day: Saturday, especially when it falls on 8, 9 and 17 of the month

Lucky colors: All shades of green and purple

Birthstone: Amethyst

January 26

27 January

the birthday of early development

The unique spirit and outstanding creative talents of people born on January 27 are often evident early in their lives, typically before they reach the age of thirty, and much of the rest of their lives is spent developing these gifts to their full potential.

Financial reward is not likely to be the motivating force of people born on this day; their motivation is more a personal desire to prove themselves and push themselves to their limits. They love the journey more than the arrival and the thrill of the chase rather than the prize. Unusually creative and intelligent, they often pick things up very quickly, an ability they demonstrated in their childhood or their teens. Sometimes their talent for adapting so quickly to the new can distance them from others with a more slow-moving approach, but it can also turn them into trendsetters. Their original perspective can also inspire them to make improvements to systems that are long past their sell-by date. Rarely will these people be on the sidelines; they are decision makers and life's movers and shakers.

The biggest challenge for those born on this day is to learn to slow down and discriminate. Because they are capable of moving so fast ahead of others, their ideas may take off prematurely. They need to develop a disciplined work ethic that matches their versatility and helps them achieve the success they deserve. This doesn't mean they should repress their exuberance; it just means they need to be more realistic in their approach to life. If they are unable to do this they may find themselves unable to hold down a job or a relationship. Fortunately, from the age of twenty-four there is a turning point which offers them opportunities to become more emotionally mature and show the world that their early promise can be fulfilled.

Above all, those born on this day have the ability to astonish everyone around them. Their energetic and sometimes childlike approach to life can mean that they are wrongly dismissed as lightweights, but once they learn concentration they are capable of great accomplishments.

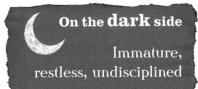

On the **dark** side

Immature, restless, undisciplined

At your **best**

Gifted, enthusiastic, intelligent

Power Thought

❝ I will learn to finish what I start ❞

Love *Erratic, but exciting*

The love life of people born on January 27 is never boring. Falling in love is a big adventure for them, and they love to flirt, often being surrounded by admirers. They like to be physical and need a partner who can be equally affectionate. Unfortunately, they also have a temper which means they can suddenly explode over the smallest of things, so it is important for them to learn to take things a little more calmly.

Health *The importance of taking responsibility*

People born on this day do have a tendency toward self-absorption and if things aren't going well they may be prone to stress and anxiety. It is important for them to eat a varied diet and to get plenty of moderate exercise, as this not only keeps them well grounded but also keeps their spirits high. Taking responsibility for their health is also an issue, and when sick they can be needy and demanding patients who expect others to run after them. Sometimes they feel as if they lack energy, and this could be because others are expecting so much of them. Spending time meditating will help protect them from fatigue, as will carrying an amethyst crystal in their pocket.

Career *Born students*

These people have the keen intelligence and potential to rise to public office and power in high places. They love to study and learn and can use their creative mind with the desire to increase their knowledge and help others. Social welfare, and the helping, counseling, teaching, academic, and healing professions would gain much from their presence. Being independent, they may prefer to work for themselves as an entrepreneur or to express their individuality and creativity in the arts, theater, or music.

Destiny *To make others feel special*

The life path of people born on this day is to learn the importance of patience and dedication. Once they are able to commit themselves to a chosen path, their destiny is to make others around them feel as special as they are.

Signs & symbols

Sun sign: Aquarius

Ruling planet: Uranus, the visionary

Symbol: The Water Carrier

Birth date ruler: Mars, the warrior

Tarot card: The Hermit (inner strength)

Favorable numbers: 1, 9

Lucky days: Saturday and Tuesday, especially when these days fall on 1 and 9 of the month

Lucky colors: Sky blue, scarlet red, purple

Birthstone: Amethyst

28 January

the birthday of the star performer

Your greatest challenge is ...

managing your constant need to be admired

The way forward is ...

to understand that seeking reassurance from others will never give you real fulfillment; the happiness, joy, and inspiration you are looking for lie within you.

You're drawn to people born on ...

July 24 to August 23

You share a mutual passion for creativity and originality, and this creates an irresistible appeal.

Luck maker

Stop trying so hard.

Trying to be noticed is not a recipe for success; in fact it often chases it away. Stop trying so hard, learn to trust in yourself and notice how your luck improves.

Charming and attractive, those born on January 28 know how to project a confident image to others. They are star performers who don't really care what other people think and their creative potential is as strong as their desire to impress others. Impressing others means as much to them as their achievements, and more often than not their achievements are so special that others have every reason to be impressed.

People born on this day will be themselves and follow their own path no matter what. They prefer to think independently, and when their rebellious streak is properly channeled it can help them forge ahead of the rest. Although they do love to be the center of attention and to be admired, they also have great depth and a shrewd insight into the motivations and feelings of others. This can help them achieve their goals, earning them friends along the way.

Sometimes those born on this day may find themselves sitting on the sidelines watching others, perhaps because they are too outrageous to be included; but sooner or later their creativity and individuality pull them back into the action where they belong. Despite their star quality, those born on this day do understand the importance of hard work and their desire to achieve something great never obscures for them the need to put in the hard work. And this combination of courage and individuality with practicality and discipline makes them the pioneer they were born to be.

Those born on January 28 run the risk of needing to be told over and over again how special they are. They may also make foolish, unrealistic decisions in their attempt to be noticed. Fortunately, around the age of twenty-three and again around the age of fifty-three there is a powerful shift toward greater emotional maturity; this emphasis on intuition will serve them well. Once people born on this day learn to listen to their intuition, not only will they attract amazing opportunities to show the world just how brilliant they really are, but their life will feel more complete.

At your **best**
Curious, progressive, hardworking

Power Thought
" I am what I seek "

Love *Please say no*

People born on January 28 tend to have a rather complicated love life and this is due to the fact that they want everybody to be in love with them. They flirt terribly and may acquire a reputation for being too easy. This isn't in fact the case, as their motivation is simply a desire to please others and make them happy. However, for their own sake they need to learn to spread themselves a little less thinly and to find a partner they love enough to be able to say both yes and no to.

Health *Take a step down*

People born on this day tend to be quite excitable and they would benefit enormously from mind–body techniques, such as yoga or martial arts, that teach them the importance of mental control. They should also not let their determination to stand out elevate them to a superhuman status where they neglect their health. Regular physical check-ups are important, as are a healthy diet and plenty of exercise to burn off some of their energy. As long as they are not allergic to them, the soothing scent of strawberries or vanilla will help bring calm and grounding.

Career *Born designers*

These people have a flair for anything artistic, as well as design, architecture and property development. Music has a strong appeal, even if it is just an interest or hobby. Their gift with words and need to be seen or heard mean that they can do well in careers that involve communication, such as writing, public relations or the media. High achievers with the ability to lead and motivate and inspire others, they could also do well in management or the business world, as well as fighting for a social or a political cause.

Destiny *To make a positive difference in the world*

The life path of people born on this day is to learn the importance of self-belief that comes from within rather than without. Once they have learned to develop real confidence, their destiny is to be noticed and to use their star quality to make a positive difference in the world.

Signs & symbols

Sun sign: Aquarius

Ruling planet: Uranus, the visionary

Symbol: The Water Carrier

Birth date ruler: Sun, the individual

Tarot card: The Magician (will-power)

Favorable numbers: 1, 2

Lucky days: Saturday and Sunday, especially when these days fall on 1 or 2 of the month

Lucky colors: Sky blue, copper, gold

Birthstone: Amethyst

29 January

the birthday of
the mystic warrior

Your greatest challenge is …

dealing with confrontation

The way forward is …

not to withdraw but to calmly state your opinion and be true to yourself. Whenever you start compromising your identity and beliefs you reduce your chances of both success and happiness.

You're drawn to people born on …

June 22 to July 23

You share a sensitive approach to life and to love and this can create a match made in heaven.

Luck maker

Be proactive

Reactive people make choices on impulse; they are like reeds blowing in the wind. Proactive people are lucky people because they recognize that they can't always control what happens to them but they can control the way they react.

People born on January 29 are highly intuitive but also very persuasive in their approach to others. They always say what they think, being direct and forceful without being offensive. Their generous nature and strong belief that there is good in everyone earn them not just the respect but the love of all who cross their path.

People born on this day may use their creative, quietly rebellious streak to support the rights of others. Their excellent communication skills serve them well in both their work and social life. The keys to their success as a negotiator and as a person are their intuitive power and their desire to work cooperatively rather than independently. They have the ability to sense what others are thinking and feeling, and when the moment is right to make a move. They also understand the power of synergy and how a group of people working toward a common goal is the greatest force of all.

Although they are open-minded and generally tolerant of the viewpoints of others, they may occasionally withdraw into unassertive behavior and—in extreme cases—into inertia; once they are able to trust their ability to make the right decision they can, however, reach for the stars. Fortunately, around the ages of twenty-two and fifty-two there are powerful turning points in their lives when they develop a greater degree of self-awareness. Life generally becomes much easier for them in their early thirties and beyond, as they start to realize that within them is the power to achieve almost anything.

Once people born on this day have developed their self-belief, their formidable determination to right wrongs can evoke extreme reactions from others; when the reaction is positive they grow in courage, but when negative they may feel hurt. It is important for them to understand that it is impossible to please everyone; sometimes there is a need to be cruel to be kind. And when they learn this they can fulfill their role as the mystic warrior: strong-willed and with the ability to inspire others and gather support for their chosen cause.

Power Thought

"My best relationship is the one I have with me"

Love *Late bloomers*

There is a tendency for people born on January 29 to hold back or withdraw from confrontations in a relationship; this will have a negative impact both on themselves and on their partner. Once in a secure relationship they are generous and giving, and they need to make sure they are in a relationship where they are able to take as well as give. Although relationships can be intense when they are young, they tend to find true love later in life when their sense of self-worth has been allowed to flower to its full potential.

Health *Sensitive to the environment*

People born on this day are sensitive not just to others but to the environment they are in. As a result they may be prone to unexplained mood swings, fatigue, headaches, or allergies or food sensitivities. They need to be extremely careful about their diet, because digestive troubles may occur; they thrive best on a wholesome, down-to-earth diet rich in natural produce and low in meat, dairy, and refined, sweet foods. Regular exercise will benefit their circulatory system as they may be prone to stiff muscles and joints, particularly in the lower body. Time spent catching up with friends or stimulating their mind with a good book will bring them much pleasure. Regular cups of cinnamon herbal tea may help their circulation and their digestion, and reading, meditating or surrounding themselves with shades of blue may help calm their mood.

Career *Born campaigners*

The compassionate, sensitive nature that marks out these people leads many to politics, law, and humanitarian and social reform; since they are intellectual and artistic as well, this could lead them to a career in the media or entertainment world, or to lecturing, teaching, or writing. When inspired, these people also make excellent campaigners and negotiators, and their strong people skills could also attract them to people-related careers, such as sales, marketing, personal relations, or advertising.

Destiny *To believe in themselves*

The life path of people born on this day is to learn to trust their gut instincts and to believe in themselves. Once they are able to do this, their inner voice will guide them toward the important things they are destined to do with their life.

Signs & symbols

Sun sign: Aquarius

Ruling planet: Uranus, the visionary

Symbol: The Water Carrier

Birth date ruler: Moon, the intuitive

Tarot card: The High Priestess (intuition)

Favorable numbers: 2, 3

Lucky days: Saturday and Monday, especially when these days fall on 2 and 3 of the month

Lucky colors: Sky blue, silvery white, purple

Birthstone: Amethyst

January 29

30 January

the birthday of assurance

Your greatest challenge is …

coping with being left alone while others enjoy the companionship you long for

The way forward is …

to learn to accept people the way they are, and not find too much fault in them or expect them always to agree with you.

You're drawn to people born on …

November 23 to December 21

The principled and idealistic but also light-hearted and adventurous people born on these days are good for you and you are good for them.

Luck maker

Don't have the last word

Every time you find yourself following someone's story with your own or pontificate, ask a question instead and listen for the answer. Know-alls aren't lucky because they isolate themselves from other people.

People born on January 30 are confident in their convictions and beliefs and like to put their personal mark on things. They live their life according to their own moral code and are always on the side of the underdog or those less privileged. Their strong social conscience, combined with their determination, charm and intelligence, means they are born to take control.

Everybody who knows people born on this day will be in no doubt of where they stand on the important issues. They have a talent for bringing like-minded people together; living in a commune on the edge of society would not be unacceptable to them if it meant they could live according to their all-important ideals. Although they arrive at their position of certainty through reasoned judgment, they do also rely heavily on their instincts. This ability to combine intuition with logic will mark them out as exceptionally gifted leaders.

Although self-assured and with strong convictions, people born on this day are prone to worry and to acting impulsively just like everyone else. A need to win the approval of others can lead them to fudge the truth if they feel it will get others on their side. It is important for them to find some sort of balance between their convictions and reality, and to know when to stick to a plan regardless of opposition or difficulties. Once they understand that their determination to succeed, if channeled positively, will always help them win, they will be less prone to anxiety and mood swings. Fortunately, around the age of twenty-one and then again at the age of fifty-one there are significant turning points which make them more confident and assertive.

Highly ambitious and strong-willed people born on this day like to give rather than take orders, and although they give orders extremely well they should learn to value the viewpoints of others. Once they have learned to discover their humility and to listen for and trust their inner guidance, they can move mountains with both their convictions and their generosity of spirit.

Love *Comrade*

People born on January 30 don't just want a partner; they want a comrade, someone who shares their convictions, their ideas and their plans. They are more than likely to meet their partner in community affairs which provide the perfect outlook for their social needs and leaderships skills. They need to be careful, however, that their relationship doesn't take second place to a cause. They do best with partners who can make them laugh and take them out of themselves every now and again.

Health *Take it easy*

People born on this day are extremely energetic and it is important for them to schedule time for regular rest and relaxation and even the odd afternoon nap. As far as diet is concerned, they need to cut back on meat and alcohol; for exercise, jogging or brisk walking is particularly recommended as it can help tone the body and calm the mind at the same time. Waking up every morning to the smell of hot water and lemon rather than coffee will help revitalize and re-energize their system.

Career *Born campaigners*

These people have the potential to succeed in careers that are people related and which require them to lead and inspire or educate and inform. They may also find themselves in executive positions or in management or negotiation. Routine doesn't really suit them unless it is for a higher purpose, and they could do well as airline personnel, pilots, navigators, or consultants of any kind, be it head of a department, doctor, social worker, psychologist, or even a producer or director.

Destiny *To transform empathy into direct action*

The life path of people born on this day is to learn to respect and value the input of others without seeing it as a threat to their convictions. Their destiny is to transform feelings of empathy into direct action and, by so doing, make a real and positive difference.

Signs & symbols

Sun sign: Aquarius

Ruling planet: Uranus, the visionary

Symbol: The Water Carrier

Birth date ruler: Jupiter, the philosopher

Tarot card: The Empress (creativity)

Favorable numbers: 3, 4

Lucky days: Saturday and Thursday, especially when these days fall on 3 and 4 of the month

Lucky colors: Sky blue and all shades of purple

Birthstone: Amethyst

January 30

31 January

the birthday of the bright spirit

Your greatest challenge is ...

to stop losing interest quickly if others don't give you their heartfelt support

The way forward is ...

not to try something else but to trust your instincts and make your own decision about what is or is not right for you.

You're drawn to people born on ...

January 21 to February 19

The two of you enjoy defying and surprising public opinion; this will create a magnetic and mutually supportive bond.

Luck maker

Take a stand

Lucky people are certain about what they want. It is this certainty (and not the approval of others) that gives them the strength and determination they need to achieve their dreams.

People born on January 31 have an overwhelming need to be noticed, heard and taken seriously. And because more often than not these bright, appealing people achieve this goal with ease, they are admired by others for their creativity, vision, and originality.

Strong will-power, steadfastness and an emphasis on self-expression define people who are born on this day. They may also be quite progressive, with a touch of the genius about them. Although they can appear absent-minded and chaotic at times, this is only because their thoughts are always on fast-forward, their mind being filled with original and ingenious ideas and concepts.

When they feel they have made some kind of breakthrough they run the risk of getting over-excited, but others tend to find this endearing rather than annoying. In fact people born on this day are generally well liked for being so inventive and entertaining in their never-ending quest for knowledge. They are magnetic personalities but harbor a tendency to be occasionally oversensitive, reading hidden meanings into the actions and words of others. When they feel upstaged, put upon or let down they may overreact and either withdraw completely and become depressed, or startle others with their sharp tongue. They need to learn to be a little less intense in their relationships and to accept that sometimes other people want to share the limelight.

Occasionally people born on this day may feel pressured to conform to others' expectations of them in order to be liked; by so doing they run the risk of losing their unique charm. Fortunately, around the age of twenty there is a turning point which suggests they are able to develop greater self-reliance; at the age of fifty there is another turning point which highlights their fighting spirit and emotional resilience.

Above all, people born on January 31 are bright spirits who have the ability to light up the world with their bubbly personalities and brilliance. Once they learn to truly value themselves they have the potential not only to bring great happiness to the world but also to influence and inspire.

On the **dark** side
Uncertain, suspicious, groveling

At your **best**
Appealing, original, strong

Love *Bubbling over*

People born on January 31 throw themselves into relationships with bubbling enthusiasm. They make endlessly fascinating and entertaining partners but also incredibly supportive and loyal ones. Their partner may find it hard to get a word in, and it is important for them to learn to calm down and listen from time to time. If they can find a lover who encourages them to show their serious as well as their fun side, a passionate and intense connection is possible.

Health *The color blue*

Difficulties with their emotional life, in particular with friends and loved ones, can affect the health of people born on this day and manifest in depression, low self-esteem or insecurity. It is important for them to learn to feel comfortable with and to express their feelings to family and friends; they could benefit from counseling or alternative therapies, such as meditation, that stress the potential of the mind to alter the way they feel both emotionally and physically. They need to make sure they eat a healthy, balanced diet, as they are also prone to eating disorders. They would also benefit from fairly energetic exercise, such as aerobics or jogging, as it will help calm their mind. Meditating, wearing or surrounding themselves in the color blue will help stabilize their mood and bring feelings of calmness.

Career *Born consultants*

These people work well as philosophers, teachers, consultants, healers, writers, academics, as they have a love of gathering knowledge and are expert at communicating it to others. Once they have learned to master their own insecurities they also make outstanding counselors and instigators of social or humanitarian reform. They may also choose to channel their creativity into the entertainment world or the arts, in particular poetry or song writing.

Destiny *To bring great joy to the world*

The life path of people born on this day is to learn to rely less on the reaction they get from others and more on their own instincts. Once they have learned to trust themselves, their destiny is to bring great joy to the world with their charm, wit, and insight.

Signs & symbols

Sun sign: Aquarius

Ruling planet: Uranus, the visionary

Symbol: The Water Carrier

Birth date ruler: Uranus, the visionary

Tarot card: The Emperor (authority)

Favorable numbers: 4, 5

Lucky days: Saturday and Sunday, especially when these days fall on 4 and 5 of the month

Lucky colors: Sky blue, silver and pale green

Birthstone: Amethyst

January 31

1 February

the birthday of the spectacular turnaround

Your greatest challenge is …

coping with feeling unsure about what to do with your life

The way forward is …

to analyze your emotions like a scientist. Once you can identify what gives you joy, you are closer to finding your answer.

You're drawn to people born on …

July 24 to August 23

You share a passion for honesty and fun and this can create an intense and magical bond.

Luck maker

Just do something

Sometimes when you can't decide what to do you simply have to do something and stop dithering. If it doesn't work out, at least you will have learned about yourself from the experience.

Those born on February 1 tend to be multi-talented individuals who refuse to conform to traditional ways of thinking or doing things. Despite the fact that others are often swayed by their conviction, it is not uncommon for them to make a spectacular turnaround a month or so later.

This unique combination of originality, intuition and flexibility means that people born on this day have an ability to attract and keep success. They can assess a situation quickly and formulate an appropriate course of action but they are also capable of dramatically changing direction as long as it takes them in the direction they want to go. They can do this with ease because they have the maturity to understand that there will always be different viewpoints. They have values and beliefs to guide them but they never shut out options that could potentially bring good fortune their way.

The willingness to learn and adapt that people born on this day favor means that they are a unique mixture of seriousness and fun, easily able to relate to and influence everyone they meet. The only danger is that by accommodating themselves to others they can lose touch with who they are. It is especially important for them to shift their focus more toward greater self-understanding and to become more aware of the effect others can have on them. Fortunately, from around the age of nineteen there is a turning point which places the emphasis firmly on developing and understanding their goals in life; at around the age of forty-nine there is a shift toward even deeper self-awareness.

With their ability to adapt and strike out in any new direction, people born on this day are often trail-blazers. Although it can sometimes be tough for them to decide what to do, once they know where they are heading and, more importantly, who they want to be, their powers of communication, combined with their versatility and charisma, have the potential to attract more success than they could ever have dreamed of.

Love *Heart on sleeve*

People born on February 1 tend to wear their heart on their sleeve and prefer relationships that are honest and open. They are never short of admirers, but they also long for the security of a relationship that allows them to be truly themselves. As long as their lover respects them with an honest approach they make loyal, entertaining and loving partners.

Health *Breathe in and out*

Those born on this day often have complicated emotional lives and this can predispose them toward nervousness and sensitivity, and unhealthy lifestyle choices that can increase their chances of poor health. They may also be prone to hypertension and heart problems. It is extremely important for them to avoid stimulants, alcohol, smoking, drugs, and the temptation of numerous sexual partners, and to find more positive ways to work through their emotions, such as vigorous exercise. A sensible diet, low in refined sugar and rich in nutritious fresh food, such as whole grains, nuts, seeds, fruits, and vegetables, is highly recommended. Regular breathing exercises, such as yoga and ch'i kung, can also help reduce stress and prevent oversensitivity.

Career *Born firefighters*

Careers that require action or the ability to think or react quickly, for example paramedics, pilots, fire fighters, doctors, or nurses, may appeal to these people. They may also be drawn to management or executive positions in large companies, or sales and promotion. With their love of change they would do well to stay away from routine jobs, and their inventive and original ideas may also draw them toward humanitarian work or setting up their own business or excelling in media, writing and the arts.

Destiny *To break new ground*

The life path of people born on this day is to discover who they really are and what they want out of life. Once they are able to do that their destiny is to break new ground and to reach further than any have reached before with their determination and drive.

Power Thought

❝ The secret of my success is self-understanding ❞

Signs & symbols

Sun sign: Aquarius

Ruling planet: Uranus, the visionary

Symbol: The Water Carrier

Birth date ruler: Sun, the individual

Tarot card: The Magician (willpower)

Favorable numbers: 1, 3

Lucky days: Saturday and Sunday, especially when these days fall on 1 and 3 of the month

Lucky colors: Aqua, orange, lilac

Birthstone: Amethyst

February 1

2 February

the birthday of elegance

Your greatest challenge is ...

learning how to let down your guard

The way forward is ...

to develop your self-awareness and to understand that trust and intimacy are not weaknesses but strengths.

You're drawn to people born on ...

June 22 to July 23

You share a refined and creative approach to life and love and this can create a transcendental and loving bond.

Luck maker

Learn your intuitive language

Your intuition may come in a dream, it may speak through other people, or it may speak to you in a quiet, gentle knowing.

Those born on February 2 tend to be sophisticated people with their own elegant style, dress code and mode of behavior. They often resist any attempt to impose rules and regulations on them but, despite their fierce need to do things their own way, they are also extremely open-minded. This makes them very easy to get along with and their presence is soothing and reassuring for others when they are troubled. They also possess the ability to stick to something to the bitter end; this determination and conviction give them a formidable energy and power.

Although people born on this day are often surrounded by admirers, they tend to keep close emotional relationships at arm's length. This could be because they can get so absorbed in their work, their ideas or their projects that they place close human contact at the bottom of the list. Their focus is often the universal, the social, the bigger picture or the group, and they are in many respects the wounded healers of this world. They are the politicians, doctors and social reformers who make great changes for the good of others but have little time for the welfare of their own family. They are the counselors and psychologists who can help others work through their emotional traumas but are unable to identify their own. They are the mystics and psychics who can see the bigger picture but can't see their own loneliness. It is crucial for their own psychological growth that they become more self-aware and respect themselves enough to let others get close to them. Fortunately, around the age of eighteen and then again around the age of forty-eight there are opportunities for them to develop stronger emotional bonds with others.

Above all, people born on this day are perceptive and unique individuals. If they can learn to apply the same level of intuitive understanding to themselves as they apply to others and the world around them, they have the potential to be not just rare and elegant, but truly inspirational individuals.

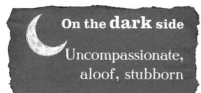

On the dark side

Uncompassionate, aloof, stubborn

At your best

Elegant, stylish, dynamic

Love *Higher love*

People born on February 2 don't just want to fall in love; they want a higher, celestial love where the earth and stars move when they are with their partner. This makes them extraordinarily romantic lovers but it can also place enormous pressure on a partner when the routine of sharing life with someone else inevitably come through. It is important for them to understand that love is not just a heavenly but also an earthly emotion, and that truly falling in love is about sharing and celebrating not just the soul of another person but also their all-too-human imperfections.

Health *The scent of roses*

People born on this day tend to be very concerned about their appearance and need to be careful that they don't take things to extremes if they don't like what they see in the mirror. They need to make sure they eat a sensible balanced diet and don't let fussy eating habits rob them of vital health-boosting nutrients. They would benefit from social forms of exercise such as sports and aerobics, fresh air in the countryside or by the sea, and more time spent relaxing and unwinding with family and friends. Rose essential oil or rose-scented perfume will help them feel more passionate toward others and warmer inside, as will wearing, meditating on and surrounding themselves with the color orange.

Career *Born designers*

These people may well be attracted to technical careers, such as engineering or computer programming, or careers in fashion or design. Their charm and elegance will also help them succeed in any careers where they need to deal on a regular basis with the public. Their curious personality may lead them toward psychology, sociology and politics, and their sensitivity and intuitive understanding of others may also lead them to careers in the arts and teaching, or healing and the spiritual side of life.

Destiny *To make the world more elegant*

The life path of people born on this day is to learn to open up to others and let them into your heart. Once you have learned to do this your destiny is to play up your exquisite taste and use it to make the world a more refined and elegant place.

Signs & symbols

Sun sign: Aquarius

Ruling planet: Uranus, the visionary

Symbol: The Water Carrier

Birth date ruler: Moon, the intuitive

Tarot card: The High Priestess (intuition)

Favorable numbers: 2, 4

Lucky days: Saturday and Monday, especially when these days fall on 2 or 4 of the month

Lucky colors: Aqua, white, purple

Birthstone: Amethyst

3 February

the birthday of new frontiers

Your greatest challenge is …

dealing with boredom

The way forward is …

to think of boredom as an opportunity to relax, unwind and spend time thinking about what you really want from life.

You're drawn to people born on …

November 23 to December 21

The two of you share a passion for exploration and discovery and this can create an adventurous and supportive bond.

Luck maker

Rest rather than run

Some of life's greatest achievements happen not when we are actively engaged in trying to make things happen but when we are simply open and available to what shows up.

People born on February 3 have a probing and inquisitive mind that thrives on variety and constant change. They are boundary breakers and nothing excites them more than a challenge or a new experience. What makes them unique, however, is that when they are actively involved in a task they can give it their undivided attention.

Once people born on this day have broken things down and learned all they think they can, they will immediately move on to something else. There is a danger that this approach to life can lead to flitting from one subject to another without acquiring any real depth. However, when they do find something that really challenges them they will probe into every minute aspect of it with an incomparable eye for detail.

These people don't just enjoy challenges, however, they need them to feel alive; if there are none to engage their active mind they may attempt to make their life more difficult. For example, they may set themselves impossible deadlines at work or push themselves to the limits physically. It is therefore important for them to learn to find ways to deal with their boredom.

Their greatest fear is to have their personal freedom to explore new frontiers taken away. This could result in a fear of commitment to partners and family, and unreliable or erratic behavior. This isn't to say they are incapable of closeness; they simply need to feel that their personal freedom has not been sacrificed. Between the ages of seventeen and forty-six there are opportunities for them to develop greater emotional closeness; after the age of forty-seven there is a turning point that gives them the emotional confidence to handle commitment.

People born on this day will achieve greater happiness when they understand that when others try to seek to be close to them they are not necessarily trying to trap them. In fact, once they have learned to resist the tendency to back off when things get intense, there are very few problems or situations that the adaptable nature of these strong individuals cannot resolve.

Love *Catch me if you can*

People born on February 3 do have a fear of commitment and until they find "the one" they may flit from partner to partner. Ironically, despite their fear of emotional closeness, when they are in a relationship they tend to be the one who throws themselves into it with an intensity that can backfire. It is important for them to understand that just as they need personal freedom in a relationship they need to allow their partner that very same freedom.

Health *Go with the flow*

Fortunately, most people born on this day have the intelligence to understand the importance of taking care of their health, but they can easily get sidetracked. They also need to make sure they don't miss out on regular health check-ups and understand that freedom to experiment should never be at the expense of their health. A routine approach to diet and exercise rarely works for people born on this day but they should make sure that most of what they eat is healthy and incorporate lots of spontaneous exercise into their lives. To help themselves stay the vibrant, full-of-life person they can be, a few drops of grapefruit, lemon, orange, rose, sandalwood, or ylang ylang essential oil sprinkled into a handkerchief to breathe in now and again may well do the trick.

Career *Born technicians*

These people are great technicians, and careers in science and technology may have great appeal. However, with their natural gift for words they may also be drawn to writing, lecturing, teaching, sales, counseling, or social work. Whatever field they choose, be it technical, scientific or creative, the originality, courage, and determination to succeed and master new talents that set people born on this day apart from others will greatly help them.

Destiny *To walk untrodden paths*

The life path of people born on this day is to learn to value the personal as much as they value the interpersonal; once they can do that, their destiny is to boldly strike out into new frontiers and to walk previously untrodden paths.

Signs & symbols

Sun sign: Aquarius

Ruling planet: Uranus, the visionary

Symbol: The Water Carrier

Birth date ruler: Jupiter, the philosopher

Tarot card: The Empress (creativity)

Favorable numbers: 3, 5

Lucky days: Saturday and Thursday, especially when these days fall on 3 and 5 of the month

Lucky colors: Aquamarine, purple, violet

Birthstone: Amethyst

February 3

4 February

the birthday of the bedazzler

Your greatest challenge is ...

understanding the feeling that you are different

The way forward is ...

to understand that everyone is unique and gifted in their own way; you just happen to be a little more unique than others.

You're drawn to people born on ...

January 21 to February 19

You share a love of adventure and boundary-breaking, and this exciting relationship is inspiring and exciting.

Luck maker

Be true to yourself

Lucky people never try to be something they are not. They understand that the only way to find true fulfillment and the respect of others is to open up and allow others to know you properly.

People born on February 4 often try to fit in but, however hard they try, they will always stand out. They have the ability to bedazzle others with their original thoughts and flashes of brilliance. Their methods may not always be orthodox but their thought-processes are always original and their problem-solving techniques always effective.

Although people born on this day are often admired for their sincerity, discipline and ability to work extremely hard, the logic behind their thoughts and actions is often incomprehensible not just to others but sometimes to themselves. Their speed of thought and energy may also exhaust those around them and they may find that people respond to them with bewilderment rather than bedazzlement. Feeling that they are a square peg in a round hole can make them feel insecure and confused; they may try to ward off feelings of difference and aloneness by attempting to fit in. This is a mistake because they shouldn't try to win the admiration of others by limiting their greatest strength: their originality.

People born on this day do often feel as if they are different from other people but they are at their happiest and most bedazzling when they are able to be themselves. Because there is often so much going on in their heads they may pay little attention to their emotions; analyzing their feelings is not easy for them. As a result they can be incredibly harsh on themselves, expecting more from themselves than anyone else. They can also be impatient and impulsive without thinking through the impact of their actions on themselves and others. Fortunately, between the ages of sixteen and forty-five there are opportunities to become more emotionally self-aware; after the age of forty-five a significant turning point comes when they become bolder, more self-accepting and assertive.

If people born on this day can understand that others will respect and admire them far more if they are themselves, they have the potential to bring about real innovations in both their personal and their professional lives.

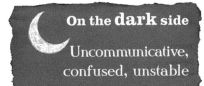

On the **dark** side

Uncommunicative, confused, unstable

At your **best**

Imaginative, unconventional, sincere

Love *Explorers*

People born on February 4 may be difficult to understand, but when it comes to affairs of the heart they are original, adventurous and exciting. They love to explore all aspects of a relationship and their partner will experience great intimacy with them. They are attracted to courageous and strong-willed people. Timid and unadventurous people do not usually attract them, unless there are smoldering passions lurking beneath.

Health *New doesn't always mean better*

People born on this day are attracted to innovation. Most alternative medicine and holistic health practices will probably appeal to them. But they need to distinguish between what is credible and what is quackery. Their love of innovation also applies to diet and exercise; they are typically the first to jump on the bandwagon, only to drop off a few weeks later for something new. Although they have incredible energy, they are prone to neglecting eating and sleeping when they are on one of their mental adventures. It is important for people born on this day to remember that sometimes traditional health advice—for example, eat little and often, and try to get enough sleep—is sensible advice. Meditating, wearing or surrounding themselves with the colors rose or green will help create balance and harmony.

Career *Born innovators*

The originality of these people will enable them to be successful in a wide variety of careers. They may be drawn toward cutting-edge science and technology, or toward the stage or politics. They may also specialize as a therapist, psychologist, counselor, or natural-health practitioner; their humanitarian focus could draw them toward charity work or social reform. They also make fantastic artists, photographers, designers, architects, sculptors, or painters, as these are excellent outlets for their unusual take on life.

Destiny *To amaze others with their original approach to life*

The life path of people born on this day is to celebrate rather than try to curb their originality. Once they are able to do that, their destiny is to amaze those around them with their honest, direct, if occasionally incomprehensible, but always brilliant and original approach to life.

Signs & symbols

Sun sign: Aquarius

Ruling planet: Uranus, the visionary

Symbol: The Water Carrier

Birth date ruler: Uranus, the visionary

Tarot card: The Emperor (authority)

Favorable numbers: 4, 6

Lucky days: Saturday and Sunday, especially when these days fall on 4 or 6 of the month

Lucky colors: Purple, silver, blue

Birthstone: Amethyst

5 February

the birthday of the smooth operator

Your greatest challenge is …

to open up about what you really feel

The way forward is …

to understand that emotions should never be repressed or ignored. If you aren't in touch with your feelings you can never be truly happy.

You're drawn to people born on …

May 22 to June 21

You share a passion for communication and this creates an intellectually and emotionally stimulating bond.

Luck maker

Admit you have fears too

If you admit you have the same fears as others you will get people on your side. When you show your vulnerable side you bring people closer to you.

People born on February 5 are often admired by others for their quiet confidence, razor-sharp wit and ability to undertake almost any task with ease. They are smooth operators with the gift of the gab and an ability to deliver the goods.

Although people born on this day may seem to be extremely capable, sometimes to the point of over-confidence, underneath they are no less insecure than anyone else. They have simply learned to mask their insecurities with a smooth, articulate and daring façade. The admiration of others means a lot more to them that they would admit, which is why they relish the role of caretaker or educator of others.

Incredibly bright, these people express themselves with ease and are at their happiest when surrounded by equally witty and intelligent people. If they are starved of intellectual stimulation there is a danger of their alienating others with a lofty and intimidating manner. Fortunately, between the ages of fifteen and forty-four their emotional sensitivity toward others becomes more emphasized; after the age of forty-four there comes a turning point which suggests they feel even greater empathy for others.

People born on this day can be exceptional thinkers as well as speakers, and nothing thrills them more than philosophy, psychology, mystery, and intrigue. With an ever-curious mind, if they are able to develop their unique ideas they have remarkable potential to excel in their chosen field. They need to be careful, however, not to become too detached in the process. It is important for them sometimes to think a little less and feel a little more, as they have the tendency to over-analyze rather than acknowledge feelings.

February 5 people work particularly well in a team or for a cause where their need for intellectual stimulation and flair for management can be fully utilized. When they learn to hold back less, trust a little more and allow others to catch up with their frenetic pace, the compelling charm of these smooth operators can take them all the way to the top.

At your best

Articulate, versatile, daring

Love *Born nurturers*

People born on February 5 have a strong desire to be needed, so they may often find themselves the caretaker of their family, friends and anyone else who strays into their territory. They love to nurture but need to be careful that they don't just offer practical rather than emotional help. They thrive best with a partner who can match their wit but who also doesn't outsmart them.

Health *See red*

People born on this day tend to be generally healthy but if health problems do occur they may find these hard to talk about or admit to. Regular health check-ups are therefore advised so that a trusting relationship can be built up with their doctor. They need to steer clear of smoking, drugs and large amounts of alcohol, and cut down on saturated fat in their diet. As far as exercise is concerned, team sports are recommended but they may also enjoy cross-country running, horse riding, or other forms of exercise that give them plenty of variety and challenge. Wearing, meditating on or surrounding themselves with shades of red will encourage them to open up emotionally as well as intellectually.

Career *Born guardians*

These people are guardians or caretakers by nature and this could open doors in medicine, education, counseling, psychology, the clergy, consultancy, finance, management, or social work. Their curiosity may also lead them toward careers in the arts, design, film, science, writing, journalism, or academia. Fierce individuals, those born on this day may also prefer to work on their own or set up their own business.

Destiny *To make the impossible seem possible*

The life path of people born on this day is to place as great an importance on feelings as on thoughts. Once they are able to develop their emotional sensitivity, their destiny is to make the impossible seem possible and by so doing to influence and inspire others toward great things.

Power Thought

66 Today I will smile and let others in on the secret 99

Signs & symbols

Sun sign: Aquarius

Ruling planet: Uranus, the visionary

Symbol: The Water Carrier

Birth date ruler: Mercury, the communicator

Tarot card: The Hierophant (guidance)

Favorable numbers: 5, 7

Lucky days: Saturday and Wednesday, especially when these days fall on 5 and 7 of the month

Lucky colors: Turquoise, green and lavender

Birthstone: Amethyst

February 5

6 February

the birthday of the charmer

Your greatest challenge is …

to moderate your desire to be needed by everyone

The way forward is …

to understand that people will like you for who you are and not because you are accommodating.

You're drawn to people born on …

April 21 to May 21

Sensuality and the thrill of seduction and togetherness excite you both, and when the two of you are together sparks can fly.

Luck maker

Be loyal and true

Don't talk about other people behind their back in order to gain popularity. It will backfire on you and repel rather than attract luck.

People born on February 6 are generous, accommodating individuals who are generally liked by everyone they meet. It's almost impossible not to like them because they have such a winning manner and enthusiastic personality. As a result they are often extremely popular and respected.

Positive feedback and approval from others really matters to people born on this day, but this need for affection isn't a one-way street; in many ways life is one big love affair for them. The only downside to this approach to life is that when things don't go their own way, or when love and generosity are met with contempt and selfishness, they can get hurt and emotional. Sometimes disappointment and disillusion can make them behave in dramatic or insecure ways which can irritate rather than endear them to others.

Although they are insecure at times, the generous and positive nature of people born on this day attracts plenty of love, admiration and success their way. They do need to be careful, however, that in their role as people pleaser they don't become too accommodating and lose touch with their own emotional needs or act inappropriately. They need to understand that friendship is not just about accommodation but also about trust, respect, generosity, and boundaries. There is a turning point around the age of forty-four when they become more assertive and aware of their own character.

The flexible nature of these people also applies to their thought processes. They are never wrong-footed by the unexpected, always being willing to explore new territory. They can sometimes be guilty of courting popularity for popularity's sake, but more often than not the unpretentious nature of these people earns them respect and praise in good and bad times alike. As long as they don't take the respect of others for granted, remembering that their self-worth needs to be based on more than popularity, these charming and thoughtful people pleasers want life to be good to them, and more often than not it is.

On the **dark** side

Needy, uncertain, insecure

At your **best**

Loving, generous, likable

Love *Swept off your feet*

People born on February 6 are in love with the idea of love itself and as a result they have a tendency to jump from one lover to the next in search of greater passion, intimacy and excitement. They are forever seeking an elusive high. When they do find someone as clever and as informed as they are, incredible loyalty and commitment can follow.

Health *Look inside*

The tendency for people born on this day is to be extremely concerned about their appearance. Often there is little need to be concerned as they tend to be blessed with good looks, but this doesn't stop them obsessing. They need to avoid fad diets and should stick to regular healthy meals and snacks. They probably enjoy competitive, vigorous forms of exercise but would benefit equally from gentler pursuits and activities, such as long walks in the countryside. They would also benefit from mind–body therapies such as meditation, which can take their focus away from the exterior to the interior. If they do find themselves feeling negative, they should spend more time with family and friends. Wearing or carrying a crystal amethyst will also help to lift their mood.

Career *Born charmers*

Any career that allows these people to use their fantastic people skills will bring them great success; for example, public relations, entertainment, media, public speaking, politics, sales, marketing, and promotion. They may also be drawn toward careers in teaching, research, science, and—for the more physically inclined—sport. They may also choose to put their ability to captivate an audience to humanitarian use and their strong sense of justice may well steer them toward human rights.

Destiny *To inspire others with their personality*

The life path of people born on this day is to make sure their own needs are not ignored while they cater to the whims of others. Once they are able to do that, their destiny is to lead others to an exciting new world of opportunity.

Power Thought

" I also flourish with love and care "

Signs & symbols

Sun sign: Aquarius

Ruling planet: Uranus, the visionary

Symbol: The Water Carrier

Birth date ruler: Venus, the lover

Tarot card: The Lovers (choices)

Favorable numbers: 6, 8

Lucky days: Saturday and Wednesday, especially when these days fall on 6 and 8 of the month

Lucky colors: Turquoise, pink and violet

Birthstone: Amethyst

February 6

7 February

the birthday of the prophet

Your greatest challenge is ...

to get others to take you seriously

The way forward is ...

to prove you mean business by acting out rather than talking about your ideals.

You're drawn to people born on ...

February 20 to March 20

Your hearts are free of greed and full of idealism, and this can create a loving and tender relationship.

Luck maker

Don't take it all personally

Just because people reject your ideas doesn't mean they are rejecting you. Lucky people have the resilience to take criticism on board without it affecting their self-esteem.

People born on February 7 are progressive individuals with a keen intellect and an inherent sense of justice. It is impossible for them to witness injustice or cruelty without speaking out. Above all, they are prophets with a vision and a burning desire to change social attitudes and right wrongs.

They have a wonderful imagination and a youthful approach to life, but also have a tendency to exaggerate or embellish things. This, together with their openness and spontaneity, can sometimes make them appear naïve or childlike. Others may dismiss them or take them for granted but this is a mistake. Although they like to share their dreams with others, the difference between them and other dreamers lies in their ability to turn dreams into reality.

Quick to identify solutions to problems, these people often pursue their goals with zest and enthusiasm, sometimes with fanatical zeal. This approach makes others sit up and take notice, but occasionally they haven't thought through their plans. Although their great communication skills easily win them supporters, when things don't run smoothly and others start to find fault, February 7 people can hide their disillusionment behind a wall of cynicism. They must understand that life is too complex to be seen in terms of right or wrong or quick-fix solutions. They need to learn to accept that there will always be viewpoints differing from their own and that there are many paths—not one—to the greater good. Around the age of forty-three there is a significant turning point which helps them fine-tune their relationship skills and become more open minded.

People born on this day like nothing better than to help others; one thing they will not accommodate, however, is authority. They have little patience for enforced conformity and if forced into a corner they may resort to subversive or disruptive behavior. As well as a rebellious streak they also have great determination; once they can find an outlet for their self-expression and fully commit to it, these modern-day prophets really can make the world a better and fairer place.

Love *High expectations*

The high expectations that people born on February 7 have can be quite daunting for potential partners. They are more than likely to live up to them themselves but if others are unable to do the same they can become bitter. It is important for them to allow their partner to have their own ideals rather than imposing theirs on them, and to be clear about what is real and what is fantasy.

Health *Stress-proofing techniques*

People born on this day tend to take care of their health and to eat healthily and exercise regularly, but they do need to make sure that they don't develop unhealthy eating patterns when under stress. Mind–body therapies such as yoga, tai chi and physical therapies such as massage or even thumping a punch bag should help them unwind when the going gets tough. If stress is a constant part of their life they might want to try burning a chamomile-, lavender-, or sandalwood-scented candle. These, like wearing, meditating on and surrounding themselves with the colors blue or green, produce a calming effect.

Career *Born storytellers*

These people have the ability to present their thoughts in a compelling way and can make excellent writers or storytellers as well as actors, journalists, politicians, teachers, and lecturers. It is best for them to avoid routine office work, and careers that offer plenty of variety, travel and challenge will appeal. Self-starters they may also find fulfillment working for themselves or they could use their analytical ability in the world of science or research. Finally, humanitarian and social causes as well as the world of conventional or alternative health care will almost certainly appeal, if not as a career than as a passionate outside interest.

Destiny *To lead the way to social reform*

The life path of people born on this day is to learn to accept that not everyone will agree with them all of the time. When they can be tolerant of divergent viewpoints, their destiny is to persuade rather than dictate to others the need for social reform.

Signs & symbols

Sun sign: Aquarius

Ruling planet: Uranus, the visionary

Symbol: The Water Carrier

Birth date ruler: Neptune, the speculator

Tarot card: The Chariot (resilience)

Favorable numbers: 7, 9

Lucky days: Saturday and Monday, especially when these days fall on 7 and 9 of the month

Lucky colors: All shades of blue and purple

Birthstone: Amethyst

February 7

8 February

the birthday of the hypnotist

People born on February 8 may not necessarily be able to see into the future but they have the ability to shape it with their thoughts and words. They have an intuitive understanding of people and situations, and are often able to spot future trends and then point everybody in that direction.

The hypnotic power that they possess gives them tremendous influence over the people and situations in which they find themselves. This influence often astounds those who may have made more obvious efforts to move things forward and who may have dismissed them as dreamers.

Perhaps because they are aware of their influence over and responsibility toward others, those born on this day can come across as grave or serious. They can tolerate but don't really enjoy chit-chat and much prefer to get their teeth into life's problems. As a result they often find themselves the treasured confidant of friends and loved ones. On the downside, in personal relationships there is both a passive side to them, as well as a shadow side that draws them toward people who aren't good for them. Fortunately, although there are opportunities earlier, in their early forties there is a significant turning point which can help them become more self-aware and assertive.

The profound sensitivity and intuitive powers of these people mean that they can effortlessly tune into the moods of others. They also run the risk of over-identifying with another person's problems and can easily fall into the worry trap, although few people will notice as they tend to conceal their true feelings to avoid being hurt. It is important for them to learn where other people end and they begin.

When people born on this day find a project that captures their interest they have all the drive and determination they need to succeed; procrastination will become a thing of the past. They can think on a grand scale, and once they learn how to project success they may well find that their bright ideas lead to great progress and reform.

Love *Learn to let one person in*

People born on February 8 may find it hard to give their all in a relationship as they can often be preoccupied with their thoughts and with the problems of others. Their partner may feel as if they are being excluded since these people can tend to live in a world of their own ideas. Once they find a partner who can nurture them as much as they nurture others, they can become an extremely loyal, loving and happy partner.

Health *Avoid self-destructive behavior*

People born on this day can sometimes take an irresponsible approach to their health; indulging in too much rich food, partying and sensual pleasures. They may also be a little lazy and should learn that too much sleep can be as bad for their health as too little. They also need to learn that too much pleasure and not enough responsibility can lead them toward weight problems, drug problems and infections. A healthy, balanced diet and plenty of exercise along with meditation to help them become aware of their self-destructive tendencies are highly recommended. Wearing, meditating or surrounding themselves with the color green and listening to upbeat music will help bring calm, chasing worries and anxieties away.

Career *Born psychics*

These people may not become psychics but they will have great intuitive powers to put to use in their chosen career, although they tend to thrive best in careers where they are allowed a lot of freedom. Their ability to see the bigger picture and project ahead makes them excellent designers, property developers, stock market traders, and architects. They may also be intellectuals, planners, or weather forecasters. Their empathy and communication skills may draw them toward careers in education, advertising, the media, or even the arts, where they can excel in writing, acting, and music.

Destiny *To bring greater harmony and understanding to the world*

The life path of people born on this day is to learn to set clear boundaries between themselves and others. Once they understand the impact they have on others and the impact others have on them their destiny is to bring greater harmony and understanding to the world.

Power Thought

" The universe runs through me, giving me direction "

Signs & symbols

Sun sign: Aquarius

Ruling planet: Uranus, the visionary

Symbol: The Water Carrier

Birth date ruler: Saturn, the teacher

Tarot card: Strength (passion)

Favorable numbers: 1, 8,

Lucky day: Saturday, especially when it falls on 1 or 8 of the month

Lucky colors: Dark blue, dark green, crocus

Birthstone: Amethyst

9 February

the birthday of the winning attitude

Your greatest challenge is ...

learning not to beat yourself up for some perceived weakness

The way forward is ...

when you do mess up to talk to yourself as though you were a small child; be positive, supportive and gentle.

You're drawn to people born on ...

March 21 to April 20

You share a passion for intensity and the unconventional, and this creates an exciting match.

Luck maker

Keep your cool

Keeping your cool creates luck because others will respect you, meaning you are less likely to have enemies; lucky people, by definition, have few enemies.

People born on February 9 are independent and generous individuals with their own unique and at times non-conformist perspective on life. They are shrewd observers of human nature and capable of enormous understanding of others' problems. Above all, though, they are fighters; life may have given them a few knocks but they have managed to bounce back with resilience, and this winning attitude can lead them to great achievements.

The remarkable ability of people born on this day to understand people and situations, even those they have not met themselves, makes them much sought after for advice and support. They make great teachers and leaders, and they influence and inspire not so much by technique but by example, showing others through their own actions how to rise above challenges with a winning attitude.

Yet when it comes to applying that same penetrating insight to their own lives and relationships they tend to be overly critical, measuring themselves by an impossibly high ideal. It is important for them to learn to be as tolerant and supportive of themselves as they are of others. Before the age of forty the needs and approval of others tend to be dominant but at the age of forty there is a turning point which places a greater emphasis on self-awareness and acceptance, as well as a need to take the initiative in all areas of their lives, possibly with a new relationship or venture.

The strong presence of people born on this day can sometimes make people think of them as aggressive, but behind this they possess a soft side that takes rejection and criticism to heart. They also have a tendency to act rashly; they need to remain calm under pressure and not allow their good will to be exploited. Once they are able to regard themselves more positively—and to be less harsh in their self-criticism—they will be able to achieve the high goals they set themselves, in the process becoming an inspirational model to everyone lucky enough to wander across their path.

At your best

Powerful, generous, resilient

Love *In for the long haul*

People born on February 9 have the charisma to attract people from all walks of life, but they feel happiest with someone whose intelligence matches their own. In a relationship, they are loyal and passionate partners with a clear idea of where the relationship should be heading. They don't give up easily on a relationship if it starts to flounder, because they believe that with the right attitude almost any kind of problem can be ironed out.

Health *Time for you*

People born on this day are often blessed with boundless energy so, unless they give in to cravings for comfort food or don't take enough care of themselves, they are unlikely to have problems with their weight. If they do have weight problems it is because they have been neglecting themselves or have dipped into depression or anxiety. It is important for them to eat little and often, and to make sure they stay away from too much alcohol and mood-altering drugs. A regular exercise routine is also recommended to keep their metabolism high. They would also benefit from breathing exercises and meditation, and if they are feeling low or uptight a few drops of jasmine essential oil on a handkerchief to breathe in will help them see the sunnier side.

Career *Born mentors*

These people are natural mentors and messengers and they make great teachers, advisors, counselors, consultants, therapists, and psychologists. Their multi-talented personality may, however, lead them into many different careers and in many cases they will have more than one career. Science and social reform will allow them freedom and growth but other possible career choices include the arts, theater, design, property development, and technology. They also thrive in careers that involve travel and change, and may be drawn toward careers in aviation, navigation, and international business.

Destiny *To inspire others to worthwhile causes*

The life path of people born on this day is to be less self-critical. When they can learn to be more positive about themselves, their destiny is to lead and inspire others with their positive attitude, devoting their energies to a worthy cause.

Power Thought

"I will always seek the possible, not the obligatory"

Signs & symbols

Sun sign: Aquarius

Ruling planet: Uranus, the visionary

Symbol: The Water Carrier

Birth date ruler: Mars, the warrior

Tarot card: The Hermit (inner strength)

Favorable numbers: 2, 9

Lucky days: Saturday and Tuesday, especially when these days fall on 2 and 9 of the month

Lucky colors: Turquoise, red, mauve

Birthstone: Amethyst

10 February

the birthday of achievement

Your greatest challenge is ...

to learn to give others a chance

The way forward is ...

to understand that giving others a chance to prove themselves is an important part of their psychological development.

You're drawn to people born on ...

July 24 to August 23

If you can learn to fulfill your mutual need for admiration and closeness, this can be an extraordinarily intense union.

Luck maker

Quiet down and slow down

Just 10 or 15 minutes of quiet time a day can make quite a difference in connecting with your intuitive or luck-making power.

People born on February 10 have a clear picture of what they want to achieve and how they want to get there. The pursuit of their goals is likely to take precedence over anything else. Achievement matters greatly to them, as do the approval and recognition of others. Their clear-sighted recognition of their aspirations, along with their ability to concentrate, means that they are more than likely to surpass their professional goals.

Once they settle on a chosen course, the drive these people are blessed with can take them right to the top. They do need, however, to be careful that they don't thereby become obsessive. It is important for them to look deep within to identify and hold onto the real motivation for their determination. They may well find that it is not material success but rather making their mark on the world and winning the approval of others.

Although the ambition and drive of people born on this day is explosive, it never leads them to stab others in the back. Intuitive, honest and decent, their ideal is to achieve success in the right way without harming or hurting others in the process. Unfortunately, though, there are people they are capable of hurting without realizing it; these are the people closest to them whom they tend to neglect when their goals take precedence over everything and everyone else. If they aren't careful, this can leave them emotionally isolated and, in extreme cases, alone. Fortunately, between the ages of twenty and thirty-nine there are many opportunities for them to open their hearts and turn the spotlight from themselves onto others. At forty there is a turning point where they feel the need to be more assertive but at the same time more passionate in their relationships with other people.

As long as people born on this day remember that admiration is no substitute for affection, and can learn from any setbacks they experience, their considerable achievements will earn them both personal fulfillment and a large number of fans.

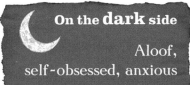

On the **dark** side
Aloof, self-obsessed, anxious

At your **best**

Positive, creative, bold

Power Thought
66 Today I will notice what is going on around me as well as in me 99

Love *Heartbreakers*

People born on February 10 have a charismatic charm which draws others to them. When it comes to affairs of the heart, they are very good at knowing how to win someone else's heart but they can have problems keeping it. It is important for them not to neglect those closest to them as the loving support of a partner gives them the kind of security and sense of perspective they need to be truly successful.

Health *Honor life's reflective moments*

Because people born on this day tend to be so driven they are often prone to disorders associated with stress and anxiety, especially if there are problems at work or their career path has been thwarted in some way. Insomnia may be a particular concern and it is important for them to make sure that there is a clear divide between home and work. Home should be a calm, restful place; they would also benefit from plenty of exercise in the fresh air, as well as hobbies, interests and a wide mix of friendships outside the workplace. Wearing, meditating on or surrounding themselves with the color purple will help them calm down and honor the simple pleasures and reflective moments in their life.

Career *Born workers*

These people have the drive, ambition and determination to succeed in almost any career that they choose. They could be a lawyer, actor, agent, politician, civil servant, charity worker, entrepreneur, sportsperson, artist, researcher, photographer, pilot, or director. In fact it might be better for them, as they have a tendency to tunnel vision, to have not one but several careers in their lifetime.

Destiny *To be recognized for their dedication and integrity*

The life path of people born on this day is to learn to look outside themselves to reach out to others, as well as inside themselves to understand their true motivation. Once they are able to unite both the external and the internal their destiny is to attract recognition for their hard work, dedication and integrity.

Signs & symbols

Sun sign: Aquarius

Ruling planet: Uranus, the visionary

Symbol: The Water Carrier

Birth date ruler: Sun, the individual

Tarot card: The Wheel of Fortune (change)

Favorable numbers: 1, 3

Lucky days: Saturday and Sunday, especially when these days fall on 1, 3 and 10 of the month

Lucky colors: Dark blue, orange, purple

Birthstone: Amethyst

February 10

11 February

the birthday of the upgrader

People born on February 11 feel they were sent to this world for one purpose only; to improve the lives of those around them. In their minds, both people and things are always in need of improvement or an upgrade. They often have an earnest quality about them, and an energy and drive that makes others want to learn from them. They also have a talent for invention and enjoy finding new ways to make life easier for others around them. They do this not for material benefit or even recognition but because they believe that the less stress and discomfort people have, the more they can devote themselves to more meaningful and spiritual pursuits.

Although they prefer to motivate by example rather than words, people born on this day have a knack for making others feel good about themselves. Their curious and inventive mind means they have a great need for intellectual stimulation; their current absorption in a project or social group should not, however, make them neglect close personal relationships. Thinking of themselves as improvers and educators, they should understand that not everyone appreciates or wants their help. Some people like to work out for themselves what will make their life easier and they may get resentful if another person tries to point things out, especially if they do so in a blunt manner. It is important for people born on this day to develop their intuition and sensitivity toward others. Fortunately, between the ages of nineteen and thirty-eight there is an emphasis on emotional sensitivity; but after the age of thirty-nine directness toward others takes center stage and it is more important than ever that they learn to channel this directness positively and sensitively.

With their inventive mind and sharp insight into what a situation or a person needs, there is little doubt that people born on this day (as long as they can master the art of diplomacy) will make a mark on the world by helping and educating others.

84

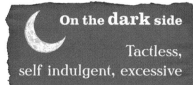

On the **dark** side
Tactless, self indulgent, excessive

At your **best**
Progressive, inventive, knowing

Love *Loyalty and trust*

People born on February 11 value their personal freedom and need space to breathe in a relationship but they are also firm believers in loyalty and trust. They are easygoing and entertaining and their need for intellectual stimulation will often lead them toward unorthodox or unusual individuals. People born on this day love tenderly and passionately and will use their strong will to help and support those they love.

Health *The high life*

People born on this day often find it tough to understand why people don't agree with their point of view; this can cause them considerable psychological stress. The support of partner, family and friends will help them work through this problem but they may also benefit from counseling. There is also a danger that their love for the high life can lead to weight problems and sexual adventures that can be damaging to their health. Although they may find a healthy diet and regular exercise routine difficult to maintain, they need to understand the strong links between mental, emotional and physical health. Meditating on an amethyst crystal or wearing or surrounding themselves with the color violet will help keep their mood balanced and their step lively.

Career *Born inventors*

These people are attracted toward any career that involves education, or personal and social development. They are inventive and progressive, making great inventors, computer programmers, and architects. In business, employers will appreciate their willingness to embrace new ideas and they also work well as advisors, specialists, or freelancers. Alternatively, they may devote themselves to charity work, or psychology, philosophy, or spirituality where they can make a difference to people's lives.

Destiny *To break new ground and experiment*

The life path of people born on this day is to understand that everyone—including themselves—needs to mess up now and again as it is an important part of the human experience. Once they have learned to become less critical of themselves and others, their destiny is to break new ground and experiment with original concepts.

Power Thought
" I am aware that what I do not want to change is what I need to change "

Signs & symbols

Sun sign: Aquarius

Ruling planet: Uranus, the visionary

Symbol: The Water Carrier

Birth date ruler: Moon, the intuitive

Tarot card: Justice (discernment)

Favorable numbers: 2, 4

Lucky days: Saturday and Monday, especially when these days fall on 2 or 4 of the month

Lucky colors: Dark blue, silvery white, violet

Birthstone: Amethyst

12 February

the birthday of the bold integrator

Your greatest challenge is ...

to focus your energy on one project alone

The way forward is ...

to understand that developing concentration is essential to anyone who aspires to take charge of their lives. An essential skill for success, its absence means our efforts get scattered.

You're drawn to people born on ...

November 23 to December 21

Both fun-loving and focused on achievement, the two of you love to communicate, creating an intense and loving bond.

Luck maker

Learn to meditate

Meditation is a luck maker because it not only helps ease stress, it also helps you learn to direct and focus your thoughts so that they can attract success your way.

Those born on February 12 have a talent for integration; they have the ability to marshal all the available information, evaluate opposing viewpoints and then bring everything and everyone together in a united front. Nothing matters more to them than the status quo and if need be they will boldly and courageously defend it. This makes them highly valued in both their professional and their personal lives.

People born on this day like to see themselves in the role of peacekeeper, pointing others in the right direction; that direction is, of course, the one they believe to be correct. This isn't to say that they are stubborn and inflexible, but they possess the tendency to ignore what others think and to believe that the best course of action is always their own. It is important for them to recognize the importance of consensus and to understand that although their ability to see and evaluate the bigger picture more than qualifies them to take the lead, great leadership is not about dictatorship but about motivating others in the direction you want them to go.

As well as being able to unite others and see the way forward with single-minded tenacity, people born on this day have a host of other talents, including confidence, originality and creativity. They do need to be careful that their talents don't cause them to squander their energies in many different directions. Until their late thirties there are opportunities for them to develop greater self-awareness, but in their forties and beyond there is a focus on personal integration and purpose; in many ways, this is when these people really come into their own.

People with a February 12 birthday have strong convictions and a progressive instinct, both of which have been developed through their powers of original thought, and high moral and ethical standards. They have the courage and charisma to lead and inspire others, and more often than not others will find them living out their mission to make the world a better and more peaceful place.

Love *Fun loving*

Although people born on February 12 have no trouble falling in love, they do need to be careful that their work and goals do not eclipse their relationships or that they take them for granted. They prefer to get involved with people who are mentally stimulating and who are interested in self-improvement, as well as having a good time. Their detached exterior can make it hard for them to open up but once they are able to do that they are sensitive, loyal and (when they aren't working too hard) fun-loving partners.

Health *Health before habit*

People born on this day are often creatures of routine when it comes to their health, diet and exercise, and although this means they are generally in good health the downside is that experimenting a little can give them more energy and more fun. It is important for them to try out a wide variety of nutritious foods rather than sticking with old-time favorites and to experiment with different types of exercise instead of sticking with one. When they are feeling stressed or anxious instead of alcohol or chocolate they should try a warm bath with a few drops of their favorite aromatherapy essential oil to soothe frayed nerves. They would also benefit from meditation and breathing techniques to focus their energy and thoughts.

Career *Born politicians*

These people may well consider politics or social reform as their chosen career. Whatever they choose, they are bound to become the head of something along the way, perhaps the principal of a school or a group leader. Their good people skills and business sense may also draw them toward management careers. Other career choices that might work include counseling, publishing, advertising, accountancy, science, or invention. Anthropology and archaeology, as well as careers in writing or the arts, may also appeal.

Destiny *To create harmony in all environments*

The life path of people born on this day is to learn to beware of their tendency to dismiss viewpoints differing from their own. Once they have learned to be more open-minded, their destiny is to create harmony in any environment in which they find themselves.

Power Thought

" The equilibrium of my mind is mirrored in my life "

Signs & symbols

Sun sign: Aquarius

Ruling planet: Uranus, the visionary

Symbol: The Water Carrier

Birth date ruler: Jupiter, the philosopher

Tarot card: The Hanged Man (reflection)

Favorable numbers: 3, 5

Lucky days: Saturday and Thursday, especially when these days fall on 3 and 5 of the month

Lucky colors: Dark blue, light purple, pink

Birthstone: Amethyst

13 February

the birthday of the enigmatic extrovert

Those born on February 13 are difficult to ignore. They are open and uninhibited in almost all that they undertake and bursting with energy, originality and fun. Often regarded as trendsetters, they are at their best when performing to an audience.

People born on this day have a unique approach to life, and their ideas and plans have the potential to make them a fortune. Because they are rebellious and more than a little wild, they will almost certainly encounter criticism and rejection in their life, in particular their teens and early twenties. It is important for them to hold fast to their individuality and to resist the urge to fit in. They just need to find the right path and the right goals to devote their considerable energy to—and the right people to encourage them to be themselves—and their success is assured.

Exuberant, original and daring, these people see a world of possibilities and potential around them. Sometimes in their enthusiasm to move forward they can come across as bossy or eccentric; they do need to learn to slow down and look before they leap. They are often guilty of following their hearts before their heads and this can also get them into trouble, leading them to hurt other people in the process. After the age of thirty-seven there is a turning point, suggesting that they will become more aggressive and focused in pursuit of their goals. It is more important than ever for them to learn to center themselves and find a sense of inner security.

February 13 people have a flair for the dramatic and although their uninhibited nature relishes being the center of attention, there are certain aspects of themselves that they keep strictly private. This gives them a fascinating enigmatic quality and complexity that only serves to intrigue and delight their audience even more. Once they are able to control rather than repress their exuberant spontaneity, these elusive but extrovert individuals can often be found entertaining, educating and intriguing their adoring fans.

Love *In and out of love*

The address book of people born on February 13 is often packed with friends and admirers, but they may find it difficult to let one person get close to them. Falling in and out of love a lot, they may find it hard to stick to relationships as they enjoy their freedom too much. But when they do find the right person it often tends to be an elusive and dramatic individual like themselves; when this happens, their love is for keeps.

Health *Not so fast*

People born on this day have a tendency to take risks with their body and their health, being prone to accidents and injuries, particularly in their legs and ankles. They need to learn to take things a little more steadily and to remain calm in difficult situations. They would benefit enormously from mind–body exercises such as yoga, tai chi and meditation techniques. When it comes to diet they also need to make sure that they avoid rich food and excessive amounts of alcohol, red meat and dairy. Moderate to mild physical exercise is preferable to vigorous exercise. Wearing, meditating on or surrounding themselves with shades of blue and green will help them handle challenges with calmness, objectivity and optimism.

Career *Born entertainers*

These people have a love for variety, adventure and acclaim, together with the versatility to handle sudden changes, so they are ideally suited to the world of entertainment. Other careers that might appeal include astronomy, meteorology, aviation, scientific research, and education. Their ability to charismatically lead campaigns could also draw them toward politics and social reform, or setting up their own business.

Destiny *To encourage others to express themselves*

The life path of people born on this day is to learn to follow both their heart and their head. Once they have learned a measure of self-control, their destiny is to express themselves and by so doing to influence and inspire others.

Power Thought

"Today is my bridge to greater self-knowledge and joy"

Signs & symbols

Sun sign: Aquarius

Ruling planet: Uranus, the visionary

Symbol: The Water Carrier

Birth date ruler: Jupiter, the philosopher

Tarot card: Death (change)

Favorable numbers: 4, 6

Lucky days: Saturday and Sunday, especially when these days fall on 4 or 6 of the month

Lucky colors: All shades of blue, silver and light green

Birthstone: Amethyst

February 13

14 February

the birthday of the vulnerable wit

Your greatest challenge is ...

to keep confidential information to yourself

The way forward is ...

to understand that the trust and respect of others are far more rewarding than the short-lived thrill of being the center of attention.

You're drawn to people born on ...

May 22 to June 21

You both have piercing insight and if you remain honest with each other this can create an intense and fulfilling union.

Luck maker

Don't have enemies

Lucky people regard everyone they meet as potential luck makers. You never know who could eventually be of help. There should always be time for politeness, sensitivity, decency, tact, and trust.

Charming, intelligent and warm-hearted, people born on February 14 are shrewd observers of human foibles. They think quickly and analytically, tending to express themselves succinctly in great one-liners.

The incisive wit of these people can work both for and against them. Their biting sense of humor can make them wonderful and entertaining company, and formidable allies in the workplace, but they can also be blunt to the point of sarcasm, driving others away with deeply wounding comments. Their sarcasm tends to surface most when they feel impatient or frustrated because others aren't attending to their demands. And because other people tend to reveal personal information to them, they need to be careful that they don't become gossips.

Jovial banter can be a way for people born on this day to camouflage their true emotions. They are typically the first to cry when a sad song is being played or to feel heartbreaking empathy with those in the world who are suffering misfortune. This vulnerability can often surprise those around them as they often expect someone with such a cool and incisive wit to be emotionally stronger.

Those born on this day should apply some of their penetrating insight to themselves as well as others, and understand that their emotions bubble quickly to the surface because they have an important message to deliver. They should listen to that message because the strong reactions they have to the misfortunes of others are often a sign of their own repressed emotion searching for an outlet. Fortunately, around the age of thirty-six there is a turning point, emphasizing that they should become more self-aware and assertive regarding their own emotions.

A lamb in wolf's clothing, people born on February 14 may appear tough but they don't take themselves too seriously. This isn't to say they are superficial; there is great emotional depth behind their banter. It simply means they are great company to keep because, whenever they are around, life always seems easier, lighter and much, much happier.

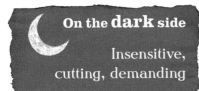

On the dark side

Insensitive, cutting, demanding

At your best

Witty, astute, engaging

Love *Mischievous flirt*

Not surprisingly, people born on February 14 have the ability to seduce others with humor and their live-for-the-moment approach to life. They will probably have quite a few relationships before they finally settle down with someone who can rise to their verbal challenges but who can also offer them loyalty, honesty and loving security.

Health *See green*

People born on this day may give the appearance of being cool and in control of their lives but they can often become stressed because they are repressing their insecurities behind a tough exterior. It is important for them to find ways to work through their insecurities, such as exercise and chats with friends and loved ones, and to find ways to calm their mind. Breathing exercises and meditation are recommended to help them to do this. It goes without saying that they should make sure they eat a healthy diet and get plenty of exercise. They should also make sure they stay away from too much alcohol and nicotine. If they try to maintain their relaxed image by taking mind-altering drugs, they may become susceptible to addictive substances. Meditating on, wearing or surrounding themselves with the color pale green will help them manage their emotions.

Career *Born talk-show host*

These people make ideal interviewers, magazine editors, radio and TV hosts, or networkers in large organizations. Alternatively banking, insurance or the stock market may appeal, as might writing, publishing or the entertainment world. Their ability to empathize with the suffering of others may also draw them toward social reform, humanitarian work or work in education. In business, whether self-employed or working for others, they will use their verbal skills and personality to promote themselves, sometimes to the very top.

Destiny *To use words to inspire others*

The life path of people born on this day is to learn to use their excellent communication skills positively rather than negatively. Once they understand this, their destiny is to influence and inspire those around them with the power of their words.

Signs & symbols

Sun sign: Aquarius

Ruling planet: Uranus, the visionary

Symbol: The Water Carrier

Birth date ruler: Mercury, the communicator

Tarot card: Temperance (moderation)

Favorable numbers: 5, 7

Lucky days: Saturday and Wednesday, especially when these days fall on 5 and 7 of the month

Lucky colors: Blue, green

Birthstone: Amethyst

15 February

the birthday of
the enterprising adventurer

People born on February 15 are full of vitality, adventure and fun. They like to walk on the wild side of life, and have great enthusiasm and ingenuity, especially when it comes to exploring novel things. When faced with a challenge, it is impossible for them to sit on the sidelines; they have to jump in and offer a solution—their solution.

The charming, energetic people born on this day have the ability to master skills quickly, using their enterprise and ingenuity to raise a skill, craft or project to undreamed-of heights. They like to live life in the fast lane and have no intention of slowing or calming down. Although this approach means they are often a powerful force to be reckoned with, it can also mean that they sometimes find it hard to know when to stop.

Those born on February 15 value their intellectual freedom above all else and they like to experience or investigate just about anything. This can lead, however, to burnout or information overload; when this happens, they may come across as chaotic or irresponsible rebels without a cause. Their moods may also swing from high to low for no reason; this is a result of living in too heightened a state. It is important for these people to understand that sometimes discipline and limits have great value. Fortunately, they tend to grow more self-disciplined when they are older; around the age of thirty-five they can become extremely assertive, so they should channel that dynamic energy positively rather than negatively.

As long as they learn the importance of self-discipline and goal setting—and others allow them to explore the wonders of the world—these multi-talented individuals have the potential to realize their original and intelligent dreams. They may have an alarming wild streak that often lands them in trouble but they are genuinely motivated by a desire to make the world a happier and more exciting place. With them around, life can be many things but it is never dull.

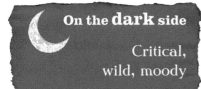
Love *Sticky situations*

People born on February 15 love adventure and variety in their relationships and they are more than likely to have numerous sexual partners, sometimes at the same time. This can get them into all sorts of sticky situations. Those born on this day who are more self-disciplined have it within them to commit to one person, as long as that person is as willing to experiment and to have fun as they are.

Health *Spontaneity*

People born on this day are prone to mood swings, so it is important for them to learn coping techniques to deal with their emotions. They would almost certainly benefit from mind–body therapies such as meditation, yoga and tai chi, as these would help them slow down and calm down. As far as diet is concerned, they need to watch out for food allergies and insensitivities; vigorous exercise, preferably outdoors, will help work off some of that manic energy. Wearing, meditating on or surrounding themselves with the color blue will help stabilize their mood, bringing calmness and a sense of promise.

Career *Born mountain climbers*

These people have many talents and are capable of success in many careers, but their wild physicality will attract them to careers in extreme sports, mountaineering, dancing, skating, aviation, space travel, nature trekking, and stunt work. On the safer side, they may be drawn to careers in teaching, writing (especially science fiction and fantasy), art, and psychology. As a nature lover, they may also be drawn to work in conservation, farming or with animals.

Destiny *To encourage others to a life of adventure*

The life path of people born on this day is to learn self-discipline without it crushing their wonderful spontaneity. Once they have been able to do that, their destiny is to encourage others by their own example to have a more adventurous and open-minded spirit.

Power Thought

❝ The harmony and balance in my mind is reflected in my life ❞

Signs & symbols

Sun sign: Aquarius

Ruling planet: Uranus, the visionary

Symbol: The Water Carrier

Birth date ruler: Venus, the lover

Tarot card: The Devil (instinct)

Favorable numbers: 6, 8

Lucky days: Saturday and Friday, especially when these days fall on 6 and 8 of the month

Lucky colors: Sapphire blue, pink

Birthstone: Amethyst

February 15

16 February

the birthday of the alchemist

Your greatest challenge is …

to resist being a know-all

The way forward is …

to understand that just as you have learned from your mistakes, sometimes other people need to learn from theirs.

You're drawn to people born on …

February 20 to March 20

This relationship is powerful and passionate because you both have an intuitive understanding of what the other needs.

Luck maker

Send your inner critic on holiday

Every time you hear your inner critic, visualize it resting in a deckchair on a sunny beach. The more you send your inner critic on holiday, the more you start to love and value yourself.

People born on February 16 have the ability to transform even the most difficult of experiences into something positive. There is a touch of the alchemist about them in their ability to see the bigger picture, bring together all the relevant information and cut right to the essence or truth of a situation.

It is likely that people born on this day have at some point in their lives experienced some form of upheaval, trauma or setback. Whatever the nature of this was, they have taken it in their stride, learned from it and grown stronger. The positive side is that it has given them great confidence; even if they sometimes appear quiet on the outside, underneath one can sense an inner strength and brightness. They also have an astute understanding of others and how the world works; rarely, if ever, do they miss a trick. The downside is that they can sometimes appear cold and detached, and their bluntness or impatience with the weaknesses of others may come across as arrogance. Others may at times resent the imperious manner that these people possess, but more often than not people end up admiring their cleverness and ability to know exactly what to say, what to do and how to do it.

If they can learn to control their bossiness, their tremendous capacity to be realistic and intuitive, both in their assessment of others and their own abilities, makes them potentially great leaders. Around the age of thirty-four there is a turning point when their ambition and focus take center stage. It is particularly important at this point in their life that they become more conscious of their emotions, rather than masking them with a bossy or imperious manner or, in some cases, with emotional reserve and detachment.

When people born on this day are able to strike a balance between their inner and outer life, they really are capable of striking gold both personally and professionally, which is after all every true alchemist's dream.

At your **best**
Realistic, intuitive, confidence

Love *Let past hurts go*

People born on February 16 need to move on from past hurts, disappointments or experiences that may have made them wary of falling in love. They need to learn to trust their hearts more, because in their hearts they still do believe in the possibility of love even if their heads don't. They also need to start believing that they deserve to be loved, because they certainly do.

Health *One tough cookie*

People born on this day are mentally and physically tough but they can sometimes push themselves too hard and this can lead to stress-related conditions such as headaches and insomnia. It is important for them to make sure they have regular health reviews. It is also important for them to eat an energy-boosting diet with plenty of nutritious meals and snacks, and make sure they keep fairly active during the day as they thrive best when they are on the go. Lazing about doesn't suit them, although they do need to make sure they get plenty of rest and relaxation. They would benefit considerably from meditation and breathing exercises to help them strike that important balance between their inner and outer life.

Career *Born reviewers*

These people have a fantastic eye for detail and an ability to see the bigger picture; this makes them fantastic editors, journalists, reviewers, film critics, lecturers, or teachers. Alternatively, they may be drawn toward a career in business, banking and the stock market or careers in which they can express their intuitive creativity such as art, entertainment, charity work, and social reform.

Destiny *To help others see the positive in life*

The life path of people born on this day is to learn to accept that they deserve all the love and goodness the world can give them. Once they have worked on their self-esteem, their destiny is to help others focus on the positives in a situation or experience.

Signs & symbols

Sun sign: Aquarius

Ruling planet: Uranus, the visionary

Symbol: The Water Carrier

Birth date ruler: Neptune, the speculator

Tarot card: The Tower (breakthrough)

Favorable numbers: 7, 8

Lucky days: Saturday and Monday, especially when these days fall on 7 and 8 of the month

Lucky colors: All shades of blue, lavender

Birthstone: Amethyst

February 16

17 February

the birthday of self discipline

People born on February 17 often figure out early in their life that the key to success in life is discipline. They are determined, ambitious people with a clear idea of where they want to go and what they need to do to get there. These qualities, combined with their remarkable self-discipline, can give them the appearance of invincibility.

Although they may appear superhuman and extraordinary, others generally warm instantly to them, respecting their honesty and ability to be true to themselves and their beliefs. Underneath their tough exterior they really are sensitive souls who can be profoundly hurt by the careless words or actions of others. In fact, neglect or criticism may have been a feature of their early life, leading them to the realization that if they are to survive in the world they need to develop a tough exterior. Occasionally, they can make their defenses so strong that others find it impossible to break through. When this happens, they run the risk of becoming emotionally detached and inflexible in their approach to others.

People born on this day have a tunnel-vision approach to their goals and objectives, giving them the potential to rise to the top. They are the athletes who train relentlessly, the entrepreneurs who sacrifice everything for their shot at success, the artists or scientists who devote their lives to their art or research. The downside, however, is that anything that hinders their quest for fulfillment will be ignored; all too often this is personal relationships. They should make sure that their emotional happiness does not take a backseat to their professional, especially after the age of thirty-three when they often become even more determined and aggressive in their approach to life.

The incredible endurance, intelligence and stamina of people born on this day mean they are able to achieve a level of self-mastery and resulting satisfaction to which others can only aspire. Once they figure out what they are best at, there is nothing that can stop them achieving remarkable things with their life.

At your best

Disciplined, determined, appealing

Love *Cool and controlled*

People born on February 17 can be distant and inflexible in close personal relationships. If they are to have a chance of success and happiness in relationships they need to address this. Although they have no problem attracting admirers, they do find it hard to open up to others. But once they find a partner who can encourage them to give as well as take, they are loyal, caring and endlessly fascinating partners.

Health *Athletes*

People born on this day push themselves hard in all areas of their life and the physical is no exception. Whether or not they are sportsmen or women, they tend to regard themselves as athletes in training and will often take great care of their physical health through attention to diet and exercise. Some people born on this day are sometimes guilty of pushing themselves so hard that their body can't take the strain. Others may be neglectful of their health when there are deadlines to consider, so moderation is just as important as self-discipline. They would benefit from a healthy diet low in saturated fats and sugar to reduce the risk of circulatory problems, and an exercise routine in which they can clearly monitor their improvement, such as weight-training. Wearing, meditating on or surrounding themselves with shades of green will help remind them of the importance of balance in their personal and professional lives.

Career *Born detectives*

These people love to unravel a mystery and can be drawn to careers in law or the police. They also have a talent for writing and self-expression and may be drawn to careers in journalism, writing or education. They also make great athletes, artists and scientists and, because they generally thrive in careers which demand great self-discipline and self-motivation, they may also be attracted to management, charity work, social reform, or self-employment.

Destiny *To inspire others with their vitality*

The life path of people born on this day is to learn to place as much importance on their personal happiness as the pursuit of their goals. Once they have learned a sense of balance, their destiny is to influence and inspire others with their considerable vitality and self-discipline.

Power Thought

66 Today I will look at life in a different way 99

Signs & symbols

Sun sign: Aquarius

Ruling planet: Uranus, the visionary

Symbol: The Water Carrier

Birth date ruler: Saturn, the teacher

Tarot card: The Star (hope)

Favorable numbers: 1, 8

Lucky day: Saturday, especially when it falls on 1 or 8 of the month

Lucky colors: Sky blue, maroon,

Birthstone: Amethyst

18 February

the birthday of the eternally young

Whatever their age, people born on February 18 never grow old in their minds and hearts. With a charismatic energy about them, they never fail to brighten up their surroundings with their infectious optimism and enthusiasm for new ideas and projects, however far-fetched and impossible.

Those who are born on this day are also courageous risk-takers. They will always be the first to volunteer or put themselves forward, loving nothing better than to live life on the edge. There is of course a danger with this reckless approach to life; it can lead them into serious trouble and on more than one occasion it will do just that. They are never happier than when they are pushing things one degree harder, higher or faster, but they do need to ask themselves why they feel the need to live like this. More often than not deep-seated fears and insecurities are hidden behind their mask of indestructibility.

With their youthful spirit and the endearing vulnerabilities that go with it, these people don't really understand that other people will be drawn to their sunny optimism. They may even find that others look to them for leadership but they aren't always happy in that role as it hinders their freedom to experience and explore the wonders of the world. Although their life does sparkle with variety and adventure, there is a price to pay. One day they may find themselves looking at their life and wondering why they haven't got a sense of real achievement. It is important for them to learn to focus their energies rather than scattering them; fortunately, after the age of thirty-two they become more assertive and self-disciplined in their daily affairs.

As long as people born on this day avoid looking in the wrong direction for a sense of risk and adventure, and understand that showing off isn't the most fulfilling or grown-up way to gain supporters, they have the potential to win the admiration and respect of others, and most important of all a sense of pride in themselves and their achievements.

At your best

Youthful, dynamic, charismatic

Love *Superstar*

People born on February 18 tend to have an immature approach to love, believing that showing off or being the center of attention is a way to win hearts. They need to learn that being calm and in control is a far more effective approach to relationships, as it puts other people naturally at ease. Once they do find a partner, one thing is assured: their partner will never be bored.

Health *Something's cooking*

The relentlessly upbeat and youthful approach to life that people born on this day are blessed with helps them keep illness and aging at bay. They don't grow old, they just get better or some might say crazier. The biggest risk to their health is their addiction to thrill seeking and they should avoid overindulgence in extreme sports, as well as addictive pastimes such as gambling, drinking and drug-taking. Knowing when to stop is an important lesson for them to learn in all aspects of their life, diet, exercise and general health included. Learning to cook properly would not only improve their diet, which tends to be irregular, but it would also be extremely therapeutic as it encourages them to slow down and think about what they are putting into their bodies. Wearing, meditating on or surrounding themselves with the color blue will help bring calmness and control into their lives.

Career *Born DJs*

These people need to have careers that give them plenty of freedom to express their original thoughts. Multitalented, they will therefore flourish in any career, provided they can follow their own path but may be particularly drawn to business, public relations, publishing, writing, journalism, the leisure industry, music, acting, and the world of entertainment.

Destiny *To motivate others with their enthusiasm*

The life path of people born on this day is to learn the importance of self-discipline. When they have learned a degree of calm, their destiny is to motivate others with their enthusiasm and crazy energy.

Signs & symbols

Sun sign: Aquarius

Ruling planet: Uranus, the visionary

Symbol: The Water Carrier

Birth date ruler: Mars, the warrior

Tarot card: The Moon (imagination)

Favorable numbers: 2, 9

Lucky days: Saturday and Tuesday, especially when these days fall on 2 and 9 of the month

Lucky colors: Sky blue, red, lilac

Birthstone: Amethyst

February 18

19 February

the birthday of
wonderlust

Your greatest challenge is ...

to finish what you started

The way forward is ...

to understand that your ability to share the load and finish what you started determines whether you will be labeled a leader or a loser.

You're drawn to people born on ...

July 24 to August 23

You share a passion for adventure and experimentation and this can create a bond with explosive potential.

Luck maker

Be a role model

Be a role model for your loved ones, children and friends. Do you want them to learn selfishness or compassion from you?

There is only one way for people born February 19 to do things and that is their way. They value their independence above all else and don't like to be ordered around, particularly by their parents. They want to find their own way in life, even if that means making mistakes along the way. As a result, they often have a lust for travel, thriving on new situations and new people.

With their independent spirit and need to stamp their individuality on everything they undertake, these people can often be found at the cutting edge of their chosen field. Although they perform best alone, they can also make inspirational leaders or enthusiastic team players; those who work alongside them will find themselves surprised by the strength of their whole-hearted commitment to success.

People born on this day quickly make a name for themselves wherever they go—and they tend to go to a lot of places. Their appetite for life and new situations is huge, and even when they appear to be settling down in a career or a relationship, their eye is always on the horizon, wondering what else might be out there for them. The danger with this inquisitive approach to life is that they might appear reckless at times or, at worst, selfish. They should learn that their go-it-alone approach to life can prevent them connecting with the needs of others. At around the age of thirty-one their ambition becomes more apparent and they may start new projects or pioneer new ideas. It is particularly important for them at this stage in life and beyond not to scatter their energies selfishly.

The life path of people born on this day will always be littered with opportunities because they have a knack of knowing where to find them. Along the way their fiercely individual approach to life may encounter setbacks or rejections; but they never let these disillusion them. In their mind and their life, the only way is their way and that way is always up.

At your **best**

Inspiring, wholehearted, independent

Love *Born to be worshiped*

Once people born on February 19 are able to balance their desire for independence and adventure with empathy for others, they have the potential to hypnotize everyone they meet with a wonderfully sexy mixture of vulnerability and excitement. Although it may take a while for them to find that special someone, they don't find it difficult to fall in love and people don't find it hard to fall in live with them. In fact, everybody loves them—children in particular—and they make great parents.

Health *Not all rules are made to be broken*

People born on this day will generally resist any attempt to have a diet or exercise regime imposed on them, preferring to go their own way. But they do need to understand that for their body to keep up with their free-spirited lifestyle it needs to be taken care of properly. It is particularly important for them to eat a healthy diet rich in energy-boosting nutrients and to make sure they stay hydrated with six to eight glasses of water a day, avoiding too much coffee to keep them alert. They should also make sure they get plenty of exercise so they remain fit for their high-octane lifestyle, but they do need to watch out for injuries to their legs, feet and ankles. As for everyone, regular rest and relaxation are important; if they have trouble sleeping, unwinding with a glass of chamomile herbal tea before bedtime may help.

Career *Born explorers*

These people may be drawn to social work or the caring professions but they also make outstanding environmental campaigners and gifted artists and performers. Other careers that might appeal include sales, promotion, design, acting, dancing, singing, and comedy as well as science, astronomy, philosophy and exploration.

Destiny *To move themselves and others forward*

The life path of people born on this day is to learn to take into account the needs and feelings of others in their quest for fulfillment. Once they have learned to develop greater empathy toward others, their destiny is to test the limits with their original thoughts and boundless energy and by so doing move themselves and everyone else one step forward.

Signs & symbols

Sun signs: Aquarius/Pisces

Ruling planets: Uranus, the visionary/Neptune, the speculator

Symbols: The Water Carrier/Two Fishes

Birth date ruler: Sun, the individual

Tarot card: The Sun (enthusiasm)

Favorable numbers: 1, 2

Lucky days: Saturday and Monday, especially when these days fall on 1 and 2 of the month

Lucky colors: Blue, orange, gold

Birthstone: Amethyst

February 19

20 February

the birthday of the perceptive charmer

Your greatest challenge is ...

learning to say no

The way forward is ...

to understand that only after you give to yourself can you give to others. If you neglect yourself, you can't be a real help to others.

You're drawn to people born on ...

June 22 to July 23

The two of you are highly sensitive and intuitive individuals, and this can create an exceptionally close and loving bond.

Luck maker

Treat yourself

Try to devote at least one day a week to something you really want: a book, a film, a haircut. Ensure it makes you feel good; the better you feel, the greater your chances of attracting luck.

People born on February 20 are often thoughtful and receptive personalities, with the ability to immediately tune into the moods of those around them, adjusting their reactions instantly. Highly ambitious, they are sure to stand out in their career, at home, or on the social scene. They have an appealing personality and an easy charm, but it's impossible to dismiss them as superficial because behind their looks and charm there is always great intelligence.

People with a February 20 birthday have a great deal of compassion, instinctively dealing with anyone—whatever their background or social status—with great understanding and warmth. In some cases they can become over-sensitive and impressionable, unable to separate their own emotions from the emotions of other people. This is because they identify so much with the viewpoint of others that they risk losing their own perspective in the process. It is vitally important for them to learn to protect themselves from over-identification. Before the age of thirty, this tendency to merge completely with other people is emphasized, but after the age of thirty they become more assertive, confident and self-protective.

There is a danger when people born on this day do become more aware and confident of their ability to instinctively relate to others that they can misuse it. It is important therefore for them to learn not to compromise themselves or take advantage of others in the single-minded pursuit of their goals.

Those people born on this day who remain true to their principles and who learn to make their receptivity work for and not against them have remarkable potential to make a difference and to be highly valued by others. They are rarely happy to sit on the sidelines and desperately want to make their mark; although they have all the drive, intelligence and charisma they need to climb right to the top, what they don't often realize is that simply being themselves already makes a huge difference; this is because when they are around, people just feel better about themselves.

Love *Little flower*

People born on February 20 can be extremely sensitive when it comes to affairs of the heart and they need to find a partner who understands this. Every detail is important to them and a missed phone call or a few misplaced words can send them into a downward spiral. When they do fall in love they make understanding and passionate lovers. There can be a tendency to put their lover on a pedestal and it is important for them to understand that everyone has faults.

Health *Learn to say no*

It is important for people born on this day to avoid become drained, anxious, stressed, depressed, or burned out because they are giving so much to others or taking on board the emotions of others. They should also find ways to avoid turning to drink, drugs and comfort eating as an escape, and would benefit considerably from substituting relaxation techniques such as meditation, natural remedies and herbal teas for those tranquillizers and copious amounts of alcohol. As well as moderate to vigorous exercise several times a week, plenty of sleep is also recommended for the sensitive people born on this day. Wearing, meditating on or surrounding themselves with the color yellow will build their self-confidence and encourage optimism.

Career *Born healers/givers*

The giving personality of people born on this day may draw them toward careers in medicine or entertainment, music or the arts where they can give to an audience. Being receptive and versatile, they tend to thrive in whatever career they choose but music, dancing, health and healing work, and all kinds of public relations roles have particular appeal.

Destiny *To inspire others by giving*

The life path of people born on this day is to learn to set boundaries. Once they have become more self-aware and assertive, their destiny is to inspire and influence others with their giving presence.

February 20

Signs & symbols

Sun signs: Pisces/Aquarius

Ruling planets: Neptune, the speculator/Saturn, the teacher

Symbols: Two Fishes/The Water Carrier

Birth date ruler: Moon, the intuitive

Tarot card: Judgment (responsibility)

Favorable numbers: 2, 4

Lucky days: Thursday and Monday, especially when those days fall on 2 or 4 of the month

Lucky colors: Sea green, silver, lavender

Birthstones: Amethyst and aquamarine

21 February

the birthday of the dominating presence

People born on February 21 have a creative, individual mind and a dominating presence. They feel most comfortable when taking the lead and least comfortable when required to follow. Their fierce independence may be a result of a tough childhood where rules, regulations or expectations often took precedence over real intimacy.

People born on this day may spend many years trying out various occupations or roles, often feeling that they don't quite fit in and occasionally reacting childishly as a form of rebellion. It is only when they understand that the key to their success is to be themselves and to lead and inspire others with their forceful presence that they truly come into their own. Fortunately, around the age of twenty-nine they tend to become more assertive and adventurous, and begin to enjoy greater self-awareness.

Although they may have developed a tough outer shell to protect them from the outside world, those who know them well will know that they can also be extremely sensitive, even shy. This sensitivity can in part explain their need to push themselves forward, as they may have suffered disappointments at the hands of others. It is important that they learn to be true to themselves—it is also important that they do not become too aggressive or cynical in the process, for their emotions lie at the center of their being and it is their sensitivity that can give them sudden flashes of inspiration.

People born on this day have great dreams, and once they learn to listen to their hearts as well as their heads and to respect the ideas of others there is little that can prevent them getting exactly what they want out of life. Wherever they go, others tend to regard them as a tower of strength and will often look to them for motivation and inspiration. This is because when they have settled on a chosen course they are a shining example of how it is possible to rise above challenges and criticism by respecting your own judgment.

On the dark side

Immature, detached, inflexible

At your best

Creative, influential, honest

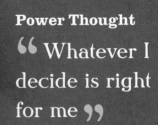
Love *Rescue me*

People born on this day need both freedom and commitment in a relationship. They love the thrill of the chase and will probably have numerous partners but a part of them also longs to feel safe in one committed relationship. They have powerful emotions and a sensitive heart with a lot of love to give; they long to be rescued by that special someone who can provide them with both excitement and stability.

Health *Go Green*

February 21 people can be prone to mood swings and—if these aren't properly handled—depression. It is extremely important for them to eat a healthy balanced diet, packed full of the mood-boosting nutrients found in oily fish, nuts, seeds, leafy green vegetables, legumes, and whole grains. They should avoid drugs, alcohol, nicotine, and any addictive or toxic substances. Plenty of exercise, preferably in the fresh air so they get the mood-boosting effects of daylight, is highly recommended as are breathing exercises, meditation or perhaps counseling if they find themselves unable to deal with feelings of anger, fear, guilt, or disappointment. Reading, wearing or meditating on the colors green and blue will help restore natural balance and healing.

Career *Born composers*

People born on this day make great leaders and any career that allows them to motivate, inspire or lead others will appeal; for example, management, politics or teaching. They may also be drawn toward careers where they can make their own rules, such as music, arts and entertainment. They can also make especially good conductors. Often rather dexterous, they may also be interested in working with their hands, so careers in design, especially costume design, construction or building, may appeal.

Destiny *To inspire others to reach their full potential*

The life path of people born on this day is to trust themselves to be able to take on board the advice of others. Once they are able to do that, their destiny is to motivate and inspire others by their own example to reach their full potential.

Signs & symbols

Sun signs: Pisces/Aquarius

Ruling planets: Neptune, the speculator/Saturn, the teacher

Symbols: Two Fishes/The Water Carrier

Birth date ruler: Jupiter, the philosopher

Tarot card: The World (fulfillment)

Favorable numbers: 3, 5

Lucky day: Thursday, especially when it falls on 3 or 5 of the month

Lucky colors: Sea green, purple

Birthstones: Amethyst and aquamarine

February 21

22 February

the birthday of the investigator

Your greatest challenge is ...

to be less self-critical

The way forward is ...

to understand that perfection is an impossible ideal; our failures sometimes propel us toward success and our vulnerabilities bring others closer to us.

You're drawn to people born on ...

January 21 to February 19

You share a passion for the mystery of love, and this creates a stimulating and intense union.

Luck maker

Get a kick out of being you

Only when you are comfortable with yourself can you be confident with your skills and talents, and deal positively with negative criticism. Recognize your own value and others will soon see it too.

People born on February 22 love nothing better than a good mystery. They are born problem solvers with an inquisitive, intuitive mind and a natural talent for unearthing the truth.

The chances are people born on this day don't have a conventional career or if they do their hobbies or interests reflect their eclectic tastes. They may have many different ideas about their life path, trying to do opposing things at once; this can confuse and frustrate others while also fascinating them. There is always method in the "madness" of these dynamic people. They believe that people are defined not by what they do but by how they do it. Whatever activity they pursue, one thing remains paramount: they can indulge their passion for investigation and problem solving.

Although these people are particularly good at uncovering information and proposing a solution, one area of their life is often neglected—their own inner life. Because they tend to be self-reliant individuals, they often expect others to be the same. They deny themselves emotional security by not sharing their anxieties with those closest to them. They also have rather high standards; when others don't live up to these they can become overly critical and pessimistic. They should learn to open up to others, and be more understanding of those who can't meet their high standards, including themselves. They can be extremely self-critical if they don't find an answer immediately, and will benefit from a more compassionate approach to themselves and others.

The tendency of these people to experiment with lots of different directions is highlighted between the ages of twenty-eight and fifty-seven. After the age of fifty-seven they may focus their energies in one direction. But whatever age they are and whatever goal they are currently choosing to focus on, one thing is sure. It will always be a fascinating one that may take them a step closer to their ultimate goal of making their own life—and the lives of others—a little less complicated and a whole lot more truthful.

On the **dark** side

Detached,
over-critical, pessimistic

At your **best**

Dynamic, problem
solving, articulate

Love *Falling in and out of love*

People born on February 22 tend to be a bit fickle when it comes to close personal relationships, blowing hot one day and cold the next. This can be terribly confusing for those close to them and they need to learn the importance of commitment and honesty in a fulfilling relationship. Once they do learn to place a value on emotional honesty, they make endlessly fascinating and exciting lovers.

Health *Keep it steady*

It is likely that people born on this day will neglect their health, especially when they are passionately engaged in their current hobby or interest. It is vital for them to make sure they eat regular meals and snacks, leaving no more than three hours between eating to keep their energy levels high and to give a regular supply of glucose to their constantly hungry brain. They might also benefit from a vitamin and mineral supplement. As far as exercise is concerned, vigorous or competitive—preferably social—sports are recommended. Reading, meditating on or surrounding themselves with the colors pink or green will encourage them to be more nurturing and less detached.

Career *Born investigators*

People born on this day thrive in careers that give them plenty of variety and utilize their problem-solving skills. They make great accountants, secret agents, detectives, scientists, and politicians. Their good communication skills also suggest success as a writer or journalist, or as a musician or actor. The side of them that is interested in the bigger picture may attract them to the clergy, the caring professions, alternative healing, social reform, or the world of medicine.

Destiny *To help and heal others*

The life path of people born on this day is to understand that diversity and problem solving are their gifts. Once they have been able to accept themselves as they are, their destiny is to help and heal others.

Signs & symbols

Sun signs: Pisces/Aquarius

Ruling planets: Neptune, the speculator/Saturn, the teacher

Symbols: Two Fishes/The Water Carrier

Birth date ruler: Uranus, the visionary

Tarot card: The Fool (freedom)

Favorable numbers: 4, 6

Lucky days: Thursday and Sunday, especially when those days fall on 4 and 6 of the month

Lucky colors: Sea green, chrome, purple

Birthstones: Amethyst and aquamarine

February 22

23 February

the birthday of the capable front runner

People born on February 23 have an optimistic, positive, can-do approach to life, and this is the key to their success. They are quietly rather than openly confident, believing that their accomplishments will speak for themselves. Because they aren't flashy, pretentious or showy in any way, other people tend to be drawn to them.

February 23 people take great care in every aspect of their lives and have an analytical approach to problems, but they most certainly aren't ponderous in their approach. They can be incredibly efficient, capable of delivering quality results for any task that they undertake. They often find great joy in the work itself rather than the reward. They believe that, having weighed up the alternatives, they are the best person for the job, with the best approach to it. The confident certainty they project can appear uncompromising but it is also infectious. More often than not, others believe exactly what they say and put enormous trust in them.

Another strength of people born on this day is their power of self-expression. Not only are they extremely articulate, they are also excellent listeners, an unusual combination that distinguishes them from other great speakers. They often find themselves in the position of confidant, this can sometimes give them an unfair advantage; they should beware of becoming manipulative when things aren't going their way. They should use their verbal skills and their empathy for others positively, especially between the ages of twenty-seven and fifty-six, when they become more confident and ambitious, and are likely to start many new ventures.

Above all, these people pride themselves on being the best person for the job. They will devote much effort to making everything in their lives, including themselves, the very best that it can be, and as a result it often is. As long as they are able to accept that life isn't—and wasn't meant to be—perfect, these capable front runners have the potential to earn great respect and affection from all those who cross their path.

Love *Take your time*

People born on February 23 have the ability to seduce others with a few carefully chosen glances and words. They are looking for someone with whom they can share their lives and build a future; one-night stands don't really appeal. They tend to be dazzled by looks first, and hearts and minds second, so it might help if they applied the same pragmatic approach to relationships as they do to their professional life, taking their time before rushing headlong in.

Health *Hands on*

Wanting to stay young and fit, people born on this day should eat carefully and have plenty of exercise to keep them looking toned and healthy. They regard their bodies in the same way they regard everything else: as an opportunity to fine tune and improve. There is a danger, however, that they can push themselves too hard, and so they need to make sure they find ways to relax and unwind and—above all—have fun. Plenty of sleep is important and they should make sure their bedroom is a comforting and peaceful place, perhaps painted in the color green to promote harmony and balance. They may also benefit from regular massage or reflexology as they can be prone to aches and pains, especially in their feet, as a result of their hard-working approach to life. The hands-on approach suits their sensual nature.

Career *Born analysts*

These people make great advisors, agents, negotiators, analysts, planners, and expert advisors in any field. Their communication skills ensure their success in any people-related career, and they may find themselves drawn to artistic, musical or dramatic forms of expression. Whatever career they choose, the capable and determined approach that people born on this day are blessed with will push them into the forefront of any area of expertise.

Destiny *To encourage others to do things the right way*

The life path of people born on this day is to learn to be the vibrant person they are. Once they learn to take themselves a little less seriously, their destiny is to encourage others to do things the right way.

Signs & symbols

Sun sign: Pisces

Ruling planet: Neptune, the speculator

Symbol: Two Fishes

Birth date ruler: Mercury, the communicator

Tarot card: The Hierophant (guidance)

Favorable numbers: 5, 7

Lucky days: Thursday and Wednesday, especially when those days fall on 5 and 7 of the month

Lucky colors: All shades of green

Birthstone: Aquamarine

February 23

24 February

the birthday of the romantic bard

Your greatest challenge is …

learning to assert yourself

The way forward is …

to take charge of your life, say no when you need to, express your true feelings and don't let others treat you like a doormat.

You're drawn to people born on …

September 24 to October 23

You mutual passion for art, romance and poetry can create an intense and fulfilling bond.

Luck maker

Believe that you deserve the best

If you don't believe that you deserve the best, you won't allow good things into your life. Believe that you deserve the best right now and you will get it.

People born on February 24 have an intuitive, generous and loving spirit that makes them a much-sought-after friend, acquaintance or partner. Highly romantic, they sometimes see the world through the eyes of a poet blinded by the power of love. Intimacy is extremely important to them—without it they can wither and pine away like the hero or heroine in a romantic novel.

Those born on this day are highly sensitive to their environment and they are constantly tuning into the moods of others and the situations going on around them. This makes them good peacemakers and valuable members of a team or family, as they can often spot trouble or find ways to resolve a situation without offending anyone. The danger lies when they concentrate on the emotional needs of others rather than on their own. It is vital for them to set boundaries in their interpersonal relationships. This won't be easy for them, and they may even bend the truth if they think it will avoid an argument. In the long run, this kind of evasive and dishonest behavior can make them feel anxious and uncertain. Fortunately, between the ages of twenty-six and fifty-six there are opportunities for them to develop their assertiveness and to be more straightforward in their relationships. Then, after the age of fifty-six, they become even steadier and more mature.

The longing for intimacy or emotional connection possessed by these people always rules their life in some way. They may have tried to suppress emotional traumas in the past, but, whatever their background or experience, these will somehow manifest themselves, perhaps in a quest for the perfect partner or in a passionate devotion to a cause.

People born on this day have a desire to use their energies selflessly on behalf of others. Once they have learned that love isn't just about pain, but also about joy, and that intimacy is not just about sacrificing and giving, but also about receiving and gaining, they will discover within themselves the tenacity and vision to achieve just about anything.

On the dark side

Needy, moody, passive

At your best

Loving, generous, altruistic

Love *Born to be in love*

People born on February 24 throw themselves wholeheartedly into relationships and may end up giving too much with very little in return. For their relationships to be satisfying, they need to learn to love themselves first. Once they are able to do that, they will find the soul mate they are pining for.

Health *Weak at the knees*

People born on this day need to be careful that they don't relax into a life of sensual pleasure, rich food, addiction, and very little exercise. They may have disorders involving the legs, feet and circulatory system; most of these could be avoided with an active lifestyle. It is very important for them to find ways to incorporate more exercise into their lives; for example, taking the stairs instead of the lift, walking around the block in their lunch hour, carrying rather than pushing their shopping, and so on. They should also watch their intake of red meat, alcohol, saturated fats, and sugar, especially chocolate. To stop cravings for sweet foods they should try smelling vanilla essential oil; wearing or meditating on the color blue will help calm and soothe them when they feel emotional.

Career *Born poets*

These people often find themselves drawn to art, music, writing, dance, poetry, and the entertainment world in general. Sensitive to color and pattern, they may also express themselves through design, in particular costume design, styling or the beauty business. Because they are so talented in dealing with people, any career which sees them in the role of mediator, adviser, counselor, agent, manager, or negotiator will suit, as will social reform, humanitarian or charity work, teaching and health careers.

Destiny *To help and heal others*

The life path of people born on this day is to learn to love and give to themselves as much as they are willing to give to others. Once they can do that, their destiny is to help and heal others and—by so doing—make the world a more loving and giving place.

Signs & symbols

Sun sign: Pisces

Ruling planet: Neptune, the speculator

Symbol: Two Fishes

Birth date ruler: Venus, the lover

Tarot card: The Lovers

Favorable numbers: 6, 8

Lucky days: Thursday and Friday, especially when those days fall on 6 and 8 of the month

Lucky colors: Turquoise, pink

Birthstone: Aquamarine

February 24

25 February

the birthday of the guru

Although people born on February 25 have a high degree of self-confidence and are fiercely individualistic, they often believe that the collective is more important than the personal. They can be radical in their desire to right social wrongs, being selfless in the pursuit of their goals. There is a touch of the guru about them, in that they desire not only to master their own destiny but to help others master theirs.

People born on this day never try to be anything by themselves. They have a simple, unaffected style that can cross boundaries, helping them relate to people from all walks of life. Everyone they meet is impressed by their honesty, optimism and desire to make a difference. As a result, they are good team players, preferring to take the role of advisor or guru rather than leader. They are the consultants with the winning formula, the brilliant teachers guiding and inspiring the next generation, the coaches who dedicate themselves to the welfare of the team, the directors with their eye on what the camera and the world see.

These people are often found working their magic on the sidelines; nothing gives them more satisfaction than engineering success for others. They can come across as silent and detached, but to those who know them well they are capable of making the most profound and helpful observations. They should beware, however, that they do not turn their greatest strengths into weaknesses by becoming so lost in the world of thought that they become secretive, negative and out of touch with reality. Fortunately, between the ages of twenty-five and fifty-four they become more self-assertive, experiencing an occasional need to step from the shadows onto center stage. Then, after the age of fifty-four, they seek more calm and steadiness in their lives.

Above all, February 25 individuals have a team-player mentality, a profound sense of justice and a desire to help the worthy win. This is a powerful combination that can inspire others to transform difficult circumstances into something better.

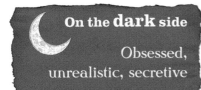

On the **dark** side

Obsessed, unrealistic, secretive

At your **best**

Intense, spiritual, ambitious

Love *Don't stay cool*

There is a tendency for people born on February 25 to play it quite cool when it comes to affairs of the heart, perhaps because they have been hurt or let down in the past. It is of vital importance for them to experience passion, and to learn to give and take in a relationship. Playing it safe, for once, isn't recommended. When they see an opportunity for love and intimacy, they should embrace it.

Health *Remember you are human!*

People born on this day are capable of great self-sacrifice and discipline and as a result they may neglect their health and well-being in the process. It is important for them to remember that the physical aspect of life is just as important as the mental. They should make sure their diet contains a wide variety of healthy foods and that they get plenty of moderate exercise, such as cycling, running and swimming. They also need to make sure they get plenty of rest to give their overactive brains a period of quiet reflection. Wearing, meditating on or surrounding themselves with the color red will help make them feel more passionate and energetic.

Career *Born lecturers*

These people are born teachers, gurus, guides, coaches, advisors, counselors, psychologists, mentors, and any other career that involves inspiring and guiding others toward success. If they wish to explore their creative potential, they may find themselves drawn toward careers in writing or art; if they wish to explore their spirituality, they may be drawn toward careers in religion or philosophy. Other careers that might suit include health care, administration and social reform.

Destiny *To inspire and guide others to a better place*

The life path of people born on this day is to learn to get involved more. Once they feel comfortable leaving the sidelines, their destiny is to teach, inspire and guide others to a better place.

Signs & symbols

Sun sign: Pisces

Ruling planet: Neptune, the speculator

Symbol: Two Fishes

Birth date ruler: Neptune, the speculator

Tarot card: The Chariot (resilience)

Favorable numbers: 7, 9

Lucky days: Thursday and Monday, especially when those days fall on 7 and 9 of the month

Lucky colors: Turquoise, indigo, lavender

Birthstone: Aquamarine

February 25

26 February

the birthday of the wise soul

Your greatest challenge is ...

to take yourself a little less seriously

The way forward is ...

to understand that humor, when used positively, can be a powerful force for good.

You're drawn to people born on ...

September 24 to October 23

You are both tough on the outside but warm on the inside; this can create a close and tender bond.

Luck maker

Show the world your teeth

Open your mouth wide when you smile. Being a wise soul you should know better than anyone that the old saying, "Smile and the world smiles with you," really does make sense.

People born on February 26 may often be described by others as old souls because they seem comfortable in their own skin. They often have great insight into how the world works and what the motivations of other people are.

When the great insight of these people is combined with their somewhat impersonal and detached persona, this can make others stand back in awe. In fact, they have quite a hypnotic power over others; people tend to do what they say or follow their example. It is important for them that they don't abuse this power—fortunately they rarely do as they also have a powerful sense of integrity and social justice. They like to find something to like in everybody and in every situation, and their unfailing optimism is truly enlightening.

One danger for people born on this day is a tendency to preach and rant, or be rigid or harsh in their opinions. They will often be unaware when they are showing this side of their personality, which is emphasized between the ages of twenty-four to fifty-four. During these years they should surround themselves with close friends or loved ones who can warn them when they are heading off track. Fortunately, they respond extremely well to constructive criticism, possessing the ability to change their ways. If someone reaches out to them emotionally and opens their heart, they will more often than not transform themselves into a more fully rounded human being.

Often blessed with great wisdom, their ability to arouse and inspire others will help them achieve worldly success. Although they do enjoy social recognition, part of them feels more comfortable as an outsider looking in. They will sometimes feel an urge to be alone with their thoughts or to sacrifice themselves to a higher cause. Being wise souls, however, they will have also learned the importance of emotional connection with others, so when they do feel the need to withdraw it will not be to isolate themselves but simply to recharge before they take the next step forward.

On the **dark** side

Dogmatic, moody, harsh

At your **best**

Insightful, hypnotic, honest

Love *Throw caution to the wind*

People born on February 26 tend to see love as a threat either to their enormous self-discipline or to their work, and as a result they may not allow others to get too close. This is a mistake, as they have a huge heart with so much love to give and they need to allow that love to express itself fully. Once they are able to open up, they make loyal, passionate and supportive partners.

Health *Food is not the answer*

The optimism of these people tends to keep them in good health but if their need for love and closeness is denied they may find themselves seeking it in food, drugs or other addictions. Diet can be a real problem for them and they need to make sure they watch the amount of fat, sugar, cream, and refined foods they eat, otherwise their blood-sugar levels could go sky high, setting themselves up for future problems with their weight and with their heart, not to mention diabetes. It is also important for them to take plenty of gentle to moderate exercise, especially later in life, when there is a tendency for them to slow down. Wearing, meditating on or surrounding themselves with the color orange will help them feel warmer and more secure. It might also lift their love life.

Career *Born judges*

These people have the wisdom and determination to be great judges or lawyers. They may also be drawn toward careers in teaching, lecturing, politics, counseling, consultancy, or social reform, where they can speak on behalf of others. Their need for artistic expression may be satisfied through art, design, music, writing, poetry, or drama.

Destiny *To follow their conscience and right social wrongs*

The life path of people born on this day is to learn that their need for love is not a weakness but a great strength. Once they are able to both give and receive love, their destiny is to follow their conscience and right social wrongs.

Power Thought

66 Today I will try to laugh at everything, myself included 99

Signs & symbols

Sun sign: Pisces

Ruling planet: Neptune, the speculator

Symbol: Two Fishes

Birth date ruler: Saturn, the teacher

Tarot card: Strength (passion)

Favorable numbers: 1, 8

Lucky days: Thursday and Saturday, especially when those days fall on 1 and 8 of the month

Lucky colors: Turquoise, brown, violet

Birthstone: Aquamarine

February 26

27 February

the birthday of hypnotic allure

People born on February 27 have the ability to turn heads and win hearts wherever they go. There is a magnetic and striking intensity about them that can hold others spellbound.

These people like to be in the limelight, and sooner or later they will be. Others admire them, not just for their hypnotic personality but because they stride confidently and with purpose through life, achieving their goals with ease and grace. They have a mind forever open to the new but they are also able to analyze in depth. By devoting a great deal of their energy to understanding how things work, their knowledge base increases steadily until it becomes so solid that it can see them through from one ambitious project to the next, taking them to the very top. There is one area of their lives, however, unlikely to be envied by others: their personal lives.

Although this may appear contradictory—given their cool and charismatic image—February 27 people often have a chaotic emotional life, with broken relationships littered around them. The reason is that they have a deeply emotional nature; although they have learned to control it when it comes to impersonal relationships, their own personal relationships are threatened by their impulse to follow their heart. It is extremely important for people born on this day to apply discipline to personal relationships and to stop making unreasonable, childish demands on others, especially between the ages of twenty-three and fifty-two when they will become even more active and adventurous. If self-discipline isn't learned during this period, the result could be emotional and personal chaos.

At their worst, people born on this day can be social-climbing attention seekers. At their best, however, they are lovable and spontaneous creatures who can both intoxicate and inspire others with their presence. They may often be described as a little crazy by those who know them, but once they invest their energy into a worthwhile cause they can achieve great things and enjoy the limelight they seem destined for.

On the **dark** side
Confused, highly strung, social climber

At your **best**
Magnetic, creative, versatile

Love *High maintenance*

People born on February 27 expect total commitment and support from others but need to learn to give it in return. They can be incredibly inconsistent lovers and those in a relationship with them will need to learn how to avoid head-on confrontations. When they do finally feel able to commit to a relationship, however, they can be spontaneous, passionate and vulnerable lovers; a little high maintenance, perhaps, but well worth the effort.

Health *Stay cool and in control*

People born on this day are full of energy and so a vigorous exercise program is recommended to prevent them working off their energy or seeking a high in an unhealthy direction, such as chasing numerous sexual partners, drinking or gambling. As far as diet is concerned, simple and natural is recommended, with reduced amounts of red meat and dairy and saturated fat. They would also benefit from breathing exercises, meditation and yoga to help them develop the self-discipline to keep their passions under control. Meditating on, wearing or surrounding themselves with the colors blue and lavender will help them stay cool and logical when passions flare.

Career *Born actors*

These people seem destined to be in the limelight, and careers on the stage, in the movies or anywhere where people will be watching them perform in some way have great appeal. If they work in business, they will be attracted to sales, advertising and marketing, but they can also make inspirational teachers and lecturers. They are also ideally suited to life as an entrepreneur and may well find satisfaction in building up their own business.

Destiny *To enchant others with their magic*

The life path of people born on this day is to learn self-discipline in their personal relationships. Once they have learned to keep their cool, their destiny is to enchant others in some way with their unique brand of magic.

Power Thought

"Today I will put love before all else"

Signs & symbols

Sun sign: Pisces

Ruling planet: Neptune, the speculator

Symbol: Two Fishes

Birth date ruler: Mars, the warrior

Tarot card: The Hermit (inner strength)

Favorable numbers: 2, 9

Lucky days: Thursday and Tuesday, especially when those days fall on 2 or 9 of the month

Lucky colors: Turquoise, red, violet

Birthstone: Aquamarine

28 February

the birthday of
the original charmer

Your greatest challenge is ...

learning to rein in your impulses

The way forward is ...

to understand that you can replace addictions with preferences.

You're drawn to people born on ...

July 21 to August 23

Your share a love of adventure and glamour; this can create a loving and energetic bond.

Luck maker

Want what you already have

Luck follows those who appreciate and are grateful for what they already have. If you appreciate what you have or acknowledge how far you have already come, you will be much more positive in your attitude.

People born on February 28 have a warm glow about them and can light up their lives of others with their energy and originality. They love to be center stage and are often in just that spot at social gatherings. Natural performers, they are never short of admirers and are blessed with the ability to charm just about anyone they meet.

Articulate and entertaining, people born on this day will go out of their way to get a laugh or reaction from others, even if this involves exaggerating the truth. They thrive on being noticed, but attention seeking isn't what drives them. Their motivation is a thirst for adventure and they will enthusiastically follow wherever their impulses direct them. Underlying their restlessness, however, is a deep-seated fear of standing still; the fear of it will drive them toward sensation-seeking and sometimes self-destructive behavior.

They won't ever lose the glint in their eye, but underneath their bravado they do secretly long to find a real purpose and achieve lasting success in the eyes of the world. This won't be possible until they discover that self-esteem is not created by thrill-seeking but by being the person they are. It is important for these people to learn to be more comfortable with being rather than doing, because until they can reach this level of awareness their life may hurtle chaotically from one situation to another and one person to another. They should learn to cultivate an inner calmness between the ages of twenty-two and fifty-one, when there is an emphasis in their life on new directions and ventures.

Because people born on this day live in such a vibrant and wholehearted way, they will experience life more intensely than others. They do, however, need to rein in their compulsion to indulge their every whim and learn greater self-control. They should never suppress their optimism and curiosity, but if they can just try to look before they leap, they can become far more than original charmers; they can become life's pioneers, boldly going where none have gone before.

118

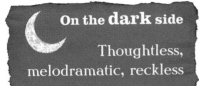
Love *Step back*

People born on February 28 can find it hard to stay committed to one relationship. They can be big flirts, which can upset a partner. To enjoy all the fulfilling rewards of a loving relationship it is important for them to learn greater self-control and to step back every now and again to let their partner take center stage. They tend to stick with partners who are loyal, energetic and glamorous.

Health *Life in the fast lane*

Life in the fast lane can take its toll on the health of people born on this day and it is important for them to set aside days of peace and rest to stop them burning out. There is a tendency for them to neglect their health as they jump from one adventure to another; regular health check-ups are therefore recommended. They often enjoy cooking, so this will encourage them to eat more healthily; as far as exercise is concerned, they would benefit most from those with a mind–body approach, such as yoga or tai chi, although swimming and running also suit them. Wearing, surrounding themselves with or meditating on shades of purple will encourage them to look within rather than without for a sense of self-esteem.

Career *Born travelers*

These people need to find careers which will allow them to channel their energy and curiosity. They are ideally suited to careers in tourism and travel, as well as arts and sports. Their sharp mind and desire to explore mentally may also draw them to science, teaching, research, and philosophy, and they can also thrive in careers which allow them to take the lead, such as management or business, or working for themselves. Later in life they may be drawn toward helping others, and their love of the dramatic may also draw them to the arts, writing and entertainment world.

Destiny *To be life's pioneer and adventurer*

The life path of people born on this day is to look within as well as without for a sense of fulfillment and adventure. Once they are able to find inner peace, their destiny is to be the pioneer and adventurer of this world.

Signs & symbols

Sun sign: Pisces

Ruling planet: Neptune, the speculator

Symbol: Two Fishes

Birth date ruler: Sun, the individual

Tarot card: The Magician (willpower)

Favorable numbers: 1, 3

Lucky days: Thursday and Sunday, especially when those days fall on 1 and 3 of the month

Lucky colors: Turquoise, orange, orchid

Birthstone: Aquamarine

February 28

29 February

the birthday of wistful vivacity

In their early years people born on this day may find it hard to be taken seriously. They may also sense something different about themselves, since they only celebrate a real birthday every four years.

Those born on this unusual day are likable and diplomatic, the latter skill perhaps learned early in life when they had to compromise over the date of their birthday. They have great social skills and the ability to relate to just about anyone. In addition, they have an ethereal quality that makes them appear less resilient than they really are. Although others may dismiss them as dreamers or social butterflies, they are in fact surprisingly tough and ambitious.

They may feel driven to aggressively validate their self-perceived differences by working harder to achieve their goals—a strategy that they may take to self-destructive extremes, especially between the ages of twenty-one and fifty-one, during which there is an emphasis on being assertive and ambitious. They should understand that over-promoting themselves is more likely to alienate than impress others.

People born on this day often have great insight into what makes people tick but others are unlikely to understand what motivates them, although their motivation is simple. They simply want to fit in, to feel needed and—above all—to feel no different from everyone else. Thus they tend to be very caring and nurturing toward the problems of others and sincere in their desire to help in times of crisis. However, being rather sensitive, if their efforts do not receive the response or gratitude they expect, they can withdraw into immature or indulgent behavior.

They do have a tendency to over-compensate for their feelings of difference and they should try to avoid extremes of behavior. Once they realize their powerful intuition and youthful vivacity are strengths not weaknesses, these special individuals will find that others not only accept but highly value their unique qualities.

At your **best**

Youthful, intuitive, offbeat

Love *Put the focus on want, not need*

People born on February 29 want a loyal and affectionate partner who is always there for them, but they do need to beware of becoming too dependent on their partner. Being insecure or needy in a relationship can destroy the security they desperately want. They need to cultivate an independent perspective and keep some part of their life separate from their relationship.

Health *Forever young*

The natural tendency of people born on this day is to indulge their hedonistic impulses, so it is important that they stay level-headed when it comes to their health and don't take any unnecessary risks. They have great physical and mental energy, and in their mature years others will admire their vigor and their children will hope to inherit it. They may even take up a youthful sport like skateboarding, parachuting, disco dancing, or rock climbing in their middle age, but they do need to be careful of injuries to the lower part of their body. Because they often love cooking, they tend to eat healthily although they do need to make sure they don't overindulge. Wearing, meditating on or surrounding themselves with shades of blue will be good for them when they want to appear cool or do some logical thinking.

Career *Born competitors*

People born on this curious day thrive in careers which allow them to indulge their competitive spirit and where they can harness their instincts and prove their worth. They may be drawn to careers in sport, business, and the stock exchange, or to the world of art, design, poetry, writing, and music. Their natural sympathy for others may also draw them toward humanitarian work or politics.

Destiny *To talk directly to the souls of others*

The life path of people born on this day is to learn to value rather than regret their uniqueness. Once they are able to develop enough self-confidence, their destiny is to find outlets for their optimism and creativity and, by so doing, talk directly to the souls of others.

Signs & symbols

Sun sign: Pisces

Ruling planet: Neptune, the speculator

Symbol: Two Fishes

Birth date ruler: Moon, the intuitive

Tarot card: The High Priestess (intuition)

Favorable numbers: 2, 4

Lucky days: Thursday and Monday, especially when those days fall on 2 and 4 of the month

Lucky colors: Turquoise, silver, ash blue

Birthstone: Aquamarine

1 March

the birthday of the practical visionary

People born on March 1 have a talent for lifting the moods of others and for transforming concepts or thoughts into solid achievements. They tend to have an eye for beauty, seeing the world with the vision of an artist. However, they can also be extremely practical and level-headed; anyone who dismisses them as lightweights will be making a big mistake.

When the strong will-power of people born on this day is focused, they can accomplish miracles through their determination and conviction. Unfortunately, despite this incredible potential to succeed, they are also prone to panic, negative thinking and lack of confidence. When in a state of anxiety, they are easily influenced and likely to attract people who will take advantage of their talents. It is important for them to build up their self-esteem so they can steer their life in the right direction instead of others jumping into the driving seat.

Until the age of nineteen it is likely that their plans for the future will be fairly vague or constantly shifting; this is the period when they are at their most vulnerable to negative influences or causes that aren't worthy of them. Fortunately, between the ages of twenty and forty-nine they enter a phase when they became more assertive and self-assured, if a little controlling, selfish or impatient when things aren't going their way. After the age of fifty they will feel a need to establish themselves and to devote themselves either to their loved ones or to a variety of humanitarian causes. In fact, throughout their lives they often feel a deep concern for the well-being of others, although it may not be until later in life that they inject practicality into those concerns and get going with them.

Despite their tendency to self-doubt, these people have great intelligence, charisma and originality. Once they learn to take responsibility for their decisions, they often find themselves in the position of a leader making a difference and paving the way for others less fortunate through the power of their personality.

At your **best**

Refined, artistic, ambitious

Love *Room to breathe*

People born on March 1 tend to be drawn to strong and controlling individuals, but to feel fulfilled in a relationship they need to have plenty of freedom and space. Until they find a relationship which offers them security but also gives them room to breathe, their love life may be somewhat chaotic.

Health *Time to daydream*

People born on this day tend to be a bit careless when it comes to their health and it is important for them to keep in regular touch with their doctor, to eat healthily and exercise every day. They may find it hard to incorporate a regular exercise routine in their life as it contradicts their dreamy nature, but brisk walks in the park or countryside will allow them both to get fit and to daydream. As sensuous individuals, they will almost certainly enjoy regular massages, in particular aromatherapy massage. If they have a load of work or study in front of them, a ginger-scented aromatic candle is a good choice. Ginger scent is also helpful when they feel confused or lacking in purpose.

Career *Born creative directors*

These people are born creative directors, channeling their imaginative thoughts and original ideas into constructive projects. Although they have the skills to succeed in business, they tend to be happier when using their imagination. As a result they may be drawn toward writing, drama, art, design, or music, or working for themselves in some way. Later in life they may also be drawn to social reform, charity work or humanitarian causes.

Destiny *To transform ideas into achievements*

The life path of people born on this day is to learn to balance the emotional extremes of negativity to which they are prone. Once they can learn to do that, their destiny is to transform their own and the ideas of others into solid achievements.

Signs & symbols

Sun sign: Pisces

Ruling planet: Neptune, the speculator

Symbol: Two Fishes

Birth date ruler: Sun, the individual

Tarot card: The Magician (will-power)

Favorable numbers: 1, 4

Lucky days: Thursday and Sunday, especially when these days fall on 1 and 4 of the month

Lucky colors: Turquoise, orange, pistachio green

Birthstone: Aquamarine

March 1

2 March

the birthday of personal vision

Your greatest challenge is …

dealing with confrontation

The way forward is …

to be more relaxed and pragmatic in your approach and not to shy away from conflict; conflict is inevitable, but it can encourage creativity, change and progress.

You're drawn to people born on …

June 22 to July 23

You both like to put your partner on a pedestal. Take turns doing this to create a loyal, satisfying union.

Luck maker

Keep making new friends

Not only will this promote your self-esteem, but having lots of friends and acquaintances, all with their own ideas, contacts and talents to offer, is also a great way to increase your chances of luck.

People born on March 2 have strong convictions and their own personal vision which they will pursue with undying loyalty, regardless of the opinions of others or the changing climate around them. They are truly independent thinkers with the ability to inspire and occasionally alarm others with their intensity.

Once those born on this day have committed to an ideal or decided on a course of action, they will hold fast to it. They can occasionally take this to an extreme, blocking out everything and everyone else. Although others have much to learn from their dedication, they can have a one-track mind and a tendency to deny themselves opportunities that could potentially enrich their work. It is important for these people to make sure that their personal convictions neither exclude the possibility of change nor alienate them from the closeness and security of personal relationships. They need to be especially careful of this tendency between the ages of eighteen and forty-eight, during which period there is an emphasis on assertiveness and activity, and their personal vision is most likely to dominate their lives.

The personal vision March 2 people dedicate themselves to so passionately is often one that tries to make positive changes to their world or environment. This is challenge enough, but by far the greatest test for these devoted souls is that of balancing their personal needs with the needs of the world. If they are unable to find that sense of balance, the people most likely to suffer are those closest to them. They are the politicians or the campaigners devoted to their party who are never there for their loved ones; the artists or writers absorbed in their work but neglectful of their family, especially their children. If, however, people born on this day find a way to bring harmony both to their own personal lives and to the wider world, their unwavering dedication to their personal vision gives them the potential to be powerful and potent forces for positive change and progress.

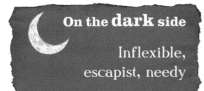

On the **dark** side

Inflexible, escapist, needy

At your **best**

Loyal, trusting, purposeful

Love *Only for you*

When people born on March 2 fall in love it is an undying and devoted love, but their unstinting adoration of their partner, children or any other person who inspires them can run the risk of stifling them. It is therefore important for these people to learn to develop a more detached and independent attitude not just toward their work, but also toward their personal lives.

Health *Get out there*

People born on this day have a tendency to isolate themselves and this can have a negative effect on their health and well-being. They need to make sure they get out into the world, as they have a lot to offer it. All kinds of exercise that involve other people, such as team sports or aerobics classes, will benefit them. As far as diet is concerned they need to steer clear of too much alcohol and to make sure they eat plenty of fresh, natural whole grains and vegetables. Wearing, meditating on or surrounding themselves with the color orange will encourage them to seek out warmth and physical contact with others.

Career *Born charity worker*

These people need to make career plans that include their natural sense of vision. The medical and healing professions may be of interest to them, as might teaching, politics, writing, social reform, or charity work. They may also choose to express their creative vision of the world in music, theater or art.

Destiny *To use their vision to make the world a better place*

The life path of people born on this day is to learn to give more of themselves to others. Once they are able to reach outside themselves, their destiny is to translate their personal vision into a reality and by so doing to make the world a better and more enlightened place.

Signs & symbols

Sun sign: Pisces

Ruling planet: Neptune, the speculator

Symbol: Two Fishes

Birth date ruler: Moon, the intuitive

Tarot card: The High Priestess (intuition)

Favorable numbers: 2, 5

Lucky days: Thursday and Monday, especially when these days fall on 2 and 5 of the month

Lucky colors: Turquoise, silver, pale green

Birthstone: Aquamarine

March 2

3 March

the birthday of proposal

Your greatest challenge is ...

building your self-esteem

The way forward is ...

to write a success list that includes everything that is meaningful to you personally. Keep adding to the list every day.

You're drawn to people born on ...

November 23 to December 21

A love of debate and communication draws you to each other and this can create a stimulating and supportive union.

Luck maker

Believe in your success

Believe in yourself, especially in times of misfortune, because this will inspire others to believe in you too and to want to help you.

People born on March 3 may feel from an early age that they were destined for something great. Intelligent, determined and versatile, there is no question that they have great potential. The question is more about where to begin; they may find themselves taken up with plans and proposals for the best step forward.

Extremely pragmatic without being pessimistic, people born on this day feel the need to prepare carefully. They are quick to recognize any defects and potential problems in their preparation, and although they are aware of the bigger picture they have a eye for detail and nothing escapes their attention. In fact, they love the preparation stage, often enjoying it more than the actual presentation or execution of a project. This approach has both its upsides and downsides. The upside is that they are fully focused on the present. The downside is that they can get bogged down in details and planning and lose momentum, direction and spontaneity.

It is important for them to work on their decision-making skills and to stop holding themselves and others back with an endless succession of "what ifs." Fortunately, between the ages eighteen and forty-seven there is an emphasis on assertiveness, activity and courage. After the age of forty-eight they may feel an increased need for calm and stability.

It is probably better for these people to make a decision about which course they want to pursue in life and stick to it. If they remain uncommitted or in the planning stage for much of their life, they need to examine why they fear commitment or execution. If fear of failure holds them back, they need to learn that it is who they are and not what they do that is a mark of success. And those March 3 individuals who do settle on a course need to be careful that they don't get so lost in their activities that they lose touch with who they are because who they are is a remarkable person with the ability to achieve great things.

On the **dark** side
Moody, compulsive, lazy

At your **best**
Generous, intelligent, determined

Love *Don't be a pushover*

People born on March 3 need to be careful that their sensitive and generous nature isn't taken advantage of and they need to be alert to the warning signs. They are often attracted by intelligent partners and their relationships tend to be linked to work or shared interests. Once they are able to avoid insecurities and an over-eagerness to please others by developing their self-confidence, they can make charming and fun-loving partners.

Health *Don't miss out on fun*

People born on this day need to make sure that they are not too inflexible in their approach to health. They may expend a lot of effort planning their meals and exercise routine, losing a sense of spontaneity in the process. They also need to be careful that they don't lower their immunity by pushing themselves too hard. Like everyone else, they should cut down on junk food and alcohol, but not to the extent that they miss out on spontaneity. As far as exercise is concerned, moderate to mild activities such as cycling and walking, preferably in the fresh air, are recommended; these will take their focus off the task in hand and let them see what is going on around them. Wearing, meditating on or surrounding themselves with the color yellow will increase their optimism and creative confidence.

Career *Born scriptwriters*

These people have the observational skills to be great writers, especially scriptwriters for film, radio and TV. They like to earn their money though a job which has some kind of message to deliver or that can make other people's lives easier, and so careers in drama, arts, counseling, and teaching may appeal, as might social work, politics and humanitarian causes.

Destiny *To uplift others by their ideas*

The life path of people born on this day is to learn to like themselves more. Once they are able to do that, their destiny is to express their original ideas and talents, inspiring, entertaining and uplifting others in the process.

Signs & symbols

Sun sign: Pisces

Ruling planet: Neptune, the speculator

Symbol: Two Fishes

Birth date ruler: Jupiter, the philosopher

Tarot card: The Empress (creativity)

Favorable numbers: 3, 6

Lucky day: Thursday, especially when it falls on 3 and 6 of the month

Lucky colors: Turquoise, purple,

Birthstone: Aquamarine

March 3

4 March

the birthday of inspired aloneness

Your greatest challenge is ...

learning to express your feelings

The way forward is ...

to understand that if you don't say what you mean or ask for what you want, people won't understand you or be able to help you.

You're drawn to people born on ...

January 21 to February 19

A relationship of opposites, you can learn much from each other about the importance of balancing inner and outer worlds.

Luck maker

Overcome shyness

Lucky people aren't necessarily the life and soul of the party but they know how to overcome shyness to get others on their side. Instead of thinking about yourself when you walk into a room, think about the people in the room.

People born on March 4 tend to come across as self-contained individuals with an ingenuity that does not require outside stimulation and a creativity that is self-generated. They are able to work and, if need be, live alone. It's not that they are antisocial or seek to cut themselves off from the outside world; it's just that striking out alone is a dominant trend in their lives, often leading to success.

For people born on this day, being alone isn't scary; it's a liberating experience and an opportunity for them to concentrate and be productive. Extremely comfortable with themselves, they often feel confined or trapped by social pressure and conformity. When they are alone they feel free rather than isolated; even when given the option to interact more, they will often choose to go it alone. This can come across as shyness or fear of involvement, but this misses the point about these gentle people.

Although they hate confrontation and will withdraw at signs of conflict, they aren't shy or passive but aware that they are most productive when living and working within guidelines set by themselves. They have an innovative and ingenious mind that works best when left alone and an ability to explore concepts with tenacity. Between the ages of seventeen and forty-six there is an emphasis on daring new ventures and, along with this, many opportunities for them to develop their assertiveness; these people need to ensure that others don't take all the credit.

The big danger for these people is that they indulge their natural tendency for self-involvement so much that they cut themselves off from reality, and from the joys and rewards of close personal relationships. It's unfortunate if this happens, as they do love to share the results or benefits of their work with others, despite their natural reserve. They also have a great empathy for others, and when they choose to reveal or share their talents to the outside world they have the potential to influence, intrigue and inspire others with their vision.

Love *Give me space*

People born on March 4 really need space in a relationship and they will suffer if a partner tries to control or crowd them in any way. They tend to be attracted to people who are free-spirited and self-contained like themselves. Although they may have long gaps between relationships, when they find the right person they are capable of deep and lasting love and commitment.

Health *Having a good time*

Those born on this day need to make sure they don't cut themselves off too much—or even completely—from the benefits of socializing. All activities that involve working or dealing with others are therefore recommended. Social forms of exercise and team sports are particularly beneficial as in these they can experience the joys of synergy. Having said that, it is equally important for people born on this day to have plenty of space to do and think their own things; having regular time out, rest and relaxation, especially outside in the fresh air, is important. Wearing, meditating on or surrounding themselves with the color red will encourage them to come out of themselves more.

Career *Born magicians*

These people are naturally suited to setting up and running their own business, preferably from their own home or office. They may also be attracted to writing in any form or to teaching, education, psychology, academia, research, the Church, the secret service, or computer programming. They may also be drawn to music, magic and the arts, and can make exceptional magicians or illusionists, conductors or DJs.

Destiny *To educate and inspire with their ingenuity*

The life path of people born on this day is to understand that they have just as much right to be heard as anyone else. Once they have worked on their assertiveness skills, their destiny is to educate, motivate and inspire others with their ingenuity.

Power Thought

❝I can always learn something from others❞

Signs & symbols

Sun sign: Pisces

Ruling planet: Neptune, the speculator

Symbol: Two Fishes

Birth date ruler: Uranus, the visionary

Tarot card: The Emperor (authority)

Favorable numbers: 4, 7

Lucky days: Thursday and Sunday, especially when these days fall on 4 and 7 of the month

Lucky colors: Turquoise, grey

Birthstone: Aquamarine

5 March

the birthday of agony and ecstasy

On the surface people born on March 5 are smooth and charming individuals with the gift of the gab, but troubled waters lie below. Their easy style conceals a complex personality that is as fascinating as it is frustrating.

The emotional current that flows beneath the light-hearted exterior of people born on this day is extraordinarily powerful. One moment they're entertaining and empathetic companions who can put everyone about them at their ease with their sharp wit and incisive mind. The next moment, however, when their emotional equilibrium is unbalanced, they can dissolve into insecurity, negativity and fits of temper. Given the instability of their emotional life, it is very important for these people to learn to manage their emotions, especially between the ages of sixteen and forty-five when they become more aggressive, assertive and determined to make their mark. After the age of forty-seven there is another turning point which sees them slow down a little, searching for stability in all areas of their lives.

Underneath the sociable and confident façade of people born on this day is a highly sensitive soul that desperately needs regular time out in quiet and solitary reflection. Inside they may have many hidden fears and insecurities to deal with; if they don't allow themselves time to acknowledge these demons, they are the mercy of their impulses and there is no telling in what direction they will go. People born on this day may worry that becoming more balanced and stable will result in a loss of intensity or edge, but they need to understand that cultivating personal will-power and self-control will not lessen but strengthen their creativity and the impact they have on others.

With their emotional honesty, March 5 people have the ability to bring out both the best and the worst in themselves and others. If they can learn to find balance and use their power over others responsibly, the world will always be a brighter place with these impulsive individuals around.

Love *Blowing hot and cold*

People born on March 5 can fall passionately in love one day, only to change their mind and blow cold the next day. Given the extremes to which they are prone, they need to receive unconditional love and support from those who are close to them, although they also need firmness. Once they know what they can and cannot get away with, they are much less likely to test the waters and will remain stable in a relationship.

Health *Highs and lows*

When people born on this day have a good time they may have trouble knowing when to stop. This can have a negative effect on their health, especially when that good time includes alcohol, rich food, nicotine, sugar, and multiple sexual partners. They may also find it difficult to sleep; if insomnia is a problem, making sure their bedroom is light and airy, taking an aromatherapy bath or a cup of chamomile tea may help, as will avoiding the stimulation of TV, conversation or exercise. Regular exercise is highly recommended, as are vitamin and mineral supplements. Because they are prone to mood swings it is especially important that they learn to connect with their inner peace and calm, perhaps by regular meditation, being in nature or listening to beautiful music.

Career *Born movie directors*

The impulsive nature of these people draws them toward the world of movies—where they can make great directors—as well as acting, music, drama, and the entertainment world. Their love of adventure and excitement may also lead them toward careers involving travel, politics, design, the fashion world. They may also be drawn toward social reform and charity work, but they are likely to excel in whatever career they choose because of their intelligence and superior communication skills.

Destiny *To make lofty dreams a reality*

The life path of people born on this day is to learn to work with both their head and their heart. Once they've learned to rein in their impulses, their destiny is to make their lofty vision and dreams for the future a reality.

Signs & symbols

Sun sign: Pisces

Ruling planet: Neptune, the speculator

Symbol: Two Fishes

Birth date ruler: Mercury, the communicator

Tarot card: The Hierophant (guidance)

Favorable numbers: 5, 8

Lucky days: Thursday and Wednesday, especially when these days fall on 5 and 8 of the month

Lucky colors: Turquoise, green, light blue

Birthstone: Aquamarine

March 5

6 March

the birthday of refinement

Your greatest challenge is ...

to avoid searching for perfection

The way forward is ...

to understand that in life there are no exact measurements for what is right because we are not statistics and geometry.

You're drawn to people born on ...

August 24 to September 23

You share a passion for beauty and refinement, and this can create a match made in heaven.

Luck maker

Allow yourself room for improvement

It's okay to have weaknesses, to be unpredictable, to make mistakes and to misunderstand. The issue is keeping a balance so that neither these, nor the search for perfection, make your life unhappy or unlucky.

People born on March 6 are at their happiest when they are searching for or surrounded by beauty. They find themselves pulled irresistibly toward ideals of loveliness, perfection and refinement that appeal to their senses and, although they are unlikely to realize it, they also have a strange beauty of their own.

They have the gift of being able to open the eyes of others to the beauty of the world around them and to teach them to appreciate every nuance of nature. They really can see eternity in a grain of sand, and the childlike wonder that they project is one of their most endearing qualities. There is a danger, however, that in their idealization of everything and everyone around them they can lose touch with what or who is actually there. Others may feel that they are more in love with the idea of romance and beauty than with the reality. And when reality does finally bite and their initial intensity fades, disenchantment may be the cruel result.

It is important for people born on this day to learn to be a little more objective in their assessment of situations and people, especially between the ages of fifteen and forty-four, during which are likely to become more active and assertive but also more vulnerable to disillusionment. Fortunately, after the age of forty-five they often become more emotionally steady and practical.

Above all, these people are motivated by a desire to experience and be uplifted by the ideal of true beauty. Much of their lives will be devoted to a never-ending quest to translate this perfect ideal into reality. Others may see this as pleasure seeking or superficiality, but there is real depth and originality under their often charming and sensuous exterior. They do need to learn to develop a more realistic and less demanding attitude, accepting that their lofty standards may not always be attained. In their search for true excellence, however, they are a constant source of energy, inspiration and beauty for all those who cross their path.

At your **best**

Youthful, refined,
sensual

Love *Strong romantic streak*

People born on March 6 are made to love and to be loved. In fact they seem perpetually in love and have a powerful romantic streak. The only danger is that they can sometimes mistake sex for love and love for sex; this can confuse both them and potential partners. It is important for them to find a partner who can share their love of beauty and sensual pleasure.

Health *Nature lovers*

People born on this day need to be careful that their love of sensual pleasures does not lead to overindulgence in rich fattening food and sexual experimentation, as these will negatively affect their health and their waistline. Fortunately, as lovers of beauty they are likely to be nature lovers and will be drawn to long walks in the countryside which is an especially good form of exercise for them. They would also benefit from a more structured exercise routine that includes regular muscle toning sessions, such as push-ups, sit-ups, etc., or gym work. Yoga and tai chi are also recommended, as these can provide great physical and emotional satisfaction. Wearing, meditating on or surrounding themselves with the color green will encourage them and others to seek harmony and balance.

Career *Born sculptors*

These people may find themselves drawn toward the beauty, fashion or health industries, but they may also be interested in the world of music and art, wanting to create sublime pieces of art, poetry, sculpture, or music. They may also have a natural affinity for the world of politics and social reform as well as the leisure and beauty industries, but whatever career they choose they will invest their considerable talents to achieve extremely high standards.

Destiny *To inspire others with their ideals of beauty*

The life path of people born on this day is to understand that perfection is not a natural or even an attainable human state. Nevertheless, they will always inspire others with their ideals of beauty.

Power Thought

" Today I will appreciate others for who they are and not as I want them to be "

Signs & symbols

Sun sign: Pisces

Ruling planet: Neptune, the speculator

Symbol: Two Fishes

Birth date ruler: Venus, the lover

Tarot card: The Lovers (choices)

Favorable numbers: 6, 9

Lucky days: Thursday and Friday, especially when these days fall on 6 and 9 of the month

Lucky colors: Turquoise, pink, lavender

Birthstone: Aquamarine

March 6

7 March

the birthday of extraordinary vision

Your greatest challenge is ...

learning to assert yourself

The way forward is ...

to be as encouraging and as positive as you can be when trying to get a point across. Be critical of people's ideas, not people themselves.

You're drawn to people born on ...

October 24 to November 22

You share charm, creativity and sensitivity, and this can create an intense and loving bond.

Luck maker

Learn to deal with criticism

If the criticism is just, see it as an opportunity to learn and grow. If, however, the criticism is unjust, take it as a compliment—it often means that the critic feels jealous or threatened by you.

Despite their ability to instantly establish rapport with anyone they meet, people born on March 7 often have an otherworldly quality about them. This is because they have a tendency to live in an abstract world of thoughts and ideals produced by their own vivid imagination.

People born on this day possess the gift of extraordinary vision and their minds love to roam far and wide. Typically, they can manifest these ideas in practical form by analyzing situations, experiences and people. Along the way, they will do their best to ensure that they get the support of colleagues, friends and loved ones, taking great care to make sure everyone feels involved. At work they never forget a name or a personal detail about their colleagues; at home they will ensure everyone can voice their opinions.

Even though they are often surrounded by friends and admirers, there is a haunting loneliness about these people; because they dislike conflict, they tend to withdraw when there is heated discussion or criticism of their methods. In their self-imposed isolation, they may also become insecure about themselves and their abilities, and secretive and suspicious of others. People born on this day should find other ways to cope when they feel under pressure; although they are unlikely to become close to large numbers of people, they should make sure they have the love and support of their family and/or a few good friends. Up to the age of forty-three they are active and assertive, a positive sign for them with their natural tendency to withdraw. After the age of forty-four there is an emphasis on greater emotional and financial stability.

Because they are so receptive to all kinds of intellectual pursuits, these people may take a while to settle on their chosen aim. However, once they are able to focus their vision and energy in a worthwhile direction, their intelligent and sensitive approach assures success. A part of them will always remain untouchable but this doesn't make them appear or feel lonely—it just adds to their magic.

At your **best**

Thoughtful, generous, intelligent

Love *Easily hurt*

Charming and generous, people born on March 7 have no problem finding friends or lovers. They do, however, hate conflict, and an argument with a partner can make them feel low for days; instead of expressing what they feel, they will simply withdraw into resentment, leaving their partner not knowing why. It is very important for these people to learn to be more honest in their relationships and try to reach agreement through compromise.

Health *See more red*

People born on this day can often be prone to food allergies and sensitivities, so it is important for them to pay attention to their diet and to discuss what might be a trigger food so that they can limit their consumption of it. In general their diet should include a wide variety of foods and, to make sure they don't miss out on nutrients, a multi-vitamin and mineral supplement is also advised as these people can be prone to lowered immunity during times of stress. Moderate exercise, in particular swimming and diving and all forms of dance, is recommended as well as enjoying plenty of fresh air by taking walks in the park or countryside. Wearing, meditating on or surrounding themselves with the color red will encourage them to assert themselves more.

Career *Born photographers*

Whatever career these people choose—be it business, politics or sport—they will mount a determined campaign to assure their success. They do have a strong need to express themselves and may be especially drawn to careers in film, art, music, photography, or dance, as well as teaching, social work and the healing professions.

Destiny *To realize their visionary goals and ideals*

The life path of people born on this day is to learn to be more honest with others. Once they are able to assert themselves, their destiny is to realize their visionary goals and ideals.

March 7

Signs & symbols

Sun sign: Pisces

Ruling planet: Neptune, the speculator

Symbol: Two Fishes

Birth date ruler: Neptune, the speculator

Tarot card: The Chariot (resilience)

Favorable numbers: 1, 7

Lucky days: Thursday and Monday, especially when these days fall on 1 and 7 of the month

Lucky colors: All shades of blue

Birthstone: Aquamarine

8 March

the birthday of the uncompromising rebel

People born on March 8 are fiercely uncompromising spirits. They may sometimes hide their non-conformity behind an agreeable exterior but anyone who knows them well will know that deep down they are independent thinkers filled with the courage of their convictions.

These people resent being told what to do, probably demonstrating their feisty nature from an early age, much to the frustration of their parents. They often have an innate distrust and in some cases a complete lack of respect for authority; they passionately believe that everybody deserves the right to think for themselves. Their somewhat subversive approach to life can wear others out but it is not usually prompted by a need to be difficult for the sake of it. More often than not their rebellion is prompted by an ability to easily spot the flaws or weaknesses in a situation that has been previously unchallenged and to identify a better approach. In fact, these people are outstanding lateral thinkers with great empathy toward others, and this marks them out as potentially great reformers in whatever field they choose to specialize.

March 8 people have a great zest for life and a need for challenge and variety. They often feel the need to strike out or break away, not just from their background, but from the current situation they are in. They are capable of commitment and loyalty, however, and may even stay in the same field for many years, but sooner or later the aggressive and uncompromising aspect of their personality demands change and progress. Their uncompromising tendencies tend to be emphasized before the age of forty-two and in this period their lives are likely to be stormy. Then, after the age of forty-three, there is a turning point which suggests a need for more emotional and financial stability.

Although these people have a knack of alienating people with their forceful opinions, they are also blessed with considerable charm; they should understand the hypnotic, addictive power they can have over people and use it wisely.

On the **dark** side

Disrespectful, irresponsible, demanding

At your **best**

Independent, honest, magnetic

Love *Craving intimacy*

People born on March 8 are often adored by others but real closeness can elude them, especially in their teens and twenties. They crave intimacy but can have problems with it as they tend to be loners. They can be passionate but are afraid of losing control, and for their relationships to be fulfilling they need to learn to be more spontaneous and to take more risks.

Health *Accident-prone*

People born on this day need to avoid stimulants like caffeine and nicotine when they are pushing themselves hard. It would be far better for them to eat an energy-boosting diet rich in nutrients and to get plenty of refreshing sleep. Fortunately, their assertive manner serves them well when it comes to their health, as they are not afraid to approach their doctor if something is troubling them; they do, however, need to take special care of their health especially when traveling, because they tend to be accident-prone. Adding a few drops of ginger essential oil to a handkerchief to breathe in whenever they feel in need of a pick-me-up can help clear their head and improve productivity.

Career *Born reformers*

Potentially great trailblazers, these people excel in academic, scientific, artistic, and social spheres, and they make good academics, researchers, scientists, chemists, musicians, painters, writers, artists, and designers. They may also be drawn toward careers in politics and social reform, as well as public relations. Alternatively, they may decide to set up their own business.

Destiny *To lead others to new ways of thinking and doing*

The life path of people born on this day is to learn the art of compromise. Once they have learned to temper their unconventional nature so that it does not alienate others, their destiny is to lead others toward new ways of thinking and doing things.

Signs & symbols

Sun sign: Pisces

Ruling planet: Neptune, the speculator

Symbol: Two Fishes

Birth date ruler: Saturn, the teacher

Tarot card: Strength (passion)

Favorable numbers: 2, 8

Lucky days: Thursday and Saturday, especially when these days fall on 2 and 8 of the month

Lucky colors: Electric blue, red and green

Birthstone: Aquamarine

March 8

9 March

the birthday of the bold explorer

People born on March 9 are innovative explorers who are always willing to take risks and venture boldly into the unknown or to experiment with new ideas and concepts. Their courageous style is often admired by others and, because they are so independent, their lives are often packed with excitement and suspense.

Despite their colorful and independent approach to life these people can be over-sensitive to the opinions of others, easily getting hurt when criticized. With a tendency to take things personally, it is important for them to learn to calm down between the ages of fourteen and forty-one, a period when their lives are full of aggression, assertiveness and new ventures. After the age of forty-two they often have a need for greater calm and emotional steadiness.

People born on this day are often bursting with energy and enthusiasm, moving so fast it can wear themselves and others out. They can quite easily flit from one job or relationship to another, as they love variety and challenge. Although others may regard them as reckless, they are in fact far less impulsive than they appear. From an early age they have learned to trust themselves because their intuition frequently leads them in the right direction. They have an ability to see the world from an unusual viewpoint and for this reason they make great advisors and friends, upon whom people can become dependent. The dependency of others, however, can cause feelings of frustration in them when others can't or won't stand on their own two feet.

A part of people born on this day always longs to fly away but, once they have found a way to balance their need for responsibility with their need to rush headlong into uncharted lands, they have the perception, charisma and enthusiasm to push forward social reforms. Although capable of great commitment once they have found a cause they believe in, they should make sure that they never lose touch of the key to their personality and success—their adventurous and curious spirit.

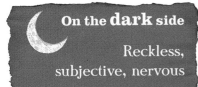

On the **dark** side
Reckless, subjective, nervous

At your **best**
Bold, innovative, intuitive

Love *Fireworks*

The dynamic drive and energy of people born on March 9 can always gain them plenty of admirers and they tend to fall in love quickly. Although they are capable of great commitment in a relationship, there will always be a part of them that wants to spread its wings. For this reason, any partner they are involved with needs to learn to avoid routine and adapt to their need for excitement, romance and adventure in a relationship.

Health *Foot massage*

People born on this day push themselves hard and, as a result, can place themselves under incredible and unnecessary pressure. Learning to recognize the signs of stress before they slip into depression is crucial. As far as diet is concerned, plenty of variety is important as these vibrant people will suffer if they are forced to stick to a regimented dietary regime. Regular moderate to vigorous exercise is recommended to help them release pent-up stress and tension, and also to keep their weight under control. Foot massages before they go to bed will help calm them down, and clary sage essential oil will be helpful when they feel low or in need of a confidence boost.

Career *Born social campaigners*

These people have a profound sense of justice and empathy for the underdog and this makes them natural social reformers or campaigners. Indeed whatever career they enter into—be it sport, art or politics—they will always show a marked interest in humanitarian concerns. Their ability to advise and influence others may also draw them to counseling, psychology, teaching, writing, and management, and because they also have great intuitive powers the world of psychic development may appeal.

Destiny *To commit to making the world a better place*

The life path of people born on this day is to learn responsibility and commitment toward others. Once they have been able to do that without losing their sense of adventure, their destiny is to commit themselves to humanitarian concerns and by so doing make the world a better and a fairer place.

Power Thought

"My intuition will always show me the best way forward "

Signs & symbols

Sun sign: Pisces

Ruling planet: Neptune, the speculator

Symbol: Two Fishes

Birth date ruler: Mars, the warrior

Tarot card: The Hermit (inner strength)

Favorable numbers: 3, 9

Lucky days: Thursday and Tuesday, especially when these days fall on 3 and 9 of the month

Lucky colors: Turquoise, red

Birthstone: Aquamarine

March 9

10 March

the birthday of sensitivity

Your greatest challenge is ...

building your self-esteem

The way forward is ...

to understand that just because you think something about yourself does not mean it is true.

You're drawn to people born on ...

July 24 to August 23

Opposites attract, as you both have qualities that balance each other's vulnerabilities; this can create a rounded and fulfilling relationship.

Luck maker

Enjoy yourself more

Spend time with people who make you feel good about yourself and stop taking yourself so seriously. The more relaxed and happy you are, the more likely you are to attract luck your way.

People born on March 10 have a fragile, vulnerable quality about them however successful they may appear on the world's stage. This is because a part of them is always searching for greater self-understanding or knowledge. Although they can be highly driven and energetic individuals, it is the inner world of ideals that defines and occupies people born on March 10. They are also extremely empathetic toward others, particular the underdog or those less fortunate.

Because they are constantly aware of their own feelings and tuned into the feelings of those around them, these highly sensitive people tend to experience life intensely and deeply. They have the capacity to show tremendous kindness and love toward others, but they do need to be careful that they don't become self-sacrificing, overprotective and jealous in the process.

Although they are highly perceptive and insightful in their relationships, they can also get deeply hurt by the words or actions of others. Instead of facing their pain when they are wounded, they are more likely to withdraw into their own private world of torment. It's important for these people to find ways to balance their sensitivity with their need to make a difference in the world. Fortunately, before the age of forty there is an emphasis in their life on assertiveness and a desire to be more active in the world. This can help them express themselves more outwardly. After the age of forty-one they often gravitate toward greater material and emotional stability, and this will help them stave off uncertainty and vulnerability.

Preoccupied with their inner conflicts, there is always a danger for these people to become self-involved; but, if they can learn not to use their sensitivity as a way of escaping responsibility and confrontation, the emphasis they place on internal rather than external fulfillment marks them out as very special people. Caring, contemplative and visionary, they will direct their intelligent and original thoughts toward the common good and, by so doing, positively influence and inspire all those who encounter them.

Love *Learn to let go*

People born on March 10 rarely have problems attracting partners; problems are more likely to occur when they are within a relationship. They need to be careful that they don't become too nurturing or overprotective, as it can suffocate others. Being easily wounded, they also need to guard against jealously. Despite the emphasis they place on togetherness, there is also a part of them that needs to retreat within themselves every now and again for private reflection.

Health *Put yourself first, for once*

People born on this day need to take extra special care of their health as their extreme sensitivity—combined with the fact that they are likely to put the needs of others way ahead of their own—makes them vulnerable to the negative energies of others. It is vital that they work on their self-esteem, to strengthen themselves not just emotionally, but also physically; otherwise they are likely to suffer from stress, depression, compassion overload, or burnout. It goes without saying that they should make sure they eat a healthy diet rich in whole grains, fruits and vegetables and low in saturated fat and refined or processed foods. Moderate exercise, preferably activity they can perform alone to recharge their batteries such as jogging, walking or yoga, is highly recommended. Wearing, meditating on or surrounding themselves with the color yellow is good for their ego, and for increasing their confidence and optimism.

Career *Born healers*

These people are well suited to the caring or healing professions, to social work, or to careers where they can bring enlightenment or happiness to others such as education, the arts, music, dance, or drama. Other work options include advertising, international business, sales, medicine, and counseling.

Destiny *To devote themselves to the happiness of others*

The life path of people born on this day is to learn that they need to take care of their own emotional needs as well as the needs of others. Once they have worked on their ego, their destiny is to devote their considerable talents to bringing happiness or comfort to others.

Signs & symbols

Sun sign: Pisces

Ruling planet: Neptune, the speculator

Symbol: Two Fishes

Birth date ruler: Leo, the individual

Tarot card: The Wheel of Fortune (change)

Favorable numbers: 1, 4

Lucky days: Thursday and Sunday, especially when these days fall on 1, or 4 of the month

Lucky colors: Turquoise, orange, mellow green

Birthstone: Aquamarine

11 March

the birthday of the magician

Your greatest challenge is ...

to learn to relax the need to control everyone and everything

The way forward is ...

to understand that however important you are, no one, including yourself, is indispensable.

You're drawn to people born on ...

June 22 to July 23

You share a passion for imaginative debate and speculation, and this can create an intense and exciting bond.

Luck maker

Be here now

If you are so organized that you are busy planning and living in the future, you are missing the true pleasure of the moment. The power to attract luck your way is always in the moment.

Individuals born on March 11 are progressive individuals with one foot lightly placed in the present and another firmly placed in the future. The key to their success is their intuition. They use this not in a dreamy but in a highly productive way to increase their chances of success. Magician-like, they have learned to harness its power to achieve their goals.

The keen mind and visionary ability of these people gives them an uncanny knack of seeking out opportunities and people that will help them progress. They always seem to be one step ahead and, if they are not the source of a trend, they will use their imagination and energy to work with that trend or, better still, move beyond it. The upside of all this is that they are often right at the cutting edge; the downside is that they can lapse into selfish or manipulative behavior if it will help them get what they want.

Although they do possess strong ambition and a powerful influence over others, their goals are generally personal rather than global. Once they set out to achieve a goal, they will work tirelessly until they it is theirs. Their emphasis on looking ahead is highlighted in their lives from childhood until the age of thirty-nine; these are the years in which they develop their self-confidence. After the age of forty, however, they become more relaxed about their goals, less focused on change and more on recognition and stability.

The key to their success lies in an ability to get their powerful intuition to work for, rather than against, them. It is their intuition that values objects, situations or people and their intuition which eventually teaches them to value their own judgment over everything else. Once they have settled on a course that is worthy of them, understanding that there are some things they can never control, they often use their intuition and strong will-power not only to successfully predict the future but also to play a part in creating it.

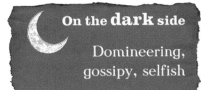

On the dark side

Domineering, gossipy, selfish

At your best

Progressive, intuitive, powerful

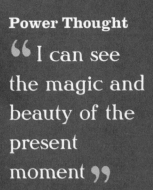

Love *Lively and fun*

Fortunately, people born on March 11 tend to be more relaxed in their relationships than they are in their working lives. They understand the importance of downtime and spending time with loved ones, enjoying nothing better than conversation with family and friends. Life is always fun and lively when they are around, and their partner needs to understand that discipline and routine in a relationship doesn't suit them well.

Health *Look at me*

People born on this day tend to be quite concerned about their appearance and may spend at lot of time shopping for new clothes, at the hairdressers or beautician, or having treatments of some kind. Although they often look stylish and well presented, they need to remember that the foundation for good looks lies not in the mirror but in a healthy diet and exercise program. They should make sure they eat a diet rich in anti-aging nutrients and antioxidants—in other words, a diet rich in fruits, vegetables and other unrefined and unprocessed foods—and take regular exercise, such as walking, swimming, jogging, cycling, or dancing. Wearing, meditating on or surrounding themselves with the color purple will help them focus less on what the future holds and more on spiritual or higher things.

Career *Born investors*

These people often make good investors or stock market traders, as they have an instinct for what will work and what won't. They also make great antique collectors. Alternatively, their love of good food may lead them toward a career in catering or nutrition, and their ability to predict the need for reform may push them toward politics, public service, labor unions, or education, as well as music, arts, entertainment, healing, or alternative therapies.

Destiny *To make their work the best it can be*

The life path for people born on this day is to learn to value both the present and the future. Once they have learned to make their intuition work for them and harnessed their creativity, their destiny is to make whatever they are working on or involved in the best and most effective that it can possibly be.

Signs & symbols

Sun sign: Pisces

Ruling planet: Neptune, the speculator

Symbol: Two Fishes

Birth date ruler: Moon, the intuitive

Tarot card: Justice (discernment)

Favorable numbers: 2, 5

Lucky days: Thursday and Monday, especially when these days fall on 2 and 5 of the month

Lucky colors: Turquoise, silver, pale blue

Birthstone: Aquamarine

March 11

12 March

the birthday of
the untamed spirit

People born on March 12 have tremendous spirit and a desire to explore as many aspects of life as they can in order to gain knowledge and test themselves in increasingly demanding challenges and adventures. Others may fear for their safety or warn them to be more responsible but it's impossible for these untamed spirits to listen, let alone heed this advice.

Although they thrive on competition, these people are not generally motivated by a need to score points over others. The motivation is to challenge themselves and see how far they can go with their own natural abilities. In their work life they think nothing of leaving a secure job to start a new venture; in their personal lives they are attracted to people with an air of danger about them. Sometimes their exploits will land them in big trouble, but they will usually have considered the risks beforehand so that they know what they are letting themselves in for. Because they are so courageous, they tend to be resilient enough to withstand any setbacks, learn from their mistakes and bounce back even stronger.

The danger for these people is a lack of direction; they need to settle on a course that is worthy of their courage and resilience. Since they are often multi-talented it can be hard for them to find focus but it is important for them to specialize in a particular field if they are to come into their own. Up until the age of thirty-eight there is an emphasis on change and new ventures. Then, after the age of thirty-nine, there is a turning point when they tend to slow down, feeling a greater need for stability and financial security.

Strong believers in an afterlife and fate, these people have a profoundly intuitive and reflective side which they would do well to cultivate. Whatever they end up doing, one thing is sure: wherever these creative and courageous spirits are to be found, there will always be an element of danger, controversy and excitement swirling about them.

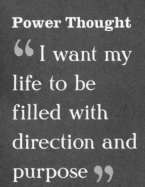
Love *Dangerous*

People born on March 12 have an air of danger about them and are attracted to people who are equally gorgeous and edgy. They love to play games and set traps in relationships and will often attract steady and genuinely loving people who are drawn to their craziness. They need to steer clear of exploiting those more vulnerable than them and to seek out people who are their match in energy, daring and eccentricity.

Health *Inner conflicts*

Despite their outward show of courage and daring, people born on this day may be prone to great emotional instability, perhaps from hardships as they were growing up. They need to learn to deal with their inner conflicts and face up to their insecurities, perhaps with the help of a counselor or therapist if family and friends are not an option. As far as diet is concerned, people born on this day tend to have a fast metabolism and can eat virtually what they want, but if weight problems occur they should cut down on saturated fat, and refined and processed comfort foods. Vigorous exercise and competitive sport to work off some of that manic energy is highly recommended. Wearing, meditating on or surrounding themselves with shades of blue and green will induce calm and encourage greater harmony and balance.

Career *Born stockbrokers*

These people have the potential to succeed in any career which requires them to take risks. If the world of business appeals, they may be drawn to stockbroking, investment or setting up their own business. They may also be interested in police work, especially that of a detective or secret agent, as well as careers in art, music, comedy, writing, journalism, and dance. Promotion, publishing and the media may also suit, as would education and lecturing.

Destiny *To lead others in radically new directions*

The life path of people born on this day is to find a sense of balance and stability in their lives. Once they are able to focus their energies, their destiny is to pursue radical quests and by so doing lead others in radically new directions.

Signs & symbols

Sun sign: Pisces

Ruling planet: Neptune, the speculator

Symbol: Two Fishes

Birth date ruler: Jupiter, the philosopher

Tarot card: The Hanged Man (reflection)

Favorable numbers: 3, 6

Lucky day: Thursday, especially when it falls on 3 and 6 of the month

Lucky colors: Turquoise, purple, apricot

Birthstone: Aquamarine

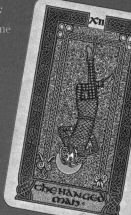

13 March

the birthday of otherworldly possibilities

Your greatest challenge is ...

steering clear of cynicism

The way forward is ...

to understand the power of your thoughts. If you think of something often enough, there is an increased likelihood of it becoming a self-fulfilling prophecy.

You're drawn to people born on ...

January 21 to February 19

You share a passion for the unconventional and a longing for trust and intimacy; this can create a lasting bond.

Luck maker

Expect good luck

Why do lucky charms sometimes work? Because people expect that they will. A positive attitude about luck attracts luck; that's the way it works.

People born on March 13 seem to have come into this world with an unshakable belief in their own fatalistic view. They are multitalented, curious and intelligent individuals instinctively drawn to what is unconventional and unexplained. Whether they are religious or not, they often believe in fate and otherworldly possibilities.

These people like to study the world and the people around them, often making predictions and judgments with wise finality. They have a talent for public discourse, and others tend to value their insights and come to them for advice. From an early age they probably challenged conventional thought and exhausted their parents and teachers with endless hows and whys. This insatiable curiosity seems to grow stronger as they grow older.

While it is important for these people to carry on exploring and understanding the unknown, they need to have a more pragmatic approach to the world. If they don't, they can get lost in esoteric or metaphysical worlds, never realizing their potential and not being taken seriously by others. There is also a risk that because they believe so strongly in predestination, they unwittingly steer events a certain way so that they become self-fulfilling prophecies. This is especially dangerous as they are prone to cynicism or negative expectation when life disappoints them. This tendency tends to be highlighted after the age of thirty-seven when there is greater inflexibility in their life. It is therefore important for people born on this day, especially when they grow older, to keep the spirit of optimism alive.

However tough things get for them, these people will always have an unshakable belief that there is more to life than has yet been discovered. This belief can help them overcome challenges and criticism that others would find overwhelming. They are often greatly admired for their resilience and incredible insight and as long as they aren't side-tracked by self-importance or negative expectation these people are capable of truly unique thoughts and achievements.

Love *Let others get to know you*

People born on March 13 need to resist the temptation to be cynical about relationships or write them off before they have had a chance to flourish. There is a strongly sensual and romantic side to them, and they need to find someone who admires them enough to express it, steering clear of people who criticize them or who don't recognize their strengths. They thrive best with a partner who is intelligent and open-minded.

Health *Lighten up*

People born on this day need to make sure that they don't get so caught up in the world of thought that they forget the importance of having fun; spending time relaxing with friends and loved ones is essential for them. As far as diet is concerned, they should experiment with a wide variety of foods but with an emphasis on what is fresh and natural, choosing whole foods rather than refined and processed ones. They should get plenty of exercise, preferably in the fresh air, and would enjoy mind–body therapies such as yoga and tai chi. Dancing is especially recommended as it is an opportunity for them to exercise and let their hair down. They are likely to be attracted to alternative medical therapies but need to make sure they can distinguish the genuine from the quack. Wearing, surrounding or meditating on the color yellow will encourage them to feel more optimistic about themselves and the world around them.

Career *Born diplomats*

Because they have a talent for public speaking, these people may be attracted to careers in politics, journalism or diplomacy. They also have the gift of dealing with the public and their good communication skills can be put to work in sales, marketing or publishing. Science and research might appeal, as might education, writing and the study of philosophy, religion, metaphysics, astronomy, and astrology.

Destiny *To lead others toward previously unknown insights*

The life path of people born on this day is to make sure they don't lose touch with the real world. Once they are able to unite their visionary tendencies with the realities of everyday life, they have the potential to lead others toward previously unknown insights.

14 March

the birthday of dazzling inventiveness

Your greatest challenge is ...

making a decision

The way forward is ...

to weigh up the pros and cons and follow your instincts. Making a decision keeps you moving forward because you can learn from your experience.

You're drawn to people born on ...

May 22 to June 21

You share a passion for discussion and intellectual stimulation, and this can create an intense and satisfying bond.

Luck maker

Step out of your comfort zone

We all like to stay in our comfort zone, where everything is possible and all options are kept open; as comforting as this place is, it is not the place to go for opportunity.

The potential for success for people born on March 14 lies in their intelligence, versatility and open-mindedness. They have the mental dexterity to jump from one idea to another without losing track of the bigger picture.

The universal attitude that people born on this day possess encourages a humanitarian outlook. Abhorring intolerance and bigotry, they are extremely sensitive to the feelings of others; this makes them extremely popular at home and at work. They have the ability to take what is familiar and transform it into something new by presenting it in an unexpected way.

Although there is a dash of brilliance about them, these people can have problems making decisions. This is not the result of a lack of direction; quite the opposite, as these people often have a very clear vision. Because they have such a universal outlook—visualizing countless future scenarios—they can sometimes find it hard to decide on a single course of action that takes into account all viewpoints.

The only danger with this approach is that it can lead to information overload, so they should find a stance they can champion or a direction they remain faithful to, even if it means disagreeing with other viewpoints. If they can't do that, the risks they run are confusion and lack of direction. Until the age of thirty-six the emphasis tends to be on swift changes of mind and direction. Fortunately, after the age of thirty-seven these people are able to make a stand; by the age of forty most of them find their focus and really come into their own.

As well as indecisiveness, people born on March 14 also need to overcome their tendency to be self-effacing. To fulfill their potential they need to trust what they feel, allowing their minds to take them to unfrequented places. Once they have learned to be bold, making decisions if life demands it, the uncommon intellectual gifts and daring inventiveness they are blessed with ensure that there will be no end to the wonders they can create.

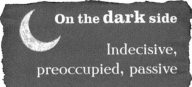

On the **dark** side

Indecisive, preoccupied, passive

At your **best**

Inventive, curious, affectionate

Love *Throw caution to the wind*

People born on March 14 often work hard to please their partners but they should also recognize their own needs and not shy away from expressing them. Slow and careful before offering their heart, they can come across as over-serious and need to learn sometimes to throw caution to the wind to keep their love life alive.

Health *Stand up*

People born on this day don't enjoy routine or the mundane so they need to make sure their diet and exercise plan has plenty of variety. As far as diet is concerned, because they are often excellent cooks and enjoy nothing better than an evening with good food and friends, they tend to eat healthily but they do need to make sure they don't over-indulge and eat for the sake of eating; this can lead to weight problems. Sitting around talking or working for long periods can also lead to problem with circulation, especially in the legs, so they need to make sure they get plenty of exercise. If their work is sedentary, they should do some stretching or walking every half-hour or so. In fact, regular walking and swimming, and exercise that is moderate rather than vigorous, are highly recommended. Wearing, meditating on or surrounding themselves with the color red will help them be more assertive in their decision making, and yellow will help boost their optimism and self-confidence.

Career *Born lecturers*

These people are excellent with words and can explain clearly and precisely what they think. They may therefore be drawn to careers in education, lecturing, debating and politics. They may also have a gift for science, accountancy, law or writing, and their humanitarian concerns may lead them to careers in social reform or the healing professions. Alternatively, they may express their creativity and inventiveness through music and the arts.

Destiny *To discover startling new insights*

Their life path is to find a direction or a focus that they can commit to. Once they are able to make a stand, their destiny is to reinvigorate the familiar by discover startling new insights.

Signs & symbols

Sun sign: Pisces

Ruling planet: Neptune, the speculator

Symbol: Two Fishes

Birth date ruler: Mercury, the communicator

Tarot card: Temperance (moderation)

Favorable numbers: 5, 8

Lucky days: Thursday and Wednesday, especially when this day falls on 5 and 8 of the month

Lucky colors: Turquoise, green, lilac

Birthstone: Aquamarine

15 March

the birthday of the mountain climber

People born on March 15 are adventurous and determined individuals with the potential to become leaders in whatever area they choose to focus on. They have great personal magnetism and others tend to follow where they lead. They might, however, be arrogant and competitive in their race to get ahead, but once they reach the summit they can keep this in check, making intelligent and benevolent leaders. They should be careful not to alienate friends and loved ones, as they depend on the support of those they really care about.

Progress in their chosen line of work tends to be rapid for people born on this day. Although they are adventurous they aren't reckless, and have the ability to weigh up positives and negatives, form a plan of action and concentrate on achieving their aims. This is a winning combination, especially when allied to their enthusiasm and lovable personality. Before the age of thirty-five they may experiment with various different directions; during this time they are most likely to place greater emphasis on getting ahead than the goal itself. This can impact their personal happiness but fortunately after the age of thirty-six they seek a meaningful direction for their ambition. This is when they really come into their own, although they should watch out for a streak of obstinacy during these years.

Given their desire to scale the heights in their chosen field, people born on this day are often attracted to activities that can, quite literally, take them higher, such as mountain climbing, skiing and flying. Those who are more timid may well find that it is failure in their chosen field that terrifies them more than high places.

Potential leaders of others, these people need to learn not to overwhelm themselves and others with their restless drive to succeed. Once they have learned to ground themselves with the support of others and a goal worthy of their intelligence and courage, they have all the originality and dynamic power they need to reach their place of destiny—the very top.

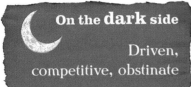

On the **dark** side

Driven, competitive, obstinate

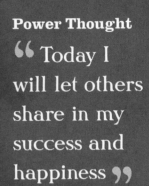

At your **best**

Charismatic, ambitious, enthusiastic

Love *Variety is the key*

People born on March 15 need to learn to place just as much importance on their personal as their professional life, as without the love of the people they care about their achievements will seem empty. They may have problems staying faithful, but once they find someone who shares their love of variety and adventure they are loyal, faithful and exciting lovers.

Health *That elusive high*

People born on this day need to be careful that in their search for variety and adventure they don't become addicted to sex, drugs, gambling, and alcohol. It is important for them to understand that addictions are ultimately for people who feel unfilled in their personal and professional life; there are more satisfying and healthy ways of finding that elusive high, such as the love of a partner, a walk in beautiful countryside or the satisfaction of a job well done. As far as diet is concerned, people born on this day need to increase their intake of natural foods and decrease their intake of processed foods and saturated fat. Regular exercise on a daily basis is also recommended, as are stretching exercises to encourage them to be flexible in body and mind. If stress or anxiety is a constant part of their life, they might want to try to burn a chamomile-, lavender- or sandalwood-scented candle. These produce a calming effect.

Career *Born pilots*

These people are often attracted to careers that can take them physically higher, such as aviation, mountain guiding or skiing. Other careers that might interest include management, advertising, law, banking, music, or being their own boss, but whatever career they choose, people born on this day tend to rise to the top.

Destiny *To blaze a spectacular trail in life*

The life path of these people is to make sure that as they rise to the top they do not become competitive, arrogant and insensitive to the needs of those who care about them. Once they are able to ground themselves, their destiny is to use their adventurous spirit to blaze a spectacular trail in life.

Power Thought

" Today I will let others share in my success and happiness "

Signs & symbols

Sun sign: Pisces

Ruling planet: Neptune, the speculator

Symbol: Two Fishes

Birth date ruler: Venus, the lover

Tarot card: The Devil (instinct)

Favorable numbers: 6, 9

Lucky days: Thursday and Friday, especially when this day falls on 6 and 9 of the month

Lucky colors: Turquoise, pink, pale blue

Birthstone: Aquamarine

16 March

the birthday of equilibrium

People born on March 16 generally appear to others as well-balanced personalities who manage to combine their imaginative potential with a practical, grounded approach. Their talent for maintaining equilibrium or seeking the middle way is the secret of their success.

People born on this day are at their best when they can find a sense of balance; they have a great talent for negotiation and for making people pull together as a team. Their love of balance also displays itself in their personal life. At work they are paragons of ambition and discipline but at home they know how to unwind and reflect. They have a dreamy, intuitive side that is sensitive to the needs of others but they are not impractical and can use their common sense to make sure everyone feels important. Their homes and workplaces are tidy and elegant but not obsessively so; as a result, people often feel instantly comfortable when visiting.

Because of the high value they place on balance, there is often a kind of wholesomeness about these people. There is a danger, however, that their balanced outlook sometimes overlooks the possibility of unexpected setbacks; they need to learn to pay attention to warning signs before trouble actually hits. They also need to be careful that their own views or values don't become so muted that they disappear altogether, especially after the age of thirty-four when they can express a need for less change and conflict, and more stability and security in their lives. They need to be careful during this time not to let their practical, hedonistic side overshadow their idealistic and intuitive side.

Above all, these people are multi-talented individuals who can channel their imagination and originality into schemes that are both visionary and practical. Once they are able to accept rather than deny their own changeable nature and take on responsibilities with excitement rather than apprehension, they will not only find a true sense of balance and equilibrium, but also the exhilarating sense of achievement and fulfillment that goes with it.

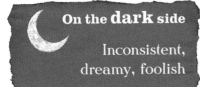

On the dark side

Inconsistent, dreamy, foolish

At your best

Practical, imaginative, insightful

Power Thought

"I am constantly moving forward in the direction of my principles"

Signs & symbols

Sun sign: Pisces

Ruling planet: Neptune, the speculator

Symbol: Two Fishes

Birth date ruler: Neptune, the speculator

Tarot card: The Tower (breakthrough)

Favorable numbers: 1, 7

Lucky days: Thursday and Monday, especially when this day falls on 1 and 7 of the month

Lucky colors: All shades of blue

Birthstone: Aquamarine

Love *For keeps*

People born on March 16 have a talent for making and keeping friends, often putting the needs of others above their own. This is also true of long-term relationships, if they are able both to overcome past hurts that inhibit deep commitment and refrain from being overly sensible about everything. Once they learn to philosophize less and laugh more they make wonderful partners.

Health *Personal responsibility*

People born on this day are likely to be sensible when it comes to their diet and exercise routine, taking great care to ensure they eat healthily and exercise regularly. This is because they understand that looking after their health is all part of taking personal responsibility for their lives. What might be lacking in their approach, however, is a sense of fun, so they should make sure they dine out more with good company, experiment more in their cooking and eating, and get plenty of exercise, preferably in the outdoors. Vigorous exercise, perhaps with an element of risk, such as ice hockey, diving, or horse riding, is recommended. Wearing, meditating on or surrounding themselves with the color red will encourage them to be more daring in their approach to life.

Career *Born mediators*

These people will flourish in situations in which they can lead and inspire, and they make great teachers or business leaders. Imaginative and sensitive to color but also practical in their application, they make great designers and image consultants, as well as art dealers or critics. They also make excellent diplomats or mediators as well as counselors, therapists, social workers, or reformers.

Destiny *To improve the lives of others with their vision*

The life path of people born on this day is to learn to place as much emphasis on their own values as those of others. Once they have learned to express themselves, their destiny is to put their energy into visionary and progressive concepts that can practically improve the lives of others.

17 March

the birthday of magical sparkle

People born on March 17 have an ethereal quality about them and often appear to others to be floating through life. This isn't to say that they are lazy or never experience setbacks and difficulties; quite the contrary, as they are incredibly hardworking with their fair share of frustrations. Yet however tough life gets, they always seem able to transcend the mundane, endowing all their actions with a lightness and sparkle.

Often charismatic with creative talents, people born on this day are also imaginative, optimistic and receptive, making enchanting company both at home and at work. Their difficulty lies in their drifting from one interest to another; rather than facing a challenge, they prefer to avoid or flow around it. There are many possible reasons for this: lack of self-confidence, dislike of confrontation and, above all, a fear of commitment and responsibility.

When properly channeled, their curiosity and sense of optimism can bring great rewards, and the admiration and support of others. However, the more they evade conflict and difficult situations when a project or relationship encounters setbacks, the more they might be considered irresponsible, flighty and unreliable. It is important for these people to learn to face up to tedious or difficult situations; this will provide them with greater satisfaction than drifting lightly but aimlessly through life. Before the age of thirty-three there is an emphasis on change and new ventures, but thereafter they often become more secure, responsible and less flighty.

Blessed with a caring nature, these people are often in a position to help others. The responsibility of this may be a struggle for these sparkling souls, but the ability to be patient and reliable in their relationships with others and in their professional life forms a vital part of their self-confidence. Once their butterfly nature has learned that touching the ground doesn't mean the death of their creativity and optimism but rather the making of it, they have the potential to lead not just exciting and creative lives but truly magical ones.

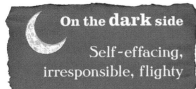

On the dark side

Self-effacing, irresponsible, flighty

At your best

Inspired, hardworking, adaptable

Power Thought

66 Today I will confront my fears with boldness 99

Love *In love with love*

People born on March 17 are often surrounded by admirers but they may resist having their wings clipped by long-term commitment and responsibility. The mundane and routine aspects of relationships unsettle them, but if they find a partner who indulges their need for independence of thought and action, their love of love will often win out and they can thrive in a committed relationship.

Health *Don't neglect warning signs*

People born on this day have an optimistic approach to life that is excellent for both their physical and emotional health; they should, however, guard against over-optimism and should pay attention to warning signs before they develop into major illnesses. They may have physical problems relating to their joints and should make sure their diet is rich in lubricating Omega-3 foods such as oily fish, nuts and seeds. They also need to take plenty of exercise to keep their bones, muscles and joints strong. Jogging as well as swimming, cycling and dancing are recommended. Wearing, meditating on or surrounding themselves with the color blue will encourage them to do some serious thinking and face up to their responsibilities.

Career *Born dancers*

These people often find themselves drawn toward design, art and crafts where they can delight others with their sensitive interpretation of the magic they see around them. They may also be interested in education, travel, public service, politics, law, philosophy, aviation, and religion. Being creative, they may also express their emotions through the light and graceful movements of dance, or through music or drama.

Destiny *To encourage others to feel more inspired and optimistic*

The life path of people born on this day is to learn to finish what they have started. Once they are able to deal with responsibility and learn from their mistakes, their destiny is to lead others toward a lighter and more optimistic approach to life.

Signs & symbols

Sun sign: Pisces

Ruling planet: Neptune, the speculator

Symbol: Two Fishes

Birth date ruler: Saturn, the teacher

Tarot card: The Star (hope)

Favorable numbers: 2, 8

Lucky days: Thursday and Saturday, especially when this day falls on a 2 and 8 of the month

Lucky colors: Turquoise, maroon, violet

Birthstone: Aquamarine

18 March

the birthday of spiritual strength

Your greatest challenge is ...

spending enough time with loved ones

The way forward is ...

to understand that as satisfying as personal ambition is, it can never replace the rewards and fulfillment of close personal relationships.

You're drawn to people born on ...

April 21 to May 21

You share a passion for adventure and surprises, and this can create an intense and exciting bond.

Luck maker

Go out of your way

Offer your help when people are down on their luck. This is the time they most need your help, and you will have the luck and happiness that friendship brings with it for life.

People born on March 18 are blessed with great courage, resilience and the ability to recover from adverse circumstances not once but time after time. They have remarkable physical, emotional and spiritual strength and, if they can learn the lessons from each setback, they've the potential to become inspirational motivators and leaders.

People born on this day are intelligent, multi-talented and resourceful. They will use their considerable energy and will-power to overcome all obstacles. Their life may have been particularly challenging during their youth and these early knocks have given them the resilience they need to succeed. They have a knack of being in the right place at the right time, a great sense of humor and an optimistic outlook; as a result, people find them appealing but also exhausting, as they tend to live at a fast pace.

The danger for these people is that their preoccupation with moving forward or bouncing back can cause them to neglect not just important details but also the feelings of others. It is important for them to pay greater attention to details so these don't create problems later and to make sure the demands of those close to them are met. Before the age of thirty-two they are likely to be more confident and assertive but also more obsessive and chaotic in their approach to their goals. After the age of thirty-three they are likely to slow down a little and become more through, secure and settled.

The recuperative powers of people born on this day are remarkable. This is partly due to their spiritual strength and patience; they have an unshakable belief that however tough things are now they will be better tomorrow. More often than not, life rewards this positive attitude and things improve significantly. Once these generous, courageous and resourceful people learn to avoid a tendency toward ruthlessness, they can earn the admiration and support of others. Whatever field they choose to work in, the lives of those they touch will be changed forever by their intensity and bravery.

Love *Thrill of the chase*

People born on March 18 like an element of danger in their relationships, tending to be attracted to individuals who will challenge them physically, mentally and emotionally. Because they love a challenge, partners should let them do most of the pursuing and be prepared for plenty of surprises. Once they are in a committed relationship, however, they treasure their partner's loyalty and return it in full.

Health *Family atmosphere*

People born on this day generally enjoy life and this is reflected in their health, which tends to be good. They do, however, run the risk of becoming self-obsessed, which can alienate them from friends and family. It is important for them to make sure they spend enough time relaxing and unwinding in the company of people they care about. As far as diet is concerned, they tend to eat on the go and would benefit from sitting down at a table, preferably with company, as this, along with chewing their food properly, will help them digest their food and its nutrients and also give them time to slow down. Vigorous exercise, preferably team sports—to work off energy and encourage them to flourish in a team—is also recommended. Wearing, meditating on or surrounding themselves with the color green will restore their energies, encouraging greater harmony in themselves and others.

Career *Born arbitrators*

These people have an ability to see the bigger picture and multiple points of view; for this reason they can make great mediators, agents, negotiators, debaters, and arbitrators. They may also be suited to careers in which their resilience will serve them well: the entertainment world, politics, business and teaching. Careers that involve travel and working with the public will also suit them, as will movie-making, design and architecture.

Destiny *To inspire others by their own courageous example*

The life path of people born on this day is to put the focus less on their own personal goals and desires and more on the needs of others. Once they have learned to temper their ruthless streak, their destiny is to influence and inspire others to rise above challenges and achieve personal success.

Signs & symbols

Sun sign: Pisces

Ruling planet: Neptune, the speculator

Symbol: Two Fishes

Birth date ruler: Mars, the warrior

Tarot card: The Moon (imagination)

Favorable numbers: 3, 9

Lucky days: Thursday and Tuesday, especially when this day falls on 3 and 9 of the month

Lucky colors: Turquoise, scarlet

Birthstone: Aquamarine

March 18

19 March

the birthday of true grit

Your greatest challenge is ...

learning to listen to the viewpoints of others

The way forward is ...

to understand that by listening to others you will learn far more than by clinging to your beliefs.

You're drawn to people born on ...

July 24 to August 23

Your mutual passion for achievement and need for security make this a fulfilling and satisfying bond.

Luck maker

Keep your eyes and ears open

You must explore new possibilities if you want to strike lucky. Lucky people are always hungry for new information, alternative viewpoints and fresh experiences.

People born on March 19 are blessed with considerable motivation and vitality. Others are often drawn to them because they possess a childlike energy and openness. Although they may give the appearance of being dreamy at times, they are extremely practical and determined.

Once they have settled on a goal, these people will work tirelessly to achieve it. They are a brilliant combination of imagination and action, creating a mental image of what they want and then taking assertive, methodical and practical steps to achieve it. In fact, they are virtually unstoppable when they have put their action plan in place, and however difficult, mundane or repetitious things are, they will see it through.

This determined approach is a recipe for success and—if directed toward a worthy goal—can take them not just to the top but to new ground. It can, however, also backfire. When their goals can't be realized, it can leave them feeling disappointed and depressed. Part of the problem is that many of their goals and dreams are based on material success and the recognition of others. They need to learn that fulfillment does not just come from outward things but also from inner contentment. Only when they are able to look within and understand the importance of both personal and professional satisfaction will they achieve lasting happiness and success.

Until the age of thirty-one there is a tendency for these people to be active in the pursuit of their goals. From the age of thirty-two to sixty-two they may be more relaxed but may also show signs of stubbornness. These are the years in which they should not neglect the importance of their inner life or stop sharing their feelings with their numerous friends.

The blend of vision and action that people born on this day possess is a powerful and seductive combination. As long as they remember to keep their ego in check and acquire a degree of self-knowledge, they have both the fantasy and the fire to make their dreams come true.

Love *Goal-focused*

Romance and intimacy are essential to people born on March 19. They can put their relationships at risk by appearing to place more importance on their professional goals but, once they understand how important it is for them to share their feelings with loved ones, they make loyal and imaginative partners. Their ideal lover would be someone who believes in their goals and their ability to make them come true.

Health *Soothe stress away*

Because people born on this day tend to be outwardly focused and success- or goal-orientated, they are often prone to stress-related disorders such as headaches, fatigue, comfort eating, and insomnia. They will probably need to find ways to ease the tension; regular massages, walks in the fresh air as well as soothing herbal teas, such as chamomile, will be beneficial. As far as diet is concerned, they should make sure they don't neglect to eat healthily. Plenty of nutritious snacks, such as fruit and a handful of nuts during the day, are recommended to keep their energy levels constant. Vigorous exercise isn't recommended because so much of their life is competitive, but moderate to mild exercise, such as jogging, walking and swimming, will help them feel and sleep better. Wearing, meditating on or surrounding themselves with soothing shades of purple will encourage them to look within for answers.

Career *Born movers and shakers*

Whatever career they choose, once these people devote their prodigious energies and powers of organization to it they have the potential to be highly successful. It may not be their first choice (business or management may initially appeal) but they are often at their happiest when working in fields in which they know they can do some good, such as politics, the military, science, social reform, the arts, the healing professions, or education.

Destiny *To effect social improvements*

The life path of people born on this day is to learn to get to know themselves better. Once they have acquired a degree of self-knowledge, their destiny is to use their prodigious determination and talents to effect social improvements.

Signs & symbols

Sun sign: Pisces

Ruling planet: Neptune, the speculator

Symbol: Two Fishes

Birth date ruler: Sun, the individual

Tarot card: The Sun (enthusiasm)

Favorable numbers: 1, 4

Lucky days: Thursday and Sunday, especially when this day falls on 1 and 4 of the month

Lucky colors: Turquoise, orange, green

Birthstone: Aquamarine

March 19

20 March

the birthday of the insightful wanderer

Your greatest challenge is ...

putting your needs first

The way forward is ...

to understand that only after you know how to give to yourself can you give to others.

You're drawn to people born on ...

June 22 to July 23

You are both compassionate and mature souls, and this can create a physically, emotionally and spiritually rewarding union.

Luck maker

Take care of yourself

Creating luck requires both a giving nature and self-love. Lucky people know how important self-care is for their well-being, so they integrate it into their lives.

People born on March 20 were born on the last day of the Zodiac wheel, and in many ways they are the most insightful and fully evolved individuals of the year. They possess such a wealth of gifts that it is hard to pinpoint one, but underneath their versatility lies their great compassion for others, a gift that can bring them great rewards, but at a price.

Those born on this day can feel overwhelmed by their feelings for others and therefore prone to depression and feelings of helplessness. They are also natural optimists, believing in the basic goodness of people, with a talent for boosting morale and getting people to work together. The danger for these people is that they can become confused to the point of indecision when they empathize too strongly with others' emotions.

Although they should never repress their sensitivity—it is one of the greatest assets—they should strive to become emotionally stronger. Until the age of thirty, if they don't learn to protect themselves, others will sometimes try to take advantage of their vulnerability and generosity. After thirty-one they have the potential for greater emotional stability; this is when they become more effective instruments for good. After the age of sixty-one they are more interested in communication and the exchange of ideas.

There is a deep longing within these people to make the world a better place. There may be many changes of direction as they experiment with different roles, and their experiences will help them discover who they really are and what they really want from their lives. Once they do settle on a goal, often to improve the lives of others in some way, they will achieve their dreams because they are both practical and idealistic. They will also find that the older they get, the more confident they become. In their later years they will draw on their rich experience of life to become a wise elder with a wealth of invaluable advice to offer the next generation.

On the **dark** side
Indecisive, unsure, oversensitive

At your **best**
Optimistic, compassionate, versatile

Love *Duty bound*

People born on March 20 can have problems distinguishing between loyalty and love and they may as a result stay in a passionless relationship out of a sense of duty. This reveals the maturity and strength of their character, but they do need to remember that their first responsibility should be to their own happiness. They should ask themselves who is really benefiting if they remain in a place from which love has departed.

Health *Get physical*

People born on this day tend to live in their head and to neglect their physical needs, so it is important for them to place more emphasis on the physical. They should make sure they eat a healthy diet rich in nutritious and tasty whole foods, fruits and vegetables and, instead of bolting down their food with their minds on something else, take the time to really taste the subtle flavors and amazing textures that all good foods possess. Moderate to mild exercise, preferably outdoors so they get plenty of sunshine and fresh air, is also recommended. Wearing, meditating on or surrounding themselves with the color blue will help them stay cool when all those around them are losing their heads.

Career *Born counselors*

These people often make excellent counselors, psychologists, advisors, consultants, managers, coaches, diplomats, and teachers. Their sensitivity for what is going on around them may also find expression in the world of art, music, drama, writing, and dance as well as photography, design and movie-making. They also excel in any career which involves dealing with the public.

Destiny *To help others reach their full potential*

The life path of people born on this day is to find out what they really want. Once they know in which direction they should be heading, their destiny is to help others overcome challenges and reach their full potential.

March 20

Signs & symbols

Sun signs: Pisces/Aries

Ruling planets: Neptune, the speculator/Mars, the warrior

Symbols: Two Fishes/The Ram

Birth date ruler: Moon, the intuitive

Tarot card: Judgment (responsibility)

Favorable numbers: 2, 5

Lucky days: Thursday and Monday, especially when these day fall on 2 and 5 of the month

Lucky colors: Turquoise, scarlet, silver

Birthstone: Aquamarine

21 March

the birthday of clear sightedness

Your greatest challenge is …

learning to be more tactful

The way forward is …

to understand that compromise or softening your focus or your words to accommodate others does not mean you have sold out on your values.

You're drawn to people born on …

November 21 to December 23

You share a passion for adventure and non-conformity, and this can create an exciting and intense bond.

Luck maker

Learn to handle your impatience

When you are in an impatient or angry state you can't create luck. Remove your tendency to exaggerate your own needs and you will begin to feel more relaxed, and luckier.

People born on March 21 have their own set of values and refuse to compromise in any way. In keeping with the pivotal significance of their birthday—the beginning of Spring and the Zodiac year—they are powerful, free-thinking individuals with an iron will to succeed whose single-mindedness almost always works.

People born on this day do not care much for convention. They are honest and direct in all their dealings and opinions; their thoughts are often so transparent that they don't need to say much to make their feelings known. They are clear-sighted in their beliefs and other people know exactly where they stand with them. This isn't to say they are aggressive and overbearing; quite the opposite, as they are often quiet in their confidence. They simply live according to their own values and if other people don't understand these, they aren't prepared to explain themselves, much preferring to go it alone.

Although remarkably clear-sighted and independent, these people can come across as inflexible, passive and antisocial when they choose to withdraw and live in splendid isolation. They also have an inclination to be stubborn and can become argumentative and blunt to get their own way. They should learn not to alienate others when pursuing their goals, accepting that success does not always result from following a direct path. Between the ages of thirty and sixty their stubborn tendencies are likely to be highlighted. During these years they need to make sure they work on transforming their way of thinking so that it takes into account the viewpoints of others.

Once they learn to moderate their impatience and their tendency to isolate themselves when things aren't going their way, they have the potential to become exceptional leaders, utilizing their powers of perception, intuition and considerable energy to great effect. When these people find themselves in a position to impress others with their talents and free-thinking action, all who come into contact with them will be more spontaneous and clear-sighted about who they are and what they want.

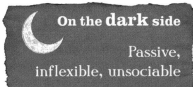

On the **dark** side
Passive, inflexible, unsociable

At your **best**
Perceptive, honest, powerful

Love *In search of an equal*

People born on March 21 do have the tendency to prefer their own company to the company of others but ultimately they are at their happiest when they find a partner who is their equal in intelligence and independence. They prefer the hunt to the chase but when they do give their heart to someone it is usually forever.

Health *Don't go it alone*

People born on this day tend to be extremely self-sufficient when it comes to their health. They prefer to take care of themselves when sick and to cheer themselves up when they feel low. Although they understand the importance of taking responsibility for their own well-being, they do need to make sure that they don't shut themselves away from the joys and rewards of receiving the love and attention of those close to them. As far as diet is concerned, they tend to have simple tastes but they can get stuck in a rut eating the same things on a weekly or sometimes even daily basis. They should try increasing their nutrient intake by experimenting with a variety of different foods. Moderate exercise, in particular dancing, aerobics and team sports, is recommended for the physical and the social benefits. Wearing, meditating on or surrounding themselves with the color orange will help them open up to others more.

Career *Born commanders*

These people have great leadership potential which they can put to use in military, police, or business careers as well as education, business management, and law. With their honest approach they are also particularly good in sales and marketing, and, if they choose to develop their creative skills, they may be drawn toward careers in advertising and the arts. And because they are so good at working alone, they may also turn their attention toward setting up their own business.

Destiny *To blaze an inspirational trail*

The life path of people born on this day is to learn to work with others as part of a team. Once they are able to do that, their destiny is to blaze an inspirational trail with their determination and conviction.

Signs & symbols

Sun signs: Aries/Pisces

Ruling planets: Mars, the warrior/Neptune, the speculator

Symbols: The Ram/Two Fishes

Birth date ruler: Jupiter, the philosopher

Tarot card: The World (fulfillment)

Favorable numbers: 3, 6

Lucky days: Tuesday and Thursday, especially when these days fall on 3 and 6 of the month

Lucky colors: Red, mauve, green

Birthstone: Diamond

March 21

22 March

the birthday of frankness

Your greatest challenge is ...

learning to show tact

The way forward is ...

to understand that sometimes directness comes across as self-importance. Being tactful is presenting the truth in a way that considers the feelings of others.

You're drawn to people born on ...

January 21 to February 19

You share a passion for openness, honesty and romance, and this can create an intense and loving bond.

Luck maker

Don't interrupt other people

Don't immediately jump in with your views when someone is talking. Listen to their views and ask them questions. You might hear something really important. Lucky people know how to listen; unlucky people don't.

People born on March 22 tend to be frank, confident individuals without a hidden agenda. They really are an open book, soon gaining the respect, protection and support of almost everyone they meet. Their honorable nature and reliability may even earn them a well-deserved following or, at the very least, a small group of ardent admirers.

Although they possess a powerful desire to achieve their goals, it is never at the expense of their personal values. They are the sort of people who always speak their minds because they value truth above all else. Although this can sometimes offend and wound others, more often than not others find themselves assimilating what these people say. The power and influence they have over others is an awesome responsibility for them and, if they can learn to channel it sensitively, they really can help others search for the truth or see the facts of a situation.

People born on this day may be uncompromising, and occasionally overbearing and proud, but they are not stubborn or inflexible when it comes to learning something new. They are often full of a curiosity that can draw them toward diverse experiences, and nothing fascinates them more than new technology and scientific discoveries. Their wondering mind may also be responsible for the many changes of direction in their lives, especially in their twenties. After the age of twenty-nine, however, there may be less emphasis on change and new ventures and more on stability and security, and this is when they really come into their own.

These people can get carried away by heroic images of themselves and by their enthusiasm for their current project or ideal; but generally, when they find a goal that is worthy of them, their refusal to be diverted from their chosen course of action gives them enormous potential for success. And when that success is achieved—which it inevitably is—there will be few who begrudge them it or feel that these honest, reliable and honorable individuals do not deserve every second of it.

On the dark side

Overbearing, unaware, proud

At your best

Reliable, confident, curious

Love *Surprises*

People born on March 22 find it hard to deal with indirectness in relationships and can get very impatient if others don't tell them directly what is concerning them. Surprisingly, despite being extremely reliable in their professional and social lives, when it comes to close personal relationships they may be more unpredictable, blowing hot one minute and cold the next. It is important for them to get in touch with their feelings and be as honest in love as they are in life.

Health *The middle way*

When it comes to diet and exercise, people born on this day can go in two directions. They are either people who like to eat what they want, especially sugary, fatty foods and generally take their health and their weight for granted; or they are people who become obsessive about their diet, exercise routine and weight. It is important for them to find some kind of middle ground regarding health and appearance, and this means eating a healthy, balanced diet, taking regular exercise for thirty or so minutes a day and not letting the scales rule their life. Wearing, meditating on or surrounding themselves with the color green will encourage them to find both inner and outer balance.

Career *Born lawyers*

People born on this day often see life in black and white terms so they may be drawn to careers in law, science, technology, or medical research. Their search for truth and beauty may also draw them to the arts, in particular dance, as well as sculpture, music and art criticism. They also possess natural abilities for leadership and management, and may have a talent for spotting opportunities and setting up their own business.

Destiny *To enlighten and inspire others*

The life path of these people is to learn not to dismiss the feelings of others in their frank discussion of an issue. Once they have learned the art of compromise, their destiny is to uncover the real nature of a situation and—by example—to encourage others to do the same.

Signs & symbols

Sun signs: Aries/Pisces

Ruling planets: Mars, the warrior/Neptune, the speculator

Symbols: The Ram/Two Fishes

Birth date ruler: Uranus, the visionary

Tarot card: The Fool (freedom)

Favorable numbers: 4, 7

Lucky days: Tuesday and Sunday, especially when these days fall on 4 and 7 of the month

Lucky colors: Red, silver, purple

Birthstone: Diamond

23 March

the birthday of
the eternal student

Your greatest challenge is ...

to pay attention to your emotional needs.

The way forward is ...

to understand that if you aren't in touch with your feelings, your self-knowledge and self-esteem will be poor.

You're drawn to people born on ...

October 24 to November 22

You share a passion for adventure, variety and communication and this can create a rewarding and intense bond.

Luck maker

Get in touch with nature

To lead a balanced life you need sometimes to be able to stop thinking and doing and just be; one of the most effective ways to calm your mind is to get in touch with nature.

People born on March 23 are fascinated by everyone and everything. They are driven by a desire to learn not just how and why things work, but also what makes people tick. To this end they tend to draw toward them as many people as will feed their insatiable curiosity.

When these people learn that a good mind and education are the keys to success, their intelligence and versatility can take them to the top of their chosen field. They have great insight into the strengths and weaknesses of others, yet can sometimes be lacking in empathy. Often too emotionally detached to be fired up by compassion for others, they tend to rely on encyclopedic knowledge, rather than personal experience. Even though they have the ability to make friends easily and are often surrounded by fellow debaters, they do run the risk of becoming observers rather than participators.

Eternal students of human nature, the issues that most interest them—the meaning of life, the hows and whys of human emotion and behavior—are those that they could most benefit from applying to themselves. Their information-gathering approach has both its strengths and its weaknesses; it does not take into account the importance of a person's inner life and how that can provide meaning and comfort. Their tendency to observe and over-analyze is most pronounced between the ages of twenty-eight and fifty-eight, when it is important that they learn to recognize their own and other people's emotional and spiritual needs. If they aren't able to, they may be prone to sudden and, to their frustration, unexplained bouts of insecurity and sadness.

These perceptive, inquisitive and eager-to-learn people are wonderfully entertaining and stimulating to have around and they never fail to surprise and delight others with their insights. Once they have learned to look within as well as outside of themselves for stimulation, they have all the enthusiasm and determination they need not only to make startling observations but also to act upon them with dramatic and often life-enhancing benefits.

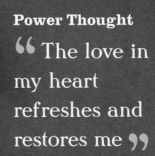

Love *Listen to your heart*

Until they develop a true sense of self-worth, people born March 23 are prone to unfaithfulness. They also need to make sure they don't apply their predilection for impartial analysis to personal relationships, as it will have disastrous consequences. Once they learn to search with their heart as well as their head they can, however, be generous and affectionate lovers.

Health *Individually tailored*

People born on this day may be prone to headaches and eye strain, especially if they stay up late studying or reading, or work long hours at a computer. They will probably have a fairly good idea of how their body works and the most effective way to take care of it with the correct diet and exercise routine, but they need to learn that each person is an individual and what might work for one person may not work as well for them. They need to make sure they drink plenty of water, leaving no more than three to four hours between meals and snacks to keep their brain adequately nourished. As far as exercise is concerned, the more vigorous the better is recommended, so as to give their minds a break from their relentless questioning. If they feel sad for no apparent reason, a bergamot-scented candle may be able to lift their mood, as would wearing the colors yellow or orange.

Career *Born surgeons*

These people are clearly well equipped for careers in medicine, science, engineering, computer or video-game design, teaching, and psychotherapy. They may, however, find that their gift for analysis and observation draws them toward the arts, acting in particular. They may also be drawn to careers in writing or publishing, but whatever career they choose, their intellect and ability to be objective will help them succeed.

Destiny *To make new discoveries*

The life path of people born on this day is to acquire self-knowledge. Once they are able to get in touch with their feelings, their destiny is to study the facts and make new discoveries, observations or hypotheses for others to work with.

Power Thought

66 The love in my heart refreshes and restores me 99

Signs & symbols

Sun signs: Aries/Pisces

Ruling planets: Mars, the warrior/Neptune, the speculator

Symbols: The Ram/Two Fishes

Birth date ruler: Mercury, the communicator

Tarot card: The Hierophant (guidance)

Favorable numbers: 5, 8

Lucky days: Tuesday and Wednesday, especially when these days fall on 5 and 8 of the month

Lucky colors: Red, light blue

Birthstone: Diamond

March 23

24 March

the birthday of stormy tranquility

Your greatest challenge is ...

dealing with your anger

The way forward is ...

to deal promptly with minor threats so anger doesn't build up. Think about what is worth getting angry about and what isn't.

You're drawn to people born on ...

August 24 to September 23

You both have qualities that balance out the other's vulnerabilities, and this can create an exciting and fulfilling bond.

Luck maker

Improve your self-esteem

If you feel good about yourself, you significantly increase your chances of attracting good luck; because like always attracts like. So challenge negative thoughts by replacing them with positive ones.

Externally, people born on March 24 appear tranquil and uncomplicated, even to the point of childlike innocence. They take great pleasure in the simple things of life, but there is often a dark cloud of stormy malcontent underneath their calm exterior.

These captivating individuals do prefer simple solutions to complicated alternatives and their nature is strictly no fuss, no frills. With the ability to take swift and decisive action, they will rarely be found dithering with indecision. They are at their happiest and best when their achievements are recognized and when their private life is simple and steady. Despite their childlike charms, their lives are often far removed from the tranquility they dream of. In fact, difficult situations and challenges seem to be attracted to them; these will continue to test them until they come to terms with their own inner conflicts.

These people should neither ignore nor suppress the dark feelings they have about themselves and life, learning to face them head-on. When they are able to do this, they will find there is far less to fear than they thought. Negative emotions, such as fear, anger, jealousy, and insecurity, exist to alert them to areas of discomfort in their lives, signaling a need for change. It is important for them to listen to the messages their emotions convey, especially between the ages of twenty-seven and fifty-seven, during which there is an emphasis on material or outward success, stability and security.

Other people may find it hard to understand why these lovely people with an army of admirers so often get themselves into trouble or occasionally explode with rage. As such, they present an enigma. Their optimistic approach to life and willingness to believe the best in others can make them vulnerable and easily exploited. As well as learning to face their inner demons, they need to take a more realistic approach to life. This should not, however, be at the expense of their simplicity and sweetness, since their most powerful strength is to light up the lives of others.

At your best

Warm, trusting, direct

Love *The full spectrum*

Relationships with people born March 24 tend to run the full spectrum; one minute they are passionate, the next they show the cold shoulder. Despite intense highs and equally intense lows, once they find a partner who is as sweet, intelligent and charming as they are, and who understands that their moods swings are a sign of insecurity and vulnerability, they can become intensely loyal and devoted lovers.

Health *Talk it over*

People born on this day may suffer from depression and low immunity if they don't learn how to express their hidden fears and insecurities. It is extremely important for them to spend time relaxing with friends and loved ones, and they may also benefit from counseling and psychotherapy to help them engage with their feelings. As far as diet is concerned, they should avoid stimulants like caffeine, alcohol and nicotine and avoid a diet high in animal products and saturated fat. A daily exercise routine would help keep their physical and emotional health in balance and they would also benefit from regular meditation or breathing exercises to help them calm down when they feel a sudden outburst of anger. Wearing, meditating on or surrounding themselves with light green will help them feel more balanced.

Career *Born motivators*

These people are often multi-talented individuals who will find fulfillment in any career that allows them to act independently and achieve results. Their ability to elevate the mood of others can help them excel as teachers, social workers, counselors, healers, therapists, or clergy. Their quick way with words may attract them to law, writing, movie-making, and entertainment, and their leadership potential will put them at the forefront of any career they choose to pursue.

Destiny *To make even the most cynical smile*

The life path of people born on this day is to learn to accept and manage their emotions. Once they have gained emotional confidence, their destiny is to make even the most cynical smile.

Power Thought

"I am positive in my outlook and life brings me good things in response"

Signs & symbols

Sun sign: Aries

Ruling planet: Mars, the warrior

Symbol: The Ram

Birth date ruler: Venus, the lover

Tarot card: The Lovers (choices)

Favorable numbers: 6, 9

Lucky days: Tuesday and Friday, especially when these days fall on 6 and 9 of the month

Lucky colors: Red, pink, light green

Birthstone: Diamond

25 March

the birthday of electric energy

Your greatest challenge is ...

learning to keep a lid on your temper

The way forward is ...

to understand that when you lash out in frustration or uncontrolled rage, it's often because your inner equilibrium is disturbed.

You're drawn to people born on ...

October 24 to November 22

A match of great potential, you both need the security of togetherness and the space to daydream alone.

Luck maker

Give others a break

When you get angry with other people, the part of you available for luck is unused. So give others the benefit of the doubt when they annoy or upset you; they may have had good intentions.

People born on March 25 like to be where the action is, and that is where they are often found. They have bags of enthusiasm and an endless supply of energy, never being afraid of taking an independent position when convinced it is necessary. Their dynamism marks them out as natural leaders as others tend to follow when they show the way; but their natural preference is often to go it alone.

These people are resilient individuals but are also compassionate and imaginative. They may have developed a tough skin to protect themselves from life's knocks but they have a sense of natural justice and strong protective instincts toward the vulnerable. Quirky and original with a rich imaginative life, what really distinguishes them is their boundless energy.

They are daring, independent and direct with an active mind and body and bright ideas. Making hasty decisions without proper plans, sometimes their spontaneity gets them into trouble. Adopting a more mature, reflective attitude will help them make smoother progress. Until the age of twenty-five they tend to be daring and carefree but after the age of twenty-six there is greater emphasis on the need for direction, consistency, security, and stability. In their thirties, forties and beyond they really come into their own.

Although much of their electric energy is externally directed, these people also have a profound need for periods of solitude and reflection; these help them avoid mood swings and temper tantrums. This need for a private life where they can be allowed to daydream can confuse those who regard them as whirlwinds of constant energy; but others need to understand that it is vital for them. It is important for them to have supportive and caring friends but these friends have to give them the freedom to be alone and recharge. If they keep a lid on their temper and give themselves those regular times out, the electric and highly creative energy and imagination of people born on this day will help them surge right to the front of their chosen field.

Love *The one that got away*

Close relationships aren't always easy for people born on March 25 as they do have an absolute requirement for solitude or aloneness every now and again. They need to find someone who can keep up with their energy and give them security but who will also allow them to be alone and to think independently. Because they are so imaginative, they also love to fantasize about the one that got away or the one they may never have.

Health *Time out*

People born on this day do seem to have limitless supplies of energy but the key to their dynamism is that they also need regular periods of rest and solitude to recharge their batteries. It is vital that they allow themselves these periods and don't neglect them in the race to get ahead; if they do it will have disastrous consequences for their physical and emotional health. As far as diet is concerned, they should stay away from too much red meat, alcohol, saturated fat, and nicotine, as these will slow them down. Their diet should be rich in energy-boosting fruits, vegetables and whole grains instead. Both vigorous and mild exercise are recommended for people born on this day; these can help speed them up when they need to direct their energy outward and slow them down when they feel the need to withdraw. People born on this day often respond well to the cooling color of indigo as it tends to calm their exuberant fire.

Career *Born propagandists*

These people may be drawn to careers in education, sales, writing, promotion, public relations, social work, the stock market, law, music, and the arts. They also make excellent propagandists or fighters for their chosen cause. Whatever career they choose, their dynamic energy and originality of thought will take them to the top.

Destiny *To highlight and reverse social wrongs*

The life path of people born on this day is to learn to balance their inner and outer life. Once they are able to recognize the importance of finding this balance, their destiny is to highlight and reverse social wrongs.

Power Thought

" I can only direct what is happening within me not around me "

Signs & symbols

Sun sign: Aries

Ruling planet: Mars, the warrior

Symbol: The Ram

Birth date ruler: Neptune, the speculator

Tarot card: The Chariot (resilience)

Favorable numbers: 1, 7

Lucky days: Tuesday and Monday, especially when these days fall on 1 and 7 of the month

Lucky colors: Red, sea green

Birthstone: Diamond

March 25

26 March

the birthday of honesty

People born on March 26 are astute, determined and courageous, with the intensity and power to achieve much in life. They can appear easygoing and unassuming; to a certain extent this is true. But they are not lazy or unmotivated; rather, they like to cut straight to the heart of the matter, not wishing to make things more complicated than they are. They don't have much time for small talk or window dressing; directness, both intellectual and emotional, is their goal.

A desire for honesty dominates the personality of these people, encouraging them to confront and explore situations others might avoid. It also helps them get things done quickly and efficiently; because they are so bold, clear-sighted and practical, they have a knack of making even the hardest of tasks seem easy. The only problem with their straightforward approach is that they can sometimes become too relaxed or detached, putting them behind those who are more aggressive and passionate.

They also have a tendency to make judgments based on their insight and then to close their mind to alternative viewpoints. It is important for them to keep their minds open and to understand that the less-is-more approach to life isn't always appropriate. Until the age of twenty-four they are likely to be active and adventurous but from the age of twenty-five to fifty-five there is an emphasis on stability and security. It is important during these years that they discover ways to express their creativity and passion.

True satisfaction for people born on this day often comes through achievements based on their own efforts. They like to work at their own pace, trusting their own impeccable judgment. Easily bored and dissatisfied when relying on the efforts and opinions of others, they are usually the best judge of what does or does not work for them. As long as they don't lose touch of their spontaneity and wry sense of humor, they are capable of producing work of great quality and, surprisingly for someone with such as laid-back exterior, incredible depth.

Your greatest challenge is …

to speak your mind when the situation demands it

The way forward is …

to understand that holding back isn't always the right approach. It can make people feel that you aren't sufficiently committed.

You're drawn to people born on …

August 23 to September 22

You have so much to learn and love about each other, making this a creative and fulfilling union

Luck maker

Discover your passion

Lucky people are passionate about what they do and say. It is this passion which gives them the strength, energy and determination they need to achieve their dreams.

Love *For better or for worse*

In love, people born on March 26 need to learn to be a little more gentle and spontaneous. They are accustomed to having things their own way and being obeyed; this is not the way to create harmony in a relationship. However, once they do fall in love they are loyal, generous and supportive in both the good and the bad times. They may not have a large circle of friends, but the ones they do have are friends for life.

Health *Don't go it alone*

People born on this day are good at self-diagnosis but when it comes to their health they should seek the advice of experts. Because they value simplicity they may feel bewildered if they find themselves suffering from depression or negativity, and again, instead of trying to work though these feelings alone, they should seek outside help and support. As far as sport is concerned, competitive, physically and mentally challenging activities, ranging from gymnastics to martial arts, appeal; they should, however, beware of injuries to the head. When it comes to diet, they should aim for consistency. They should avoid big meals and then going for long periods of time without food, as this will confuse their metabolism. Wearing, surrounding themselves with or meditating on the color green will help restore their energies and encourage balance.

Career *Born managers*

These people may be drawn to military careers, as well as diplomacy or other professions that stress organization, in particular time management. Their need for self-expression may tempt them toward arts, music and the entertainment world and, because they are never happy being told what to do, management opportunities, or setting up their own business, will appeal.

Destiny *To simplify what is complicated*

The life path of people born on this day is to learn to be more spontaneous. Once they have learned to follow their instincts, the destiny of people born on this day is to simplify what is complicated and by so doing to help others cut to the heart of the issue.

Power Thought

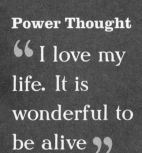

66 **I love my life.** It is wonderful to be alive 99

Signs & symbols

Sun sign: Aries

Ruling planet: Mars, the warrior

Symbol: The Ram

Birth date ruler: Saturn, the teacher

Tarot card: Strength (passion)

Favorable numbers: 2, 8

Lucky days: Tuesday and Saturday, especially when these days fall on 2 and 8 of the month

Lucky colors: All shades of red and green

Birthstone: Diamond

March 26

27 March

the birthday of the individual

There is something about people born on March 27 that is wholly endearing. They are true individuals with their own inimitable style of dress and behavior, attracting attention wherever they go. They don't just have star quality; they have something far more special: the likability factor.

Despite always being in demand, these strongly independent and individualistic people are more concerned with following their own unique path than gaining the approval of others. Their work is important to them; any success they achieve is earned because they understand the importance of discipline and will push themselves single-mindedly to achieve their goals. This determination and refusal to fit in often results from youthful struggles and setbacks; although this gives them resilience and a unique persona, it can also make them unsympathetic to the feelings of others. Other people may be attracted to them but deep down March 27 people aren't that interested in other people at all; it is their work that fascinates them.

Occasionally the driven personality and tendency to lack empathy for others can make these people appear tense, aloof or self-absorbed. As wonderful and as fascinating as they are, it's important for them to learn to step outside themselves every now and again, and they should realize there is a whole world out there. This tendency toward self-absorption is especially highlighted between their mid twenties and mid fifties; during these years they need to make sure they get in touch with the feelings and concerns of others.

These people often have great courage and strength, and in times of crisis they are the ones who instinctively take control, typically saving or helping others before themselves. Ironically, it is during periods of stability and security that they struggle most to find meaning and purpose, and may lapse into bouts of inaction. It is important for these multi-talented, charismatic individuals to understand that they don't actually need to wait for a crisis to make their mark. They can start to make a contribution that is wonderfully and uniquely their own right now.

On the **dark** side

Aloof, tense, difficult

At your **best**

Dynamic, stylish, imaginative

Love *Show your softer side*

People born on March 27 tend to be preoccupied with their work and their goals; this can make it difficult to achieve harmony in a relationship. They need to learn to open up, share their feelings with their partner and experience the softer side of pleasure. When they find a partner who can help them relax and unwind, however, they are passionate, faithful and devoted companions.

Health *Don't soldier on regardless*

People born on this day are energetic, impulsive and accident prone and should watch out for insomnia and migraines. If they get ill, they tend to try to soldier on regardless, but this approach is counter-productive as inattention to minor health concerns can lead to full-blown illnesses or disorders. As far as diet is concerned, they should make sure they eat healthily and don't get so over-involved with work that they forget to eat. If they learned the basics of cooking it would encourage them to take greater interest in the importance of nutrition for mental, physical and emotional health. Vigorous exercise is likely to appeal but they would benefit more from moderate to mild exercise, particularly with a mind–bond emphasis, such as yoga. This can help them calm down and unwind. Carrying a malachite crystal or having malachite ornaments around their house will help balance their emotions and bring calmness and a sense of ease.

Career *Born paramedics*

These people have the gift of the gab and can make excellent news anchors or public relations officers, as any employer would like to have them at the front of any storms. They also make gifted academics, lawyers, politicians, and scientists, and their individualism may find creative expression in design, music, writing, art, or drama. Because they cope so well in times of crisis, careers in medicine and the emergency services may also appeal.

Destiny *To blaze a unique trail*

The life path of people born on this day is to learn not to neglect their own emotional needs or to isolate themselves from others. Once they are able to do that, their destiny is to blaze a trail in their own unique way.

Power Thought

" Every day is filled with chances to feel happier and more fulfilled "

Signs & symbols

Sun sign: Aries

Ruling planet: Mars, the warrior

Symbol: The Ram

Birth date ruler: Mars, the warrior

Tarot card: Strength (passion)

Favorable numbers: 3, 9

Lucky day: Tuesday, especially when it falls on 3 or 9 of the month

Lucky colors: All shades of red

Birthstone: Diamond

March 27

28 March

the birthday of magnificent remoteness

Your greatest challenge is ...

to stop doubting yourself

The way forward is ...

to change the way you talk to yourself. Most of your negative beliefs aren't founded in reality, so train yourself to believe positive things.

You're drawn to people born on ...

July 24 to August 23

You share a passion for freedom and a need for affection, and this can create an understanding and supportive bond.

Luck maker

Be your own best friend

When you feel good about yourself, it's much easier to attract luck; so become your own best friend, saying reassuring and comforting things to yourself when things aren't going well.

Although people born on March 28 tend to be independent loners at heart, they often find themselves at the center of others' attention. This is because of their sunny and commonsense approach to life, as well as their morality, compassion and generosity toward others. They also have the ability to respond brilliantly in a crisis and, whether they like it or not, a recurring theme in their life will be offering their advice and support to others.

These people often have a burning desire to create something special in their chosen field. Their work is very important to them and a source of great fulfillment. With an incredible ability to focus, they remain calm and emotionally detached during the most difficult of situations. Despite their serenity and obvious intellectual talents, they may find that they don't advance as fast or as high as they deserve. There is a reason for this: their lack of self-confidence and self-belief.

Although their modest, self-effacing nature is endearing, they should find ways to build their self-esteem. Until they do so, they will doubt their abilities and will move forward with difficulty. From their early twenties to their early fifties it is important for them to work on building their self-confidence, as they need to establish security and stability. They also need to make sure that they don't settle for second best, sacrificing their personal fulfillment in the process. After the age of fifty-three there is a turning point in their life that highlights communication skills and the need for greater self-expression.

Charming, inspirational and popular, these people need privacy, and others should not try to impose restrictions or limitations on them as their remoteness is in many ways the key to their success. They need regular downtime and a degree of solitude to gather their strength and protect themselves from feeling vulnerable. Then, when they feel ready, they can rejoin the world, bringing to it their unique brand of humor, optimism, courage, and magnificent calm in the face of adversity.

On the dark side

Unaware, vacillating, unrealistic

At your best

Independent, optimistic, focused

Love *Childlike*

March 28 people can be spontaneous and emotional when it comes to affairs of the heart but they don't often reveal deeper feelings that lie beneath the surface. They may also resent the limitations and restrictions that a close relationship can bring and, instead of opening up about their concerns, may suddenly disappear, leaving the other person confused as to the reason. They need to find a partner who is as strong-willed and as independent as they are, yet also capable of being loyal and dependent.

Health *Make positive changes*

People born on this day may be prone to sudden and unexplained bouts of depression, but they should see these low moods as opportunities to figure out what isn't working in their life and to make positive changes, as their depression tends to be reactive. As far as diet is concerned, they should try to make cooking and eating more fun and less of a chore. The same applies to exercise; it should be a pleasure rather than a duty. They are prone to blood-sugar disorders and hypertension, so they need to make sure their diet is rich in fruit and vegetables and low in refined foods, sugar and salt. Wearing, meditating on or surrounding themselves with the color yellow will help build their confidence.

Career *Born police officers*

Because of their ability to stay calm in a crisis and remain emotionally detached, these people are well suited to careers in the police force and the military, as well as in medicine, law, sport, education, social work, business, and the building trades. They may also use their creativity to forge ahead in careers in architecture, photography, art, entertainment, and movie-making.

Destiny *To motivate others with their proactive approach to life*

The life path of people born on this day is to learn to believe in themselves. Once they have developed their self-confidence, their destiny is to motivate others by presenting a positive, can-do and in-control face to the world.

Signs & symbols

Sun sign: Aries

Ruling planet: Mars, the warrior

Symbol: The Ram

Birth date ruler: Sun, the individual

Tarot card: The Magician (will-power)

Favorable numbers: 1, 4

Lucky days: Tuesday and Sunday, especially when these days fall on 1 and 4 of the month

Lucky colors: Red, orange, gold

Birthstone: Diamond

March 28

29 March

the birthday of
the discerning presence

Your greatest challenge is ...

asserting yourself

The way forward is ...

to understand that being assertive is not the same as being aggressive or rude. You are simply making sure your valuable contribution is recognized.

You're drawn to people born on ...

June 22 to July 23

You are both genuine and open individuals, and this can create a lasting union of rare honesty.

Luck maker

Expect good luck

Don't hope for good fortune, expect it. People who are lucky believe with absolute certainty that they will succeed, even when life doesn't go according to plan. We tend to get what we expect.

Undoubtedly intuitive, people born on March 29 like to observe everything that is going on around them, carefully considering all aspects of a situation before making a decision. This slow and steady approach to life often proves highly successful. Others may criticize them for being overly cautious or for lacking focus, passion and commitment, but they are the ones with the knack of winning in the end.

These people are often polite and genuine in every aspect of their life. Not to be so would imply rudeness or insincerity; their intellect, sensitivity and honesty would not stand for this. They are not driven by personal ambition but by a desire to make a positive difference in the world through their intellect and perception. In fact, they are perhaps a little too wise at times, which can lead them to being disillusioned if they are not careful, especially when it comes to close personal relationships.

The danger for people born on this day is that their caution can lead to negativity or pessimism; it is important for them not to spiral into depression if people do let them down. They need to understand that human beings are complex creatures with both strengths and weaknesses and that it is far better to believe the best of people than the worst. People have a tendency to live up to the expectations we have of them. Between the ages of twenty-one and fifty-one they need to be especially careful not to sink into cynicism and inflexibility, as there is an emphasis in their life on security and stability and establishing themselves.

Although they do like to keep themselves to themselves, when in public their discerning presence has a calming and soothing influence on those around them. Their self-containment can also—much to their surprise—thrust them into the limelight. These authentic, loyal and coolly intelligent individuals, with their own enigmatic purity and beauty, when put into positions of authority and leadership, are more than qualified to assume the reins of power.

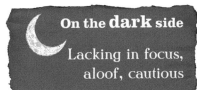

At your **best**

Creative, genuine, perceptive

Love *At first sight*

When it comes to relationships, March 29 people are extremely romantic and intense. They believe in love at first sight but are unlikely to throw themselves into a love affair without first weighing up the pros and cons. Once they have made up their mind, however, that they have found "the one," they rarely meet any resistance, remaining loyal and deeply affectionate partners for life.

Health *Highly sensitive*

People born on this day are prone to hormonal imbalances, skin problems and food allergies. Being so sensitive, it is important for them to make sure they eat a healthy diet and avoid foods high in sugar, saturated fat, salt, additives, and preservatives. They don't generally have weight problems if they keep active but there may be problems with bloating and weight gain around the middle, especially in mid life; again this can be avoided with healthy eating and with a daily exercise program. Making sure they get plenty of time to relax, unwind and recharge their energy is important for people born on this day, as is spending time with a close circle of friends. Wearing, meditating on or surrounding themselves with the colors orange and yellow will encourage them to be more optimistic.

Career *Born producers*

Whatever career these positive and multi-talented individuals choose they are likely to be successful, but the fields of education, publishing, law, business, computing, engineering, medicine, and social reform may particularly appeal. If they choose to express their creative side, they may be drawn to music, art, and dance as well as photography, film production and photography.

Destiny *To inspire, comfort and influence others*

The life path of people born on this day is to learn to be more assertive so that others do not take them for granted or assume credit for their work. Once they have been able to ensure they do not go unrecognized, their destiny is to inspire, comfort and influence others with their loyalty, steadfastness, calmness, and courage.

Signs & symbols

Sun sign: Aries

Ruling planet: Mars, the warrior

Symbol: The Ram

Birth date ruler: Moon, the intuitive

Tarot card: The High Priestess (intuition)

Favorable numbers: 2, 5

Lucky days: Tuesday and Monday, especially when these days fall on 2 and 5 of the month

Lucky colors: Red, pink, silver

Birthstone: Diamond

March 29

30 March

the birthday of irresistible conviction

Your greatest challenge is ...

learning how bide your time

The way forward is ...

to understand that the very impulsiveness that drives you can also sabotage your efforts. You need to consider the effects of your words and deeds.

You're drawn to people born on ...

November 23 to December 21

You share a passion for independence and a need for closeness, and this can create an understanding and enduring bond.

Luck maker

Sleep on it

When things don't go according to plan it is sometimes better to chalk it up as a rough day. What you can't solve now, you may be able to solve tomorrow.

People born on March 30 are an irresistible combination of dynamic confidence and courage, and touching earnestness and vulnerability. Although their conviction is strong enough to help them bounce back from setbacks and criticism, it's impossible for them to hide their pain, bewilderment and disappointment. For this reason they can both antagonize and endear themselves to people, more often than not at the same time.

These people are at their happiest and best when allowed the freedom to work alone and set their own agenda. They may appear selfish to friends and colleagues, but they are not. They simply love to absorb themselves in their personal goals, fearing that if they allow others to distract them from their vision they might never attain it. It is important for them, however, to take the time to unwind; otherwise they run the risk of becoming driven at work and isolated in their personal life. They should not neglect their emotional and social needs between the ages of twenty and fifty, during which there is an emphasis on acquiring wealth, status and material security. After the age of fifty they may feel a need to communicate and exchange ideas; this is when their talents are most likely to mature and gain recognition.

With a hint of the dramatic and the irresistible in their make-up, these people have an attractive, energetic but mild manner which masks a hidden sensuality and complexity. Because they are so upbeat, passionate and focused about their goals in life, they may find that they have more than their fair share of good luck. If, however, they surrender their natural optimism the opposite may be true, so it is important for them to keep as positive as possible.

As long as these people don't allow themselves to become buried by their ambitions or their tendency toward perfectionism—and others allow them the freedom to pursue their highly creative vision—they have the potential not just to achieve outstanding success but to provoke feelings of adoration in others.

Love *Simply irresistible*

People born on March 30 are irresistible and will often attract partners who want to help and support them, as well as adore them. Their ideal mate will be someone who has an independent streak as strong as their own and a mind as inquisitive and far reaching. Sometimes their insecurities and driven nature can damage a relationship, but if they are able to make it work they make warm and endlessly fascinating partners.

Health *Watch your stress levels*

The biggest risk to the health of people born on this day is stress. Some stress is good for them as it makes them feel alive, but too much can lead to headaches, insomnia, hormonal imbalances, weight gain, forgetfulness, insecurity, and a host of other emotional, mental and physical disorders. Eating a healthy diet rich in nutritious whole grains, fruits and vegetables and low in refined and processed foods, and getting plenty of fresh air and exercise, will help ease stress, as will regular time out with friends and loved ones. Mind–body therapies and deep-breathing techniques such as meditation and yoga are highly recommended, as are massage and aromatherapy. A soothing cup of herbal tea, such as chamomile, before bedtime will encourage restful sleep; wearing, meditating on or surrounding themselves with the colors blue and purple will help quell their exuberant fires.

Career *Born interior designers*

Because of their determination and creativity, these people have the potential to achieve great success in arts, music, design, theater, and the entertainment world. Their pleasure in mental pursuits may also lead them to careers in teaching, lecturing, research, or writing, as well as management, sales, business, and public affairs. Alternatively they may choose to set up their own business.

Destiny *To inspire others with their fearless energy*

The life path of people born on this day is to place as much importance on their personal as on their professional goals. Once they have learned to get in touch with their feelings and the feelings of others, their destiny is to influence and inspire others with their fearless energy and passion for what they believe in.

Signs & symbols

Sun sign: Aries

Ruling planet: Mars, the warrior

Symbol: The Ram

Birth date ruler: Jupiter, the philosopher

Tarot card: The Empress (creativity)

Favorable numbers: 3, 6

Lucky days: Tuesday and Thursday, especially when these days fall on 3 and 6 of the month

Lucky colors: Red, purple, lavender

Birthstone: Diamond

March 30

31 March

the birthday of the commanding presence

People born on March 31 are often stable individuals with a profound sense of who they are. Their presence is commanding and the force of their authority unquestioned. They have little time for small talk but plenty of time and energy for action and common sense.

There's a calmness and steadiness about these people, making them highly valued in both professional and personal environments. With a pragmatic and determined approach, they are also capable of compromise if life demands it, because they value making progress in an orderly and direct manner. If, however, they feel that others are standing in the way or complicating matters, they can be extremely argumentative and demanding.

The air of authority of these people marks them out as potential leaders but they tend to feel comfortable when they are contributing ideas or working within a team where their contagious energy motivates others to go along with them. They aren't great risk-takers as they prefer security to gambling, but it's important for them not to let opportunities to express their talents pass them by. They are most likely to favor a steady and pragmatic approach to life between the ages of twenty and fifty; during this time they should get out of their comfort zone every now and again, taking the odd calculated risk. After the age of fifty there is a greater emphasis on experimentation and new ventures.

These people do tend to be led by their head rather than their heart. Emotional control is important to them. When they feel threatened by their emotions, cynicism or sudden outbursts of temper are often their ways of avoiding dealing with them. Recognizing their need for greater emotional expression, life has a way of forcing them to get in touch with their feelings, through either the people they meet or the situations they experience. Once they learn to listen to their emotions as much as their common sense, these resourceful, realistic, energetic, and remarkably influential people are destined for a rare combination of success in every aspect of their lives.

Love *Loyal and true*

People born on March 31 are extremely loyal and faithful lovers once they have found the person who is right for them. Because trial and error is not their style and they want to get things right first time, they may spend many years on their own, possibly even marrying late. Great displays of affection are not for them, but tenderness and togetherness are.

Health *Express yourself*

People born on this day need to make sure they don't repress their feelings so much that it affects their physical and emotional health, making them prone to stress, depression, lowered immunity, and high blood pressure. It is important for them to find a way to express themselves, and time spent with friends and loved ones is essential. Vigorous exercise, such as rock climbing, or exercise that is expressive, such as dancing, are highly recommended as these will help them open up. As far as diet is concerned, they need to ensure they make meals more a social occasion, limiting their intake of alcohol and saturated fat. Wearing, meditating on or surrounding themselves with the color orange will encourage them to open up more, as would hobbies such as art, writing and pottery.

Career *Born business people*

These people have the determination and the flexibility to achieve great success in the worlds of business, politics, education, and public service, but their commanding presence will serve them well in any field. In their choice of career they should make sure that they don't get stuck in a rut and miss out on opportunities for travel, change and promotion.

Destiny *To encourage others to work alongside them*

The life path of people born on this day is to learn to relax their expectation of constant control. Once they are able to recognize the need to express themselves emotionally, their destiny is to encourage others to work alongside them and follow their energetic and determined example.

Signs & symbols

Sun sign: Aries

Ruling planet: Mars, the warrior

Symbol: The Ram

Birth date ruler: Uranus, the visionary

Tarot card: The Emperor (authority)

Favorable numbers: 4, 7

Lucky days: Tuesday and Sunday, especially when these days fall on 4 and 7 of the month

Lucky colors: Red, silver

Birthstone: Diamond

March 31

1 April

the birthday of quiet confidence

Your greatest challenge is ...

coping with work and the requests of others

The way forward is ...

to learn to delegate your responsibilities and to stop expecting so much from yourself.

You're drawn to people born on ...

July 24 to August 23

You both have qualities which the other needs to learn and develop to feel truly fulfilled.

Luck maker

Take care whom you help

If you are exhausted because you have taken on too much, you will block luck from your life. Anger and negative thoughts may take over or you may be too tired to seize opportunities.

Despite the reputation of their birthday, people born on April 1 are far from being April Fools. They often display wisdom and a quiet confidence way in advance of their years. They were the children on whom parents and teachers knew they could rely and in their adult life they continue to be dependable, the ones who show up punctually, always giving one hundred per cent.

Although they have a reputation for being reliable and responsible, these people are rarely plodding or dull as they have a youthful and wholesome appeal that draws others to them. Incapable of hiding their emotions, their emotional spontaneity earns them many admirers; their natural shyness and reserve may, however, make it hard for them to respond and appreciate this attention. They also have a great need for privacy and personal space, loving to sit thinking for long hours and coming up with highly original plans and projects.

The aura of quiet confidence and honesty with which these people are blessed is capable of inspiring enormous faith and trust in others. They make excellent leaders but their motive is never a desire for self-aggrandizement as it is the work itself rather than being the center of attention that inspires them. All they really want is to be allowed to get on with their work, as a job well done gives them enormous satisfaction. Although their outstanding ability to focus on their work assures their success in virtually any field, they do need to be careful that in the process they don't become isolated workaholics, especially between the ages of nineteen and forty-nine, during which they seek stability, security and routine. After the age of fifty, however, they move toward new interests, learning and communication.

The one similarity between the archetypal jester and these mature souls may be the sense of affection they inspire in others. Their responsible and quietly confident approach to life and lack of desire to promote themselves—unless thought necessary for the task in hand—is a true joy to behold.

Love *An open heart*

People born on April 1 have an extremely warm and open heart that is incapable of deception but they do need to be careful that they don't put their relationships at risk because of their obsession with work. They tend to be attracted to intelligent people who can give them the mental stimulation they need; but they thrive best with someone who can give them affection and warmth.

Health *Keep active*

Regular exercise is extremely important for people born on this day as they have a tendency to choose professions that keep them mentally active but physically sedentary. They should try to schedule in at least half an hour of activity a day; walking, jogging, swimming, and cycling are all activities that would suit, as they can also use this time to be alone and to gather their thoughts. As far as diet is concerned they need to remember to eat regularly and healthily as well and not to get so carried away with their current project that they eat on the go or forget to eat at all. Wearing, meditating on or surrounding themselves with the color red will encourage them to open up and respond more freely to others.

Career *Born teachers*

These people command respect with their quiet confidence, insight and brilliant organizational skills; for this reason they would excel in politics, education, management, administration, merchandising, or the military. They have a sharp business sense but they may use their great imagination to excel in art, music or drama. So varied are their talents, however, that they usually excel in any career they choose.

Destiny *To find practical solutions to problems*

The life path of people born on this day is to learn to trust and to speak their mind. Once they have learned to open up, their destiny is to find practical solutions to problems and to see others benefit from these solutions.

Signs & symbols

Sun sign: Aries

Ruling planet: Mars, the warrior

Symbol: The Ram

Birth date ruler: Sun, the individual

Tarot card: The Magician (will-power)

Favorable numbers: 1, 5

Lucky days: Tuesday and Sunday, especially when these days fall on 1 and 5 of the month

Lucky colors: Red, orange, yellow

Birthstone: Diamond

April 1

2 April

the birthday of utopia

Your greatest challenge is ...

listening to different viewpoints

The way forward is ...

to understand that one of the best ways to win the respect and support of others is to listen and make them feel included.

You're drawn to people born on ...

June 21 to July 22

You are both intuitive and creative, and this can be a loving and supportive union.

Luck maker

Be realistic

People who are lucky don't get everything that they want but they get most of what they want. They don't set themselves up for failure by setting unrealistic goals, they value what they know they can achieve.

People born on April 2 have a fresh, youthful outlook and a utopian view of the world. The purity of their intentions and genuine belief in their dreams of a better world can earn them great respect. They are also extremely compassionate and never fail to be moved by the suffering of others.

These people love to talk about their dreams and vision of a better future. These dreams, however, often don't take into account the possibility of obstacles or complications, so this idealism can test the patience of those with a more realistic approach to life. They may also become so passionate in their convictions that they are unable or unwilling to see differing viewpoints, which may alarm others.

When they have problems inspiring a similar level of zeal in others, these people may alienate themselves from a group with their inability to compromise. It's important for them to have a more objective view of the impact their ideals have on others and to try to find less aggressive ways of enlisting others' support. Between the ages of eighteen and forty-eight their tendency to express their convictions too forcefully is heightened, so they should learn to accept differences of opinion, tempering their idealism with realism; this will increase their chances of success and protect them from disappointment. After the age of forty-nine they become more flexible and more willing to entertain different viewpoints.

These people with a strong sense of justice do possess a subtle power and once they have learned to discipline and direct it positively, they have enormous potential to overcome almost any obstacle. Their motives may be misunderstood and criticized as naïve and futile, but this is unlikely to deter them. What matters to them isn't what others think but their personal vision and being true to themselves and their beliefs. As long as they direct their passion to goals that are worthy of them, their honesty, single-mindedness and determination to see the best in everybody can help even the most cynical believe in undreamed-of possibilities.

Love *Hard work but worth it*

People born on April 2 are very idealistic when it comes to love and can make demanding and attention-seeking lovers but they are so warm, pure and generous that they are well worth it. As long as they don't alienate their partner with their extreme views and learn to confront emotional difficulties in a relationship rather than run away from them, they make loyal, loving and endlessly fascinating lovers.

Health *Regular check-ups*

People born on this day need to make sure they pay attention to any warning signs their bodies are sending them, as they do have a tendency to live in their heads and in their daydreams rather than the real world, thereby ignoring their health. They may be prone to headaches, insomnia, gum disease, and dental health problems. A healthy diet rich in nutrients, perhaps with a multi-vitamin and minerals, is essential, as is regular exercise to help keep them physically and mentally fit. They should make sure that their bedroom is a place of peace and calm, and that the TV and other electrical appliances are removed, as this will help them have the refreshing sleep they need to function optimally. Wearing, meditating on or surrounding themselves with the colors green and brown will help keep them balanced and grounded.

Career *Born movie directors*

These people have the potential to be excellent politicians, photographers, designers, artists, musicians, actors, and movie directors, as this kind of work gives them a medium in which to project their idealism or personal vision to the world. Alternatively they may be drawn to people-related careers in the media, public relations, psychology, counseling, and social work, or to careers in which they can express their humanitarian concerns, such as social reform and charity work.

Destiny *To encourage others to realize their full potential*

The life path of people born on this day is to learn to accept their limitations and the limitations of others. Once they are able to do that without losing their sunny optimism their destiny is to inspire others and encourage them, by example, to realize their full potential.

Signs & symbols

Sun sign: Aries

Ruling planet: Mars, the warrior

Symbol: The Ram

Birth date ruler: Moon, the intuitive

Tarot card: The High Priestess (intuition)

Favorable numbers: 2, 6

Lucky days: Tuesday and Monday, especially when these days fall on 2 and 6 of the month

Lucky colors: Scarlet, silver

Birthstone: Diamond

April 2

187

3 April

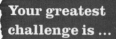

the birthday of the keynote

Your greatest challenge is ...

to learn to work independently

The way forward is ...

to understand that working in a team gives tremendous rewards but the greatest adventures often occur when you strike out on your own.

You're drawn to people born on ...

November 23 to December 21

You are both wild and spontaneous spirits, and this can create a union with electrifying energy.

Luck maker

Keep moving

When you hear the word "no," don't make rude phone calls, slash clothing or sit in a depressed stupor. Instead see rejection as information; information you can use to increase your future chances of success.

People born on April 3 are at their happiest and best when they can occupy the key position at home or at work. It gives them enormous satisfaction to feel indispensable; and with their remarkable creativity and energy, they often are.

Because they like to be at the center of things, life is seldom dull for these people. They have strong motivation and excellent communication skills; these, plus their outgoing and generous nature, give them great powers of persuasion. They thrive on challenges, but if they feel left out on the action they can become moody. Fortunately, this doesn't happen often since people value their contribution and love having them around.

These people don't dislike being on their own but they often flourish in a group. With the ability to gather a diverse collection of people together and transform them into a team, they like to occupy the key position. The only danger with this approach is that team members and friends tend to become too dependent on them, which can also create frustrations when they want to change direction.

Change is a theme for people born on this day. Their childhood and early teens may have been quite restless and reckless; their adult life will continue to see changes, some positive, some negative, because although they are highly intuitive they can sometimes be naïve. Despite these changes, however, their enthusiasm and motivation will ensure that some, if not all, of their dreams are fulfilled. In fact, the challenge and variety offered by change is essential for them because staying in one role limits the discovery and development of their vision and enthusiasm.

They make great leaders because they like to feel needed and because their natural charisma is so strong it tends to attract less energetic people. As long as they learn to respect the viewpoints of others and not to become oversensitive when they encounter criticism, their ability to energize and orchestrate others toward a common goal is second to none.

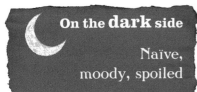
Love *Easy to fall in love*

People born on April 3 tend to fall in love very easily but sometimes their choice of partner is not ideal. They need to find someone who can match their energy, creativity and sense of adventure. When they are in a relationship they are loyal and loving partners but need to be careful that they don't forgo their own independence.

Health *Little and often*

People born on this day tend to be more concerned or interested in the health of others than in their own and this can be extremely negative for their health. Although they tend to be fit and energetic, they need to make sure they don't take their good health for granted. As far as diet is concerned, they may be susceptible to blood-sugar imbalances and, when they find themselves feeling moody or irritable for no reason or suffering from poor concentration, unexplained weight gain or headaches, they may be suffering from blood-sugar problems. To even themselves out they should eat little and often and go for small, well-balanced low-sugar meals as frequently as six times a day. Moderate to mild exercise, such as jogging or aerobics, is recommended, and wearing, meditating on or surrounding themselves with the color blue will help them stay calmer and cooler, and think more logically.

Career *Born promoter*

These people have the persuasive skills to make great sales people, politicians, movie directors, actors, promoters, and motivational speakers, but their capabilities are such that they have the potential to achieve success in virtually any career that they choose. Careers involving travel and variety, such as airline personnel, journalism, business, and transport may also appeal. Whatever career or careers they choose, it is extremely important for people born on this day to find a job that keeps their adventurous spirit alive.

Destiny *To promote a worthy cause*

The life path of people born on this day is to learn to react in a more mature and objective way when things are not going their way. Once they have learned to control their temperamental outbursts, their destiny is to win others over to a cause that is worthy of them.

Power Thought

❝I have full faith in my inner resources❞

Signs & symbols

Sun sign: Aries

Ruling planet: Mars, the warrior

Symbol: The Ram

Birth date ruler: Jupiter, the philosopher

Tarot card: The Empress (creativity)

Favorable numbers: 3, 7

Lucky days: Tuesday and Thursday, especially when these days fall on 3 and 7 of the month

Lucky colors: Scarlet, green

Birthstone: Diamond

April 3

4 April

the birthday of the catalyst

Those born on April 4 are catalysts—people who affect the lives of others in a profound way. Their creative energy is explosive, and both at home and at work they have little trouble initiating projects and inspiring others to join their cause.

When they are inspired, these people will typically throw their considerable energy, tenacity and organizational skills into a project, giving them huge potential for outstanding success. Above all, they like to initiate; they also have tremendous courage, happy to strike out in a completely new direction. Too often, however, they move on to the next crusade before the previous one has been completed, leaving those who are less impulsive to reap the rewards. To find true fulfillment, they should settle on a goal and see it through to the end. If they cannot slow down their shocking pace they may eventually wear themselves out, losing their unique and unusual energy.

From their late teens unto the age of forty-six there is an emphasis on security and stability; during these years their dedication and enthusiasm are likely to have a positive influence on everyone they meet or work with. After the age of forty-seven, they become interested in new learning and communication; it is important during these years that they establish their financial security before exploring any new interests.

Catalysts that they are, these people are attracted to challenges and opportunities. They are driven and inspired, and others admire them but may have trouble keeping up with their constant shifts of direction. If they aren't careful, they may end up alone because others regard them as unreliable. They should surround themselves with friends or loved ones who can gently warn them when they are heading off course. They also need to learn that perseverance and self-discipline are the keys to success. However, once they have learned to ground themselves in reality, they should always be allowed to generate and express their ideas. The world would be a less colorful place without them.

Love *Hard to pin down*

People born April 4 often find it hard to settle down in relationships. They are attracted to unusual people and it takes someone very unique and quirky to pin them down. Partners may feel confused by their constant changes of direction, but once they commit to a relationship they bring a tremendous amount of energy to it, and that more than compensates for any inconsistencies.

Health *Slow down*

People born on this day can be extremely impulsive and this is the greatest risk to their health. They may throw themselves in at the deep end without proper preparation and this can result in injuries if the activity is physical, stress if the challenge is mental and anxiety if their emotions have led them in the wrong direction. It is extremely important for them to slow down every once in a while and consider the consequences of their actions before they jump right in. As far as diet is concerned, they should eat a wide variety of foods from all the different groups, and vigorous exercise is recommended to burn off some energy, as long as they don't push themselves too hard. They would also benefit from mind–body therapies such as meditation and breathing exercises to help them feel calmer and more in control. Adding a few drops of lavender essential oil to their handkerchief to breathe in when they feel their hearts racing will help soothe their body and soul.

Career *Born organizers*

These people have excellent organizational skills, giving them great potential for success in business and finance, as well as in the literary and performing arts and the arena of social reform. They make superb managers at an executive level or possibly working for themselves. Many entrepreneurs, producers, promoters, architects, and designers are born on this day.

Destiny *To fight for the well-being of others*

The life path of people born on this day is to learn to persevere with things and see them through to the end. Once they have learned greater discipline their destiny is to fight for the rights or well-being of others.

Signs & symbols

Sun sign: Aries

Ruling planet: Mars, the warrior

Symbol: The Ram

Birth date ruler: Uranus, the visionary

Tarot card: The Emperor (authority)

Favorable numbers: 4, 8

Lucky days: Tuesday and Sunday, especially when these days fall on 4 and 8 of the month

Lucky colors: Scarlet, blue, red

Birthstone: Diamond

April 4

5 April

the birthday of the athlete

People born on April 5 have star quality, but they don't tend to seek out fame or even fortune. For them, the satisfaction and reward always lies in the work itself. Like true athletes totally dedicated to their sport, their goal is to constantly learn, improve and strive for their personal best.

These people tend to focus on work and career, valuing solid achievement but, because they are highly principled, their success will never be at the expense of others. They need to feel that they deserve their success and, given the fact that they are blessed with both creativity to inspire others and tenacity to see things through, they have great potential to succeed in life. Their manner tends to be quiet and unassuming, and they like to avoid conflict if they can. This doesn't mean they are pushovers. When their plans are threatened or their beliefs criticized, others may be surprised at their bluntness and drive to succeed. Once they have settled on a chosen course, they will stick to it and defend it passionately. Although this dedicated approach will attract success, it is important for them to understand that some change is essential for progress and development.

Their tendency toward stubbornness is highlighted between the ages of fifteen and forty-five, during which there is an emphasis in their life on security and stability. After the age of forty-six, however, they become more interested in travel, communication, learning new skills, and change. If they can take advantage of the opportunities offered to them, this can be an extremely positive period in their life.

The strong and consistent personality of these people makes them natural candidates for leadership; but because they set extremely high standards, they should be careful that they don't become too demanding of themselves and others in the process. They also have the determination to overcome the most frustrating of obstacles and, even though they don't seek or even realize it, their energy, dedication and will-power will earn them the applause of all their contemporaries.

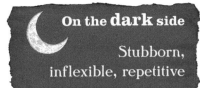
Love *Tempestuous*

People born on April 5 tend to be hard to reach emotionally and they need to find a partner who will encourage them to open up. Once in a relationship, staying faithful may be a problem because they have great charm and have no problem in attracting lovers. Their challenge is to learn to commit, and to keep their relationships steady and harmonious.

Health *Don't go overboard*

People born on this day give so much of themselves to their work that when it comes to their personal life they tend to overindulge by eating or drinking too much, partying too often and generally being reckless. They need to make sure they don't take their health for granted or take unnecessary risks. As far as diet is concerned, the emphasis should be on fresh natural foods and they should reduce their intake of foods rich in sugar, salt and additives. Regular exercise is recommended, particularly exercise they can perform alone, such as walking or jogging, as they need this time to reflect on things and recharge their energies. Wearing, meditating on or surrounding themselves with the color green will help restore their energies, inspiring healing and inner balance.

Career *Born sports stars*

These people have a pioneering spirit and they may excel in careers in which they can test themselves constantly such as sport, music, dance, art, theater, or movie-making. They may also set up their own business or be drawn toward careers in law, the civil service, politics, business, or education.

Destiny *To motivate and inspire others to be the very best*

The life path of people born on this day is to learn to be more flexible in their goals and opinions. Once they have learned the art of compromise, their destiny is to motivate and inspire others, by their own example, to be the very best that they can be.

Power Thought

❝I take time to renew myself in silence❞

Signs & symbols

Sun sign: Aries

Ruling planet: Mars, the warrior

Symbol: The Ram

Birth date ruler: Mercury, the communicator

Tarot card: The Hierophant (guidance)

Favorable numbers: 5, 9

Lucky day: Tuesday, especially when it falls on 5 and 9 of the month

Lucky colors: Scarlet, silver, orange

Birthstone: Diamond

April 5

6 April

the birthday of irresistible curiosity

Your greatest challenge is ...

learning to trust yourself

The way forward is ...

to understand that although others can offer their insight, nobody knows you better than you.

You're drawn to people born on ...

September 23 to October 22

This is a wonderful example of how opposites attract; you have so much to learn and love about each other.

Luck maker

The importance of being earnest

Centering your life round anything else but positive values is a recipe for disaster. Living in accord with your values is the only policy if you want to improve your luck.

People born on April 6 have charisma, with lots to spare. There is a kind of wild-eyed excitement about them, ruled as they are by desire, the love of beautiful things and a restless quest for knowledge. They have an irresistible urge to discover everything about the world and the people around them, their minds always being open to new and better ways of doing things.

These people are great fun to have around. They are willing to try almost anything, with the refreshing ability to laugh at themselves. Others are often happy to help them achieve their goals because their ego never gets in the way. They are multi-talented, with a knack for finding innovative solutions in all aspects of life. This makes them the home improvement experts, the planners and organizers at work, and the life and soul of the party.

With so much going for them it's easy to see why they seem destined for great success but also why some fail to realize their full potential. Lack of discrimination is their problem both professionally and at home, and this can lead to low self-esteem. Their naïvety and openness may lead them down many wrong paths, attracting controlling individuals to them and those who haven't got their best interests at heart.

It is important for them to learn to trust their intuition more and to beware of giving too much too soon. Between the ages of fourteen and forty-four they may search for security and stability; they should use this time to develop their self-confidence and sense of direction so that they are not so easily led. After the age of forty-five they may concentrate on learning new skills and expanding their interests.

People born on this day seem to have limitless energy and the ability to visualize undreamed-of possibilities. As long as they can get in touch with their feelings and become more discriminating, they have the potential to be great innovators and to lead others to previously uncharted areas.

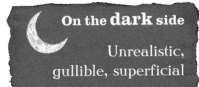
Love *Serious loving*

People born on April 6 are extremely romantic and will almost certainly enjoy experimenting sexually. However, once they have found a partner to whom they want to commit, they do make time for serious and committed loving as beneath their sensual and daring nature is a deep desire for a settled relationship.

Health *Constant motion*

People born on this day apply the same level of curiosity to their bodies as they do to everything else and they are often keen to try new diet and exercise routines and to challenge themselves with a variety of sports. As long as their experimentation does not include drugs and extreme sports, they generally enjoy good health; they do, however, need to watch that their love of good food and socializing does not lead to overindulgence and that their eyes don't suffer from long hours spent studying or learning. Because they are constantly on the go both physically and mentally, they need more sleep than most to avoid burnout and should aim for at least seven to eight hours a night, minimum. Wearing, meditating on or surrounding themselves with the color yellow will help to boost their self-confidence and optimism.

Career *Born investigators*

These people have the potential to be great scientists, investigators and researchers, although they are such good all-rounders that they can also make great musicians, philosophers, lawyers, and writers. Other careers that might appeal include sales, negotiation, diplomacy, public relations, charity work, politics, acting, and any career that involves plenty of travel and change.

Destiny *To discover as yet unknown truths*

The life path of people born on this day is to strengthen their personal identity. Once they know who they are and where they are heading, their destiny is to discover as yet unknown truths.

Power Thought

❝ My life is a reflection of the positive choices I make ❞

Signs & symbols

Sun sign: Aries

Ruling planet: Mars, the warrior

Symbol: The Ram

Birth date ruler: Venus, the lover

Tarot card: The Lovers (choices)

Favorable numbers: 1, 6

Lucky days: Tuesday and Friday, especially when these days fall on 1 and 6 of the month

Lucky colors: Scarlet, green, pink

Birthstone: Diamond

April 6

7 April

the birthday of intensity

Your greatest challenge is …

to learn not to alienate others who disagree with you

The way forward is …

to understand that listening objectively to the views of others doesn't weaken your position, it strengthens it.

You're drawn to people born on …

October 24 to November 22

You share a passion for romance and stimulating conversation, and this creates an intense and exciting union.

Luck maker

Don't hold grudges

Lucky people don't have grudges or enemies. Holding a grudge may feel like you are teaching someone a lesson but what you are really doing is shutting down your positive energy and pushing luck away.

People born on April 7 are bold and forthright individuals with deep beliefs they will fight to the death to defend. When they commit themselves to an idea, a project or a person they burn with a passion and an intensity that can drive them to extremes of thought and behaviour.

There are often two sides to the personality of these people: the vibrant, positive side that inspires them to devote themselves passionately to progress; and a more negative, impatient side that can manifest in wild-eyed fury or rebellious behavior when their expectations are not met. There is no middle ground between these two extremes of behavior and they will often swing between them, alienating others when they feel disgruntled.

Although they are blessed with unlimited zeal, determination and optimism, possessing the ability and drive to get where they want to in life, it is important for these people—and to their benefit—to learn to adopt a more considered approach. Rebellion will almost certainly be a feature of their childhood, but between the ages of fifteen and forty-three they may have opportunities to adopt a more considered approach to life. After the age of forty-four they may find new areas of interest, as well as a greater desire for communication and learning new skills. If by this age they have learned the importance of finding the middle way, they are likely to come into their own.

Although they are forthright and courageous people, they also have the hearts of dreamers. They often see different futures unfolding, and this proves invaluable to their planning. They may also feel there is a meaning to their lives but as they search for it there may be setbacks; they may rush into what they believe is their destiny only to find that they lose interest or that it wasn't really for them. Their positive expectations of happiness are, however, often rewarded. This means that although they may not find their meaning and purpose until later in life, when they do find it they discover that waiting was worthwhile.

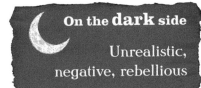

On the **dark** side
Unrealistic, negative, rebellious

At your **best**
Deep, imaginative, vibrant

Love *Hot-headed*

The energy and passion with which people born April 7 are blessed will attract many lovers, but potential partners may be scared off by their temperamental outbursts and extremes of behavior. The beginnings of their relationships tend to have a lot of heat and passion, and they need to learn that when a fire inevitably cools in a relationship it doesn't necessarily mean it is burned out.

Health *Prevention is the best cure*

When it comes to health, people born on this day need to make sure they don't take their good health and seemingly limitless energy for granted. If they don't they could be vulnerable to stress-induced stomach ulcers, immune system disorders, such as chronic fatigue syndrome, allergies as well as headaches, poor concentration, and poor health in general. Since they lack the patience needed for being a good patient, prevention really is the best medicine for them. As far as diet and exercise are concerned, they should avoid foods that are fatty, spicy and creamy, making sure they take plenty of moderate-intensity exercise; cycling and swimming are ideal. Wearing, meditating on and surrounding themselves with the color blue will help them when they need to cool down and do some logical thinking.

Career *Born interviewers*

These people have excellent communication skills and they may use this to their advantage in careers such as law, acting, directing, interviewing, and writing. They may also be drawn toward management or executive positions in business or to working for themselves. Whatever career they choose, their ability to take charge will be highly valued, especially when they learn to stay calm in a crisis.

Destiny *To make their own and others' dreams a reality*

The life path of people born on this day is to learn to be calmer and more considered in their approach to situations and people. Once they are able to control their impulses, their destiny is to make their dreams and the dreams of others a reality.

Signs & symbols

Sun sign: Aries

Ruling planet: Mars, the warrior

Symbol: The Ram

Birth date ruler: Neptune, the speculator

Tarot card: The Chariot (resilience)

Favorable numbers: 2, 7

Lucky days: Tuesday and Monday, especially when these days fall on 2 and 7 of the month

Lucky colors: Scarlet, aquamarine, sea green

Birthstone: Diamond

8 April

the birthday of
noble intention

Your greatest challenge is ...

learning to give to yourself

The way forward is ...

to understand that until you have met your own physical and emotional needs, you can't muster sufficient resources for helping others.

You're drawn to people born on ...

August 24 to September 23

You share a passion for self-improvement and original thought, and this can create a stimulating and rewarding union.

Luck maker

Feel good about yourself

Find ways to feel good about yourself and your life. If you don't feel good about yourself, how can you expect others to feel good about you and offer you opportunities to improve your luck?

People born on April 8 have a passionate sense of right and wrong, with a strong focus on humanitarian concerns. Their intentions are extremely noble, being motivated by a deep passion for the underdog or those who haven't been given a chance to develop their potential. The admiration or respect of others is not their main concern; what matters to them is the well-being of others.

Despite their compassion, there is a tendency for these people to see things in black and white; as a result they run the risk of becoming intolerant or dismissive. They passionately believe that everyone is equal, and if they see any form of injustice they can become extremely critical. In the process, they can gain more enemies than friends. It is therefore important for them to learn to control their impulses and find more effective ways of getting their point across.

Since they often find it hard to express their emotions freely they can appear somewhat detached or reserved. When there is a crisis, however, they are a tower of strength. Despite their apparent steadiness they may also alternate between being warm and responsible, and cold and indifferent.

Beneath their self-confidence lie fears of inadequacy that can manifest in self-sacrificing behavior; but if they can overcome these fears, their enormous determination, combined with their incisive and methodical mind, can help them achieve almost anything. Before the age of forty-two there is an emphasis on establishing security and stability, but after that age their focus is on new interests and on communication. These are the years when their self-confidence tends to flower and they really come into their own.

As well as being noble in their intentions, they are independent and daring, keen to express themselves with originality. Their drive to succeed is great but not usually selfish, as they prefer to express their uniqueness through humanitarian deeds that benefit many people. This is what gives these enigmatic but lovely people the potential to bring harmony to the world.

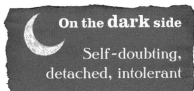
At your best

Compassionate, intense,
responsible

Love *Avoid power games*

People born April 8 have a tendency to become jealous and insecure when it comes to relationships, and they need to learn to let those they love fly free as this will strengthen rather than weaken their relationship. Fortunately, their charm, generosity and people-skills ensure that they are never without friends or admirers. They are attracted to partners who are intelligent and altruistic, but who also have the potential for success.

Health *Put your health and well-being first*

People born on this day tend to be more worried about the health of others than their own, and it is important for them to make sure they put their health and well-being first; otherwise they will be prone to stress and depression. As far as diet is concerned, they need to make sure they avoid going for long periods without eating and should eat four to six small meals and snacks during the day. Red meat and foods high in saturated fat, sugar, salt, and additives should be avoided. Exercise is a must as they enjoy energetic pursuits, and solitary pursuits such as walking, jogging, and cycling suit their need for time alone or time out. Wearing, meditating on or surrounding themselves with the color pink will encourage them to take better care of themselves.

Career *Born reformers*

The ideals those born on this day promote make them well suited to careers in law, the military, politics, humanitarian activity, and social reform, but because they also enjoy physical activity, sporting careers may also appeal. Being natural psychologists, they may also be interested in counseling or healing, and they may choose to express themselves through journalism, writing, drama, music, and art.

Destiny *To become a righter of wrongs*

The life path of people born on this day is to learn to become neither too self-sacrificing nor intolerant of others. Once they have developed these skills, they have the potential to turn their noble intentions into reality and become a righter of wrongs.

Signs & symbols

Sun sign: Aries

Ruling planet: Mars, the warrior

Symbol: The Ram

Birth date ruler: Saturn, the teacher

Tarot card: Strength (passion)

Favorable numbers: 3, 8

Lucky days: Tuesday and Saturday, especially when these days fall on 3 and 8 of the month

Lucky colors: Scarlet, dark blue, blood red

Birthstone: Diamond

April 8

9 April

the birthday of the whirlwind

People born on April 9 have fantastic stamina. They live and love like a whirlwind, possessing an insatiable appetite for all the pleasures of life. Although they love to have a good time, they can also work very hard. Blessed with prodigious energy, originality and single-mindedness, they have great potential to achieve their ambitions.

These people have a strong personality and don't like to be in a subservient position. In their professional life, their understanding of what people need can make them accurate predictors of social trends. They have the ability to turn their ideas into reality, and by so doing they not only enrich the lives of others, they can also profit themselves.

Others are often seduced by their charm, although some find their out-spokenness somewhat excessive. They have to win every argument, often somewhat bluntly, and they also don't take kindly to criticism, regarding any such comment as a form of betrayal. Their fondness for pushing the limits by indulging in physical pleasures can alarm others, especially when their lavish lifestyle attracts those who do not have their best interests at heart.

Until the age of forty-one they may concentrate on material stability; it is important during this time that they base their life around positive rather than negative values. After the age of forty-two they may broaden their horizons, becoming more interested in furthering their own spiritual and psychological growth. It is during these years that their generosity, openness and warmth are most likely to be offset by their lack of reliability.

Although people born on this day can be erratic and extreme, their drive and strength of purpose can sweep others off their feet, carrying them along in a whirlwind of enthusiasm. There's little time for quiet reflection along the way but there will be plenty of excitement. This is because life rarely stands still for these people; it's an action-packed adventure with many surprises and opportunities. If they can put these opportunities to good use, they can become energetic campaigners for greater self-expression and for progress.

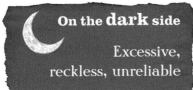
Love *Insatiable*

When it comes to relationships, people born on April 9 are hungry for all sorts of romantic adventures and they are likely to enjoy experimenting in this area. They have fantastic energy and can be a lot of fun in a relationship, although their lack of dependability can be a problem. They are attracted to quietly confident people who can stimulate their natural creativity.

Health *Less is definitely more*

People born on this day are their own worst enemies as far as their health is concerned, as they are prone to indulge in rich food, drink, partying, and excess in general. They need to learn that moderation in all things is central to health and well-being. As far as diet is concerned, they should avoid fasting for long periods followed by bingeing as this will trigger blood-sugar and weight problems. Exercise should be moderate to mild, rather than vigorous, and activities such as brisk walking or light jogging can give them time to gather their thoughts and be alone. They should also make sure they schedule regular periods of relaxation into their lives, such as aromatherapy baths, massage, chatting with friends and so on. Carrying a malachite crystal or having a malachite ornament around their house will help balance their emotions, bringing with it a sense of calmness and ease.

Career *Born freedom fighters*

These people have the pioneering spirit, leadership skills and courage to excel in a wide range of careers but they are often attracted to careers in business, the military, engineering, and politics, or to leadership in labor union organizations. They may also be drawn toward careers in management or social reform as well as philosophy, art, music, retail, and antiques.

Destiny *To organize their ideas and the ideas of others*

The life path of people born on this day is to learn to relax, as their overindulgence can alienate others and lead to health problems. Once they have learned to temper their impulses, their destiny is to organize their ideas and the ideas of others, and put them to good use.

Power Thought

❝ I understand the principle of less is more and will incorporate it in my life ❞

Signs & symbols

Sun sign: Aries

Ruling planet: Mars, the warrior

Symbol: The Ram

Birth date ruler: Mars, the warrior

Tarot card: The Hermit (inner strength)

Favorable numbers: 4, 9

Lucky day: Tuesday, especially when it falls on 4 and 9 of the month

Lucky colors: Scarlet, orange, red

Birthstone: Diamond

April 9

1O April

the birthday of
the shrewd hero/heroine

People born on April 10 have a dazzling personality that likes to do courageous and daring things. Their life tends to be a roller-coaster but, although they do take considerable risks both professionally and personally, they are neither foolish nor reckless. Without a doubt they are action heroes and heroines, but shrewd ones.

While those who do not know them well may be taken aback by their daring or radical approach, these people are in fact confident of success, secure in the knowledge that they have carefully evaluated the risks. They may appear impulsive but behind the scenes there is always a soundly considered plan of action to realize their ambitions. This combination of pragmatism and adventure, combined with their undoubted intelligence and enormous energy, augurs well for success.

It can sometimes be difficult for them to slow down, even with their closest friends. Restless and action orientated, they have a tendency to race through life as if they are afraid of missing out on something. It is important for them to learn to relax. Until the age of forty they may concentrate on security and stability, but after this age they will want to learn new skills; it is important that they learn to slow down and reflect on their progress.

Curiously the private lives of these bold people may be marked by a certain degree of detachment from others, as well as by attacks of anxiety or even phobias. These private fears might indicate a fear of failure or rejection; these can be resolved once they learn to connect with their feelings, experiencing the joys of sharing and intimacy with others.

Since people born on this day find it easier to compete than to cooperate, they are excellent self-starters with real leadership potential. Naturally charming, their non-conformist perspective often attracts many admirers. Once they are able to balance their restlessness with sensitivity and patience, there is no doubt that these warriors, with their ability to plan and complete a project, will go far.

On the **dark** side

Workaholic, detached, unstable

At your **best**

Daring, competitive, dedicated

Love *Reticence*

Although people born on April 10 have no problem attracting friends and potential partners, they can sometimes find it hard to open up to those close to them. They need a partner who can gently coax them into doing so, because they are at their happiest and their best when they are able to experience close and supportive relationships with loved ones.

Health *Relax!*

People born on this day must learn to relax more, as it is essential to their health and well-being. If they don't allow themselves time to unwind, they may be prone to mood swings, headaches, stress, and depression. They would benefit greatly from mind–body therapies such as meditation, yoga and tai chi, as these will help them calm down and learn greater self-control. As far as diet is concerned, they should avoid excessive amounts of alcohol and steer clear of smoking and drugs. Their exercise routine should not be restrictive, and instead of focusing on one activity, such as running, they should aim for plenty of variety; cross-training is ideal. Wearing, meditating on or surrounding themselves with the color green or purple will encourage them to relax.

Career *Born stuntmen/women*

Methodical and adventurous, these people can excel in careers in advertising, surveying or marketing, as well as sales, negotiation, publishing, law and banking, and stunt work. Their need for self-expression may also lead them to drama or the entertainment world; alternatively, they may choose to strike out alone and work for themselves.

Destiny *To encourage others to step outside their comfort zone*

The life path of people born on this day is to learn to occasionally step back when necessary. As soon as they have understood the importance of relaxation, their destiny is to encourage others by their example to challenge themselves and step outside their comfort zone.

Signs & symbols

Sun sign: Aries

Ruling planet: Mars, the warrior

Symbol: The Ram

Birth date ruler: Sun, the individual

Tarot card: The Wheel of Fortune (change)

Favorable numbers: 1, 5

Lucky days: Tuesday and Sunday, especially when these days fall on 1 and 5 of the month

Lucky colors: Scarlet, yellow, orange

Birthstone: Diamond

11 April

the birthday of the mediator

The assertive but warm-hearted individuals born on April 11 have the ability to see problems in both an emotional and a practical way, making them excellent problem solvers and mediators. They are capable of bringing even the most divergent of opinions into harmony with great charm and tact.

If there is a good cause to promote, these people are often the first to volunteer to help. They are eternally optimistic, with the ability to devote their energy and interpersonal skills to a plan of action, then promoting it with tenacity. They are also realistic enough to know that the support of others will benefit them; so they set out to charm and convert any opposition to their cause by means of skilled diplomacy.

Although they often find themselves the center of attention, these people do not purposely seek the limelight, preferring to be a part rather than a focus of the action. In their professional life, they are more concerned with ideas than image, working tirelessly to find common ground for agreement.

Unfortunately, they aren't always as diplomatic in their private lives and at times they can be unresponsive to the needs of those closest to them. They often have plenty of admirers, loving nothing better than planning get-togethers where large numbers of people can mingle; but to their nearest and dearest they can be cool. Fortunately, around the age of forty they are likely to focus their energies less on financial security and popularity, and more on close friends and loved ones.

They also are great communicators, working particularly well when given charge of a team with the opportunity to inspire and encourage others. They run the risk that in knowing what is best for the common good they refuse to consider alternative viewpoints, so it is important for their psychological growth to keep their minds open to other, perhaps better, ways of doing things. Once they have learned greater flexibility, they can use their powers of persuasion, tenacity and clear-sightedness to champion justice, creating a more nurturing and peaceful world.

Power Thought

66 Today I will consider both sides of every argument 99

Love *Bit of a tease*

Never short of potential partners, some might consider the charming and popular people born on April 11 a bit of a tease; but often their coolness is because they don't give their heart until they are absolutely certain that affections will be returned. When they do commit to a relationship, however, they are warm, loyal and romantic.

Health *Time out*

People born on this day need to make sure they give themselves plenty of time to relax and unwind as they suffer from a tendency to push themselves too hard, especially mentally. They would benefit enormously from nature walks where they can observe the magical workings of the natural world. Sleep is also of great importance as they need more than most, and they should avoid burning the midnight oil as this will have a negative impact on their health. As far as diet is concerned they are unlikely to have problems with their weight, but if they do they should eat more nutritious foods, such as fruits, vegetables and whole grains, and cut back on refined and processed foods rich in sugar, salt and additives. Regular exercise will also boost their thinking skills and encourage them to take time out. Wearing, meditating on or surrounding themselves with the color green will help restore natural healing and balance in their lives.

Career *Born judges*

People born on this day are ideally suited for careers in which they can help others find common ground, such as negotiation, translation and diplomacy. They also make great agents, teachers, counselors, psychologists, politicians, judges, and social workers. They have the business skills and charm to succeed in sales and marketing, and the communication skills needed for careers in management, the clergy and charity work.

Destiny *To enlist others to their progressive ideals*

The life path of people born on this day is to recognize the importance of relaxation and quiet emotional fulfillment. Once they are able to do that, their destiny is to enlist the support of others to their progressive ideals.

Signs & symbols

Sun sign: Aries

Ruling planet: Mars, the warrior

Symbol: The Ram

Birth date ruler: Moon, the intuitive

Tarot card: Justice (discernment)

Favorable numbers: 2, 6

Lucky days: Tuesday and Monday, especially when these days fall on 2 and 6 of the month

Lucky colors: Scarlet, silver, blue

Birthstone: Diamond

April 11

12 April

the birthday of the enigmatic interviewer

People born on April 12 are often surrounded by a fascinated group of listeners. They are well liked for their ability to get others to open up to them, possessing the knack of making people laugh at their own insecurities, offering others an opportunity thereby to rise above themselves.

Stimulating, witty and fun, they are interested in everyone and everything. Their inquisitive minds are forever on the alert, looking out for the latest news or research to inform or entertain. Curiously, they find it hard to share their feelings, being more comfortable in the role of interviewer, entertainer or informer than of confidant. This elusiveness can cause tension both at home and at work; it is important for them to learn to open up about their own feelings.

These people don't like to miss a thing and they may therefore spend a great deal of their twenties and thirties wandering from job to job or even country to country in search of a satisfying profession. While this would prove disastrous for most, for them it can work because every experience they have, even the ones that disappoint and frustrate, is regarded as a learning opportunity. Then, some time in their forties, through this process of trial and error, they find a goal or purpose which can make use of the vast store of knowledge and experience they have thus far accumulated.

Keen observers of the human condition, people born on this day prize knowledge above all else and love to share what they have learned with others. There is a danger that they can become judgmental in the process or heavily influenced by the opinions of others; it is important for them to stay curious and open-minded, and not become dogmatic. Getting to know who they are and what they, not others, think about things is central to their success. This is because when they get in touch with their own feelings, as well as those of others, they can not only entertain and inform, but inspire as well.

Love *Lucky star*

People born on April 12 tend to be fortunate when it comes to affairs of the heart, often stumbling into the perfect situation with the minimum of effort. Once in a relationship, however, their tendency to remain elusive and hide their feelings can cause friction, so they need to learn to open up if they want their love to last.

Health *Inner balance*

It is extremely important for people born on this day to learn to spend time alone; not with a book or with the TV or radio on, but with just themselves, so that they can check in with their thoughts and feelings. As far as diet is concerned, they often like to make eating a social occasion in which they can entertain others, but they do need to watch that they don't overeat as a result. Taking time to chew their food so that it can be digested properly is important. Regular exercise is essential, as is sufficient sleep—although their health is generally good, they should not take it for granted. Wearing, meditating on or surrounding themselves with the color purple will encourage them to look inward and think of higher things.

Career *Born investigative journalists*

These people have excellent communication skills and can excel in careers in journalism, reporting, politics, research, show business, and the arts. Being progressive and original in their thought, they may also be attracted to professions such as public relations, design, science, and the healing professions as well as police work, law, business, and finance.

Destiny *To invigorate others with optimism and wit*

The life path of people born on this day is to uncover the truth about themselves. Once they are able to get in touch with who they are and what they want, their destiny is to invigorate and inspire others with their optimism, originality and wit.

Signs & symbols

Sun sign: Aries

Ruling planet: Mars, the warrior

Symbol: The Ram

Birth date ruler: Jupiter, the philosopher

Tarot card: The Hanged Man (reflection)

Favorable numbers: 3, 7

Lucky days: Tuesday and Thursday, especially when these days fall on 3 and 7 of the month

Lucky colors: Red, deep purple, geranium

Birthstone: Diamond

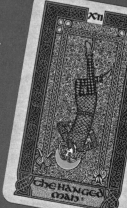

13 April

the birthday of the reformer

Your greatest challenge is ...

learning not to lose faith in yourself

The way forward is ...

to draw on the strength and support of those closest to you and to remind yourself that there is only one you with your unique contribution.

You're drawn to people born on ...

January 21 to February 20

You are both strong-minded individuals who need personal space and stability, and this can create a loving and supportive union.

Luck maker

Be an encourager

Look around you and find someone who needs inspiration. Encourage them to do what they can, rather than think about what they can't. When you start to encourage another person, you feel encouraged yourself.

People born on April 13 are born reformers, willing to work tirelessly to make changes they consider crucial. They are an endless source of new ideas and, although some of these might be considered eccentric, people appreciate their unusual approach to problem solving.

These highly intelligent people can often handle tasks that most others find exacting. They excel at resolving problems and coming up with a better way of doing things. Mental stimulation is essential to them and if they don't feel challenged they can get easily bored and restless, with a tendency to fidget. They don't like sitting still and try to inject as much activity as they can into every moment. Their propensity to seek out new challenges is particularly highlighted after the age of thirty-seven, when their focus changes from that of material stability to intellectual curiosity.

These people don't actively seek out the company of others because they are essentially private, preferring to connect with the world and make their mark through their work. Their greatest satisfaction comes from moving humanity forward or from employing their considerable talents in projects that benefit others. They derive great satisfaction from the comfort and support of a few close friends and family, preferably those who validate their vision and provide them with support when their ideas are criticized. Although skeptical of convention and compelled to seek out alternative solutions, they are nonetheless deeply sensitive to the opinions of others; even if these opinions hurt, they are rarely deflected from their chosen course.

Because people born on this day value their solitude, often feeling the need to withdraw from scrutiny, especially when working on a project, they can often be criticized for being remote, distant or in extreme cases weird. But the truth is that they are highly sensitive individuals with a need for privacy. But when the time feels right they can overcome any fear or hesitation they might have and, like the true pioneers they are, can step out with boldness, often breaking new ground in the process.

Love *Alone together*

People born on April 13 are at their happiest and their best when they are in a stable, loving relationship, preferably with someone who understands their need for independence within a relationship and who can keep up with their fast pace. To get really close to someone, however, they need to work on slowing down their fast pace.

Health *Don't hide away*

People born on this day need to resist their tendency to hide away when their feelings overwhelm them; because if they don't find ways to manage these feelings, they can easily spiral into depression or depression-related illnesses, such as eating disorders or self-harm. They must also make sure they don't use their intense need for privacy as an excuse to avoid personal responsibilities and commitments. They should avoid excessive consumption of alcohol and other escapist pastimes, such as watching too much television or staying too long in bed. Exercise is a great way for them to become more externally focused; they would benefit greatly from social forms of exercise such as dancing and aerobics, although they will tend to prefer solitary pursuits such as walking. Wearing, meditating on or surrounding themselves with the color orange will encourage them to feel more optimistic and friendly.

Career *Born politicians*

People born on this day tend to be attracted to careers in which they can translate their reforming vision into reality, making great politicians, judges and military commanders, as well as musicians, writers and actors. They may also be attracted to any career that offers them opportunities for management, supervision or leadership, or to be a pioneer in some way.

Destiny *To turn their progressive vision into a reality*

The life path of people born on this day is to learn to cope positively with discouragement. Once they are able to turn rejection into resolve, their destiny is to turn their progressive vision into a reality.

Power Thought

" Today I will feel the fear and do it anyway "

Signs & symbols

Sun sign: Aries

Ruling planet: Mars, the warrior

Symbol: The Ram

Birth date ruler: Uranus, the visionary

Tarot card: Death (change)

Favorable numbers: 4, 8

Lucky days: Tuesday and Sunday, especially when these days fall on 4 and 8 of the month

Lucky colors: Scarlet, violet, amethyst

Birthstone: Diamond

April 13

14 April

the birthday of respect

People born on April 14 often have outstanding communication skills and a wonderful way with people. Their obvious leadership skills earn them the admiration of others. Whatever situation or line of work they find themselves in, others tend to listen to and respect them.

The respect of others matters greatly to these people, as they themselves have great respect for the past and a strong desire to follow in the footsteps of others. Creating new systems or methods doesn't interest them as much as reaching the heights others have already scaled. This doesn't mean they're stuck in the past; quite the opposite, as they will always put a unique stamp on their work. It just means they have a powerful sense of tradition and great respect for the work of others. As a result, conservative methods will often be preferred to more radical ones.

These people are at their happiest and best when their home and work lives are stable, giving them the feeling of security they need to excel in their chosen field. It is therefore important for them not to take the love and support of those closest to them for granted. Until the age of thirty-six they concentrate on material security, building a solid foundation. After the age of thirty-seven they enter a period of new ideas and increased productivity during which they may use their excellent communication skills to become a mouthpiece for an organization or group.

These people like to be in control, both at work and at home, but despite this autocratic tendency they are also intuitive, often quick to realize when they have crossed the line, adjusting their behavior accordingly. Their respectful attitude toward others serves them well, their success rarely being resented. Even though they do suffer from bouts of anxiety and uncertainty—manifested in their obsession with details—it is important that they put their talents to good use because all forms of communication invigorate their lives, so they not only follow in the footsteps of the great, but become great themselves.

On the dark side

Fussy, anxious, autocratic

At your best

Respectful, ambitious, disciplined

Love *Sensitive souls*

Other people tend to see those born on April 14 as self-assured and confident, but underneath they can be quite vulnerable, needing someone who can cherish and protect them. They are sensitive souls at heart and it may take a while for them to be able to trust another in a relationship; but once they do, they are spontaneous and fun-loving partners.

Health *Mirror, mirror on the wall*

People born on this day are often extremely concerned with the way they look and their appearance matters greatly to them. It may take them a long time to get ready in the morning or to decide on exactly the right outfit for a specific occasion. Rather than succumbing to an endless round of beauty treatments or surgery, it is important for them to understand that the best way to stay fit and young looking is to eat a healthy diet, avoid yo-yo dieting and take regular moderate-intensity exercise. They may also have ear and eye problems, and issues with facial blemishes. Wearing, meditating on or surrounding themselves with the colors orange or yellow will help build their confidence and self-esteem.

Career *Born writers*

These people are great communicators so any career that utilizes this skill, such as journalism, writing, law, politics, acting, music, dancing, or the arts and entertainment industry, would appeal. Because they love creating order and have excellent people skills, tourism, the retail trade, the leisure industry, and all kinds of business will also appeal.

Destiny *To follow in the footsteps of the greats*

The life path of people born on this day is to learn not to take other people, especially those closest to them, for granted. Once they have learned to do this, their destiny is to follow in the footsteps of the greats.

Signs & symbols

Sun sign: Aries

Ruling planet: Mars, the warrior

Symbol: The Ram

Birth date ruler: Mercury, the communicator

Tarot card: Temperance (moderation)

Favorable numbers: 5, 9

Lucky days: Tuesday and Wednesday, especially when these days fall on 5 and 9 of the month

Lucky colors: Scarlet, sky blue

Birthstone: Diamond

April 14

15 April

the birthday of intellectual incisiveness

The charismatic individuals born on April 15 are sensitive and charming, yet ambitious and powerful. The key to their complex and seemingly contradictory personality is their intellectual incisiveness which enables them to formulate well-structured strategies in response to almost any challenge.

The powerful intellect they are blessed with can make them extraordinarily sensitive to what is going on around them. Sometimes they can take their skills of observation to the extreme; this can become a source of friction with loved ones, who want to be seen for who they actually are, not for what they could be. It can also contribute to feelings of anxiety and insecurity, as people born on this day may hear or observe something out of context and draw the incorrect conclusions. Their passion for detailed observation and analysis may make them take themselves and everyone else a little too seriously, so they forget the importance of relaxing and simply having fun. On the plus side, and it's a big plus, their acute intellect and powers of observation enable them to detect a vital piece of information or the missing link needed to remedy or explain a situation. The compassionate, wise side of their nature also means that others often turn to them for support, encouragement and advice.

Their ability to see life in broad rather than specific terms may be regarded by others as unrealistic or impossible and it may be that the world is not yet ready for their sweeping and imaginative ideas. Until the age of thirty-five the emphasis in their life is on practical considerations, but after the age of thirty-six they are likely to place more significance on knowledge, communication and mental exploration, and these are the years when people born on this day really come into their own.

These people long to make their mark on the world and, if they can learn to channel their rare combination of great imagination, brilliant organization and tenacity into a direction that others find acceptable, they have the potential to be truly inspirational.

Power Thought

❝ Today my happiness will inspire my creativity ❞

Love *Don't give too much away*

People are often drawn to those born on April 15 because they are powerful and dependable, yet when they fall in love there is a tendency for them to give too much of their power away, and to become needy and possessive. It is important for them to make sure they keep their relationships on an equal footing and to learn to love others for who they are, and not for what they want them to be.

Health *Laughter is the best medicine*

People born on this day are keen observers of the human condition and therefore likely to know a great deal about health. The trouble is they don't always practice what they preach and need to be careful that they don't take their health for granted. They should avoid any kind of extreme diet or going for long periods without food, as this will unsettle their metabolism and set them up for weight problems. They should also give themselves plenty of time to relax and unwind, and the best way for them to do this is to have more fun. In fact, laugher is the best medicine for these people. Wearing, meditating on or surrounding themselves with the color orange will increase feelings of warmth, physical enjoyment and security.

Career *Born designers*

These people tend to be multi-talented and so it is likely they will have several career changes in their life. Many things inspire them but they have a gift for working with their hands, especially when they can be creative as beauticians, gardeners, chefs, artists, decorators, designers, and caterers. Being broadminded and philosophical, they may also be drawn to careers in teaching, law or research, but whatever field they enter they will want to pioneer new projects.

Destiny *To find ways for their talents to be admired*

The life path of people born on this day is to learn to take themselves a little less seriously. Once they have learned to be more relaxed, their destiny is to find ways for their talents to be admired by more conventional types.

Signs & symbols

Sun sign: Aries

Ruling planet: Mars, the warrior

Symbol: The Ram

Birth date ruler: Venus, the lover

Tarot card: The Devil (instinct)

Favorable numbers: 1, 6

Lucky days: Tuesday and Friday, especially when these days fall on 1 and 6 of the month

Lucky colors: Scarlet, lime, pink

Birthstone: Diamond

April 15

16 April

the birthday of the truth seeker

Your greatest challenge is ...

not being exploited

The way forward is ...

to think carefully about who you want to help or be with. You should make sure you don't give to people who are lazy or self-destructive.

You're drawn to people born on ...

October 24 to November 22

You share a passion for philosophy and a need for closeness, and this can create an intoxicating and passionate union.

Luck maker

Look within

Turn your gaze around from the world and other people, and realize that the happiness, inspiration and luck you search for are already within you.

People born on April 16 love to talk about the meaning of life, being fascinated by life's mysteries. At the same time they are seductive, charming and very amusing. They know how to make other people smile, and friends, loved ones and colleagues will often regard these humorous and dreamy individuals with great affection.

Although they have the ability to see the humor in almost any situation, they are not superficial individuals. Quite the opposite; they have a deep awareness of life's tragedies, which gives them the insight to understand that humor is one of the best and most cathartic responses. Despite being wise and insightful, they can be generous to the point of stupidity; others often take advantage of their willingness to share. They also tend to over-indulge in everything they enjoy, easily slipping into irresponsible behavior.

In general, strong emotions make these people feel uncomfortable and they like to lighten intense moments with humor. This can make their contribution invaluable during times of stress, as it teaches others how to deal effectively with setbacks. It can, however, also work against them; instead of facing situations that need to be resolved, they avoid them. It is important for them to resist the temptation to sidestep conflict, as this can lead to hidden resentments in the future.

These people can appear as if they are living in a world of dreams. While it is true that they are visionaries, they are able to translate their dreams into reality. Until the age of thirty-four they focus on building a secure foundation for their dreams. Then, after the age of thirty-five, they have a greater interest in interpersonal relationships and communication skills. This is a positive development for them, as becoming more aware of the dreams and ideals of others—and not just their own—aids their psychological growth. Once they strike a healthy balance between their inner and outer selves, others will admire them not only for their humor and gentle presence, but also for their inspirational strength of purpose.

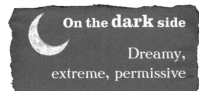

On the **dark** side
Dreamy, extreme, permissive

At your **best**
Entertaining, kind, generous

Love *Spiritual union*

People born on April 16 believe in the possibility of a soul mate and dream of a once-in-a-lifetime emotional, physical and spiritual union. Highly idealistic, they often enter into a relationship with high expectations and an ability to sink into the depths of their partner. They need to make sure they find someone with a fine mind who shares their interests; otherwise their intensity may be more scary than exhilarating.

Health *Down to earth*

People born on this day don't tend to worry too much about their health, and this optimistic attitude more often than not ensures that their health is good. They do, however, need to make sure they don't take it for granted. They are more likely to suffer from psychological rather than physical problems, such as stress, anxiety and feeling depressed when it seems that others are not on their wavelength. As far as diet is concerned, they should not ignore their hunger signals, eating little and often to keep their energy levels high. Regular exercise, such as aerobics, running, swimming, and cycling, is important for them as it will help them relax more. Wearing, meditating on or surrounding themselves with the color green will help them feel more grounded.

Career *Born comedians*

These people have a talent for making others smile and would make excellent comedians, tour guides, entertainers, clowns, actors, writers, photographers, artists, designers, and architects. Because they also have great organizational skills, they would also excel in careers in science and research, and their love of action may draw them to careers in travel and sport.

Destiny *To use humor in their fight for issues*

The life path of people born on this day is to learn that it is impossible to please everyone. Once they have learned not to take on too many burdens, their destiny is to fight for the issues that motivate them in a way that entertains but also intrigues others.

Signs & symbols

Sun sign: Aries

Ruling planet: Mars, the warrior

Symbol: The Ram

Birth date ruler: Neptune, the speculator

Tarot card: The Tower (breakthrough)

Favorable numbers: 2, 7

Lucky days: Tuesday and Monday, especially when these days fall on 2 and 7 of the month

Lucky colors: Scarlet, blue, green

Birthstone: Diamond

April 16

17 April

the birthday of will-power

People born on April 17 are confident, ambitious and opportunistic individuals. When knocked down, they have the will-power and resilience to bounce right back. They know their own mind, having a clear idea of where they are going and how to get there. Determined to succeed, they also have a talent for spotting opportunities, not just for themselves, but for others.

Despite often being quietly spoken, the impression these people make on others is often strong because they promote their ideals with absolute conviction. They expect others to agree with them and, because of their intense will-power, others often do. They also have the ability to translate their ideals into action and may find themselves leading those who are less determined. Although it can seem as if they were born to be successful, they do have to work hard to get to the top. This isn't a problem for them, though, as they do whatever it takes to make their mark. They thrive on challenge and love a good battle and, in the process, make either loyal friends or resentful enemies.

These people are prone to mood swings and like to spend time alone when dark moments are upon them. Although this can be beneficial in their professional relationships, in their personal relationships it can be detrimental; refusing to share their ups and downs limits the depth of close bonds. Their tendency is to divide everything into positive and negative; just as it's important for them to appreciate the complexity of their emotional life, they also need to acknowledge the complexities in the world around them. Until the age of thirty-three they strive for security and certainty, but after the age of thirty-four they may move toward a more flexible world view.

It is important for them to ensure that their amazing will-power does not make them too judgmental or serious. Once they inject a little light-heartedness into their lives, they will discover that their authority isn't weakened but strengthened, and that wherever their dreams take them, others will gladly follow.

On the **dark** side

Moody, judgmental, harsh

At your **best**

Purposeful, opportunistic, resilient

Love *Take a risk*

People born on March 17 can be passionate and loyal lovers but it can take a while for them to open up in relationships and be truly themselves. They like to feel in control and, when another person makes them feel vulnerable or needy, their response is often to withdraw or to flirt with other admirers. It is important for their psychological growth to take a risk and share their feelings with loved ones.

Health *Go dancing*

People born on this day can sometimes feel lonely and misunderstood, and it is important for them not to try and seek comfort in food, drugs, alcohol, and sex. The best therapy for them when they feel low is to spend time with close family and friends. They would also benefit from regular exercise, in particular walking or dancing, which will encourage them to be more sociable and spontaneous. As far as diet is concerned, they should avoid as much as possible foods that are refined, processed or high in saturated fat, salt, sugar, and additives. Mind–body therapies such as meditation and yoga would appeal to their interest in thought control. Carrying a rose quartz crystal or placing one around their house or office will help them release pent-up stress and tension, providing a calming space for emotional wounds to heal.

Career *Born politicians*

These people have a highly developed sense of justice and so careers in humanitarian-related fields such as politics, law and the military will appeal, although they may also put their organizational skills to good use in careers in business, banking or accountancy. Alternatively, they may work as self-employed people in their own right or express their ideals in music or the arts.

Destiny *To become a great leader*

The life path of people born on this day is to learn to be less judgmental of themselves and others. Once they are able to do that their destiny is to become a great leader.

Power Thought

66 Today I am prepared to look at myself and the world differently 99

Signs & symbols

Sun sign: Aries

Ruling planet: Mars, the warrior

Symbol: The Ram

Birth date ruler: Saturn, the teacher

Tarot card: The Star (hope)

Favorable numbers: 3, 8

Lucky days: Tuesday and Saturday, especially when these days fall on 3 and 8 of the month

Lucky colors: Scarlet, green, red

Birthstone: Diamond

April 17

18 April

the birthday of dignity

Your greatest challenge is …

learning to let down your guard

The way forward is …

to understand that being yourself is the best and only way to earn the respect of others, even if that means appearing ungainly or vulnerable.

You're drawn to people born on …

March 21 to April 20

You are both strong-willed and highly romantic individuals, and this can create a passionate and stimulating union.

Luck maker

Age doesn't matter

Don't let anyone convince you that age is a handicap. You are never too old or too young to get lucky—unless you think you are.

People born on April 18 are powerful, strong, dependable and influential. They stand firm in their beliefs, possessing boundless energy and conviction. Often taking the lead in conversations or projects, they like to think of themselves as confident and dignified; this is exactly how they come across to others.

In some ways similar to a comic-book superhero, they are bold, hardworking and dignified, and also like to defend the underdog. Sometimes, though, their views are so lofty and their standards so high that they set themselves up for frustration and disappointment. This can manifest itself in sudden and unexpected outbursts of temper or, even worse, disdain.

The respect of others is extremely important for them and they take great care how they present themselves to others. They are particularly vulnerable to attacks on their dignity or performance but, because they are so well prepared, these rarely occur. Generally, they have an extremely positive effect on others, their main problem being recognition of their own and others' limits. They need to be careful that they don't become extreme or fanatical, especially before the age of thirty-two. During this period, the influence of either their mother or father over their choice of career may be strong. After the age of thirty-three they may develop a desire to become more knowledgeable and communicative, and therefore more flexible and independent. Around the age of sixty-two there is another important shift, which accentuates their emotional needs, home and friends.

Despite the seriousness of their ideals, most people born on this day understand the importance of relaxation, and this can help them avoid becoming obsessive. They may even have a slightly mischievous streak and they should never seek to repress that positive energy. This is because when they are able to become more spontaneous in their words and deeds, they have the potential to earn both the respect of others, and their loyalty, admiration and affection.

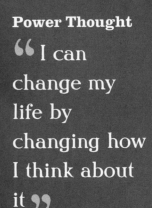
Love *Hearts, flowers and violins*

In love, all the toughness that defines people born on April 18 completely disappears when they find a suitably challenging partner. They need someone who is an individual but also highly romantic, as they love to indulge the softer side of their personality. They also enjoy the thrill of the chase and are not excited by people who make things too easy for them.

Health *Structure is key*

People born on this day are at their happiest and healthiest when their life is structured and ordered. They need to make sure their lifestyle routines are regular and that their time is used constructively. Sleep is important for them as they are so mentally active, and they should go to bed and wake up at roughly the same time, even at the weekends. As far as diet is concerned, they should make sure that they eat healthily, avoiding saturated fat and ensuring that their main meal is before 8 p.m.; otherwise the quality of their sleep may be compromised. Daily exercise should be scheduled into their routine, even if it gets them sweaty and a little disheveled. Mental stimulation is vital and they get great satisfaction from studying, in particular from learning new languages. Wearing, meditating on or surrounding themselves with the color green will restore their energies, inspiring harmony in themselves and others.

Career *Born philanthropists*

These people will thrive in careers where they can affect tangible benefits or improvements from their concerns: politics, for example, or the military, the judiciary, public services, or the healing or caring professions. They may also choose to share their original and gifted ideas in the arts. A philosophical leaning may draw them toward humanitarian causes and philanthropy.

Destiny *To achieve their humanitarian and personal ambitions*

The life path of people born on this day is to learn to recognize their own limits and not to take on too much. Once they have learned not to become obsessive about their ideals, their destiny is to achieve their humanitarian and personal ambitions.

Signs & symbols

Sun sign: Aries

Ruling planet: Mars, the warrior

Symbol: The Ram

Birth date ruler: Mars, the warrior

Tarot card: The Moon (imagination)

Favorable numbers: 4, 9

Lucky day: Tuesday, especially when it falls on 4 and 9 of the month

Lucky colors: Scarlet, crimson, orange

Birthstone: Diamond

19 April

the birthday of magnetic self-sufficiency

Liberally endowed with originality, stamina, intelligence, and ambition, people born on April 19 possess unlimited faith in their own knowledge. This means they will also take some knocks but much of their confidence is gained through their experience of victory and defeat.

Possessing a strong competitive streak, if something isn't difficult or nearly impossible, these people are not interested. With the ability to turn weaknesses into strengths, they are often the unqualified workers who soar up through the ranks. Although career focused, they are rarely materialistic, often being generous with both their time and their money. Their goal is not necessarily to be rich but to be self-sufficient, as in their eyes dependency on another is a sign of weakness. Learning to accept financial support—or any type of support for that matter—from family and friends may be difficult, given the high value they place on self-sufficiency, but reaching out will take them a step forward in personal development.

It is important for them to learn to step back now and again, and let others take the lead. Until the age of thirty-one there is an emphasis on security and routine in their life and they need to be careful not to be over-controlling or to ignore the feelings of others. After the age of thirty-two, however, they may widen their interests, placing more emphasis on learning, knowledge and new skills. If they can teach themselves and others to experiment with new and untested approaches to situations this period in their lives can be extremely productive.

Nothing gives them more satisfaction than knowing that the success they have achieved has been of their own making. They instinctively take control, providing vision and direction in cooperative ventures; others tend to look to them for leadership because their confidence and poise under fire make their advice difficult to ignore. Once they have learned to delegate, to listen more and talk just a little less, their stamina, mental acuity and personal magnetism can help them succeed in virtually anything.

At your best

Committed, skillful, charismatic

Love *Only you*

Once people born on April 19 have fixed their sights upon a potential partner, the matter is usually settled as their sex appeal is irresistible. However, this is not to imply that their judgment is always perfect and their high sex drive can frequently lead to hasty and unhappy marriages, or affairs and lots of children. Although they do not find it hard to attract partners, they really do fare best with a steady stream of love from one special person.

Health *Empty yourself out*

A healthy, balanced diet, quality sleep and regular sex are the keys to good health for people born on this day. Sports provide a positive and healthy outlet for their competitive instinct. Both individual challenges, such as jogging, and group sports such as baseball and soccer will be worthwhile. These people often have a secret yearning to relinquish the daily battles of the world and tend to do best when they allow themselves to recharge—through gardening, massage, a vacation, or simply taking themselves less seriously. Wearing, meditating on or surrounding themselves with the color purple will encourage them to look inward and think of higher things.

Career *Born freelancers*

Their excellent communication skills mean that careers involving people and persuasion are ideal, such as public relations, advertising, law, politics, project management, or construction. Their creativity may also draw them toward careers in fashion, performing arts, journalism, design, or being an intermediary or agent. They are born self-starters, so working for themselves may appeal and, because their idealistic nature yearns to accomplish something that will benefit others, they may be drawn toward medicine, teaching, charity work, or work that serves the community.

Destiny *To introduce efficient, smoothly running and progressive systems*

The life path of people born on this day is to learn to cooperate with, as well as take charge of, others. Once they have learned the importance of being part of a team, their destiny is to introduce efficient, smoothly running and progressive systems into the world.

Signs & symbols

Sun sign: Aries

Ruling planet: Mars, the warrior

Symbol: The Ram

Birth date ruler: Sun, the Individual

Tarot card: The Sun (enthusiasm)

Favorable numbers: 1, 5

Lucky days: Tuesday and Sunday, especially when these days fall on 1 and 5 of the month

Lucky colors: Scarlet, orange, gold

Birthstone: Diamond

April 19

20 April

the birthday of the hypnotic personality

Your greatest challenge is ...

dealing with negative feedback

The way forward is ...

to understand that any kind of feedback, positive or negative, is helpful. The secret is to learn from it.

You're drawn to people born on ...

June 22 to July 23

You share both a passion for romance and nurturing instincts, and this can create a supportive and loving bond.

Luck maker

Master the art of quiet contentedness

Don't brag when life goes your way, as people will resent you, increasing your chances of bad luck. Master the art of quiet contentedness and you'll get a lot further and feel a lot happier.

People born on April 20 often have a hypnotic personality; others willingly follow their lead, sometimes even blindly. They are hungry for success and the admiration of others, with a burning desire to see their goals realized. Fortunately, they also have a highly developed sense of fair play; only rarely will they use their hypnotic powers for personal gain or unworthy causes.

Once they find a cause or a goal to inspire them, these people will often identify with it. Despite identifying strongly with group values there is, however, a side to them that remains deeply private, sensual and sensitive. In tune with all their senses, physical touch is their sustenance; to break down barriers, they will often be the first to kiss, hug or hold hands. This combination of ambition and sensitivity can occasionally make them moody and needy, but it also gives them an enigmatic and compelling quality.

When these determined and charismatic people set their minds on something, they will allow nothing and no one to stand in their way. Such ambition and tenacity suggest that they have the potential for outstanding success in all areas of their lives. The danger with their clarity of vision and purpose is that it can inspire strong opposition. Since they find it hard to accept criticism of any sort, they have a tendency to block out alternative opinions and viewpoints, often dominating others. They also have a tendency, if thwarted, to retreat into a fantasy world far removed from the reality of others.

It is important for people born on this day to recognize the importance of maintaining an open mind and to accept that, despite their personal magnetism and ability to inspire others, they may not always be right. This tendency to be inflexible is highlighted in their first thirty years, but after the age of thirty they become more interested in learning and communication. If they can take advantage of this opportunity to become more open-minded, there is nothing to stop them achieving the ambitions that inspire them.

On the **dark** side

Egotistical, isolated, stubborn

At your **best**

Sensual, charismatic, inspirational

Love *Hugs and kisses*

People born on April 20 are very tactile and like to show their affection physically, so if they are not holding their partner's hand at the movie theater something may be wrong. They can be highly strung at times, but when they find a partner who enjoys being as busy as they are, they make loving, understanding and deeply sensual lovers.

Health *Pass on the sugar*

People born on this day need to make sure their diet is not too high in sugar or saturated fat, as there is a tendency for them to comfort eat when they are feeling low; this will have a negative effect on their blood-sugar levels, their waistline and their health in general. Their diet should be as rich as possible in fresh, natural, unprocessed foods such as whole grains, fruits, vegetables, lean meats, nuts, and seeds. Such a diet will not only keep their health in balance, but also their moods. As far as exercise is concerned, they should avoid competitive sports and choose activities that help them take time out from competition and getting ahead, such as walking, swimming, cycling, or dancing. Mind–body therapies such as yoga, meditation and tai chi are also recommended. Wearing, meditating on or surrounding themselves with the color green will help restore their energies and inspire trust in others.

Career *Born project managers*

These people have the focus, determination and tenacity to become excellent negotiators, agents, project managers, consultants, or advisors. They also possess natural leadership qualities, particularly as a manager, executive or entrepreneur. A strong creative ability may lead them to the world of arts and entertainment or setting up their own business as a freelancer.

Destiny *To lead and inspire others toward progressive ideals*

The life path of people born on this day is to learn to open their mind to alternative visions of the future. Once they are able to accept the possibility of other realities apart from their own, their destiny is to lead and inspire others toward progressive ideals.

Power Thought

" Today, and every day, I will make a point of getting curious about one thing "

Signs & symbols

Sun signs: Aries/Taurus

Ruling planets: Mars, the warrior/Venus, the lover

Symbols: The Ram/The Bull

Birth date ruler: Moon, the intuitive

Tarot card: Judgment (responsibility)

Favorable numbers: 2, 6

Lucky days: Tuesday and Monday, especially when these days fall on 2 and 6 of the month

Lucky colors: Scarlet, silver, lilac

Birthstone: Diamond

April 20

21 April

the birthday of graciousness

Your greatest challenge is …

learning how to accept help from others

The way forward is …

to understand that other people have just as great a need for help and support as you have; don't deny them that opportunity.

You're drawn to people born on …

November 23 to December 21

You share a passion for life's good things and meaningful connection, and this can create an intense and fulfilling union.

Luck maker

Treat yourself more often

Lucky people know the importance of feeling good about themselves and their lives. When people feel happy and relaxed, they are more likely to attract luck their way.

The majestic people born on April 21 often inspire others with their graciousness and hard-working approach. Willing to push themselves hard, they often end up way ahead of others. Financial reward and getting ahead of others are not their motivation, however; what motivates them is a desire to push themselves as far as they can go.

They like to set themselves high standards, and so strong is their self-knowledge that only the most unforeseen of circumstances will prevent them from achieving their goals. They are dignified and self-assured people whose reliability, tenacity and sensitivity to alternative viewpoints earn them the respect of others, who tend to regard them as noble, gracious, loyal individuals. Never afraid to voice their opinions, they will only do so in a positive, constructive way.

Although they are highly driven, they know how to relax and make themselves and others laugh. They also have a love for the good things in life and, although this is in keeping with the regal or privileged inclinations of their personality, it can provoke addictions to sex, food, drink, and other "pleasurable" pastimes. They are especially vulnerable when their reputation at work is criticized. Fortunately, after the age of thirty, when they put greater emphasis on clear communication and new interests than on material things, they become more resilient and less at risk from losing themselves in these ways.

These people love nothing better than to help others reach their full potential, and can be generous with their time and love. They should be careful not to become too controlling and to give those in their charge the chance to make their own mistakes. There may be some chopping and changing in their professional life, particularly in their thirties and early forties, but when they do find their feet their single-mindedness and endearing desire to see others progress will help them realize their ambitions and, like the gracious nobles they are, earn them the respect and loyalty of others.

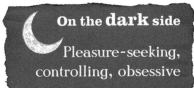

On the dark side

Pleasure-seeking, controlling, obsessive

At your best

Honest, regal, energetic

Love *Give and take*

People born on April 21 tend to be the givers in relationships and it is important for them to learn to receive as well. Fear of becoming vulnerable may also make some of them retreat into isolated self-sufficiency. Once in a relationship, they are loyal and faithful but may sometimes stay in it too long out of a sense of misguided loyalty; so it is important for them to stay in touch with their emotional needs.

Health *Naturally slim*

Although naturally slim, people born on this day often have a great love for fine food and wine, and are prone to over-indulgence; as a result they may suffer from fluctuating weight. They may also suffer from disorders to the neck and throat, such as sore throats and thyroid disorders. A healthy, balanced diet rich in natural, unprocessed foods, as well as oily fish, nuts and seeds, will help balance their hormones and their weight. Regular exercise is essential, as it will help them beat food and other cravings, keeping them fit and slim at the same time. Because they are so sensual, they may be attracted to physical therapies such as massage and aromatherapy, all of which will benefit them greatly. Wearing, meditating on and surrounding themselves with the color purple will help them focus less on physical pleasures and more on finding inner fulfillment and satisfaction.

Career *Born motivators*

Any career which allows these people to motivate or encourage others, such as teaching, coaching, consultancy, management, or counseling, will appeal. They may also have an affinity with all things artistic and be drawn toward art, music, dancing, singing, writing, or acting. Other careers that might appeal include law, social reform and garden design.

Destiny *To encourage and inspire others to reach their full potential*

The life path of people born on this day is to avoid extremes of behavior. Once they have learned to tread the middle way, their destiny is, by example, to encourage and inspire others to develop their full potential.

Power Thought

" Today I bless and wish others well, and they do the same for me "

Signs & symbols

Sun signs: Taurus/Aries

Ruling planets: Venus, the lover/Mars, the warrior

Symbols: The Bull/The Ram

Birth date ruler: Jupiter, the philosopher

Tarot card: The World (fulfillment)

Favorable numbers: 3, 7

Lucky days: Friday and Thursday, especially when these days fall on 3 and 7 of the month

Lucky colors: Lavender, pale blue, pink

Birthstone: Emerald

April 21

225

22 April

the birthday of quality

The charismatic people born on April 22 tend to devote their considerable skills to the pursuit of quality; they want the best job, best car and best home. They often exude power but in a quiet, understated way, and friends and family rarely resent their ambitions because they are likely to lavish praise and recognition on others. They also have a hypnotic charm and the ability to make others change their minds about almost anything.

They believe that they are born to create something of quality with their lives. Their talents and imposing physical presence express themselves best in their organizational skills and ability to motivate others to work toward a common goal. Those who work alongside them respect their down-to-earth approach and ability to offer positive encouragement. These people are altogether confident and charming, so life really should be easy for them, but their stumbling block is their intense desire for power. There is a real danger that they can be controlling, opinionated, overbearing and, in extreme cases, unkind and critical of others.

To avoid alienating themselves from the goodwill of others, these people need to make sure that they use their imposing presence wisely and don't become enslaved by materialistic concerns. Up to the age of twenty-eight they are most likely to be concerned with power and establishing themselves financially, but after the age of twenty-nine they develop an interest in education and learning new skills. This will continue until their fifties, when there is a shift toward their feelings, and the growing importance of friends and family.

It is extremely important for these people to reject values, goals and people that are inconsistent with moral and social justice. Developing their spiritual side will help them to become more aware of their own power without the need for external validation. Once they find a goal, and a technique for attaining that goal, their clear-sighted vision, pragmatic outlook, excellent communication skills, and fierce resilience will help them make their own very special mark on the world.

Love *Suspicious minds*

People born on April 22 do tend to be suspicious when it comes to affairs of the heart and will only open up to a potential partner after a long and sometimes disheartening getting-to-know-you period. However, they are worth the wait because once they find someone who can inspire them to love and give of themselves they are loyal, devoted and relentlessly charming lovers, for as long as they are in love.

Health *Only the best*

When it comes to their health, people born on this day expect only the best; they enjoy searching for the best foods, wines and restaurants and the best gyms and holiday locations. This serves them well, but they do need to be careful they don't become too controlling and should ease up on themselves every now and again. They may be prone to food intolerances and allergies as well as problems affecting their voice. Regular exercise is important for them, as they have a tendency to gain weight, especially around the waist; they also have a high sex drive and enjoy physical pleasures like massage. Wearing, meditating on or surrounding themselves with the color purple will encourage them to develop their spiritual side.

Career *Born executives*

These people do crave material reward and the recognition of others for their efforts, and so careers in business, management, finance, banking, and commerce will appeal. They prefer to be in a leading position, so they may set up a business of their own, and their communication skills also make them great politicians, teachers and lawyers. Conversely, the more creative of those born on this day may be attracted to music, drama, singing, and art.

Destiny *To help and inspire others to achieve progress*

The life path of people born on this day is to learn to use their power wisely. Once they are able to do that, their destiny is to direct their energies toward helping and inspiring others in a quest to achieve progress.

Power Thought

66 Wonder and discovery are the keys to unlocking my spirit 99

Signs & symbols

Sun signs: Taurus/Aries

Ruling planets: Venus, the lover/Mars, the warrior

Symbols: The Bull/The Ram

Birth date ruler: Uranus, the visionary

Tarot card: The Fool (freedom)

Favorable numbers: 4, 8

Lucky days: Friday and Sunday, especially when these days fall on 4 and 8 of the month

Lucky colors: Pale blue, silver, pink

Birthstone: Emerald

April 22

23 April

the birthday of the elusive guide

Your greatest challenge is ...

not getting stuck in your ways

The way forward is ...

to understand that change is essential to your psychological growth. Without it, you won't learn, grow or reach your full potential.

You're drawn to people born on ...

October 24 to November 22

You share a passion for romance and communication, and this can create an exciting and rewarding relationship.

Luck maker

Keep innovating

To get what you want in life you must keep moving, generating action and new opportunities.

There's an elusive quality about people born on April 23 and they tend to be known only to their most intimate friends. This is because, although they are non-conformist, they like to make others feel comfortable and so others can form a false image of them. Being misread, however, is unlikely to bother them, as they have enough self-awareness to allow others to think of them what they will.

Although they have the confidence to be accommodating, this doesn't mean they are always compliant. Quite the opposite; from an early age they are likely to have had a strong desire to establish their individuality and make their mark on the world. They would prefer to act as a guide to others rather than follow in someone else's footsteps. As innovators, they are often able to sense future trends, but their visionary talents never cut them off from practical reality.

Their progressive outlook puts them ahead of their contemporaries but they do have an odd tendency to become set in their ways, favoring routine and control over spontaneity. There is also a possessive and anxious streak to their nature. They should try to overcome reservations, especially regarding close relationships, because they tend to be at their happiest and best in the security of one loving union. Until the age of twenty-seven they may cling to the safety of routine and be set in their ways; after the age of twenty-eight they are more receptive to new ideas, ways of thinking and doing things. This process continues until the end of their fifties, when there is a positive shift toward their emotional needs, especially those concerning home and family.

Compassionate and popular on the one hand, blessed with great insight, originality and tenacity on the other, they can achieve great things. Once they can free themselves from routine and allow themselves to become the innovators that they really are, they can not only make their mark on the world but also act as a guide and source of hope to others.

Love *Old-fashioned and romantic*

People born on April 23 are often old-fashioned and romantic when it comes to relationships; they enjoy the process of courtship and seduction, sometimes more than the relationship itself. Although popular and never short of admirers, they do have a tendency to set their sights on someone unattainable. Once in a relationship they need to be careful that they don't become too possessive or controlling.

Health *Don't get stuck in your ways*

It's easy for people born on this day to settle into a routine when it comes to their health and to get stuck in their ways. They need to understand that what worked in their twenties may not necessarily work in their forties, and they should constantly adapt and modify to increase their chances of good health. For example, if they have always eaten three meals a day they may find that later in life changing to five or six small meals and snacks works better for them. They also need to make sure that they don't do the same workout year in year out, and that they experiment with cross-training. Arthritis or back problems could be a big concern, so it is important for them to eat healthily and keep flexible with regular stretching and/or yoga. Wearing, meditating on or surrounding themselves with the color orange will encourage them to be more spontaneous.

Career *Born writers*

These people thrive best in careers in which they can express their talent for innovation and interpersonal communication, such as drama, music, art, writing, choreography, movie-making, and photography. Their charm and communication skills could also be put to good use in mediation, management, business, sales, promotion, negotiation, real estate, public relations, law, and politics.

Destiny *To make an uncontroversial mark on the world*

The life path of people born on this day is to learn to be as spontaneous in their emotional life as they can be in their professional life. Once they are able to do that, their destiny is to make a mark on the world without incurring the envy, anger or disappointment of others.

Signs & symbols

Sun sign: Taurus/Aries

Ruling planet: Venus, the lover/Mars, the warrior

Symbol: The Bull/The Ram

Birth date ruler: Mercury, the communicator

Tarot card: The Hierophant (guidance)

Favorable numbers: 5, 9

Lucky days: Friday and Wednesday, especially when these days fall on 5 and 9 of the month

Lucky colors: All shades of blue

Birthstone: Emerald

April 23

24 April

the birthday of devotion

Your greatest challenge is …

resisting the need to respond to every request

The way forward is …

to understand that there is a difference between generosity and stupidity. Don't give to people who are capable of helping themselves.

You're drawn to people born on …

September 24 to October 23

You share a passion for romance and a desire for care, and this can create an intense and loving union.

Luck maker

Stop saying "yes" to others

Saying "no" more often to others and "yes" to yourself allows you to put your energies where they belong. If you spread yourself too thinly, you may miss an opportunity to contribute to the world.

Nothing gives people born on April 24 greater satisfaction that knowing they have inspired or guided the lives of others. They have enormous hearts, and devoted and protective friends who believe the world should be a place of universal love and equality.

They can have a strong protective instinct toward those they love, but the parental role they like to assume can be alternately endearing and exasperating. Others are grateful for their attentions but may also find them draining and restrictive. They can be the nurturing parent who finds it hard to let go when a child wants to spread their wings or the lover who cannot think of a world outside their relationship. They can also feel let down when those they love fall from the lofty pedestal by somehow failing to obey their directions. They should learn to allow others the chance to follow their own hearts and, if need be, make their own mistakes.

As well as being devoted to close relationships, they can also become completely dedicated to their career, often fully identifying with it. It can be enormously painful for them if there is a conflict between commitment to work or family, and they may agonize over maintaining a balance. This is because they find it hard to separate their heart and their lives; but if they learn to give a little less and sometimes put themselves first, they may find that it is possible to be more accommodating.

Until the age of twenty-six their lives are often centered on a need for affection and material security; after the age of twenty-seven there are opportunities for them develop more interests. There is another turning point after the age of fifty-seven, placing more emphasis on fulfilling their emotional needs. Throughout their lives, learning to confidently use the word "no" will help them feel less torn between career and family. It will also allow them to make their unique mark on the world and to put their organizational capabilities, creative energies and single-mindedness to their best possible use.

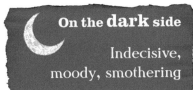
Power Thought

❝ I am in charge of my life. I reclaim my power ❞

Love *Love-struck*

People born on April 24 have great magnetism when it comes to affairs of the heart but they need to be careful that they don't become so love-struck that they are blind to the faults of their partner. They also should avoid becoming too smothering in a relationship, as it will drain the romance out of it.

Health *A good clear out*

Stability and domestic harmony are extremely important for people born on this day and they may end up sacrificing a great deal of their individuality to achieve it; this can manifest in stress, depression and comfort eating. It is crucial for them to learn to say "no" to the constant demands put upon them and to put themselves first more regularly. There may also be a tendency for them to suffer from hormonal problems or fertility issues. Moderate to light exercise, in particular brisk walking, will increase their fitness levels and also give them much-needed time and space to think and be alone. As far as diet is concerned, they need to avoid routine and choose a varied but light diet, rich in fruits, vegetables and whole grains. Their houses are likely to be cluttered with things from the past and having a good clear out now and again will help them feel freer and lighter. Wearing, meditating on or surrounding themselves with the color red will boost their energy and encourage them to be more confrontational.

Career *Born educators*

These people have excellent communication skills and a desire to protect and guide others. They can make excellent teachers, nurses, coaches, doctors, and counselors. Writing is also a skill that comes naturally to them, and because they are attracted to public life they can become involved in politics, acting, music, or entertainment. They may also be drawn to environmental concerns, philosophy or mysticism.

Destiny *To guide, motivate and inspire others*

The life path of people born on this day is to learn to draw a clear dividing line between their personal and professional lives. Once they are able to be more diverse in their approach to life, their destiny is, by example, to guide, motivate and inspire others.

Signs & symbols

Sun sign: Taurus

Ruling planet: Venus, the lover

Symbol: The Bull

Birth date ruler: Venus, the lover

Tarot card: The Lovers (choices)

Favorable numbers: 1, 6

Lucky day: Friday, especially when it falls on 1 and 6 of the month

Lucky colors: Blue, pink, coral

Birthstone: Emerald

April 24

25 April

the birthday of imposing vigor

People born on April 25 are hard to ignore. Whatever their physical size, their presence and energy are dynamic and imposing. Strong-minded, they are more interested in action than reflection, and their drive to succeed inspires awe in those who are less self-assured.

When they employ their remarkable energy, intellectual focus and steadfast determination, they have enormous potential to achieve all their aims. Despite their unwavering sense of purpose they can, however, unwittingly sabotage their own efforts by making snap decisions and putting themselves unnecessarily at risk. They don't seek danger but they are courageous and, if presented with a demanding challenge, they are unlikely to avoid it but rather face it head on.

They tend to concentrate their energies on the practical; the subtle aspects of life are often lost on them. This can-do approach with little time for ideas, theories or small talk means that there is nothing vague or undefined about them; indeed they often establish themselves fairly early in life. The danger, however, is their lack of interest in the spiritual or abstract side of life. When things are going well they are unlikely to notice this area of their life is limited, but when things are going badly or they feel in need of comfort, they will feel a sense of loss, confusion and bewilderment.

Fortunately, after the age of twenty-six there are opportunities for them to communicate and exchange ideas, stretching themselves mentally with new kinds of study. They should ensure that the emphasis is not just on the practical but also on the theoretical or spiritual. After the age of fifty-six they are likely to feel the need to be closer to those they love and care for. This again is significant, as until then the focus of their energies is likely to have been their career.

Above all, they have the ability to effortlessly command respect and, as long as they remember to check their impulsiveness and nurture their spiritual self, there is little that they cannot accomplish.

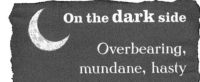

On the **dark** side

Overbearing, mundane, hasty

At your **best**

Energetic, imposing, steadfast

Power Thought

"I am protected by the spirit that flows through and inspires me "

Love *Take the lead*

Curiously, although people born on April 25 are commanding and sensual outside of a relationship, when they are in one they can let their partner take the lead completely. If they can overcome the worry that another person will ever love them, they can settle into a relationship that is both stable and passionate.

Health *Earthy sensuality*

People born on this day are blessed with an earthy sensuality and physical grace, and few are as likely to feel as comfortable in their bodies as they are. They love exercise in all its forms, in particular dance. Any health problems they have are likely to be physical—such as injuries, or high blood-pressure or cholesterol—rather than emotional or mental, such as stress or depression. As far as diet is concerned, they should eat a heart-healthy diet rich in vitamin E and essential fats to boost their circulation. They would also benefit greatly from mind–body therapies such as yoga and meditation. Carrying a moonstone crystal around with them will encourage them to connect with their intuition. Wearing or meditating on the color purple will encourage them to think of higher things.

Career *Born lawyers*

The sense of purpose and single-mindedness with which these people are blessed will serve them well in many careers, but they may be drawn to politics, law, business, science, and art. Their humanity and compassion may also lead them to social reform and charity work, and their creative side may draw them to design, drama and music.

Destiny *To take practical and positive steps forward*

The life path of people born on this day is to learn to take care of their spirit. Once they are able to do this, their destiny is to take practical and positive steps in the direction of progress.

Signs & symbols

Sun sign: Taurus

Ruling planet: Venus, the lover

Symbol: The Bull

Birth date ruler: Venus, the lover

Tarot card: The Chariot

Favorable numbers: 2, 7

Lucky days: Friday and Monday, especially when these days fall on 2 and 7 of the month

Lucky colors: pale blue, sea green

Birthstone: Emerald

April 25

26 April

the birthday of beautiful logic

Your greatest challenge is …

learning there are no exact moral measurements

The way forward is …

to understand that people, yourself included, are not statistics or geometry. In human terms, perfection is about being imperfect.

You're drawn to people born on …

August 24 to September 23

You share a passion for beauty and a need to nurture, and this can create a loyal and fulfilling union.

Luck maker

Be all you can be

Lucky people value what they know they can achieve, they don't set up unattainable goals for themselves that lead to failure. The more realistic and attainable your goals, the more likely you are to achieve them.

Although those born on April 26 can be bold and visionary in their plans, one of their defining characteristics is a meticulous attention to detail. Making sure everything is cut to the right size and shape matters greatly to them. They instinctively understand that, for a project to be successful, logical planning and careful preparation is essential. They are pillars of logic and common sense.

Having considered and worked through all the possibilities and contingencies without losing focus on their ultimate objective, it's no surprise that they are often found presiding over smooth-running projects. They are often greatly admired for their dependability, efficiency and, as great self-starters, their independence. They are highly confident in their abilities; there is a risk, however, that they become rigid in their beliefs and dismiss any other way but their way. This controlling tendency can have a damaging effect on personal and professional relationships; they need to learn to respect diversity of opinion and the individuality of others.

Until the age of twenty-five, their stubbornness is likely to dominate; but after the age of twenty-six they may become more flexible in their thinking and in their approach to life by studying and communicating. After the age of fifty-six they feel the need to be close to those they love and care for.

Throughout their lives they need to make sure that their love of logic, order and detail does not estrange them from their heart. They need to understand that perfecting themselves is not the way to a fulfilling life. The sooner they can start getting in touch with their feelings and the feelings of others, the sooner they can enjoy a more balanced and healthy life. In their dedication to perfection they can become isolated from others. Learning to embrace and enjoy the inconsistencies of others will help them feel less lonely.

Once they understand that human beings aren't perfect or logical there is no reason why their inspired and productive strategies can't help them achieve and even exceed their goals.

On the dark side

Isolated, stubborn, controlling

At your best

Rational, dependable, independent

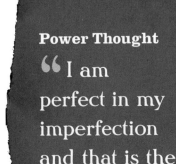

Love *High ideals*

People born on April 26 have a tendency to seek out "beautiful" people who are out of reach or unsuitable. It is best for them to look for those who can pamper them and appreciate their hard work and dedication. They do have high ideals in a relationship and want someone who will be as faithful and loving as they are.

Health *The lighter side of life*

People born on this day have a wonderful sense of humor and it would benefit their health and well-being to express it more. There is a tendency for them to become rigid and stuck in their lifestyle habits, and it is important for them to learn to be more flexible. Because physical activity does not figure strongly in their life, they can be at risk from problems with their weight or with weight-related issues such as diabetes or heart disease. As far as diet is concerned, they should avoid saturated fat and excess sugar. Regular exercise, preferably every day, is essential for their health and well-being. If joining a gym doesn't appeal, brisk walks, jogging and cycling, together with simple lifestyle changes like taking the stairs instead of the lift, will all benefit. Wearing, surrounding themselves with or meditating on the color yellow is good for increasing their optimism, sense of humor and confidence.

Career *Born gardeners*

These people like to nurture and tend things, and careers that allow them to constantly check on or oversee progress, such as gardening, landscaping, farming, education, manufacturing, social work, charity work, photography, movie-making, medicine, and real estate, will appeal. They may also be drawn toward business, banking and stockbroking, and, because they are creative and good with their hands, design, writing, painting, and music.

Destiny *To pay meticulous attention to detail*

The life path of people born on this day is to stop the notion of perfection from getting in the way of their psychological development. Once they are able to be more objective and flexible in their approach to life, their destiny is to ensure quality is produced by meticulous attention to detail.

Power Thought

"I am perfect in my imperfection and that is the way it should be "

Signs & symbols

Sun sign: Taurus

Ruling planet: Venus, the lover

Symbol: The Bull

Birth date ruler: Saturn, the teacher

Tarot card: Strength (passion)

Favorable numbers: 3, 8

Lucky days: Friday and Saturday, especially when these days fall on 3 and 8 of the month

Lucky colors: Pale blue, burgundy, brown

Birthstone: Emerald

April 26

27 April

the birthday of charming self-reliance

People born on April 27 tend to direct a lot of their energies inward, often preferring the inner world of ideas over the distractions of social activity. They like to spend time alone but they are hardly ever lonely. This is because they are self-reliant individuals who don't feel the need to seek the approval or validation of others. Despite their natural reserve and inward focus, when they do find themselves part of a social group others often find them both charming and fascinating.

More outgoing people may regard them as shy or antisocial but they are highly intuitive and compassionate individuals who will willingly offer their help and support to others if needed. In fact, they really come into their own in a group setting; they will often amaze others who have only previously interacted with them on a one-to-one basis with their gregariousness, willingness to give almost anything a go and highly developed sense of humor. They can get frustrated at times when others don't offer as much support as they do, but it is important that they don't take their bitterness to extremes and cut themselves off from the benefits of being with others.

There will always be a tendency for these reflective people to favor the world of concepts and knowledge over everything else. They may also be tempted by some form of fundamentalism or extremism; this will impede their psychological growth. Fortunately, between the ages of twenty-four and fifty-four they experience an increased need to communicate and exchange ideas. This can be an extremely positive and productive time during which they expand their ideas, learn new skills or take up new areas of study.

Their tendency to withdraw into their private world, coupled with their sensitivity and strong sense of realism, gives them with great potential for creativity and innovation. As long as they make sure they remain emotionally open and live in the present and not some distant future, they can achieve considerable success, at the same time inspiring and improving the lives of others.

Love *Devoted to you*

People born on April 27 may spend long periods living alone, but when they do meet the right person they often blossom intellectually, physically and spiritually. They make devoted and endlessly fascinating partners and are attracted to enterprising, resourceful and intelligent individuals who can offer them the same devotion.

Health *Develop your wonderful sense of humor*

People born on this day have a nature that is reflective and inward. Although they are resilient when life knocks them back, they are also prone to reactive depression, especially during challenging phases in their lives such as parenthood, the menopause or retirement. The best therapies for them are regular exercise, preferably every day in the fresh air so they get all the mood-boosting benefits of sunlight, and laughter. People born on this day have a highly developed sense of humor and they need to focus more on that and incorporate as much fun as they can into their lives. As far as diet and lifestyle are concerned, they should avoid saturated fat, sugar, salt, nicotine, and excessive amounts of caffeine and alcohol. Wearing, meditating on or surrounding themselves with the color orange will increase feelings of warmth and security.

Career *Born researchers*

These people can excel in careers related to law, research and education. Because they have good technical skills, careers in computing or various types of engineering may also appeal. Alternatively, they may be interested in psychology, humanitarian or social work and the medical profession.

Destiny *To share their knowledge and their skills*

The life path of people born on this day is to demonstrate greater emotional openness, especially in their private life. Once they are able to do that, their destiny is to improve the lives of others by sharing their knowledge and their skills.

Power Thought

❝ Love is the thread that joins everyone together ❞

April 27

Signs & symbols

Sun sign: Taurus

Ruling planet: Venus, the lover

Symbol: The Bull

Birth date ruler: Mars, the warrior

Tarot card: The Hermit (inner strength)

Favorable numbers: 4, 9

Lucky days: Friday and Tuesday, especially when these days fall on 4 and 9 of the month

Lucky colors: Pale blue, red, lilac

Birthstone: Emerald

237

28 April

the birthday of the conductor

Your greatest challenge is ...

learning to let go

The way forward is ...

to understand that great leadership is about empowering others to take charge of their own destinies.

You're drawn to people born on ...

August 24 to September 23

You share a desire for creativity and security, and this can create a dramatic and a passionate union.

Luck maker

Master the art of delegation

Taking responsibility for everyone and everything will just make you feel exhausted and stressed, blocking out the possibility of luck. To improve your chances of luck, master the art of delegation.

When people born on April 28 have decided on a chosen course of action, nothing can divert them from it. Energetic and radiant people, they can motivate others with their imposing emotional, physical and psychological presence. Life is a dance or an orchestra and they are the choreographer or conductor.

Among the most focused individuals of the entire year, they never give up until they see the light at the end of the tunnel. Others instinctively recognize their strength and dependability, and they are often the first to be called on for help during a crisis. They immediately take charge of situations, encouraging others to take positive action and coming up with workable solutions. They try to be as honest as they can be with everyone they meet. Some people may find them too blunt, but they would rather risk offending someone than be involved in any kind of deception.

They take great care to always look the part, and you will rarely find them looking anything less than their best. They are also able to stay in tune with what others are thinking and feeling; this helps them guide and direct others with sensitivity and respect, rather than with overbearing authority. Occasionally they can lapse into stubbornness, but this is often a manifestation of their fear of not being needed. They should learn that the greatest leaders, parents and guides are those who can give their charges or children the confidence and skills they need to survive without their support.

Cultivating a wide range of interests outside the home and learning to take themselves less seriously will help them develop the psychological strength to let others take control of their own lives. Fortunately, from the ages of twenty-three to fifty-three the pace of their life increases; they find new interests, skills and forms of communication. If they can take advantage of these opportunities for growth and diversification, they can use their powers of pragmatism, resourcefulness and creativity to single-mindedly work toward the fulfillment of their goals and their dreams.

Love *Power games*

Love comes naturally to people born on April 28 and they are often surrounded by admirers. They do like to take the lead and have all the power in a relationship, but it is important for them to have a partner who can challenge them and take that power away from time to time. Security is important to them, and when they can learn to take as well as give direction in a relationship they are dynamic and sensitive lovers.

Health *Take better care of your soul*

People born on this day are extremely energetic and it is important for them to find outlets for their energy. Competitive sports will appeal, as will all forms of exercise, in particular dance. They do tend to be prone to weight gain, high blood pressure and problems with the thyroid gland, so they need to make sure that their diet is healthy and balanced. Because they love dining out and experimenting with different kinds of foods, they need to make sure that they don't overeat. Wearing, meditating on or surrounding themselves with the color purple will encourage them to look inward, think of higher things and develop their spiritual side which, in their haste to accomplish, direct and resolve, may often get neglected.

Career *Born advisors*

These people have a great understanding of human nature, indicating that they may be drawn to careers in teaching, therapy, counseling, or advising. They also like to take charge of large projects or groups of people, and careers in management, advertising, the media, or publishing will appeal. Their natural flair for creativity, form and color may also inspire them to become a designer or draw them to theater, music and the arts.

Destiny *To direct and encourage others*

The life path of people born on this day is to learn to be more flexible in their approach to life. Once they are able to listen to alternative viewpoints and take on board the advice of others, their destiny is to direct and encourage others with their dedication, focus, honesty, and dependability.

Signs & symbols

Sun sign: Taurus

Ruling planet: Venus, the lover

Symbol: The Bull

Birth date ruler: Sun, the individual

Tarot card: The Magician (will-power)

Favorable numbers: 1, 5

Lucky days: Friday and Sunday, especially when these days fall on 1 and 5 of the month

Lucky colors: Pale blue, orange, yellow

Birthstone: Emerald

April 28

29 April

the birthday of impeccable manners

Your greatest challenge is ...

learning to let your hair down

The way forward is ...

to understand that those with the ability to laugh at themselves are more likely to get others on their side and lead a satisfying life.

You're drawn to people born on ...

June 22 to July 23

You are both intuitive and loving individuals and this can create a generous, supportive and enlightened relationship.

Luck maker

Do some cloud spotting

Gaze at the sky and the slow-moving clouds. This can help create a restful atmosphere that helps your luck-creating intuition to surface.

The dignified but warm individuals born on April 29 devote a considerable amount of their energy to the image they present to the world. With their impeccable manners and appreciation of the finer things in life they prefer the company of equally poised people, but they have the flexibility to alter their behavior according to the company they keep. This doesn't mean they are insecure. Quite the contrary; they have a clear self-image. It's just that the positive opinion of others, from whatever walk of life, matters greatly to them.

Friends and co-workers are unlikely to find them unprepared for any situation they are in. They will do their utmost to present themselves as positively as possible and to perform to the best of their ability. And because they are so reliable, they often find themselves in positions of responsibility. The downside of this is that constantly presenting a perfect, self-assured image can be exhausting, especially as they love nothing better than to occasionally relax and let their hair down.

It is vital for them to make sure they do find time to enjoy the lighter side of life as always being counted on by others may give them an exaggerated sense of self-importance. Fortunately, between the ages of twenty-two and fifty-two there are many opportunities for them to increase the tempo of their lives with new interests and new skills. Around the age of fifty-two they may concentrate on emotional security.

They tend to be givers rather than takers, always having an interest in and a kind word for others. There are times, however, when they might feel deeply insecure for no apparent reason; this is usually because they aren't paying sufficient attention to their feelings. If they can learn to tap into their hidden creativity and get their sensitivity to the moods and feelings of others to work for, not against them, they will discover an unlimited resource for guidance, transformation and self-empowerment, and the key to unlocking outstanding potential for success in all aspects of their lives.

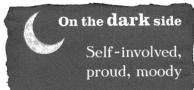
On the **dark** side

Self-involved,
proud, moody

At your **best**

Dignified, meticulous,
dependable

Love *Throw caution to the wind*

People born on April 29 love to shower their partners with gifts, advice and adoration, and they demand similar treatment. If they can learn to hold back a little, their chances of finding lasting happiness in a relationship will improve significantly. They are attracted to people who will share their hopes and dreams, and who can help them throw caution to the wind every now and again.

Health *Sturdy constitution*

People born on this day are highly sensitive to their environment, and learning to offer others support without over-identifying with their feelings will help them avoid mood swings. As far as diet is concerned, they are likely to have a hearty appetite for traditional, earthy foods such as whole grains, stews, soups, and potatoes. They often have a sturdy constitution and shapely figure, not because they diet or exercise religiously, but because they believe in moderation in all things when it comes to their health and lifestyle. There may, however, have problems with their voice or their thyroid gland. Wearing, meditating on and surrounding themselves with the color purple will encourage them to connect with their intuition.

Career *Born image consultants*

These people understand the importance of image and presentation, and this will serve them well in careers in fashion, design, marketing, promotion, public relations, and business. Those who are artistically gifted might perhaps succeed as writers, journalists, actors, musicians, and artists. They may also choose to devote themselves to education, humanitarian concerns and the study of religion or spirituality.

Destiny *To make the world a more harmonious place*

The life path of people born on this day is to learn to relax more, as it is during these times that they are really themselves. Once they are able to connect with their powerful intuition, their destiny is to make the world a more harmonious place by bringing out the caring and polite instincts in others.

Signs & symbols

Sun sign: Taurus

Ruling planet: Venus, the lover

Symbol: The Bull

Birth date ruler: Moon, the intuitive

Tarot card: The High Priestess (intuition)

Favorable numbers: 2, 8

Lucky days: Friday and Monday, especially when these days fall on 2 or 8 of the month

Lucky colors: All shades of blue

Birthstone: Emerald

April 29

30 April

the birthday of commitment

Your greatest challenge is ...

not feeling burdened by responsibility

The way forward is ...

to understand the need to remove yourself temporarily from the demands of others, to recharge your batteries and to concentrate on your own needs.

You're drawn to people born on ...

November 23 to December 21

You respect each other's need for freedom, and this can create an independent but understanding and supportive union.

Luck maker

Let yourself off the hook

Feeling guilty because you don't think you are doing enough will do little to improve your self-esteem or your luck-making potential. Let go of guilt and positive change will enter your life.

People born on April 30 often give the impression of being calm and collected. They love the good things in life, approaching others with affection. They can be extremely funny, as long as the joke is not on them, and their natural good cheer ensures they are the center of attention. However, contrary to their relaxed exterior, such is their intelligence and drive that they will feel unfulfilled unless they can devote themselves to their work or another person.

They tend to value commitment, responsibility and duty above all else; this is why they present a hardworking, cheerful and reliable front to the world. They are extremely capable practically and intellectually, trying their hands at almost any task. As pillars of the community, they may feel inclined to take up a charitable cause or generally do good deeds in the neighborhood.

There is a danger that their commitment to their boss, family or friends is so powerful it can become unquestioning and they end up performing tasks or running errands unworthy of them. They should not to be blind in their devotion or let the rank of a person intimidate them into compliance. They should also be careful that their dedication to a method, cause or project does not turn into stubbornness and obstinacy when alternatives are presented. Any form of aggression or criticism is likely to be met with anger or veiled threats; they need to learn to take criticism for what it is: someone else's opinion. Fortunately, between the ages of twenty-one and fifty-one they may concentrate on new interests and acquiring knowledge; during this period they should try to treat criticism as a learning experience.

These charming, multi-talented and reliable people have the potential to make their mark on whatever project or goal interests them. They should be careful, however, that in their need to feel committed they don't relinquish their objectivity. But when they do commit themselves to a worthwhile cause, they can surprise everyone with their spontaneity and ability to bring about progress.

Love *Personal space required*

People born on April 30 are incredibly devoted and loyal in a relationship but they do need to take breaks every now and again. Their partners need to understand this and not interpret it as a problem within the relationship. Those born on this day therefore need to be clear about what makes them feel happy in a relationship and seek out someone who isn't clingy.

Health *Tender, loving care*

People born on this day often neglect their own needs for those of another, in particular aging family members. It is crucial for their health and well-being that they take regular time out and make time for themselves and their interests; if they don't, they may find themselves victims of stress, depression or, in extreme cases, cancer. Regular exercise is essential as long as their devotion to a particular training method is not taken to extremes. As far as diet and lifestyle are concerned they need to make sure they don't over-indulge in rich food, drink, nicotine, and drugs. There are healthier ways to indulge their sensual nature, such as exercise, massage or mind–body therapies such as yoga or tai chi. Wearing, meditating on or surrounding themselves with the colors pink or orange will encourage them to attract some tender, loving care and put their own needs first.

Career *Born officers*

These people have the potential to make their mark on any career they choose, as they are highly valued for their intelligence and reliability. They may be drawn toward careers in education, law enforcement, the army, commerce, promotions, advertising, or sales. Alternatively they may be attracted to the caring professions, to humanitarian concerns or to social work. If they are creative, the world of the arts or entertainment, especially production or design, will appeal.

Destiny *To demonstrate the importance of respect and dedication*

The life path of people born on this day is to make sure they are as committed to the development of their own talents as they are to those of others. Once they are able to find that balance, their destiny is to move the world forward by demonstrating the importance of respect and dedication.

Signs & symbols

Sun sign: Taurus

Ruling planet: Venus, the lover

Symbol: The Bull

Birth date ruler: Jupiter, the philosopher

Tarot card: The Empress (creativity)

Favorable numbers: 3, 7

Lucky days: Friday and Thursday, especially when these days fall on 3 and 7 of the month

Lucky colors: Pale blue, indigo, purple

Birthstone: Emerald

April 30

1 May

the birthday of perspicacity

There is little that escapes the attention of people born on May 1. Blessed with remarkable powers of intellectual perception, they are calm and insightful but often aren't talkative. When they do speak, their few but well-chosen words have considerable impact because they are based on close observation.

Perspicacity is the greatest strength and driving force of these people. Because they are highly intuitive they notice what is going on around them and also what is being implied; this enables them to rely on their instincts, and then apply logic and reason to establish an effective plan of action. Their calm and considered approach to life can, however, become a handicap as others tend to rely on them to maintain a sense of perspective; this can keep them from pushing themselves forward. They should use their emotional intelligence to their own advantage as wel as others'.

These people need to have more faith in their own abilities. In most cases they are capable of achieving far more than they realize. They are highly imaginative, with natural leadership abilities, even though some may not appreciate their bluntness or their satirical and cleverly observed humor. They tend to like the familiar; change or new situations may alarm them, even if they don't show that fear on the surface. It is important for them, however, to embrace change as this offers them opportunities for psychological growth. Between the ages of twenty and fifty they have an increased desire to relate more with their immediate environment; this is extremely positive as it will encourage them to diversify, experiment and step out of their comfort zone. After the age of fifty there is an emphasis on emotional stability.

The deceptively calm people born on this day have a lot going for them; they just don't always realize it. However, once they wake up to their huge potential they will surprise themselves and others with their creativity and the passion through which that creative spirit can manifest.

On the **dark** side

Cautious, tactless, passive

At your **best**

Witty, insightful, calm

Power Thought

66 Today I will go further than usual 99

Love *Slow and steady*

People born on May 1 prefer slow and steady relationships to complicated and intense ones. They may sometimes feel as if they need to be more spontaneous but they feel more comfortable knowing what to expect. In a committed relationship they appreciate a partner who can help them unwind, especially if that partner is optimistic, intelligent and kind.

Health *Weighty issues*

People born on this day may have problems with their weight, but with due care and attention to a healthy diet, rich in fruit and vegetables, and regular exercise (preferably on a daily basis), they can easily manage the situation. There may be problems associated with their neck, voice and vocal chords so they need to take extra special care that they don't allow colds to linger for long as this could lead to complications. Highly sensual massages and sex will help them unwind and boost their energy. Wearing, meditating on or surrounding themselves with the color red is physically stimulating; it will encourage them to be less cautious and take more risks.

Career *Born psychiatrists*

These people may be drawn to careers such as psychiatry, counseling or medicine where they can develop their powerful skills of observation. Less altruistic types may be drawn toward sales, promotion, real estate, banking, and catering; those who wish to nurture their creativity may excel in writing, singing and the arts in general.

Destiny *To make the world a happier and more productive place*

The life path of people born on this day is to use their incredible insight to their own advantage. Once they have learned to express their own needs, their destiny is to help create harmonious situations and by so doing to make the world a happier and more productive place.

Signs & symbols

Sun sign: Taurus

Ruling planet: Venus, the lover

Symbol: The Bull

Birth date ruler: Sun, the individual

Tarot card: The Magician (will-power)

Favorable numbers: 1, 6

Lucky days: Friday and Sunday, especially when these days fall on 1 and 6 of the month

Lucky colors: Pale blue, orange, gold

Birthstone: Emerald

May 1

2 May

the birthday of inquisitive honesty

People born on May 2 have a no-nonsense approach to life, believing in results not theories. Although others admire them for their intellectual gifts and ability to organize their original thoughts with logical coherence, they do have a tendency to express themselves bluntly. Fiercely honest, they don't ever set out to wound others as they are naturally inclined toward cooperation and harmony; they simply believe that the best way to effect improvement is to tell others exactly how it is.

These people are blessed with inquisitiveness and great insight into the workings of the human mind. It's not easy to fool them and they don't believe in pulling the wool over anyone's eyes. They will be respected for their intelligence and honesty but their bluntness may sometimes come across as insensitivity, earning them unnecessary enemies. They should use their intelligence and insight into human nature to avoid this. They also should avoid gossiping; even though this is not fueled by malice but more by their natural curiosity, it can upset others. Respecting the privacy of others is important between the ages of nineteen and forty-nine, during which there is an emphasis on communication and exchanging ideas. After the age of forty-nine they may feel the growing importance of getting in touch with their own feelings as well as those of others.

As perfectionists, they often shine in whatever task is set them and motivate others to emulate their fantastic organizational skills. Although they can work well in a team, they are at their most productive when they are making an individual contribution. This desire to work alone can cross over to their personal life; and their private life is exactly that—private. Despite their reticence, they are at their happiest when they feel supported by friends and family.

These people are, above all, intelligent and caring; if they can listen to the honest advice they give others and apply it to themselves, they have the potential to achieve outstanding success, whatever path in life they choose.

Love *50/50*

In relationships there may be a tendency for people born on May 2 to hold back or keep a part of themselves hidden. They may choose to mask this by behavior that is controlling, smothering or self-sacrificing. They often fall for the underdog or people with problems, but to feel fulfilled in a relationship they need to aim for a 50/50 partnership in which both partners give and take equally.

Health *Vacations are a must*

People born on this day need to be careful that they don't work themselves too hard in their quest to achieve results as this will cause them stress and damage their personal relationships. As important as their work is to them, they will be more productive if they learn to identify less with it and seek out opportunities to explore other interests. Regular vacations or time off work are a must and they should resist the tendency to work through their holiday. As far as diet is concerned, they need to make sure they eat plenty of whole grains, fruits, and vegetables and get their mood-boosting essential fats from oily fish, nuts, and seeds. Regular exercise is essential, and they will find walking or jogging particularly beneficial. Wearing, meditating on or surrounding themselves with the color yellow will encourage them to feel more optimistic and self-confident.

Career *Born surgeons*

These people have a marked potential for success in the technical side of the caring professions, such as medicine or scientific research, but also in advertising, media and writing and acting. Social reform, building and management will also appeal, but in whatever field they choose to specialize, their luck and opportunities will often come through work.

Destiny *To work for the common good*

The life path of people born on this day is to learn to become more aware of the impact their words and deeds can have on others. Once they have become more self-aware, their destiny is to work for the common good.

Power Thought

❝ The more kind and gentle I am, the more positive energy I have ❞

Signs & symbols

Sun sign: Taurus

Ruling planet: Venus, the lover

Symbol: The Bull

Birth date ruler: Moon, the intuitive

Tarot card: The High Priestess (intuition)

Favorable numbers: 2, 7

Lucky days: Friday and Monday, especially when these days fall on 2 and 7 of the month

Lucky colors: Pale blue, silver, green

Birthstone: Emerald

May 2

3 May

the birthday of spectacular efficiency

Your greatest challenge is ...

learning to trust

The way forward is ...

to understand that if you expect to be let down, the chances are you will be. Change your expectations to more positive ones.

You're drawn to people born on ...

November 23 to December 21

You share a passion for intellectual stimulation and fun, and this can create a rewarding and creative bond.

Luck maker

The world's full of luck

Unwavering belief is the one absolutely essential element in lucky people. Expect luck and it will change your life.

People born on May 3 are not just well-organized; they are spectacularly efficient. Their houses and offices are often tidy, and their natural charm and politeness earn them many friends and admirers.

The lives of these people reflect their efficient approach; they are often the ones others count on to keep things running smoothly, both at home and at work. Slow but steady improvements are a feature of their lives rather than sudden changes of fortune. In their teenage years they may feel restricted in some way but any setbacks they experience pave the way for two good things: determination and patience. As long as they keep pushing steadily forward, life will reward them with success and happiness.

Between the ages of eighteen and forty-eight there will be a big need to communicate; this can be an extremely positive time for them if they allow their natural potential to blossom and don't smother it with routine or fear of change. After the age of forty-nine they will feel an increased need for emotional security. Again this can be extremely positive if they accept the fact that feelings can't be categorized and controlled.

Stubborn and strong willed, these people may find themselves in conflict with less systematic individuals. They may judge people and situations harshly and they need to avoid becoming rigid, negative or demanding in their objectivity. They also have a tendency to worry too much and work too hard to prove themselves or their ability. Fortunately, they are perceptive individuals and their lives will improve if they can occasionally take an honest look at themselves, their behavior and the effect they have on others.

Above all, people born on this day are valued by others for their rare gift of objective insight and their ability to organize and lead with spectacular efficiency. They have much to teach others and as long as they remember to curb their tendency to detach emotionally—especially when it comes to those closest to them—and to listen to their heart as well as their head, they have the potential to make their big dreams of reform and progress a reality.

Love *Head or heart?*

Others are attracted to people born on May 3 for the pleasantness they create but they can have great difficulty committing themselves to one person; this is a result of their tendency to judge with their head rather than their heart. When they do fall in love, however, they fall deeply, and give their heart and soul. They are attracted to individuals whom they can mold or organize but will feel happier with someone who can encourage them to unwind.

Health *Worry less, live more*

People born on this day are worriers and it is important for them to find ways to manage their negativity. There is also a hedonistic side to their nature and they need to avoid going to extremes when it comes to diet. Overeating could be a problem, as could their number of sexual partners. They should eat a healthy, balanced diet and avoid any kind of excess, especially when it comes to sugar, saturated fat and alcohol. Exercise will also be extremely beneficial; solitary pursuits such as jogging, cycling and hiking will appeal, particularly when they find themselves trapped in a vicious circle of worry. A physical routine that soothes their mind as well as their body, such as yoga, will work wonders. Carrying a small titanium quartz crystal will help them pull themselves together when they feel "all over the place."

Career *Born horticulturalists*

These people have the necessary emotional detachment to become excellent counselors, psychologists and psychiatrists. Their ability to think coolly and logically equips them well for careers in politics and business, in particular banking, real estate and commerce. Scientific research and law may also appeal, and their affinity with nature could lead them to careers in agriculture and horticulture. Alternatively they may choose to develop their creativity in writing, interior design and decorating.

Destiny *To maximize the strengths of others*

The life path of people born on this day is to avoid over-analyzing relationships, as this will restrict their happiness. Once they have learned to get in touch with their feelings, their destiny is to help others maximize their strengths.

Power Thought

"I now respect my body, my mind and my emotions. I feel wonderful"

Signs & symbols

Sun sign: Taurus

Ruling planet: Venus, the lover

Symbol: The Bull

Birth date ruler: Jupiter, the speculator

Tarot card: The Empress (creativity)

Favorable numbers: 3, 8

Lucky days: Friday and Thursday, especially when these days fall on 3 and 8 of the month

Lucky colors: Lilac, lavender, green

Birthstone: Emerald

May 3

4 May

the birthday of sparkling goodness

Your greatest challenge is …

not becoming worn down serving others

The way forward is …

to understand that the best way to help others become self-sufficient is to be an example of someone who can support themselves.

You're drawn to people born on …

January 21 to February 19

This is a meeting of minds and hearts, and is in many ways a perfect match.

Luck maker

Strengthen yourself

Lucky people understand that before you can take care of others, you need to take care of and strengthen yourself. Sacrificing yourself on the altar of altruism sets a poor example, and drains your energy and optimism.

Even though their manners are often gentle and reserved, those born on May 4 often have an easy charm and hypnotic sparkle that draws those to them who are seeking guidance, direction or support. Whatever situation they are in, they frequently end up in the position of teacher and guide, and rightly so; others have much to learn from them.

These people are acutely perceptive but not judgmental. Though they are affectionate and quick to perceive goodness in everyone, they possess a strong will-power and inner strength. These can sometimes translate into stubbornness, especially when their opinions or ideals are called into question. Because they appear calm and stable, people who need practical and emotional guidance will seek them out. It is therefore important for them not to become too self-denying.

Many of these people do find themselves giving a lot of themselves to others, particularly friends and family. This should not stop them following their own dreams, which could leave them resentful of their responsibility toward others. Their home life is likely to be very important to them but again they need to make sure that they don't allow those closest to them to take over their lives completely.

They prefer to encourage or help others through deeds, and the example of dependability and compassion they set, rather than through words or theories. Their calm and common-sense approach to life earns them many fans but surprisingly there is a deep need within them to take more risks. They should not repress this need but confront it; when the time comes for them to make big changes—typically between the ages of seventeen and forty-seven, during which there is an emphasis on new directions—they need to make them. This will not damage their sense of responsibility or their sparkling reputation, it will enhance it, because to feel truly fulfilled, these perceptive, nurturing and inspiring individuals need to do more than dream about their hopes and ideals; they need to live them.

On the **dark** side

Unfulfilled, stubborn, self-sacrificing

At your **best**

Giving, supportive, warm

Love *Inside out*

What people think and feel matters more to people born on May 4 than what they look like, and their choice of partner may often surprise those closest to them. Though they are affectionate and loyal, they need to be careful not to analyze a relationship too much as it can make others feel uncomfortable.

Health *Brisk walking*

People born on this day are likely to devote a lot of time to nurturing or supporting others, especially if they have children. It is important for them to make sure that their own needs do not get neglected as it will lead to poor health and resentment. They also have a love of food and, if they don't make sure that their diet is healthy and their lifestyle is active, they are prone to mild weight gain. Brisk walking and cycling are excellent ways for them to get in shape; they also need to make sure they get enough sleep, as lack of quality sleep can trigger not just weight gain but mood swings. Wearing, meditating on and surrounding themselves with the colors pink and green will restore their energies and attract some well-deserved tender loving care from others.

Career *Born counselors*

Whether they make a career in counseling or not, these people will often find that their advice or guidance is sought regardless of the profession they choose. They may be drawn to charity work or working with the disadvantaged, and, if attracted to public life, could do well in careers in politics, sport or public relations. Those who yearn to develop their creativity may be attracted to music, singing, acting, and photography.

Destiny *To reach for their dreams*

The life path of people born on this day is to learn to pay just as much attention to their own dreams and goals as they do to the goals of others. Once they are able to do that, their destiny is to reach for their dreams and by so doing inspire others by their steadiness, empathy and optimism.

Power Thought

❝I am learning to love and take care of myself❞

Signs & symbols

Sun sign: Taurus

Ruling planet: Venus, the lover

Symbol: The Bull

Birth date ruler: Uranus, the visionary

Tarot card: The Emperor (authority)

Favorable numbers: 4, 9

Lucky days: Friday and Sunday, especially when these days fall on 4 and 9 of the month

Lucky colors: Lilac, copper, green

Birthstone: Emerald

May 4

5 May

the birthday of motivating energy

People born on May 5 are often full of original and innovative solutions, and know the best way to implement them. Others rely on them to offer ideas when things have ground to a halt or to inject their special brand of motivating energy. They have enough energy for everyone and, unless they feel undermined or threatened, they never seem to tire.

They have excellent communication skills and the ability to impart knowledge or insight to others. This isn't to say they are know-alls; it is just that they love nothing better than to motivate and inspire others toward action. They do this by getting to the heart of the matter; in some cases this may involve pointing out some uncomfortable home truths. Their aim is not to wound but to help others progress, although their interpersonal skills might improve if they learned the importance of listening a bit more.

They may find it hard to sit back when they witness a lack of awareness in others, and will quickly assume the role of parent or mentor. They do take this role extremely seriously and, if it is threatened in any way, they can become jealous, manipulative and aggressive. They should learn to be less possessive and more accepting of the need of others to make their own mistakes, especially between the ages of sixteen to forty-six during which there is an emphasis in their lives on communication in all forms. After the age of forty-six they may become more sensitive toward their own feelings and the feelings of others.

Hidden beneath the knowledgeable but practical exterior of these people there is a highly idealistic individual. To stop them becoming overly serious, they need to learn to use their unusual sense of humor; to feel more fulfilled they need to trust more in their instincts. This sense of their own power will give them the self-confidence and spontaneity they need to focus their energy not just on guiding others but on motivating themselves to express and develop their own highly creative potential.

Love *Love means everything*

For people born on May 5 the love and support of a partner mean everything, and they will do whatever it takes to keep a relationship alive. They are not afraid of commitment, romance or sentiment, but do need to be careful that they don't see their partner as an extension of themselves. Their ideal partner will share their sense of commitment.

Health *All a question of balance*

The greatest risk to the health of people born on this day is their tendency to go overboard in one area of their life, be it diet, exercise, sex, or work. They need to find ways to balance their incredible energy and to make sure that their lives are structured. As far as diet is concerned, they may have a sweet tooth and will need to make sure they limit their intake of sugar and refined and processed foods. Regular exercise, preferably on a daily basis—even if it is only a walk around the block—will help them keep a sense of perspective and balance. They are sensual people so will benefit greatly from regular massage. Placing a few drops of geranium essential oil on their handkerchief to breathe in when they feel overwhelmed will help them feel more balanced and upbeat.

Career *Born politicians*

With their motivating energy, these people have a gift for sales, promotion, advertising, and marketing. Careers in the retail trade also augur well, as do careers in politics and academic fields such as philosophy and medicine, as well as the arts, for which they have a natural affinity. Naturally sensual, they may also be attracted to catering, and the beauty and health industries.

Destiny *To inspire others with their energy*

The life path of people born on this day is to learn to guide and support others without dominating them. Once they have learned to be less authoritarian, their destiny is to influence and inspire others with their tremendous focus and energy.

Signs & symbols

Sun sign: Taurus

Ruling planet: Venus, the lover

Symbol: The Bull

Birth date ruler: Mercury, the communicator

Tarot card: The Hierophant (guidance)

Favorable numbers: 1, 5

Lucky days: Friday and Wednesday, especially when these days fall on 1 and 5 of the month

Lucky colors: Lilac, cobalt blue, green

Birthstone: Emerald

May 5

6 May

the birthday of
the sensitive star

The highly imaginative and intuitive people born on May 6 are often acutely sensitive to the feelings, dreams and hopes of others, especially those less fortunate. Fascinated by the human psyche and keen to learn what it is that motivates and inspires others, they often feel compelled to pass their wisdom on to others. If they aren't guiding and directing others, they will be inspiring them by living out dreams and fantasies that most of us repress.

As well as being finely tuned to the feelings of others, they are highly sensitive themselves; this can lead to misunderstandings and hurts that really aren't necessary. They should learn to be objective in their dealings with others; otherwise they will experience insecurity, uncertainty and disappointment. Between the ages of fifteen and forty-five there is an emphasis on communication and the exchange of ideas, so they should not take everything so personally. After the age of forty-five these people focus more on emotional closeness, family and security.

Their interest in human nature can take them beyond social interaction and business to a deep desire to do something meaningful in the world. This may involve fighting for a cause in the world and will stop them feeling unfulfilled. The most common block to their progress is a lack of faith in their own abilities; this can trigger sudden changes of mood and bouts of indecision. Being prone to excessive highs and lows, they need to turn the understanding they have of unpredictable behavior in others upon themselves. If they can do this, they will see that much of their emotional instability stems from their lack of self-belief.

Their self-doubt may also result in their taking a secondary role rather than making full use of their creative potential. They do, however, respond extremely well to advice and encouragement; reading self-help books or biographies about people they admire will help them gain control of their lives. They should remember that every step they take toward fulfilling their ambitions and dreams works to inspire and motivate others.

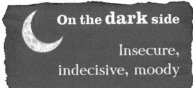
At your **best**

Sensitive, artistic, astute

Love *Waiting*

People born on May 6 are unwilling to commit to a relationship unless they feel it has the potential to be a perfect union. This means that they may spend many years searching and waiting, but when they finally find their soul mate they are at their happiest and their best, because love and giving to others is a strong motivating force in their lives.

Health *Boosting your self-esteem*

People born on this day tend to suffer from a lack of self-confidence and they need to find ways to build their self-esteem. Food is a passion, so they should keep an eye on what they are eating and make sure that they do not seek refuge in comfort eating. Listening to their hunger signals, and putting their knife and fork down between mouthfuls, will help them feel more in control. Regular exercise is also essential, not just because it will boost their immune system and sense of well-being but also because it can help them cope with excessive worry. Wearing, surrounding themselves with or meditating on the color orange will boost their self-esteem and encourage them to feel more positive, as will mind-training therapies such as cognitive development therapy or hypnotherapy.

Career *Born doctors*

People born on this day will often find career fulfillment in the medical, psychiatric or caring professions but they may also be well suited to politics and the arts, both areas in which they can use their sensitivity and desire to help or inspire others. Whatever career they choose, be it public affairs, caring or the world of entertainment, their natural psychological skills will be of great assistance.

Destiny *To inspire others with their energy*

The life path of people born on this day is to learn to believe in themselves. Once they have developed greater self-confidence, their destiny is to direct their prodigious energy toward the progression of others, be that in a practical or an inspirational way.

Signs & symbols

Sun sign: Taurus

Ruling planet: Venus, the lover

Symbol: The Bull

Birth date ruler: Venus, the lover

Tarot card: The Lovers

Favorable numbers: 2, 6

Lucky day: Friday, especially when it falls on 2 or 6 of the month

Lucky colors: Lilac, pink, green

Birthstone: Emerald

May 6

7 May

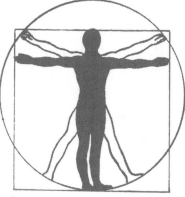

the birthday of absolute perfection

People born on May 7 are a curious mixture of inward-looking spirituality and outward-orientated concern with personal image. Although they are able to recognize that the most important values are non-materialistic, they also have a great desire to make an impression on others. This combination of inner and outer expectation is, however, in keeping with their quest for absolute perfection in all areas of their lives.

As well as being deeply sensitive and compassionate, they are also elegant and gifted communicators who can inspire others with their ideals. Often devoted to these ideals, they are willing to give them every ounce of their mental, physical and spiritual energy. This can develop into a tendency to give too much of themselves, but most of them are self-aware enough to know where and when to draw the line. They should ensure they retain a sense of perspective in their twenties, thirties and early forties, when there is an emphasis on change, communication and learning new skills. After the age of forty it is vital for them not to lose a sense of self, because this is a turning point when they are likely to focus more on emotional relationships, family and their instinctual understanding of others' needs.

It is their search for perfection, however, that best defines these people. There is always a danger that this will manifest in unrealistic fantasies and expectations, and they need to focus on making some of their high ideals a workable reality. Materially, their intelligence and drive will help them succeed; making money is not a problem for them, although—because they like enjoying and sharing the good things in life—keeping it sometimes is.

As far as spiritual or inner goals are concerned, they have to come to terms with the fact that finding their spirituality or inner meaning will be a lifelong mission. They should use their natural intuition to get in touch with their wisdom and creativity which, if allowed to express themselves freely, will be able to satisfy their deepest yearnings for fulfillment.

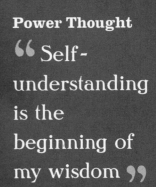
Love *Higher love*

People born on May 7 have a deep need to experience a spiritual union but a part of them may doubt if this is possible with another human being. They need to remain open to the fact that it can be. Their ideal mate is likely to be intelligent and creative, with a deep hunger for a spiritual dimension in their lives.

Health *Strike a balance*

People born on this day must strive to achieve balance in all areas of their lives as they are prone to neglect themselves for the sake of others or for the demands of work. If they don't take care of themselves and give themselves regular periods of rest and relaxation, they will suffer from stress, anxiety and—in extreme cases—depression. They do have a tendency to gain weight, especially around the waist during midlife, but this can be easily remedied by healthy eating and daily exercise. In fact exercise is highly therapeutic for these people, as long as they don't take it to extremes and push their bodies too hard. Regular meditation and spiritual or religious pursuits are also important for their mental and emotional health and well-being. Wearing, meditating on or surrounding themselves with the color green will encourage them to take better care of themselves and keep a sense of balance and perspective.

Career *Born composers*

People born on this day have excellent communication skills and the potential to excel in the artistic sphere, not just as poets, composers and writers, but as spiritual or even political evangelists. Other careers that might appeal include advertising, business, art dealership, education, and social or humanitarian reform.

Destiny *To make the world a more beautiful place*

The life path of people born on this day is to learn to understand their inner conflicts better. Once they are more self-aware, their destiny is to put their high ideals and devotion to good use by making the world a more beautiful place.

Power Thought

❝ Self-understanding is the beginning of my wisdom ❞

Signs & symbols

Sun sign: Taurus

Ruling planet: Venus, the lover

Symbol: The Bull

Birth date ruler: Neptune, the speculator

Tarot card: The Chariot

Favorable numbers: 3, 7

Lucky days: Friday and Monday, especially when these days fall on 3 and 7 of the month

Lucky colors: Lilac, blue, green

Birthstone: Emerald

May 7

8 May

the birthday of the irresistible messenger

Your greatest challenge is ...

listening to alternative viewpoints

The way forward is ...

to understand that by listening to what people have to say, you earn their trust and respect.

You're drawn to people born on ...

December 22 to January 20

You both desire loyalty, commitment and trust, and this can create a happy and fulfilling union.

Luck maker

Walk in someone else's shoes

Take a look at the world from the point of view of someone different. Lucky people understand that, however much you know, there is always more to learn.

P eople born on May 8 are strong-willed individuals who rarely back down. They are totally dedicated to their ideals, often stepping forward as spokesperson for a group. Their extraordinary self-belief is so irresistible that others find it impossible not to be moved or inspired by their message.

They will typically possess powerful convictions, striving to promote these as persuasively as possible. When they are particularly impassioned, they may sometimes come across as too forceful, judgmental and harsh. Diplomacy isn't one of their strengths but they have the potential to be excellent communicators. Once they have learned the art of getting their message over using gentle persuasion, they instinctively understand and successfully exploit the value of converting rather than alienating others.

Although their conviction earns them the admiration of others, it can also make people slightly afraid of them. But underneath their tough exterior lies a gentle, caring and generous side which—as they tend to regard any kind of vulnerability as a weakness—they will only reveal to their nearest and dearest. It is important for them to understand that strength and power can be found in gentleness. They can sometimes be too strong willed and serious, and often need to be more flexible and take a lighter approach. Between the ages of thirteen and forty-three there will be many opportunities for them to discover their playful side as there is an emphasis on communication and diversification. After the age of forty-three they will focus on emotional connections with others, and again, if they can learn to lighten up, happiness and fulfillment are within easy reach.

With an innate appreciation of beauty, they will often feel a strong connection with the natural world or their immediate man-made surroundings. They may therefore devote themselves to environmental concerns, to preserving historical buildings or simply to improving their homes or local neighborhood. Wherever they decide to devote their energies, the art of diplomacy will make it easier for them to realize their ambitions.

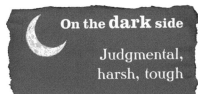

On the dark side

Judgmental, harsh, tough

At your best

Outspoken, caring, persuasive

Love *Faithful and true*

People born on May 8 tend to be very faithful partners. Love is a serious business for them, but to keep the flame of passion alive they need to learn that love should also be a laughing matter. They need to be careful that they don't end up with someone who is weaker than them because they are at their happiest and best when they are in a committed relationship with someone who is their equal.

Health *Go green*

People born on this day tend to have strong views about health and well-being, and will often challenge the wisdom of conventional medicine, preferring to self-medicate with supplements and herbs. Although this approach can work wonders for them, they need to remain open to the possibility of seeking advice from their doctor if they do fall seriously ill, as independence and will-power are not miracle cures. As far as diet is concerned, they need to make sure they eat at least five or six meals and snacks a day instead of three larger meals, as this will keep their energy levels constant and their minds alert. Regular exercise is also a must, as long as they don't punish themselves with grueling regimes, keeping the emphasis on recreation and fun. Listening to music and wearing the color green will be extremely therapeutic for them.

Career *Born conservationists*

These people possess the charisma and persuasive skills to excel in careers in promotion, negotiation and sales. They may also be drawn to sales, publishing, advertising, law, politics, real estate, farming, and conservation work. Their strong leadership qualities also suit them to management, and their creativity may well draw them to music, writing, radio, and movies, as well as design and architecture.

Destiny *To be the spokesperson for their cause*

The life path of people born on this day is to learn to be more diplomatic in the expression of their ideas. Once they have learned to be gentle in their approach to others, their destiny is to be the spokesperson for their cause, neighborhood or generation.

Signs & symbols

Sun sign: Taurus

Ruling planet: Venus, the lover

Symbol: The Bull

Birth date ruler: Saturn, the teacher

Tarot card: Strength (passion)

Favorable numbers: 4, 8

Lucky days: Friday and Saturday, especially when these days fall on 4 and 8 of the month

Lucky colors: Lavender, claret, green

Birthstone: Emerald

May 8

259

9 May

the birthday of the activist

Your greatest challenge is …

dealing with your anger

The way forward is …

to understand what triggers your anger and have a plan ready to counteract it.

You're drawn to people born on …

October 24 to November 22

You are both brave and true individuals with a positive disposition, and this can create a supportive and passionate relationship.

Luck maker

Turn regret into resolve

Your luck-making potential is strongest when you are compelled by guilt, and a need to pay back and set things right. So resolve any guilt you have by making a positive difference.

People born on May 9 may appear calm and steady on the surface, but to those who know them well they radiate energy and drive. They possess a clear-cut sense of morality and fair play, and are compelled to place themselves in the role of reformer, protester or activist if they witness any kind of injustice or abuse.

Above all, their desire is to be a support to those who are less fortunate or to play a part in highlighting their cause or reversing their fortunes. Occasionally, they have such a strong sense of honor that they seem to belong to a more civilized age. When responding to a humanitarian cause or championing the rights of the oppressed, they draw on their powers of compassion, steadfastness and courage which may have developed as a result of hardships or difficulties they have struggled to overcome in their past, perhaps in their childhood or teenage years. Until the age of forty-two there is an emphasis on sudden changes of direction and this may involve learning through struggle and setback; but after the age of forty-three life tends to get easier for them and they can concentrate on security, both emotional and financial.

Because people born on this day are so committed to their progressive visions, they can find it hard to forgive the failings of others, expecting them to live up to their own lofty standards. When they do experience disappointment or disillusionment at home or at work, they can astonish with their sudden flashes of temper. It is important for them to learn to manage their anger, because all the support and respect their charisma, focus and persuasive power may have gathered can vanish in an instant when their temperamental tendencies surge to the fore.

Once they learn to be more flexible and to respond in more constructive ways when they see something that upsets them, their success, and more important to them the success of the ideals they believe in, are virtually guaranteed.

Love *For life*

The charismatic individuals with strong convictions born on May 9 are never short of admirers. When they fall in love, however, it is for life, even if the relationship runs its course. They are fiercely protective of their partner and extremely generous and tactile but they need to make sure they take into account their partner's feelings and don't become too domineering.

Health *Self-control*

People born on this day have temperamental tendencies and they need to make sure that this does not cause them to suffer injuries or stress-induced disorders such as fatigue and headaches. Self-control and learning to be more tolerant of the weaknesses and vulnerabilities of others will enhance all areas of their health. As far as diet is concerned, they should monitor their intake of sugar and alcohol, ensuring that they eat little and often to avoid blood-sugar imbalances and mood swings. Moderate to mild exercise is recommended, in particular non-competitive activities such as walking or dancing. They would also benefit greatly from mind–body therapies such as yoga, meditation and tai chi. Wearing, meditating on or surrounding themselves with the color blue will encourage them to be more objective and to stay cool, calm and in control.

Career *Born politicians*

These people have all the qualities they need to excel in careers in politics, law, acting, and the caring professions. Their undoubted charm could draw them toward people-orientated careers, such as promotions and sales and marketing, and their natural business sense and leadership could draw them toward management or to working for themselves.

Destiny *To inspire others with their passion and commitment*

The life path of people born on this day is to learn to manage their emotions successfully. Once they are able to distance themselves emotionally from situations that provoke their anger, their destiny is to lead or inspire others with their passion and commitment.

Power Thought

"I am ready to release myself from the habit of criticism"

Signs & symbols

Sun sign: Taurus

Ruling planet: Venus, the lover

Symbol: The Bull

Birth date ruler: Mars, the warrior

Tarot card: The Hermit (inner strength)

Favorable numbers: 5, 9

Lucky days: Friday and Tuesday, especially when these days fall on 5 and 9 of the month

Lucky colors: Lavender, red, green

Birthstone: Emerald

May 9

1O May

the birthday of
natural rhythm

Your greatest challenge is ...

finding time or energy for others

The way forward is ...

to understand that relationships with other people are not incompatible with single-minded dedication to a project; all that's needed is to find balance.

You're drawn to people born on ...

August 24 to September 23

You share a passion for adventure and action, and this can create a passionate and intense union.

Luck maker

Be willing to give selflessly

If you focus on what you can give, not on what you can get from others, in time luck will reward you well.

People born on May 10 follow their own natural rhythm. They often glide rather than struggle through life. They intuitively seem to know when to make a move, when to step back, when to quicken their pace and when to slow it down; their intuitive approach is more often right than wrong.

These people like to go their own way and, although their suggestions are often innovative, they tend to work best as an individual rather than as part of a team. They can become wholly absorbed in projects that fuel their imagination and are willing to take a lone stand when necessary. Although they have the communication skills and tenacity to enlist the support of others, they have an impulsive, thoughtless and occasionally self-indulgent side that can make them enemies or lead them into trouble.

They should always learn to look before they leap, making sure that they devote their great tenacity and energy to a worthy cause. Before the age of forty-two they risk getting involved in questionable pursuits; during this period they may need to be guided by those close to them or by a mentor who has their best interests at heart. After the age of forty-three they may concentrate on emotional security and they need to take advantage of this opportunity to connect more deeply with their own and others' feelings. If they don't open up and ignore the seemingly trivial obligations of close relationships, they are likely to become alienated from the joys of interaction.

Movement and activity are extremely important to these people and they may even get depressed if they don't take enough exercise. They have enhanced sensual qualities and these make them fine lovers; they do, however, need to beware of over-indulgence in any form. With a highly developed imagination, sensibility and intelligence, they enjoy looking at the world with a perspective that is often way ahead of their time. All these qualities endow people born on this day with the potential to make their mark on the world as far-sighted innovators.

Love *Beauty is only skin deep*

People born on May 10 are sensual, highly charged and extremely charismatic. As a result they can be very tactile and flirtatious. They do have a tendency to go for looks over personality, but fortunately when they grow older they learn to be less superficial in their choice of partner. When they find someone new they can be inspired and passionate, and will make a tremendous effort to include their loved one in their private world.

Health *Regular health checks*

People born on this day run the risk of becoming so involved in a project or passion that they forget about their own health. Therefore it is important for them to eat healthily and have regular check-ups with their doctor. As far as exercise is concerned, it is essential that they engage in it often, as plenty of movement keeps them happy and fulfilled. If they are one of those born on this day that doesn't do much exercise they should try it, as it will change their lives. Personal relationships are also crucial for their physical and emotional well-being, and they should make sure they spend plenty of time with family and friends. Wearing, meditating on or surrounding themselves with the color green will restore their energies and encourage them to find more balance.

Career *Born dancers*

These people generally have a strong affinity with the arts, in particular music and dance, but they may also be drawn to sports, business, politics, or working for themselves, as these are all areas which allow scope for their imaginative and ambitious urges to achieve success. Other careers that might appeal include teaching, science, medicine, and alternative health.

Destiny *To look at things from a fresh perspective*

The life path of people born on this day is to make sure they don't neglect relationships with others. Once they are able to develop their empathetic feelings, their destiny is to lead and inspire others toward progress by encouraging them to look at things from a fresh perspective.

Signs & symbols

Sun sign: Taurus

Ruling planet: Venus, the lover

Symbol: The Bull

Birth date ruler: Sun, the individual

Tarot card: The Wheel of Fortune (change)

Favorable numbers: 1, 6

Lucky days: Friday and Sunday, especially when these days fall on 1 and 6 of the month

Lucky colors: Lavender, orange, yellow

Birthstone: Emerald

11 May

the birthday of distinctive flair

People born on May 11 are blessed with a highly developed and independent aesthetic sense that refuses to be constrained by the rules, regulations and ideals of others. They live in a world of their own creation and enjoy adding their colorful, light-hearted but extremely distinctive flair to any situation they are in.

These highly creative people excel at making what is seemingly mundane or routine appear entertaining or new. They are the people who can turn household chores into games or study assignments into exciting challenges. With a burning desire to learn the truth for themselves, their approach causes them to challenge, side-step or walk all over conventional thinking. Their questing and imaginative powers are supplemented by their powers of perception, originality and stubborn tenacity.

Among the many gifts with which people born on this day are blessed is their ability to make life more colorful and exciting, and for that they earn the gratitude of others, but unfortunately not always their respect. This is because, although they are brilliant at inspiring and entertaining, they can get so immersed in their dream world that they lose touch with reality. Although some have a talent for making a profit from their unusual thoughts, others with less self-mastery often struggle to make their dreams and imaginations work. They should never lose touch of their audience when expressing their unique creativity. If they don't stick to the facts and what is realistically workable, they may be branded highly intelligent but ineffective.

Until the age of forty they will focus on change and new interests. This is often a period of study and experimentation, and they need to be careful not to lose themselves in exaggeration or fantasy. After the age of forty-one their sensitivity increases and they place more emphasis on home and family life. They need to understand that they have the potential to achieve something better than the admiration of others; that is, the respect and undying loyalty of all those lucky enough to wander across their path.

On the dark side

Unrealistic, eccentric, detached

At your best

Creative, distinctive, fun-loving

Love *Enchanted realm*

People born on May 11 have the ability to add youthfulness and sparkle to their relationships. They also love to be around children and are perfect playmates for them. Because of their tendency to become immersed in work, they may have long periods alone but they are at their happiest and their best when they are in a loving and supportive relationship.

Health *Hypochondriac tendencies*

People born on this day are highly imaginative and if they are prone to worry they may feel anxious about their health when they have no reason to be. It is important for them to stay as real as possible and, if they have any health concerns, to discuss them with their doctor instead of endlessly worrying about them. As far as diet is concerned, they would thrive best on a diet based on whole grains, nuts, seeds, fruit and vegetables, lean meat, and oily fish, as diets high in sugar, salt, saturated fat, dairy, and refined and processed foods could trigger food allergies or intolerances. Moderate to mild exercise is recommended, as it will help boost their immune system and help them feel more grounded in the real world. Wearing, meditating on or surrounding themselves with the color orange encourages them to attract much-needed warmth, physical enjoyment and security.

Career *Born entrepreneurs*

These people may be drawn to careers in research but they are also sensitive creatures with an interest in the human condition and this may draw them toward the judiciary or politics. Highly imaginative and creative, they may also find ways to make a success of their original ideas in business or by working for themselves. This birthday also suggests musical, creative or dramatic talent which can be a commercial success.

Destiny *To blaze an innovatory trail through life*

The life path of people born on this day is to make sure they don't lose sight of what is real in their life. Once they are able to stay more objective, their destiny is to blaze an innovatory trail through life that entertains, inspires and informs others.

Power Thought

"I am respected by everyone because I respect myself"

Signs & symbols

Sun sign: Taurus

Ruling planet: Venus, the lover

Symbol: The Bull

Birth date ruler: Moon, the intuitive

Tarot card: Justice (discernment)

Favorable numbers: 2, 7

Lucky days: Friday and Monday, especially when these days fall on 2 and 7 of the month

Lucky colors: Lavender, silver, green

Birthstone: Emerald

May 11

12 May

the birthday of lucidity

Your greatest challenge is …

to be tactful when expressing your opinions

The way forward is …

to understand that people generally respond better to you when you make them feel good about themselves.

You're drawn to people born on …

November 23 to December 21

You share a passion for information and adventure, and this can create a playful and intense union.

Luck maker

Be generous with your compliments

Lucky people know how to pay compliments. Compliments that are sincere make other people feel good; when people feel good they are more likely to want to help you.

People born on May 12 may appear steady and sensible on first acquaintance but past the small-talk stage a witty and engaging person emerges. In fact, their wealth of intelligent perspectives often takes other people by surprise.

They have tremendous energy and will-power and although they do not necessarily seek leadership, they often find themselves promoted to that position because of their hard work and dedication. Independent and self-assured but also easy to approach, they inspire confidence in the people they live and work with. They are also extremely observant and their well-honed critical faculties can work to their advantage. Although they use humor and the element of surprise to question and challenge conventional thinking, this can degenerate into criticism and sarcasm. They do need to learn to curb their biting observations and avoid alienating those close to them.

Until the age of thirty-nine there is an emphasis on study and developing their communication skills; during this time they should learn to soften their sharp tongue with humor. After the age of forty they perceive the importance of home and the need to care emotionally for themselves, as well as others. During these years they need to show their generous side by highlighting the strengths of others as well as their weaknesses, and by praising as much as they criticize. Once they understand that the more they give, the more they get back, there is nothing to stop them reaching for their dreams.

When it comes to their own ideas and dreams, however, there is a tendency for these people to be reticent. As a result, others may sense something in them that always remains distant and a mystery. There is nothing wrong with keeping a part of themselves private; the only danger is that by not revealing what they think and criticizing what others think, others may accuse them of only finding problems and not solutions. This, however, is unjust as they have a unique perspective on the world that has tremendous potential to motivate and inspire others with its expansive optimism.

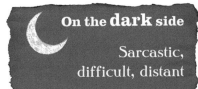

Love *Feelings are worth sharing*

People born on this day can put their partners in a relationship under scrutiny but, once they learn to back down, they can become their lover's greatest supporter. They are passionate and energetic lovers although there will always be a tendency for them to hold back emotionally when it comes to their own feelings. They need to understand that their feelings, however insignificant or trivial they may seem, are worth sharing.

Health *Just say Om!*

The highly energetic people born on this day often have a fast metabolism that keeps them in good shape. If they do struggle with their weight this may be because they have confused their metabolism with yo-yo dieting, unhealthy eating and lack of exercise. They can get things back on track by making sure they always eat breakfast, by eating little and often (five or six small meals and snacks instead of three large meals a day) and by taking moderate to mild exercise for at least 30 minutes, preferably on a daily basis. Meditation is recommended to help them be more objective in a situation and focus an equal amount of attention on the positive as well as the negative. Wearing, meditating on or surrounding themselves with the color yellow will encourage them to express themselves more optimistically.

Career *Born movie critics*

With their love of observation and ability to get to the point quickly, these people thrive in careers which allow them to analyze and dissect situations, such as movie or theater critics, or consultants or advisors of any sort. The caring side of their nature may surface with an interest in education, counseling, charity work, or healing. The side of them that wishes to express their creativity may also draw them toward careers in design, music and the arts.

Destiny *To offer the world their fresh perspective*

The life path of people born on this day is to learn that the more you give in life, the more you get. Once they are able to look for the positives as well as the negatives in a situation, their destiny is to offer the world their fresh, optimistic and innovative perspective.

Power Thought

“Today I will make compassion the heart of my life ”

Signs & symbols

Sun sign: Taurus

Ruling planet: Venus, the lover

Symbol: The Bull

Birth date ruler: Jupiter, the philosopher

Tarot card: The Hanged Man (reflection)

Favorable numbers: 3, 8

Lucky days: Friday and Thursday, especially when these days fall on 3 and 8 of the month

Lucky colors: Lilac, green

Birthstone: Emerald

May 12

13 May

the birthday of the wild child

Your greatest challenge is ...

learning to control your impulses

The way forward is ...

to understand that self-control is the key to success in your life; without it you are like a reed blown about by the wind.

You're drawn to people born on ...

January 21 to February 19

You share a passion for adventure and excitement, and this can create a colorful and intense union.

Luck maker

Think before you act

It sounds simple, but taking time out to think about the pros and cons before you make a decision shows that you are prepared and therefore less likely to attract bad luck.

Other people find themselves instantly drawn to the natural charisma and playful charm of people born on May 13. These untamed spirits follow their instincts and, although they often clash with the conventions and restrictions placed upon them by society, their wild-child presence always has an electrifying effect on others.

These people are often self-taught in some way and their approach to situations and people is easy and natural. They have the ability to win friends quickly and easily and, as a result, to attract good fortune. Unfortunately, this can sometimes make them the object of envy or resentment. They should be aware of the effect their success and popularity have on others; if necessary they should tone down their lighthearted approach or find the appropriate level of intensity for their audience.

In keeping with their wild-child personality, they find practical concerns and routine boring and unfulfilling. With a love of movement, change and variety, if they do find themselves stuck or restricted in any way, they may get depressed or behave recklessly. Although this butterfly approach makes them fascinating individuals with a wealth of knowledge and experience, if those born on this day delved more deeply into subjects or situations they would discover how enriching and enlightening a more intense knowledge or commitment can be. Before the age of thirty-seven they should deepen their approach and outlook; after the age of thirty-eight they may be more concerned with emotional commitment.

Although they appear to breeze through life, it's highly likely that at some point a significant event, generally one with unpleasant or painful consequences, will have given them the impetus to focus on their more serious side and have concern for the welfare of others. When this newfound earnestness and sense of purpose is combined with the enthusiastic enjoyment of life that is their defining feature, the possibilities for them to achieve success in all areas of their lives are limitless.

Love *In too deep*

People born on May 13 love deeply and romantically; although they believe that a relationship should be for life, they often forget that relationships need work. They are usually very fortunate in attracting admirers but, as with everything in their lives, they do need to exercise a certain amount of discrimination before they take the plunge.

Health *Body talk*

People born on this day don't tend to have major problems with their health because they are often very much in tune with their bodies, eating only when they are hungry, exercising when they feel the need to be active and so on. If they do suffer from weight problems or poor health, learning to listen to their body's signals and seeking medical advice on diet and exercise will get them back on track. They need to steer clear of recreational drugs, as these will have an extremely damaging effect on their health and well-being. The best kind of therapy for people born on this day, apart from fresh air and exercise, is committing to study or increasing their knowledge in one specific area. Wearing, meditating on and surrounding themselves with the color blue will encourage them to be less impulsive and more logical in their approach.

Career *Born designers*

These people have the independence and impulsive creativity to excel in careers in the arts, music, dance, and design. Their natural charm may also attract them to people-related careers such as sales, public relations, teaching, and law; but whatever career they choose, their chances of success are high.

Destiny

The life path of people born on this day is to learn to commit themselves on a deeper level to people and situations. Once they can find it within themselves to delve deeper, their destiny is to invigorate, inspire and—if necessary—shock others into progressive ways of thinking and doing things.

Power Thought

❝I can choose how I will respond to every situation in my life ❞

Signs & symbols

Sun sign: Taurus

Ruling planet: Venus, the lover

Symbol: The Bull

Birth date ruler: Jupiter, the philosopher

Tarot card: Death (change)

Favorable numbers: 4, 9

Lucky days: Friday and Sunday, especially when these days fall on 4 and 9 of the month

Lucky colors: Lilac, pale green, light blue

Birthstone: Emerald

May 13

14 May

the birthday of the progressive outlook

The articulate individuals born on May 14 are progressive in their outlook and are intellectually far in advance of other members of their generation. Their forward-thinking, progressive outlook allows them to see potential and opportunities that those who are less imaginative may miss.

They are extremely energetic, being propelled forward by their nervous energy and unlimited curiosity. Proud and independent self-starters, they are unlikely to seek help from others but such is the power of their vision that influential people are often standing by to offer assistance if they ask. With the ability to lift whatever enterprise they undertake to the next level, the only way for them to feel more fulfilled is to take on the mantle of progress in some way.

As indefatigable workers who strive for excellence in all areas of their lives, they usually achieve this excellence but there's a price to pay. Physical and emotional burnout and a high degree of stress and nervous tension are very real dangers for them. It is important that they recognize their limits and, as fascinating as the future is, all they really have is the present moment. This tendency to drive themselves too hard or be extremely critical of their performance is a theme throughout their lives but is especially strong before the age of thirty-six. At the age of thirty-seven they may concentrate on the growing importance of home, family and emotional needs. Then, after the age of sixty-six, they become far more confident and self-assured.

Because people born on this day always have their eye on the future, there may be times when their opinions or visions are misinterpreted or, worse still for them, ridiculed. This can cause them great distress, but if they learn to back down and bide their time, more often than not others will eventually come around to their way of thinking. And once they learn to be less critical of themselves and more patient with others, these progressive souls may well be the ones who come up with ground-breaking ideas capable of changing the world.

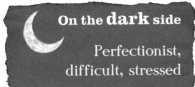
Power Thought

" Today I live in the moment "

Love *Don't try too hard.*

People born on May 14 often put a lot of effort into their relationship and are the first to blame themselves if something goes wrong. They need to understand that if they are trying too hard to win someone's affection and admiration, something in the relationship isn't working. Prone to mood swings, they thrive best with partners who respect their need for freedom but who can also share their interests and keep them mentally active.

Health *Stress relief*

Stress and related problems such as insomnia and headaches are the biggest risk to health for people born on this day. It is very important for them not to take themselves too seriously and to ensure they have plenty of time for fun and relaxation. They also have a tendency to be extremely stubborn when it comes to their health; accepting that they might be ill can be a serious problem for them. They may also suffer from digestive disorders and from swollen glands, particularly around the throat. As far as diet is concerned, they need to make sure they don't overindulge in sweet, refined foods and focus on a diet rich in whole grains and natural products. A daily exercise routine will help them feel more in control of their health and their weight. Wearing, meditating on or surrounding themselves with the color green will help them feel more grounded in the present and inspire confidence in others.

Career *Born social scientists*

These people have the vision to excel in careers in politics, social science, travel, space research, information technology, science, advertising, and investment. They may also be drawn to artistic and creative pursuits such as music, drama, literature, and painting or sculpture. With their love of variety they need to choose a career that does not involve routine, and the media, photography, journalism or working for themselves will all appeal.

Destiny *To predict future trends*

The life path of people born on this day is to learn to focus just as much of their energies on the present as they do on the future. Once they are able to find that balance, their destiny is to predict future and potentially groundbreaking trends.

Signs & symbols

Sun sign: Taurus

Ruling planet: Venus, the lover

Symbol: The Bull

Birth date ruler: Mercury, the communicator

Tarot card: Temperance

Favorable numbers: 1, 5

Lucky days: Friday and Wednesday, especially when these days fall on 1 and 5 of the month

Lucky colors: Lilac, all shades of blue

Birthstone: Emerald

May 14

15 May

the birthday of delightful introspection

People born on May 15 are blessed with intelligence, charm and a rich and powerful imagination. Young at heart, they have the ability to touch the hearts and minds of all those lucky enough to wander across their path.

What makes people born on this day so special is their creativity. They are the ones with the brightest solutions or magical ideas and when they are around the world always seems a fresher and more colorful place. They often live in their dreams, so their plans frequently come to nothing while they are sitting back expecting others to come forward or to seek their advice. At work they may see a way forward but they are unlikely to volunteer this information to their boss unless asked for it; in their personal life they may expect others to make the first move. It is important for them to put themselves forward and take responsibility for their creativity and talent, because this is the only way they will be able to reach their potential and fulfill their dreams.

From about the age of six to the age of thirty-six, there is an emphasis on education, communication and new interests; this is one of the reasons why their imaginative faculties are so advanced and why they may opt to stay in school longer or train longer than others. Around the age of thirty-six, however, home and family life present opportunities for them to shake off their passivity and become more confident of themselves and their abilities.

They are often seen by others as being rather otherworldly or living in a world of their own; in many respects this assumption is correct as they do have an irresistible urge to acquire knowledge, oftentimes mystical knowledge. Despite the dreamy image they present, once they learn to take responsibility for their talents they are rarely isolated from others. This is because others will always be drawn to their capacity to present the inspirational fruits of their mental adventures and, by so doing, bring great happiness and illumination to the world.

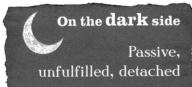
At your **best**

Imaginative, intelligent, charming

Love *Make the first move*

People born on May 15 are never short of admirers but they may miss out on opportunities for romance because they are reluctant to make the first move. Once in a relationship they also need to guard against passivity and should try to take the initiative more, especially when it comes to showing affection; their undemonstrative nature may be interpreted by others as indifference.

Health *Don't isolate yourself*

People born on this day need to avoid isolating themselves from social contact. All activities that bring them out of themselves should be encouraged, as should spending more time with friends and loved ones. Exercise is highly recommended, especially activities that involve social contact, such as dancing, aerobics and team sports. As far as diet is concerned, they have a tendency to overindulge in foods they enjoy. One of the best ways to counteract this is to make sure that boredom and loneliness are not the real causes of their overeating. The same applies to sex and drugs, in which they may also be tempted to indulge. Addiction of any kind is extremely negative and unhealthy for them, so if they can't fight it alone they need to seek help from their doctor or a counselor. Wearing, meditating on or surrounding themselves with the color orange will encourage them to feel warmer and more secure in the company of others.

Career *Born webmasters*

These people have the potential to inspire others and succeed in just about every career, from scientific research to business to something more artistic and creative. They may also choose to work from home or devote themselves to web design, finance or accountancy. Their birthday shows excellent work opportunities and a strong awareness of responsibility, but they need to guard against becoming stuck in a job that does not fulfill them.

Destiny *To share their innovative ideas*

The life path of people born on this day is to make sure they don't cut themselves off from others. Once they are able to find a balance between their creativity and their responsibility to the world, their destiny is to share their innovative ideas and by so doing inspire others.

Signs & symbols

Sun sign: Taurus

Ruling planet: Venus, the lover

Symbol: The Bull

Birth date ruler: Venus, the lover

Tarot card: The Devil (instinct)

Favorable numbers: 2, 6

Lucky day: Friday, especially when it falls on 2 or 6 of the month

Lucky colors: Lilac, pink, pale blue

Birthstone: Emerald

May 15

16 May

the birthday of bright color

People born on May 16 are blessed with a wild energy that manifests itself in diverse, hidden or outrageous ways. Early in life they may have recognized in themselves a need to fly in the face of convention or rebel in their own distinctive and often flamboyant way. They are colorful and expressive, and life may be unpredictable when they are around but it is never boring.

Some of these people are less extrovert and perhaps quieter in their approach to life, but this tendency toward flamboyance will still express itself when their passions are aroused or their interests are threatened. In fact, whether introvert or extrovert, they can be extremely volatile and others soon learn to tread carefully around them. If they can't learn to control their wildness, they run the risk of wasting their energy and their potential on dramatic but ultimately futile displays of temper. If, however, they learn to harness their energy and passion, their potential, especially for creative ventures, is limitless.

Life for these people is often one of extremes. It is important for them to take charge of their emotions, learning to be less reactive so that when the bad times come they have better coping mechanisms to rise above them. Until the age of thirty-five there is an emphasis in their lives on learning and education; this would be the ideal time for them to learn to manage their emotions better as they are then at their most receptive to new ways of thinking and doing things. After the age of thirty-six they will focus on emotional security, home and family life; for their professional and personal lives to be a success during this time, self-discipline again must be a priority.

Although self-mastery is the key to their success, this should never be at the expense of their colorful and expressive personality. It is through their dynamic style of expression and passionately held convictions that they are able to impress others. By so doing, they add a touch of the colorful or exotic to the world around them.

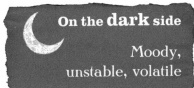
Love *Rapidly changing moods*

People born on May 16 are warm and affectionate, and are never short of admirers because they are exciting and sensual partners; their rapidly changing moods, however, can strain even the closest of relationships. They need to learn to balance their volatility by making their relationship and their home as secure and as stable as possible.

Health *Stability is key*

People born on this day are prone to mood swings; these can put a strain on their relationships and their health. They need to find ways to keep their lives more in balance. One way to do this is to ensure they eat a healthy diet full of fresh, natural foods rather than foods rich in sugar, salt, saturated fats, additives, and preservatives; these are known to affect brain function negatively and dampen mood. Regular exercise is a must; it will help them feel more in control of their bodies and their weight, and will also be a healthy way for them to release pent-up tension. Dressing in shades of green and blue will encourage them to feel calmer and more in control, inspiring harmony in themselves and others.

Career *Born performers*

These people have a flair for the dramatic and can excel in careers in the theater, entertainment, music, dance, and the arts. They are also likely to be successful in sporting careers or careers such as negotiation, banking, property speculation, interior design, or management. A humanitarian leaning may draw them toward charity work or philanthropy.

Destiny

The life path of people born on this day is to learn to control their emotions. Once they are able to find a sense of balance and objectivity, their destiny is to direct their prodigious energy to influencing, inspiring and entertaining others.

Signs & symbols

Sun sign: Taurus

Ruling planet: Venus, the lover

Symbol: The Bull

Birth date ruler: Neptune, the speculator

Tarot card: The Tower (breakthrough)

Favorable numbers: 3, 7

Lucky days: Friday and Monday, especially when these days fall on 3 and 7 of the month

Lucky colors: Lilac, sea green, pale blue

Birthstone: Emerald

May 16

17 May

the birthday of profound simplicity

Your greatest challenge is ...

asking for help

The way forward is ...

to understand that if you want to make something happen, you must dare to ask for what you want.

You're drawn to people born on ...

December 22 to January 20

You share a passion for devotion, commitment and respect, and together you can create a fulfilling and intense union.

Luck maker

Create a luck network

Many big breaks come from the least likely contacts, so make an effort to network and stay in touch with as many people as you can.

People born on May 17 have a clear-cut code of personal behavior which guides them through every decision they make. Straightforward and to the point, they have a talent for making simple but profound comments on situations.

With little time for small talk, they say what they mean and mean what they say. They are an inspiring example to others but don't have much patience with those who try to shirk their responsibilities; if they notice someone slacking or not pulling their weight, they are likely to tell them straight out. This clear-cut approach can, unfortunately, win them as many enemies as supporters and so they might benefit from learning more tact. Their insightful and original approach, combined with their refusal to be diverted from their chosen course, would appear to be a recipe for success. Where this is not the case it is because they have a tendency to overestimate the power of what they can achieve through determination and will-power alone. They often prefer to go it alone, but if this works against them they should recognize the power of a group of people working together to achieve a goal.

Until their mid thirties there is an emphasis in their lives on learning in all its forms and they need to take advantage of these opportunities to communicate and exchange ideas with others. After the age of thirty-four they may focus more on emotional intimacy and security. If they can learn to get in touch with their own feelings and the feelings of others during this period, it promises great fulfillment and happiness.

There is no denying that these people often have fixed views on things. This can hold them back as life is not as black and white as they think it is. However, if they learn to develop a more tolerant approach it will not only help them achieve their aims and attract a following, it will also open up within them the compassion and determination to improve the lives of others and a creativity that might otherwise have remained dormant.

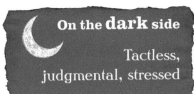

On the dark side

Tactless, judgmental, stressed

At your best

Dedicated, honorable, insightful

Love *Inside out*

People born on May 17 value personality, integrity and a strong will over good looks, and would rather be alone than with someone they can't respect. Although they may try to suppress it, they have an extremely sensual nature and a voracious romantic drive; releasing some of that energy into a committed relationship will help mellow and soften them.

Health *Give yourself a break*

People born on this day are extraordinarily determined and at times this can make them drive themselves too hard and become prone to headaches or digestive upsets. Ideally they should surround themselves with close friends and loved ones who can encourage them to relax and unwind. Those who find themselves alone might find training and owning a dog extremely beneficial. As far as diet and lifestyle are concerned, they should stay away from drugs and alcohol as their body is extremely sensitive to toxins of any kind. Moderate to mild exercise, especially brisk walking, is encouraged to help them blow away the cobwebs, keep their weight under control and boost their immune system. Wearing, meditating on or surrounding themselves with the color orange will encourage them to be warm and open in the company of others.

Career *Born artists*

People born on this day have the creativity and focus to excel in the world of art and music. Alternatively education, science, research, and law, as well as working for themselves, may appeal. Once they appreciate the importance of working cooperatively with others, they may be drawn toward sales, promotion, public relations, finance, negotiation, social work, and banking.

Destiny *To inspire others with their creative and organizational talents*

The life path of people born on this day is to learn the power of synergy. Once they are able to open up to others, their destiny is to inspire them with their creative and organizational talents.

Signs & symbols

Sun sign: Taurus

Ruling planet: Venus, the lover

Symbol: The Bull

Birth date ruler: Saturn, the teacher

Tarot card: The Star (hope)

Favorable numbers: 4, 8

Lucky days: Friday and Saturday, especially when these days fall on 4 and 8 of the month

Lucky colors: Lilac, green, brown

Birthstone: Emerald

May 17

18 May

the birthday of the brave stance

People born on May 18 care deeply about the world they live in. Their greatest desire is often to alleviate the suffering of others and improve social systems. When convinced of their moral position, they will not flinch from taking a brave stance until their views have been heard or the challenge has been overcome.

As well as being progressive in their thought, compassionate in their desire to right wrongs and unwavering in their defense of what they believe to be right, they are also extremely practical. Presenting a logical, rational approach to situations, they are much-sought-after business allies or co-workers, although their black-and-white approach to life and inability to back down can at times make them seem stern and insensitive. They are the bosses who forget that trainees have a lot to learn or the parents who unintentionally stifle their child's creativity with relentless rationalism. They should learn that not everyone is as practical or capable as they are and that humility, mystery and wonder have their special place in life.

These people often have a passion of some kind; this can take any form, from charity work to archeology. They also tend to mix with people who share their passion and would benefit from meeting people from other walks of life, as they may give too much of themselves to their passion. Until the age of thirty-three they may focus on learning, communication and study but are still unsure of themselves and the direction in which they want to head. Typically, by the age of thirty-four they have settled on their chosen course as they see a need for more security and stability. At this stage they need to be on their guard against their tendency to become over-zealous or fanatical when promoting their chosen cause.

Above all, whatever path in life they choose, these people are energetic campaigners for human progress. They have tremendous courage, vigor and steadfastness, and these, combined with their considerable compassion, sets them apart as the true movers and shakers of this world.

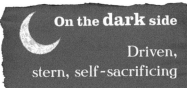

On the dark side

Driven, stern, self-sacrificing

At your best

Progressive, energetic, principled

Love *Put your heart first*

People born on May 18 are often drawn to people who share their passions and interests, but they thrive best with those who can offer them love and commitment but also a fresh perspective on life. Although love may not be their highest priority, when in a relationship these people are at their happiest and their best as it offers a great mental release for them.

Health *More than meets the eye*

People born on this day need to make sure that they allow themselves to get in touch with their feelings and express their sensual, loving side. If they don't, they are likely to fall victim to stress, anxiety and sudden bursts of anger. Spending time with loved ones is extremely important as it will offer them a way to release pent-up tension. Regular massages are also recommended to indulge their sensual side and help them relax and unwind. As far as diet is concerned, there could be problems with meat and dairy products so they need to increase their intake of whole grains, fruits and vegetables, finding other sources of protein from legumes, nuts, seeds, or oily fish. Exercise, preferably outdoors so they can get all the mood-boosting benefits of sunshine, is also recommended. Wearing, meditating on or surrounding themselves with the color purple will help them think of higher things.

Career *Born martial artist*

These people enjoy initiating projects and taking the lead, so careers in law and order or government may appeal. Since they are good at promoting their cause, careers in sales, promotion, marketing, negotiation, charity work, fund raising, or working with products of the land would also be appropriate. Alternatively, they may express their creativity in the arts, music or dance and their extraordinary focus will help them excel as dancers, coaches or martial arts teachers.

Destiny *To inspire others with their direct action*

The life path of people born on this day is to learn to recognize the merit of conflicting viewpoints. When they are able to be more tolerant, their destiny is to inspire others with their ability to take direct action.

Signs & symbols

Sun sign: Taurus

Ruling planet: Venus, the lover

Symbol: The Bull

Birth date ruler: Mars, the warrior

Tarot card: The Moon (imagination)

Favorable numbers: 5, 9

Lucky days: Friday and Tuesday, especially when these days fall on 5 and 9 of the month

Lucky colors: Lilac, red, rose

Birthstone: Emerald

May 18

19 May

the birthday of
the convincing candidate

People born on May 19 have a highly developed sense of fair play and an ability to put forward their case convincingly and credibly. They will speak out eloquently when they notice any injustice and act decisively to ensure positive changes are made.

One of the greatest strengths of these people is their natural ability to convince others that changes need to be made and action needs to be taken. Such is their persuasive power that after spending time with them others often find themselves feeling energized, focused and ready to commit themselves to a new course of action. There is a danger, however, that their magnetic and inspiring communicative skills can be used for unworthy causes. When this is the case, their charisma and eloquence can slip into dishonesty; they should avoid this path at all costs as it will only lead to frustration.

Until the age of thirty-two there is an emphasis in the lives of people born on this day on learning, writing, speech, and study, and, because this coincides with their student years, their talent for communication will be given plenty of opportunities to express itself and develop. In fact, education in some form is vital to bring out the best of their potential. During this time they will also begin to appreciate the powerful effect they have on others; as a consequence, they need to ensure they don't become manipulative or overbearing. After the age of thirty-two they become more focused on emotional intimacy, family and security; these years can be highly fulfilling and rewarding.

Inventive and original, people born on this day have a progressive philosophy in life and whatever they choose to focus their energies on, their arguments and ideals are always worth listening to. Once they learn to strike a balance between standing up for their own ideas and being receptive to the ideas of others, not only are able to persuade others of the importance of their ideals, they can also become excellent representatives for others less fortunate than themselves.

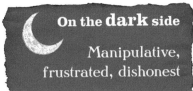
At your **best**

Persuasive, fair, energetic

Love *Examine your motives*

People born on May 19 have a great deal of charisma, and there will be no shortage of admirers. Problems may arise, however, when social status, popularity or appearance govern their choice of partner rather than their heart. It is important for them to examine their motives for becoming overly concerned with their own material status and that of others.

Health *Exercise caution*

People born on this day have a wild streak about them and as a result can be accident prone. They need to be cautious when it comes to sports and exercise, and also when traveling. This doesn't mean, however, that they should avoid exercise. Quite the opposite, as exercise is essential for these energetic people and without it they can become stressed or depressed. It just means they should listen to their bodies and not push themselves or take unnecessary risks. As far as diet is concerned, they may be among those fortunate people who can eat what they like but if they aren't getting plenty of exercise, eating five or six lighter meals and snacks a day instead of two or three big meals will help keep their weight under control. Herbal infusions, such as chamomile tea, are highly recommended to help them relax and should be preferred to caffeine, which they tend to consume in excess.

Career *Born songwriters*

These people thrive in careers in which they can motivate, inform and inspire, such as education, politics and the caring professions. Their original mind may also draw them into careers in philosophy or scientific research, and humanitarian aspirations may steer them toward social reform or religion. Their way with words may express itself through speaking, writing, singing, or the world of entertainment in general.

Destiny *To become a representative for their peers*

The life path of people born on this day is to learn to use their persuasive talents wisely. Once they have learned to strike a balance between their own needs and the benefits of others, their destiny is to become a representative for their peers and perhaps their generation.

Signs & symbols

Sun sign: Taurus

Ruling planet: Venus, the lover

Symbol: The Bull

Birth date ruler: Sun, the individual

Tarot card: The Sun

Favorable numbers: 1, 6

Lucky days: Friday and Sunday, especially when these days fall on 1 and 6 of the month

Lucky colors: Lavender, orange, yellow

Birthstone: Emerald

May 19

20 May

the birthday of continuous momentum

Your greatest challenge is ...

learning to pace yourself

The way forward is ...

to understand that your desire to constantly seek out the new will lead you into random and inconsistent behavior, ultimately causing frustration not fulfillment.

You're drawn to people born on ...

June 22 to July 23

You share a passion for communication and a need for stability, and this can create a rewarding and expressive relationship.

Luck maker

Finish what you start

Lucky people understand the importance of discipline. They finish what they start, even if it means doing things they don't like in order to reach their goals.

People born on May 20 tend to be versatile, communicative and inventive. They generally respond to people and situations quickly and openly. When one of their highly original impulses strikes, not only do they talk about it a lot and update the whole world on their progress—they act on it.

However safe and serene they may appear, underneath they crave change, diversity and freedom of expression. When their fertile imagination has been activated they find it impossible to keep it to themselves, provoking both awe and exhaustion in others. The awe comes from their ability to convey excitement; the exhaustion from the speed with which they talk and move from one thing to another. They tend to stay up late and get up early, so there is never enough time in the day for them to do everything they want; but they will try regardless.

Outwardly focused with a huge range of interests, they run the risk of exhausting themselves when their pace becomes too manic. Others may also accuse them of only skimming the surface of life, rather than getting to grips with it. Until the age of thirty-one—when they are most likely to be constantly on the move, physically and mentally—they focus on learning, study and communication. After the age of thirty-two, however, they will concentrate more on emotional depth, family, home, and security. Although they should never lose their wonderful energy, this would be the ideal time for them to get to know themselves better and commit to a project, person or place.

These people may often feel as if they simply can't switch off. It is important for their psychological growth, however, to learn that they don't constantly need to be on the go to find the fulfillment and excitement they crave. Once they learn to strike a balance between being and doing, these pioneering and stylish adventurers have the potential to be both a quick-witted energetic jack of all trades *and* an accomplished master of one; and this is a very rare combination indeed.

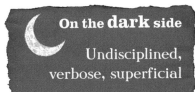

On the dark side

Undisciplined, verbose, superficial

At your best

Innovative, expressive, communicative

Power Thought

Love *Stylish*

People born on May 20 are often stylish and fashion conscious, and they like their partner to be the same. It is important for them, however, to understand that true quality in a person can never be determined by their outward appearance. Although they may appear flirty and flighty, committed relationships are extremely good for them because these give them the secure foundation they need to spread their wings.

Health *Time out required*

People born on this day sometimes neglect their health because they are constantly on the go. Establishing a regular sleeping pattern—preferably one where they are asleep by midnight—will help them feel more refreshed and in control. Sitting down to cooked meals and getting plenty of exercise to work off some of their pent-up energy are also essential. They would benefit from regular meditation or quiet time where they can stand still and objectively examine their thoughts and feelings. If they fail to take care of their physical and mental health in this way, there is a real danger that they may become exhausted and prone to headaches, anxiety, disorders such as ME or chronic exhaustion, and stress-related digestive disorders such as irritable bowel syndrome. Wearing, meditating on or surrounding themselves with the color purple will encourage them to connect with the stillness and peace within.

Career *Born firefighters*

The humanitarian, philosophical or artistic spheres are especially propitious for these people and they may be drawn to careers in social work, education, counseling, politics, scientific research, the arts, and the healing professions. Their way with words may inspire them to express themselves though music, singing or writing; careers in travel, rally driving, fire fighting and rescue, and extreme sports or stunts, may also appeal.

Destiny *To energize others with their sparkling perspective*

The life path of people born on this day is to appreciate the importance of self-discipline and restraint. Once they are able to maintain a balance in all areas of their lives, they desire to energize others with their sparkling and original perspective.

Signs & symbols

Sun signs: Taurus/Gemini

Ruling planets: Venus, the lover/Mercury, the communicator

Symbols: The Bull/The Twins

Birth date ruler: Moon, the intuitive

Tarot card: Judgment (responsibility)

Favorable numbers: 2, 7

Lucky days: Friday and Monday, especially when these days fall on 2 and 7 of the month

Lucky colors: Lavender, silver, green

Birthstone: Emerald

May 20

21 May

the birthday of the can-do attitude

Your greatest challenge is ...

learning to balance giving and receiving

The way forward is ...

to understand that offering help to others and receiving support back is fundamental to psychological growth.

You're drawn to people born on ...

November 23 to December 21

You share a passion for adventure and a need for a co-adventurer; this can create an intense and committed union.

Luck maker

Perform random acts of kindness

Try it for a week and notice how generous behavior not only makes you feel great, it also brings you luck.

People born on May 21 are defined by their courage in the face of opposition and by their can-do attitude in the pursuit of their dreams. Their natural confidence may inspire jealousy in those who feel less in control of their lives but it gives them the head start they need to achieve their goals.

People born on this day have a refreshingly upbeat approach to life and when they are around things always seem much easier and challenges less daunting. In fact no challenge seems to be too much for them. This is because not only do they have wonderful ideas and talents, they also have the discipline to persevere. They are not just dreamers but also doers who roll up their sleeves and do whatever it takes to get the job done.

Whatever line of work these courageous people are involved in they are unlikely to be standing on the sidelines because they are at their happiest and their best when they are battling their way physically, mentally and emotionally toward progress. Less evolved types born on this day who find themselves unable to translate their dreams into reality are destined for unhappiness and frustration. It is very important for them to get into the driving seat of their lives because if they can find the strength to take action the chances are extremely good that they will succeed.

Until the age of thirty there is an emphasis in the lives of people born on this day on learning, study and communication and because of this they will probably have been an alert and quick learner at school or college. Their ability to learn quickly may have worked against them as they may have found themselves restless or bored with formal education or training and their early years may have been difficult as a result because others could not relate to their ingenious turn of mind. After the age of thirty, however, there is a turning point which shifts their perspective toward emotional security and stability and it is during these years that they are most likely to come into their own. As long as they are careful that their confidence does not turn into conceit there is very little that can stand in the way of their success.

On the **dark** side

Egoistic, defensive, frustrated

At your **best**

Bold, capable, confident

Love *Too busy for love*

Socially inclined and extremely popular, in affairs of the heart people born on May 21 have a tendency to expect others to fall in line with their demands. Once they have learned the importance of give and take in a relationship, however, they make generous and committed partners. They like devoted relationships and are happiest when in one.

Health *Human dynamos*

People born on his day are often human dynamos and, although their energy and optimism may seem limitless, they need to recharge their batteries with healthy food, regular but moderate exercise and plenty of sleep. If they don't take care of themselves and keep imposing unnecessary pressures on themselves, they will be increasing their risk of stress and heart disease and, in extreme cases, reducing their life expectancy. They may also be prone to disorders of the throat or voice. It is extremely important for them to take regular vacations and to make sure that they have at least two clear days away from work a week. They would benefit greatly from mind–body therapies such as meditation, yoga, tai chi, and aromatherapy massages. Geranium is an essential oil that is an ideal uplifting and balancing scent for them. Wearing, surrounding themselves with and meditating on the color purple will encourage them to slow down and focus on higher things.

Career *Born inventors*

Their visionary and practical tendencies augur well for finance-related careers but also for the more unusual realm of technical invention. Their sensitivity may also draw them toward humanitarian work and their desire to improve the human condition to careers in social reform, politics, law, and educational research. Their creativity may also draw them to a wide range of artistic endeavors, in particular art, music, writing, and journalism.

Destiny *To investigate, develop and implement their ideas*

The life path of people born on this day is to learn to take time out to recharge their mental and physical health. Once they are able to take stock of their motivations and behavior, their destiny is to tenaciously investigate, develop and implement their stunning ideas.

Signs & symbols

Sun signs: Taurus/Gemini

Ruling planets: Venus, the lover/Mercury, the communicator

Symbols: The Bull/The Twins

Birth date ruler: Jupiter, the philosopher

Tarot card: The World (fulfillment)

Favorable numbers: 3, 8

Lucky days: Friday and Thursday, especially when these days fall on 3 and 8 of the month

Lucky colors: Lavender, purple, orange

Birthstone: Agate

May 21

22 May

the birthday of
the inventor

**Your greatest
challenge is …**

avoiding obsessive or
controlling behavior

The way forward is …

to understand that the more
you try to control people or
situations, the more they want
to break free.

**You're drawn to
people born on …**

January 21 to February 19

You are both intelligent and
curious free spirits; with ample
breathing space, this can create
an exciting and rewarding
union.

Luck maker

Focus on what you want

Lucky people have goals they
want to achieve. It sounds
morbid but if you aren't sure
what your goals are, writing
your obituary can help you
organize your thoughts about
what you want from life.

People born on May 22 have exceptionally inquisitive and productive minds. Not only can they concentrate on one area in minute detail; they also abhor intellectual stagnation. This is an unusual and unique combination that gives them the potential to invent or discover something unique.

There is no doubt that people born on this day are creative and original thinkers; their biggest challenge is often deciding what it is that they want to create. It can sometimes take years for them to make up their minds; their twenties and much of their thirties are likely to be spent in intellectual exploration and experimentation. When they are involved in a specific project it will often take over their lives and, if their concentration is interrupted, they can become extremely irritable or unsettled, which may lead others to accuse them of being obsessive. It is extremely important that others give them the space to experiment and explore, and refrain from criticism, because before the age of thirty total devotion to one project is essential for their psychological and intellectual growth.

Typically by the age of thirty these people will have calmed down and learned to be less touchy when their concentration is disturbed. The late thirties and beyond are also the years when they are most likely to decide on what they want to contribute to the world and back it up with action. Once they have decided on a course of action, their single-mindedness will give them the drive, resilience and focus needed to realize their ambitions.

With a tendency to overreach themselves, they should never tone down their vision or ambition, but for their own happiness and fulfillment they should devote as much energy to finding ways to play to their strengths and minimize their weaknesses. This is because once they understand themselves better and are able to be more realistic in their quest for illumination and success, they have the potential to pioneer new and potentially life-changing, but also soundly researched, ideas.

Love *Born free*

People born on May 22 are likely to be attracted to people who are as unique, independent and insatiable in their search for knowledge as themselves. Once in a relationship, it is important for them to avoid becoming controlling or smothering; they should remember that what attracted them in the first place was their partner's freedom and independence.

Health *Make fitness a priority*

People born on this day have a tendency to become obsessive or compulsive in their professional and personal lives, and they need to watch that they don't drive themselves too hard and become stressed or ill as a result. As long as they don't go overboard, a positive way for them to channel their energy would be to make physical fitness a priority as they have the will-power to eat healthily and tone their body into fine, athletic shape with regular exercise. If they do find themselves feeling constantly exhausted, making sure they get enough quality sleep and short naps is recommended. They may also benefit from mind–body therapies such as meditation, yoga and tai chi; these can help them direct their focus positively. Wearing, meditating on or surrounding themselves with the color green will encourage their bodies, hearts and minds to feel more in balance.

Career *Born inventors*

These people have the potential to be great innovators, explorers or inventors in whatever field they choose to work. In addition to artistic, research and scientific fields, they may find satisfaction in such arts-related business activities as journalism and advertising, as well as politics. Their quick mind also points to success in business as an analyst or troubleshooter.

Destiny *To pioneer new ideas and methods*

The life path of people born on this day is to get to know themselves better. Once they know how to play to their strengths, their destiny is to pioneer new ideas and methods in a leadership or mentoring role.

Signs & symbols

Sun signs: Gemini/Taurus

Ruling planets: Mercury, the communicator/Venus, the lover

Symbols: The Twins/The Bull

Birth date ruler: Uranus, the visionary

Tarot card: The Fool (freedom)

Favorable numbers: 4, 9

Lucky days: Wednesday and Sunday, especially when these days fall on 4 and 9 of the month

Lucky colors: Yellow, silver, orange

Birthstone: Agate

May 22

23 May

the birthday of the seductive solution

Your greatest challenge is ...

learning to say no

The way forward is ...

to understand that people will respect and approve of you more if you set down clear boundaries and let them know what your limits are.

You're drawn to people born on ...

June 22 to July 23

You share a passion for communication, intellectual discovery and intimacy, and this can create a passionate and fulfilling union.

Luck maker

Just do it!

When lucky people long to do something they find ways to do it, even when they feel afraid. So if there is something you long to do, go ahead—just do it! You will feel fantastic.

There is something radiant about the positive and seductive energy of people born on May 23 that others find impossible to ignore. Their defining feature, however, isn't their charisma and sex appeal, but their ingenuity. They are gifted problem solvers who generously give a lot of their time and energy to help others resolve their problems in both practical and emotional ways.

As well as being inventive problem solvers, they are natural communicators. They can present a case convincingly and offer viable solutions. When faced with a dilemma they may find that they have brilliant eureka moments when the answer just pops into their mind. They have a natural flair for everything imaginative but instead of talking about creating, as they are prone to do, they need to get on and do it! This is because it is in activity rather than discussion that these intuitive individuals release their inventiveness.

They aren't motivated by a need to be the center of attention or to assume leadership, getting tremendous satisfaction from simply helping others solve professional and personal woes. The downside of this is that while they attack the problems of others with great energy and insight, they often neglect their own affairs. This can have negative consequences when others take advantage of their generosity and willingness to help. It is vital for their psychological growth that they learn to speak up for their own needs and interests; if they don't, this can lead to frustration and lack of fulfillment.

Until the age of twenty-nine there is an emphasis on information gathering, communication and learning; after the age of thirty they are likely to become more sensitive and security conscious. It is important during this turning point that they learn to say "no" to the demands of others and avoid sacrificing their needs completely to home, family and loved ones. They need to accept that people can and do value them for the energetic, innovative, positive, and inspiring person that they are, and not for what they can do for them.

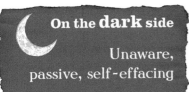
At your **best**

Sensual, ingenious,
convincing

Power Thought

" What I
desire from
others I
already
possess "

Love *Meeting of minds and hearts*

People born on May 23 are attracted to people who are their equal intellectually. Unfortunately, though, they often neglect the importance of emotional compatibility and may find that their generosity of spirit and willingness to subordinate their needs to their loved one are taken advantage of. They need to be in a relationship where minds and hearts meet and where both parties are willing to give and take.

Health *Home cooking*

People born on this day need to make sure that they don't neglect their health and well-being for the sake of others. As far as diet is concerned, they should make sure it is healthy and balanced. If they live alone, rather than eating erratically or on the go, they should make sure they nurture themselves with home cooking and foods that are as fresh and natural as possible. Exercise will be vital to boosting their immune system, their self-esteem and body image, and fast-paced sports such as tennis, squash, football, and netball are highly recommended, as well as individual sports such as jogging, brisk walking, swimming, and cycling. Wearing, surrounding themselves with and meditating on the color yellow will increase their confidence and self-esteem.

Career *Born advisor*

These people are often drawn to the caring and healing professions but the performing arts, teaching and diplomacy may also appeal, as they are gifted communicators. They are likely to be skilled with their hands, so may be involved in creative and artistic pursuits. Law, counseling or psychology could also provide an outlet for their talent in offering advice and information.

Destiny *To be at the service of progress*

The life path of people born on this day is to learn to focus on their own needs as much as they do on others. Once they have learned to be more self-nurturing, their destiny is to place their prodigious energy at the service of progress, both their own and others'.

Signs & symbols

Sun signs: Gemini/Taurus

Ruling planets: Mercury, the communicator/Venus, the lover

Symbols: The Twins/The Bull

Birth date ruler: Mercury, the communicator

Tarot card: The Hierophant (guidance)

Favorable numbers: 1, 5,

Lucky day: Wednesday, especially when it falls on 1 and 5 of the month

Lucky colors: Orange, violet, yellow

Birthstone: Agate

May 23

24 May

the birthday of
the incisive commentator

Your greatest challenge is ...

not being a gossip

The way forward is ...

to understand that although gossip gets the attention of others, they will not respect and admire you unless you talk about others in a positive way.

You're drawn to people born on ...

September 23 to October 24

You share a passion for communication and intimacy, and this can create a haven of love, security and respect.

Luck maker

Become an apprentice

Lucky people understand that nobody likes a know-all. Demonstrating a sincere willingness and openness to learn will draw other people to you and they will want to help you.

People born on May 24 have a gift for expressing what others feel and for getting to the heart of the matter. Incredibly observant, they are commentators on what they see going on around them and will rarely hesitate to broadcast their often profound and insightful views.

With their love of observing and commenting, people born on this day often have a wealth of information about human nature. They are often obsessed with talking about the relationships of others, and others love their company and highly entertaining tales. Although they will always champion the underdog, they do need to be careful that they don't betray the confidences of others and that their witty insights don't dissolve into gossip. Despite being so eloquent about the affairs of others, they are often strangely reticent about discussing their own lives.

Their gift for incisive observation attracts the admiration of other sharp-witted people but they need to watch their tendency to alienate others with one cutting comment too many. They may also close their minds to conflicting opinions so it is important for them to learn the art of diplomacy and to respect the opinions of others. Until the age of twenty-eight they focus on learning and communication but around the age of twenty-nine they may prefer to look for emotional and professional security; the following thirty or so years are when they are likely to come into their own. Around the age of fifty-eight there is another turning point when they enter a period of increased authority, strength and confidence.

As long as these clever and witty people don't drain their energies with negative criticism and keep their minds positive and inquisitive, their natural vitality, drive, creativity, and ability to clarify the most complicated of situations will keep them investigating new projects and invigorating old ones. They can see possibilities and connections that others might miss and this can take them far; and they will always be fascinating conversationalists.

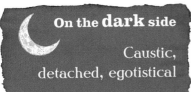
Love *Inquisitive*

People born on May 24 love to explore the inner recesses of their partner's mind but also the minds of everyone they meet, so any partner may find themselves in the role of diplomatic ally. They need to learn to be more open about their own feelings in a relationship, but when they meet someone they feel comfortable enough to open up to they can be loyal, loving and highly entertaining partners.

Health *Not too hot or too cold!*

People born on this day don't tend to complain much about their health; except when they are too hot or too cold, which they can't tolerate. They are prone to coughs, colds, circulation problems, and physical exhaustion, generally as a result of their fast-paced life. If they can't find a satisfactory way to relax and unwind, stress or nervous exhaustion could also be a problem. They may have an urge to escape their busy social life and hide away; they should not repress this as they would benefit significantly from time out alone when they can read, relax and connect with their intuition. As far as diet and lifestyle are concerned, they should keep it varied and avoid smoking and alcohol. Exercise should be moderate to vigorous and if possible it should be a structured part of their lives rather than ad hoc. Wearing, meditating on or surrounding themselves with the color purple will encourage them to connect with the peace and stillness within.

Career *Born journalists*

These people could make great journalists, in particular gossip columnists, but their ability to persuade and inspire others could also mark them out for careers in sales and politics, as well as education, art, design, acting, writing, singing, composing, photography, movie-making, law, and the world of entertainment.

Destiny *To entertain, influence and direct others*

The life path of people born on this day is to learn to accept others as they are. Once they are more relaxed and tolerant of differences of opinion, their destiny is to use their strong communication skills to entertain, influence and direct others.

May 24

Signs & symbols

Sun sign: Gemini

Ruling planet: Mercury, the communicator

Symbol: The Twins

Birth date ruler: Venus, the lover

Tarot card: The Lovers (choices)

Favorable numbers: 2, 6

Lucky days: Wednesday and Friday, especially when these days fall on 2 and 6 of the month

Lucky colors: Orange, light green, pink

Birthstone: Agate

25 May

the birthday of the caring soldier

Your greatest challenge is ...

opening up to others about your feelings

The way forward is ...

to understand that opening up to others about the way you feel does not imply weakness or lack of moral fiber; everyone experiences inner conflicts.

You're drawn to people born on ...

September 24 to October 23

Principles and spirit come before material concerns for you both and this can create a rewarding and stimulating relationship.

Luck maker

Feelings should follow behavior

Lucky people don't always feel happy but they have learned that the power of their lives lies in positive action and behavior, no matter how scared or resistant they feel.

Intelligence, imagination, compassion, and courage are associated with those born on May 25. They are a study in paradox, sometimes being as much a puzzle to themselves as they are to others.

These people know how to fight for what they believe in. They have a strong sense of honor and personal responsibility to which they will cling regardless of the pressures imposed by those less principled. This does not mean they are intellectually rigid, for they often possess a sharp and inquisitive mind, allowing them to embrace new ideas. They are bold and courageous, but are also sensitive and willing to devote their energy and communication skills to improving the lot of those less fortunate. Although they have more than enough courage to go it alone, their favored approach is to inspire a group of like-minded individuals who are equally enthusiastic, principled and progressive.

With a tendency to be philosophically inclined, when it comes to the world of feelings, however, they can come across as cool and aloof. They have high expectations not only of themselves but also of others, and do need to learn to be more flexible and tolerant. They should therefore get in touch with their feelings and the feelings of others because if they don't, however successful they are in their professional life or in their ability to encourage social reform, they are likely to feel repressed and unfulfilled.

The childhood and teens of these people may have been emotionally isolating or difficult in some way but fortunately after the age of twenty-seven they focus on their emotional life, becoming aware of the need for a foundation or center to build from. They need to take advantage of these opportunities, because once they are able to ground themselves emotionally they will feel less frustrated. They will discover that their courage in the face of opposition and their compassion for others are not incompatible but highly compatible energies, being the key to their potential for making a difference and improving human life—be it in the global or personal sense.

At your **best**

Honorable, caring, bold

Love *Lighten up a little*

Sometimes people born on May 25 can be too serious for their own good; they need to make sure they incorporate plenty of fun into their relationship to keep it alive. If they do find themselves disappointed in love, they tend to blame themselves and their lack of judgment but they need to understand that, in the world of feelings, sometimes the heart can be stronger than the head.

Health *Try a cool new look*

People born on this day tend to present a rather cold front to the world and they need to make sure that this doesn't distance them from friends and loved ones. If they can learn to express themselves more and have more fun, they can complement their cool head with a cool look. They need to make sure they don't become too fixed in their ways regarding diet, and they would benefit from greater variety and flexibility; eating small meals and snacks instead of three big meals is the way forward. They should also get out of their exercise rut and experiment with some cross-training. Wearing, meditating on and surrounding themselves with the colors yellow or orange will encourage them to feel warmer and more connected to others.

Career *Born humanitarians*

These people have pronounced leadership potential and could gain great fulfillment in blazing a political or humanitarian trail in psychology or the healing professions. They may on the other hand prefer a career that makes the most of their communication skills, such as sales, law, music, art, and journalism. Alternatively they may be drawn to careers in computers, engineering and philosophy.

Destiny *To implement their ideological convictions*

The life path of people born on this day is to learn to be less judgmental of themselves and others. Once they are able to be more tolerant, their destiny is to implement their ideological convictions with their prodigious vigor and determination.

Signs & symbols

Sun sign: Gemini

Ruling planet: Mercury, the communicator

Symbol: The Twins

Birth date ruler: Neptune, the speculator

Tarot card: The Chariot

Favorable numbers: 3, 7

Lucky days: Wednesday and Monday, especially when these days fall on 3 or 7 of the month

Lucky colors: Orange, sapphire blue, yellow

Birthstone: Agate

May 25

26 May

the birthday of
the solicitous adventurer

Your greatest challenge is ...

conforming to your own high standards

The way forward is ...

to understand that if you don't live what you preach, others will accuse you of hypocrisy, an accusation which will hurt and offend you deeply.

You're drawn to people born on ...

September 24 to October 23

You are both strong-willed individuals who need freedom of expression, and this can create an intense and rewarding union.

Luck maker

Ask for things, don't demand

Creating luck is about having preferences, not addictions. Addictions are things you tell yourself you must have at all costs; a preference is something that you really want but isn't vital.

On the surface, people born on May 26 appear to be charismatic and popular but deep down they may dream of breaking away. Publicly they uphold convention, being vocal in their promotion of social values and their concern for others. Privately they tend to be a rebel against restrictions of all kinds.

It may seem paradoxical that for people born on this day it is their own talents, which they can use so effectively on behalf of others, that can impede their own search for fulfillment. If their firmly held beliefs and restless drive for new knowledge and experiences are in harmony, they can be startlingly progressive and innovative. But out of harmony they can result in double standards or impulsive, selfish and intolerant behavior.

The dynamism of those born on this day frequently inspires the imagination and admiration of others—but also their intense dislike. The fierce need these people have to express their individuality manifests in a highly visible struggle within themselves that gives them intense charisma, but can also lead them to disreputable, occasionally dangerous, causes and to unworthy people or situations.

Life may be something of a struggle for these complicated but fascinating people but they are unlikely to want it any other way. Part of them feels that conflict is essential for their psychological growth; in some respects they are right, but they should understand that self-knowledge can be gained during times of peace and contentment as well as times of danger. After the age of twenty-six they may focus on having a strong foundation or home and there are opportunities for them to get in touch with their feelings. They need to make the most of these as, contrary to their beliefs, feeling happy and fulfilled is a distinct possibility for them. Once they are able to gain a more profound level of self-knowledge, they have the potential not just to rise to positions of leadership but to impart their strong views through inspiring words and inspirational deeds.

Love *Commitment-shy*

People born on May 26 might talk about the joys of marriage and commitment to one partner, but in their private life they may opt for the single life or for skipping from one relationship to another. They are attracted to people who are as free-spirited and as intelligent as they are, but the best person for them would be someone who has the gentleness to help them open up. They hate to show vulnerability, but vulnerability will, ironically, give them greater strength.

Health *Sweet tooth*

People born on this day are often moving too fast to be struck down by illness but nervous exhaustion is a potential problem if they can't find a satisfying way to relax and wind down. They may also be prone to injuries to the arms, hands and fingers, and should avoid smoking or passive smoking at all costs. They do have a tendency to overindulge as far as diet is concerned, and need to find ways to satisfy their sweet and savory tooth in healthier ways; for example, fruit instead of chocolate, nuts and seeds instead of salted chips. Vigorous exercise is highly recommended as it will help them work off some of their pent-up energy in a positive, health-boosting and waist-whittling way. Wearing, meditating on or surrounding themselves with the color orange increases feelings of warmth, physical enjoyment and security.

Career *Born politicians*

People born on this day love to talk about their views and would make excellent politicians, journalists, teachers, sales persons, and performers. They may need to discipline themselves to avoid scattering their energies, but once they are able to concentrate, their quick mind gives them the ability to succeed in whatever career they choose.

Destiny *To influence and inspire others with their charisma and persistence*

The life path of people born on this day is to learn to understand themselves better. Once their words are in line with their deeds, their destiny is to influence and inspire others with their charisma and persistence.

Signs & symbols

Sun sign: Gemini

Ruling planet: Mercury, the communicator

Symbol: The Twins

Birth date ruler: Saturn, the teacher

Tarot card: Strength (passion)

Favorable numbers: 4, 8

Lucky days: Wednesday and Saturday, especially when these days fall on 4 and 8 of the month

Lucky colors: Orange, navy, yellow

Birthstone: Agate

27 May

the birthday of progressive action

Although they are perceptive and creative thinkers, those born on May 27 are generally not interested in philosophical ideas but in sharing their knowledge with the wider world. Indeed their greatest desire is to find ways to benefit humanity as a whole, their favored approach being to take action to realize their progressive ideals.

Blessed with a healthy dose of self-confidence, they have the ability to keep their cool during the most difficult circumstances. Although very interested in the human condition and concerned for the well-being of others, they can detach emotionally. Others may criticize them for sometimes being cold and impersonal, but they instinctively realize that getting too emotionally involved in situations weakens their ability to offer effective help.

The steadiness of these people is complemented by their strength of purpose and infectious optimism. Their elegance and sophistication brighten every situation and they are generally well respected and liked by those they meet. Unfortunately, their close personal relationships may be less harmonious because they often devote most of their time and energy to work. Their strong self-belief draws success and opportunities to them; if self-belief is lacking, this may be because they have chosen a career not aligned to their talents. Fortunately, there are several pivotal moments in their lives which offer them opportunities to rethink their life; these will occur at age 25, age 30, age 40 and age 55. Although their greatest wish is to serve humanity, in the interests of their self-development they should take advantage of these opportunities to re-examine their motivations and strategies.

They find it hard to accept criticism, so their psychological progression depends on their being less controlling and taking on board alternative viewpoints in both their personal and their professional lives. Once they are more flexible in their approach, the prodigious energy and spirit of enterprise of these clever and passionate people will ensure their success as a guide and inspiration to others.

On the **dark** side

Detached, obsessive, selfish

At your **best**

Steady, dedicated, elegant

Love *Listen, really listen*

People born on May 27 are affectionate, seductive partners but they have a tendency to blank out anything that sounds like criticism, making them seem insensitive. It is important for them to really listen to what their partner has to say as this will make their relationship more harmonious. They are attracted to people who are as hard-working as they are, but ideally they need someone with gentleness to help them open up emotionally.

Health *Get up and go*

People born on this day can lose themselves in their work and this is dangerous as it can make them neglect their diet and health. They may smoke and drink but are strongly advised to cut down or give up both. They are also prone to depression but often it is reactive depression that occurs when they do not feel fulfilled in their professional life. Taking time out to talk to mentors, friends, family, or even a counselor would help them get back on the right track. They are naturally good at all forms of exercise; if they don't have an exercise routine already, they should set one up because it will boost their health, manage their waistline and give them an outlet for the release of tension. Wearing, meditating on and surrounding themselves with the color orange will increase feelings of warmth and security.

Career *Born doctors*

These people have the skills and personality to excel in the medical, teaching, legal, or diplomatic professions as well as the artistic or sporting realms in which they can express themselves more freely. They may change careers a number of times in their lives, but whatever they eventually settle on, the opportunity to guide and care for others in some way is essential for their fulfillment.

Destiny *To help other people achieve tangible results*

The life task of people born on this day is to make sure they do not becoming domineering or controlling. Once they have learned to admit that they have personal failings just like everyone else, their destiny is to help other people (practically and by example) achieve tangible results.

Power Thought

66 Today I will replace old habits of judgment with new habits of flexibility 99

Signs & symbols

Sun sign: Gemini

Ruling planet: Mercury, the communicator

Symbol: The Twins

Birth date ruler: Mars, the warrior

Tarot card: The Hermit (inner strength)

Favorable numbers: 5, 9

Lucky days: Wednesday and Tuesday, especially when these days fall on 5 and 9 of the month

Lucky colors: Orange, red, maroon

Birthstone: Agate

May 27

28 May

the birthday of rejuvenation

Your greatest challenge is ...

coping with boredom

The way forward is ...

to understand that feeling bored can actually be a positive experience as it can teach you vital life skills such as patience, gratitude and self-sufficiency.

You're drawn to people born on ...

July 24 to August 23

You share a passion for adventure and the new, and this can create a stimulating and intense relationship.

Luck maker

Dream for fifteen minutes daily

Set aside fifteen minutes a day, away from distractions or noise, and use it to think, imagine and dream. Tuning into your thoughts can make all the difference in helping you connect with your intuition.

People born on May 28 are active, versatile, innovative, and creative. Both at home and at work they are mentally sharp and physically agile, and they can think and act with lightning speed. They excel at concocting original schemes and are eager to see them produce results, before rushing onto the next.

Novelty, adventure and the excitement of the new are what these people crave, constantly seeking to reinvent themselves with traveling, visiting new places, meeting new people, and trying new things. Others find their silver-tongued charm hard to resist but they are doers as well as talkers, mastering any skill or discipline that is exciting enough to hold their interest. Competitive by nature, with a perfectionist streak and youthful assertiveness, they are well positioned for success.

They like to share their ideas with others but they can grow impatient when others seem slow to catch on. The problem lies in their choice of audience. They need to find a way to work independently from the mainstream in specialized areas where their flair, originality and versatility can be appreciated. It may take a while before they find their feet professionally and personally, perhaps moving from job to job or even from country to county, but when they do find their focus and an enlightened and adventurous audience, they usually succeed with spectacular flair and elegance.

Between the ages of twenty-four and fifty-four there are opportunities for them to find their place in life; after the age of fifty-five they may become more confident and creativity, allowing them to become more powerful in public positions. Throughout their lives, however, their quest for inner security will lead them to explore many avenues of knowledge and they will feel a need to constantly renew themselves with novel situations and stimuli. Even so, they will eventually find that the greatest success comes when they slow down and simplify their life. In fact, reflection and learning to savor their success might be the most rejuvenating change of all.

On the **dark** side

Restless,
impatient, hasty

At your **best**

Innovative, progressive,
versatile

Love *Not so fast*

In love, just as in other areas of their lives, rushing tends to be a problem for people born on May 28. They believe in love at first sight, and may rush into relationships and marriages too quickly, only to discover further down the line that there are basic incompatibilities. Once they learn to slow down their frenetic pace, however, they make loyal and exciting partners. Free spirits, they thrive best with partners who adore them but never try to control them.

Health *Calming lavender*

People born on this day hate to be bored and will constantly seek new challenges to test them. As a result they tend to be accident prone, but advising them to stop taking risks is impossible as it is so much a part of their personality. They would benefit, however, from the support and guidance of concerned loved ones who could encourage them to direct their energies positively and not recklessly. Since they love variety, their diet tends to be nutritious and energizing but they do need to avoid smoking and excessive consumption of alcohol. Vigorous and energetic competitive sports are recommended for exercise, although they need to beware of injuries to the arms and hands. Because they are so active, plenty of quality sleep is recommended but if their head is buzzing so much with new ideas, dropping a few drops of lavender, bergamot or jasmine essential oil on their pillow at night will ease tension and induce drowsiness.

Career *Born stage performers*

These people can make successful artists, writers, stage performers, or business entrepreneurs. They may also be drawn to careers in sales, promotion, commerce, publishing, and human resources. If they prefer to serve others, law and teaching may appeal, and if they want to become a specialist in their area they may become an advisor, psychologist or philosopher.

Destiny *To inspire with their perspective on life*

The life path of people born on this day is to learn the importance of patience and discipline. Once they have learned to slow down, their destiny is to inspire with their progressive, sometimes radical perspective on life.

Power Thought

" Today I will remember to stop and ask my intuition before acting "

Signs & symbols

Sun sign: Gemini

Ruling planet: Mercury, the communicator

Symbol: The Twins

Birth date ruler: Sun, the individual

Tarot card: The Magician

Favorable numbers: 1, 6

Lucky days: Wednesday and Sunday, especially when these days fall on 1 and 6 of the month

Lucky colors: Orange, yellow, gold

Birthstone: Agate

May 28

29 May

the birthday of the plate spinner

Your greatest challenge is ...

knowing what you want to do

The way forward is ...

to keep pushing ahead and trying out new experiences until you find what's right for you, remembering that nothing you do is ever wasted.

You're drawn to people born on ...

September 24 to October 23

You share a passion for romance and a need to be understood, and this can create an intense and loving union.

Luck maker

Mix with people you admire

Look for people who are trying to make a success of whatever they are trying to achieve and learn from them. Mix with people you admire and you will feel inspired to create your own success.

Others are often drawn to the vibrant charm of people born on May 29. They are determined to find a career or a cause that fulfills them but they also believe in sharing their talents. Exhibiting both hedonistic and altruistic tendencies, they manage to juggle these opposites extremely effectively.

They are not necessarily motivated by money, wealth or social position but they do need an audience. If they don't have a following of some kind they can become very frustrated because they are always "switched on," entertaining others with amusing observations and stimulating conversation. They have a way with people and words, and enjoy employing their diplomatic skills to resolve conflicts between others. Unfortunately, their desire to please or entertain others can lead them to repress anger, with sudden and sometimes violent outbursts becoming almost inevitable. They should learn to deal with distressing issues or situations when they appear instead of letting them fester dangerously beneath the surface.

So determined are these people to experience all that life has to offer and to win as many admirers as possible that they may find themselves with dozens of projects on the go. Remarkably, they have the creativity and versatility to keep all these projects running smoothly, and others will constantly wonder how they manage to do it. Beneath their apparently languid approach to multi-tasking lies a fierce determination and desire to be tested as often as possible.

It will take some time for these people to settle on a fulfilling career; until then they may be something of a jack of all trades. They have a tendency to spread their energies too thinly but between the ages of twenty-three and fifty-three there are opportunities for them to find their direction and focus as they search for emotional security and fulfillment. Wherever they decide to direct their energies, however, their greatest wish is to improve the lives of others; once they find a way to make this a reality, they possess the charisma and leadership skills to make the world a better place.

Love *Gregarious*

People born on May 29 are gregarious, charming, and romantic. They will rarely be short of admirers even when they are in a committed relationship, sometimes being interested in several people at one time. Once in a relationship they will put their heart and soul into it for as long as their passion lasts, but they can also suddenly and inexplicably turn cold. They need a partner who is sensitive and understanding and who has faith in their abilities.

Health *Listen to your fears*

Most people need to be told to face their fears but instead of rising to the challenge people born on this day need to pay greater attention to what their fears and insecurities are trying to tell them. They are among those rare people who could actually benefit from greater caution. They are accident prone and also prone to stress, coughs, colds, and bad circulation, so it is important for them to make sure they pace themselves, slow down if need be, and practice preventative medicine when it comes to their health. Their diet should be rich in fresh, natural produce and they need to take regular, moderate-intensity exercise to boost their immune system. Wearing, meditating on or surrounding themselves with the color blue will encourage them to stay calm and cool when important decisions need to be made.

Career *Born politicians*

These people will thrive in careers that are people orientated and which allow them to act as a mouthpiece or instrument to encourage progress or reform. Politics, law, business, and the arts will therefore all appeal. Their easy way with words may also enable them to be an author or a lecturer or to excel in sales; if attracted to business, they are likely to be successful as an agent or in the worlds of travel, technology or tourism.

Destiny *To improve and inspire the lives of others*

The life path of people born on this day is to narrow down their wide-ranging interests and discover their true vocation in life. Once they are able to find their focus, their destiny is to improve and inspire the lives of others through their words, their deeds or their legacy.

Power Thought

" Everything that happens to me helps me learn and grow "

Signs & symbols

Sun sign: Gemini

Ruling planet: Mercury, the communicator

Symbol: The Twins

Birth date ruler: Cancer, the intuitive

Tarot card: The High Priestess (intuition)

Favorable numbers: 2, 7

Lucky days: Wednesday and Monday, especially when these days fall on 2 or 7 of the month

Lucky colors: Orange, blue, silver

Birthstone: Agate

30 May

the birthday of mercurial sparkle

Your greatest challenge is ...

learning to focus your energies

The way forward is ...

to understand that scattering your energies all over the place is equivalent to scattering your potential.

You're drawn to people born on ...

November 23 to December 21

You share a passion for variety, adventure and intimacy, and this can create an exciting and intense union.

Luck maker

Improve your concentration

Developing the power of concentration is a luck-making essential because a focused mind is a powerful mind. If you find it hard to concentrate, meditation can help.

People born on May 30 tend to be versatile, talkative and expressive with a mental quickness that ensures they shine in social situations. They possess an astute and agile mind, and the insight to take advantage of opportunities.

With a thirst for knowledge and a sharp intellect, they may be involved in many diverse activities. Although they have a talent to succeed in a variety of fields, they need to guard against becoming too restless or scattering their energies with diverse interests. Their challenge is to pick only one field of interest and to commit themselves to it for the long haul. As gifted, capable, expansive, and energetic as they are, their insatiable hunger for change can lead them to neglect their commitments and let others down if they get bored with routine or want to move on without seeing things through.

These people can also change mood rapidly, sometimes in a split second. They may suddenly explode with anger, impatience or frustration, only to be laughing and teasing the next; excitable and passionate one day, they may be cold and serious the day after. Although this adds to their sparkle and appeal, it can also work against them by unnerving those who may doubt their reliability and commitment. Fortunately, between the ages of twenty-two and fifty-two they may focus on emotional security and finding a secure home base, providing opportunities for them to become more responsible and understanding in their relationships.

Thanks to their mercurial sparkle, they can be both difficult and delightful, sometimes at exactly the same time. The greatest lesson for them to learn is the commitment that is essential for success in all aspects of their lives. When a little staying power is combined with their great communication skills, limitless imaginative powers, enthusiasm, and refusal to be bound by convention, these people can be blessed with great innovatory power and the capacity to inspire others with their magical vision.

On the **dark** side

Irresponsible, flighty, nervous

At your **best**

Fast, gifted, expansive

Love *Restless*

People born on May 30 can charm others effortlessly with their enthusiasm and impulsiveness but they can also unsettle them with their restlessness. However, once they find an enthusiastic and adventurous lover with whom they can discuss their plans and dreams, they are capable of loyalty as long as plenty of fun and variety is injected into the relationship.

Health *On the run*

People born on this day have quick and sensitive minds that are easily thrown off balance and overwhelmed. They can therefore be prone to stress, insomnia, poor concentration, and other signs of overload. They would benefit greatly from scheduled windows of quiet, with minimal stimulation to allow their nervous system to recharge itself. As far as diet is concerned, they need to make sure they don't constantly eat on the go, keeping their junk food intake to a minimum. To keep up their energy and good spirits they need to make sure they eat a healthy, nutritious diet and avoid overloading themselves with caffeine, as this can make them feel more jumpy. Plenty of moderate-intensity exercise is important as it will boost their immune system and help ward off the respiratory infections to which they are prone. Wearing, meditating on or surrounding themselves with the colors blue and purple will help them feel calmer and more in control.

Career *Born day traders*

These people need careers that offer them plenty of variety and challenge, and they may be drawn to careers such as stockbroking, as well as artistic and sporting pursuits. Their talent with words may draw them toward writing, teaching, journalism, promotion, commerce, negotiating, and the world of entertainment. As natural psychologists they may also find occupations such as counseling, therapy or health care fulfilling.

Destiny *To influence, inspire and motivate others*

The life path of people born on this day is to learn to commit to people and projects. Once they have become more moderate in their approach to life, their destiny is to influence, inspire and motivate others with their enthusiasm, energy and vision.

Signs & symbols

Sun sign: Gemini

Ruling planet: Mercury, the communicator

Symbol: The Twins

Birth date ruler: Jupiter, the speculator

Tarot card: The Empress (creativity)

Favorable numbers: 3, 8

Lucky days: Wednesday and Thursday, especially when these days fall on 3 and 8 of the month

Lucky colors: Orange, deep purple, yellow

Birthstone: Agate

31 May

the birthday of clarity

Your greatest challenge is ...

coping with rejection

The way forward is ...

to understand that there is no such thing as failure if you learn from your experience. In fact, the road to success is often paved with failure.

You're drawn to people born on ...

January 21 to February 19

You share a passion for communication and uncomplicated displays of affection, and this can create an honest and loving union.

Luck maker

Turn rejection into resolve

Lucky people don't allow rejection to devastate them. However negative a situation seems, there is always something positive you can focus on or something you can learn to improve your chances of success next time.

People born on this day are often known for their strong views and no-nonsense approach to life. They carry out their work and personal life with the minimum of fuss and are capable of adapting easily to changing situations. Although the image they project is often one of toughness, their greatest desire isn't to be feared or even admired, but for their intentions and their words to be clearly understood by everyone.

Because they want their message to be understood clearly, they are extremely efficient, no detail ever escaping them. The downside of leaving no room for misinterpretation is that they can tend to repeat themselves, and this can irritate others. They can also be obsessed with doing rather than reflecting. Underneath all this, however, is often an underlying confusion; this confusion is almost what keeps them constantly on the go and can make them explode with anger and frustration. The key to their success is to find some kind of balance between their restlessness and talent for adaptation, and their need for structure and clarity. Neither constant activity nor inaction will bring them fulfillment; this lies somewhere in between.

Between the ages of twenty-one and fifty-one they are likely to have a growing need for personal intimacy and emotional security. This can often be a challenging time for them because their overpowering mind rules their lives; they need to avoid the tendency to squash any sign of weakness and should remember that they, like all people, are a combination of weakness and strength. If they can express this, their loved ones will feel closer to them and others will relate to them more easily. After the age of fifty-two there is a turning point which suggests a period of high creativity, confidence, authority, and strength.

Above all, these people have an air of authority and seriousness about them. Although they will benefit from letting their hair down occasionally, if they can direct their mind to being expansive rather than single-minded, they have the potential to achieve great success and possibly fame.

At your best

Confident, clear-sighted, capable

Love *No game playing*

In relationships people born on May 31 abhor game playing, valuing honesty and loyalty above all else in a relationship. They are very expressive and show their love with plenty of hugs and kisses, affection and love. They tend to be attracted to complicated and passionate people who will benefit from their directness and determination to make love work and work forever.

Health *Escapist*

Such is their self-confidence that failure is not an option for people born on this day; when they inevitably encounter setbacks and rejection, they can find it hard to cope and are likely to seek solace in escapist activities such as recreational drugs or alcohol. It is extremely important for them to be realistic in their approach to life, allowing themselves the possibility of failure with the understanding that dealing with disappointment is an important part of their psychological growth. There is also a tendency for them to be constantly on the go, never allowing themselves time to rest and to reflect or deal with their fears; it is important for them, therefore, to schedule enough quiet time into their lives so that their nervous system can recharge itself. A healthy, varied diet and plenty of exercise, preferably cross-training, will help them stay strong physically and emotionally. Wearing, meditating on and surrounding themselves with the color purple will encourage them to step back every now and again and think of higher things.

Career *Born writers*

These people are especially attracted to every form of art, be it music, dance, singing, drama, painting, sculpture, poetry, or writing; they may also find fulfillment in humanitarian work, teaching and people-related careers, and options such as public relations and promotions.

Destiny *To inspire others with their energy and enthusiasm for knowledge*

The life path of people born on this day is to learn to be more realistic in their approach to life. Once they have learned to be less black and white, their destiny is to find inner peace by inspiring others with their prodigious energy and enthusiasm for knowledge.

Signs & symbols

Sun sign: Gemini

Ruling planet: Mercury, the communicator

Symbol: The Twins

Birth date ruler: Uranus, the visionary

Tarot card: The Emperor (authority)

Favorable numbers: 4, 9

Lucky days: Wednesday and Sunday, especially when these days fall on 4 or 9 of the month

Lucky colors: Orange, grey, silver

Birthstone: Agate

1 June

the birthday of
the enigmatic student

Your greatest challenge is ...

understanding yourself

The way forward is ...

to understand that acquiring self-knowledge is a lifetime's task, and there will be good days and bad days.

You're drawn to people born on ...

July 24 to August 23

You share a passion for conversation and adventure, and this can create a stimulating and intense relationship.

Luck maker

Follow your own star

Lucky people believe in their own uniqueness and they attract all they need to discover to fulfill their life's purpose. You are the one and only you; only you can make the contribution you came here to make.

People adore the wit and humor of those born on June 1. They are often chatty, entertaining and fun to be around and even those who are less talkative will still have a mischievous sparkle in their eyes.

At work and in social settings they possess mercurial inquisitiveness, rarely concentrating on one subject alone because details bore them. There is one subject that never fails to fascinate them: human behavior. In all parts of their lives they tend to keep the focus on other people, often studying and imitating the styles of those at the top in the hope of achieving their success. Since feelings often follow behavior, this approach is often successful, leading them to success. The downside, however, is that they never get to know themselves or what their own talents, hopes and dreams are.

Their positive energy will attract many admirers; the danger is that they can be quite vain and may be tempted to flit from one admirer to another depending on who flatters them the most. This need for flattery is often the result of deep feelings of uncertainty and confusion. Despite their compulsive interest in others, they are private individuals who rarely reveal their deeper thoughts or feelings to others. They do need to get in touch with their own feelings and find what they want out of life; if they don't, they will find it impossible to attain their creative potential. Between the ages of twenty and fifty there will be opportunities for them to establish a sense of their own individuality; it is crucial during this time that they don't scatter their energies on causes and people unworthy of them. After the age of fifty they become more confident, assertive and self-assured.

If they can find the courage to trust their instincts they will be able to unite the enigmatic and melancholic aspects of their personality with those parts of themselves that are impulsive and charismatic. This will give them the focus and concentration they need to stop imitating others and realize their own unique potential.

On the dark side

Scattered, impatient, vain

At your best

Discerning, popular, sociable

Love *Fickle*

People born on June 1 will often have many admirers but few of them will really know them well. They will only open up in a secure relationship with an accepting mate. Love does come easy to them but they can easily get bored and there is a tendency for them to be fickle. They are attracted to complicated people but would thrive best with those who are more self-assured.

Health *Preventative medicine*

People born on this day simply don't have time to get ill because they are always on the go. They often have a distrust of doctors and an intense dislike of hospitals, but if they push themselves too hard and don't have regular health check-ups they could suffer from circulation problems, nervous exhaustion, respiratory infections, and lowered immunity. Because they are so impatient and find illness frustrating, the best advice for them is to practice preventative medicine, eating a healthy, varied diet and taking plenty of exercise, preferably in the fresh air. To clear their active mind whenever they feel stressed, they may want to put one drop of lemon onto a tissue and inhale the scent because it will help clear their brain and act as an antiviral protector. Wearing, meditating on or surrounding themselves with the color purple will help them focus on higher things.

Career *Born detectives*

These people have the potential to achieve success in such fields as marketing, advertising, the media, politics, and perhaps psychology or detective work. With their natural communication skills they also make great sales people and may be drawn to careers in writing, music or the theater. Whatever career they choose, there must always be an emphasis on change and variety.

Destiny *To bring a touch of glamour, magic or flair*

The life path of people born on this day is to find out what it is that they want. Once they have learned to look within, their destiny is to bring an inspiring touch of glamour, magic or flair to every enterprise they are involved in.

Signs & symbols

Sun sign: Gemini

Ruling planet: Mercury, the communicator

Symbol: The Twins

Birth date ruler: Sun, the individual

Tarot card: The Magician (will-power)

Favorable numbers: 1, 7

Lucky days: Wednesday and Sunday, especially when these days fall on 1 and 7 of the month

Lucky colors: Orange, sunflower yellow, gold

Birthstone: Agate

June 1

2 June

the birthday of ingenuity

Your greatest challenge is ...

enjoying the ordinary

The way forward is ...

to understand that a fulfilling and happy life is not one of extremes but of steady, positive feelings about every aspect of your life, even chores and routine.

You're drawn to people born on ...

January 21 to February 19

You share a passion for adventure, and this can create an exciting and intense union.

Luck maker

Make every day special

Lucky people understand that every day in their lives, including those that are without highlights, is unique and special; they never waste an opportunity to feel positive and upbeat about their lives.

Analytical and intense, people born on June 2 have a talent for unraveling complicated situations. Their lives are rarely problem-free, but they would have it no other way. They are at their happiest when they are testing their ingenuity; if life won't present them with problems to overcome, their natural response is to seek them out.

Their lives rarely run smoothly but they thrive during times of crisis; as quick-witted individuals who can readily analyze and adapt to a situation, they often devise an effective solution or course of action. They can be the life-savers who restore order, but their addiction to new stimuli or challenges can also work against them by unnecessarily complicating their lives and their relationships when things are running smoothly. Co-workers, for example, may resent their habit of playing devil's advocate and injecting difficulties into simple procedures; when a close relationship is going well they may develop bad habits like lateness or disorganization that threaten it.

The enthusiasm they have for problems and complications can attract them to people and causes that are troubled or unworthy. It is important that they remember the greatest challenge of all for them does not lie in the outside world but in getting to know themselves better. Between the ages of nineteen and forty-nine there are numerous opportunities for them to become more emotionally aware and tuned into themselves. They should take advantage of these because they offer great potential for fulfillment. After the age of fifty they enter a period of growing vitality and confidence.

If they can learn to focus less on external stimuli for a sense of fulfillment and more on their own talents and imaginative powers, their potential for success in whatever area of life they choose to focus on is limitless because they have highly developed intuitive powers. When directed to a cause that is worthy of them, these intuitive powers will lead them toward the satisfying sense of fulfillment that can only be gained from accessing their own unique and potentially spell-binding creativity.

Love *Don't try to change others, change yourself*

People born on June 2 may find themselves involved in difficult or testing relationship after relationship, but the only way for them to break out of this cycle is to understand that they cannot change others, they can only change themselves. When they do find a partner they love and who loves them back in turn, they must resist the temptation to cultivate excitement by creating tension.

Health *Bon appétit!*

People born on this day may have a tendency to gain weight and, because they love to dine out regularly, this can be extremely frustrating for them. Instead of going on fad diets, the best approach is to cut down on saturated fat, sugar, salt, processed and refined foods, and increase their intake of natural foods, particularly fruits and vegetables, whole grains, nuts, seeds, and oily fish. If this healthy, natural diet is combined with regular moderate to vigorous exercise, they will find that they can continue to entertain, dine out and party without the pounds piling on; although they should stay away as much as possible from rich sauces and red meat. Like many people born in early June they are prone to nervous exhaustion, so regular vacations and periods of rest and relaxation are essential. Wearing, meditating on and surrounding themselves with the color green will encourage them to feel more harmonious and balanced.

Career *Born troubleshooters*

These people thrive in careers that allow them autonomy in thought and action. They may find themselves drawn to the artistic sphere—especially as performers—and also to scientific research or as corporate troubleshooters or consultants. They also make excellent buyers, agents or negotiators, and their humanitarian streak may draw them to counseling.

Destiny *To inspire others with their resilience, ingenuity and flair*

The life path of people born on this day is to learn that change begins from the inside out. Once they are able to understand that life-changing fact, their destiny is to influence, motivate and inspire others with their resilience, ingenuity and flair.

Power Thought

" Every day offers me an opportunity to learn something new about myself "

June 2

Signs & symbols

Sun sign: Gemini

Ruling planet: Mercury, the communicator

Symbol: The Twins

Birth date ruler: Moon, the intuitive

Tarot card: The High Priestess (intuition)

Favorable numbers: 2, 8

Lucky days: Wednesday and Monday, especially when these days fall on 2 and 8 of the month

Lucky colors: Orange, pearl, silver

Birthstone: Agate

3 June

the birthday of original wit

Those born on June 3 have a wonderful way with words and their superb communication skills are the keys to their success, both personally and professionally. At work they use their persuasive powers to influence business negotiations and in social situations they use their sparkling wit to impress and entertain others, winning them many admirers.

Their ideas are always innovative and progressive; so much so that others may sometimes have problems understanding them. Not feeling understood can be an incredibly frustrating experience for them because they have plenty of important things to say and hate feeling misunderstood. Free spirits who need to express their individuality, if they feel their position is compromised or misrepresented they will defend their position passionately.

With a sharp wit and a fantastic sense of humor, their feelings run deep and they have a strong belief in the equality of all. But when disputes occur they are not afraid of using biting sarcasm to get their point of view across. Sometimes unaware that their comments can be so insensitive that they can greatly hurt others, it is important for them to become more sensitive to the effect their extreme words have on others. If they don't, others will shy away from them, a terrible punishment because one of their biggest fears is being ignored. Fortunately, between the ages of eighteen and forty-eight there are opportunities for them to become more sensitive to the feelings of others as there is an accent on personal relationships. After the age of forty-nine they have a strong need for self-expression and assertiveness.

Once they have learned to be more aware of the impact their words have on others and, ironically for such talented communicators, the impact that the seductive words of others have on them, there is very little to stop them reaching for the top. They will always be slightly eccentric or unconventional in their approach, but this originality is their driving force. Deep down they know that when they are true to themselves, life is infinitely more rewarding and fulfilling.

Love *Unique spirit*

People born on June 3 are attracted to those with high ideals and aspirations. They need to be careful, however, that they don't draw to them those who want to dampen their unique spirit in any way. They need deep intimacy and can be extremely warm and loving at times, but there may be conflicts between love and work.

Health *Regular check-ups*

People born on this day are often reluctant to visit the doctor, preferring to self-medicate or take the natural and holistic approach if they feel unwell. Generally their health is sound, but they are still advised to take regular check-ups and to listen to their doctor's advice if their health gives them a reason to do so. Regular exercise is highly recommended, as there is a tendency for these people to prefer mental to physical activity. As far as diet is concerned, plenty of variety, especially when it comes to fruits and vegetables, is recommended. Wearing, meditating on or surrounding themselves with the color orange encourages warmth, physical enjoyment and security.

Career *Born lecturers*

These people have the potential to excel in teaching, lecturing, research, and the performing arts, in particular music. A mentally challenging career is essential, and if research or education does not appeal they may find themselves drawn toward sales, writing, publishing, commerce, and industry.

Destiny *To inspire others with their original ideas*

The life path of people born on this day is to learn to be more lucid and sensitive in the presentation of their arguments. Once they are able to find this balance, their destiny is to express their original ideas, inspire others to participate in them and by so doing make their unique mark on the world.

Power Thought

❝I now choose to release every negative thought from my mind and my life❞

Signs & symbols

Sun sign: Gemini

Ruling planet: Mercury, the communicator

Symbol: The Twins

Birth date ruler: Jupiter, the philosopher

Tarot card: The Empress (creativity)

Favorable numbers: 3, 9

Lucky days: Wednesday and Thursday, especially when these days fall on 3 and 9 of the month

Lucky colors: Orange, purple, yellow

Birthstone: Agate

June 3

4 June

the birthday of the apprentice

Your greatest challenge is …

acknowledging your emotions

The way forward is …

to understand that every emotion, even so-called negative ones such as anger, fear and envy, has something important to tell you.

You're drawn to people born on …

January 21 to February 19

You both have intelligence and a inquisitive approach to life, and this can be a fulfilling and loving union.

Luck maker

Put first things first

Lucky people put first things first and last things last. Although work is important, the physical and emotional well-being of themselves and the people they care about is more so.

The intellectual powers of those born on this day are spectacular. The key to their success is an education or apprenticeship that can help nurture their quick minds and they are at their best when they are in the role of student acquiring new knowledge.

With an intense desire to learn and perfect themselves, they are always hungry for novel information or new challenges. Their natural curiosity is one of their greatest strengths but it can also turn into a weakness if they rely on it too much and neglect their emotional side. If trapped in the learning stage, they run the risk of losing some of their flexibility and identity by becoming totally absorbed with the project in hand. They can, moreover, explode with anger if their work is interrupted.

It is important for them to place more of an emphasis on the perceptive, feeling part of their nature, especially in close personal relationships. Fortunately, between the ages of seventeen and forty-seven there are plenty of opportunities for them to focus on the importance of their emotional well-being. They need to take advantage of these opportunities; if they neglect them they could end up becoming workaholics, with all the loneliness and lack of fulfillment that this lifestyle suggests. After the age of forty-eight they are likely to become more confident and there will be opportunities for them to realize their visions.

People born on this day have great leadership potential but until they grow in self-confidence they are often happiest working as part of a team, to which they will always be an asset given their excellent organizational and technical skills. Once they have learned to tune into their own and others' feelings, they will grow in confidence and discover a creative potential within themselves that may have been lying dormant. They should aim to cultivate and develop that potential, as not only will it help them progress from the apprentice stage to becoming more powerful in their own right, it is the key to their fulfillment as a human being.

Love *Develop your nurturing side*

There is a tendency for people born on June 4 to allow work take precedence over their personal life, but it is important for their psychological development that they learn to accentuate the feeling, sensitive and nurturing part of their nature. They need to understand that a relationship is about warmth, reassurance and small acts of kindness and concern as well as intellectual stimulation.

Health *Laughter is the best medicine*

People born on this day may be prone to waist gain, especially in mid-life, but they can manage the flab situation by making sure they eat healthily and get lots of vigorous exercise. Long hours studying or working will take their toll on their physical and emotional health, so they also need to make sure they give themselves plenty of opportunities to relax and unwind. A little on the serious side, they could certainly benefit from having more fun; laughter is the best therapy for those born on this day. Mind–body techniques such as meditation and yoga will also help lift their spirits and remind them that they are in control of their thoughts and their emotional well-being. Wearing, meditating on and surrounding themselves with the color yellow will encourage them to be more optimistic and creatively confident.

Career *Born researchers*

These people have an aptitude for study and would make excellent teachers, researchers and lecturers. Once they are able to get in touch with their creative side they may also be drawn to art, music, dance, and drama. They enjoy sharing their knowledge with others and working in a team so they may also excel in sales, publishing, advertising, and journalism.

Destiny *To share their knowledge with others*

The life path of people born on this day is to learn to have more confidence in their own creativity. Once they have got in touch with their intuition, their destiny is to achieve progress by sharing their knowledge with others.

Power Thought

" Today I am an open channel for original ideas "

Signs & symbols

Sun sign: Gemini

Ruling planet: Mercury, the communicator

Symbol: The Twins

Birth date ruler: Uranus, the visionary

Tarot card: The Emperor (authority)

Favorable numbers: 1, 4

Lucky days: Wednesday and Sunday, especially when these days fall on 1 and 4 of the month

Lucky colors: Orange, lavender, yellow

Birthstone: Agate

June 4

5 June

the birthday of the intellectual juggler

Your greatest challenge is …

learning to pace yourself

The way forward is …

to understand that just because you are capable of doing lots of things at once doesn't mean you have to.

You're drawn to people born on …

August 24 to September 23

You share a passion for intellectual stimulation and thoughtfulness, and this can create a fulfilling and intense union.

Luck maker

Get rid of "what ifs"

Lucky people understand that "what ifs" rob their present and distort their future. If you are always exhausted by worrying about things that aren't going to happen, you won't have the energy to go after what you want.

People born on June 5 can often be found successfully juggling ideas and projects simultaneously. They also have the ability to generate such innovative ideas that others either admire or fail to understand them. Indeed, their vision and soaring imagination seem unlimited in their scope.

With their unlimited energy, expansive mind, excellent conversation skills, and ability to get things done, they are always in demand. Born to stimulate others to think, they are always seeking to unearth some great discovery or mystery. The key to their success, however, lies in their ability to communicate effectively with others. If they are misunderstood, however, it is likely to wound them deeply and express itself in flashes of anger, irritation or nervous tension. Learning to be more patient and focused in the presentation of their thoughts and listening to what others have to say will help them get their point across more effectively.

Between the ages of sixteen and forty-six they may focus on emotional security, and security and home issues are likely to come to the fore. It is important during this time that they learn to guard against sudden anger, obstinacy and criticism in the way they communicate with others. Born worriers, they also need to learn to manage their own negativity and hold on to the dreams that inspire them when others perceive them as unrealistic or unfeasible. After the age of forty-seven there is a turning point which signals a period of growing self-confidence and strength, allowing them to become more outgoing and hopefully more measured in their approach to others.

These people have boundless energy and creativity; although they should never lose their vitality, they do need to learn how to channel it effectively. They also have the ability to multi-task, but learning to become more focused will work to their advantage. Once they are able to find balance between their intellect and their instincts, they have the imaginative gifts, technical aptitude and steadfastness of focus needed to develop their novel ideas and share them successfully with others.

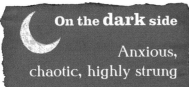

On the **dark** side

Anxious, chaotic, highly strung

At your **best**

Articulate, versatile, intelligent

Love *What lies beneath*

People born on June 5 often have plenty of friends and admirers because they are genuinely interested in people and extremely warm and generous. However, few of these people will really know them well and only after they have found the perfect partner will they start to open up and reveal their true and passionate nature within.

Health *Put it in the diary*

People born on this day are always on the go and appear to have limitless energy. Generally their health is good but they do need to be careful not to rely on caffeine, cigarettes, alcohol, and other stimulants. They also need to make sure they recharge their batteries with plenty of rest and relaxation with friends and loved ones. As far as diet and exercise are concerned, a routine approach is recommended to help keep their hectic lifestyle balanced. For example, mealtimes and snacks should be regular and sessions of exercise should be put into their diary. They would benefit from meditation techniques to help control their tendency to think negatively; wearing, meditating on and surrounding themselves with the color blue will encourage them to stay cool and in control.

Career *Born comics*

These people have a talent for using language and possess the originality of thought to become great comics, writers, poets, and lyricists. The realm of science and technology will also allow their talents to flourish, and their verbal skills may serve them well in law, diplomacy, business, advertising, merchandising, art administration or dealership, and healthcare.

Destiny *To inspire and even shock others with their ideas or approach*

The life path of people born on this day is to learn to worry less and live more. Once they are able to manage their negativity, their destiny is to refresh, inspire and occasionally shock others with their innovative ideas or approach.

Power Thought

" Today I let go of my worry and uncertainty "

Signs & symbols

Sun sign: Gemini

Ruling planet: Mercury, the communicator

Symbol: The Twins

Birth date ruler: Mercury, the communicator

Tarot card: The Hierophant (spiritual guidance)

Favorable numbers: 2, 5

Lucky day: Wednesday, especially when it falls on 2 and 5 of the month

Lucky colors: Orange, cobalt blue, red

Birthstone: Agate

June 5

315

6 June

the birthday of anticipation

Your greatest challenge is ...

avoiding feeling misunderstood by others

The way forward is ...

to put yourself in your audience's shoes and to tailor the presentation of your vision to the interests of your audience.

You're drawn to people born on ...

September 24 to October 23

You share a passion for communication, adventure and commitment, and this can create a close and happy union.

Luck maker

Be flexible

We all want things on our own terms, but lucky people know that if they are flexible life can be more satisfying and enjoyable.

Whenever people born on June 6 enter the room there is a sense of excitement and anticipation. They are people who know how to make things happen and others instinctively sense this. They have no problem communicating their progressive ideals and will work steadfastly to make them a reality, often gaining a following with their commitment to improve the lives of everyone.

Although these people are movers and shakers, they can take their ideals or vision to an extreme; this can manifest in unusual or dangerous behavior. More conventional people may find their wilder side expresses itself in extreme hobbies, unusual relationships, or strange and wonderful fantasies. Sometimes their dreams and ideals are so far-reaching that others may find them opaque; this can be deeply distressing to them as they live to share, inspire and reform. Learning to express themselves with greater simplicity will help them get their point across.

Although they should never rein in their wonderful energy, they should find some kind of balance so their more bizarre tendencies do not alienate others and isolate themselves. Fortunately, between the ages of fifteen and forty-five they are likely to be more restrained and security conscious, with a strong focus on their family, home and intimate personal life. However, when they reach the age of forty-six there is an increased need for self-expression and leadership; during this time they are likely to become more assertive and confident, taking more of a public role. It is important at this time that they understand how their actions serve as a role model for others and that a more balanced approach to life will help others relate to them.

Once they have found an audience they can relate to and who can relate to them, they more than live up to the anticipation that their progressive visions have created. The relief that they feel in finally being understood will encourage them to express their caring nature and, in their typically extreme way, their revolutionary determination to change the world.

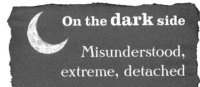

On the **dark** side

Misunderstood, extreme, detached

At your **best**

Idealistic, visionary, artistic

Love *Born to love*

Love and friendship come easily to people born on June 6. Friends can sometimes find them stubborn and inflexible in their views, but they more than make up for it with their compassion, vivaciousness, enthusiasm, and madcap humor. Their chosen partner will be someone who can share many adventures with them but who is also hardworking, reliable and able to give them a sense of security.

Health *Going to extremes*

The greatest threat to the health of people born on this day is themselves. They will often take their far-reaching ideas to extreme lengths, putting themselves in danger in the process. This may involve excessive overwork but also endurance tests, dubious schemes, extreme behavior, mind games, or other destructive acts. If family and friends are not available, counseling or psychotherapy might be advised to help them get in touch with their feelings and to understand why they have the need to push the limits. As far as diet is concerned, they need to avoid extremes, sticking with a healthy and varied diet that can keep their moods balanced and their active minds well nourished. Moderate to mild exercise, such as brisk walking or swimming, is recommended to help them feel calmer and more centered. Wearing, meditating on or surrounding themselves with the color blue will encourage them to feel more rational and in control of their lives.

Career *Born event organizers*

These people are likely to excel in careers that allow their unusual ideas to flourish, and they may be drawn to design, art, writing, music, drama, dance, advertising, sales, journalism, education, and entertainment. They may also make great wedding or party planners and, if they can develop the ability to enquire rationally and logically, scientists and technologists.

Destiny *To inspire others with their independence of thought*

The life path of people born on this day is to learn the importance of compromise. Once they have managed to strike a balance between their minds and their hearts, their destiny is to influence and inspire others with their independence of thought.

Signs & symbols

Sun sign: Gemini

Ruling planet: Mercury, the communicator

Symbol: The Twins

Birth date ruler: Venus, the lover

Tarot card: The Lovers (choices)

Favorable numbers: 3, 6

Lucky days: Wednesday and Friday, especially when these days fall on 3 and 6 of the month

Lucky colors: Orange, pink, yellow

Birthstone: Agate

June 6

7 June

the birthday of the seduction

Many people think that the colorful individuals born on June 7 live in a land of make-believe; in fact it is an inner world full of great ideas and potential. Their enchanting verve and style captivates people's imagination and, more often than not, these seductive individuals are fashion icons or trendsetters.

Whatever they decide to do, it will be slightly ahead of its time. They instinctively know how to reach people with their creative energy; they enjoy the process of seduction and invest much energy in non-verbal signals. They often take great pains over their appearance and in many social situations their clothes, body language and eyes do the talking for them—sometimes too much talking, as they are not afraid of being shocking or sensational. They also have a fantastic sense of humor and fun, and life is always entertaining when they are around. Instinctively grasping the seductive powers of surprise and humor, they delight in shocking people and making them smile.

If they don't get in touch with their feelings, however, they run the risk of living life on a superficial level. When this happens, instead of being captivating and enchanting, others may start to think of them as unreliable, forgetful and unfocused and they could find themselves alone. Often possessing an instinct to run away, it is important therefore for them to try and probe their lives more deeply. Fortunately, before the age of forty-four there are significant opportunities for them to focus more on their inner life. After the age of forty-five there is a turning point which encourages greater self-expression and assertiveness; as long as they guard against self-absorption, these are the years they can really come into their own.

People born on this day have a rich inner life and they need to make sure that they don't subordinate this to material concerns or refuse to acknowledge or express it because they fear others might think them odd. They aren't odd—they're just full of unique and special potential.

Love *Thrill of the chase*

People born on June 7 will endlessly fantasize about love. They have a passionate nature and strong desire, together with the charm and charisma to easily draw admirers to them. Because they love the thrill of the chase, commitment to one person may be a problem; but a close, loving relationship with one special person is the secret to their emotional fulfillment and an ideal they should work toward.

Health *Mirror, mirror on the wall*

People born on this day are often fascinated by their own appearance and will do as much as they can to enhance or change it if the fancy takes them. Personal grooming is essential for them but they need to be careful not to take this to extremes, becoming too self-absorbed and vain in the process. As far as diet is concerned, they understand the connection between junk food, weight problems and poor health; they are therefore likely to eat healthily but they do have a sweet tooth and may occasionally indulge in binges, although it won't be long before they get things back under control. They enjoy exercise and can benefit greatly from it as long as they don't take it to extremes. Wearing, meditating and surrounding themselves with the color purple will encourage them to think more of higher things, as would spiritual or self-help books and practicing meditation.

Career *Born entertainers*

These people love to enchant an audience, and are natural performers and entertainers. They also make great party planners, sales people and publishers. Other career choices that might appeal include teaching, lecturing, writing, marketing, advertising, commerce, or law.

Destiny *To enchant the world with their charisma and magic*

The life path for people born on this day is to learn to look within themselves for a sense of fulfillment. Once they have been able to look at their lives more deeply, their destiny is to enchant the world with their special brand of charisma and magic.

Signs & symbols

Sun sign: Gemini

Ruling planet: Mercury, the communicator

Symbol: The Twins

Birth date ruler: Neptune, the speculator

Tarot card: The Chariot (resilience)

Favorable numbers: 4, 7

Lucky days: Wednesday and Monday, especially when these days fall on 4 and 7 of the month

Lucky colors: Orange, sky blue, yellow

Birthstone: Agate

June 7

8 June

the birthday of
expectation

Your greatest challenge is ...

knowing how to relax

The way forward is ...

to understand that time out is not time wasted but time gained; you will return to your work with greater enthusiasm, energy and clarity.

You're drawn to people born on ...

April 21 to May 21

You are both loyal, hardworking and romantic individuals, and this can be a rewarding and fulfilling relationship.

Luck maker

Anchor your goals in reality

Lucky people affirm clear goals for themselves but they make sure these goals are within reason. So be realistically optimistic in your goal setting.

People born on June 8 are honest and direct in their approach to life. They speak their mind and, because they have such high expectations of themselves and others, despise laziness or injustice in any form.

Although highly independent and quite happy to work alone, people born on this day will often find themselves in the position of leader. This is because they have a strong sense of fair play and understand the importance of adhering to rules—as long as these rules are their own. They also make great leaders because they set an inspiring example in their wholehearted dedication to their life's work, be that running a business, heading a team or raising a family. There is a danger, however, that their dedication and industriousness can tip over into workaholism.

Until the age of forty-three they focus on home and their emotional life. Their basic nature is to be personable and fun, so it is important during this time that they don't let their spontaneity disappear. In their attempt to be just, they should also make sure they don't become harsh or judgmental, placing impossible expectations of loyalty and dedication on themselves and others. After the age of forty-four they become more self-expressive and assertive, but they need to make sure that they do not become preachy toward others and overly zealous in their attitude to work. The key to their success and fulfillment both personally and professionally is to balance their emotional needs with their strong sense of responsibility. As they approach the age of seventy, they start to become more practical and analytical, and the emphasis turns toward serving others.

The integrity, industriousness and devotion that they are capable of enable them to blaze a pioneering trail through life and build a wide social circle. Once they can develop empathy and a greater tolerance for their own vulnerabilities and those of others, the high expectation of fulfillment that they have always had will be realized in their own success and happiness.

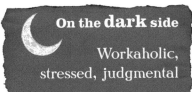
At your **best**

Independent, honest, dedicated

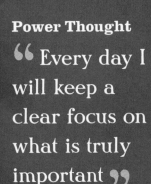

Power Thought

❝ Every day I will keep a clear focus on what is truly important ❞

Love *Fun to be around*

People born on June 8 are great fun to be around, but their long absences and commitment to work may put their friendships and relationships at risk. They need to make sure that they set enough time aside for their relationships and cultivate a sense of play. They also need to find ways to express their feelings to others and not allow hidden insecurities to manifest in quarrelsome or judgmental behavior.

Health *An active life*

Exercise is vital for people born on this day, and if they don't already have an exercise routine in place they are strongly advised to make one. This is because exercise will not only boost their immunity and self-esteem and keep their weight down; it will force them to take time out to concentrate on their well-being. There is a tendency for them to become workaholics and, if this isn't checked, they could become victims of stress and depression. Exercise, a healthy diet rich in mood-boosting fruits, vegetables, oily fish, nuts, and seeds, together with time spent relaxing with loved ones, will help them feel more in balance. Wearing, meditating on and surrounding themselves with the color orange will increase feelings of warmth, physical enjoyment and security.

Career *Born architects*

These people are especially well equipped for science-related careers, such as research and computer programming, but design-related careers such as architecture, landscaping and planning are also favored. Other careers that might interest them include law, education, banking, or accountancy. This date also shows potential for success in show business, art and music.

Destiny *To influence and guide others with their powers of perception*

The life path of people born on this day is to learn to balance their sense of integrity and fair play with a more liberal approach to life. Once they are able to find this balance, their destiny is to influence and guide others with their incisive powers of perception.

Signs & symbols

Sun sign: Gemini

Ruling planet: Mercury, the communicator

Symbol: The Twins

Birth date ruler: Saturn, the teacher

Tarot card: Strength (passion)

Favorable numbers: 5, 8

Lucky days: Wednesday and Saturday, especially when these days fall on 5 and 8 of the month

Lucky colors: Orange, hunter green, yellow

Birthstone: Agate

June 8

9 June

the birthday of unexpected opportunity

Your greatest challenge is …

being consistent

The way forward is …

to understand that consistency and responsibility are not limiting energies but extremely creative ones; without them, no project stands a chance.

You're drawn to people born on …

Mary 21 to April 20

You are both fiery, passionate and gentle, and this can create an intense and exciting union.

Luck maker

Don't give up so soon

Lots of people miss out on good fortune because they aren't patient enough to wait for it; lucky people are patient people.

People born on June 9 have a wonderful zest for life. They have limitless energy and others may find it hard to keep up with their ever-changing thoughts, feelings and emotions. Although they have quick minds and a logical orientation, everything about them is unexpected.

They have a quick temper but are quick to forgive. In their world view they are forthright and strong-willed, but in personal relationships they can be surprisingly passive and reserved. They are unconventional in their behavior but respectful toward authority. They are sympathetic and generous to those less fortunate, but sometimes insensitive and neglectful to their loved ones. Because they have so many different faces to present to the world they are endlessly fascinating individuals.

Action is a key word for them and they thrive on challenges and variety. Life can be a mad rush between one activity and another; they have little spare time, so great is their hunger for all that life has to offer. It is important for them occasionally to slow down and catch their breath. If they don't they may find that their lives descend into chaos. They should also aim to bring all aspects of their personality into an integrated whole; if they don't their lives will be governed by impulse rather than a clear sense of direction or purpose. Until the age of forty-two they focus on home, security and family; it is likely that they will spend longer than normal living with their parents or near their parents' home, being unwilling to branch out on their own. Around the age of forty-two, however, there is a turning point which emphasizes energy, power and self-confidence; these are the years when they can really come into their own.

Above all, people born on this day are spectacularly colorful and versatile individuals; if they can learn to harness their primitive instincts and channel their energies into mature goals that are worthy of them, they will find that life offers them a series of unexpected but well-deserved opportunities for happiness, success and fulfillment.

Love *Don't rush into love*

People born on June 9 fall in love easily but, as with everything else, they can rush into love and make the wrong decisions in the heat of passion. They can also put their relationships in jeopardy by not investing enough time and energy in them; they need to understand that relationships, like flowers, need work and tender care for them to flourish and grow into something beautiful.

Health *Love to move*

People born on this day love to move and they are often naturally good at sports of all kinds. They particularly enjoy competitive sports and athletics. If exercise has faded from their lives, it is important for them to incorporate it back as it is an endless source of enjoyment for them. As far as diet and lifestyle are concerned, they need to keep things simple and as fresh and natural as possible, steering clear of alcohol, smoking and recreational drugs of all kinds. Mind–body therapies such as massage, yoga and tai chi are also extremely beneficial for them, as these all encourage them to relax and get in tune with their inner selves. Wearing, meditating on or surrounding themselves with the color yellow will encourage them to be more self-aware and self-confident.

Career *Born rock climbers*

These people generally prefer careers that are active or hands-on to those that are administrative; they would excel in a multitude of professions ranging from writing, music and drama to medical research, politics or computing. They may be particularly drawn to careers that involve plenty of fresh air and activity, such as sport, rock climbing, tourism, and farming. Journalism may also appeal, as would careers working with children or being self-employed.

Destiny *To inspire others to reach for their dreams*

The life path of people born on this day is to learn to get to know themselves better. Once they have been able to bring all the different parts of their personality together, their destiny is to stay young at heart and by so doing to inspire others to reach for their dreams.

Signs & symbols

Sun sign: Gemini

Ruling planet: Mercury, the communicator

Symbol: The Twins

Birth date ruler: Mars, the warrior

Tarot card: The Hermit (inner strength)

Favorable numbers: 6, 9

Lucky days: Wednesday and Tuesday, especially when these days fall on 6 and 9 of the month

Lucky colors: Orange, crimson, yellow

Birthstone: Agate

June 9

10 June

the birthday of dichotomy

People born on June 10 are gifted but extreme individuals with strongly held views they are not afraid to express. They have an abundance of talent and ideas, and boundless energy to put them to good use. Everything about them exudes vitality, confidence and charisma but, despite this, they can suffer from bouts of crippling insecurity and self-doubt.

They are experts at keeping up a happy front in both their professional and personal lives but underneath they have a serious and intense mind prone to negativity and worry. This dichotomy between public persona and personal fears splits their personality, making it hard for them to feel truly happy and fulfilled. They are unwilling to acknowledge their insecurities to others because it would mean admitting them to themselves. They would rather run, hide or lose themselves in either the confident persona they have created or in sex, passion or violence. But if they faced their inner demons and acknowledged them, they would find a sense of contentment and inner peace.

Until the age of forty-one they may focus on emotional security, home and family life; they should take advantage of these opportunities to get in touch with their feelings and build up a network of close friends to whom they can open up. After the age of forty-two they enter a period of increasing self-confidence, authority, strength and self-expression. If during this period they make sure they don't avoid problems or let other people walk all over them, these are the years where they are most likely to develop their talents successfully and really come into their own.

Above all, people born on this day should not underestimate their ability to cope in life because they are capable of bold and daring action once they confront their obstacles directly. The greatest challenge for them will be confronting their inner fears. Once they find the courage to do that, they will discover within themselves a powerhouse of creativity and star potential to achieve not just one, but all of their amazing dreams.

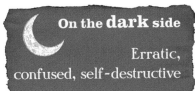

On the **dark** side
Erratic, confused, self-destructive

At your **best**
Gifted, warm, daring

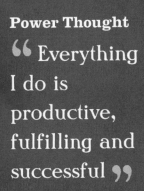

Power Thought
" Everything I do is productive, fulfilling and successful "

Love *Make up your mind*

People born on June 10 do have a tendency to have more than one love interest hanging around, but for the sake of their own happiness they need to learn to make up their mind and commit to one special person. They are often attracted to intelligent personalities who can help teach them to develop a more serious attitude to love.

Health *Self-destructive tendencies*

People born on this day have self-destructive tendencies and they need to make sure that they stay away from recreational drugs, drink, alcohol, and violence. Depression is another danger, and the way to avoid that is to make sure that they surround themselves with optimistic and positive people, not those who will flatter them insincerely and ultimately drag them down. As far as diet is concerned, they need to aim for variety and as many cooked meals as possible instead of eating on the go. Exercise is essential as it will help them release pent-up anger and frustration, boosting their mood. Brisk walking is particularly recommended, as are dancing, swimming and cycling. They are prone to respiratory infections and should also watch out for injuries to their arms and hands. Wearing, meditating on and surrounding themselves with the color green will help them feel less split and more in balance.

Career *Born theater stars*

These people have tremendous energy and stamina, being well suited to careers in live theater as well as the military or the police. They may also excel at public relations, diplomacy, sales, education, journalism, photography, or any career that involves plenty of variety and change, as they do not like routine.

Destiny *To develop their innovative and inspirational potential*

The life path of people born on this day is to learn to deal with their fears. Once they have found the courage to be themselves, their destiny is to develop their innovative and inspirational potential.

Signs & symbols

Sun sign: Gemini

Ruling planet: Mercury, the communicator

Symbol: The Twins

Birth date ruler: Sun, the individual

Tarot card: The Wheel of Fortune (change)

Favorable numbers: 1, 7

Lucky days: Wednesday and Sunday, especially when these days fall on 1 and 7 of the month

Lucky colors: Orange, silver, white

Birthstone: Agate

June 10

11 June

the birthday of expansion

Your greatest challenge is ...

dealing with domestic responsibilities

The way forward is ...

to understand that great fulfillment can only be found when all areas of their lives, including the domestic, are harmonized.

You're drawn to people born on ...

September 24 to October 23

You share a passion for progressive ideas, but also a need to feel nurtured and secure within a relationship.

Luck maker

Diversify your goals

Studies have shown that happiness is greater among those whose lives are generally positive in many areas rather than in simply one area.

Disciplined, energetic, perceptive, and optimistic, the ambitious people born on June 11 will often push their way toward their goals with surprising force, tearing down any obstacles in their path. Their driving force is always to push ahead, test their limits and expand their knowledge and experience.

With the enviable ability to lose themselves wholly in their work, their aim is to learn as much as possible in one specialist area and then move the goal posts by pioneering a breakthrough. Their sense of fair play and willingness to get their hands dirty makes them a much-sought-after team player. Less evolved individuals born on this day who find themselves lacking the support of others may find their self-absorption has slipped into arrogance or egotism. If they can change their approach to one of sensitivity and humility, they may find that others are more willing to seek them out.

Their remarkable zest for life and outstanding potential to make the important breakthrough means they have little time for those with less energy or enthusiasm. They despise being around negative or depressed people because they instinctively understand that a positive attitude increases their chances of success. But happiness and success are not always enough for them because their greatest desire is excellence; this is why they will often be found pushing their work or lifestyle to new heights. Although this winning attitude can take them to the very top, it can lead to emotional isolation when co-workers or friends find their constant pushing to be exhausting.

Fortunately, before the age of forty-one there are opportunities for them to develop a sense of emotional security. They should ensure they take advantage of these and don't neglect their friends and family. After the age of forty-two they become more confident and aggressive in their approach; if they have learned to recognize the damaging effect their obsessive tendencies can have on themselves and others, this is the period when they have the potential to achieve truly great breakthroughs not just in their careers but in their lives.

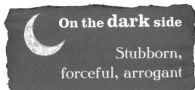

At your **best**

Progressive, positive, disciplined

Love *Personal charm*

People born on June 11 have great personal charm, and a desire to protect and nurture those they love. Having said that, they can also find it hard to sustain their family life. It's not that they don't care; it's simply that the lure of outside interests draws them away from domestic chores and responsibilities. They need an intelligent partner who can give them a sense of security but also plenty of personal space.

Health *Work to live*

People born on this day tend to live to work, not work to live, and this can lead to obsession if taken to extremes. Fortunately, they often enjoy their work so the negative effects of being a workaholic are limited. Even so, they do need to establish a more healthy work–life balance, because if they don't they will end up feeling emotionally isolated. As far as diet is concerned, more time and care need to be taken in its preparation as they tend to eat on the go. Regular exercise will be beneficial since it will encourage them to have a more balanced perspective on life. Too busy to be ill, they may also neglect the importance of regular health check-ups and are advised to see their doctor if anything concerns them. Wearing, meditating on and surrounding themselves with the color orange will increase feelings of warmth, physical enjoyment and emotional security.

Career *Born marathon runners*

These people are attracted to the realms of scientific research, artistic innovation and sport. They are bright and versatile, with excellent communication skills, so could thrive in any career; but they may find themselves drawn toward social work, politics, business, law, and the civil service. If they develop their innate creativity, they may also be drawn to film, painting or music.

Destiny *To pioneer significant breakthroughs*

The life path of people born on this day is to learn to sustain a settled and happy family or social life. Once they have learned not to sacrifice their personal to their professional lives, their destiny is to push the boundaries and pioneer significant breakthroughs.

Signs & symbols

Sun sign: Gemini

Ruling planet: Mercury, the communicator

Symbol: The Twins

Birth date ruler: Moon, the intuitive

Tarot card: Justice (discernment)

Favorable numbers: 2, 8

Lucky days: Wednesday and Monday, especially when these days fall on 2 and 8 of the month

Lucky colors: Orange, buttermilk, beige

Birthstone: Agate

June 11

12 June

the birthday of realistic positivity

Your greatest challenge is ...

facing your fears and insecurities

The way forward is ...

to understand that acknowledging you have fears and insecurities actually reduces their power over you. Once the enemy is understood, it is far easier to manage.

You're drawn to people born on ...

November 23 to December 24

You both share a cheerful disposition, and this can be an exciting and fulfilling union.

Luck maker

Ask your intuition questions

Lucky people interact with their intuition or inner wisdom as if it were a palpable force in their lives. They ask questions and expect to receive answers that will improve their good fortune.

People born on this day tend to have a cheerful disposition and their optimistic, positive approach to life serves them well. Their strong belief in the power of good also has an uplifting effect on those around them, helping other people change for the better.

Extremely generous and supportive of others, their positivity is always tempered by realism. They support or value what they know they can achieve or what they believe others can achieve. Their aim is not to make things perfect, but better in the belief that the best way to help someone is to encourage them to help themselves. Occasionally this can manifest in judgmental words but their cruel-to-be-kind approach generally works.

The sunny disposition that the self-contained people born on this day present to the world bestows upon them the capacity not only to achieve great things but also to be pioneers in many aspects of their lives. They can't bear inertia and will push themselves to their limits, even devising new activities for friends and family or learning a new language or skill. The downside to all this cheerfulness is that it can sometimes be irritating to others, who may see them as lacking in depth. Although they can give the appearance of being superficial, inner conflicts often lie beneath their cheerful exterior. It is important for them not to try and bury these conflicts with external activities; if they do, it will lead to deep unhappiness.

Until the age of thirty-nine they focus on emotional security and need to take advantage of opportunities to learn about love and understanding. After the age of forty they become more self-confident and their personal capabilities are often recognized. During this time they need to make sure they surround themselves with people who challenge them intellectually or emotionally, and who encourage them to focus inwards. Once they have learned to understand themselves and others better and connect with their intuition, their infectious dynamism and creativity will be validated by remarkable achievements in all aspects of their lives.

Love *Self-knowledge*

Pursuing self-knowledge and deepening their emotional awareness will help people born on June 12 become lucky in love. They need to understand that loving someone else is impossible if they don't love themselves first. They need to make sure they avoid cynical, manipulative and superficial people, and find a partner who is as intelligent, positive, loving, and giving as themselves.

Health *You are not invincible*

People born on this day have an extremely positive attitude toward their health and this generally serves them well, but they do need to remember that they are not invincible and regular health check-ups are advised. As far as diet is concerned, they should aim for variety and food that is as fresh and natural as possible. Regular exercise, in particular solitary activities such as running, swimming and cycling, is recommended as not only will it boost their immunity, it will also give them time alone to think and gather their thoughts. Wearing, meditating on and surrounding themselves with the color purple will encourage them to look within and find inner peace.

Career *Born motivational speakers*

These people would make excellent motivational speakers or personal coaches. Their strong organizational skills also suit them to work in a variety of professions, from outdoor physical work to administrative jobs. Occupations such as travel and tourism may suit their adventurous spirit; their love of action may attract them to careers involving sport or leisure, and their sensitivity may draw them to careers in medicine, drama or music.

Destiny *To encourage, motivate and inspire others by their example*

The life path of people born on this day is to learn to understand themselves better. Once they have become more self-aware, their destiny is to lead, encourage, motivate, and inspire others by their example or their words.

Signs & symbols

Sun sign: Gemini

Ruling planet: Mercury, the communicator

Symbol: The Twins

Birth date ruler: Jupiter, the philosopher

Tarot card: The Hanged Man (reflection)

Favorable numbers: 3, 9

Lucky days: Wednesday and Thursday, especially when these days fall on 3 or 9 of the month

Lucky colors: Orange, mauve, lilac

Birthstone: Agate

June 12

13 June

the birthday of the wild dreamer

Your greatest challenge is ...

being sensible

The way forward is ...

to understand that sensible does not always mean being boring; it can also mean maximizing your chances of success by being focused and realistic about your objectives.

You're drawn to people born on ...

January 21 to February 19

You share a passion for discovery and adventure, and this can create a surprisingly secure union.

Luck maker

Quieten down and slow down

Just a few minutes a day of quiet time when you are just "hanging around" not doing anything in particular can make a huge difference in connecting with your intuitive power.

People born on June 13 live life according to their own rules and values. Often way ahead of their time, they can't bear routine and the everyday, and their wild streak will take them to places no one else would dare to visit.

Although following their highly creative and vivid imagination can lead them into danger, it can also make them great innovators and pioneers. They love to travel and explore, both externally and internally; their thirst for adventure can take them all over the world to exotic places or it can manifest itself in total absorption in their intellectual discoveries. They truly believe that the world is theirs for the taking and that they can achieve virtually anything they set their mind and heart on.

Many of these people realize their wild dreams and become highly successful in their chosen field. Those who are less evolved, however, may struggle to translate their dreams into reality. It is important for them to get in touch with their intuition as this will tell them which risks are achievable and which are likely to end in frustration. They also need positive people who encourage them to dream but who provide a healthy dose of realism and objectivity. Until the age of thirty-eight they focus on emotional security and should take advantage of opportunities to develop greater self-awareness and understanding. After the age of thirty-nine they will have more self-confidence and a greater recognition of their capabilities. During this period they should ensure their appetite for adventure does not endanger them; they need to think long and hard about what their wild schemes really entail.

Above all, people born on this day are adventurers and they should never try to dampen their powerful imagination and boundless energy with routine and repetition. However, if they are to maximize their potential to not just dream but actually realize the impossible, they should weigh up the pros and cons, studying what is possible and what is not *before* they leap in at the deep end.

On the **dark** side

Rash, unrealistic, dangerous

At your **best**

Imaginative, intelligent, adventurous

Power Thought

❝ My intuition is waiting for me to simply ask it for guidance ❞

Love *Surprise me!*

People born on June 13 can get easily bored in relationships and hate to feel trapped or restricted in any way. If they do find themselves in a relationship that is too comfortable, they may want to end it. They need to find someone who is as unusual and as capable of surprise as they are.

Health *Accident prone*

People born on this day like to take risks and are often accident prone, suffering injuries to their arms and hands. They can also be susceptible to depression when their fantasies become so wild that they can't be expressed in real life; if this is the case, some form of counseling or therapy is advised. As far as diet and lifestyle are concerned, they should steer clear of alcohol and recreational drugs, and put the emphasis on fresh, healthy produce rather than refined or processed foods. Regular exercise is extremely important to them and they love walking, running and climbing. There is a tendency for them to push their bodies to extremes, so again they need to exercise caution. Wearing, meditating on and surrounding themselves with the color blue will encourage them to be cool, calm and collected in their approach.

Career *Born meteorologists*

These people have the curiosity and the determination to excel in any career but they thrive best in professions that involve study, travel and plenty of variety. Careers that might appeal include science, research, tourism, weather forecasting, journalism, writing, sales, media, and the world of entertainment.

Destiny *To explore and uncover new insights*

The life path of people born on this day is to learn to be more realistic and objective in their approach to life. Once they have learned to avoid extremes, their destiny is to explore and uncover new insights or universal truths.

Signs & symbols

Sun sign: Gemini

Ruling planet: Mercury, the communicator

Symbol: The Twins

Birth date ruler: Uranus, the visionary

Tarot card: Death (choices)

Favorable numbers: 1, 4

Lucky days: Wednesday and Sunday, especially when these days fall on 1 and 4 of the month

Lucky colors: Orange, amber, silvery blue

Birthstone: Agate

14 June

the birthday of
the supervisor

Your greatest challenge is …

resisting the urge to take charge

The way forward is …

to understand that sometimes the only way for people to learn and grow is for them to make their own mistakes.

You're drawn to people born on …

August 24 to September 23

This is a classic case of opposites attract. You both have so much to learn and gain from each other.

Luck maker

Treat everyone with respect

Treat important people as if they are important and treat less important people as if they were important too. You never know who might hold the key to your good fortune one day.

The bold individuals born on June 14 often have a powerful desire to take charge of people or situations, whether these are co-workers, friends or family, or projects that need to be supervised. Their instinctive urge to take control stems from their ability to observe what is going on around them and sum up quickly what needs to be done and who needs to do it.

The supreme confidence they have in their convictions is the result of their strong self-belief and their inability to stand on the sidelines when work needs to be done. It's no surprise that they often make inspirational and dynamic leaders, but their actions can sometimes be perceived as bossy and abrupt by those who prefer to make their own minds up. Unfortunately, when their methods or behavior are challenged they can become impatient and confrontational, and this can work against them, especially in their personal relationships. It is important for them to make a real effort to anticipate the reactions that their forcefulness can arouse in others.

Until the age of thirty-seven they may focus on their emotional security, and it is important during these years that they take advantage of opportunities to develop a greater awareness and consideration of the feelings of others. After the age of thirty-eight they enter a period of increased strength and confidence and, given their already well-developed self-confidence, they need to make sure that their direct approach does not tip over into arrogant certainty as this will alienate others from them.

Above all, they have clear-cut and strong opinions, together with a compulsion to take uncompromising direct action to achieve their far-sighted visions. They are also willing to work very hard, making considerable sacrifices for the people or causes close to their heart. Once they learn to respect the sensitivities of others, they have the potential not just to be outstanding supervisors but to make outstanding leaders and contributors to whatever field they choose to devote their prodigious energies, forthright opinions and powerful intellect.

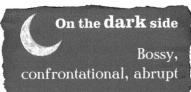
Love *Loners*

People born on June 14 can be loners, not because they are short of admirers but because their lives are so full of activities, interests and people that there is no time for a special relationship. Although personal space is important to them there is a part of them that needs emotional security; should they fall in love, they will remain hopelessly devoted to their chosen partner.

Health *Pace yourself*

People born on this day can be impatient not just with other people but with themselves. If they are ill, they will often go back to work before they are better or simply refuse to take time off at all. Although their positive attitude does mean that they shake off illnesses more easily than others, they also need to realize that when illness strikes, in particular the colds and flu to which they are prone, their bodies are trying to tell them that they need a period of rest. They should ensure that they allow themselves more time to relax and unwind, and that they take vacations instead of working through them. A healthy diet, instead of eating on the go, is also recommended, as is plenty of moderate intensity exercise, preferably outdoors. The zesty aroma of lemon will help keep their energy levels high. Wearing, meditating on or surrounding themselves with the color green will encourage them to be more sensitive to the feelings of others.

Career *Born CEOs*

These people love the written word and all things to do with the media, and they would therefore excel in careers in publishing, film, journalism, or television. They also make gifted CEOs and business leaders, and their strongly competitive nature might also draw them to the world of sport, sales, commerce, and business in general.

Destiny *To lead, motivate and inspire others*

The life path of people born on this day is to learn that their opinion is just an opinion and that others have valuable contributions to make as well. Once they have learned to take the views and feelings of others into consideration, their destiny is to do what they do best: lead, motivate and inspire others.

Signs & symbols

Sun sign: Gemini

Ruling planet: Mercury, the communicator

Symbol: The Twins

Birth date ruler: Mercury, the communicator

Tarot card: Temperance (moderation)

Favorable numbers: 2, 5

Lucky day: Wednesday, especially when it falls on 2 and 5 of the month

Lucky colors: Orange, emerald green, yellow

Birthstone: Agate

June 14

15 June

the birthday of irresistible charm

June 15 people are blessed with natural charm. They can easily bring others around to their point of view, often using their seductive power to win the support of co-workers, friends and family and indeed anyone they meet. Their charm and their appeal are so strong that even the most cynical and suspicious of people find it hard to resist them.

What makes these people so charming is their genuine interest in others and their remarkable ability to guess what they are thinking or feeling. This makes others feel good, in that they feel they are on the same wavelength as these attractive individuals. Their outstanding people skills will often fast-forward them into positions of influence; if they do find themselves in such positions, they should devote their persuasive powers to worthy causes. If they don't, others may resent being conned into questionable courses of action. They also need to ensure they don't give others the wrong impression and charm them into believing a friendship exists when it doesn't. In all their dealings they should observe a strict code of ethics.

Until the age of thirty-six they may focus on emotional security; during this time they should ensure they are as honest with themselves and others as possible, and don't place being popular, wealthy or attractive over a sense of personal achievement. After the age of thirty-seven they become more confident and this may encourage them to use their people skills in a more assertive way. It is important during these years that they keep on the straight and narrow; if they do, they can direct their energy, intellect and inner power to influence others in productive and positive ways.

They have the potential to make great contributions to partnerships, groups and society as a whole, as long as they are aware of the power they have over others and make sure they are not manipulating them. If they truly believe in the cause they are promoting, their ambition and personal charm virtually guarantee their popularity, happiness and success.

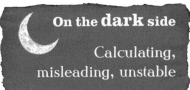

On the dark side

Calculating, misleading, unstable

At your best

Seductive, attractive, intelligent

Love *Irresistible*

People born on June 15 are powerfully attractive as romantic partners and enjoy winning others' hearts with their charming words and smiles. They are attracted to beautiful, intelligent people and enjoy a good debate but need to be careful that they don't value outer over inner beauty, and get caught up in arguments and power games. Once they find the perfect partner, however, they can be loyal, gentle and loving.

Health *Moderation is key*

Their physical appearance matters a great deal to people born on this day and this can either manifest in careful attention to diet and exercise or in extreme, obsessive behavior. They should learn that true beauty comes from within and, instead of buying creams or exercising relentlessly, they may find that inner peace and contentment work wonders instead. Some of these people, however, neglect their physical appearance and live their lives in pursuit of pleasure; this can lead to weight problems and unhappiness. Moderation is key. As far as diet is concerned, they need to make sure they eat little and often to keep their energy levels boosted. Regular exercise is also important, as it will boost their self-esteem because, despite appearances to the contrary, they can suffer from nerves and insecurity. Wearing, meditating on and surrounding themselves with the color purple will encourage them to focus less on the material and more on higher things.

Career *Born advertisers*

These people will often find fulfillment in artistic careers, in particular drama, art or music, where they can gather a following and bring enjoyment to others. They may also be drawn to advertising, marketing, the retail trade, law, public relations, promotion, consultancy, agency work, and the leisure and beauty industries.

Destiny *To uplift, inspire and motivate others*

The life path of people born on this day is to learn to use their people skills wisely and productively. Once they have a found a cause worthy of them, their destiny is to use their considerable powers of intuition and perspicacity to uplift, inspire and motivate others.

Signs & symbols

Sun sign: Gemini

Ruling planet: Mercury, the communicator

Symbol: The Twins

Birth date ruler: Venus, the lover

Tarot card: The Devil or (instinct)

Favorable numbers: 3, 6

Lucky days: Wednesday and Friday, especially when these days fall on 3 or 6 of the month

Lucky colors: Orange, cerise, green

Birthstone: Agate

June 15

16 June

the birthday of far-sighted astuteness

Your greatest challenge is ...

not being suspicious of everyone and everything

The way forward is ...

to understand that being too cautious can sometimes block creativity and spontaneity, key ingredients for your fulfillment and success.

You're drawn to people born on ...

September 24 to October 23

This is a very natural combination, and the relationship will be full of intellectual stimulation and happy chat.

Luck maker

Pay attention to meaningful coincidences

Think of all the people you have met by chance or the situations you have found yourself in that went on to change your life in pivotal ways. You never know when good luck is about to strike.

Those born on June 16 combine within their personalities a unique blend of adventurousness and caution. Although they have a vivid imagination and innovative inclinations, they are also extremely astute, possessing a willingness to be flexible without losing their vision.

Often having big plans and an uncanny ability to pick up on lifestyle trends before they happen, they rarely throw caution to the winds by speculating wildly. They are far more likely to plot their course in life carefully, laying firm foundations for the future one brick at a time. They are at their happiest when they can take risks within a controlled environment where their goals are clear and where they can receive constant updates or feedback on their progress. They are at their least productive, however, when they fail to find a balance between their enterprising and prudent qualities, and suppress their risk-taking tendencies in order to play safe.

Until the age of thirty-five, emotional security is likely to play an important part in their lives; they need to remember to leave some room in their structured lifestyle for fun and games. After the age of thirty-six, they grow in confidence and often become more assertive and self-expressive. It's important during this period that they don't block their incredible enthusiasm, will-power and determination with indecision. They should be sure of what they wish for, as this is the time in their life when they are most likely to have the power to make their ideas a reality.

Equally practical and imaginative, they tend to derive the greatest comfort and satisfaction from non-material pleasures, such as strong relationships or the beauty found in nature and the arts. They often live their life according to a strict humanitarian code, giving them compassion for those less fortunate and contempt for those who abuse their power. When they have learned to be neither too impulsive not too cautious, the strength of their desire for progress can be a remarkable power for good, not just for themselves but for all whose lives they touch.

336

On the **dark** side

Inflexible, indecisive, anxious

At your **best**

Earnest, patient, original

Love *Intelligent and restless*

People born on June 16 have a tendency to swing between being demonstrative and detached; this can drive their partner crazy because they never know where they are. They need to make it clear to their partner that although they are in a close relationship, they still need to feel free and independent at times.

Health *Preventative medicine*

With their eye always on the future, people born on this day understand the importance of taking care of their health and they are likely to make sure that their diet is healthy, and their exercise routine is regular and challenging. There will be some less-evolved souls born on this day who ignore their bodies and their health, but the only way for them to feel truly energized is to take an active interest in their well-being. As far as diet is concerned, they need to stay away as much as possible from refined and processed foods and those high in sugar, as eating too much of these can lead to weight problems. All forms of exercise, in particular cross-training, are recommended. Wearing, meditating on and surrounding themselves with the colors yellow and orange will encourage them to incorporate more fun and relaxation into their structured lifestyle.

Career *Born doctors*

These people have natural communication skills and could excel in careers in teaching, lecturing, education, the media, journalism, commerce, and financial advice. Alternatively they may get involved with humanitarian, healing or charitable organizations and work for worthwhile causes. Their individuality may also find expression in the creative world, where they are likely to be an original and accomplished writer, artist, photographer, film-maker, painter, or designer.

Destiny *To inspire others with compassion and far-sighted vision*

The life path of people born on this day is to strike a balance between their need for security and their need to take risks. Once they have found this balance, their destiny is to influence and inspire others with their compassion and far-sighted vision.

Power Thought

" Today I will act with speed, good judgment and resolve "

Signs & symbols

Sun sign: Gemini

Ruling planet: Mercury, the communicator

Symbol: The Twins

Birth date ruler: Neptune, the speculator

Tarot card: The Tower (breakthrough)

Favorable numbers: 4, 7

Lucky days: Wednesday and Monday, especially when these days fall on 4 and 7 of the month

Lucky colors: Orange, blue, yellow

Birthstone: Agate

17 June

the birthday of the influential example

People born on June 17 are often strong and inspirational individuals who believe everyone has it within them to follow their dreams. A fascinating combination of creativity and structure, they know how to conform but also have a vivid imagination that they want to explore and, if possible, profit from.

Demanding a lot of themselves and the people they live and work with, whatever situation they are in they are likely to be excellent performers and a forceful presence. Although they set a terrific example to others and people are drawn to their vitality and masterful demeanor, if they find themselves in the role of mentor they may struggle. This is because they are often too wrapped up in their own goals, lacking the patience and understanding to listen to others.

There is a danger that they might stretch the truth if they feel it serves their purposes. This isn't motivated by a desire to deceive but simply so their arguments sound more plausible. But if they don't control this tendency to manipulate the truth, they can become known as untrustworthy. Such is their influence, however, that even if their exaggeration is uncovered, others may still continue blindly to follow their lead. It is important therefore for them to impose a strict ethical code upon themselves. Until the age of thirty-four they may focus on emotional relations, security and family; for their own happiness they need to ensure that they take advantage of opportunities to discover their feelings and learn how to express them to others. After the age of thirty-five they enter a period of strength, power and confidence; these are the years when they come into their own as inspirational leaders or pioneers.

Above all, the forceful but imaginative and progressive individuals born on this day are fired by progressive ideals. Once they develop an understanding of the effect that their intensity has on others, not only will this give their ideals a better chance of gaining acceptance, it will also bring them greater emotional fulfillment.

Love *Aloof*

Although they are often surrounded by potential partners, establishing a close relationship may prove difficult for people born on June 17 as they tend to be physically undemonstrative and emotionally aloof. They are attracted to people who are successful or living their dreams and, once they do find that special someone, they can open up to they make faithful, protective and loving partners.

Health *Will-power needed*

People born on this day often have a strong physical presence and they need to make sure they don't succumb to addiction of any kind, be it drink, recreational drugs, sex, or food. Although they have terrific will-power professionally, when it comes to their personal life they don't show nearly the same resolve. It is important that they take charge of their well-being by eating healthily, exercising regularly and refraining from activities that give them a temporary high followed by a prolonged low. Once they do get their diet and lifestyle on track, they will find that their need for stimulants fades away. Wearing, meditating on and surrounding themselves with the color purple will encourage them to look inward and think of higher, purer things.

Career *Born conductors*

These people have a quick mind and the ability to lead; this offers them many career opportunities where they can rise to prominent positions. Alternatively, they may prefer to work for themselves. They are well suited to intellectual professions such as law, research or writing, and to careers where they can be involved in humanitarian or social reform, whether in society, religion or health care. A desire for creativity may lead them to express their individuality in the arts, the theater, and particularly music or conducting orchestras.

Destiny *To inspire others to fight for their values*

The life path of people born on this day is to learn to get in touch with their feelings so that they can express them outwardly. Once they are able to be less detached in their dealings with others, their destiny is to inspire others with their courageous ability to fight for their values.

Power Thought

❝I don't need external force or validation to feel at harmony with myself❞

Signs & symbols

Sun sign: Gemini

Ruling planet: Mercury, the communicator

Symbol: The Twins

Birth date ruler: Saturn, the teacher

Tarot card: The Star (hope)

Favorable numbers: 5, 8

Lucky days: Wednesday and Saturday, especially when these days fall on 5 and 8 of the month

Lucky colors: Orange, coffee, sunset

Birthstone: Agate

June 17

18 June

the birthday of perceptive congeniality

Your greatest challenge is …

dealing with boredom

The way forward is …

to understand that the answer to boredom is not in external stimulation but in the sense of excitement and change generated within.

You're drawn to people born on …

March 21 to April 22

You are both passionate and adventurous individuals, and this can be a powerful and intense union.

Luck maker

Focus on what is good

Gratitude is the foundation stone of a lucky life, so instead of looking over the horizon for excitement or happiness, try thinking about all that is good in your life right now.

People born on June 18 often have a charming manner and a likable vitality that uplifts everyone they meet. Their instant likability, however, conceals an insightful mind and a serious head for responsibility and business. They place as high a priority on meeting their personal, financial and professional goals as they do on being popular.

Whether they realize it or not, their personality has a lasting effect on others and, even if not physically present, their influence will be felt in some way. They possess a perceptive and highly intuitive mentality, and when this is combined with their sharp wit and quirky sense of fun they manage to get their point across effectively without causing offence. This makes it hard for others to forget them. Their ability to leave a lasting impact gives them potential for leadership, although they need to be careful that they don't abuse this power and become manipulative.

Although they enjoy attention, and popularity comes naturally to them, they are also good at reciprocating it, especially when it comes to helping others. They will often be indefatigable fighters for the rights of others and make witty and dramatic speakers and doers who refuse to tolerate injustice. Despite their sincerity and intelligence, they need to be entertained and can get easily bored. Their need for constant change, challenge and excitement can make them behave erratically and occasionally selfishly. They need to learn to be more consistent and disciplined in their approach to people and situations.

Until the age of thirty-two they may focus on emotional security but after the age of thirty-three they become more self-expressive and assertive. They should ensure that they don't fritter away their considerable talents during these years by a "grass is always greener" mentality. Once they learn to be grateful for what they already have, they will discover a capacity for spiritual achievement. This is the key to their creativity and their ability to make a positive impression on all those lucky enough to cross their path.

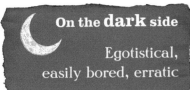
Love *Confusing*

People born on June 18 tend to be slightly erratic when it comes to affairs of the heart; sometimes they are very devoted and passionate, while at other times they can be detached. This can obviously be confusing to potential partners. They also have a tendency to drop partners at a moment's notice, thinking they will have no problem finding someone better. It would be good for everyone concerned if they learned to appreciate what they already have.

Health *Spiritual orientation*

People born on this day usually understand the importance of investing time and energy into taking care of their health, and because they are spiritually orientated they may be attracted to mind–body therapies such as meditation, hypnotherapy, yoga, and tai chi. As far as diet is concerned, they should avoid saturated fat and refined and processed foods, as these could lead to mood swings and weight problems. Regular exercise, in particular walking, swimming, cycling, and body toning, is recommended. Wearing, meditating on and surrounding themselves with color green will encourage them to be more consistent and balanced in their approach to life.

Career *Born lyricists*

These people have the potential to make their mark in the performing arts, in particular music, poetry and writing, but they may also blaze a trail as scientific researchers or entrepreneurs. They may be attracted to law, education and the media, as well as politics, labor union leadership, counseling, charity work, and social and humanitarian reform.

Destiny *To influence, inspire and encourage progress*

The life path of people born on this day is to learn that much of what they seek already lies within them. Once they become more self-contained their destiny is to influence, inspire and encourage progress with their ideas, visions and humanitarian concerns.

Signs & symbols

Sun sign: Gemini

Ruling planet: Mercury, the communicator

Symbol: The Twins

Birth date ruler: Mars, the warrior

Tarot card: The Moon (imagination)

Favorable numbers: 6 or 9

Lucky days: Wednesday and Tuesday, especially when these days fall on 6 and 9 of the month

Lucky colors: Orange, red, yellow

Birthstone: Agate

June 18

19 June

the birthday of the activator

Your greatest challenge is …

with being too confrontational

The way forward is …

to understand that the direct approach simply won't work in every situation. The best way to get people on your side is often to approach them gently.

You're drawn to people born on …

July 24 to August 24

You are both courageous, outgoing and sensitive, and this can be a passionate and exciting relationship.

Luck maker

Make others feel special

Lucky people understand that the more special you make people feel by listening to them and complimenting them when they do things well, the more likely they are to listen to and support you.

People born on June 19 are blessed with the ability to stimulate and uplift others. Their resolve and courage, along with their patience, tolerance and generally good intentions, serve as an inspiring example. Whether they realize it or not, they are catalysts spurring others into action and moving situations forward in the process.

They may choose to fight vociferously or to quietly hold firm, but whatever strategy they choose they rarely crumble under pressure. Their resolve comes from their most outstanding characteristic: their self-belief. They are rarely beset by feelings of doubt which can arouse both admiration and irritation. Indeed their huge personality can intimidate those less confident; however, their single-minded determination is not the result of blinkered obstinacy but rather of supreme confidence engendered by the knowledge that they have evaluated every viewpoint and arrived at the best conclusion. And their confidence is well founded, as they are blessed with incisive analytical skills, intellectual inquisitiveness and profound intuition.

Less evolved types born on this day may express themselves in controlling or dictatorial behavior, but life usually ends up teaching them the benefits of a less confrontational approach. Until the age of thirty-one they may focus on emotional security, home and family. After the age of thirty-two, however, they enter a period of greater self-expression and creativity, with added assertiveness and boldness. It is important during this period that they learn the art of diplomacy; if they do, these are the years that they come into their own. At the age of sixty-two they may feel a desire to be more methodical and to offer practical service to others.

Above all, people born on this day have the ability to empower others with their compassion, sparkling wit and youthful vitality. They may have a tendency to push themselves too hard, but as long as they maintain a sense of balance and perspective they have the potential to make their mark on the world by guiding, improving and energizing others.

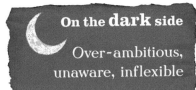
Love *Young at heart*

Young at heart and outgoing, people born on June 19 are often sociable and popular. They are passionate and committed lovers but they can also be stubborn, vain and argumentative at times. However, should their partner face problems, there is no one more loyal or understanding than they are.

Health *Burnout*

People born on this day have a tendency to drive themselves too hard and, because they perform well under stress, they may not notice how run down they really are until poor health forces them to take time out. It is therefore important for them to make sure they include plenty of rest and relaxation in their lives and to practice stress-management techniques such as deep breathing, meditation, chatting with friends, or simply having a long soak in an aromatherapy bath. As far as diet is concerned, they should avoid eating on the run and go for plenty of wholesome, preferably home-cooked food. Exercise should be moderate to mild and low impact to help them stay healthy, calm and centered. Wearing, meditating on and surrounding themselves with the color green will help them feel more in balance, and carrying a rose quartz crystal can help them release pent-up stress and tension.

Career *Born teachers*

People born on this day have the ability to inspire and motivate others and may therefore be drawn to careers in education, counseling, consultancy, or lecturing. Other careers that might appeal include sales, commerce, promotion, negotiation, business training, writing, research, social reform, and politics. Alternatively, their need for self-expression may draw them to art, design, advertising, and the media.

Destiny *To share their sense of purpose and their vision of progress*

The life path of people born on this day is to become aware of the influential effect they have on others and not abuse it. Once they have learned to be more tolerant and diplomatic, their destiny is to encourage others to share their sense of purpose and their vision of progress.

Signs & symbols

Sun sign: Gemini

Ruling planet: Mercury, the communicator

Symbol: The Twins

Birth date ruler: Sun, the individual

Tarot card: The Sun (enthusiasm)

Favorable numbers: 1, 7

Lucky days: Wednesday and Sunday, especially when these days fall on 1 and 7 of the month

Lucky colors: Neon orange, red, yellow

Birthstone: Agate

June 19

20 June

the birthday of excitement

People born on June 20 are affectionate and spontaneous with everyone they meet, because expressing their emotions comes naturally to them. Indifference is something they simply don't understand since, above all else, these people love and thrive on excitement.

Life is never dull when these popular people are around since everything elicits a passionate reaction from them. They are dramatic, charismatic, outgoing charmers who love to talk and adore being the center of attention. Excellent communication skills and an innovative mind crammed with insights make them vibrant, witty conversationalists. However, because they love excitement, they can sometimes provoke an argument for the sake of it. They can also be a little too needy of praise and if they don't get the reinforcement they crave, they may respond with attention-seeking or irrational behavior. It is important for them to surround themselves with warm-hearted but level-headed people who can give them the balance they need.

Until the age of thirty there is an emphasis on home, family and emotional security, and they should take advantage of opportunities to find a sense of inner balance. After the age of thirty-one, however, they will become more creative and confident, developing the assertiveness to be more adventurous. If they can get a grip on their passionate responses to situations and their ability to churn up strong emotions in others, these are the years when they can really come into their own.

Although people born on this day can sometimes create fireworks unnecessarily, more often than not they are a positive force. The atmosphere seems lighter when they are around because they help bring out the repressed emotions of others. Excitement and passion seem to follow them wherever they go and they also have considerable intuitive powers, helping them to enchant, persuade and influence others. If they can find a worthy cause and ensure that they occasionally check in with their reason as well as their emotions they can transform their creative and exciting dreams into reality.

On the **dark** side
Insecure, irrational, hypersensitive

At your **best**
Dynamic, exciting, rousing

Love *Make time for love*

People born on June 20 are often so popular that they simply haven't got time for that special someone. However, once they do fall in love they find the experience incredibly fulfilling and so they should always remain open to the possibility of love. They are drawn toward intelligent and level-headed individuals who can help calm and balance them.

Health *Cool, calm and collected*

People born on this day tend to attract people and situations into their lives that are stressful and demanding; they need to find out why this is the case. Getting in touch with their own feelings and increasing their depth of self-understanding will help them attract more positive energy. They would benefit enormously from mind-control therapies such as meditation, yoga and counseling. They would also benefit from more quiet time alone thinking, reading or simply being in the moment. As far as diet is concerned, they need to make sure that they structure fixed meal and snack times into their day as this will help ground them. The same applies for their exercise routine; it should be timetabled into their weekly diary. Sticking to regular going-to-bed and rising times is also recommended. Wearing, meditating on and surrounding themselves with the color blue will encourage them to be more cool, calm and collected.

Career *Born investigative journalist*

People born on this day have the ability to think on their feet and sense the potential drama or opportunity in a situation; this will make them excellent problem solvers, investigative journalists, politicians, teachers, and researchers. Their easy charm and organizational skills will also help them succeed in people-orientated careers, whether in business or the public sector. Creative outlets are likely to be through the media, theater or music.

Destiny *To encourage others to be more open and receptive*

The life path of people born on this day is to learn to temper their restlessness and thirst for stimulation with a streak of realism and self-discipline. Once this is achieved, their destiny is to draw people to them with their sympathetic nature, encouraging others to be more open and receptive themselves.

Signs & symbols

Sun signs: Gemini/Cancer

Ruling planets: Mercury, the communicator/Moon, the intuitive

Symbols: The Twins/The Crab

Birth date ruler: Moon, the intuitive

Tarot card: Judgment (responsibility)

Favorable numbers: 2 or 8

Lucky days: Wednesday and Monday, especially when these days fall on 2 and 8 of the month

Lucky colors: Orange, milky white, yellow

Birthstone: Agate

June 20

21 June

the birthday of rhapsody

People born on June 21 tend to be intense, exciting and sensual individuals. Born on the longest and perhaps most magical day of the year, they are gregarious, sociable and relentlessly busy. They love every aspect of their lives with rarely the time to meet all their goals.

Fiercely individualistic, they detest pigeonholing of any kind and believe they can be a sex symbol, researcher, athlete, devoted parent, and talented artist all at the same time. Since it is almost impossible to achieve so much in one lifetime, they run the risk of driving themselves and others to exhaustion. They would not have it any other way, so determined are they to experience all the riches the world has to offer. They have terrific enthusiasm and determination to exceed, giving them the power and momentum not just to overcome obstacles but to grow stronger after surmounting them.

These highly sensual people take great delight in all that the world has to offer but they are not only devoted to physical and material pleasures; their thoughts and feelings are intense and passionate too. The big danger is that they can go to extremes, losing themselves in a world of sensation or obsession; they need to learn greater self-control. Until the age of thirty they may focus on emotional security, home and family, and they need to make sure they don't become too dictatorial and impatient with others. After the age of thirty they become more creative and confident, developing the assertiveness to be more adventurous. If they can learn to keep a sense of balance and focus, these are the years when they will realize that they can have it all—just not all at once.

Their inexhaustible thirst for adventure and external stimuli makes them not only interested but also extremely interesting individuals. Blessed with natural charisma, if they can learn to develop their introspective gifts of empathy and understanding, and avoid becoming obsessive about what excites them, their capacity for original and creative thought gives them genius potential.

On the **dark** side

Excessive, dictatorial, extreme

At your **best**

Sensual, exciting, intense

Love *Don't set the bar too high*

People born on June 21 are often highly sensual and will attract many admirers. They do, however, set themselves extremely high standards when it comes to potential partners, and this can make them dictatorial and controlling. They need to stop looking for perfection because it does not exist and appreciate the qualities that make others special.

Health *Look within*

People born on this day will often take things to extremes and push themselves rather hard so they need to make sure they have a more balanced and moderate approach to life. Addictive behavior is a concern and they should guard against this. They would benefit enormously from meditation, cognitive therapy or counseling, as well as more time spent with family and friends to give them a sense of healthy perspective. As far as diet is concerned, they should steer clear of alcohol and limit their intake of sugar, salt, processed and refined foods, although they should avoid extreme dietary measures as eating disorders are a potential risk. Moderate to mild exercise, preferably in the fresh air, is recommended. Wearing, meditating on and surrounding themselves with the color purple will encourage them to look within for comfort and a sense of fulfillment.

Career *Born reformers*

Whatever career these people choose they will have a need to express their creativity. They also need jobs that offer them variety, travel and human contact. Often humanitarian by nature, they may be drawn to education, counseling, healing, or social reform. Their love of knowledge may also attract them to law, religion and philosophy. Usually good with their hands, they may excel in design, and with their communication skills they may make excellent writers, journalists, advertisers, presenters, and promoters.

Destiny *To share their vision and intensity with others*

The life path of people born on this day is to learn to avoid excessive extremes and to cooperate with others. Once they have learned this, their destiny is to make their mark on the world by sharing their vision and their intensity with others.

Power Thought

66 Every moment contains an opportunity for me to feel inspired 99

Signs & symbols

Sun signs: Gemini/Cancer

Ruling planets: Mercury, the communicator/Moon, the intuitive

Symbols: The Twins/The Crab

Birth date ruler: Jupiter, the speculator

Tarot card: The World (fulfillment)

Favorable numbers: 3 or 9

Lucky days: Wednesday and Thursday, especially when these days fall on 3 and 9 of the month

Lucky colors: Orange, lilac, purple

Birthstone: Agate

June 21

22 June

the birthday of breathless anticipation

The romantic, affectionate and sensitive individuals born on June 22 tend to greet each new day, however ordinary, with breathless anticipation. For them every day is an optimistic new beginning where anything could happen; their imagination infuses everyday events and situations with excitement and potential.

Whether or not they realize it, people born on this day are constantly seeking their personal nirvana, be it the perfect love affair, lifestyle or a combination of both. Although they can be practical and will often excel in their careers, personal happiness typically takes precedence over professional success because they feel that if they have the love of a soul mate they can achieve virtually anything. Finding true love is therefore of paramount importance to their emotional and professional well-being, and they may sometimes pick unusual partners.

Until the age of thirty they focus on security, and if they don't marry young they may prefer to stay at home or build up a network of supportive friends. After the age of thirty, however, they will usually gain in confidence and perform with skill in their chosen field. In their middle years, if they have not already used the powerful energies of their birthday, they will get another opportunity to achieve success.

Although they can keep romance alive long after the routine of daily life has stripped away much of its mystery, they do need to look at the surface as well as the depths of the people they are attracted to. If they don't keep their feet on the ground by listening to other people's perceptions, they may find that they are left feeling isolated in their fantasy world and doomed to disappointment in love. However, such is their zest for life and enthusiasm for intellectual and sensory stimulation that they will not stay down for long, finding consolation in their professional interests, friends, hobbies, and, of course, their belief that today may just be the day when something or someone wonderful enters their lives.

Your greatest challenge is ...

dealing with disillusionment

The way forward is ...

to understand that disappointment is likely if you credit others with qualities that they do not actually possess, so don't place unrealistic demands on yourself or others.

You're drawn to people born on ...

September 24 to October 23

You are energetic and exciting individuals with a love of beauty, and this can create an intense and fabulous union.

Luck maker

The power is within you

Lucky people understand that ultimate fulfillment can never be found in the perfect relationship or lifestyle. True fulfillment can only come from within.

On the dark side

Naïve, dreamy, confused

At your best

Imaginative, sensitive, romantic

Love *Affectionate and attractive*

Since they are often affectionate and attractive individuals, people born on June 22 rarely have trouble attracting potential partners. There is a danger, however, that some of them will remain unsatisfied because their romantic visions are too unrealistic or because the intensity of their emotions frightens off potential partners who feel they can not live up to the ideal personality projected on them.

Health *Serious thinking*

Serious illnesses tend to creep up on people born on this day without anyone noticing until they have slumped into a profound depression or become so stressed that they simply can't function. It is therefore important for them to make sure that they make plenty of opportunities for rest and relaxation and don't burn the candle at both ends. They may be prone to digestive disorders, anemia and lowered vitality. Boosting the intake of iron in their diet, switching to low fat, cutting down on saturated fat and dairy products, and getting plenty of bone-strengthening exercise, such as walking and swimming, will help get them back on track. And because they also need to guard against emotional insecurity with objectivity and rational thinking, wearing, meditating on and surrounding themselves with the color blue will help them when they want to appear cool or need some time out to do some serious thinking.

Career *Born designers*

The sensitivity of people born on this day suits them well for careers in the arts where they can live their fantasies, and they may be drawn to writing, music or the theater. Other careers that appeal include interior design, photography, film-making, counseling, medical or alternative health, education, social work, and law.

Destiny *To bring happiness to those around them*

The life path of people born on this day is to learn to see the world not just from their point of view but from the point of view of others. Once they are able to be more realistic in their assessment of people and situations, their destiny is to use their imagination, sensitivity and boundless enthusiasm for life to bring happiness to those around them and to the world at large.

349

Power Thought

" I already have all the wisdom and power I will ever need "

Signs & symbols

Sun signs: Cancer/Gemini

Ruling planets: Moon, the intuitive/Mercury, the communicator

Symbols: The Crab/The Twins

Birth date ruler: Uranus, the visionary

Tarot card: The Fool (freedom)

Favorable numbers: 1, 4

Lucky days: Monday and Sunday, especially when these days fall on 1 and 4 of the month

Lucky colors: Silver, white, chrome

Birthstone: Pearl

June 22

23 June

the birthday of the improver

People born on June 23 tend to be highly sensitive and loving individuals who yearn to make the world around them a more beautiful place. With the vision of a peaceful world to inspire them, they devote their energy and intelligence to identifying areas that need improvements and then improving them.

They are extremely interested in the lives of others and are eager to help them in any way, be it emotionally, financially or practically. Not surprisingly they place great value on interpersonal relationships, treating both loved ones and strangers with great respect, consideration and warmth. Unfortunately, in their eagerness to connect with others they tend to become interfering and to repeat confidences. Although this is never done with malicious intent, it can make them appear untrustworthy, which they are not.

Up to the age of twenty-nine, they will be concerned with their home, family and their own emotional security; but after the age of thirty they are likely to be drawn into public situations which require them to be strong and confident. These are the years when they are likely to come into their own, realizing their dreams of improving the world in some way by enriching it with artistic endeavors or by bringing greater harmony, compassion and peace within human relationships.

They don't just love to study other people; they also love to share their ideas about how life can be improved in some way. Some of these ideas may be particularly wacky, especially those about love and sex, but generally such is their insight and charisma that others often find their lives improved or changed after spending time with them because they have an ability to make others feel secure and loved. They should, however, resist the tendency to pry uninvited into the affairs of others; but once they are able to be more discreet and open-minded, they have the creative potential and the practicality to implement their romantic ideals and to effect not just their own emotional fulfillment, but the happiness of all they meet.

Love *Love is all around*

Love makes the world go round for people born on June 23 and few can match their intensity when it comes to one-on-one relationships. They are prone to fall in love easily and may put their partner on a pedestal that is impossible to live up to. Although their need for absolute devotion may scare away potential partners, once in a secure relationship they have an extraordinary ability to keep romance and passion alive.

Health *Home alone*

People born on this day tend to be happiest when they are in a loving relationship or surrounded by friends and loved ones. They can suffer terribly if life forces periods of solitude upon them, but if they can learn to be as happy in their own company as they are in that of others, their potential for happiness and personal fulfillment increases significantly. As far as diet is concerned, they would be wise to steer clear of too much alcohol, and spicy and fatty foods, as these can irritate their digestive system and cause stomach upsets. All forms of exercise are recommended, especially when they feel their mood is in need of a boost. Wearing, meditating on and surrounding themselves with the color purple will encourage them to feel happier in their own company.

Career *Born psychotherapists*

Their natural orientation toward helping others draws these people to careers in health care, policing, counseling, and social work, as well as politics and law. They may also be drawn to the performing arts, poetry, writing, music, and painting. Other areas that might interest them include education, computer technology, research, catering, and commerce.

Destiny *To influence, inspire and improve the lives of others*

The life path of people born on this day is to learn to step back every now and again and resist the tendency to become over-involved in problems that are not really their own. Once they have learned to be more objective, their destiny is to influence, inspire and improve the lives of others.

Signs & symbols

Sun signs: Cancer/Gemini

Ruling planets: Moon, the intuitive/Mercury, the communicator

Symbols: The Crab/The Twins

Birth date ruler: Mercury, the communicator

Tarot card: The Hierophant (reflection)

Favorable numbers: 2, 5

Lucky days: Monday and Wednesday, especially when these days fall on 2 and 5 of the month

Lucky colors: Cream, white, silver blue

Birthstone: Pearl

24 June

the birthday of
inspired proficiency

Your greatest challenge is ...

learning to rely on others

The way forward is ...

to understand that a totally independent state of existence is impossible because no man or woman is an island.

You're drawn to people born on ...

September 24 to October 23

You both have much to learn about love and this relationship might just teach you that perfect love does exist.

Luck maker

Ask for help

Lucky people understand that luck is a two-way street; if they want something to happen, they increase their chances of success significantly if they ask other people to help or support them.

People born on June 24 are often ambitious, hard working and strikingly independent. Leaders not followers, they like to choose their own path and will often be so successful that others follow their example. On whatever they choose to focus their energies, be it work, a cause or their family life, they tend to be extraordinarily proficient.

Blessed with keen intellects as well as innovative imaginations, the visions of these people can be startlingly original and their problem-solving ability inspired. Colleagues, friends and family know they can count on them because their approach is thorough. In addition, they are capable of remarkable feats of concentration and focus; when all this is combined with their energy and drive, they have enormous potential for success.

Despite the inspirational effect they have on others, they often perform best when they are largely undistracted. Although they recognize that they cannot obtain their objectives single-handedly, they tend to immerse themselves in work and neglect their personal life. They can also be remarkably insensitive to the emotional needs of others. It is important for them to become more self-aware and be alert to this tendency, because it will hinder their psychological growth and emotional fulfillment.

Up to the age of twenty-eight, issues relating to financial and emotional security can dominate their lives. However, after the age of twenty-nine they become more daring in their power and creativity. Crucial to their potential for success and happiness during this time is a need to curtail their urge for complete independence and apply empathy and sensitivity toward those closest to them. They should also choose a worthy career or vocation and not devote themselves to a cause that is ethically questionable. This is because if they choose a career that makes them feel they are making a positive, valuable or progressive contribution to the world, not only will they get the recognition they need and deserve from all those who play a part in their lives; they also will achieve something far more rewarding: personal fulfillment.

Love *Large doses of solitude*

People born on June 24 are extremely charming and rarely lack potential admirers. They are, however, also extremely independent and need large doses of solitude to formulate their plans. This can be difficult for loved ones to understand and deal with, especially when they go for long periods without seeing them, so it is important for these people to reassess their priorities every now and again.

Health *The mind–body connection*

People born on June 24 can completely neglect both their emotional and physical health when they are wrapped up with their work, and this is dangerous as it could lead to weight problems, heart problems and gastric disorders. Mind–body therapies such as meditation and yoga can help remind them of the importance of a healthy mind in a healthy body. As far as diet is concerned, they need to make sure they avoid foods high in sugar, salt, saturated fat, additives, and preservatives, as their constitution thrives best on simple, natural foods. Regular exercise is recommended, again to provide them with a healthy mind–body balance. Wearing, meditating on and surrounding themselves with the color orange will increase feelings of warmth, physical enjoyment and security, helping them relate better to others.

Career *Born management consultants*

Careers as scientists, technical researchers, managers, or management consultants, where they can combine their talent for analysis with the opportunity to see their goals realized, appeal to these people. Sporting and artistic pursuits are also highlighted. Their interest in mental pursuits could lead them to careers in teaching, research and writing, and they could also excel in business, particularly sales and promotion. Alternatively, they may decide to go it alone and set up their own business from home.

Destiny *To achieve their visions of progress and reform*

The life path of people born on this day is to learn to be less preoccupied with work and to make their emotions more explicit. Once they are able to develop their interpersonal skills, their destiny is to achieve their visions of progress and reform.

Signs & symbols

Sun sign: Cancer

Ruling planet: Moon, the intuitive

Symbol: The Crab

Birth date ruler: Venus, the lover

Tarot card: The Lovers (choices)

Favorable numbers: 3, 6

Lucky days: Monday and Thursday, especially when these days fall on 3 and 6 of the month

Lucky colors: Cream, pink, light green

Birthstone: Pearl

25 June

the birthday of original sensitivity

People born on June 25 tend to be highly creative and sensitive. They react strongly to external influences, using their powerful intuition to draw clear-sighted conclusions or solutions. Others, however, don't just value them for their problem-solving abilities, but also for their fine minds and stunning originality of thought.

The sensitivity of these people makes them valuable team players because they sense what others need and enjoy helping them. Their heart definitely rules their head, and most of their actions are closely allied to their feelings and emotions; this can make them appear vacillating or contradictory. It is important for them to reconcile their emotional and mental responses because, if they do, they have the originality and ability to be effective instruments of progress. However, when their minds and hearts are unbalanced, it can result in insecurity, confusion, hypersensitivity, or inconsistent motivations.

This sensitivity will become less of a problem after the age of twenty-seven, when they become bolder and more self-assured in all areas of their lives. During this period, opportunities to develop greater self-awareness will arise and, if they can build their self-esteem and rely less on the approval of others, these are the years when they are capable of making outstanding contributions to the world. After the age of fifty-seven they are likely to apply greater patience and precision to their life skills, taking a more practical approach to life and fine-tuning their skills and creativity.

To achieve success, it is crucial for them to find a subject or cause that really captures their imagination, one that will keep them focused and perhaps help them develop as a specialist. If they fail to keep themselves mentally challenged, they run the risk of scattering their energies and suffering from frustration. However, if they learn to develop patience and discipline, they will soon see that along with their inspired creativity and powerful intuition, they also possess depth of thought and a mind capable of producing not just great, but truly inspirational work.

At your best

Creative, empathetic,
sensitive

Love *Aim for equality*

People born on June 25 usually have many admirers and friends but there is a tendency for them to please others before they please themselves. This is a disastrous strategy because it will lead to unhappiness and frustration, it is important to aim for greater equality in all their relationships.

Health *Protective bubble*

It is vital for the physical and emotional well-being of people born on this day that they pour less of themselves into the lives of others. Highly sensitive to the moods of others, they need to protect themselves by imagining some kind of protective bubble around them that screens them from negative emotions. They also need to distance themselves more by cultivating greater objectivity. If they are unable to do this, they may suffer from mood swings, stress, anxiety and, in extreme cases, depression. Regular periods of quiet and solitude will help them regain a sense of self, as will surrounding themselves with people who are not in any way needy or negative. In general they should eat a nutritious and mood-boosting diet rich in fruits, vegetables, whole grains, oily fish, nuts, and seeds. Moderate to mild exercise, such as walking or swimming, is recommended on a daily basis. Wearing, meditating on and surrounding themselves with the color blue will encourage them to be cooler and more objective toward others.

Career *Born commercial artists*

The sensitivity that these people possess, as well as their natural affinity for art, suggests great success as designers and commercial artists. A need to express their individuality may also draw them to journalism, architecture, art, and music. In their choice of career they need to guard against boredom, as it is important for them to have a career where there is plenty of variety and opportunities to learn.

Destiny *To act as a sensitive and compassionate force for good*

The life path of people born on this day is to develop their capacity for objectivity and setting priorities. Once they have learned to be realistic about what really matters to them, their destiny is to act as a sensitive and compassionate force for good.

Signs & symbols

Sun sign: Cancer

Ruling planet: Moon, the intuitive

Symbol: The Crab

Birth date ruler: Neptune, the speculator

Tarot card: The Chariot (resilience)

Favorable numbers: 4, 7

Lucky days: Monday, especially when these days fall on 4 and 7 of the month

Lucky colors: Cream, marine blue, white

Birthstone: Pearl

June 25

26 June

the birthday of energetic fortitude

Your greatest challenge is ...

letting others fend for themselves

The way forward is ...

to understand that sometimes the best way for people to learn and grow is for them to make their own mistakes.

You're drawn to people born on ...

December 22 to January 19

You share a respect for family and tradition, and you have much you can learn to love about each other.

Luck maker

Don't feel guilty about receiving

If you have problems receiving help or guidance from other people, ask yourself why and how you are blocking good things from happening to you. Why do you always prefer to be the giver?

People born on June 26 tend to have an energetic, sturdy, resilient approach to life. They stand up well to attack and want those they love to lean on them; as a result others often wholly rely on them. Warm and sensual, they have great compassion and are good at taking control of people in need of guidance. They love life's comforts and are willing to work hard to provide these for themselves and those they love.

Another trait of these people is their prodigious energy, physical strength and stamina. Enjoying all kinds of physical, preferably sporting activity, their energetic approach will manifest itself in other areas of their lives, such as their work or hobbies. The area to which they will always devote most of their energy, however, will be the people around them. They are truly empathetic individuals whose intuitive response to the feelings of others arouses their urge to protect, guide and nurture. Not surprisingly, this tendency is pronounced if they have children; but whether they have a family or not, they will assume a mentoring role for colleagues and friends.

Whatever path in life they choose, they are at their best when they are part of a team or community. Their strong social orientation is perhaps their defining feature, but it has the potential to bring them both enormous fulfillment and enormous pain. This is because others may perceive their advice as an attempt to control their independence. It is extremely important for them to control their well-intentioned directional tendencies before it alienates others and smothers their own emotional needs.

Curiously, when it comes to their own personal life, hidden insecurities may manifest in unusual or compulsive behavior, such as an obsession with order and cleanliness. Fortunately, especially after the age of twenty-six, when there are opportunities for them to connect with their own emotions, they are able to discover courage and confidence within themselves. Once they have achieved this, they can display their own strong ideological beliefs and inspirational vision in a positive and self-assured way.

At your **best**

Energetic, resilient,
sensual

Love *Warm and caring*

Committed, loyal and steadfast, people born on June 26 take their relationships very seriously, and since they are affectionate and sociable they are
likely to have many friends, staying in touch with them all. They make wonderfully warm and caring lovers, but they need to make sure that they don't
become over-protective or stifling in their compassion.

Health *Physical stamina*

People born on this day often enjoy exercise and sports of all kinds because they
love to test their physical stamina and match themselves against their oppo-
nents. They do, however, have a tendency to push themselves too hard and
need to guard against accidents and injuries of all kinds, particularly to their
chest, stomach and rib cage. Although they are able to work productively on
their own, they function much better when part of a team or group. Staying
close to their family and friends both emotionally and physically also con-
tributes to their happiness. As far as diet is concerned, they need to make sure
they eat little and often to keep their energy levels consistent, not leaving long
periods between meals or snacks. Any form of exercise is recommended, as
long as it is not taken to extremes. Wearing, meditating on and surrounding
themselves with the color yellow will increase their self-confidence and creative optimism, turning the spotlight away from others on to them.

Career *Born governors*

People born on this day will often be drawn toward careers in which they
can make a practical contribution to the common good, for example social
work, charity work, education, economics, politics, and lecturing. They may
also flourish in such diverse professions as research, technology, the performing arts, sales, promotion, catering, psychology, and counseling.

Destiny *To promote the common good*

The life path of people born on this day is to learn to be as protective and
nurturing of their own emotional needs as they are of others. Once they have
learned to place self-care at the top of their list of priorities, their destiny is
to make their valuable contribution toward promoting the common good.

Power Thought

❝ Everything
in my life
works better
when I love
and take care
of myself ❞

Signs & symbols

Sun sign: Cancer

Ruling planet: Moon, the
intuitive

Symbol: The Crab

Birth date ruler: Saturn, the
teacher

Tarot card: Strength
(passion)

Favorable numbers: 5, 8

Lucky days: Monday and
Saturday, especially when
these days fall on 5 and 8 of
the month

Lucky colors: Cream,
burgundy,
white

Birthstone:
Pearl

June 26

27 June

the birthday of protective conviction

Your greatest challenge is …

dealing with criticism

The way forward is …

to remember that constructive criticism can be enormously helpful because it can help you learn, improve and fine-tune your strategies.

You're drawn to people born on …

March 21 to April 20

You both have a strong will and bags of energy; this can create a hot, fiery but intensely rewarding relationship.

Luck maker

Open your eyes and ears

You must explore new possibilities if you want to strike lucky. Lucky people are always hungry for experiences, knowledge and new insights because they have learned that they will eventually find something wonderful.

People born on June 27 tend to be watchful, diligent and very capable of defending themselves and their interests from attack. They are competitive, driven and persuasive,and those who dare to criticize or argue with their convictions may find themselves out of their depth.

They feel they have a duty to guide and, if necessary, force others to follow the same uncompromising moral convictions that they themselves hold. The profound empathy they feel for those less fortunate arouses their fiercely protective instincts and a burning desire to effect social improvement. Such steadfastness does, however, have its drawbacks: they have a tendency to become inflexible and overly defensive when others try to offer their opinions or criticize them. If this happens, their favored response is to withdraw, shutting out everyone and everything in the process.

Emotions and family matters may occupy them into their mid-twenties, and they should take advantage of opportunities to become more sensitive to the feelings of others. Although they may appear self-assured, they may find that the solid confidence they seek is not forthcoming until after the age of twenty-five. It is important during these years that they keep their minds and hearts open, avoiding becoming too defensive or inflexible in their convictions, which could provoke unnecessary rifts in relationships and problems in their working life. After the age of fifty-five they become more practical, analytical and discerning. Remaining inquisitive and open-minded is the key to their happiness and success during this period.

The single-mindedness of these people can also mean that they miss out on opportunities to develop new assets or relationships. It is crucial for their psychological development that they remain open to the debates that their actions will engender, because learning to become more accommodating is the key to their personal happiness and fulfillment. It will unlock their intuition, giving them the inspiration they need to fulfill their progressive urge to effect real and significant improvements in the human condition.

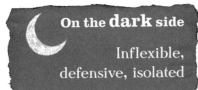
Love *Fluctuating moods*

Charming and friendly with a warm and caring personality, people born on June 27 are often loyal and devoted partners, as well as being loving parents. Although they find it easy to make friends and attract admirers, they can have fluctuating moods and be quick to take offence at any form of criticism, and this vacillating touchiness can affect their relationships negatively.

Health *Limber up*

People born on this day have a tendency to be inflexible in both mind and body, and this can manifest itself in physical discomforts such as joint pain, backache, sciatica, and headaches. They would benefit enormously from all forms of stretching, such as yoga and dance, or any form of exercise that encourages them to be more flexible. As far as diet is concerned, they need to optimize their intake of health-boosting nutrients. In addition, they need to make sure they include a wide variety of foods in their meal plans and don't just keep repeating the same menu week after week. Wearing, meditating on and surrounding themselves with the color yellow will encourage them to be more open, optimistic and confident.

Career *Born charity workers*

People born on this day may express their humanitarian concerns in a range of careers, including nursing, teaching, therapy, social work, or charity work. Alternatively, they may choose to spread their message more overtly via the arts in music, acting or writing, although their theatrical side conjoined with their idealism may also lead them into politics.

Destiny *To devote their energy to helping and inspiring others*

The life path of people born on this day is to learn to be more open-minded in their approach to people and situations. Once they have become more flexible, their destiny is to devote their considerable energy to helping and inspiring others.

Power Thought

"My understanding is clear, but my opinions are flexible"

Signs & symbols

Sun sign: Cancer

Ruling planet: Moon, the intuitive

Symbol: The Crab

Birth date ruler: Mars, the warrior

Tarot card: The Hermit (inner strength)

Favorable numbers: 6, 9

Lucky days: Monday and Tuesday, especially when these days fall on 6 and 9 of the month

Lucky colors: Cream, volcanic red, white

Birthstone: Pearl

June 27

28 June

the birthday of the sprite

Your greatest challenge is …

not always feeling you need to perform or deliver

The way forward is …

to understand that you alone teach other people what to expect from you, so teach them to treat you with respect.

You're drawn to people born on …

July 23 to August 23

You are both fiercely individualistic and inquisitive individuals, and this can be a warm and fulfilling relationship.

Luck maker

Trust in yourself

Unwavering belief in their own potential is the one essential element in lucky people. It generates the ability and enthusiasm necessary to attract luck and become a winner in life. Believe you can succeed and you will.

People born on June 28 are often focused and driven individuals, but they also have a sense of fun and lightness that permeates their lives. They can also laugh at themselves if the joke is on them and don't take themselves too seriously. Motivated and enterprising, they eagerly latch onto every opportunity to further their plans and endeavors.

They can typically be counted on to break the tension at any social gathering, their sharp wit turning the spotlight on them and winning them many admirers. Occasionally they can block their good fortune by taking easy shots that offend their targets, but they mainly aim to surprise and delight. Although they have a light-hearted quality about them, it's a mistake to underestimate their ability in the competitive world as underneath their fun-loving exterior they have an iron will and a facility to turn their visions into reality.

Sometimes they may be accused of disorganization because they like to be on the go; if they aren't moving, dancing or running they will probably be fidgeting, but the quality of the work they produce is anything but chaotic. Others will wonder how someone so lighthearted makes difficult tasks look so easy. What others don't realize is that they have worked as hard as everyone else, sometimes harder, but instead of complaining or reminding others of how tough things are, they simply get on with it and "effortlessly" generate quality results.

There is no denying that these people like to be the center of attention; their mischievous good humor well suits the spotlight. They do need to be aware, however, that their longing to be noticed may be the result of hidden fears and insecurities. In their early life they may have been painfully shy but after the age of twenty-three they gain a much-needed boost of strength and confidence. If they can take advantage of the opportunities to build their self-esteem, they have within them the determination to become an advisor or authority figure that others admire, respect and hope to emulate.

Love *Share the spotlight*

Being witty, friendly and charming, people born on June 28 don't often have problems attracting partners, but anyone who wants to share their life may have to be content with playing a supporting role. Finding someone who can share their stimulating intellectual interests and sense of fun is likely to create the ideal relationship.

Health *Serious thinking*

People born on this day understand the importance of plenty of fun, laughter and love in their lives, and their physical and emotional health and well-being benefits as a result. They need to be careful that they don't get over-involved in the problems of their friends and families, because this will drag some of the lightness and humor out of them. As far as diet is concerned, they may have problems with their weight so they need to eat healthy, nutritious food and avoid fad diets, as these will just make problems worse. Regular exercise is highly recommended but even if they don't exercise they will burn off plenty of energy with their constant fidgeting and need to be on the move. They would benefit from meditation techniques that can help them travel internally rather than externally and wearing, meditating on and surrounding themselves with the color blue will encourage others to take them more seriously.

Career *Born celebrities*

These people have a yearning to be instruments of progress, and this may draw them toward the caring professions or humanitarian projects. Being natural psychologists, they may also excel in careers that involve personal contact such as counseling, personnel, promotions, or public relations. Teaching and lecturing may also appeal, and a desire to be creative may draw them toward catering, design, acting, music, and the world of entertainment, or setting up their own business as an entrepreneur.

Destiny *To share their happiness and inspiration with others*

The life path of people born on this day is to discover that people can and do love them for who they are and not for their ability to entertain. Once they have worked on their self-esteem, their destiny is to share their happiness and inspiration with others.

Signs & symbols

Sun sign: Cancer

Ruling planet: Moon, the intuitive

Symbol: The Crab

Birth date ruler: Sun, the individual

Tarot card: Magician (will-power)

Favorable numbers: 1, 7

Lucky days: Monday and Sunday, especially when these days fall on 1 and 7 of the month

Lucky colors: Cream, orange, yellow

Birthstone: Pearl

29 June

the birthday of the altruistic visionary

Your greatest challenge is ...

not giving too much of yourself

The way forward is ...

to understand that only after you know how to take care of yourself can you take care of others.

You're drawn to people born on ...

June 22 to July 23

You both have much to give and take from each other, and this can be a dynamic and satisfying relationship.

Luck maker

Treat yourself

Treat yourself to something that you really want: a book, a film, a new outfit, a haircut. Make sure it's something that makes you feel good, because when you feel good your chances of attracting good luck increase.

People born on June 29 are often highly intuitive and sensitive. They have a knack for anticipating other people's words, actions and reactions. This is because they have the rare ability to put themselves into another's shoes. As well as being intuitive, they also possess a dazzling imagination and the practical ability to transform their progressive visions into reality.

With their unique combination of altruistic intuition and imagination, these people give much to others and share their burdens. They are the people who will be a shoulder for their friends to cry on, a morale booster at work and a charity worker in their spare time. They will often be drawn to people who are lonely and insecure because they hope that offering their friendship will reinforce the self-esteem of those who feel fragile.

They often present a lighthearted, youthful and energetic face to the world, and others will love the fact that they rarely complain or drag people down with negativity. Their aim is always to uplift and help others, and while they may be accused of superficiality, underneath their charm and innocence they have all the drive and competitive edge they need to achieve their goals. They often have a talent for making money, and lots of it, although their competitive drive is motivated by a desire to share their vision and happiness with others, rather than gain personal success.

Although their dedication to bringing pleasure to others is admirable, they occasionally need to give themselves a boost as well. If their behavior becomes too self-sacrificing, they may suffer from bouts of indecision and anxiety about their own personal focus and motivation. Before the age of twenty they may be inclined to be shy or reserved but after twenty-three they will enjoy opportunities to develop their personal power and creativity. It is vital that they take advantage of these because in this period their intellect, imagination and understanding of the needs of others can help them make their own dreams, as well as the dreams of others, a practical reality.

Love *Exceedingly generous*

People born on June 29 can easily attract people with their optimistic, upbeat, caring approach and they usually think in twosomes. They may be drawn toward partners who are insecure in some way but since they are prone to insecurity themselves, they might be better choosing someone less needy. Once in a relationship they are often exceedingly generous with those they love and may need to temper their giving impulse to allow their partner or children to stand on their own two feet.

Health *Self-care*

People born on this day have a tendency to put others before themselves, and although this is commendable they need to remember to take care of themselves as well. They are also prone to taking on the burdens of others and this can sometimes result in emotional difficulties or even co-dependent relationships. As far as diet and lifestyle are concerned, they may have a craving for sweet foods, foods high in fat, alcohol, or recreational drugs; they need to counteract this with a healthy, balanced diet and plenty of exercise. Any form of aerobic exercise is recommended as it will boost their cardiovascular and respiratory health. Wearing, meditating on and surrounding themselves with the color red will increase their self-confidence and help them distance themselves from those who might drag them down.

Career *Born charity workers*

These people are well suited to careers in education, the fashion, leisure, and beauty industries, and careers connected to the home and family. They also have natural skills in working for a charitable cause. Their imagination and quick intelligence may draw them to science, medicine, alternative healing, or business, and their need for creative expression may draw them to writing, music and art.

Destiny *To inspire others with their generosity*

The life path of people born on this day is to learn to find a balance between their own needs and those of others. Once they have found that balance, their destiny is to influence and inspire others with their generosity and their ability to make the impossible seem possible.

Power Thought

66 I owe it to myself to develop my many talents and abilities 99

Signs & symbols

Sun sign: Cancer

Ruling planet: Moon, the intuitive

Symbol: The Crab

Birth date ruler: Moon, the intuitive

Tarot card: The High Priestess (intuition)

Favorable numbers: 2, 8

Lucky day: Monday, especially when it falls on 2 and 8 of the month

Lucky colors: Cream, silver, white

Birthstone: Pearl

June 29

30 June

the birthday of mystery

Your greatest challenge is ...

dealing with your insecurity

The way forward is ...

to understand that you are not alone. Everyone has doubts and fears, and building self-esteem is a lifetime's work-in-progress for all of us.

You're drawn to people born on ...

October 24 to November 23

You are both hungry for love and closeness, and, if you are both honest, this union has incredible potential.

Luck maker

Never give up on yourself

Lucky people understand that the darkest time is just before dawn. So when the going gets rough, never give up on yourself, knowing that you can and will feel happy and joyous again.

To those who don't know them well, people born on June 30 present something of a mystery. On the one hand they are driven and imaginative with a quirky sense of humor and flashes of fire when challenged; on the other hand, their tendency to keep their feelings to themselves puts them in the introvert category.

These people are indeed complicated, often appearing to be something they are not. It isn't just others who find it hard to second-guess them; they are often a mystery to themselves and unsure of their true identity. Despite their elusiveness, they have two distinctive personality traits. First, they are ambitious and highly motivated individuals with all the intelligence, imagination and tenacity to take them right to the top. Second, although they dislike public displays of affection, they are extremely giving and loving to their small group of friends.

They may incline more toward introversion in their early life, but around the age of twenty-two they may undergo a transformation of their power, creativity and confidence. Once they understand that strong emotional bonds of intimacy—so important to their feelings of self-worth—cannot be forged unless they open themselves up to others, these are the years when they are likely to achieve their personal and professional ambitions. After the age of fifty-two they tend to use their abilities to provide practical and inspirational service to others.

Often working hard to fulfill the expectations of others, be they employers, partners or family members, they may surprise people with bouts of apparent laziness. It's important that others allow them this time out and don't try to push them back into action prematurely. They need to recharge their batteries, and when they feel ready they will get back in the driving seat. When they reconcile the diverse aspects of their personality they have the potential not just to achieve outstanding personal and professional success, but to empower others with a sense of confidence and creativity.

Love *Not in public*

People born on June 30 easily attract people with their wit and social skills but tend to prefer people who are genuinely intelligent, hardworking and caring. They prefer to focus their energies on a small number of close friends rather than a large number of acquaintances. Partners will know them as affectionate and loving in private but less demonstrative in public.

Health *Balance is important*

People born on this day have a tendency to worry needlessly about their health, although upsets of the digestive system and lungs are common. They may also be prone to bouts of depression when they don't allow themselves the time and space to reflect on their motivations. Self-examination is crucial to their emotional health and they might benefit enormously from counseling and therapy. As far as diet is concerned, they should aim for a balanced diet, rich in fresh, natural products such as fruits, vegetables, whole grains, nuts, seeds, and oily fish. Mild to moderate exercise, such as brisk walking, ballroom dancing, low-impact aerobics, swimming, and cycling, is recommended. Wearing, meditating on and surrounding themselves with the color purple will encourage them to look within themselves for answers.

Career *Born trainers*

These people have a flair for the dramatic and are well suited to careers in the world of art, music, writing, theater, film, or design, but they may also become leading teachers, trainers, lecturers, athletes, agents, or promoters, as well as excelling in public relations and the world of entertainment. Their intelligence may also draw them toward science, medicine, alternative healing, or business, and their natural humanitarianism may incline them to counseling and community or charity work.

Destiny *To motivate and inspire others with compassion, commitment, affection and loyalty*

The life path of people born on this day is to try to understand themselves and their motivations better. Once they have learned the importance of self-examination, their destiny is to motivate and inspire others with their compassion, commitment, affection and loyalty.

Power Thought

66 When I listen to my inner wisdom I find the answers I need **99**

Signs & symbols

Sun sign: Cancer

Ruling planet: Moon, the intuitive

Symbol: The Crab

Birth date ruler: Jupiter, the philosopher

Tarot card: The Empress (creativity)

Favorable numbers: 3, 9

Lucky days: Monday and Thursday, especially when these days fall on 3 and 9 of the month

Lucky colors: Cream, purple, lilac

Birthstone: Pearl

June 30

1 July

the birthday of delicate equilibrium

Your greatest challenge is ...

being consistent

The way forward is ...

to understand that when you're ruled by your impulses you're not in control of your life.

You're drawn to people born on ...

July 24 to August 23

You share a love of excitement and a need for security, and this can create a passionate but secure union.

Luck maker

Stop self-destructive behavior

Lucky people don't destroy their own chances of success and happiness with self-sabotaging behavior, so begin to notice when you are doing things that do not promote positive results.

Charismatic, enterprising and determined to get ahead in life, people born on July 1 possess an adventurous spirit, a shrewd mind and a remarkable memory. Insightful, intuitive and imaginative, many of them are also great humanitarians capable of making tremendous sacrifices for others and for society as a whole.

Although they have the ability to be extroverts and are often genial and outgoing in public, in private they can be more moody and changeable than most realize. Balancing the introvert and extrovert, or feminine and masculine energies, within them, they are equally solitary and gregarious. They also have an unusual empathy for the issues, conflicts and insecurities experienced by the opposite sex, and as a result will be sought out by both male and female friends for their opinions or friendship. They love to give advice and offer support, especially if it's for those less fortunate; other people love them for their spontaneous generosity. Their volatile, artistic temperament can, however, cause them to act on impulse, alienating them from others when they say or do things they later regret.

Until the age of twenty-one they are likely to be extremely shy and lacking confidence in their own abilities, but after the age of twenty-two there are many opportunities for them to develop their strength, creativity and self-expression. They need to take advantage of these opportunities because if they don't, they may start to torture themselves with worry, anxiety and self-doubt. After the age of fifty-one their focus changes to a more pragmatic desire to be of service.

In many ways it could be said that they are their own worst enemies. They need to learn to reconcile their inner and outer selves so that they don't get trapped in only one half of their lives. When they do reach this delicate balance they will discover within themselves a rare and exquisite magic that can not only reach out and inspire others, but also enhance their own potential for happiness, success and good fortune in all areas of their lives.

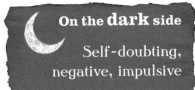

On the dark side

Self-doubting,
negative, impulsive

At your best

Warm, ambitious,
charismatic

Power Thought

" The only
constraints I
have are the
constraints I
decide to
believe in "

Love *The big issue*

Love for people born on July 1 is the big issue of their lives, and they need a partner who is solid and secure and of whom they can feel proud. Loyalty and trust play an important role in their relationships, but they need to make sure that passion and love are the price they pay for safety and security.

Health *Happy inside*

People born on this day don't always have a positive relationship with their body and their health and well-being may suffer as a result. They are prone to eating disorders, or to exercising and dieting obsessively to get into shape. It is extremely important for them to learn to get a sense of balance and perspective, remembering that until they feel happy inside no amount of exercising or dieting is going to make any difference. Depression is another major health risk for them and they would benefit from counseling or therapy. Listening to music may also be extremely therapeutic, as would plenty of mild mood-boosting aerobic exercise such as walking, dancing and swimming. Carrying a titanium quartz crystal with them will help them pull themselves together when they feel all over the place, and wearing the color yellow will help boost their self-confidence.

Career *Born actors*

These people like to be in control so they may succeed in management or executive positions. They may also prefer to work for themselves. Other careers that might suit them include politics, theater, film-making, fashion, acting, directing, art, music, dance, the caring professions, the leisure industry, sport, social work, teaching, and working with children.

Destiny *To help alleviate suffering in the world*

The life path of people born on this day is to learn to give and receive. When they reach this balance, their destiny is to turn the spotlight on injustices and help alleviate suffering.

Signs & symbols

Sun sign: Cancer

Ruling planet: Moon, the intuitive

Symbol: The Crab

Birth date ruler: Sun, the individual

Tarot card: The Magician (will-power)

Favorable numbers: 1, 8

Lucky days: Monday and Sunday, especially when these days fall on 1 and 8 of the month

Lucky colors: Cream, ginger, gold

Birthstone: Pearl

July 1

2 July

the birthday of emotional intensity

Your greatest challenge is ...

addressing your own deepest needs

The way forward is ...

to understand that while the love of others may temper feelings of insecurity, the way to feel really fulfilled is to address your deepest needs.

You're drawn to people born on ...

October 24 to November 22

You are both big on feelings, and a match between you is likely to be deep and intimate.

Luck maker

Stop doubting yourself

When you feel bad about yourself you block luck, attracting people and situations that will continue to make you feel bad about yourself.

People born on July 2 are deeply intuitive and imaginative individuals with the ability to utilize their marked determination, organizational skills and tenacity to great effect. They may, however, have often felt overwhelmed by their own emotional intensity and the key to their success or failure is the way they choose to deal with it.

They are also defined by their extraordinary sensitivity, a quality that leads them to empathize with those around them—especially those less fortunate—and which arouses in them strong feelings of natural justice that they are inclined to champion. They have a knack of reaching out to others and making them feel like family, but although their public persona is often colorful and capable, they may be plagued by private insecurities. They also constantly support friends and co-workers but find it hard to accept the support and praise they richly deserve from others.

It is important for them to get to grips with their fragile feelings and understand what motivates their self-sabotaging behavior; building their self-esteem is a crucial requirement for their psychological growth. Until the age of twenty they may be reserved but after the age of twenty-one they have opportunities to become more dynamic, positive and self-assured. They need to take advantage of these; if they do, their confidence will extend over the next thirty years, helping them achieve the positions of leadership or authority for which they are well qualified. After the age of fifty they become more discriminating and may desire to be practically useful and inspirational to others.

People born on this day can get carried away with unfounded emotions and fantasies either leading to introversion and an inability to express themselves, or to an exuberance that sometimes alarms others with its intensity. If, however, they can devote more time and energy to self-examination, looking at the effect their behavior has on themselves and others, they will find ways to balance their emotions, and this new-found stability will bring them greater happiness, success and fulfillment.

Love *Just the way you are*

Though people born on this day can effortlessly attract potential partners, they never feel sure that their partner loves them for who they are. Whoever falls in love with them needs to be able to handle their fragile feelings and offer them plenty of reassurance, but they will be rewarded by deep devotion and romance.

Health *Nervous tension*

People born on this day don't just feel things, they feel them intensely, and as a result they may be prone to stress, anxiety and nervousness. Those who are more introverted can damage their emotional well-being by suppressing their emotions; if this is the case, counseling is recommended. Those who are more extroverted need to make sure that their desire for intensity does not lead them to recreational drugs and alcohol. As far as diet is concerned, the emphasis should be on consistency, and balance; eating on the run or skipping meals should definitely be avoided. Moderate to mild exercise, in particular brisk walking, is recommended to boost their physical health and also to give them much-needed time to gather their thoughts. Wearing, meditating on and surrounding themselves with the color green will restore their balance and help calm their frayed nerves.

Career *Born psychiatrists*

These people are well suited to careers in psychiatry, therapy, counseling, and similar branches of medicine, as well as the arts, writing, drama, or music, in all of which they can find a creative outlet for their emotional intensity. They may also have a talent for business and do especially well in management positions, particularly in areas such as real estate, media or advertising.

Destiny *To support, inspire and motivate others*

The life path of people born on this day is to examine their internal conflicts to discover what their motivations are. Once they are able to work on their own self-development, their destiny is to use their formidable practical skills, energetic determination and powerful imagination to support, inspire and motivate others.

Power Thought

"I am as fulfilled, successful and self-confident as I decide to be"

Signs & symbols

Sun sign: Cancer

Ruling planet: Moon, the intuitive

Symbol: The Crab

Birth date ruler: Moon, the intuitive

Tarot card: The High Priestess (intuition)

Favorable numbers: 2, 9

Lucky day: Monday, especially when it falls on 2 and 9 of the month

Lucky colors: Cream, silver, rose

Birthstone: Pearl

July 2

3 July

the birthday of the surveyor

People born on July 3 are keen observers of everything that is going on around them. Their approach to life, however, is not that of the critic but of the philosopher or judge surveying what they see and coming up with an authoritative conclusion.

People born on this day have a very rational mind that helps them manage their emotions effectively. They want the world to be a better place but they usually conclude that emotions tend to hinder rather than help people progress, so they prefer to hide theirs. Although endlessly fascinated by people and the workings of the world, they tend to keep themselves detached because without emotions to cloud their judgment they think they can be more effective. They can charm virtually anyone with their calm, mild manner, and when they believe in a cause their progress is virtually unstoppable.

They are always curious to discover something new, but they should ensure this doesn't earn them the reputation of being interfering or nosy. Their curiosity may also lead them toward dubious or questionable people or causes but their rationality will help them steer clear of any wrongdoing or extremes of behavior. Until the age of nineteen they may focus on security and family, but after the age of twenty they may be offered opportunities to develop in confidence and to strengthen their performance in their chosen field. This can be an exciting time for them but they should remember that they belong to the same species as the creatures whose actions they love to survey. After the age of forty-nine they are likely to develop a more discriminating attitude and, although service to others is highlighted, they should make sure they don't become cynical or superior in their approach to others.

Once these people have been able to find a balance between detachment and involvement, they will find that their intuitive and intellectual talents combine to endow them with outstanding potential to become effective instruments of reform and progress.

At your **best**

Observant, insightful, committed

Love *Don't play games*

People born on July 3 rarely jump head first into a relationship and they may keep potential partners on hold until they determine what they really want. Anyone who tries to sweet talk them or play games with them is more likely to earn their contempt rather than their respect, but when they do find lasting love they accept both their partner's gifts and flaws, and don't try to change them.

Health *Getting involved*

People born on this day have a tendency to withdraw from social interaction or to cast themselves in the position of observer or commentator on the action. For their psychological growth it is important that they overcome their reluctance and participate more fully in what is going on around them. If they don't seek human contact, they are likely to feel unfulfilled, lonely and insecure. Spending plenty of time with family and friends is beneficial for them, as is getting involved in charity work or humanitarian causes. As far as diet is concerned, cooking for or eating out with loved ones and friends is highly recommended. Exercise that is socially orientated, such as dancing, competitive sports or joining a gym, will also be beneficial. Wearing, meditating on or surrounding themselves with the color orange will help lift their social life and increase feelings of physical enjoyment, warmth and security.

Career *Born psychologists*

These people are well suited to careers in psychology and psychiatry as well as medicine and education. Their imaginative powers also augur well for careers in art or entertainment. They are likely to shine in positions of authority as they can be fair and just, and this makes them excellent managers or administrators. Other careers that might interest them include charity work, labor unions, antiques dealer, chef, caterer, art dealer, or administrator.

Destiny *To inspire others with their visions of progress*

The life path of people born on this day is to learn to engage emotionally with the world around them. Once they are able to participate fully, their destiny is to influence and inspire others with their talents and their visions of fairness and progress.

Signs & symbols

Sun sign: Cancer

Ruling planet: Moon, the intuitive

Symbol: The Crab

Birth date ruler: Jupiter, the philosopher

Tarot card: The Empress (creativity)

Favorable numbers: 1, 3

Lucky days: Monday and Thursday, especially when these days fall on 1 and 3 of the month

Lucky colors: Cream, amethyst, lavender

Birthstone: Pearl

July 3

4 July

the birthday of dedication

People born on July 4 tend to identify strongly with groups and organizations, be they their family, co-workers, local community, country or even humanity as a whole. The creation of shared human bonds and goals is extremely important to them, and they will often dedicate themselves to defending people's wider interests.

Whatever path in life they choose, they will be at their happiest when they are surrounded by those who are working toward a common goal. Ironically, though, for those so focused on communal identification, they are also quite private individuals and prefer to keep their own feelings to themselves; opening up to others won't be easy for them. Despite their reserve, it's no coincidence that these people were born on US Independence Day. Their dedication and loyalty are matched only by their courageous spirit and desire to defend and protect those less fortunate. They are also extremely intuitive, but because this gift can make them feel as if they are different they may choose to repress it or only reveal it to those who know them well.

In the years leading up to the age of eighteen they will be concerned with home, family and security; after they age of nineteen they may find that they are increasingly drawn into public positions that require strength and confidence. During these years they should guard against inflexibility and uncritical belief in their cause. After the age of forty-eight they enter a new phase which brings practical issues to prominence, and they are likely to become more analytical, observant and methodical.

If they devote themselves to a cause that is worthy of them, they have the potential to rise all the way to the top, helping others rise to the top with them. The opposite is true if they make the wrong choice, so learning to make the right choices and decisions will be their major challenge. They will, however, be able to make the right choice with ease if they work with their intuition, investing time and energy to listening to their inner voice.

At your best

Principled, courageous, generous

Love *Always knows best*

The mild-mannered charm of people born on July 4 will often attract admirers but when in a relationship they need to watch their tendency to always know what's best for everyone, especially as they tend to be attracted to enterprising, successful people who are determined to succeed. Once in a loving relationship, however, they can be extremely affectionate, generous, loyal, and loving.

Health *Don't neglect the gift of health*

People born on this day have a tendency to neglect their own health and well-being for the sake of the family or the group they are working with, so it is important for them to make sure that their own personal well-being takes center stage. They would benefit greatly from scheduling regular exercise into their diary to make sure they don't decide to give it a miss. Team sports and regular fitness classes are ideal ways for them to keep in shape, but they may also benefit from a running, swimming or cycling schedule. As far as diet is concerned, they need to increase their intake of fresh produce, in particular fruits and vegetables. Mind–body therapies that encourage them to get in touch with their intuition such as meditation, hypnotherapy and yoga would be extremely beneficial. Wearing, meditating on and surrounding themselves with the color purple will encourage them to focus more on their inner life.

Career *Born firefighters*

These people will thrive in any job that involves people and an element of risk. They might make great firefighters, paramedics, police officers or emergency care workers. They may also be drawn to sales, negotiation, promotion, law, publishing, banking, or politics. Any occupation that deals with items for the home, food or caring would also be a possibility, and their love of the dramatic may lure them to the world of art and entertainment.

Destiny *To devote their talents to the common good*

The life path of people born on this day is to understand that some of the answers they are looking for can only be found by searching within. Once they are able to connect with their intuition, their destiny is to devote their considerable talents to the common good.

Power Thought

❝ I bring good to others by discovering the good in me ❞

Signs & symbols

Sun sign: Cancer

Ruling planet: Moon, the intuitive

Symbol: The Crab

Birth date ruler: Uranus, the visionary

Tarot card: The Emperor (authority)

Favorable numbers: 2, 4

Lucky days: Monday and Sunday, especially when these days fall on 2 and 4 of the month

Lucky colors: Cream, cobalt blue, lavender

Birthstone: Pearl

July 4

5 July

the birthday of fireworks

Whatever situation they are in or whatever person or group of people they are with, people born on July 5 have a flair for injecting sparkle, energy and excitement into the atmosphere. Everything about them is vivid and colorful, and their charming manners and interesting conversation light up the workplace and social gatherings.

Thriving on constant variety and stimulation, their life never seems to stand still, and even if they are in a routine of some kind because of work or family commitments they will make sure that they have a hobby or interest to absorb them. They can, however, alienate others with their boundless energy and enthusiasm. Although they tend to have many admirers, some people may have trouble keeping up with their explosive pace; their wild shifts in mood may also frustrate those who admire them but doubt their reliability.

Before the age of eighteen, they may often have problems or difficulties with school or study. This is because their restless nature makes it hard for them to concentrate for long periods or conform to a schedule. Their vivid imagination may also make them feel different in some way, but they should cherish rather than repress it as later in life it may offer them an endless source of inspiration. After the age of eighteen their confidence increases; these are the years they are most likely to be adventurous and creative. It is important during this period that they learn to maintain a sense of stability, not frittering their energy and away in too many directions. After the age of forty-seven they may become more discriminating and efficient.

The key to their success is education and learning, as these will help develop the discipline and awareness they need to reach their true potential. Their desire to keep busy will always be a key characteristic, but when it is combined with a more centered existence their explosive ideas will finally come down from the drawing board and transform into accomplishments or achievements that are progressive and lasting in their impact.

On the dark side

Wild, erratic, unreliable

At your best

Exciting, entertaining, imaginative

Love *Someone very special*

People born on July 5 may often resist attempts to make them settle down, and it will take someone special to hold their attention for long and add much-needed stability to their life. They prefer to be associated with people who are charismatic, exciting and influential like themselves, but they would benefit more from associating with those who have a calmer, gentler and more centered approach.

Health *Experimental*

People born on this day love to experiment in all aspects of their life, emotionally, intellectually and physically. Their diet is likely to be varied and interesting and, as long as they make sure they don't go for long periods without food, when they are absorbed in their work they are likely to be eating healthily; as their life is often hectic and they are prone to coughs and colds, however, they might benefit from a multi-vitamin and mineral pill every day. Regular exercise is recommended, especially activities and sports that involve other people in a competitive or social way. Mind-training therapies that encourage them to slow down, calm down and focus their minds such as meditation, hypnotherapy and cognitive therapy are highly recommended. An ideal way for them to unwind after a hectic day would be in a warm bath with one drop of juniper essential oil. Wearing the color blue will also help them feel calmer and more centered.

Career *Born inventors*

These people have creative flair that may express itself in careers in design, invention, technology, art, music, film-making, and dance. Multi-talented, they may also excel in a variety of occupations including sales, promotion, banking, counseling, and the world of entertainment. A dislike for taking orders often leads them into positions of authority, and a love of variety may provoke them to work on their own.

Destiny *To realize their visionary sense of purpose*

The life path of people born on this day is to learn to maintain stability in their relationships and their lives. Once they are more grounded, their destiny is to innovate and reform and, by so doing, realize their vision.

Signs & symbols

Sun sign: Cancer

Ruling planet: Moon, the intuitive

Symbol: The Crab

Birth date ruler: Mercury, the communicator

Tarot card: The Hierophant (spiritual guidance)

Favorable numbers: 3, 5

Lucky days: Monday and Wednesday, especially when these days fall on 3 and 5 of the month

Lucky colors: Cream, indigo blue, silver

Birthstone: Pearl

July 5

6 July

the birthday of passionate attachment

Your greatest challenge is …

avoiding tunnel vision

The way forward is …

to understand that human beings have complex emotional, physical, and intellectual needs; happiness and fulfillment can never be found through one avenue alone.

You're drawn to people born on …

April 21 to May 21

You are both passionate and sensual, but also have a need for security and trust within a relationship.

Luck maker

Don't rely on one thing

Lucky people never allow their happiness to depend on one person or thing alone because they know that the more broad and well rounded their life is, the greater their chances of success and happiness.

People born on July 6 are filled with infectious energy, vibrant optimism and dedicated enthusiasm about every aspect of their lives. It is impossible for them to be anything but passionate and intense about their relationships, responsibilities or career.

Compromise just doesn't make sense for these people. More than anything else they yearn to achieve their ideals and will dedicate themselves passionately to their personal quest, be it for the perfect love, career or lifestyle. Although they are reliable and dedicated, the passionate attachment that they have to their own ideas and plans can lead to problems with others. In some cases they can become so single-minded in their pursuit of their dreams that work may take over their life, their love life may dominate all their decisions, or they may devote every ounce of their energy to a cause. This is potentially dangerous as their happiness may depend on just one thing; if that is unachievable or there are setbacks, their behavior may become needy or obsessive. It is extremely important therefore that they learn to be less obsessive, broadening their interests and horizons to include not just one, but several potential sources of fulfillment.

After the age of sixteen they may have opportunities to become bolder and more self-assured; they need to take advantage of these to broaden their perspective. After the age of forty-six they are likely to become more health conscious, precise and discriminating; during these years it is important for them to manage their financial assets well as their passionate nature means that they may have a tendency to spend money faster than they make it.

Above all, people born on this day need to learn not to devote all their energy and enthusiasm to one area of their life. This is because when they finally manage to cultivate a more well-rounded approach to life they will find that they have all the talent and personal magnetism they need to see most of the passionate dreams that inspire them transformed into reality.

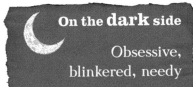
Love *Don't fall in love too easily*

People born on July 6 are passionate and loyal romantic partners but they need to be a bit more cautious and give themselves plenty of time before pledging their love. They can also be a little too needy and should give their partners enough room to breathe. When they are able to let go in this way, they will find love a much easier game to play.

Health *Avoid dependency of any sort*

People born on this day have a tendency to be addictive or intense in their approach to life, so it is very important for them to avoid dependency on alcohol, cigarettes, recreational drugs, sugary or fatty, food and any other substance that can temporarily induce a high. Cultivating a well-rounded approach to life with a number of potential sources of fulfillment rather than just one will help manage that potential problem. As far as diet is concerned, the emphasis should be on a balanced diet with plenty of variety so that they don't get stuck in a particular food routine. Regular exercise, especially cross-training where a variety of disciplines are combined, is recommended. Wearing, meditating on and surrounding themselves with the color yellow will encourage them to feel more creative and open-minded.

Career *Born image makers*

These people have the intellectual insight, determination and focus to succeed in any career, but they may find themselves drawn to teaching, lecturing or self-employment where they can have the freedom to work in their own way. Other career options might include banking, business, the stock market, show business, the arts, charity work, image making, the healing professions, or work in the community.

Destiny *To raise standards*

The life path of people born on this day is to learn to find fulfillment in all areas of their lives, not just one. Once they learn to be more open-minded and realistic, their destiny is to use their remarkable charisma to recruit others to their own highly idealized standards.

Signs & symbols

Sun sign: Cancer

Ruling planet: Moon, the intuitive

Symbol: The Crab

Birth date ruler: Venus, the lover

Tarot card: The Lovers (intuition)

Favorable numbers: 4, 6

Lucky days: Monday and Friday, especially when these days fall on 4 and 6 of the month

Lucky colors: Cream, pink, crimson

Birthstone: Pearl

July 6

7 July

the birthday of
the beautiful dreamer

People born on July 7 are the type of individuals whose soaring imagination will cause them to support projects deemed unfeasible and then surprise and confuse others showing that they are indeed feasible. The key to their ability to achieve the impossible is their rare combination of imagination and fierce determination.

They are beautiful dreamers in every sense, blessed with the creativity and idealism that many others lose when they become adults. People may describe them as naïve, not because they are unintelligent but because any form of deception is alien to them. Their openness and honesty is touching and endearing, but it will limit their rise professionally and socially. This is unlikely to bother them, however, because for them a life that isn't honest or where they can't be creative is a life not worth living.

Shyness and sensitivity may become less of a problem for them after the age of sixteen, when there are opportunities for them to become bolder and more assertive in all areas of their lives. At the age of forty-five they are likely to become more analytical and discriminating. They will never lose their remarkable imagination but these are the years when they are likely to fine-tune their creative talents, using their creative approach to life to lift others out of the mundane. Crucial to their success or failure, however, will be their willingness to step out from their dreams every now and again and see the world for what it really is.

The big threat to their happiness is the way they react to criticism or to those who misunderstand them. Instead of accepting that there will always be differences of opinion or learning from feedback, they may react strongly by crawling into a shell of resentment, self-pity and defeatism that is not conducive to psychological growth. However, once they develop the emotional maturity to be more objective, they have all the potential and passion not only to generate ambitious plans and see them realized, but to earn the support and admiration of others.

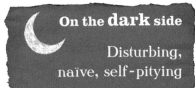
At your best

Imaginative, determined, creative

Love *Give everything*

People born on this day have a tendency to fall in and out of love quickly and they need a partner who can maintain their interest and keep them feeling grounded and secure. Since they attract partners easily, they need to become aware of becoming too demanding or emotional in their love life, but once in a steady relationship they give everything to the one they love.

Health *Calm down*

People born on this day have a low stress threshold so they need to make sure they give themselves plenty of rest and relaxation. A happy home life will be extremely beneficial to their emotional health and well-being because it will give them a place to shelter when they feel vulnerable, and a place to sit and dream. Music and spending time by the sea or sailing are particularly good healers for them, but they may also find that other stress-management techniques such as aromatherapy, massage and meditation work wonders. As far as diet is concerned, they need to be careful with fatty and heavily processed and refined foods high in additives, because these can trigger digestive disorders. Mild to moderate exercise, preferably outdoors to give them more freedom and plenty of mood-boosting sunshine, is also recommended. Wearing, meditating on and surrounding themselves with the color yellow will help boost their self-confidence.

Career *Born painters*

People born on this day are often drawn to careers in the arts such as music, painting and acting but they can also use their energy and intuition effectively in the business world or the world of science and technology. Other possible career options include law, banking and publishing.

Destiny *To touch the lives of others with ingeniousness and creativity*

The life path of people born on this day is not so much to toughen up emotionally but to become more objective and realistic in their approach to life, without losing their wonderful creativity. Once they are able to do this, their destiny is to touch the lives of others with their ingeniousness and creativity.

Signs & symbols

Sun sign: Cancer

Ruling planet: Moon, the intuitive

Symbol: The Crab

Birth date ruler: Neptune, the speculator

Tarot card: The Chariot (resilience)

Favorable numbers: 5, 7

Lucky day: Monday, especially when it falls on 5 and 7 of the month

Lucky colors: Cream, sea green, emerald

Birthstone: Pearl

July 7

8 July

the birthday of mysterious pragmatism

Your greatest challenge is …

learning to switch off or relax

The way forward is …

to understand that regular down time is an essential ingredient for success, as it allows you to recharge your batteries and come back refreshed and re-energized.

You're drawn to people born on …

April 21 to May 21

You are both sensual, passionate individuals who need security and honesty, and this can be a stunning match.

Luck maker

Take a natural break

When you feel pressured and tense, you block your chances of luck. A good way to calm your mind is to take a walk in the park or escape the city for a few hours.

People tend to admire those born on July 8 for their impressive pragmatism, fixity of purpose and dynamic energy, but the admiration they earn tends to be more of the respectful, awed variety rather than that born of affection. Such is their strength of will and uncompromising determination that they will stop at nothing to achieve their progressive aims.

They are often strong willed and motivated by the desire to make their mark on the world, tending to devote themselves to one single purpose and stick with it through thick and thin. Sometimes this one-track approach backfires, but more often than not they invest their time and energy wisely, bringing them considerable financial success. This sense of purpose can be so strong that it overrides their sense of right and wrong, so it is crucial for them to decide what their principles are and stick to them.

Despite their steadiness and fixity of purpose they are anything but an open book. Quite the opposite; they will often remain a mystery even to those closest to them. Of the many reasons for this one may be that they may have grown up never feeling quite good enough; because of this they may have grown emotionally defensive and doubly determined to achieve success in their career and relationships. This determination may lead to controlling or domineering behavior whenever they feel threatened or vulnerable. It is therefore important for their psychological growth that they get in touch with their emotions.

After the age of fifteen there are opportunities for them to use their talents and skills in a more confident way but they should ensure their driving interests don't alienate those closest to them. After the age of forty-four practical considerations become more important and these are the years when they are capable of achieving great things professionally and personally. If they can become more aware of the forceful influence they have on others, they can earn not just the respect but also the loyalty and affection of those they live and work with.

Love *Sincere concern*

People born on July 8 often have a wide circle of friends. In relationships they make devoted partners willing to make great sacrifices for those they love. Though others may appreciate their sincere concern there may also be times when they resent their interference. It is important for them not to treat their partners as children because it will block passion and spontaneity in the relationship.

Health *Get up and move*

People born on this day have controlling tendencies and may prefer to sit on the sidelines guiding and directing others rather than getting their hands dirty. As a result they may neglect physical exercise, so they should ensure that they get up and move about more in their daily lives, not sitting for long periods at their desk or in their favorite armchair. In addition to becoming more active in their daily lives, they should sign up for three or more vigorous exercise sessions every week to work off some of their pent-up energy. As far as diet is concerned, they should take a more active interest in buying, cooking and preparing food rather than just expecting it to be served. Wearing, meditating on and surrounding themselves with the colors pink or green will restore natural healing and balance, and inspire harmony in others.

Career *Born scientists*

These people have the imagination and tenacity to excel in scientific or commercial careers, as well as in artistic careers that require detailed preparation and research. They may also be drawn to business management, teaching and counseling, or to work that is of benefit to the community. Alternatively, they may prefer to be self-employed.

Destiny *To influence and improve the lives of others*

The life path of people born on this day is to understand that their priorities may not always be the same as everyone else's. Once they have learned to place equal value on their own interests and the concerns of those close to them, their destiny is to implement their progressive aims and improve the lives of others in the process.

Signs & symbols

Sun sign: Cancer

Ruling planet: Moon, the intuitive

Symbol: The Crab

Birth date ruler: Saturn, the teacher

Tarot card: Strength (passion)

Favorable numbers: 6, 8

Lucky days: Monday and Saturday, especially when these days fall on 6 and 8 of the month

Lucky colors: Cream, chocolate brown, white

Birthstone: Pearl

July 8

9 July

the birthday of the lovable opportunist

Your greatest challenge is ...

accepting the word "no"

The way forward is ...

to understand that "no" can be an awful word to hear but the only way to move onward is to find ways to turn rejection into direction.

You're drawn to people born on ...

March 21 to April 20

You are both expressive and energetic, and this can be a passionate and stimulating relationship.

Luck maker

Ask why

When they hear "no," lucky people do everything they can to find out why. They focus on the reasons they didn't get what they want, and learn to move on from their mistakes.

People born on July 9 are often a powerhouse of energy and enthusiasm. They love to taste all that life has to offer and put their heart and soul into everything that they do, whether it is work or a relationship. Endearingly curious and eager to learn, their wide-eyed wonder has an energizing and motivating effect on everyone they deal with.

The opportunist streak that they possess, when combined with their questing imagination and boundless energy, gives them great creative and innovative potential. Indeed, their conviction that there is so much yet to be discovered may lead them to explore concepts that others may dismiss as totally unfeasible or unacceptable. Despite their fierce originality, however, they are not unrealistic about the possibility of success and are able to supplement their intellect and intuition with persistence and effective practical skills. When their optimism and charisma are added to this combination, it's no surprise that they are often attractive and popular individuals.

Although they do tend to have a healthy self-esteem, they are not always so good at dealing with rejection or setbacks and they can also suffer from exhaustion. When they are feeling low, they may withdraw into bitterness, frustration or disillusionment; it is vital for their self-image that they find more constructive ways to deal with disappointment, using it as an incentive or a learning experience. When they hit their teenage years they will be presented with opportunities to develop more confidence to display their talents and skills; it is important for them to take advantage of these, ensuring that they believe in their potential for success, regardless of the setbacks they encounter. After the age of forty-three they are likely to become more discriminating, practical and perfectionist.

These people really do believe that anything is possible; if they can just learn to try another approach if the first fails, their enduring interest in investigating, exploring and pushing the boundaries of human knowledge gives them outstanding potential to blaze truly innovative trails throughout life.

On the **dark** side

Disillusioned, unrealistic, withdrawn

At your **best**

Vital, imaginative, persistent

Power Thought

❝ Every obstacle in my life is an opportunity for me to learn and grow ❞

Love *High expectations*

People born on July 9 are blessed with natural charm and this makes them extremely popular. They have high expectations of relationships and give a lot to those they love, but they do need to be loved and appreciated themselves in return. Their choice of romantic partners tends to be those who share their curiosity and who come from different backgrounds to their own.

Health *Energy dips*

For the benefit of their emotional and physical health, people born on this day need to learn to pace themselves because they have a tendency to throw themselves wholeheartedly into whatever they do and this can lead to energy dips and exhaustion. Making sure they have plenty of time for rest and relaxation is recommended, as are periods of solitary meditation. They may not like to spend time alone but the need to recharge is part of their nature and they will damage their health if they don't. As far as diet is concerned, they are likely to go for variety so their nutritional intake is probably sound, but they might benefit from daily multi-vitamins and minerals as an insurance policy. Extreme forms of exercise should also be avoided although moderate-intensity exercise, such as jogging, dancing, or cycling, should not. Wearing, meditating on and surrounding themselves with the colors orange and yellow will give them a confidence and energy boost when they feel low.

Career *Born pioneers*

These people are innovators and they will often be found pioneering artistic or scientific theories, or even psychic phenomena, mysticism and spirituality. Their gift with people also makes them ideal for working with the public and their interest in humanitarianism may lead them to the healing professions, law, social work, and counseling. Other careers that might appeal include writing, public speaking, sales, promotion, publishing, interior design, or theater, art, and music.

Destiny *To blaze an innovative trail through life*

The life path of people born on this day is to learn how to handle rejection and setbacks positively. Once they have learned how to deal with challenges, their destiny is to blaze an innovative trail through life.

Signs & symbols

Sun sign: Cancer

Ruling planet: Moon, the intuitive

Symbol: The Crab

Birth date ruler: Mars, the warrior

Tarot card: The Hermit (inner strength)

Favorable numbers: 7, 9

Lucky days: Monday and Tuesday, especially when these days fall on 7 and 9 of the month

Lucky colors: Cream, cherry red, white

Birthstone: Pearl

July 9

10 July

the birthday of the dark horse

Your greatest challenge is ...

overcoming your shyness

The way forward is ...

to forget what you're thinking and feeling, and find out what others are thinking and feeling. When you put the attention on others, shyness will soon disappear.

You're drawn to people born on ...

September 24 to October 23

You share a passion for art, beauty and harmony, and this can be an intensely fulfilling relationship.

Luck maker

Find ways to express passion

To get a lucky break you need to let people see how much you want something. Revealing your passion can be a good-luck strategy because it shows others you're committed.

People born on July 10 learn lessons from the successes and defeats of those around them and plot their actions accordingly. Others may regard them as passive but they're not; they're steady and purposeful, only making a move when certain it will be successful or well received.

Sensitive to everything going on around them, once they have secured the background data they need for the best chance of success, they will embark on the quest to realize their goals with tenacity and determination, drawing upon their intellectual and organizational skills. Although motivation and perseverance are vital to their success, they are also quick learners with the self-confidence to be flexible in their approach.

People born on this day may often lead modest, steady lives but they are neither predictable nor dull. Quite the opposite; when people get to know them better, everything about them has the potential to surprise. For example, they are never afraid to speak their mind but when they do it is with tact and sensitivity. They may also surprise others with their incisive wit or devote their considerable energy to one specific goal, stepping aside at the last minute to allow others to take the credit. At certain points in their lives, their early forties especially, they are also likely to astonish people with a total change of lifestyle, but even though the change may come as a shock to others, to themselves it will all be part of a well-planned strategy.

It's not that they don't like to be in the limelight; they do. It's just that they will only step into it if it serves a purpose or highlights a cause they are promoting. Others may sometimes see them as shy and sensitive but beneath lies a steely determination to succeed that will reveal itself when the time is right. When they finally do decide to invest their energy into a worthy cause, everyone will wonder how they could have underestimated the creative and dynamic energy of this dark horse hiding behind a mild-mannered exterior.

On the dark side

Withdrawn,
passive, insecure

At your best

Curious, purposeful,
receptive

Love *Mystery*

People born on July 10 may size up potential partners from a distance before they make the first move or declare their intentions. Even their long-term partner may find them something of a mystery, finding it hard to know what they are thinking and feeling. It is wise for them to look before they leap but they need to make sure they don't linger and observe for so long that they spend their life forever weighing up the pros and cons on the sidelines.

Health *Experiment*

Although they are quick to observe the negative effects of poor diet and exercise on other people, when it comes to themselves they can be surprisingly passive and detached. It is therefore important that they experiment with their diet until they find one that maximizes their nutrient intake without leading to weight gain. They also need to experiment with various forms of exercise to find which one they truly enjoy because this will increase their chances of sticking to it. Soaking in an aromatherapy bath and regular massages will help them feel more connected with their bodies. Surrounding themselves with the color red will encourage them to be more open and self-confident when socializing with others.

Career *Born psychiatrists*

People born on this day may often be drawn to careers as psychologists or psychiatrists, but they can also excel as actors, writers, painters, and athletes. Other possible career options include photography, counseling, tourism, and working for themselves.

Destiny *To surprise others with their progressive vision*

The life path of people born on this day is to learn to participate more in life and occasionally let their heart rule their head. Once they are able to be more impulsive, their destiny is to surprise and delight others with their clear sense of purpose and progressive ideals.

Power Thought

❝ I express my feelings in joyous, positive ways ❞

Signs & symbols

Sun sign: Cancer

Ruling planet: Moon, the intuitive

Symbol: The Crab

Birth date ruler: Sun, the individual

Tarot card: The Wheel of Fortune (change)

Favorable numbers: 1, 8

Lucky days: Monday and Sunday, especially when these days fall on 1 and 8 of the month

Lucky colors: Cream, orange, yellow

Birthstone: Pearl

July 10

11 July

the birthday of
the innovative chameleon

People born on July 11 have an easy-going charm that appeals to other people, putting them at their ease. With the ability to effortlessly blend in no matter where they are or who they're with, they always seem to have the inside knowledge both professionally and socially.

The diplomatic skills of these people are extraordinary and they are often excellent at working around problems and sidestepping confrontations; this doesn't necessarily mean they are fickle or lazy. Quite the opposite. Although they are amiable and sensitive to the moods of others, they can be fiercely innovative and ambitious, with more than enough energy, intelligence and resourcefulness to reach their personal goals. It is just that, whether they realize it or not, their personality is defined by an intense interest in interpersonal relationships; this compels them to put the maximum effort into creating successful relationships with others.

Through their teenage years their confidence and creativity will gradually increase. During their twenties and thirties they will often find that they have unique access to information or insights into situations. If they choose to be discreet and stick to the truth, they will earn the respect and support of others; but if they choose to spread disinformation or fool others, they will earn a reputation for unreliability. After the age of forty-one there are opportunities to become more patient and discriminating; these may include providing practical service for others. They need to take advantage of these opportunities because the only way for them to find emotional fulfillment is through honesty, discretion and compassion toward others.

Throughout their lives they will find themselves in situations where their ability to put others at ease guarantees their popularity, giving them access to inside information. As long as they remember to center their lives on positive values such as honesty, respect, love, and responsibility, steering clear of play-acting or game-playing, these multi-talented individuals have the potential and versatility to produce excellent work, whatever they decide to do.

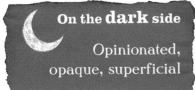
Power Thought

❝ I follow my inner light. I am a shining example of love and clarity ❞

Love *Romantic and sensitive*

Being part of a couple is a key personal goal for people born on July 11 because they prefer to plan joint activities rather than to pursue their interests alone. Romantic and sensitive, they have a lot of love to give but they may become restless if they feel too restricted in a routine, so keeping active is a prerequisite for their happiness in relationships.

Health *Steer clear of fads*

As long as people born on this day have plenty of company, security and affection, they are likely to stay fit and healthy. Health problems, such as digestive upsets, coughs and colds, fatigue, aches and pains, are likely to arise through worry when they feel themselves to be alone. As far as diet is concerned, they will probably be well aware of the latest fads or trends but need to steer clear of any form of crash diet or diet that excludes certain food groups. They should ensure that they eat a balanced, well-rounded diet as it will give them the nutrients they need to stay fit, slim and healthy. Regular physical exercise, preferably team sports, is a must because it helps to make them feel more grounded. Wearing, meditating on or surrounding themselves with the color blue will encourage them to be free, creative and truthful in their self-expression.

Career *Born journalists*

These people have a natural affinity for the arts and may make drama, art or music their career, but they will also be found making their mark in commercial enterprise, politics or sports. Other careers they may be drawn to include journalism, banking, law, sales, public relations, carpentry, cookery, and design.

Destiny *To motivate, uplift and inspire others*

The life path of people born on this day is to learn to be honest with themselves and others. Once they find the courage to base their lives on love and integrity, their destiny is to use their optimism and empathy to motivate, uplift and inspire others.

Signs & symbols

Sun sign: Cancer

Ruling planet: Moon, the intuitive

Symbol: The Crab

Birth date ruler: Moon, the intuitive

Tarot card: Justice (discernment)

Favorable numbers: 2, 9

Lucky day: Monday, especially when it falls on 2 and 9 of the month

Lucky colors: Blue, silver, white

Birthstone: Pearl

July 11

12 July

the birthday of the subtle initiator

Your greatest challenge is …

accepting you may be wrong

The way forward is …

to understand that truly great leaders are truly great because they have learned to adjust their opinions if life gives them reason to do so.

You're drawn to people born on …

October 24 to November 22

You are both sensitive and intense, and this can be a deep and intimate relationship.

Luck maker

Think like a mirror

A mirror doesn't judge or give advice. It reflects. Sometimes people just need to be heard, and mirroring their words back to them makes them feel that they are understood.

Those born on July 12 are characterized by their dualistic nature. On the one hand, they are profoundly empathetic and gentle creatures keenly sensitive to the emotions of those around them; on the other, they possess a compelling urge to initiate and direct the actions of others. Although these two aspects seem to conflict, they both stem from their intense altruism.

It's a mistake to dismiss these people as a pushover, because they hold profound convictions and refuse to redefine them. Their loyalty isn't limited to their convictions; they are a steadfast and generous friend, although their tendency to try and orchestrate the lives of others can become annoying. Sometimes they plant their suggestions in such a subtle way that other people will believe that they themselves have originated them. As a result they often have a powerful influence over others; the key to their success is whether they decide to exert this influence in a positive way that encourages others to grow independently, or in a negative way that fosters dependence.

They are such insightful and capable individuals that they will often step in without giving others a chance to get involved; this can earn them a reputation for being controlling, difficult and stubborn. However, if they can learn occasionally to take a step back and give others a turn, they will find that their chances of success and happiness increase. This isn't to say they should hide their talents. It's just that they are such strong-willed individuals that there's a tendency for others to be guided rather than inspired by them.

Until the age of forty there will be many opportunities for them to demonstrate their creativity and strong convictions. After the age of forty-one they may become more pragmatic and discerning. As long as they ensure that they nurture others without smothering them, this is the period when these empathetic but progressive individuals will do what they do best: initiate action that ensures the welfare of others and, by so doing, make their own special mark.

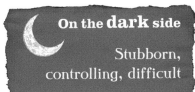

On the **dark** side

Stubborn, controlling, difficult

At your **best**

Persuasive, capable, disciplined

Love *Who takes the lead?*

Romantic partners who let people born on July 12 take the lead will appeal at first, but for a relationship to be successful in the long term it would be far more exciting and better for them to find someone who is their equal. Staying spontaneous and independent is the key to developing their inner power while still enjoying loving relationships.

Health *Personal organizer*

One of the best things people born on this day can do for their health is to organize their lives so that there is enough time for regular health check-ups, a daily exercise routine, and buying, cooking and preparing healthy fresh food. This is because they tend to lose themselves in their work and projects, and their health suffers as a result. They would also benefit from regular periods of peace and solitude where they can get in touch with their own feelings instead of constantly focusing on the feelings and concerns of others. An ideal way for them to relax would be to soak up the scent in an aromatherapy bath. One drop of juniper oil should do the trick. Wearing the color orange will also attract more positive people and influences into their lives.

Career *Born advisors*

These people don't like to follow the herd so they may prefer to work alone. Apart from national and civil politics or social work, other career choices might include writing, counseling, education, and all forms of advice-giving, such as sales, negotiation and promotion. Their excellent communication skills and sharp mind indicate tremendous potential to achieve, although they do need to avoid scattering their energies in self-doubt.

Destiny *To lead, guide, advise, and inspire others*

The life path of people born on this day is to learn to trust and let go as far as their relationships with others are concerned. Once they are able to manage their urge to take control, their destiny is to lead, guide, advise, and inspire others.

Signs & symbols

Sun sign: Cancer

Ruling planet: Moon, the intuitive

Symbol: The Crab

Birth date ruler: Jupiter, the philosopher

Tarot card: The Hanged Man (reflection)

Favorable numbers: 1, 3

Lucky days: Monday and Thursday, especially when these days fall on 1 and 3 of the month

Lucky colors: White, purple, blue

Birthstone: Pearl

July 12

13 July

the birthday of action man/woman

Your greatest challenge is ...

believing in yourself

The way forward is ...

to understand that like attracts like; self-doubt will attract misfortune and unhappiness. Change the way you think about yourself and you will attract joy, success and good fortune.

You're drawn to people born on ...

March 21 to April 20

You are both energetic, adventurous and expressive, and this relationship has the potential to be intense and fulfilling.

Luck maker

Just imagine

Lucky people understand that their imagination is the key to unlocking their success. You can't accomplish anything without it first being pictured in your mind. The way to success is to visualize yourself succeeding.

People born on July 13 tend to be courageous and daring risk-takers with a resilience that ensures they will always bounce back with their energy redoubled no matter how hard life knocks them down. This isn't to say they are blind optimists; rather their imagination never fails them, and if things can't or won't happen in one particular way they look for a new approach or strategy.

Fearless and focused, there is little that can intimidate them, except perhaps when it comes to affairs of the heart where they can be a little unsubtle and awkward. Their approach to life is action orientated, endowing them with an irresistible urge to achieve their targets. When their sharp mind, originality, inventiveness, and prodigious energy are added, it results in an outstanding capacity to recognize a potentially advantageous opportunity, seize the moment and act incisively. Sometimes their risk-taking strategy backfires, but their refusal to admit defeat and willingness to look at alternative approaches maximizes their chances of success.

Taking risks and achieving success comes naturally to them because they tend to be blessed with self-confidence. There may, however, be those less evolved who lack this self-belief, and this is probably because they have taken a risk that backfired, affecting their confidence. It is vital for their personal fulfillment that they do not allow their negative self-belief to become a self-fulfilling prophecy. Getting involved may be their strength, but to be true to themselves they first need to change their thoughts about themselves. When they truly believe in their own potential, their chances of fulfillment and good fortune will increase significantly.

At the age of thirty-nine they come to a turning point; this is the time when they are most likely to be plagued by self-doubt. If, however, they can make this turning point work for rather than against them by becoming more orderly, discriminating and practical in their approach, they will find that their creativity and optimism return.

On the **dark** side

Reckless, inflexible, self-doubting

At your **best**

Daring, opportunist, resilient

Power Thought

❝ I am now free from self-doubt ❞

Love *Try a more subtle style*

People born on July 13 are often uncomfortable and unsubtle when it comes to affairs of the hearts. They are so action-orientated that they seldom appreciate the need for a more subtle approach by winning someone over with beautiful words or gestures. They are also incredibly restless and may tire quickly of their partners. Part of the problem is that they aren't really sure what they want from a relationship, but once they make up their mind they will find it.

Health *Watch your stress levels*

Because people born on this day are such risk-takers they may suddenly make major lifestyle changes or decisions, and may not appreciate how greatly this can impact their health and well-being. Stress and insomnia could be problems, as could digestive upsets and fragile immune systems. It is important for them therefore to give themselves plenty of time to adjust to new routines or situations, making sure they get enough rest, relaxation and fun. Improving their diet by eating plenty of fruits and vegetables, nuts, seeds, and oily fish will help them cope with stress, and regular exercise, preferably mild to moderate such as swimming or cycling, is also highly beneficial. Mind-control techniques such as cognitive therapy or hypnotherapy are recommended if self-esteem is a problem, and wearing the color blue will help them approach people and situations in a calm, controlled way.

Career *Born entrepreneurs*

These people may be drawn toward careers where they can work for the welfare of others such as social work or teaching, although their talents may suit them equally well to becoming entrepreneurs, performers or artists. Other careers that might suit include public relations, sales, catering, landscape gardening, or real estate.

Destiny *To surprise and inspire others with daring originality*

The life path of people born on this day is to learn to trust their good judgment, and weigh up the pros and cons before taking a risk. Once they have learned to believe in themselves, their destiny is to surprise and inspire others with their originality and courage.

Signs & symbols

Sun sign: Cancer

Ruling planet: Moon, the intuitive

Symbol: The Crab

Birth date ruler: Uranus, the visionary

Tarot card: Death (change)

Favorable numbers: 2, 4

Lucky days: Monday and Sunday, especially when these days fall on 2 and 4 of the month

Lucky colors: Cream, light blue, silvery white

Birthstone: Pearl

July 13

14 July

the birthday of
the illusionist

Your greatest challenge is …

reliability

The way forward is …

to understand that however great is your ability to charm, the best way to earn the respect of others is to prove that you're honest, reliable and committed.

You're drawn to people born on …

August 24 to September 24

An excellent combination; you have much to learn from each other about balancing your emotions with a need for stability.

Luck maker

You can't please everyone

One of the fastest ways to chase luck right out of your life is to make other people's approval your first priority. The need to make everyone happy is neither in your own nor others' best interest.

People born on July 14 tend to be seductive individuals blessed with intelligence and personal magnetism. They have the ability to cast a spell over others with their intense presence and excellent communication skills. Their charm can be gentle and subtle or bold and entertaining, but it will always match the occasion perfectly.

Whether they are talking to a large group or a small circle of close friends, these people know how to inspire confidence and, regardless of what cause or career they choose, they aim to convince and inspire others. They are masters of the art of illusion and their talent for developing believable and fascinating theories, strategies and stories is awesome. Possessing the drive and enthusiasm to make things happen, they can, despite their obvious gifts, get depressed or melancholy for no apparent reason.

Despite these sudden and unexplained episodes of melancholy, others tend to regard them with great affection and admiration. If they direct their thoughts and talents to a cause they believe in, they have the potential to achieve success. However, if they choose to manipulate the truth or devote themselves to an unworthy cause, they can become unscrupulous and untrustworthy. It is important, therefore, for them to understand the influence they have on others and not misuse their powers.

Until the age of thirty-eight, they are likely to grow steadily in confidence and creativity. Although winning the hearts of others by sensing their hidden motivations and promising to fulfill their desires will earn them popularity, if they want to hold the affection of others they must learn to balance this seductive gift with solid results. After the age of thirty-nine they will develop a more methodical and discriminating attitude, together with a desire to be of service to others; these are the years when they have opportunities to turn the illusions they create into reality. They need to take advantage of these because when they use their dynamic and seductive will-power to achieve rather than talk about their objectives, they are a force to be reckoned with.

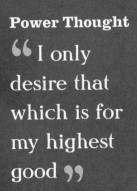

On the **dark** side

Misleading, dark, unscrupulous

At your **best**

Persuasive, interesting, seductive

Love *Root your relationships in fact not fantasy*

Although they effortlessly attract admirers, people born on July 14 can try too hard to please in a relationship. It is important that they let others know who they really are, so that their relationships are rooted in fact not fantasy. They are sensitive, caring and willing to support those they love and admire. Their ideal partner would be someone loving and dynamic who can keep them constantly interested.

Health *Darkness before dawn*

People born on this day are prone to sudden dark moods or bouts of anxiety and depression. It is important that they don't try to deny these or put on a brave front; they should treat these as an opportunity to connect with their feelings and see the process as a new beginning. If they can regard their suffering as a sign that certain aspects of their lives need to change, it gives it a meaning and a purpose for them. As far as their physical health is concerned, they need to be especially careful about digestive disorders, skin problems and respiratory difficulties, such as asthma. Their diet should be varied and wholesome with an emphasis on fruits and vegetables, and their exercise routine should be regular. Wearing, meditating on or surrounding themselves with the color blue will encourage them to be honest in their communication with others.

Career *Born social campaigners*

These people are often found in careers concerned with humanitarian goals such as social campaigning or politics but they may also devote their talents to improving the lives of others through artistic pursuits such as theater, art, music, and dance. Other careers that might appeal include commerce, finance, management, education, social work, or working for themselves as an entrepreneur.

Destiny *To influence, inspire and improve the lives of others*

The life path of people born on this day is to find and devote themselves to a cause they believe in. Once they have found their own truth, their destiny is find ways to influence, inspire and improve the lives of others.

Signs & symbols

Sun sign: Cancer

Ruling planet: Moon, the intuitive

Symbol: The Crab

Birth date ruler: Mercury, the communicator

Tarot card: Temperance (moderation)

Favorable numbers: 3, 5

Lucky days: Monday and Wednesday, especially when these days fall on 3 and 5 of the month

Lucky colors: Cream, sky blue, white

Birthstone: Pearl

July 14

15 July

the birthday of stimulus

Your greatest challenge is …

not being selfish

The way forward is …

to understand that being selfish only brings short-term satisfaction; taking the feelings of others into consideration brings both short- and long-term satisfaction.

You're drawn to people born on …

September 24 to October 23

You share a passion for art, beauty and intellectual pursuits, and this can create an intense and creative union.

Luck maker

Learn to read people better

Lucky people are always sensitive to how they are perceived by others because they know that their chances of attracting luck improve significantly if they come across positively.

Whether they realize it or not, people born on July 15 have a powerful effect on others and a rare ability to exert their influence positively to help others move forward with their lives. When others do achieve impressive results, they do not hold back their praise, which only serves to increase their popularity: a wonderfully virtuous circle.

These people manage to combine their highly developed intellectual powers with an affinity and sensitivity toward both their environment and all those who live and work with them. This combination of emotional empathy and intellectual perspicacity, when combined with their strong powers of imagination and the profound effect they tend to have on others, endows them with the potential to bring about progressive change, enriching the lives of others.

From about the age of seven or eight, people born on this day are likely to begin manifesting their characteristic self-confidence and magnetic charm, but at around the age of thirty-seven there is a turning point which sees them becoming more pragmatic and realistic; they may find that their desire to be of service to others grows more intense, and these are the years when they can really come into their own. If they can learn to direct their prodigious energy and creativity toward the greater good, they are likely to bring about considerable change for the better.

An inner ambition or desire to achieve and make a positive difference in the world can extend to all parts of their lives, and their determination can be compelling and inspirational. If, however, they become materialistic or selfish and use their influence to manipulate others, they can be ruthless and disruptive. It is absolutely crucial for them, therefore, not just to think about what they want to accomplish in their lives, but also to consider what effect their behavior and their actions will have on others. To truly utilize their outstanding potential for leadership, they may have to recognize the awesome power of their commanding disposition.

At your **best**

Influential, motivating, exciting

Love *Emotional honesty*

People born on July 15 have the magnetic charm to effortlessly attract admirers but they also have a tendency to take advantage of the vulnerabilities of others. Once in a committed relationship they will do anything to help and encourage their partner, but they need to watch their tendency to become controlling or domineering. It is crucial for them to ensure that they are emotionally honest and direct in all affairs of the heart.

Health *Higher things*

People born on this day are prone to excess in all areas of their lives and their love of material pleasures may lead them to overeating and drinking too much. Their love of life's material pleasures may lead them to gambling and a money-orientated approach to life. For their physical and emotional fulfillment it is therefore crucial for them to connect more with their emotions and their spirituality. Meditation is highly recommended, as is quiet time alone reading, thinking and dreaming. Diet should be wholesome and balanced, and low in sugar, salt, additives, and saturated fat. Team sports and competitive forms of exercise are a great way for them to deal with pent-up frustrations. Wearing, meditating on and surrounding themselves with the color purple will encourage them to think of higher things.

Career *Born businessmen/women*

These people have the ruthless streak needed to make it big in business or commerce but they may prefer to reach out to the world through creative and expressive endeavors, such as acting, music, art, writing, singing, or speaking. They may also be attracted to teaching, lecturing, journalism, the caring professions, and health care, but whatever career they choose, education of some type will be important to help them realize their exceptional potential.

Destiny *To enrich the lives of others*

The life path of people born on this day is to understand themselves and their motivations better, and to become aware of the forceful impact they have on others. Once they are able to do that, their destiny is to enrich the lives of others in some way.

Signs & symbols

Sun sign: Cancer

Ruling planet: Moon, the intuitive

Symbol: The Crab

Birth date ruler: Venus, the lover

Tarot card: The Devil (instinct)

Favorable numbers: 4, 6

Lucky days: Monday and Friday, especially when these days fall on 4 and 6 of the month

Lucky colors: Cream, pink, light green

Birthstone: Pearl

July 15

16 July

the birthday of passionate logic

People born on July 16 tend to have an impulsive, passionate nature. They dream adventurous and exciting dreams and more often than not these come true. Once they are inspired, their energy and enthusiasm is without equal, but they have another side, their logical side. This unusual combination of passion and logic makes them interesting, unusual and exceptional.

The demeanor of these people can be down to earth and pragmatic, but despite this they never lose sight of their dreams and passions. Whatever life path they choose, there will always be a conflict between their logic and their impulses, and this will come across in words that are rational but presented passionately or behavior that is impulsive but explained logically. When their logic and passion are in harmony, with neither gaining the upper hand, they are likely to feel at their happiest; but when one is more dominant than the other it can lead to unhappiness. For example, they may try to repress their emotions by becoming obsessive in their behavior; or they may try to bury their logic and become unrealistic or unfocused in their approach.

For the first thirty-five years of their lives people born on this day will often grow in confidence and capability; these are the years when emotions are most likely to take the lead. After the age of thirty-six, however, there is a shift toward logic and reason, and they are likely to have a more practical and discriminating attitude, with service to others becoming a more important part of their lives. After the age of sixty-six there is an emphasis on harmony and balance between the two conflicting sides of their personality.

The key to success and happiness for people born on this day is to allow neither their rational nor their impulsive side to take the lead. If they can find a way to balance the two, they will find that they have within them outstanding potential not just to achieve their own dreams but also to bring excitement into the lives of others.

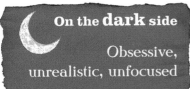
Love *Follow your heart*

People born on July 16 aim high when it comes to affairs of the heart and they often tend to pursue and succeed in capturing romantic partners whom others may consider unsuitable or out of their league in terms of wealth, appearance and educational background. This is because they are passionate, sensitive and intelligent but also determined and focused enough to get who or what they want, no matter what odds are stacked against them.

Health *Will-power alone*

People born on this day need to understand that sometimes they will need to seek the advice of their doctor and that will-power alone cannot always keep them feeling healthy. They are especially prone to illnesses of the upper digestive tract, indigestion, catarrh, coughs, anemia, and lowered vitality, so it is important for them to make sure they boost their health and their immune systems with a nutritious diet rich in antioxidants (found in fruit and vegetables) and plenty of exercise. Being so strong willed, they are unlikely to take the advice of any nutritionist or fitness instructor, preferring to devise their own health program. This is fine as long as they do plenty of research first to find the best diet and exercise routine for their hectic lifestyle. Wearing, meditating on and surrounding themselves with the color green will boost their self-esteem and help them bring balance to all aspects of their lives.

Career *Born spokesperson*

These people are particularly suited to the arts, where their innovative work can inspire others, but they may also choose to help others by becoming social or religious campaigners. Other careers they may be drawn to include education, counseling, social work, or a job that requires speaking up for others, such as labor unions, politics or law.

Destiny *To transform or better the lives of others*

The life path of people born on this day is to find ways to balance their impulsive and their rational side. Once they find this balance, their destiny is to make a positive and transforming contribution to bettering the lives of others.

Signs & symbols

Sun sign: Cancer

Ruling planet: Moon, the intuitive

Symbol: The Crab

Birth date ruler: Neptune, the speculator

Tarot card: The Tower (breakthrough)

Favorable numbers: 5, 7

Lucky day: Monday, especially when it falls on 5 and 7 of the month

Lucky colors: Cream, lagoon blue, white

Birthstone: Pearl

July 16

17 July

the birthday of the master

People born on July 17 strive to rise to the very top in their chosen field and to have others acknowledge their mastery. Their independence, confidence and discipline make them extremely capable workers in whatever task they undertake, and they often greatly impress others with their focus, tenacity and professionalism.

Tending to present a serious, sometimes harsh face to the world, within their chosen sphere they are, however, passionate and creative; to those who know them well they have a wacky sense of humor. With a tendency to focus their energies on money and material concerns, they may end up in careers or situations that waste their talents. It is important, therefore, that they pay great attention to their choice of career as they will not find true fulfillment until they devote themselves to something that inspires them or speaks to their principles. They may also be guilty of procrastination. Although they are extremely good at working their way patiently up to the top, sometimes their rate of progress is so slow that it is detrimental to their creativity. They need to find the courage to speak up for themselves so that their talents can be exposed and given the recognition they deserve.

Until the age of thirty-six they are likely to win the respect of their associates and acquaintances with their confident, cool efficiency. After the age of thirty-seven, sometimes sooner, when there are opportunities for them to become more practical and discriminating, it is important that they direct their efforts toward gaining recognition for their creativity as well, so that well-deserved promotion does not pass them by.

If they make sure that their self-sufficiency does not make them seem unapproachable, they will be well on track to attain the targets they set for themselves without forfeiting the goodwill of others. They may also find that although their wish to have others acknowledge their mastery is granted, they find greater happiness and pleasure from their ability to bring cheer and inspiration to others with their generosity and creativity.

Love *A special, close link*

People born on July 17 tend to be quite traditional when it comes to affairs of the heart but they may also be tempted to have secret love affairs. They need a very special, close link with their partners and are attracted to independent, intelligent and creative thinkers like themselves. Although they can be warm and loving, they need to be careful that the image they present is not so self-sufficient that others feel they won't be needed.

Health *Don't crawl into your shell*

People born on this day give the appearance of great self-sufficiency and they are likely to take care of their physical health by eating well and getting enough exercise. They do, however, need to pay greater attention to their emotional and psychological health. If they don't get to know themselves better they may find that their so-called independence shatters when they encounter setbacks, challenges and disappointments in life, and that instead of being resilient and upbeat they crawl into a shell of negativity and anxiety. It is therefore extremely important for them to devote more time to self-development, challenging negative thinking and building their self-esteem. Meditation, yoga, cognitive behavioral therapy, and counseling are all recommended, as is spending more time relaxing with friends and loved ones. Wearing, meditating on and surrounding themselves with the color orange will increase feelings of warmth, security and enjoyment.

Career *Born newscasters*

These people are multi-talented with outstanding potential to acquire knowledge in whatever career they choose; they may be drawn to careers in management, law, sales, promotion, and politics. Alternatively, they may choose to develop their creative side and talent with the spoken or written word in drama, education, writing, journalism, lecturing, or the media.

Destiny *To inform, entertain or inspire others*

The life path of people born on this day is to put more effort into their own creativity. Once they stop trying so hard to win people's respect, their destiny is to inform, entertain or inspire others.

Signs & symbols

Sun sign: Cancer

Ruling planet: Moon, the intuitive

Symbol: The Crab

Birth date ruler: Saturn, the teacher

Tarot card: The Star (hope)

Favorable numbers: 6, 8

Lucky days: Monday and Saturday, especially when these days fall on 6 and 8 of the month

Lucky colors: Cream, maroon, brown

Birthstone: Pearl

July 17

18 July

the birthday of the better way

Your greatest challenge is ...

recognizing your individual needs

The way forward is ...

to understand that making time for your own thoughts and interests is not incompatible with the needs of the people you are devoted to.

You're drawn to people born on ...

March 21 to April 20

You are both magnetic, expressive and emotional individuals and this can be an intense and passionate union.

Luck maker

Connect with your intuition

Ask your intuition specific, focused questions and wait for the answer. It may show up in the form of an amazing coincidence or a luck-making thought in your head.

People born on July 18 appear to have limitless energy and enthusiasm. Throwing their heart, body and soul into whatever they do, they are admired for their dedication, conviction and determination to make their voice heard. They are unlikely to follow the conventional path in their personal or professional lives, and always aim to find a better way, speaking out boldly to let others know about it.

Although they can give the appearance of being extreme, eccentric or wild, there is often a method to their madness. Independent and innovative in their thinking, they also prefer to identify themselves with a group or common cause. The reasons for this include strong feelings of empathy with others, as well as a somewhat insecure need to ground themselves in the bonds of camaraderie that come from serving a common cause and receiving recognition.

Until the age of thirty-four they will be given opportunities to develop their daring as their power, confidence and creativity increase. They will often, however, choose to invest their considerable energies, intellectual talents and emotions in shared aims; it is important during this time that they don't allow their views or opinions to become extreme or inflexible. After the age of thirty-five they may become more discriminating, businesslike and efficient. The need to work with and serve others will be as strong as ever, but this time the emphasis will be on supplying creative and progressive solutions, making these people powerful figures in the community. Another turning point comes at the age of sixty-four when issues around beauty, harmony and emotional fulfillment are emphasized.

Although they are self-disciplined, intelligent and sociable, the true inspiration they seek will lie in the realms of emotional satisfaction. They will always be gifted problem solvers able to find a better way for others; but once they understand that the best way for themselves is the inner way and trusting their highly developed intuition, they will find that they attract countless opportunities for their own happiness and true fulfillment.

Love *Make love your cause*

People born on July 18 do have a tendency to identify themselves so strongly with the cause or project they are promoting that partners can feel left out or insignificant by comparison. Although they are attracted to people who will support their pursuit of truth, to keep their relationship alive they need to turn the spotlight on their partner from time to time and make them their cause.

Health *Emotional confidence*

People born on this day need to ensure that they find ways to express their negative emotions; repressing them will lead to unhappiness and confusion. They should understand that emotions, such as fear, anger, guilt, and sadness, should not be ignored but listened to because they have something important to say. Getting in touch with their emotions is therefore crucial, and if they can't do this alone they may benefit from therapy or counseling. As far as diet is concerned, they should eat little and often to keep their energy levels high; the importance of moderate to mild exercise every day should not be overlooked as it will help them deal with pent-up emotions, boosting their self-esteem and body image at the same time. Wearing, meditating on and surrounding themselves with the color silver will encourage them to be more open and honest with themselves and others.

Career *Born politicians*

These people will often identify themselves with a group or cause and may therefore be attracted to careers in sports, politics, art, or religion. They may also excel in leadership positions in education, research, science, public relations, and philosophy. Whatever career they choose, they are never happy being told what to do, so it is imperative for them not to stay in a servile position for too long.

Destiny *To be a just and progressive force*

The life path of people born on this day is to learn to think independently and not always identify themselves with others. Once they are able to recognize the importance of individual and community needs, their destiny is to be a powerful force for justice and progress in their community and the world.

Signs & symbols

Sun sign: Cancer

Ruling planet: Moon, the intuitive

Symbol: The Crab

Birth date ruler: Mars, the warrior

Tarot card: The Moon (intuition)

Favorable numbers: 7, 9

Lucky days: Monday and Tuesday, especially when these days fall on 7 and 9 of the month

Lucky colors: White, crimson, cream

Birthstone: Pearl

July 18

19 July

the birthday of energetic self-awareness

Your greatest challenge is ...

avoiding negative thinking

The way forward is ...

to understand that negative thinking is just as irrational as positive thinking. There are always two sides to the story, so aim for more realistic thinking.

You're drawn to people born on ...

October 24 to November 23

You are both big on feelings and this relationship can be passionate and intense.

Luck maker

Believe in your own value

Lucky people understand that they are not perfect, but are just like everyone else; they have simply learned how to minimize their weaknesses and maximize their strengths.

People born on July 19 set themselves extremely high standards. From a very early age self-improvement will have been a key theme. They expect a great deal from themselves and others, but those who know them well will recognize that their harshest criticism is reserved for themselves.

These people are energetic and charming, and both physically and intellectually they need to keep their bodies and minds active. This is why they will often push themselves incredibly hard or jump from activity to activity. They need to keep moving and, above all, to feel that they are learning, growing and improving in all areas of their lives. In many ways they are among the most self-aware individuals of the year and when they have made any kind of mistake or oversight they will immediately acknowledge it, trying to find ways of improving their performance, behavior or attitude in the future. Others love them for their ability to learn and change, but their self-awareness does come at a price: a painful awareness of their own inadequacies.

People born on this day are prone to relentless self-criticism and they may often exaggerate their imagined shortcomings. When they are indulging in a bout of insecurity, mood swings and impatience are likely, so it is extremely important for their psychological growth that they understand the need to stay centered. Spending more time simply being instead of doing will help boost their self-esteem, giving them the objectivity and distance needed to manage their emotions effectively.

Until the age of thirty-three they will be presented with opportunities to develop their strength and confidence. After the age of thirty-four they are likely to become even more perfectionist in their approach to life. Because of their tendency to be harsh with themselves, they should ensure that they also bring more patience to their talents during these years, because if they do they will be able to make the most of their wonderful potential, becoming the creative and charismatic person they were always meant to be.

Love *Seductive playfulness*

People born on July 19 may be prone to mood swings and tantrums, but their charm and seductive playfulness will more than make up for these shortcomings, drawing many different potential partners to them. They have a strong need for emotional security and will often seek a close relationship with someone who is dependable.

Health *On the move*

People born on this day love to move and, if exercise isn't already a part of their lives, they should make sure it is because it offers them the opportunity to boost their health both physically and emotionally. Building their self-esteem is also of crucial importance because, although others find them fascinating and creative individuals, they are more likely to focus on their weaknesses than their strengths. Mind-control techniques such as meditation and cognitive behavior therapy may help them challenge and question irrational and negative thoughts. As far as diet is concerned, they tend to have a craving for sweet foods and chocolate, particularly when they are feeling low; so finding healthy alternatives such as fruit, or doing some exercise when the craving strikes, is recommended. Wearing, meditating on or surrounding themselves with the color yellow will boost their self-confidence and bring out their sunny potential.

Career *Born sprinters*

People born on this day are extremely energetic and this may draw them to sporting careers or the mastery of technical or artistic pursuits. Careers that offer the possibility of fulfillment include politics, social work, education, the caring professions, design, writing, music, art, poetry, dance, drama, law, business, and fundraising.

Destiny *To help humanity progress*

The life path of people born on this day is to learn to believe in their own self-worth. Once they have started to work on building their self-esteem—which is a lifelong task—their destiny is to help humanity progress, be it socially, physically, technically, or ideologically.

Signs & symbols

Sun sign: Cancer

Ruling planet: Moon, the intuitive

Symbol: The Crab

Birth date ruler: Sun, the individual

Tarot card: The Sun (enthusiasm)

Favorable numbers: 1, 8

Lucky days: Monday and Sunday, especially when these days fall on 1 and 8 of the month

Lucky colors: Orange, gold, yellow

Birthstone: Pearl

20 July

the birthday of evolution

Your greatest challenge is ...

feeling satisfied

The way forward is ...

to understand that moving onto the next challenge will not necessarily bring you the fulfillment you seek. The secret of fulfillment is within you, not without.

You're drawn to people born on ...

June 22 to July 23

You are both creative and sensitive and this can create an intense and passionate union.

Luck maker

Give luck room to breathe

Sometimes luck happens when you are not trying to make it happen but when you are simply open and available to what shows up. So just wait until the moment is right.

People born on July 20 love the journey of life. They thrive on movement, change and new experiences, being exhilarated rather than daunted by fresh challenges and situations. No matter how comfortable or secure their position in life, routine can be deadly to them and their restless spirit constantly seeks to move on and evolve.

These people rarely remain static for long, and their energy and intensity are boundless both physically and intellectually. Whether they are sporting types or not, they don't like sitting down for long; likewise whether they are academically inclined or not, they are inquisitive and constantly searching for novel experiences.

Not surprisingly, their natural exuberance and infectious optimism draw others to them, and friends may often take great pleasure in hearing about their adventures. Given the constant process of change that defines their lives, they run the risk of being unstable; but in many cases the opposite is true and they are all calmness and control. Courageous risk-takers, nothing really unsettles them but boredom, and they are far more likely to be anxious and unbalanced when their lives are too easy or stuck in a rut. Others may find their obsessive need for challenge and contrast hard to understand, but these people are at their happiest and their best when they are struggling.

Until the age of thirty-two, they will have many opportunities to use the sociable and dramatic part of their personality. Both at work and at home they are likely to be popular, poised and self-assured but slightly lacking in direction and focus. It may take them longer than normal to find their true vocation or direction in life. There is a change of emphasis after the age of thirty-two when they are inclined to be more orderly, practically motivated and methodical. During these years, if they can develop a greater sense of focus and find goals that provide them with enough adventure and challenge, they can direct their creativity and energy toward increasing their knowledge, as well as enriching the lives of others.

Love *Wild imagination*

People born on July 20 are often attracted to restless, exciting types just like themselves but they will thrive better with a partner who is stable and reliable, and who lets them go off into their wild imagination without stifling them. Mental stimulation is also extremely important for them in a relationship, so they need to find a partner who can match their intellectual curiosity.

Health *Emotional anchor*

People born on this day will often put their bodies and minds under great stress, tending to be accident prone as a result. It will be extremely beneficial for them to have a close-knit group of friends or loved ones who can offer them an emotional anchor. As far as diet is concerned, obsessive food cravings could become a problem, so to counteract this they need to make sure they eat a diet that is as varied, healthy and interesting as possible. Fad diets should be avoided completely, as should any kind of dependence on recreational drugs, cigarettes or alcohol. Regular moderate-intensity exercise is highly recommended, such as jogging, swimming, cycling, and dancing, as it will help release tension and provide them with physical challenges to overcome. Regular rest and relaxation are crucial to help them balance their being with their doing, and wearing, meditating on and surrounding themselves with the color blue will be calming and soothing to them.

Career *Born photographers*

Success in people-related careers such as counseling, education, law, medicine, and social reform is likely for these people, and their determination and creativity can help them accomplish much in the world of business. They may also have a special interest in working with children or dealing with food. Alternatively careers in film-making, photography, art, music, drama, or entertainment may appeal.

Destiny *To evolve into creative and inspirational individuals*

The life path of people born on this day is to learn to find a balance between being and doing. Once they have learned that often the most exciting challenges lie within rather than without, their destiny is to grow, learn, develop, and evolve into creative and inspirational individuals.

Power Thought

❝ The most exciting journey of all is the journey within ❞

Signs & symbols

Sun sign: Cancer

Ruling planet: Moon, the intuitive

Symbol: The Crab

Birth date ruler: Sun, the individual

Tarot card: The Moon (intuition)

Favorable numbers: 2, 9

Lucky day: Monday, especially when it falls on 2 and 9 of the month

Lucky colors: Cream, silver, white

Birthstone: Pearl

July 20

21 July

the birthday of daring

Your greatest challenge is ...

feeling that life is moving fast enough

The way forward is ...

to focus more on the spiritual aspects of your life; this will help you move into the deeper, more profound aspects of yourself.

You're drawn to people born on ...

November 23 to December 21

Relationships between people born on these days have the potential for great intimacy, intensity, and depth.

Luck maker

Less is more

Lucky people know when to draw the line. They don't overdo it and understand that too much stimulation can create confusion, blocking their chances of luck.

Those born on July 21 are not afraid to go where no man or woman has ever gone before. Highly dynamic and innovative, their curiosity and understanding of what motivates others make them extremely good at assessing people and situations, and this unique combination of shrewdness and daring ambition draws both success and controversy their way.

Above all, they love being on the cutting edge of innovative projects and activities, possessing the vitality and ambition to be successful in creative endeavors. They move fast and usually prefer to be in the thick of battle rather than sitting on the sidelines. They tend to aim high and, even if things don't always work out exactly as planned, their jovial optimism and tragicomic sense of humor act as a buffer, providing them with a resilience that is second to none.

The drama and controversy of opposite points of view appeal greatly to the daring nature of these individuals. They make great debaters and conversationalists because they can see both sides of the argument. They love excitement, conflict and explosive situations, and are likely to be attracted to action games, racing cars, theme-park rides, diving, or any high-energy, adrenalin-pumping situation that provides drama and demands courage. Until the age of thirty there are many opportunities for them to develop their strength, creativity and confidence; these are the years during which they need to make sure their love of thrill-seeking does not encourage them to stir up trouble for the sake of it. After the age of thirty their focus will change to a more pragmatic and rational approach, with a desire for a life that is still very fast moving, but slightly more settled and orderly.

The greatest strengths of these people are to be found in their daring creativity and courage, and in their generosity and empathy toward others. Sometimes these qualities will combine and result in a rare and talented individual who can be counted among the most dynamic but also the most understanding of all people.

On the dark side

Thrill-seeking, impatient, reckless

At your best

Bold, interesting, exciting

Power Thought

66 Focus and concentration are the keys to my success 99

Love *Fighting spirit*

When it comes to love, people born on July 21 top the charts in almost every area, from devotion to romance. They are attracted to creative, hard-working people who know their own mind and who are not afraid to open their hearts and express their inner feelings. The only downside is that they don't thrive in relationships where there is constant harmony; if things are going too well, they are not above stirring up trouble to keep the adrenaline pumping.

Health *Avoid excess of all kinds*

Their need for escapism, if not disciplined and channeled, can make people born on this day vulnerable to recreational drugs, drink and other addictions. It's vital for them to find activities and friends that help them keep both feet on the ground and retain a sense of perspective. As far as diet and exercise are concerned, they should avoid excess of all kinds. Their diet should be as varied and interesting as possible to decrease their chances of nutritional deficiency, and a multi-vitamin and mineral supplement may be a good insurance policy when they are on the go. An exercise routine is advised, but since they are unlikely to stick to it, getting as much fresh air and outdoor activity every day as possible is a more realistic goal. Wearing, surrounding themselves with or meditating on the color green will balance their emotions and help bring a feeling of calmness.

Career *Born film-maker*

These people are well suited to careers as teachers, scientists, social workers, or working in the caring professions, although their adventurous spirit may draw them to occupations that involve risk, such as the army and secret services. Their debating skills might attract them to politics, sales, business, philosophy, and psychology. The theater, film-making and cookery would appeal to their inherent flamboyance.

Destiny *To turn the spotlight on human progress*

The life path of people born on this day is to learn self-discipline and humility. Once they have found a sense of balance, their destiny is to inspire and encourage others to think independently and, by so doing, turn the spotlight on human progress.

Signs & symbols

Sun signs: Cancer/Leo

Ruling planets: Moon, the intuitive/Sun, the individual

Symbols: The Crab/The Lion

Birth date ruler: Jupiter, the philosopher

Tarot card: The World (fulfillment)

Favorable numbers: 1, 3

Lucky days: Monday and Thursday, especially when these days fall on 1 and 3 of the month

Lucky colors: Gold, green, white

Birthstone: Pearl

22 July

the birthday of brave compulsion

Your greatest challenge is ...

learning from your mistakes

The way forward is ...

to understand that making mistakes is an essential ingredient for success, helping you learn, grow and fine-tune your approach.

You're drawn to people born on ...

January 21 to February 19

You approach life differently but if you learn from each other this can be an extremely compatible relationship.

Luck maker

Pay attention to the details

Although lucky people never lose sight of the bigger picture, they also understand the importance of the details. It is these that often make the difference between something average and something of outstanding quality.

People born on July 22 are action orientated. They want to see progress, not talk about it. Although this compulsion to act can lead them into difficulties, it can also make them remarkable inovators.

In addition to their sharp intellect and prodigious physical and emotional energy, these people possess great sensitivity and creativity, although they sometimes take action without having fully thought through the potential consequences. However, when disaster strikes they are masters at coping with the often messy and complicated results. This is because from an early age they have realized the importance of self-sufficiency and have become extremely resilient as a result. Because they are impulse driven and action orientated, their lives will often fluctuate between periods of great success and periods of great disappointment, but so powerful are their self-belief and desire to win through that they never consider giving up.

One big problem for them is their refusal to acknowledge their own shortcomings. While their belief in the indestructibility of the human spirit is commendable, they don't take into account their vulnerabilities and the warning signs of potential problems. They may also have problems handling their anger and frustration, and this can manifest in controlling, dictatorial behavior or in repression with dangerous outbursts of rage. Until the age of twenty-nine there is an emphasis on creativity and sociability; during these years they need to make sure that they learn from both their failures and their successes. After the age of thirty there are opportunities for them to become more analytical, methodical and orderly. It is important for their psychological growth that they take advantage of these opportunities because attention to the details is the key to their success.

Above all, these people are natural optimists and, even though their actions can sometimes wear others out, their brave compulsion to re-energize and challenge themselves marks them out as inspirational leaders and survivors in their chosen fields.

On the **dark** side

Reckless, moody, inflexible

At your **best**

Bold, exciting, visionary

Love *Spot the warning signs*

People born on July 22 can be incredibly charming and as a result they are rarely short of friends and admirers. Settling into a long-term relationship may initially be difficult as there is an emphasis on emotional fluctuations and love affairs, but once they do find someone they want to commit to they can be loyal and caring. Their ideal partner will be someone who can recognize the warning signs when they are pushing themselves too hard and can encourage them to unwind.

Health *Self-awareness is key*

It is important for people born on this day to get in touch with their emotions because lack of self-knowledge or self-awareness is a potential problem that could make them push themselves too hard or devote themselves to causes and people they are not suited to. Counseling or therapy may be helpful but they would also benefit from regular periods of rest, quiet and relaxation. As far as diet is concerned they should avoid drinking too much coffee and should experiment with herbal teas instead, such as chamomile which can ease stress and promote relaxation. Moderate to mild exercise is recommended, as are a no-working-at-weekends rule and regular holidays. Wearing, meditating on and surrounding themselves with the color yellow will boost their confidence and self-awareness.

Career *Born chefs*

Their varied gifts give these people the potential to succeed in a variety of careers, but their creativity makes them particularly suited to artistic or technical pursuits in which they can take a leadership position. Other careers that might appeal include sales, diplomacy, politics, education, art, theater, writing, fashion, interior design, music, catering, cookery, engineering, counseling, and childcare.

Destiny *To combine patience and discipline with courage and vision*

The life path of people born on this day is to learn from their mistakes and turn their weaknesses into strengths. Once they are more careful in their approach, their destiny is to show others that great things can be achieved when patience and discipline are combined with courage and vision.

Power Thought

❝ I draw strength, wisdom and inspiration from the stillness within me ❞

Signs & symbols

Sun signs: Cancer/Leo

Ruling planets: Moon, the intuitive/Sun, the individual

Symbols: The Crab/The Lion

Birth date ruler: Uranus, the visionary

Tarot card: The Fool (freedom)

Favorable numbers: 2, 4

Lucky days: Monday and Sunday, especially when these days fall on 2 and 4 of the month

Lucky colors: Gold, purple, cream

Birthstone: Pearl

July 22

23 July

the birthday of the liberator

Your greatest challenge is ...

avoiding being taken advantage of

The way forward is ...

to understand that there is a difference between compassion and stupidity. You are not stupid, so make sure you are only there for those who appreciate you.

You're drawn to people born on ...

May 22 to June 21

As long as you make sure you share the spotlight, this relationship will be full of fast-paced action and fun.

Luck maker

Think of yourself

Give to others by all means but not to the point where you neglect yourself. Luck making requires you to think of yourself as well; not just as an afterthought, but all the time.

People born on July 23 are often warm and sympathetic individuals and the first choice of shoulder for others to cry on. They have a gift for helping others resolve their inner conflicts and a strong desire to help them progress—be it professionally, materially or spirituality—and are prepared to devote their considerable energies to this cause.

Above all, their greatest wish is to see others liberated from their doubts, fears, anxieties, and misfortunes. Other people recognize this selfless orientation and will gravitate readily to their warmth and compassion. For example, their office will always be the one where people stop to chat about what is going on, or their home the one where people like to congregate or settle disputes. But as well as being giving and supportive they have a quick and piercing mind. They can be a little conservative in their views, but underneath they are bursting with creativity and are excellent at learning new skills.

Sometimes, however, their approach to life can be a little too cerebral and they may hide their own feelings. Ironically, for someone who is always there to listen to others, when it comes to their own feelings they can be incredibly shy. It is important for their psychological growth that they learn to pay as much attention to their own feelings as they do to the feelings of others, because their feelings have important messages to tell them.

After the age of thirty there is a turning point when they are likely to become more practical, analytical and discerning in their approach to life. In the years ahead their lives can be positive, fulfilling and powerful if they take advantage of the opportunities presented to them to pay attention to their feelings and grow in emotional confidence. Once they stop trying to be everyone's liberator and pay sufficient attention to their own need for liberation and fulfillment, their strength of conviction, vigor, creativity, and orientation toward the common good augur well for outstanding success both personally and professionally.

Love *Hold out*

People born on July 23 will often be extremely sociable and popular, appearing to effortlessly attract potential partners. However, the ones they attract may not always be the ones who are most beneficial for their psychological growth. They need to hold on and wait for that special someone who is willing and able to give as well as take.

Health *Pamper yourself more*

Not surprisingly, people born on this day tend to put their own emotional and physical needs last, and this can lead to both physical and psychological problems. Therapy and counseling will help them get in touch with their feelings, as would more time spent reading, relaxing and pampering themselves. As far as diet is concerned, they need to make sure they avoid foods high in saturated fat, salt, sugar, additives, and preservatives, and go for foods that are as fresh, natural and rich in nutrients as possible. Alcohol, comfort eating and recreational drugs of all kinds should be avoided altogether because they have addictive tendencies. Moderate to mild exercise is recommended, especially walking, as it will give them time to think and dream. Wearing, meditating on and surrounding themselves with the color red will encourage them to be more assertive and to put their own needs first for a change.

Career *Born carers*

These people need to feel wanted and they may thrive in the caring professions, medicine, teaching, social work, the military, and politics. They may also be successful in any kind of business or management position; with their love of freedom and independence, they may wish to be work for themselves or to express their creative side through the arts.

Destiny *To guide the lives of others*

The life path of people born on this day is to learn to listen to their own feelings as well as those of others. Once they are able to place a higher value on their own needs, their destiny is to influence the opinions and the lives of others.

Power Thought

"I commit myself to the practice of reflecting in silence"

Signs & symbols

Sun signs: Leo/Cancer

Ruling planets: Sun, the individual/Moon, the intuitive

Symbols: The Lion/The Crab

Birth date ruler: Mercury, the communicator

Tarot card: The Hierophant (guidance)

Favorable numbers: 3, 5

Lucky days: Sunday and Wednesday, especially when these days fall on 3 and 5 of the month

Lucky colors: Gold, blue, orange

Birthstone: Ruby

July 23

24 July

the birthday of charismatic uncertainty

People born on July 24 are among the most original and exciting of the year. They have an invigorating presence that surprises and shocks everyone they meet, and their charisma is so intense that others find themselves irresistibly drawn in.

They are exciting and adventurous, and others tend to cluster around them in the hope of understanding them better and perhaps catching some of their magic and energy. Sometimes they may express the dangerous side of their personality by taking up an extreme sport, dating someone wholly inappropriate or accepting a job that involves a huge amount of retraining or risk to their professional status. They are able to do this because they are often more concerned with the thrill of taking on a new challenge than they are with the consequences of their actions. They are here to have an amazing time and that is what matters most to them.

Although they may give the impression of being fearless, what they fear most of all is routine, the mundane and not moving forward with their lives. They need to learn that some of the greatest adventures lie within, and that getting to know themselves better will be an endless source of excitement and discovery. After the age of thirty there is a turning point in their lives when opportunities will be presented to them to draw more pleasure from being of service and doing their job well. They need to take advantage of these opportunities because their real source of fulfillment is to motivate and help others.

Whatever they choose to devote their dynamic creativity to, they will always find themselves attracted to the far out and the unusual. Whether they realize it or not, their actions are often designed to attract the admiration or attention of others. Once they discover that others will notice and admire them just as much, if not more, when they demonstrate their quieter, but no less effective, gifts for sensitivity and creativity, they have the potential not just to motivate others but to truly amaze and inspire them.

On the **dark** side

Selfish, obsessive, fickle

At your **best**

Innovative, hypnotic, inspirational

Love *Teach me*

It won't be easy for people born on July 24 to find a partner who is as compelling, unusual and adventurous as they are, but when they do they can be loyal, passionate and endlessly exciting partners. Settling down may also be a problem as they have such a restless nature. They are attracted to those who can teach them something but who also have a fun, youthful side to their personality.

Health *Focus on higher things*

Not surprisingly, people born on this day are prone to accidents because they can be so reckless and their compulsion to seek out new and unusual experiences may lead them to experiment with activities, such as drug taking, that are detrimental to their health and well-being. They are prone to eating binges and comfort eating when they feel bored, so it is important that their diet is as varied as possible so they don't deprive themselves of foods they love. They should also find healthy ways to relieve their boredom: going for a walk, writing in a journal or chatting to a friend or loved one. Because they are generally so active, regular exercise may not be as essential as it is for other people, but in the unlikely event that they do find themselves in a sedentary job, exercise will be an excellent way to release pent-up tension. Wearing, meditating on and surrounding themselves with the color purple will encourage them to take time out to reflex and focus on higher things.

Career *Born entrepreneurs*

The creative talents of these people are so strong that they may suit a variety of professions, with the proviso that they assume a leadership role or at least act as independent agents. Being a good organizer, they can excel in commerce but they could do equally well in promotion, advertising, education, philosophy, psychology, politics, acting, and writing.

Destiny *To admire, lead, motivate, and inspire others*

The life path of people born on this day is to recognize the impact that their actions may have on others. Once they have learned to think through the consequences of their actions, their destiny is to admire, lead, motivate, and inspire others.

Signs & symbols

Sun signs: Leo/Cancer

Ruling planets: Sun, the individual/Moon, the intuitive

Symbols: The Lion/The Crab

Birth date ruler: Venus, the lover

Tarot card: The Lovers (choices)

Favorable numbers: 4, 6

Lucky days: Sunday and Friday, especially when these days fall on 4 and 6 of the month

Lucky colors: Gold, pink, green

Birthstone: Ruby

July 24

413

25 July

the birthday of pure intention

Your greatest challenge is ...

learning to like yourself

The way forward is ...

to understand that human beings weren't meant to be perfect. It is okay to have weaknesses, make mistakes and have room for improvement.

You're drawn to people born on ...

October 24 to November 23

You have much to learn and give each other, and this can be a passionate and intense union.

Luck maker

Have faith

Lucky people understand that believing you can succeed determines to a great extent whether you will succeed or not. Faith is the most powerful force in the universe, so believe in yourself and your potential.

Those born on July 25 are motivated by a passionate desire to realize their progressive ideals. Whatever their motivation may be—professional recognition or the accumulation of wealth—they will always strive to do the right thing, their actions always being governed by a personal code of conduct that forbids them from doing anything that disadvantages others.

These people have a code of honor or a set of strongly held principles which they live by. These principles give them a sense of purpose and are more important to them than success itself. They are more interested in the reasons for a person's behavior than the outcome of their actions, and winning and losing matters less to them than discipline, integrity and sincerity. Those who are success orientated may find this approach to life limiting, but to people born on this day it is liberating because it means that no experience, even the ones they fail in, is ever wasted.

With much to teach others, they have the potential to be a shining example of maturity and integrity, but curiously they are often unwilling to ask for the same level of honest commitment from others as they are willing to give themselves. This is because personal integrity is their guiding force in life and they believe that this must be the same for others. Unfortunately, this approach can be a little naïve and they may find that others often disappoint them or let them down.

After the age of twenty-eight they are likely to develop their analytical skills and to become more practical, discerning and efficient. It is important during this period that they don't become too perfectionist in their approach, because it will block their creativity. In fact, throughout their lives they need to be a little less harsh on themselves because if they learn to be more accepting of themselves they will find that it isn't just their integrity that makes others smile with appreciation; it is also their creativity, charm and unwavering devotion to their remarkably progressive vision.

On the **dark** side

Self-critical, struggling, naïve

At your **best**

Noble, dignified, warm

Love *Charming and strong*

People born on July 25 are charming and strong, attracting many admirers, but they need to be careful that they don't surround themselves with "yes" people. They are attracted to partners who can challenge them, and in a close relationship they can be loyal, supportive and loving. They do need, however, to get down from the moral high ground occasionally and be a little more lighthearted.

Health *More time laughing*

People born on this day are prone to fatigue because they tend to push themselves very hard. They are also prone to stress injuries through accidents, and muscle aches and pains. When they do find themselves feeling run down, they should not try to ignore it but welcome it as an opportunity to rest and recover; they should also make sure they don't try to get back on their feet until they have fully recovered. As far as diet is concerned, they would benefit from regular meal times; this will give their day a much-needed structure. The same applies to going to bed; they should aim for roughly the same time each night. Regular exercise is essential as it will help them burn off energy and remove toxins. Wearing, meditating on and surrounding themselves with the color green will help them relax, as will spending more time laughing with friends and loved ones.

Career *Born law enforcement officers*

These multi-talented people can thrive in any profession, but to ensure success they need to develop faith in their abilities. Naturally charming and trustworthy, they may excel in public relations, politics, business, and sales, but they may also be drawn to careers where integrity is key, such as law and police work. They are also good with words and may be drawn to writing, the media and education, as well as art and music.

Destiny *To inspire others with their integrity*

The life path of people born on this day is to learn to be less harsh on themselves. Once they have learned to accept themselves, their destiny is to inspire and motivate others with their integrity and the infectious nature of their dynamic enthusiasm.

Signs & symbols

Sun sign: Leo

Ruling planet: Sun, the individual

Symbol: The Lion

Birth date ruler: Neptune, the speculator

Tarot card: The Chariot (resilience)

Favorable numbers: 5, 7

Lucky days: Sunday and Monday, especially when these days fall on 5 and 7 of the month

Lucky colors: Gold, sea green, blue

Birthstone: Ruby

July 25

26 July

the birthday of self-assurance

Your greatest challenge is ...

not being overconfident

The way forward is ...

to understand that for self-confidence to work it needs to be appealing, not overpowering. People need to feel motivated by you, not cornered or embarrassed.

You're drawn to people born on ...

December 22 to January 20

You both share a love for the good things in life, and this can be an intense and passionate relationship.

Luck maker

Demonstrate a willingness to learn

Lucky people understand that nobody really likes or wants to help a know-all. Demonstrating a sincere and humble willingness to listen and to learn will draw people to you, and they will want to help you.

People born on July 26 tend to be charming and strong individuals with an almost unshakable belief in themselves. Without doubting their ability to judge situations and people, they will offer their opinions unstintingly as fact, expecting others to agree and acknowledge them as such.

Other people tend to listen when these dominant personalities speak because they have an air of authority and experience about them which others respect and admire. They also don't speculate widely and pointlessly on a wide variety of subjects but focus their energies on one particular field of interest in which they have immersed themselves and about which they have earned the right to speak with authority. They don't believe in fabricating the truth, and others can be sure that what they are saying is the honest and blunt truth, however painful it may be to hear.

They can also display incredible moments of insight; this can be reflected in a humorous outlook that expresses profound wisdom behind the joker's façade. Such is the astuteness, wit and insight of their pronouncements that others sometimes put them on a pedestal and more often than not they are very happy sitting there. Unfortunately, their elevated status can come at a cost; they may find that they lose touch with their spontaneity and feelings, becoming isolated from the very group whose admiration, affection and respect they crave.

From the age of twenty-seven they have an increasing desire for more practical order, efficiency and analysis in their lives. In the years that follow, it is important for their psychological growth that they don't become overconfident and should be more sensitive not just to their own feelings but to those of others. This is because once they can accept that they are a part of the world and not removed from it, and that others have feelings just like themselves, they can use their formidable intelligence, insight and passion to formulate spectacular and authoritative strategies for success in all aspects of their lives.

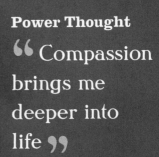

On the **dark** side
Over-confident, tactless, uncompromising

At your **best**
Honest, authoritative, confident

Love *Strong and self-assured as you are*

Romantic partners tend to be in awe of the self-assurance that people born on July 26 tend to be blessed with, but they thrive better with those who are not afraid to puncture their ego every now and again. Behind their authoritarian façade there is a youthful and playful spirit that others find highly attractive and once in a relationship they enjoy sharing with those they love.

Health *Dynamic in every way*

Just as people born on this day tend to be dynamic and authoritative in their professional and personal lives, when it comes to their health they may be impressively fit and active. Their natural vitality and shine draw them to sports, games and social activities of all kinds, and if they are not exercising regularly they should start immediately as their energetic nature requires it of them. Sex is extremely important for them and celibacy may cause great frustration. They are also extremely social and if they find that their authority alienates them from those they love, for their emotional fulfillment they need to find ways to climb down from their pedestal. As far as diet is concerned, they should not go overboard with animal and dairy products, as this can lead to digestive upsets; a diet which is rich in whole grains, legumes, fruits, vegetables, oily fish, nuts, and seeds is recommended. Wearing, meditating on and surrounding themselves with the color green will help them feel more connected to those around them.

Career *Born performers*

Natural performers, these people are especially suited to careers in the arts or in other creative areas such as media or advertising. Their excellent communication skills may also draw them to promotion, sales, writing, lecturing, psychology, counseling, public relations, and business. In the entertainment world or the film world, the director's chair may appeal to them.

Destiny *To arouse strong responses in others*

The life path of people born on this day is to learn to get to know themselves and others a little better. Once they have got in touch with their humanity and their humility, their destiny is to arouse strong responses in others.

Power Thought
"Compassion brings me deeper into life "

Signs & symbols

Sun signs: Leo

Ruling planets: Sun, the individual

Symbols: The Lion

Birth date ruler: Saturn, the teacher

Tarot card: Strength (passion)

Favorable numbers: 6, 8

Lucky days: Sunday and Saturday, especially when these days fall on 6 and 8 of the month

Lucky colors: Gold, maroon, brown

Birthstone: Ruby

July 26

27 July

the birthday of the director

People born on July 27 are blessed with energy, passion and authority as well as highly developed practical and organizational skills—a formidable combination which often casts them in the role of linchpin around which others revolve. In fact, these dynamic individuals can often be found successfully organizing, managing or directing others in some way.

They make wonderful directors of those around them, in command both of the bigger picture needed for victory and of the strategies that will make it possible. Fueled by the desire to make progress, they rarely do things by halves and will throw themselves into the pursuit of their professional and personal vision with single-minded determination and dedication. Their style is often so authoritative and powerful that it can mislead others into assuming that they are as tough as nails; but the truth is they are not.

Underneath they are actually quite vulnerable and this will manifest in their inability to make decisions on their own behalf. While they are superb at managing what is best for others, when it comes to their own concerns they can be hesitant and indecisive. They may, for example, be able to advise others on the best career strategy but be unable to decide which direction their own career should take.

After the age of twenty-six they often become more analytical, practical and efficient; it is important for them to make sure they channel this emphasis positively and don't procrastinate in an unworthy career or lifestyle that does not utilize their full creative potential. They are natural leaders, and others tend to do things the way these people want, but for their own psychological growth and emotional fulfillment it is vital that they focus their energies on making the right decisions for themselves. This is because with a little more self-awareness and honesty these creative and determined thinkers can produce original thoughts and, with a clear personal vision, they will be able to turn their wonderful ideas into a tangible reality that guarantees both personal and professional success.

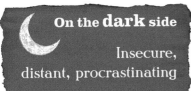
Love *Can-do attitude*

People born on July 27 show their love to others by doing rather than by talking; although partners may yearn for them to be more open, they will love their can-do attitude and willingness to offer practical help and support. Ambitious and self-motivated, they are usually attracted to hardworking and independent individuals. For happiness and long-lasting relationships they may need to overcome a tendency to be too possessive and temperamental.

Health *Your personal schedule*

People born on this day are happiest when their life is structured or organized in some way, but although they recognize this need they may find it hard to implement by themselves. Taking charge of their personal schedule to make sure they have regular meals and time for exercise will be a positive step for them as it will help them feel more in control. As far as diet is concerned, they need to make sure they eat a varied but balanced diet. Regular exercise is highly recommended to boost their health and body image. They may also suffer from sudden and unexplained bouts of depression; seeking the advice of a friend, loved one or counselor may help them get in touch with their feelings. Wearing, meditating on or surrounding themselves with the color yellow will encourage them to focus more on their own needs.

Career *Born corporate players*

The inclinations and talents of these people augur well for success as corporate players but their hidden creativity, adventurousness and love of color and beauty also equip them with outstanding artistic potential. Other careers that might appeal include sales, public relations, education, administration, management, law, counseling, and design. They also rarely miss an opportunity to keep up with the latest information and may become a collector or expert in books, magazines or computer technology.

Destiny *To realize their progressive ambitions*

The life path of people born on this day is to be honest with themselves about what they want from life. Once they have become more self-aware, their destiny is to marshal their considerable energy and creative talents, and realize their progressive personal and professional ambitions.

419

Power Thought

❝ I am willing to face up to my feelings ❞

Signs & symbols

Sun sign: Leo

Ruling planet: Sun, the individual

Symbol: The Lion

Birth date ruler: Mars, the warrior

Tarot card: The Hermit (inner strength)

Favorable numbers: 7, 9

Lucky days: Sunday and Tuesday, especially when these days fall on 7 and 9 of the month

Lucky colors: Yellow, orange, red

Birthstone: Ruby

July 27

28 July

the birthday of the independent spirit

People born on July 28 are fiercely independent and competitive. They love to work independently, and although they have superb communication skills they prefer to lead by example than by hollow words. They relish testing themselves against challenges and their urge to win is so powerful that they find it almost impossible to admit defeat.

The dominating characteristic of these people at first appears to be an urge to win at all costs, but this competitive streak is fueled by their intense desire to appear self-reliant. From an early age this independent spirit will probably have manifested itself in a refusal to conform or acknowledge authority they do not respect, and throughout their lives they will always value independence of thought and action above all else.

Other people tend to be awed by this self-assurance and although it can lead people born on this day to considerable achievements it can also lead to loneliness and, ultimately, disappointment. This is because the admiration that these people earn for their courage, confidence and willingness to break new ground is merely admiration; what they crave is the affection of others. There is often a reason for this lack. The single-minded, independent and combative approach that they are characterized by is, unfortunately, more likely to alienate those they seek to impress, who perceive them as being selfish or lacking in consideration for others. This is unfair as they can be kind, generous, intuitive, and warm; but until they forge lasting emotional connections with others, their creativity and potential may be misunderstood.

Fortunately, from the age of twenty-five there are opportunities for them to become more discriminating, practical and thoughtful with their time and energy, as well as the image they present to others. If they can take advantage of these opportunities to let others see what a modest, thoughtful and generous person they are, this will assure them the popularity and affectionate recognition they need to truly enjoy their undoubted talents and seemingly endless winning streak.

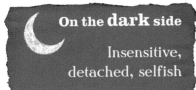
Love *Don't hide your loving nature*

People born on July 28 are effortlessly charismatic and will often be surrounded by admirers or even followers; in a close relationship, however, romantic partners may feel alienated by their reluctance to appear needy or reveal their loving nature. With their passionate temperament they may experience love at first sight but to make sure that love is long lasting they need to balance their need for independence with the necessity of cooperation.

Health *Born survivor*

People born on this day are incredibly independent and may therefore find it hard to accept the advice of their doctor but it is important for them to understand they have occasionally to relinquish control to someone with greater knowledge. They don't tend to get ill often but when they do they can be surprisingly needy of attention and affection. As far as diet is concerned, they need to make sure they eat sensibly and healthily, avoiding over-indulgence in foods high in saturated fat, salt, sugar, additives, and preservatives. Regular exercise is recommended, but not of a competitive nature; they are competitive enough already. Wearing, meditating on and surrounding themselves with the color orange can encourage feelings of warmth and security, and inspire affection in others.

Career *Born fighters*

These people are admirably equipped for professions in which confrontational tactics are important such as the military, politics and commercial enterprises, as well as the sporting or artistic spheres. They may excel in the theater as an actor or director, and with their leadership potential will rise to positions of power. Other careers that may appeal include writing, lecturing, publishing, sales, social reform, health, and charity work.

Destiny *To be the best at everything they accomplish*

The life path of people born on this day is to learn to reach out to others and share the spotlight. Once they understand that winning entails that someone loses and that trusting others does not weaken their strength but increases it, their destiny is to inspire others by being the best at everything they accomplish.

Power Thought

" My compassion produces positive energy in the world around me "

Signs & symbols

Sun sign: Leo

Ruling planet: Sun, the individual

Symbol: The Lion

Birth date ruler: Sun, the individual

Tarot card: The Magician (will-power)

Favorable numbers: 1, 8

Lucky day: Sunday, especially when it falls on 1 or 8 of the month

Lucky colors: Gold, orange, yellow

Birthstone: Ruby

July 28

29 July

the birthday of the partisan leader

People born on July 29 tend to be energetic and positive individuals dedicated to fostering community awareness. Their ambitions are directed less toward achieving their own success and more toward benefiting the social group to which they belong, be this their family, their local community, their work, their country or the world as a whole.

Within their own social group, these people tend to gravitate toward leadership positions and, because they are strong willed with clear-cut goals and the organizational talents to motivate others, they can be inspirational. Their willingness to nurture and assume responsibility for those around them—combined with the generosity, loyalty and pride they display toward those in their charge—generally earns them affection, respect and gratitude.

Although their dedication and commitment to the social group they belong to is nothing but admirable, their intense communal bias does not leave them much room for those closest to them, such as partners and family, or for their own independent interests. This is ironic considering that many of these people like nothing better than to encourage self-reliance in others, even though this self-reliance does need to be within a framework of community awareness.

It's important for them to make time for themselves and for their own psychological development, especially between the ages of twenty-four and fifty-four, during which their mental focus becomes more analytical and practical, and the desire to be of service to others takes center stage. These are the years when they are likely to make outstanding contributions to their community or even humanity as a whole, but they need to make sure they don't regard their own personal needs and ambitions as less important than those of the community. This is because by demonstrating to others that their community supports their individuality rather than suppresses it, they can give their community the most powerful and liberating endorsement of all.

At your **best**

Generous, loyal, cooperative

Power Thought

66 I take my power back. My destiny is up to me 99

Love *Don't overlook the individuals*

People born on July 29 are attracted to people who fit in with their community but they would actually benefit more from potential partners who are more individualistic in their outlook. Once in a relationship they can be positive and thoughtful lovers, and their wonderful way with words can quickly dissolve tension and create harmony.

Health *The placebo effect*

People born on this day should do some research about the placebo effect and the relationship between mind and body. This is because they tend to believe either that they will inherit illnesses from their parents or that when they reach a certain age they will be prone to age-related illnesses. It would benefit them enormously if they freed themselves from culturally accepted beliefs about aging, and focused instead on health and eternal youth. As far as diet is concerned, they should aim for variety and not be afraid to experiment with new tastes. When it comes to exercise, variety is again essential, but this time their structured approach may work for them; once they find an exercise routine that works for them, they are likely to stick with it. Wearing, meditating on and surrounding themselves with the color yellow will encourage them to focus more on their own needs.

Career *Born charity leaders*

These people make excellent teachers, and social, charity or political party workers, but they may also be drawn toward the world of entertainment, teaching or writing. Their leadership skills may make them sensitive and successful directors and businessmen. With their natural sense of authority, they don't like to be in a subservient position and are at their best when working selflessly for a cause or group they believe in.

Destiny *To dedicate themselves to the common good*

The life path of people born on this day is to remember their own individuality and the individuality of others. Once they are able to serve their community without losing themselves in it, their destiny is to become a living and inspiring example of how dedication to the common good can nurture and inspire true individuality.

Signs & symbols

Sun sign: Leo

Ruling planet: Sun, the individual

Symbol: The Lion

Birth date ruler: Moon, the intuitive

Tarot card: The High Priestess (intuition)

Favorable numbers: 2, 9

Lucky days: Sunday and Monday, especially when these days fall on 2 and 9 of the month

Lucky colors: Gold, silver, milky white

Birthstone: Ruby

July 29

30 July

the birthday of the robust explorer

People born on July 30 tend to be practical and down-to-earth individuals. They set ambitious material goals for themselves and love exploring all aspects of the physical world. Sensual and robust, they are often comfortable in their bodies, and their forceful, self-confident manner usually takes them to the top in their careers. Money and status, and all the privilege and pleasure they can bring, matter a great deal to them.

Although friends and family will often take second place to material goals, their relationships are conducted with steady equanimity and a concern for the physical and emotional well-being of friends and loved ones. They are fair and ethical in their dealings with others, and are almost always true to their word. They hate playing games of any kind and can be extremely generous with their material assets. In fact, one of the reasons they devote so much energy to increasing their earning power is that they enjoy being able to offer material support to those close to them.

Despite their morality, reliability and generosity, their target-orientated ambitions tend to exclude recognition of the importance of personal emotional and spiritual fulfillment. Unless they learn to cultivate an interest in their psychological growth, any victories they achieve in the material world will seem strangely hollow. Between the ages of twenty-three and fifty-three there is an emphasis in their lives on practicality and, given that they are already biased toward the material, it is crucial that they try to see beyond the material world they love so much. After the age of fifty-four there is a turning point which highlights their growing need for intimate relationships, creativity and harmony.

Above all, these extraordinarily robust individuals are motivated by a desire to achieve concrete progress in life, and they have all the determination and star quality they need to succeed. Their journey toward success, however, will be considerably happier and more rewarding if they can learn to appreciate and put a high value on the things in life that money can't buy.

Love *Solid dependability*

People born on July 30 are often warm, sensual and entertaining, and they tend to have a very active social life. Once in a relationship they can be incredible loyal, dependable and supportive. They need to be careful, however, not to neglect their partner or make them feel that they come a distant second to money, status and material gain.

Health *Seeking balance*

People born on this day are often very physically aware and, if they don't excel at sports themselves, they will often be interested in it. They are likely to take regular exercise and to eat healthily and, as long as they make sure they don't take things to extremes, their body-conscious lifestyle keeps their energy and spirits high. The biggest health risk for them isn't a specific illness, although they can be prone to muscle problems, high fevers and sudden illnesses, but their tendency to neglect the importance of spiritual, emotional, mental, and intuitive realities in their lives. They need to understand that happiness and success can only be experienced when all aspects of their lives—their minds, bodies, hearts, and souls—are in balance. It would be extremely beneficial for them to find ways to regularly renew and strengthen these four key areas of their lives. Wearing, meditating on and surrounding themselves with the color green will encourage them to seek this balance.

Career *Born art dealers*

The practical talents of these people, combined with their goal-orientated approach, make them well suited to careers in finance and commerce, as well as in the sporting arena. Their highly developed and inquisitive sensuality may also equip them for success in the arts as a painter, musician, writer, actor, or art collector. Other careers that might appeal include the catering and leisure industries.

Destiny *To support and enrich the lives of others*

The life path of people born on this day is to learn to open themselves up to emotional and spiritual experiences. Once they have learned to become more self-aware, their destiny is find ways to support and enrich the lives of others.

Power Thought

"Taking time to relax is my gift to myself and to my spirit"

Signs & symbols

Sun sign: Leo

Ruling planet: Sun, the individual

Symbol: The Lion

Birth date ruler: Jupiter, the philosopher

Tarot card: The Empress (creativity)

Favorable numbers: 1, 3

Lucky days: Sunday and Thursday, especially when these days fall on 1 and 3 of the month

Lucky colors: Yellow, purple, orange

Birthstone: Ruby

July 30

31 July

the birthday of
the descriptive artist

People born on July 31 are eloquent observers of the human condition. They always seem to be researching or digging around for information, possessing the ability to share or describe people and situations with remarkable accuracy and insight.

Nothing seems to escape their attention, even their own faults, which they are quick to correct. Their communication skills are superb and their insightful observations are often laced with a keen sense of humor. Those less comfortable with social interaction may prefer to use the medium of writing, music, art, or painting to make their contribution, but whether they become artists or not they often have a well-developed esthetic sense, loving to surround themselves with beautiful objects and attractive people.

Their highly developed concern for exploring, describing and occasionally idolizing aspects of human existence, combined with their logical train of thought, tenacity and devotion to their work, suggest that these people can make significant contributions to the store of human knowledge. They are not, however, the types to allow their observations to isolate them from the world around them; if they do make a breakthrough, they are often eager to share their insights and their triumphs.

Work matters greatly to them and they may throw themselves so wholeheartedly into it that they have little time to spare for friends and family. If they are to become emotionally fulfilled, they need to strike a better work–life balance. They also need to watch their tendency to think negatively. Their observations of the harsh realities of life may have led them toward pessimism but they need to ensure this does not become a destructive force in their lives, especially between the ages of twenty-two and fifty-two when there is an added emphasis on practicality and realism. If, however, they can keep their generous spirit alive with uplifting thoughts and compassion, they may be able to transform their high ideals of emotional fulfillment and dreams of beauty into reality.

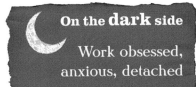

On the **dark** side

Work obsessed, anxious, detached

At your **best**

Articulate, artistic, hard working

Love *Shared goals*

Physical beauty is a high priority for people born on July 31, but for long-term satisfaction they should seek someone who shares their strong work ethic and artistic sensitivity. With their charm and ability to radiate warmth they can be attractive to others but need to be careful that their restless nature does not involve them in power plays with partners.

Health *Don't sit on the sidelines*

People born on this day love to watch and learn but they need to be careful that this doesn't leave them sitting on the sidelines or with little time for social interaction. Social interaction and participation are important for their psychological growth, helping them manage their thoughts in a more positive, uplifting direction. They also have a tendency to worry endlessly, sometimes in the small hours of the morning, and learning to make decisions about things they can change and letting go of things that they can't will benefit them enormously. As far as diet is concerned, they need to make sure that they don't neglect the importance of eating a healthy, nutritious diet because it will help boost their mood and their powers of concentration. Regular moderate exercise and sport are also highly recommended, especially those which involve social interaction such as dancing, fitness classes or team sports. Wearing, meditating on and surrounding themselves with the color orange will encourage them to be more upbeat.

Career *Born investigative researchers*

The love of observation and description that defines these people may draw them toward investigative careers such as forensic science, detective work, journalism, law, or science. They may also gravitate toward teaching. Other careers that might appeal include management, administration, politics, charity work, medicine, and art.

Destiny *To utilize their findings to help others*

The life path of people born on this day is to learn to make their thoughts work for them, not against them. Once they have managed to control their tendency toward negativity, their destiny is to make great discoveries and utilize their findings to help others.

Power Thought

" My beautiful, loving thoughts create my beautiful, loving world "

Signs & symbols

Sun sign: Leo

Ruling planet: Sun, the individual

Symbol: The Lion

Birth date ruler: Uranus, the visionary

Tarot card: The Emperor (authority)

Favorable numbers: 2, 4

Lucky day: Sunday, especially when it falls on 2 or 4 of the month

Lucky colors: Yellow, mauve, gold

Birthstone: Ruby

July 31

427

1 August

the birthday of independence

Independent in thought and behavior, people born on August 1 will often speak out passionately about their beliefs and when confronted with criticism, setbacks or disappointments they will rarely give up on those beliefs. Because they find it hard to function in a subordinate position they are best suited to roles where they can function independently or take a leadership role.

When these people see opportunities for improvement they will not hesitate to take them. Self-reliant, they hope others will see the wisdom of their ideas but they will never force others to accept their point of view, believing wisely that people need to be ready for the truth to hear it. They will, however, subtly try to influence people with their excellent, sometimes dark, sense of humor, and their insights that are merciless but accurate.

Those born on this day prize self-sufficiency above all else and, although this can help them bring about great progress through their energy and organizational skills, it can also bring them great unhappiness. They may, for example, cut themselves off from the love and support of others, a tendency which will leave them feeling emotionally isolated, wounding those who wish to offer them help. They can also take their independence to the extreme by becoming stubborn and inflexible in their beliefs; this can block their psychological growth and their chances of achieving success.

It is important, therefore, for them to learn to compromise and to be aware of the negative effect their intensity can have on others. Between the ages of twenty-one and fifty-one they will enter a period of increased emphasis on work, efficiency and order during which they are likely to gain an enhanced awareness of practical problem solving. Whatever their age, if they can recognize the need to be less detached and more sensitive to the feelings of others, so that workable compromises can be reached, these strong and independent individualists will surprise themselves and others with flashes of outstanding and truly inspired creativity.

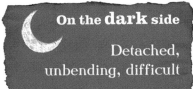
At your **best**

Independent, original,
influential

Love *Wonderful wit*

People born on August 1 can be somewhat inflexible and detached in relationships but their wonderful wit will always draw others to them. Once they learn to be more sensitive to the feelings of others they can be enormous fun; the only problem is that everyone will want a piece of them and they may find it hard to single out one potential partner. To avoid disappointment they need to take themselves less seriously when it comes to affairs of the heart.

Health *Be more flexible*

People born on this day are independent by nature, often preferring to be their own experts on issues of health, diet, and lifestyle. They believe that they are the only ones who know what is best for them, and although this is laudable it can also lead them to ignore important advice from well-meaning friends and sometimes even doctors. If they can learn to compromise, they may find that their emotional and physical health benefit. As far as diet is concerned, a structured eating plan works best. Regular exercise should also be scheduled, but to avoid getting into a rut they should consider cross-training, mixing swimming with running or brisk walking with cycling. Yoga, tai chi and all forms of stretching are recommended, and wearing, meditating on and surrounding themselves with the colors green or peach will help them be more spontaneous.

Career *Born scientists*

These people are best suited to careers, such as science or writing, where their work or research can be transformed into products. They may also be drawn toward social reform and the healing professions. With their natural executive and leadership abilities they are also well suited to careers in management, while their potential for creativity may draw them toward music, drama and art.

Destiny *To bring their talents to a wider audience*

The life path of people born on this day is to find a balance between their need for privacy and independence, and their need for social interaction and cooperation. Once they have found this balance, their destiny is to bring their talents to a wider audience.

Power Thought

66 Other
people are
meant to be
joyful, and so
am I 99

Signs & symbols

Sun sign: Leo

Ruling planet: Sun, the individual

Symbol: The Lion

Birth date ruler: Sun, the individual

Tarot card: The Magician (will-power)

Favorable numbers: 1, 9

Lucky day: Sunday, especially when it falls on 1 and 9 of the month

Lucky colors: Gold, orange, yellow

Birthstone: Ruby

August 1

429

2 August

the birthday of extreme clarity

Your greatest challenge is ...

falling in love

The way forward is ...

to stop confusing love with admiration. When it comes to affairs of the heart there are no rules or regulations, except that you and your partner should be yourselves.

You're drawn to people born on ...

June 22 to July 23

You have much to learn from each other; if you both open up there's much room for passion and fulfillment.

Luck maker

Accept help from others

Lucky people are self-reliant but they also willingly accept the help of others when it is offered because they understand that luck always comes via other people.

People born on August 2 tend to be straightforward, and their clarity of vision makes it easy for them to identify their goals in life and then direct their prodigious energy, tenacity and organizational skills to their realization. What you see is what you get with these people; developing their talents and being respected is far more important to them than being liked as a person.

Often supremely confident in their ability to reach their professional goals, rarely will they be thrown off track. Their confidence is the result of their ability to realistically assess their abilities and know exactly what their strengths and weaknesses are. And because they rarely set goals that are out of their reach, more often than not they achieve them. Sometimes in their journey toward success they may appear to change course, earning them a chameleon-like reputation, but this is just a demonstration of their flexibility and creativity. They never lose sight of their ultimate goals and are simply experimenting with different ways to get there.

Despite their toughness and determination, the more sensitive people born on this day can be hurt by the criticism of others but are unlikely to show it. Their nature is to be non-conformist and their straight-ahead vision can lead to harshness toward others. In fact, they need to be extremely careful that the hard shell with which they surround themselves does not lead to a hardening of their attitudes. Fortunately, between the ages of twenty-two and fifty-two, although there is an emphasis on order, analysis, efficiency, and logic in their lives, they may also feel the need to become more introspective. If they can use this opportunity to get in touch with their feelings and the feelings of others, their quality of life will improve immeasurably.

Blessed with a strong personality, clarity of vision and a unique approach to life, they have outstanding potential and, as long as they make sure they never lose touch with their intuition and sensitivity, their success and happiness are often assured.

Love *Pulled in two directions*

Although they are attractive to others, romance can be tough or elusive for people born August 2 because they have a tendency to place extremely high demands on those they're involved with. Once in a relationship they can be charming, loyal and passionate lovers, but they may find they are pulled by an equally strong desire for freedom.

Health *Focus on what you already have*

People born on this day tend to have action-packed lives with little time for introspection and are prone to stress and burnout as well as depression, weight gain and high blood pressure. It is important for them to make sure that they invest time and energy into building close and loving relationships with those who can warn them when they are heading off track. They also need to spend less time obsessing about what they do not have and more time being grateful for what they already have. That way they won't miss out on all the good things right under their noses. As far as diet and exercise are concerned, they need to steer clear of extreme or fad diets or intensive exercise regimes. Moderation and balance are essential to their health and well-being. Soaking up the scent of chamomile, rosemary or melissa essential oil can help fight insomnia and calm their mind, and wearing the color green can encourage feelings of warmth and security.

Career *Born playwrights*

Their independence and clarity of vision promise success as scientists or inventors. They are capable of working in a team or for a company, and may excel in business, banking or law. They may also be attracted to careers in promotion, sales, education, advertising, publishing, personal relations, media, or counseling, and their original approach to life may find expression in the arts or the theater, especially as an actor or playwright.

Destiny *To use their imaginative powers to inspire others*

The life path of people born on this day is to learn the value of cooperation and shared ideals. Once they have learned to remember the needs of others, their destiny is to use their imaginative powers and clarity of purpose to influence and inspire others.

Signs & symbols

Sun sign: Leo

Ruling planet: Sun, the individual

Symbol: The Lion

Birth date ruler: Moon, the intuitive

Tarot card: The High Priestess (intuition)

Favorable numbers: 1, 2

Lucky days: Sunday and Monday, especially when these days fall on 1 and 2 of the month

Lucky colors: Gold, red, yellow

Birthstone: Ruby

August 2

3 August

the birthday of the heroic rescuer

Your greatest challenge is ...

avoiding dangerous thrill-seeking

The way forward is ...

to understand that you don't need to put yourself at risk to feel alive. The journey within is the most exciting and fulfilling exploration you will ever undertake.

You're drawn to people born on ...

November 23 to December 21

You both share a passion for adventure and excitement, and this relationship will be full of creative fire and passion.

Luck maker

Slow down and be yourself

Concentrate on your sense of existing rather than throwing yourself into the action. You will then experience your true self, where all wisdom and good fortune lie.

People born on August 3 are fiercely energetic people primarily driven by their constant need for excitement, the stimulation from testing themselves against a variety of challenges, their desire to receive the admiration and respect of others, and last, but by no means least, their wish to cast themselves in the role of the heroic rescuer.

Their adventurous compulsion and heroic instinct to protect and rescue others can lead them to act impulsively and dangerously, but can also help them seize opportunities while others stand back and hesitate. They tend to believe that their ability to overcome risk and uncertainty gives them the right to get involved in other people's problems and offer their help, support and judgments. This is not always the case. Although friends and colleagues value their loyalty, and their willingness to throw themselves in and help out, they may tire of their constant need to give advice. These people need to learn to back off, allowing others the freedom to make and learn from their own mistakes.

Another danger for people born on this day is their susceptibility to flattery and praise, as this can lead them to an over-inflated sense of their own worth, isolating them both from others and from reality. From the age of nineteen there is an increasing desire for practical order, analysis and efficiency in their lives, and some may find that their urge to seek out danger for danger's sake eases somewhat over the years. From the age of forty-nine there is a change of emphasis in their lives when relationships and creativity are likely to take center stage.

Whatever age they are, however, they will always fantasize about rescuing or inspiring others with their heroics; if they can learn to seek a balance between their fantasies and reality—so that they don't endanger themselves for no reason or rescue others who don't actually want rescuing—their sudden flashes of insight and outstanding displays of courage can, like the heroes that they are, both impress and inspire others.

Love *Purposeful and high minded*

People born on August 3 have passionate, strong desires and their love of risk-taking makes them appear popular and attractive to others, although they can become too domineering. Loyal and loving, they prefer relationships that give them the space to feel independent and are attracted to people with the same purposeful, high-minded and direct approach to life.

Health *Love of danger*

It's no surprise that people born on this day are prone to accidents, injuries and stress-related illness of all kinds. It's important for them to be more cautious with their body, especially as the one thing they hate is being limited by poor health. Dedicating time to calm their mind and center themselves will be particularly beneficial; meditation techniques are highly recommended. As far as diet is concerned, they have a tendency to bolt down their food and not to think about its quality, so putting their knife and fork down between mouthfuls and reading food labels will boost their digestion and increase their intake of nutrients. Mild exercise to calm their mind and tone their body, such as walking, swimming and trampoline, is recommended, as are yoga and tai chi. Wearing, meditating on and surrounding themselves with the color blue will encourage them to be more calm, cool and objective.

Career *Born lifeguards*

The personal bravery and single-minded determination with which these people are blessed suggest that they may make great commercial entrepreneurs. They may also excel in careers where courage is essential, such as the emergency services. Other careers that might appeal include sales, promotion, negotiation, acting, directing, and scriptwriting. Their personal ambition and energetic personality will, however, take them to the top in almost any career, where they are likely to assume management positions.

Destiny *To be courageous, selfless and inspiring pioneers*

The life path of people born on this day is to learn to subordinate their ego to the real needs of the situation or person they are dealing with. Once they have found a balance between their own desires and those of others, their destiny is to be courageous, selfless and inspiring pioneers.

Signs & symbols

Sun sign: Leo

Ruling planet: Sun, the individual

Symbol: The Lion

Birth date ruler: Jupiter, the speculator

Tarot card: The Empress (creativity)

Favorable numbers: 2, 3

Lucky days: Sunday and Thursday, especially when these days fall on 2 and 3 of the month

Lucky colors: Gold, pale green and blue

Birthstone: Ruby

August 3

4 August

the birthday of the rebel

Your greatest challenge is ...

dealing with authority

The way forward is ...

to understand that freedom and independence are not automatically superior to acceptance, cooperation and diplomacy.

You're drawn to people born on ...

September 24 to October 23

You are both clever and elusive individuals, and this can create a powerful and intelligent union.

Luck maker

Say thank you

The more grateful you are for what you already have, the more good fortune you are likely to attract; this is because the universe responds to your gratitude and appreciation for what you already have by manifesting even more.

Those born on August 4 are rebellious free spirits who definitely prefer to take the path less traveled, even if there is nothing really wrong with the path everyone else seems to be taking. Their intense dislike of being restrained in any way, combined with their hatred of complacency and the unthinking acceptance of the status quo, often leads them to behave, think, act, or dress somewhat perversely or to defend unconventional opinions.

These people are intelligent, compassionate and strong-willed, and their resistance to any kind of restraint endows them with radical and pioneering potential. When they channel their energies positively they have the ability to enlighten and enliven others, but others should be very careful not to challenge their need for independence because autonomy of thought is of the utmost importance to them. So averse are they to submitting to the authority or directions of others that from an early age they may reject well-intentioned attempts to help them, fearing that some sinister motive lurks behind people's helpful exterior. Taken to an extreme, this can make them fiercely independent but also incredibly lonely figures.

From childhood, people born on this day are likely to have enjoyed being at the center of things. At the age of eighteen, however, they enter a thirty-year period during which there are opportunities for them to become more conscientious, thoughtful, discriminating, and efficient in their working environment. They need to take advantage of these opportunities to learn the art of diplomacy and compromise, as this will make life much easier.

When they are forty-eight they will reach another turning point that puts the emphasis on creativity and relationships. If, throughout their lives, they can learn to distinguish between independence and self-sabotaging behavior—being perverse for the sake of it—they will find that instead of becoming misunderstood, restless loners, they have the potential to become responsible rebels on whom others know they can depend for inspiration, guidance and radical but always exceptional insight.

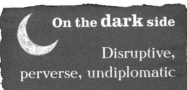
Love *Love-hate relationships*

People born on August 4 tend to have a kind of love-hate relationship with friends and loved ones, resisting their support and love yet also craving them. Despite their restlessness and need for freedom, partnerships are very important for them and they are attracted to people with whom they can share some kind of intellectual activity.

Health *Let your stress out*

People born on this day will often hide their feelings in an attempt to appear strong, but keeping problems locked inside can isolate them from others, creating unhappiness and distress. It's important for their physical and emotional health that they learn to open up and share their feelings; if they keep bottling things up it can negatively affect their health. They should ensure they listen to the advice of their doctors, understanding that sometimes it won't be possible for them to get better on their own. They are likely to have very little interest in diet and exercise, but understanding the links between what they eat, their activity levels and their health will help them make positive lifestyle changes. Carrying a turquoise crystal around will encourage them to communicate and express themselves more, as will wearing, meditating on or surrounding themselves with the color orange.

Career *Born artists*

These people are well suited to artistic, sporting or educational careers in which their talents can be used to inspire and guide others. Independent and preferring to give rather than take orders, they are best suited to leadership positions or working on their own; if in a group, they need the freedom to work in their own way. They are also good evaluators and may be drawn to real estate, banking and the stock market. Their humanitarian instincts may draw them to the healing professions, or social and community work.

Destiny *To inspire and enlighten others*

The life path of people born on this day is to learn that they can be independent within a group. Once they have learned to find a balance between their need for autonomy and their need for support, their destiny is to use their talents to inspire and enlighten others.

Power Thought

❝ I choose harmony and loving communication wherever I find myself **❞**

Signs & symbols

Sun sign: Leo

Ruling planet: Sun, the individual

Symbol: The Lion

Birth date ruler: Uranus, the visionary

Tarot card: The Emperor (authority)

Favorable numbers: 3, 4

Lucky days: Sunday, especially when it falls on 3 and 4 of the month

Lucky colors: White, yellow, silver

Birthstone: Ruby

August 4

5 August

the birthday of steely determination

The focus and steely determination people born on August 5 are blessed with, combined with their ability to keep their cool, instills in others a sense of admiration. This often turns to awe when their resolute sense of purpose, striking originality and incredible energy help them achieve their goals.

These people dream big dreams, but what makes them stand out is that they are prepared to give everything they have to make these dreams happen. At their happiest and best they are natural optimists and, although their lack of caution can lead them into trouble, they have no problems taking calculated risks or betting against the odds. Not surprisingly their fixity of purpose can antagonize others, but criticism rarely deters them, rather energizing them and spurring them on to prove everybody wrong.

They have the potential to achieve success in any sphere that holds their interest; but more often than not underneath their impressive self-discipline there are intense and powerful emotions which, if they are crossed in any way, can explode in dramatic outbursts of temper. The volatile tendency that is characteristic of these people can be unsettling to those around them, and it is important for them to be gentler with both themselves and others.

After the age of seventeen, and for the next thirty years, there is an increased need for practical order and stability in their lives and they will be more inclined to analyze things practically and look for ways to reshape their lives. The key to their success during these years will be to ease up a little on the expectations they place on both themselves and others. After the age of forty-seven there is a turning point which emphasizes the growing importance of relationships, creativity and harmony. Throughout their lives it is important for these strong and determined personalities to learn to trust rather than repress their feelings. This is because working with their intuition will help them build up the confidence and faith they need to achieve their inspired dreams.

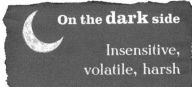
Love *Your dreams are not mine*

People born on August 5 are often very attractive to others because of their charm, sensuality and optimism, but they can be restless and indecisive about close relationships. Once in a relationship they are loyal and passionate lovers but also a bit controlling. They need to be careful not to become too bossy, understanding that their partner's dreams may not be the same as theirs.

Health *Inner health*

People born on this day should be careful not to focus on outer health to the neglect of their emotions or inner health. Generally they are fairly good at making sure they eat healthily and stay in shape, but less good at getting in touch with their feelings and those of others, despite the cool face they present to the world. Emotional confusion can lead to all kinds of health problems from the psychological—stress and depression—to the physical—lowered immunity, fatigue and hormonal imbalances. They should therefore find ways to ease their inner tension, such as meditation, breathing exercises or other stress-management techniques such as spending more time with family and friends, listening to music or pampering themselves. As far as diet is concerned, they should aim for healthy food, steering clear of foods high in salt, sugar, saturated fat, additives, and preservatives. Vigorous exercise that helps them release pent-up emotions is also recommended, as is wearing, meditating on or surrounding themselves with the color green.

Career *Born innovators*

The need to act autonomously that characterizes these people suits them to careers in music and film-making as well as to scientific, social or even philosophical innovations. Always aware of their image, they may also be attracted to the theater or the entertainment world. Other career choices that might appeal include law, sales, business, and working for themselves.

Destiny *To become impressive agents of change*

The life path of people born on this day is to learn to value simple acts of kindness and affection. Once they have learned to manage their emotions positively, their destiny is to use their fierce determination to become impressive agents of change.

Signs & symbols

Sun sign: Leo

Ruling planet: Sun, the individual

Symbol: The Lion

Birth date ruler: Mercury, the communicator

Tarot card: The Hierophant (guidance)

Favorable numbers: 4, 5

Lucky days: Sunday and Wednesday, especially when these days fall on 4 and 5 of the month

Lucky colors: Yellow, sapphire blue, light green

Birthstone: Ruby

August 5

437

6 August

the birthday of high expectations

Your greatest challenge is ...

coping with routine

The way forward is ...

to understand that routine is not always a deadening force; it can provide a safe and secure structure in which creativity can be nurtured.

You're drawn to people born on ...

September 24 to October 22

You are both sensual and thrive on mental stimulation, and this can create a passionate and creative relationship.

Luck maker

Every day's a lucky day

Lucky people understand that many days will be ordinary. Yet within these regular days there are opportunities for enjoyment, inspiration and fulfillment. Viewed this way, every day's a lucky day.

People born on August 6 have a lust for life, especially things that are uncommon and exciting. Their fascination with what is unique leads them to seek out the extraordinary and attracts interesting experiences their way.

They work hard and play hard, and big projects and grand schemes are their hallmark. If they are allowed to retain decision-making powers and the independence that is so important to them, their sharp mind, ability to take decisive action and unwavering determination augur well for professional success in whatever field they choose to devote their prodigious energies. In their private lives they understand the importance of secure bonds with friends and loved ones, but their commitment to their work may make it hard for them to live up to their ideal of devoting equal time to both work and home.

The urge for people born on this day to participate fully in every area of their lives can make it hard for them to deal with the more mundane aspects of life. This is because, whether they realize it or not, they are forever searching for something extraordinary or unusual. When life does not live up to their expectations they can become moody, despondent and restless. The key to success and happiness for them is to find ways to combine their passion for the unique and unusual with the routine of daily life.

After the age of sixteen and for the next thirty years there is an increased emphasis on order and practical problem solving, and they may become more discriminating with their time and energy. Another turning point occurs after the age of forty-six when they may focus more on relationships and the opportunity to develop any latent artistic, musical, literary, or creative talent. In fact it is in the realm of creative expression that they may eventually find the fulfillment they have always been seeking, as this will give them the opportunity to discover that the fantastic and the extraordinary really can be found in the most ordinary things.

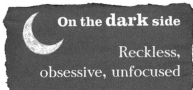

Love *Intense*

People born on August 6 are never short of admirers because they have an unquenchable interest in others and the ability to make them feel special. They can be sensual and passionate as well as reliable and kind, but their intensity can become wearing. It is important for them to understand that laughter, fun, silence and just chilling out with the person you love are a crucial part of keeping a relationship spontaneous and alive.

Health *Moderation in all things*

The lifestyles of people born on this day are likely to be chaotic and they would benefit greatly from more emphasis on the mundane activities of daily life. The key is to maintain a healthy lifestyle routine without getting bored or distracted; they should embrace moderation in all things but allow themselves the odd indulgence or wild night out. As far as their physical health is concerned, they need to be alert to the possibility of hidden health problems, such as undiagnosed high blood pressure or diabetes. Regular health checks are therefore recommended. Wearing, meditating on and surrounding themselves with the color blue will help them to plan, create and imagine with calm self-assurance and control.

Career *Born composers*

These people thrive in careers that offer them plenty of travel, variety, networking, and challenge; they might excel in business, merchandising, manufacturing, the travel industry, and banking. Creative and talented, they may also be attracted to design, art, the theater, and the world of music and entertainment, and should they decide to utilize their compassionate instincts they may be drawn to childcare, counseling, healing, or community work. They may also become talented athletes or sporting stars.

Destiny *To push the bounds of human endeavor forward*

The life path of people born on this day is to learn that they don't constantly need to seek out new and extraordinary experiences to feel fulfilled. Once they have been able to enjoy both old and new experiences and to prioritize the demands made on their time, their destiny is to push the boundaries of human endeavor forward.

Signs & symbols

Sun sign: Leo

Ruling planet: Sun, the individual

Symbol: The Lion

Birth date ruler: Venus, the lover

Tarot card: The Lovers (choices)

Favorable numbers: 5, 6

Lucky days: Sunday and Friday, especially when these days fall on 5 and 6 of the month

Lucky colors: Gold, pink, green

Birthstone: Ruby

August 6

7 August

the birthday of the undercover visionary

People born on August 7 have fascinating, many-faceted personalities with many hidden talents which they are often surprisingly reluctant to reveal. Their secretive nature allows them to surprise and amaze people with sudden and unexpected flashes of insight, or outstanding contributions and achievements.

They are attracted to what is secret or unknown, and their own life mirrors this attraction. Not only do they love to uncover mysteries or secrets—they are often fans of detective stories—there is also something secret or enigmatic about them; even their closest friends may find it hard to really get to know them. Although they are sociable, witty and charming they tend to dwell in a realm of private feelings and fantasies that they seldom, and sometimes never, share. When this is taken to extremes they can even become reclusive or antisocial in their behavior, but they are more likely to find a compromise and will assume an outwardly confident and extroverted personality while at the same time enjoying a hidden fantasy life.

After the age of fifteen they are likely to feel an increased need for practical order in their day-to-day existence, and for the next thirty years they will be more inclined to analyze things, looking for ways to restructure and improve their lives. They should take advantage of this opportunity to find a way to integrate their hidden personality into their social world. They also need to guard against lethargy and becoming too closed or fixed, and should avoid resting in some comfortable routine that does not challenge them to achieve their full potential. After the age of forty-five there is a significant turning point which sees them recognizing the growing importance of relationships, creativity and harmony; these are the years during which they are most likely to open up to others about their feelings.

However, the sooner they find the confidence to open up, the better. The hidden but potentially outstanding originality, creativity and intellect of these fascinating people should never, ever be underestimated.

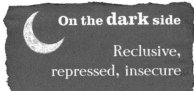
Love *Hidden passion*

Intuitive and reflective, people born on August 7 have the ability to attract others to them but they need to make sure that these people boost rather than drain their energy. They find it hard to express their feelings and vulnerability, and once they start to feel serious about someone it can take forever for them to declare how they feel. Surrounding themselves with trusted friends who give them confidence will help them open up sooner.

Health *Hug for health*

People born on this day have a tendency to lead a double life and they may be prone to anxiety, stress and depression. Counseling and therapy are recommended if the love and support of friends and family and the respect of co-workers don't boost their emotional confidence. Receiving hugs from those close to them will be surprisingly therapeutic. They would also benefit from daily exercise, preferably the socially orientated forms such as fitness classes, dancing or training with a partner. As far as diet is concerned, they should make sure they watch their salt and sugar intake to avoid the risk of high blood pressure and blood-sugar swings that can lead to hormone imbalances, low moods and poor concentration. Carrying a rose quartz crystal at all times can help them release pent-up stress, promoting love on all levels; wearing the color orange will encourage feelings of warmth and security.

Career *Born performers*

The inclinations and talents of these people suit them to careers in which they can find ways to express themselves freely without fear of disapproval or restriction from others, such as sport, writing, acting, drawing, painting, music, dancing, or the world of entertainment. Other careers that might interest them include business, law, religious ministry, and detective work, as well as charity work and social reform.

Destiny *To promote their originality with compelling determination*

The life path of people born on this day is to find a way to integrate their dreams and fantasies into their daily lives. Once they are able to be more true to themselves, their destiny is to promote their originality and vision with compelling vigor and determination.

Signs & symbols

Sun sign: Leo

Ruling planet: Sun, the individual

Symbol: The Lion

Birth date ruler: Neptune, the speculator

Tarot card: The Chariot (resilience)

Favorable numbers: 6, 7

Lucky days: Sunday and Monday, especially when these days fall on 6 and 7 of the month

Lucky colors: Gold, sea blue, orange

Birthstone: Ruby

August 7

8 August

the birthday of versatility

Other people tend to think that success comes easily to people born on August 8 because they appear to be naturally good at everything they do. Their success, however, is the result of their sharp intellect and strong work ethic. It is also a result of their exceptional versatility and ability to learn new skills from scratch.

Although they are versatile and will probably play many roles and sample many careers in their lives, they are not flighty by nature. Quite the opposite, in fact; when they are engaged in a particular project their focus is intense and their discipline inspirational. It is just that when they have learned all they feel they can learn or gained the recognition they feel they deserve, they like to move on to the next challenge, even if it is totally unrelated to the one they devoted themselves to previously. This ability to change direction and immerse themselves in different projects both confuses and surprises others, especially when these people change direction when they appear to be at the height of their success or capability.

Until the age of forty-four there is an emphasis in their lives on order, problem solving and being more discriminating with their time and energy. It is particularly important during this period that their versatility does not lead them to make career or life choices that are unrealistic or simply unsuitable. After the age of forty-four there is a significant turning point which stimulates their need for balance and harmony, and heightens their awareness of partnerships and relationships in general.

During this period in their lives the key to their happiness will be to develop more emotional depth and find ways to stamp their individuality on the world around them. Having said that, they should not try to suppress their characteristic versatility because, once they find a cause that is worthy of them, their affinity with diversity and love of fresh challenges will continue to be the key to their success.

Love *All-round excellence*

The all-round excellence of people born on August 8 may be intimidating to partners and friends alike, so for success in long-term relationships they need to ensure they allow others to see their vulnerable human qualities as well as their super-capable ones. In a relationship they work for harmony but they can become quarrelsome if they feel insecure. Learning to be more patient with others will help smooth over problems.

Health *Relax and unwind*

Without realizing it, people born on this day are likely to push themselves very hard and they need to understand that even they need to take a step back and unwind every so often. Sticking to a regular sleep, exercise and meal routine will help them feel more secure, especially when they are going through one of their many life transitions. They are often very physical and sensuous individuals, and sports of all kinds are recommended. Weight problems, especially around the middle, could be a problem later in life but they can handle this by eating a diet rich in fruits, vegetables, legumes, and whole grains, and cutting down on the amount of refined foods they eat and the amount of stress in their lives. Time spent relaxing with friends and loved ones will help keep them on an even keel, and wearing, meditating on or surrounding themselves with the color yellow will increase their creative confidence.

Career *Born travelers*

These inquisitive, imaginative and energetic people have an affinity for sporting or artistic careers, but they may also be drawn to theater, the world of media and entertainment, advertising, business, politics, and tourism. Because they are multi-talented, many careers will appeal to them and there are likely to be many changes, but their love of change means they will always be happiest in flexible careers.

Destiny *To challenge the wisdom of convention*

The life path of people born on this day is to find ways to stamp their individuality on all that they do. Once they are able to make their goals realistic and attainable, their destiny is to challenge convention with their versatility and ability to make even the hardest of challenges appear easy.

Power Thought

" True inspiration arises from the still silence within me "

Signs & symbols

Sun sign: Leo

Ruling planet: Sun, the individual

Symbol: The Lion

Birth date ruler: Saturn, the teacher

Tarot card: Strength (passion)

Favorable numbers: 7, 8

Lucky days: Sunday and Saturday, especially when these days fall on 7 and 8 of the month

Lucky colors: Yellow, burgundy, orange

Birthstone: Ruby

August 8

9 August

the birthday of the mentor

People born on August 9 are dynamic and determined achievers. Their presence is authoritative and others tend to look to them for guidance. Although they are extremely ambitious they can also be patient, inspiring and hands-on mentors to those who want to learn.

They are at their happiest and their best when they are giving advice to others. They feel qualified to take on the role of mentor because they have a good understanding of human psychology and what motivates or demotivates others. They have a wealth of ideas and insights about how people can improve or enjoy their life more, and are extremely generous with their advice and support. However, because they love to be looked up to and consulted when decisions need to be made, they can get upset if others ignore them, or assert their own independence and follow their own advice. It is extremely important for the psychological growth and emotional fulfillment of people born on this day that they ensure their concern for others does not turn into a need to control them.

Until the age of forty-three they will find that life presents them with opportunities to be conscientious, discriminating and efficient in the working environment. During these years they need to be especially careful not to let their controlling tendencies exert an unhealthy amount of influence over the lives of others. Learning to listen to others and understanding things from their point of view will help them with this. After the age of forty-four there is a turning point which brings a strong emphasis on social relationships and partnerships, and after the age of seventy their focus is on deep emotional transformation.

Whatever age they are, however, if these wise and generous individuals can learn to let go of their need to tell others what to do all the time and listen to their own inner guidance instead, they have the potential to be not just a mentor but a creative, inspiring, confident, charming, and successful role model as well.

Love *Concern not control is required*

Although they are charming and have no problem attracting admirers, there is a tendency for people born on August 9 to come on too strongly or be too assertive and controlling in relationships, frequently telling loved ones what to do or even what to think in a self-righteous manner. Though their intentions are good, if they don't allow others the same freedom they demand for themselves they could end up feeling emotionally isolated.

Health *Listen to your own advice*

Although people born on this day are excellent at dispensing health and diet advice to those around them, when it comes to their own lifestyle they may not show the same wisdom. They need to learn to listen to themselves, and put their own diet and health in the spotlight. As far as diet is concerned, they may find that, especially in later life, weight problems occur; but instead of skipping meals, which can slow their metabolism, they need to eat smaller meals every few hours to keep their metabolism and energy levels high and hunger at bay. It is especially important for them not to skip breakfast. Regular exercise is also recommended, in particular walking or jogging, because it is something they can do anytime, anywhere and will fit in with their busy lifestyle. Wearing, meditating on and surrounding themselves with the color indigo will help them feel calmer and encourage them to be less intimidating in their authority over others.

Career *Born careers advisors*

These people are well suited to careers in which they can devote themselves to guiding and benefiting others, such as teaching, counseling, lecturing, or human resources. They may also be drawn to politics and public relations. Alternatively, the world of entertainment may provide an outlet for their imagination and creativity.

Destiny *To inform and inspire others*

The life path of people born on this day is to understand that a vital part of the personal development of other people is for them to make their own decisions. When they are able to give others the freedom they need to flourish, their destiny is to inform and inspire others.

Power Thought
“ I release my need to control to the universe. I feel at peace with the world ”

Signs & symbols

Sun sign: Leo

Ruling planet: Sun, the individual

Symbol: The Lion

Birth date ruler: Mars, the warrior

Tarot card: The Hermit (inner strength)

Favorable numbers: 8, 9

Lucky days: Sunday and Tuesday, especially when these days fall on 8 and 9 of the month

Lucky colors: Yellow, red, orange

Birthstone: Ruby

August 9

1O August

the birthday of expressive charm

Your greatest challenge is ...

coping with rejection

The way forward is ...

to try to find out why things didn't work out. The answer could help you change your approach and improve your chances of success.

You're drawn to people born on ...

July 23 to August 22

You are both expressive and creative individuals, and this can be a passionate and intense union.

Luck maker

Be your own hero

As you start to imagine this winning side of your personality, you begin to change your ideas about the uncertainty of luck. You don't hope for it any more. You expect it.

People born on August 10 like nothing better than to please others or to win their approval. As a result they are often highly appreciated and admired, both at home and at work. They understand the importance of communication, utilizing their impressive vocal skills to persuade and influence others. In fact, their charming and energetic public persona is often cultivated with the sole purpose of impressing and delighting others.

Orientated toward others, these people seek to communicate their ideas to as many people as they can and, because their greatest desire is to be of benefit to others, their ideas are often progressive and original. Once they have convinced themselves of the merit of a course of action, they will pursue it with tenacity and courage. Determined to make their voice heard and to draw the attention of others to what they have to say, they are hard to ignore.

However, because they put such a high priority on what others think of them they will often put on a happy face, regardless of how they are feeling. Although this makes them very popular, it can deny others the chance to get to know the real person behind the mask. They spend very little time getting to know themselves and what they really want out of life, and their lack of self-awareness can make them place unrealistic expectations on themselves.

Until the age of forty-two they will often place great emphasis on order, work and efficiency. These are years when they are most likely to focus on how much they are appreciated and, because of this, they can suffer greatly when they encounter rejection or setbacks. Discovering what their strengths and weaknesses are will help them gain in confidence and resilience. After the age of forty-three there is a turning point which places more emphasis on relationships and creativity and, if they can learn to open up emotionally to themselves and others, these are the years when they are likely to develop the necessary self-confidence and conviction to ensure that their message becomes an effective instrument of progress.

At your **best**

Charming, convincing, attractive

Love *Striking a balance*

Although the popular and attractive people born on August 10 have no problems attracting admirers, they can have problems opening up emotionally to others and they need to understand that others will still care about them even when they are feeling low. In a close relationship their willingness to please can make them lose touch with who they are, so striking a balance between giving and taking is crucial for their success.

Health *Let your stress out*

To appear strong, people born on this day will often try to hide their struggles. The less willing they are to share their problems with loved ones, however, the more these problems are likely to overwhelm them, with a negative impact on their life and health. It is therefore important for them to cope with stress by talking more about their problems and frustrations. They also need to pay a little less attention to how they look; it is their internal rather than external health that should be their main concern. They can best take care of their internal health by opening up emotionally and also by making sure that they eat healthily and exercise regularly. This will help them cope better with stress and help them keep their weight down, so that they aren't at risk of heart disease or circulatory problems. Wearing, meditation on and surrounding themselves with the color green will help boost their self-esteem.

Career *Born speakers*

The natural sense of justice and desire to help others that are characteristic of these people may draw them to political or social campaigning or to charity work, but their considerable creativity and fine communication skills will also lead them toward acting, writing, music, or art. Whatever career they choose, their creativity, sharp intelligence, fine people skills, and capacity for hard work give them the potential to rise to the top of their careers.

Destiny *To make their voice and message heard*

The life path of people born on this day is to strike a balance between their own and others' needs. Once they have strengthened their self-awareness and self-esteem, their destiny is to make their voice and progressive message heard.

Signs & symbols

Sun sign: Leo

Ruling planet: Sun, the individual

Symbol: The Lion

Birth date ruler: Sun, the individual

Tarot card: The Wheel of Fortune (change)

Favorable numbers: 1, 9

Lucky day: Sunday, especially when it falls on 1 and 9 of the month

Lucky colors: Yellow, orange, gold

Birthstone: Ruby

August 10

11 August

the birthday of
the commentator

Your greatest challenge is …

being considered in your words and behavior

The way forward is …

to understand that just because you feel or think something does not mean you have to act on it.

You're drawn to people born on …

October 23 to November 21

This relationship has explosive potential but it can also be incredible fun.

Luck maker

Consider your impact on others

Lucky people always consider the impact their words or actions will have on others because putting yourself in someone else's shoes shows you are prepared and less likely to attract bad luck.

People born on August 11 are astute observers and communicators with a powerful desire to uncover the truth or hidden but essential knowledge or insight. In any situation they are in, both at home and at work, they have the ability to go directly to the root causes of the issues.

These people seek clarity and are always quick to detect manipulative behavior in those around them. They aren't shy about confronting others with their version of the truth either, even it if hurts. In fact, they like nothing more than to reveal to others the insights they have uncovered and are often at their happiest and their best in front of an audience. Not surprisingly, they can be harsh and judgmental at times and their sharp criticism can distance them from others; but they are also quick to point out the good in people and are as lavish in their praise as they are with their criticism, winning themselves many admirers in the process.

The clear-sighted observation with which they are blessed, when combined with their resourcefulness, courage and determination, augurs well for success, but their love of exposing hypocrisy, although refreshing, can lead them into confrontation with those who seek to maintain the status quo. In addition, their inability to accept others at face value can lead to relationship problems. Until the age of forty-one there is an emphasis in their lives on practicality and efficiency, and they need to be careful that they don't become too discriminating or critical of those around them. After the age of forty-two, however, there is a turning point when they may want to become more involved in personal matters and may move from concentrating on practical considerations to more creative, esthetic ones.

Throughout their lives if they can learn to moderate their tendency toward brutal honesty and develop greater tolerance of others' imperfections, they will not only retain the affection of those closest to them, they will also gain the attention, affection, approval, and respect of the wider audience that they crave.

On the **dark** side

Argumentative, hurtful, attention seeking

At your **best**

Insightful, powerful, intelligent

Power Thought

❝ I can pause and reflect before I speak ❞

Love *Powerful and intelligent*

People born on August 11 can be reluctant to open up emotionally to others, but once they find someone they feel comfortable with they can be loyal, generous and romantic partners. They are especially drawn toward powerful and intelligent individuals like themselves, but they need to make sure that they don't get involved in too many conflicts or arguments with loved ones.

Health *It's never too late*

People born on this day tend to think that their habits are set, and even if they could change them it would make little difference. They need to understand that improving their habits can improve their health at any age. There is no point lamenting what they did not do for themselves in the past, but there is tremendous value in thinking about what they can do for themselves in the future. Because their nature is impulsive and they are attracted to conflict, they tend to be accident prone, so they need to learn to think before they act, rather than after. As far as diet is concerned, they could have problems with red meat and dairy products; a diet rich in fruits, vegetables, whole grains, legumes, and lean meat is recommended. Regular exercise is also essential, as it will encourage them to release pent-up tension and boost their body image. Carrying a green agate crystal with them will help resolve conflicts, as will wearing or meditating on the color green.

Career *Born critics*

These people may be drawn toward careers within such academic disciplines as science and philosophy, or they may be found working as journalists, critics and law enforcement agents. In business they have a flair for sales, promotion and negotiation, and can also excel as financial and business leaders or advisors. They could also do well in the entertainment world, in writing or in music.

Destiny *To uncover and present essential truths to others*

The life path of people born on this day is to learn to think before they speak and act. Once they have learned to manage their impulses positively, their destiny is to uncover and present to others essential truths.

Signs & symbols

Sun sign: Leo

Ruling planet: Sun, the individual

Symbol: The Lion

Birth date ruler: Moon, the intuitive

Tarot card: Justice (discernment)

Favorable numbers: 1, 2

Lucky days: Sunday and Monday, especially when these days fall on 1 and 2 of the month

Lucky colors: Yellow, silver, white

Birthstone: Ruby

12 August

the birthday of the historian

People born on August 12 have a strong desire to make progress by leading others along an innovative path. At the same time they respect and value existing knowledge and convention. In some respects, they are like a historian in that they gather as much information as they can and subject it to logical evaluation before deciding on the best way to proceed.

When their intelligence and clarity of purpose are combined with their resourcefulness and tenacity, they often impress others with their abilities. They can often be virtuosos in their chosen field, whether that is conducting orchestras, writing books, raising a family, or designing a building. Not afraid of hard work and able to toil at a frenetic pace, they draw on both the latest research and traditional knowledge to create spectacular results. Not surprisingly, they have high expectations of themselves and the knowledge that they have thoroughly investigated every aspect of their belief gives them almost unshakable self-belief. Despite the potential success that such personality traits appear to offer, these people can, however, run the risk of alienating those they seek to influence by their inflated ego or harsh words of criticism. Although they should not compromise on their self-belief, learning to share will encourage others to listen to and support them more.

Until the age of forty there is an emphasis on efficiency and practicality, and they need to be especially careful during this period not to become too strict or emotionally detached from others. After the age of forty-one they may focus on relationships and a need to bring more beauty, harmony, creativity, and balance into their lives. This can draw them toward such activities as writing, art, music, or any of the creative arts.

Throughout their lives, if they can learn to assess the potentially damaging effect their forceful approach can have on others and develop greater tolerance and patience, this will not only help them achieve their aims more successfully, it will add an additional and infinitely more rewarding dimension to their lives.

On the **dark** side
Tyrannical, overly serious, judgmental

At your **best**
Energetic, innovative, knowledgeable

Love *Magnet for romantic attention*

People born on August 12 often attract admirers effortlessly but their tendency to put work before their relationships can limit their chances of happiness in love. They thrive best with a partner who can appreciate their brilliance and does not mind them stealing the limelight, but who can also equal them in intelligence and determination.

Health *Hostility hurts you*

People born on this day need to understand that positive connections between people are a source of mental and physical well-being. They need to realize that their resentment and negativity will hurt them more than it hurts the target of their anger. Learning to accept, understand and relax when people around them disobey, rebel or question is therefore crucial to their health. Having more fun and spending more time with friends and loved ones should definitely be a priority. As far as diet is concerned, they need to ensure they don't get so wrapped up in work that they forget to eat healthily. They should also exercise for at least thirty minutes every day, however busy their life gets, as this will not only boost their health and keep their weight down; it will give them much-needed time out. Wearing, meditating on and surrounding themselves with the color orange will encourage them to have fun and love life.

Career *Born historians*

These people may be drawn to careers in which logic and information gathering are essential, such as history and science, but they may also be drawn to education, business, or the world of art, writing and entertainment. Whatever career they choose, they will want the freedom to work in their own unique way, and a dislike of taking orders may encourage them to seek leadership positions or to work for themselves.

Destiny *To benefit humankind as a whole*

The life path of people born on this day is to learn to get the right balance between work and play. Once they have learned to share and relax more, their destiny is to unite the wisdom of tradition and the creativity of innovation and, by so doing, benefit humanity as a whole.

Power Thought
"I close my eyes and feel the happiness of being alive this moment"

Signs & symbols

Sun sign: Leo

Ruling planet: Sun, the individual

Symbol: The Lion

Birth date ruler: Jupiter, the philosopher

Tarot card: The Hanged Man (reflection)

Favorable numbers: 2, 3

Lucky days: Sunday and Thursday, especially when these days fall on 2 and 3 of the month

Lucky colors: Gold, yellow, green

Birthstone: Ruby

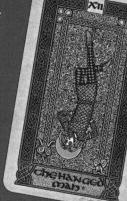

13 August

the birthday of the sharpshooter

People born on August 13 are no strangers to conflict and controversy. They are sharpshooters who always aim true, and their urge to break with convention compels them to take on challenges or make waves, whatever situation they are in.

The unconventional vision, resilience and tenacity of purpose that are key characteristics of these people can earn both the admiration and the disapproval of others. This is because despite the wounding criticism of those who regard their rebellious notions as ridiculous or fanciful, they always remain faithful to their beliefs. If life doesn't go their way, they refuse to be crushed by disappointment. And as their unusual imagination is supported by solid analytical skills, more often than not those who start out disagreeing with or disapproving of them will end up admiring their bravery, even if not agreeing with their standpoint.

Until the age of thirty-nine there is an emphasis in their lives on practical order and efficiency. It is important during these years that they keep their authoritarian tendencies and their temper in check. After the age of forty there is a significant turning point when they are likely to become more amiable and collaborative, placing greater emphasis on personal relationships. Whatever age they are, it is important for them to understand that although aiming true and flouting convention will guarantee that they are a force to be reckoned with, they will not guarantee that they always triumph.

As risk takers, they have all the courage, discipline and energy to attract success; what they sometimes lack is perfect timing. They need to learn when to cut their losses and move on, when to be patient, and when to pounce. The only way for them to learn this skill is to develop their intuition. Once they are able to recognize and connect with their intuition, they will not only be able to identify their target and take aim, they will finally be able to shoot and, by so doing, make progressive and characteristically unconventional contributions to society.

452

Power Thought

❝ My intuition is always readily available. I just need to listen ❞

Love *Zest for life*

Dynamic and sociable, people born on August 13 often have a wide circle of friends, and their deeply felt passions and zest for life are incredibly attractive to romantic partners. However, deep insecurities underneath the bravado may block their dreams of intimacy and true love. Spending more time alone so that they can get in touch with their feelings and understand themselves better will be of enormous benefit.

Health *Give yourself time*

People born on this day often feel that there isn't enough time, rushing from one thing to the next and not stopping until the day is over. Time out for themselves is advised, however, because they need to understand that time spent quietly alone is not a luxury but essential for their health and well-being. They need to ensure they give themselves time to sit, think and feel every single day, even if only for a few minutes. Sleep is incredibly important for them as dreams are often a way to connect with their hidden potential or intuition. As far as diet is concerned, they need to make sure they eat little and often to keep their energy levels high. Regular exercise is also advised, in particular competitive sports as they love to win, regardless of the odds. Carrying a titanium quartz crystal with them will help them find their true path in life, as will wearing, meditating on and surrounding themselves with the color blue.

Career *Born lawyers*

These people long to make a substantial contribution to society and may therefore be drawn to careers in law, politics, science, technology, or art that give them this opportunity. They might also be particularly interested in education, writing, publishing, advertising, and all areas of social reform. Whatever career they choose, their sharp intellect and perseverance will help them rise to positions of authority.

Destiny *To make a tangible contribution to society*

The life path of people born on this day is to learn to trust themselves more. Once they are able to find a cause that is worthy of them, their destiny is to make a tangible contribution to society.

Signs & symbols

Sun sign: Leo

Ruling planet: Sun, the individual

Symbol: The Lion

Birth date ruler: Uranus, the visionary

Tarot card: Death (change)

Favorable numbers: 3, 4

Lucky day: Sunday, especially when it falls on 3 and 4 of the month

Lucky colors: Yellow, purple, green

Birthstone: Ruby

August 13

453

14 August

the birthday of reflection

Your greatest challenge is ...

attaining self-awareness

The way forward is ...

to understand that you will never fully understand other people until you understand yourself first.

You're drawn to people born on ...

September 23 to October 22

You share a love of humor and fun, and this can create a stimulating and rewarding relationship.

Luck maker

Get to know yourself

Lucky people understand that self-knowledge is the beginning of wisdom. This is because only when you are able to recognize what makes you happy or unhappy can you start to make positive changes.

Those born on August 14 are among the most perceptive individuals of the year. Their primary focus is on what is going on around them and, because they blessed with clarity of vision, they have a gift for assessing the motivations of others and the impulses that govern their behavior. Nothing escapes their penetrating gaze. They never hesitate to say what others may be reluctant to say and in many ways become a mirror for others; through them, others see themselves as they really are.

These people are inspired by a desire to get to the truth of a situation and because they like to express their thoughts in a direct, sometimes brutally honest manner, it is not surprising that they often end up in deep water. Fortunately they understand the importance of humor, and this considerably softens the impact of their judgments, but it is important to understand the powerful influence they can have on others and to use it wisely.

Although their insights and perceptions often stimulate others to think more deeply about themselves, when it comes to their own personality they are surprisingly unaware. Instead of reflecting the views of others they would benefit enormously from some quiet reflection of their own so as to discover their own strengths and weaknesses. If they are able to do this, they will realize that they have a talent for entertaining and informing the world with the biting accuracy of their comments. They will also find out, however, that their tendency to observe rather than participate in human dramas often leaves them feeling emotionally isolated and is the cause of much of their unhappiness and confusion.

Fortunately, around the age of thirty-eight there is a turning point which places more emphasis on relationships and creativity; but throughout their lives, if they can remember that communication is not just about words, language and behavior but also about connection, their strong sense of purpose and undoubted creativity ensure that nothing can stop them from achieving their tremendous potential.

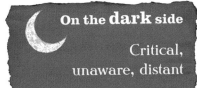

On the **dark** side
Critical, unaware, distant

At your **best**
Perceptive, honest, amusing

Love *Fast wit and humor*

People born on August 14 are charming and likely to attract admirers, but their passion for observation and analysis can alienate others. If they remember that people are not lab specimens, they can be passionate and communicative lovers always willing to offer advice and support. They thrive with people who appreciate their fast wit and humor.

Health *Choose your comparisons wisely*

Most of the feelings of uncertainty that people born on this day possess are caused by their tendency to compare themselves negatively with others. It is important for them to understand that their feelings about life can vary depending on whom they compare themselves with. To boost their self-esteem and their health and well-being, they should try to compare themselves with people who are meaningful to them and who make them feel comfortable. As far as diet is concerned, they will often be aware of the latest trends and should use their knowledge to improve their health. They may be prone to weight problems but can guard against this by eating less refined and processed food and more natural produce, and increasing the amount of exercise they do. Around 30 to 40 minutes of moderate to mild aerobic exercise, such as swimming, running and cycling, is recommended every day. Wearing, meditating on and surrounding themselves with the color blue will encourage them to become more self-aware.

Career *Born educators*

These people yearn to comment on society, so they may be attracted to journalism and politics. Other careers of interest include commerce, banking, law, writing, music, and the theater. The humanitarian side of their nature may draw them toward teaching, counseling, social work, or labor leadership. Alternatively they might be drawn toward sport.

Destiny *To influence, inform and enlighten others*

The life path of people born on this day is to get to know themselves better. Once they are able to turn their perception inward, their destiny is to influence, inform and enlighten others with their commentary or by their example.

Signs & symbols

Sun sign: Leo

Ruling planet: Sun, the individual

Symbol: The Lion

Birth date ruler: Mercury, the communicator

Tarot card: Temperance (moderation)

Favorable numbers: 4, 5

Lucky days: Sunday and Wednesday, especially when these days fall on 4 and 5 of the month

Lucky colors: Yellow, blue, green

Birthstone: Ruby

August 14

15 August

the birthday of the regal presence

Your greatest challenge is ...

coping with coming second

The way forward is ...

to understand that however much you feel you deserve it, you simply cannot come first every time. You will often learn more from your "failures" than your successes.

You're drawn to people born on ...

September 23
22 October 22

You are both attractive and upbeat individuals and this can create a strong and loving union.

Luck maker

Don't get over-confident

If you get caught up in your own brilliance it can backfire because you start to think your way is the only way. Nobody wants to help those who appear so self-sufficient that they don't need help.

People born on August 15 tend to be blessed with great self-confidence and courage, giving them a commanding or imposing presence whatever situation they are in. Others look to them for leadership and enjoy basking in their regal presence.

These people have such great self-belief that even if they find themselves in a situation where they are out of their depth they will still be able to convince others that they are the right person for the job or responsibility. Their optimism and ambition are magnanimous enough to include all those close to them, as well as co-workers, and they will never be reluctant to share their success. They are powerful role models but sometimes others may feel that they are losing themselves and their identity in the mighty shadow of these people.

It is important for them to learn to cooperate with their fellow human beings and to grant other people a chance to give their opinion or make their contribution. If they don't do this, they run they risk of becoming controlling in their domination. Until the age of thirty-seven there is an emphasis in their lives on practical order and efficiency, particularly in their working lives, and they need to make sure that their need for adoration does not lead to an inflated ego. They also should ensure that they listen very carefully to what other people are trying to tell them, as listening will earn them greater support and respect than commanding.

After the age of thirty-eight there is a turning point that highlights the importance of relationships and creativity, and this can stimulate them to develop any latent musical, artistic or literary talents. Throughout their lives, however, the key to their success will be their ability to empathize with others and to recognize that the right to personal autonomy is not their sole preserve. Once they are able to develop this awareness, not only will they be able to realize their ambitious and progressive visions, they will be able to lead and inspire others.

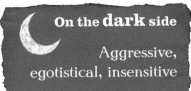
Love *Intensely passionate*

People born on August 15 are passionate and popular individuals with natural charisma. They seek a partner who can inspire them and share their interests. In close relationships they can be generous, warm and supportive, but they need to be careful that they don't become too controlling or possessive and give their partners a chance to voice their feelings.

Health *Laughter is the best medicine*

People born on this day have a tendency to take themselves a little too seriously and it is important for them to find more time for fun and laughter. This is because laughter not only helps them relax, it can also reduce the stress to which they are prone. In keeping with their regal presence, they also tend to have expensive tastes and may over-indulge in delicious foods. This can not only lead to weight gain, it can increase the risk of heart disease, so it is important for them to find other ways to satisfy cravings, such as exercise, phoning a friend or writing in a journal. All forms of exercise are recommended, including less common activities such as horse riding or rock climbing. Variety is the key to keeping their interest in activity alive and their physiques in shape. Wearing, meditating on and surrounding themselves with the colors pink and green will encourage them to be more magnanimous to others.

Career *Born leaders*

These people are, above all, natural leaders so they will flourish in any career that gives them the freedom to make their own decisions and take charge of others. Careers they may be drawn to include sales, marketing, promotion, education, lecturing, acting, performing, and public speaking. As excellent fighters for a cause, they may also be drawn to careers such as law, being a spokesperson, or labor union leadership. Similarly, their humanitarian instincts could guide them to counseling and social work, or they may prefer to be self-employed.

Destiny *To lead and inspire others*

The life path of people born on this day is to learn to combine their natural talent for leadership with compassion. Once they are able to moderate their commanding approach, their destiny is to lead and inspire others.

Power Thought

❝ Being compassionate connects me to my higher self which is my true nobility ❞

Signs & symbols

Sun sign: Leo

Ruling planet: Sun, the individual

Symbol: The Lion

Birth date ruler: Venus, the lover

Tarot card: The Devil (instinct)

Favorable numbers: 5, 6

Lucky days: Sunday and Friday, especially when these days fall on 5 and 6 of the month

Lucky colors: Yellow, pink, pale green

Birthstone: Ruby

August 15

16 August

the birthday of the powerhouse

Your greatest challenge is ...

resisting the desire for revenge

The way forward is ...

to understand that revenge isn't sweet. People don't like to be associated with those who are bitter or motivated by anger.

You're drawn to people born on ...

February 19 to March 20

This combination of mystical expressiveness with physical expressiveness can create a steamy and intense union.

Luck maker

Don't have enemies

Lucky people regard everyone they meet as potential luck makers. One of the most effective ways to avoid bad luck and increase your chances of good fortune is to have as few enemies as possible.

Seductive and magnetic, people born on August 16 are at their happiest when they can broadcast their unconventional convictions to as large an audience as possible. Their main priority in life seems to be to attract attention to themselves and, because they are such a powerhouse of energy, ambition and enthusiasm, they are often impossible to ignore.

Once they have decided on their sphere of influence, they will seek to triumph over any obstacles or people that stand in their way. Their drive to achieve power and recognition is so strong that they can be vindictive and destructive toward those that oppose them, and the desire for revenge is a destructively powerful force in their lives. Yet behind the brash and confrontational exterior that these people adopt there is a more determined self that directs their attention-seeking behavior but is entirely different to the image they project. Although their behavior appears to be geared toward material gain and career success, their more profound motivation is found in the attainment of personal happiness. As a result their private life is just that: private. This is the one area of their lives in which they can take off their public persona and be themselves.

Until the age of thirty-six there is an emphasis on being practical and building a structure for themselves, particularly in their work environment. These are the years when they tend to be at their most ruthless and they need to be careful that their enormous potential for creativity does not transform into driven exhibitionism. After the age of thirty-seven they may start to place more importance on relationships and the emphasis will be on quality rather than quantity when it comes to displaying their creativity.

Throughout their lives if they can listen to their powerful conscience and make sure their don't act in ways that are hurtful to others or lose touch with the simple pleasures of life, they have the potential not just to seduce others with their magnetic style, but to surprise them with their extraordinary achievements.

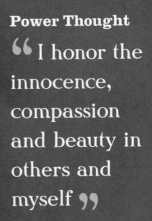

Love *The pursuer rather than the pursued*

When it comes to affairs of the heart people born on August 16 can be fiercely loyal and supportive, seeing others for who they are rather than what they would like them to be. They like to be the pursuer rather than the pursued and because they are so fiercely independent, setting goals with their partner can be a problem. If they choose a partner who is energetic, confident and strong-willed just like them, however, this will not be a problem.

Health *Cherish your friends*

It is important for people born on this day to remember that their ties to family and friends are as important to their health as good nutrition and exercise. Because they are so energetic and focused on the present rather than the future, it's not surprising that they can find it hard to stick to the routine of a well-balanced diet and an exercise program, but it is important for them to ground themselves with healthy eating habits and daily doses of moderate to vigorous exercise. This routine will help them avoid excesses, such as smoking, overeating and addictive or thrill-seeking behavior, which are damaging to their physical and emotional health. Carrying a malachite crystal will bring calmness and a sense of ease, as will wearing, meditating on and surrounding themselves with the color blue.

Career *Born chairpersons*

These people are well equipped for any field in which they can inspire or direct others, and will often find success in the arts or show business, as performers, producers or directors, or in politics or teaching. In business they will be drawn to large enterprises or the media but they may also devote themselves to charity work. Whatever career they choose, they do not thrive in subordinate positions and may decide to work for themselves if, for some reason, leadership positions are unattainable.

Destiny *To inspire or direct others*

The life path of people born on this day is to avoid extremes and excesses. Once they have found a healthy balance that allows them to serve rather than rebel against society, their destiny is to inspire or direct others.

Power Thought

❝I honor the innocence, compassion and beauty in others and myself ❞

Signs & symbols

Sun sign: Leo

Ruling planet: Sun, the individual

Symbol: The Lion

Birth date ruler: Neptune, the speculator

Tarot card: The Tower (breakthrough)

Favorable numbers: 6, 7

Lucky days: Sunday and Monday, especially when these days fall on 6 and 7 of the month

Lucky colors: Yellow, sea green, wild rose

Birthstone: Ruby

August 16

17 August

the birthday of
the dormant volcano

People born on August 17 may present a calm, composed exterior to the world but, like a dormant volcano, underneath fiery emotions fester and smolder. The quest for success for these people is relentless and, because they are so strong-willed, they either win a loyal following of devoted fans or create a legion of implacable enemies.

These people attract the attention of others with their intensity and self-sufficiency. On the one hand independent and creative types with great energy, imagination and determination not to be bound by convention, on the other they are serious thinkers with the ability to focus on progressive, occasionally idiosyncratic ideals. This combination of vigor, self-confidence and purpose ensures that any contribution they make has great impact. Although they make fine leaders, possessing the resilience and self-belief to recover from virtually any setback, their Achilles' heel is their argumentative, stubborn nature. They can be extremely defensive and aggressive, and their occasional rages can terrify those around them.

Until the age of thirty-five there is an emphasis in their lives on practicality and creating an effective working environment; these are the years when their untamed energy can be at its most explosive and undirected. Learning to think before they speak and act and listening more to the advice of others will help them gain the control and sense of direction they need to earn the respect of others. After the age of thirty-six there is a significant turning point that highlights their social relationships and partnerships; during these years their already powerful creative energies are highlighted even more, and this is the period during which they can really come into their own.

Throughout their lives the key to their success will be putting the emphasis on self-control. If they can find ways to harness and direct their incredible energies to a cause that is worthy of them, when their volcanic creativity erupts it will not cause chaos and destruction but enlighten, inspire and guide others with its dynamic originality.

Love *Passionate and intense*

People born on August 17 make passionate, loyal, generous, and loving partners; being friendly and sociable, they tend to have many friends and admirers. They are attracted to creative, intense people like themselves but would thrive best with someone who is capable of drawing out their passions but who is also calm and consistent.

Health *Avoid holding grudges*

One of the biggest threats to the health of people born on this day is their inability to control their anger. Not only can this make them more injury prone, it can also threaten their immune systems and increase the risk of stress, depression and anxiety. Learning how to forgive and to let go of angry thoughts and feelings will help their bodies return from an aroused to a normal state. Staying on an even keel allows their bodies to function at their best, so for their own good health they need to steer clear of holding grudges. As far as diet is concerned, they should avoid eating when they are feeling angry, stressed or unhappy, as this could lead to eating disorders and digestive problems. Regular exercise is highly recommended because it will help them unwind and release pent-up tension. Wearing, meditating on and surrounding themselves with the color blue will encourage them to feel calmer and in control, as will carrying a malachite crystal.

Career *Born leaders*

These people thrive best in careers where they can organize their own timetable and make an impact on others. Whatever career they choose they will climb up the ladder of success to leadership positions, but they may be drawn to politics, business, the theater or entertainment world, as well as management, writing, law, charity work, and education.

Destiny *To find success in the public eye*

The life path of people born on this day is to learn how to manage their emotions. Once they feel more in control of their lives, their destiny is to make an impact on others and find success in the public eye.

Signs & symbols

Sun sign: Leo

Ruling planet: Sun, the individual

Symbol: The Lion

Birth date ruler: Saturn, the teacher

Tarot card: The Star (hope)

Favorable numbers: 7, 8

Lucky days: Sunday and Saturday, especially when these days fall on 7 and 8 of the month

Lucky colors: Gold, hunter green, brown

Birthstone: Ruby

18 August

the birthday of the deep heart

People born on August 18 are among the most sensitive and tolerant of the year. Emotionally deep, they seem to experience both joy and pain at a more intense level than anyone else. However, this sensitivity doesn't unsettle them since they believe that feelings hold the key to their personal fulfillment.

Not surprisingly, they are not only sensitive to their own emotions but to the emotions of others, and others will often seek them out for advice and support, sensing a person who will not only listen to their problems but who will also take these on board. Not only do these people feel a pronounced sense of responsibility toward others, their urge to benevolently guide and protect others is also strong. Although this wins them many friends and supporters, it can also cause confusion about what their real needs and feelings are, limiting their potential to think and act independently. Once they have the maturity and the self-confidence to connect with their own feelings and be more objective when it comes to the feelings of others, they will discover that they have an innovative and original mindset that gives them the potential to be the masters in any chosen field.

Until the age of thirty-four there is an increasing emphasis on practicality and a need for order in their lives and it is important during these years that they find ways to connect with other people without losing themselves in them. Learning not to over-extend themselves and to find a place in their hearts for optimism alongside their realism will help them recharge their batteries. After the age of thirty-five their awareness of relationships is highlighted and they may be stimulated to develop a number of innate artistic interests.

If they can find a way to protect and nurture their sensitivity and vivid imagination without becoming self-involved, they will find that these are the years when they are most likely to inspire others with their idealism, determination, compassion, and progressive vision.

Love *Generous and sensitive*

People born on August 18 are generous and sensitive, and their warmth and insight mean they will have no problems attracting others. They thrive best in nurturing long-term relationships. In relationships it is important for them to be honest and direct, but although their sensitivity can make them tender and thoughtful, they need to guard against escapism through over-indulgence or avoidance.

Health *Keep healthy foods handy*

People born on this day are highly sensitive and when life or other people threaten to overwhelm them they may treat food as a form of comfort. Understanding this tendency will help them find healthier ways to ease their anxiety, such as going for a walk, playing a musical instrument or soaking in a warm aromatherapy bath. Being more strategic about their food choices when they are not hungry will help them be much more health orientated when they are. They should particularly avoid processed and refined foods or foods high in sugar. Because they tend to overreach themselves with work it is also important for them to ensure they have plenty of relaxation, fun and regular holidays, as well as plenty of quality sleep. Wearing, meditating on and surrounding themselves with the color blue will encourage them to be more objective in their approach to those around them.

Career *Born artists*

These people have a strong affinity for artistic disciplines and may choose to make these their career of choice. They may also be drawn toward social work, the caring professions, education, politics, law, business, and the theater, as well as merchandising, manufacturing and banking. Alternatively their sensitivity and natural healing ability may draw them toward the medical or alternative health professions.

Destiny *To arouse affection and a sense of direction in others*

The life path of people born on this day is to learn to balance their own needs with those of others. Once they have understood that until they can take care of themselves they cannot be effective in caring for or helping others, their destiny is to arouse loyalty, affection and a sense of direction in others.

Power Thought

❝ Obstacles are opportunities, and my life is more a dance than a battle ❞

Signs & symbols

Sun sign: Leo

Ruling planet: Sun, the individual

Symbol: The Lion

Birth date ruler: Mars, the warrior

Tarot card: The Moon (intuition)

Favorable numbers: 8, 9

Lucky days: Sunday and Tuesday, especially when these days fall on 8 and 9 of the month

Lucky colors: Gold, bright red, orange

Birthstone: Ruby

August 18

19 August

the birthday of the editor

People born on August 19 present a deceptively smooth façade to the world, but behind all this is a more serious person—one who has a definite agenda and will push ahead determinedly until this is achieved. The thoughts and feelings they present to others may be genuine but they never reveal the whole story, having carefully edited their ideas and opinions before presenting them.

They prefer to reveal to others only the information which they feel will impress or enlighten them. Image is extremely important—sometimes more important than performance. With such meticulous attention to detail and presentation, more often than not these people find that their work or ideas inspire enthusiasm in others, who tend to follow wherever they lead. There is a risk, however, that with such effort put into their image they lose touch with their real feelings and fall prey to delusions of grandeur or invincibility.

Deep-seated insecurities rarely lurk beneath the façade of people born on this day. Quite the opposite; they tend to be very aware of their own worth, and this is one of the reasons why they need to hide any trace of weakness. Sometimes this struggle to maintain their image can prevent them taking the risks necessary for their psychological growth and they run the risk of procrastinating when they should be moving forward.

Until the age of thirty-three there is a growing importance in their lives on paying attention to detail. It is extremely important during these years that they are more open and generous with their feelings because they will find that their complexity, rather than being a weakness, is a strength, helping others relate to them better. After the age of thirty-four there is a turning point when they are likely to become even more sociable and creative. If they can remind themselves that to err is human, these dynamic and bright individuals will find ways to combine their courage, originality, popularity, and endearing complexity to achieve brilliant and inspiring results.

On the **dark** side

Secretive, bland, indecisive

At your **best**

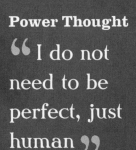

Charismatic, influential, confident

> " I do not need to be perfect, just human "

Love *Private world*

Only a few people are allowed access to the "unscripted" personality of people born on August 19 as they tend to guard their privacy fiercely. They are charismatic and seductive, and people are drawn to them instantly, but they may have problems achieving lasting intimacy if they do not learn to open up and accept that other people love them warts and all.

Health *Be a role model*

People born on this day are very aware of the image they present to the outside world and, because they have such an influence on others, not only their health but also the health of those who look to them for guidance will improve if they focus on making sure that their habits are healthy. They should make sure they have regular check-ups with their doctor, not hesitating to seek medical advice if their health is poor. It will be better for them not to wait until they get a serious illness before they learn to take their health seriously. Their diet should be well rounded with an emphasis on fresh, natural produce such as fruits, vegetables and whole grains, and their exercise routine should be mild to moderate. It doesn't matter what form of exercise they choose to commit to; the important thing is that they commit to it. Wearing, meditating on and surrounding themselves with the color orange will encourage them to be more open and generous toward others.

Career *Born politicians*

These people have the dedication and resourcefulness to succeed in any career but they are often drawn to politics, education or law. They may also prefer a career in sales, fashion, design, or the worlds of theater and entertainment, but whatever career path they tread they will probably want to be in charge and direct all the action.

Destiny *To attract and motivate others*

The life path of people born on this day is to learn that people are not—and are not meant to be—perfect. Once they have learned to celebrate their complexity rather than hide it, their destiny is to use their incisive intellectual powers to attract and motivate others.

Signs & symbols

Sun sign: Leo

Ruling planet: Sun, the individual

Symbol: The Lion

Birth date ruler: Sun, the individual

Tarot card: The Sun (enthusiasm)

Favorable numbers: 1, 9

Lucky day: Sunday, especially when it falls on 1 and 9 of the month

Lucky colors: Gold, yellow, orange

Birthstone: Ruby

20 August

the birthday of thoughtful mystery

Those born on August 20 are complex, self-contained individuals whom others often find very hard to understand. The reason for this is the air of thoughtful mystery that tends to surround them.

Although people born on this day need time alone this does not mean they are lonely. Quite the opposite, they are orientated toward and genuinely concerned for the well-being of others and their intelligent humor often lightens the atmosphere. It's just that, even in their most relaxed and happy moments, there is always a tinge of thoughtfulness about them which others may interpret as sadness. It can sometimes seem as if they are struggling with dark and deep secrets, but more often than not they aren't really sure why they find it difficult to share their complex imagination with others.

Struggling and overcoming their personal fears are therefore key driving forces for the melancholic but beautiful people born on this day, and sometimes the struggle can become so intense that they long to be able to forget themselves. They may seek solace in addictive pursuits or by losing themselves in their work, but neither approach will bring them long-term happiness and fulfillment. Although their need to understand and explore their past is a dominant and overpowering force in their lives, learning to focus their energies on the here and now will be the way forward.

Until the age of thirty-one there is an emphasis in the lives of August 20 people on order and practicality. They may find themselves continually analyzing things to improve them and their chances of happiness will improve if they shift the focus of this self-improvement from the past to the present. After the age of thirty-two there is a turning point which puts the spotlight on relationships and, if they can find ways to stand up for themselves and express their dynamic creativity and originality in the here and now, not only will they solve their personal mystery—they will also discover a magical way to live.

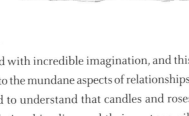
Power Thought

❝ When I focus on the here and now my life is more magical and rewarding ❞

Love *Imaginative power*

People born on August 20 are blessed with incredible imagination, and this enables them to infuse excitement into the mundane aspects of relationships. In love they want romance but need to understand that candles and roses are not always enough to keep a relationship alive, and their partner will want them to be practical and supportive too.

Health *The mind–body link*

People born on this day may put so much emphasis on their emotional or psychological health that they neglect their physical health. Reading up about the mind–body connection may help them understand that their physical well-being is often wrapped up in their emotional well-being and vice versa. Taking better care of themselves by eating healthily and exercising regularly will therefore help boost their mood and their sense of well-being. It is especially important for them to steer clear of addictive substances such as alcohol and recreational drugs. There could also be problems with digestion and with the liver and kidneys, so in addition to a healthy diet rich in fruit and vegetables they should make sure they schedule yearly or half-yearly check-ups with their family doctor. Wearing, meditating on and surrounding themselves with the color yellow will encourage them to feel more self-confident and attract vibrant, energetic people to them rather than those who are needy or damaged.

Career *Born researchers*

These people love to uncover information about themselves, but they are also naturally curious about everyone and everything; they may therefore make gifted researchers, scientists and journalists, as well as counselors, artists, writers, and musicians. Other career choices include media, publishing, diplomacy, politics, and public relations, as well as self-employment.

Destiny *To effect improvement*

The life path of people born on this day is to learn to look forward rather than back and to be grateful for what they already have. Once they have learned to struggle less and live more, their destiny is to mastermind practical programs for improvement.

Signs & symbols

Sun sign: Leo

Ruling planet: Sun, the individual

Symbol: The Lion

Birth date ruler: Moon, the intuitive

Tarot card: Judgment (responsibility)

Favorable numbers: 1, 2

Lucky days: Sunday and Monday, especially when these days fall on 1 and 2 of the month

Lucky colors: Gold, silver, white

Birthstone: Ruby

August 20

21 August

the birthday of the attention magnet

However hard they try to fit in or lose themselves in the crowd, people born on August 21 will always attract attention. Their appeal is so powerful and bright that it refuses to blend in or conform.

These people tend to stand out but not because others reject or ridicule them. They stand out because there is something incredibly likable and appealing about them; they may be beautiful to look at, they may have a seductive voice or they may be extremely athletic or intelligent. Whatever the secret of their appeal, the curious thing about these people is that a part of them longs to withdraw and not attract attention. They often resent feeling like a square peg in a round hole, but as long as they are unable to accept or embrace their uniqueness they will find that their opportunities for success and fulfillment are limited. However, once they are mature enough to celebrate who they are, they can put their natural appeal to work so that the attention they gather can be redirected as they wish.

Until the age of thirty there will be an emphasis in their lives on practically and perfectionism, and these are the years when they are most likely to deny or repress their individuality. After the age of thirty-one, however, there is a turning point that brings a growing awareness of relationships. Their creative abilities might be enhanced as well, and these are the years when they are likely to feel more comfortable with themselves and their exceptional talents.

Above all, they are extraordinarily imaginative, and because they are also blessed with resourcefulness and formidable practical skills to develop their visions they have trail-blazing potential. The only roadblock for them is their tendency to repress their deep creativity and originality, but when they realize that far more satisfaction can be gained from expression and involvement than from detachment and distance, and that people love them for being fresh and original, they have a world of opportunities for success and happiness at their feet.

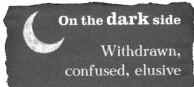
Love *Don't let the one for you slip away*

People born on August 21 are so attractive to others that they are often surrounded by admirers and will not spend long periods of their lives single. They need to be careful that their active social life does not make it hard for them to commit to the right partner for them, because they really are at their happiest and their best when in a committed and loving relationship.

Health *Seek health not perfection*

People born on this day often feel they need to prove or change themselves in some way and this may manifest in a doomed quest for the perfect body. Seeking out a healthier lifestyle is a great thing, but seeking the perfect body is not good or helpful, sometimes even leading to eating disorders and body image problems. They should be aiming for a healthy body that functions, not a perfect body that looks like the models in glossy magazines. As far as diet is concerned, they need to make sure they don't overload on dairy and meat products, nor on processed and refined foods, as these could lead to digestive troubles. The emphasis should be on fresh, natural foods such as fruits, vegetables, lean meat, oily fish, legumes, nuts, seeds, and healthy oils like olive or sunflower oil. Regular exercise is recommended as it will help boost their immunity and self-esteem. Wearing, meditating on and surrounding themselves with the color violet will encourage them to embrace their unique creativity.

Career *Born publishers*

These people may be drawn to politics, science or the arts, but whatever profession they choose they will be spurred on by their desire to make positive changes. Their lively intellect may make them choose education, publishing and writing, and their need for variety may draw them toward the travel and tourism industries. Alternatively they may excel in art, music, the entertainment world, and sport.

Destiny *To be a role model for those who feel they don't fit in*

The life path of people born on this day is to put less focus on proving themselves and more energy into accepting themselves. Once they have found a way to cope with the interest that others often have in their lives, their destiny is to become a role model for all those who feel different in some way.

Signs & symbols

Sun signs: Leo/Virgo

Ruling planets: Sun, the individual/Mercury, the communicator

Symbols: The Lion/The Virgin

Birth date ruler: Jupiter, the philosopher

Tarot card: The World (fulfillment)

Favorable numbers: 2, 3

Lucky days: Sunday and Thursday, especially when these days fall on 2 and 3 of the month

Lucky colors: Gold, green, blue

Birthstone: Ruby

August 21

22 August

the birthday of the commander

Whatever talents they are blessed with, August 22 people will not hesitate in exploiting them to full. They believe that hard work is the secret of success, not luck or fate, and they like to be the master and commander of their own destinies. Not surprisingly, for people with such remarkable self-control they are also far happier giving orders and commanding others than they are receiving them.

As well as being commanding, people born on this day are also extraordinarily creative. Their imagination is broad enough to cover a wealth of possibilities, and so powerful is their charisma that they are able to inspire others to execute their inspirations alongside them. They have a talent for making work seem exciting, bringing flair to even the most mundane chores. In keeping with their authoritative presence they typically display a tough and outspoken exterior to others, and they can be extremely stubborn in their refusal to change their opinion once it is formed. Behind their combative exterior there is, however, a surprisingly sensitive side, although they are unlikely to allow anyone to see it.

Until the age of thirty there is an emphasis in their lives on practical order, and during these years they are likely to lay the foundation stones for their far-seeing and carefully constructed game plans for realizing their ambitions. It is extremely important during these years that they remain as open to advice and suggestion as possible. After the age of thirty there is a significant turning point when their natural talent for leadership is likely to come to the fore and the urge to do things their way—sometimes regardless of the potential cost to others and themselves—will dominate. Fortunately, however, there is also an emphasis on relationships and creativity. If they can find ways to incorporate their love of discovery and adventure into their lives so that they can be creative as well as commanding they have outstanding potential, not just for leadership positions, but for fulfillment and happiness in all areas of their lives.

At your **best**

Influential, courageous, hard working

Love *The art of compromise*

People born on August 22 are warm and sociable individuals, and they will attract a number of admirers. Relationships are good for them because they help them develop their creativity and ability to compromise, but even if they find the most ideal mate they will not be happy unless they are free to pursue their own interests and go their own way from time to time.

Health *Are you moving too fast?*

People born on this day are expert at time management because it helps them feel in control of their lives but they need to understand that time management is not the only life skill they need. It is important for them to make sure that they are not so organized that they live in the future, missing out on the true pleasures of the moment. They should also allow themselves time to indulge their love of discovery, and taking up hobbies or traveling more will help unlock their creativity. As far as diet is concerned, they need to ensure they eat plenty of whole grains, fruits and vegetables to keep their digestive system healthy, and they should also not neglect the immunity-boosting importance of regular moderate exercise—such as brisk walking, jogging or cycling—that gets them slightly out of breath. Wearing, meditating on and surrounding themselves with the color orange will encourage them to get in touch with their own feelings and the feelings of others.

Career *Born managers*

These people will often find themselves in leadership or management positions whatever career they choose. In business they may well be happier working for themselves but they may also be drawn to sales, promotion or advertising. They may also excel in professions that use their mind such as education, law, and writing, as well as the theater, music or the entertainment world.

Destiny *To inspire others with discipline, originality and ambition*

The life path of people born on this way is to learn that there is never only one way to approach a situation. Once they have learned that being more open to suggestion improves their chances of success, their destiny is to inspire others with their discipline, originality and ambition.

Signs & symbols

Sun signs: Leo/Virgo

Ruling planets: Sun, the individual/Mercury, the communicator

Symbols: The Lion/The Virgin

Birth date ruler: Uranus, the visionary

Tarot card: The Fool (freedom)

Favorable numbers: 3, 4

Lucky day: Sunday, especially when it falls on 3 and 4 of the month

Lucky colors: Gold, lavender, blue

Birthstone: Ruby

23 August

the birthday of sparkling accuracy

Your greatest challenge is ...

avoiding preoccupation with your own interests

The way forward is ...

to understand that there's nothing wrong with self-involvement as long as you aren't insensitive to the feelings of others.

You're drawn to people born on ...

October 23 to November 21

You are both hard-working and determined individuals with inquiring minds who can bring out the best in each other.

Luck maker

Small things and great love

Research has shown that life satisfaction improves significantly with the level of altruistic activity. Look for ways to do random acts of kindness every day and see how this makes you feel happier and brings luck.

People born on August 23 have a tremendous store of energy, and when it is directed to something that holds their interest, their intensity and commitment sparkle. They pay as much attention to the process as the product, whether they are preparing an assignment, arranging flowers or deciding what to wear. The accurate eye, incredible focus and attention to detail that define them are invaluable to colleagues, friends and family alike, and everyone counts on them to keep everything organized and running smoothly.

The intensity of their commitment to accuracy can make them lose sight of the bigger picture from time to time. It is important for them, however, never to lose sight of their progressive and ambitious goals because they have the resourcefulness, tenacity, technical abilities and, if they trust themselves more, the creativity to see their visions realized.

Another danger for these people is that they can become so wrapped up in their interests and their work that any kind of interruption or setback can lead to outbursts of anger; others may therefore perceive them as aggressive, neglectful or in extreme cases selfish. This is unfair, as August 23 people are inherently kind and always willing to help those in need. It's just that they have a strong tendency to immerse themselves in the solitary pursuit of intellectual concerns, and although this gives them incredible potential for professional success, they run the risk of unintentionally upsetting or neglecting others.

After the age of thirty there is less emphasis on practicality, efficiency, problem solving, and order in the lives of people born on this day, and opportunities will arise to focus more on relationships, and explore the possibility of creative and artistic outlets. It is important for them to take advantage of these opportunities and not to be confused by the apparent emotional complexities they create in their lives, because, paradoxically, it is the complexities that hold the key to their fulfillment and happiness.

Love *Ultimate faith*

People born on August 23 will often be relied upon by their friends and family to keep everything organized and, as long as they are rewarded with gratitude, they are very happy to be placed in this role. They have a tendency to put their professional life before their personal life, making them sometimes restless and indecisive about relationships. Their ideal partner is someone who is intelligent and compassionate and has absolute faith in them.

Health *Money can't buy it*

Many people born on this day are very good at earning or saving money. For the sake of their emotional health and well-being they may need to remind themselves from time to time that, however rich they become, money and material possessions cannot buy self-esteem or happiness. They need to value and respect themselves more, appreciating that value and self-worth can only come from within. If they find it hard to feel good about themselves and relate to others, they may benefit from counseling. As far as diet is concerned, food allergies and sugar cravings could be a problem, although they should not forget that food is meant to be one of life's pleasures. Regular exercise, preferably outdoors in the fresh air, is highly recommended, as is any activity that encourages them to get out, explore and see more of the world. Wearing, meditating on and surrounding themselves with the color yellow will encourage them to be more optimistic and spontaneous.

Career *Born crafts workers*

These people are multi-talented but should avoid careers that are monotonous in any way. They may be drawn to teaching, sales, writing, publishing, engineering, science, art, the entertainment world, banking, information technology, real estate, or working with other people's money. Whatever career they choose, they are likely to be a perfectionist.

Destiny *To act as agents of improvement*

The life path of people born on this day is to learn to find a balance between their own needs and those of others. Once they have learned to be more sensitive to the feelings of others, their destiny is to act as highly skilled agents of improvement.

Signs & symbols

Sun signs: Virgo/Leo

Ruling planets: Mercury, the communicator/Sun, the individual

Symbols: The Virgin/The Lion

Birth date ruler: Mercury, the communicator

Tarot card: The Hierophant (guidance)

Favorable numbers: 4, 5

Lucky days: Sunday and Wednesday, especially when these days fall on 4 and 5 of the month

Lucky colors: Gold, blue, green

Birthstone: Sapphire

August 23

24 August

the birthday of
the questioning discoverer

People born on August 24 are blessed with a sharp and questioning mind that is at its best when untangling mysteries, uncovering the truth or making new discoveries. They don't like to take anything at face value, and even the opinions of experts or their most trusted friends will not stop them searching through the evidence to catch what others might have missed and to discover their version of the truth.

Their questioning mind makes them hard to manipulate, and people may rely heavily on them for advice and insight. Indeed, they often have a reputation for being someone whose opinion and approval others can trust. They could be said to mistrust anything or anyone that appears simple or straightforward, so strong is their belief that hidden complexities lie beneath the surface. Paradoxically, although their self-image is of being very simple and direct, what they do not realize is that they are just as complex as the subjects of their investigation, if not more so. Although they never miss the facts, they can have a tendency to miss out in their observations what is subtle or unspoken, and their accuracy and creativity would be enhanced if they learned to develop their intuition.

Until the age of twenty-nine there is an emphasis in their lives on practicality and efficiency, but after the age of thirty there is a turning point when they may focus on relationships and opportunities to develop their latent creative potential. They need to take advantage of these opportunities, using sharp-witted intellectual skills and their creative potential, as these will boost their chances of success professionally and personally.

Throughout their lives, intense inner forces may cause them to alternate between extremes of uncertainty and a sense of being special. If they can cultivate positive thinking, trust their deeper intuition and learn to manage worry positively, these gifted and astute discoverers, who leave no stone unturned in their quest for knowledge, have the potential to enrich the lives of others with the fruits of their observations.

On the dark side

Stifling,
over-critical, suspicious

At your best

Observant, insightful,
through

Love *A marriage of heart and mind*

People born on August 24 are always interested in new people and new places, and they struggle with routine in relationships. However, when relationships are based on mutual affinity they are usually successful. The right partner will be someone who knows how to inspire trust in them, teaching them to listen to their hearts as much as their minds.

Health *Stay super-young*

People born on this day have a fascination with the world about them; as long as they don't become self-critical, they will probably be working or thinking in some capacity for all their lives. As far as diet is concerned, people born on this day need to make sure they don't get so absorbed in their work or studies that they forget the importance of good nutrition. They also need to exercise regularly, preferably in the outdoors, so they get all the mood-boosting benefits of sunshine. Hypochondria can be a real concern, so it is important that they don't get overly concerned about their health and maintain a relaxed attitude. It is recommended that they spend more time with family and friends, and have more fun. Wearing, meditating on and surrounding themselves with the color orange will encourage them to love life as much as they love studying it.

Career *Born commentators*

These people are naturally drawn to the arts, music, painting, writing, and music, but they are also gifted and astute psychologists, therapists and commentators on human behavior and all aspects of the natural world. Other career choices that might appeal include education, lecturing, commerce, research, science, health care, and real estate.

Destiny *To inform, enlighten and enrich the lives of others*

The life path of people born on this day is to learn to observe less and feel more. Once they have balanced their urge for discovery with their psychological need to get involved, their destiny is to inform, enlighten and enrich the lives of others with their surprising and insightful observations.

Signs & symbols

Sun signs: Virgo/Leo

Ruling planets: Mercury, the communicator/Sun, the individual

Symbols: The Virgin/The Lion

Birth date ruler: Venus, the lover

Tarot card: The Lovers (choices)

Favorable numbers: 5, 6

Lucky days: Sunday and Friday, especially when these days fall on 5 and 6 of the month

Lucky colors: Yellow, rose, light green

Birthstone: Sapphire

August 24

25 August

the birthday of the live wire

Your greatest challenge is ...

resisting the need to prove yourself all the time

The way forward is ...

to understand that only you can give yourself a sense of self-worth.

You're drawn to people born on ...

October 23 to November 21

You both have inquiring, agile minds and the ability to bring the best out in each other.

Luck maker

Stop comparison shopping

Don't compare yourself with others because it will keep you feeling negative and low in self-esteem. Lucky people know that they are special, unique and irreplaceable, and this positive attitude about themselves attracts luck.

People born on August 25 are difficult to ignore. Their polished image and excellent social skills get them noticed wherever they go, success seeming to come easily to them. Others often think of them as self-assured, attractive, clever, accomplished, and charismatic. In short, they are real live wires and life always seems more interesting and dynamic when they are around.

Although they are seductive, outgoing and vital on the outside, these people seldom feel like this on the inside, and they will drive themselves extremely hard to prove to others that they are really self-assured and accomplished. They rarely let down their guard and if they feel threatened or insecure in any way they may over-emphasize their polished public image to compensate. Unfortunately, this can lead to conceited, arrogant or superficial words or behavior that can alienate the very people they seek to impress. It is vital for people born on this day to focus less on charming others to win their approval and more on cultivating their own sense of self-worth.

From childhood people born on this day may have been inclined to analyze situations practically in order to understand and improve them. As they grow older they may devote a great deal of energy to cultivating and projecting their public image. After the age of twenty-eight, however, there is a turning point and over the next thirty years they become more aware of the importance of close relationships and partnerships. Creative abilities are also enhanced during this time. After the age of fifty-eight there is another turning point which brings an emphasis on greater self-awareness and personal power. In some respects, these may be the years when they feel at their happiest and their best because the focus is on their individuality.

However, whatever age they are, if they can find the courage to discover and develop their real talents and sharp intellect, they will find that the accomplished, clever, attractive, and creative persona they have created isn't a mask any more but a reality.

Power Thought

"I know that I am good enough"

Love *Endless love*

People born on August 25 will often have many love affairs or relationships in their lives, some at the same time. They are so eye-catching that attracting partners is not a problem; the problem is relating to others on a deeper, less superficial level. Constantly falling in love may in fact be an expression of their inability to love themselves; intimacy with another will only be possible when they have worked on their self-worth.

Health *Exercise for your mind*

People born on this day tend to place too great an emphasis on physical fitness and appearance and as a result their mental and emotional fitness tends to get neglected. As far as diet is concerned, they should limit their intake of meat and dairy products, as digestive problems are indicated, and go for a more vegetarian-based diet. Regular moderate to intense exercise is recommended as it will help them release pent-up tension and boost their self-esteem. They would also enjoy the relaxing and sensual benefits of massage, and cognitive behavior therapy would help them challenge their tendency to think negatively. Wearing, meditating on and surrounding themselves with the color yellow will boost their self-esteem and sense of personal power from the inside.

Career *Born promoters*

People born on this day may be attracted to professions such as law, medicine or the caring services where they can help or support others. They may also excel as managers, team leaders or media representatives, teachers, trainers, counselors, or charity workers. They may be interested in research, science or chemistry, mathematics or engineering, or possess musical or artistic talents and a love of writing.

Destiny *To inspire and lead others*

The life path of people born on this day is to learn to trust themselves and their unique talents more. Once they feel truly confident in their insights, their destiny is to inspire others to develop their own creativity.

Signs & symbols

Sun signs: Virgo/Leo

Ruling planets: Mercury, the communicator/Sun, the individual

Symbols: The Virgin/The Lion

Birth date ruler: Neptune, the speculator

Tarot card: The Chariot (resilience)

Favorable numbers: 6, 7

Lucky days: Wednesday and Monday, especially when these days fall on 6 and 7 of the month

Lucky colors: Yellow, jade green, blue

Birthstone: Sapphire

August 25

26 August

the birthday of star potential

People born on August 26 tend to feel most comfortable when they are the power or support behind the throne. Although their star potential is undoubted, they often choose the role of understudy, second in command or advisor, gaining quiet satisfaction from the knowledge that the success of others is largely down to their support.

Usually setting high standards for themselves in whatever line of work they select for themselves, they will often master their skills so well that their work is often of an exceptionally high standard. Yet if their admirable talents are thrown into the limelight, even if the recognition is well earned and well deserved, they will feel ill at ease and may resort to self-deprecating behavior to underplay their talents. This is because nothing matters more to them than the satisfaction and happiness of everyone they are living and working with. If their own profile gets too high they feel that this might have a detrimental effect on others.

Until the age of twenty-seven the selfless tendencies of these people will be highlighted, and they need to make sure this does not lead to unhappiness and resentment. After the age of twenty-eight there is a turning point which puts the emphasis on diplomacy, partnerships and relationships; these are the years when they are most likely to step into the role of supportive advisor, guide or partner. If they are content to remain in this role they can feel incredibly fulfilled, but if they are not content and long to strike out on their own they can feel frustrated. Fortunately, during this time they are also likely to gain an enhanced sense of balance and harmony that helps them develop their creativity.

If they can learn to stand up for themselves, these are the years when their undeniable star potential and capacity for independent and original thought will finally reveal themselves to the world, to guide and inspire others in a supportive role, or enlighten and surprise others in a leadership role.

Love *Team player*

People born on August 26 will often put the happiness of their partner or loved ones above their own and they need to remind themselves that their happiness is just as important. In love, they find it easy to connect and are seldom without a partner to support, encourage and adore. They are at their best when in a relationship, but need to find a balance between their need for independence and their desire for cooperation.

Health *Helping yourself*

People born on this day are compassionate and selfless at heart and need to make sure that they don't neglect their own health for the sake of others. Prone to anxiety and insecurity, they would benefit greatly if family friends or members encouraged them to take a more proactive role in their health and well-being. This would include regular health check-ups, and due care and attention to healthy eating and a regular exercise program. Getting enough quality sleep is also important to them as they are prone to insomnia. Travel and variety when it comes to their holiday destinations are important as they will stop them getting stuck in a rut. Wearing, meditating on and surrounding themselves with the color red will encourage them to be more confrontational, and carrying a tiger's eye crystal will boost their self-confidence.

Career *Born VIPs*

These people are excellent team players and will thrive in any situation where group decisions or team work is required. Their natural business acumen may draw them to senior business positions and the world of commerce but their communication skills will also draw them to education, writing, music and law. Their love of detail will attract them to science, engineering, research or industry and their natural sympathy toward others can find an outlet in the healing or caring professions as well as in fundraising or charity work.

Destiny *To support, guide, inspire, and enlighten others*

The life path of people born on this day is to learn to balance their own needs with those of others. Once they have learned how to take the lead once in a while, their destiny is to support, guide, inspire, and enlighten others with their original thoughts.

479

Power Thought

"I give myself permission to take the lead "

Signs & symbols

Sun sign: Virgo

Ruling planet: Mercury, the communicator

Symbol: The Virgin

Birth date ruler: Saturn, the teacher

Tarot card: Strength (passion)

Favorable numbers: 7, 8

Lucky days: Wednesday and Saturday, especially when these days fall on 7 and 8 of the month

Lucky colors: Blue, hunter green, caramel

Birthstone: Sapphire

August 26

27 August

the birthday of the humanitarian spirit

Your greatest challenge is ...

to overcome negative thinking

The way forward is ...

to realize you cannot help the world by focusing on negative things. As you focus on the world's negative events you are only adding to them.

You're drawn to people born on ...

March 21 to April 19

You can teach each other much about balancing giving with receiving, and this can create a fulfilling union.

Luck maker

Tilt your thoughts toward optimism

Research shows that unlucky people tend to think negatively and lucky people tend to think more optimistically; so adopt an attitude of gratitude and positive expectancy, and you'll turn your luck around.

People born on August 27 have much to give the world and may often be found helping others or doing charity work. They have a huge humanitarian spirit and from an early age may have felt that they need to heal the world in some way. The key to their happiness will depend on whether or not they can allow the world to give back to them as well.

They are generous, special spirits and they are at their happiest and best when making others happy, or improving others' lives in some way by performing a valuable service. Self-sacrificing, they drive themselves incredibly hard and expect others to offer the same level of devotion and commitment to their ideals as they have. Their generous urge means that they are universally admired and respected, but their success can be limited by their tendency to be easily disillusioned, seeing the world as an unhappy, negative place. Developing optimism and positive thinking will help them balance giving and receiving, and turn their life from a struggle into an adventure.

Until the age of twenty-five there is an emphasis on being mentally focused and discriminating, and they can help themselves considerably during these years if they think and worry a little less about the common good and get involved more in making a difference. In fact, the positive energy that practical involvement gives them will help them find their way in life. After the age of twenty-five there is a turning point when there is an increased need for partnership or relationships with others, with the possibility of exploring literary, artistic or creative outlets in some form.

Whatever age they are, however, they are always likely to be universal in their approach to life and, if they are able to find an outlet for their humanitarianism and spirituality, they might not only find deeper fulfillment—they might also find that their generosity and kindness are repaid many times over.

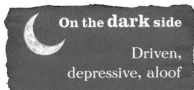

On the dark side

Driven, depressive, aloof

At your best

Generous, altruistic, hard working

Love *Generous and too giving*

People born on this day are loving, warm, generous, and giving, and unlikely to be without a partner for long. Sometimes they may feel deeply alone but this is only because they are not allowing themselves to open up to the love of others. Learning to receive as well as give in a relationship is vital for these passionate and altruistic people.

Health *Don't submerge your needs*

People born on this day need to beware that they don't submerge their physical and emotional health needs for another's, as this will not only make them less effective in their helping role, it will lead to their own unhappiness and frustration. Spending more quality time alone and pampering themselves with massages or other treats are highly recommended, as are cognitive behavior therapy and meditation if they are prone to negative thinking. As far as diet is concerned, they need to make sure they avoid alcohol, recreational drugs and other addictive substances when they feel low; comfort eating could also be a threat to their health and to their waistline. Regular exercise, preferably the kind they can perform alone, will boost their immune system, manage their weight and boost their self-esteem. Wearing the color red will help them avoid needy types who will drain their energy, and lavender essential oil as an air freshener will help lift their mood.

Career *Born charity workers*

People born on this day have the potential to excel in the fields of science, medicine, financial planning, accountancy, and investigative journalism. Although they are art lovers, they tend to be drawn to practical and intellectual pursuits that satisfy their realistic and straightforward natures, and may lean toward education, mathematics or architecture as well as humanitarian pursuits, social and charity work.

Destiny *To make the world a better place*

The life path of people born on this day is to find a balance between their own needs and those of others. Once they are able to cultivate an attitude of positive expectancy, their destiny is to set an inspiring example to others and, by so doing, make the world a better place.

Power Thought

❝I keep my thoughts positive. My future is glorious ❞

Signs & symbols

Sun sign: Virgo

Ruling planet: Mercury, the communicator

Symbol: The Virgin

Birth date ruler: Mars, the warrior

Tarot card: The Hermit (inner strength)

Favorable numbers: 8, 9

Lucky days: Wednesday and Tuesday, especially when these days fall on 8 and 9 of the month

Lucky colors: Blue, scarlet, orange

Birthstone: Sapphire

August 27

28 August

the birthday of the debater

Your greatest challenge is ...

becoming more flexible

The way forward is ...

to understand that those who are inflexible and stubborn don't tend to grow psychologically or progress as fast as those who understand the importance of compromise.

You're drawn to people born on ...

September 23 to October 22

You both have a strong intellect and a love of knowledge, and this can create a progressive and exciting relationship.

Luck maker

Consider other perspectives

Keep your mind open and listen to alternative points of view because an open mind is a prerequisite for attracting and keeping luck.

People born on August 28 are blessed with superb communication skills. They are extremely convincing speakers and know how to get others to listen to them and, even if they don't agree with them, to admire them. Although they are also skilled crafts workers with excellent organizational skills, one of their greatest strengths is their debating skill.

Their informed comments on a huge range of subjects are likely to have the backing and validation of detailed research or personal experience. This is why others don't just trust and rely upon their pronouncements, but also expect them to have a word or two to say about anything. They are highly principled, and the word dishonesty simply isn't in their impressive vocabulary. Although their knowledge is extensive and they can back it up with facts, they possess a tendency to become so convinced of the truth of their arguments that they start to believe that they alone have the answer. It is vital for their psychological growth that they don't abuse their superior intellect by shutting out alternative viewpoints or by manipulating others with the strength of their convictions.

When they reach the age of twenty-five they will enter a thirty-year period of increased emphasis on partnerships, both personally and professionally. This is the time when they may also develop a greater sense of esthetic beauty and may want to develop their latent creativity. It is important during these years for them to keep themselves motivated and their minds stimulated with constant challenges; settling into a mundane routine in which no questions are asked is damaging for them. After the age of fifty-five there is another turning point when they are likely to seek deeper meaning in their lives, becoming more reflective and thoughtful.

Whatever age they are, as soon as they can accept that there should always be more questions than answers, they have the potential not just to become convincing and influential debaters, but to be brilliant advisors with original, imaginative and innovative contributions to offer the world.

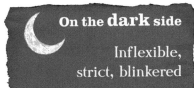

On the **dark** side
Inflexible, strict, blinkered

At your **best**
Articulate, respected, knowledgeable

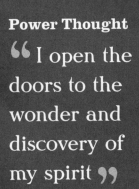

Love _Independent streak_

People born on August 28 tend to have an independent streak but their charisma tends to draw others to them. People love to hear them talk but they need to remember that a conversation is a two-way process. They are usually generous, with a charming personality that always has something interesting to say. A close relationship is extremely beneficial to them as it will help them express the side that loves all things sensuous and fun.

Health _Quality relationships_

People born on this day will often be well informed about health but they may need reminding that an often overlooked component of good health is the quality of relationships with friends and family. People who enjoy good, strong relationships are healthier because they feel less stress generally and tend to deal with stressful situations better; cherishing and strengthening their ties to others are as important to their health as good nutrition and exercise. A healthy, balanced diet is highly recommended, as is sitting down with friends and loved ones to a meal to discuss the day's events. Walking is an ideal form of exercise for them so they can enjoy the freedom it offers to think. Wearing, meditating on and surrounding themselves with the color orange encourage feelings of warmth, physical enjoyment and security.

Career _Born literary artists_

These people are well suited to careers in science or the literary arts where they can combine their creative and analytical skills, as well as using their impressive articulacy. Their gift for communication may also draw them to sales, education and editing, as well as show business or the music industry. Other careers that might suit include spokesperson, public relations, promotions, and interior design.

Destiny _To inform, benefit and inspire others with their articulacy_

The life path of people born on this day is to learn to listen more and speak a little less. Once they have learned to listen to other points of view, their destiny is to inform, benefit and inspire others with their articulacy.

Signs & symbols

Sun sign: Virgo

Ruling planet: Mercury, the communicator

Symbol: The Virgin

Birth date ruler: Sun, the individual

Tarot card: The Magician (will-power)

Favorable numbers: 1, 9

Lucky days: Wednesday and Sunday, especially when these days fall on 1 and 9 of the month

Lucky colors: Blue, yellow, amber

Birthstone: Sapphire

August 28

29 August

the birthday of the improviser

Your greatest challenge is ...

going with the flow

The way forward is ...

to understand that sometimes life can't be controlled; you simply have to relax and trust that something good will come to you.

You're drawn to people born on ...

June 21 to July 22

This is a classic case of opposites attract; you have so much to learn from and give each other.

Luck maker

Let the pieces come together

When things don't work out, relax and think of your life as a giant jigsaw. You may be desperate for luck, but nothing will make sense until all the pieces of your life come together.

People born on August 29 are blessed with an incredible imagination that can take them to the pinnacle of success in their personal and professional life. Reluctant to be confined by the limits of convention, they prefer to analyze all existing information, reappraise it and then present their findings in a new and original manner. As such, they are the great improvisers and re-interpreters of the year.

Although they are wonderfully creative and artistic in their approach, they also thrive on routine and structure. A recurring theme for them is their attempt to impose control or structure upon every situation. As such they are not just positive thinkers but also positive doers; once they have set down their ambitious goals, they move toward implementing them with a self-discipline and practicality that inspire amazement in their friends and colleagues alike. Paradoxically, the one area of their lives where they find it hard to improvise or impose structure is their emotional life. Frequently, they will subordinate their private to their professional life, preferring to devote their energies to an environment in which they don't feel so threatened. It would be beneficial for them, therefore, to reappraise their priorities.

From childhood they will probably have demonstrated their practical and analytical skills, impressing others with their ability to find their way around problems by thinking up new solutions. After the age of twenty-four there will be opportunities for them to focus on their relationships, and it is important for them to take advantage of these opportunities as their need for a fulfilling personal life is strong, however much they try to escape. There will also be an emphasis on creativity during these years.

Whatever age they are, if they can learn that sometimes the best solution to a problem is to stop trying so hard to solve or understand it and to simply trust, they will be able to present to others the fruits of their research in reinterpretations that are both innovative and inspiring.

On the dark side

Withdrawn, impatient, lonely

At your best

Innovative, structured, imaginative

Love *Excuses, excuses*

Partners often have a hard time competing with the professional priorities of people born on August 29 and may accuse them of using their work as an excuse to avoid intimacy. This is unfair as they are not afraid of intimacy, just unsure how to cope with it. If they can find a partner who can gently encourage them to open up without fear of rejection, they make charming, enthusiastic and communicative lovers.

Health *Make relationships a high priority*

People born on this day place a high priority on work as a source of satisfaction, but it would be better to emphasise their personal lives as close relationships offer them greater potential for happiness. They will also find that close relationships make them more productive at work because they give them a sense of perspective. Study after study has also shown the health-boosting effects of intimacy. As far as diet is concerned, they should not try to deal with stress by comfort eating or taking recreational drugs or other addictive substances. Regular exercise is highly recommended as it will give their day the structure they love, especially if their personal life is chaotic. Wearing, meditating on and surrounding themselves with the color orange will encourage them to be more spontaneous in their interactions, and burning lavender essential oil will help lift their mood during times of stress.

Career *Born designers*

These people may devote their energies to a variety of fields but they thrive in technology, computing or design, where they can operate unhindered and impose a sense of structure. Other careers that might appeal include management, self-employment, the caring professions, education, law, science, writing, politics, manufacturing, music and entertainment.

Destiny *To benefit others with their intellectual curiosity and sense of style*

The life path of people born on this day is to get time on their side by learning to let the pieces of their life come together. Once they are able to go with the flow, their destiny is to benefit others with their intellectual curiosity, wisdom, independence, and sense of style and structure.

Power Thought

❝ The more I trust and let go, the greater my possibilities ❞

Signs & symbols

Sun sign: Virgo

Ruling planet: Mercury, the communicator

Symbol: The Virgin

Birth date ruler: Moon, the intuitive

Tarot card: The High Priestess (intuition)

Favorable numbers: 1, 2

Lucky days: Wednesday and Monday, especially when these days fall on 1 and 2 of the month

Lucky colors: Pale blue, silver, white

Birthstone: Sapphire

August 29

30 August

the birthday of stability

People born on August 30 often play a leading and protective role in both their professional and personal lives. Friends, family and co-workers look to them for stability, guidance, support, and a sense of direction, and because they are often intelligent, capable and insightful individuals, they are well qualified to assume this responsibility.

Self-reliant and strongly focused on their goals, people born on this day seem destined for success and recognition in whatever field they choose to specialize. Their mercurial minds also bestow on them marked curiosity, as well as the desire to impose order and structure in both their professional and personal life. Because they often have such a responsible and self-possessed air about them, they run the risk of becoming a magnet for needy people. Although they relish guiding and protecting, it is important for them to understand the difference between those who genuinely need their help and those who are lazy and irresponsible. They must also ensure that their need to control others does not make others overly dependent on them.

From their childhood, they are likely to have been interested in studying situations and people in order to understand, improve and direct them. After the age of twenty-three and for the next thirty years, there is a turning point which places an increased emphasis on partnerships, both personally and professionally. This is also a time when they have an increased sense of beauty and harmony, and may want to develop their creativity. It is important during these years that they don't get obsessed with the material aspects of their lives by placing too much emphasis on money making, practical problem solving, directing, and organizing at the expense of their emotional and spiritual needs.

This is because, whatever age they are, the more they get in touch with their feelings and the feelings of others, and the more they can connect with and use the spiritual power or intuitive wisdom within them, the more power, happiness and fulfillment they will attract to themselves.

Power Thought

❝ Life shows me miracles every day ❞

Love *Find time for love*

If people born on August 30 find time in their busy schedules for love, they will find a source of great happiness. They need to make sure that they do not get involved with someone who is too dependent on them and that there is plenty of room in their relationship for freedom as well as intimacy. Although generous and giving, they can become cold or withdrawn, and should ensure that they don't get too controlling in a relationship.

Health *Avoid excesses of all kinds*

People born on this day are very sensual and must beware of excesses of all kinds when it comes to their health and well-being. Recreational drugs, alcohol and smoking should be avoided, as should overindulgence in rich or exotic food. They should make sure they eat plenty of fresh foods and as little processed and refined products as possible, because a diet rich in sugar and salt and low in nutrients could trigger digestive disorders and headaches. Moderate-intensity exercise should also be a high priority, as it will help keep their weight down and boost their immune system, and they would also benefit from mind–body therapies such as meditation or yoga. During times of stress the healing qualities of lavender essential oil can calm their nerves and boost their mood. Wearing, meditating on and surrounding themselves with the colors magenta or green will restore their energies and promote emotional healing.

Career *Born landscape gardeners*

The progressive inclinations of these people augur well in any career they choose, but they may find themselves drawn to medicine, sport, science, research, and education. Other careers might include the caring professions, writing, social reform, counseling, music, acting and, because they have a feel for nature, agriculture or landscape gardening.

Destiny *To support and inspire others*

The life path of people born on this day is to learn how to let go so others can learn independence. Once they have managed to downplay their controlling tendencies and cultivate their spirituality, their destiny is to support and inspire those with whom they live and work.

Signs & symbols

Sun sign: Virgo

Ruling planet: Mercury, the communicator

Symbol: The Virgin

Birth date ruler: Jupiter, the philosopher

Tarot card: The Empress (creativity)

Favorable numbers: 2, 3

Lucky days: Wednesday and Thursday, especially when these days fall on 2 and 3 of the month

Lucky colors: Blue, hunter green, caramel

Birthstone: Sapphire

August 30

31 August

the birthday of dynamic approval

Your greatest challenge is ...

to escape dependency on the approval of others

The way forward is ...

to understand that if you rely on the attention or approval of others for feelings of self-worth, you will not be in control of your life.

You're drawn to people born on ...

April 20 to May 20

You are both practical and energetic, and this can be a fulfilling and intense relationship.

Luck maker

Connect with your intuition

To get in touch with your luck-making potential you need quiet time. Turn off the TV or radio. Let the answering machine take messages. Make time to meditate, or simply have a cup of tea and think.

People born on August 31 are blessed with abundant energy and enthusiasm. There is often something attractive and fun about them that draws others to them effortlessly, and they typically climb the ladder of success to leadership positions with great ease.

They tend to make life appear very easy but there's a price to pay for their popularity and success. Although extremely astute when it comes to understanding what makes others tick—and therefore able to influence the thoughts and moods of others—when it comes to their personal development they may be completely in the dark. Unaware of what their real needs are, they may rely heavily on the attention or approval of others for feelings of self-worth. Ultimately this is a dangerous strategy as it puts control of their happiness in the hands of others. It is only when they are able to lessen their need for public attention that they will grow psychologically and, although they are dynamic with few problems either socially or professionally, their "success" in life may have an empty feel about it.

After the age of twenty-two there is an increased emphasis on social relationships for the next thirty years of their lives. It is important for them not to lose themselves in work or other people during this period. Their happiness and fulfillment depend on their ability to look within for guidance and approval; if they are unable to do this they may end up feeling stressed, confused and frustrated. Fortunately, there is also an emphasis during this time on developing their creativity, and they need to take advantage of the opportunities life presents them to think and act more independently.

After the age of fifty-two there is a powerful turning point that signifies a need for emotional change, making them more self-reliant and in control. Whatever age they are, the sooner they learn to depend less on the approval of others and more on their intuition, the greater their chances of finding true happiness and lasting fulfillment.

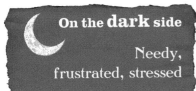

Love *Attention seekers*

People born on August 31 love to be the center of attention and if the attention fades away they can become cranky or caustic in a bid to win it back. Their partners adore their sense of humor and appetite for romance, and their ability to make their partners feel like the most important person in the world. Usually they marry for intellectual affinity and need a partner who can provide them with security, support and—of course—plenty of attention.

Health *Digestive health*

People born on this day may suffer from chronic digestive problems, headaches, and diet-related disorders such as diabetes or high blood pressure. It is important for them to limit their intake of salt, sugar, saturated fat, and processed and refined foods. The emphasis should always be on fresh and natural foods. They may seek out the advice of a variety of different experts, but they need to understand that the most treatment is not necessarily the best treatment. Exercise and walks on a daily basis are strongly advised. They would also benefit from mind–body therapies such as meditation or yoga to help them find that quiet space within. Wearing the color yellow will boost their confidence and self-esteem.

Career *Born multi-taskers*

These people are born multi-taskers and are well equipped to succeed in a variety of professions as long as they are allowed to advise, influence or take center stage. Their flair for people and natural understanding of current trends could make them excel in sales, media and business; their analytical mind may draw them toward science, research, editing, accountancy, property development, and engineering. Their latent creativity may express itself in writing, music and art, and their humanitarian spirit may draw them to charity work and the caring professions.

Destiny *To motivate others with their enthusiasm for life*

The life path of people born on this day is to seek internal rather than external guidance when finding their way in the world. Once they are able to stay in touch with their inner selves, their destiny is to inspire, motivate and energize others with their enthusiasm for life.

Power Thought

66 I trust and listen with love to my inner voice 99

Signs & symbols

Sun sign: Virgo

Ruling planet: Mercury, the communicator

Symbol: The Virgin

Birth date ruler: Uranus, the visionary

Tarot card: The Emperor (authority)

Favorable numbers: 3, 4

Lucky days: Wednesday and Sunday, especially when these days fall on 3 and 4 of the month

Lucky colors: Blue, hunter green, caramel

Birthstone: Sapphire

1 September

the birthday of the survivor

Your greatest challenge is ...

knowing when to stop

The way forward is ...

to understand the principle of less is more. Sometimes it is beneficial to hold back or quit while you are ahead.

You're drawn to people born on ...

April 20 to May 20

You are both practical and down to earth, and this can be a dynamic and creative relationship.

Luck maker

Cut your losses

Hanging on for too long in a situation that isn't working is bad for luck making. What mistakes have you made that can be remedied only by acknowledging that it is time to move on?

People born on September 1 are often obsessed with their work, but this does not mean they are boring and uninspiring. Quite the opposite; they simply find work demanding and fulfilling and will carry out their responsibilities with an infectious enthusiasm and excitement. They also like nothing more than to have their skills or abilities tested and challenged, and are very open to suggestions for improvement. In fact, they have the mental and physical toughness to survive even the most taxing of circumstances, standing their ground with pride in the face of adversity. This makes them the true survivors of the year.

With a tendency to take their work and themselves very seriously, they would benefit greatly from more fun and laughter in their lives, although their energy, enthusiasm, industriousness, and insatiable curiosity for everyone and everything more than compensate. Being so dedicated and full of enjoyment of their work, it's not surprising that many of them excel in their careers; but sometimes their love of challenge and refusal to give up can work against them. For example, they may find themselves putting up with things that they shouldn't be putting up with simply because they are unable to move on, find it hard to admit defeat or don't know when to cut their losses.

After the age of twenty-one, the following thirty years present opportunities for them to develop stronger relationships with those around them, strengthening their intuition; they should take advantage of these opportunities as these will help them improve their timing, so that they can enhance their chances of success by knowing when to hang on and when to quit. During these years they may swing between modesty and confidence, but when they are positive and enthusiastic about a project they have the ability to motivate and energize others.

Whatever age they are, however, their extraordinary mental and physical toughness and fixity of purpose in the pursuit of their goals endow them with the potential for extraordinary and inspiring accomplishments.

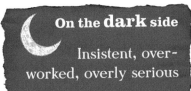

On the **dark** side

Insistent, over-worked, overly serious

At your **best**

Courageous, resilient, hard working

Love *New opportunities*

The love of discovering all they can about other people may earn people born on September 1 a reputation as a flirt, but once in a relationship to which they are committed they are straightforward and affectionate partners who demand nothing less than complete honesty from their partner. They are attracted to optimistic people who can inspire them with new ideas and new opportunities.

Health *Strong physical and mental needs*

People born on this day have strong physical and mental needs. It is important for their health and well-being that they keep themselves fit by exercising regularly, and that they keep their mind agile with regular challenges at work or by learning new skills in their spare time. They will probably be highly competitive as far as sporting activities are concerned, and may need to be reminded that a friendly game is just that: a friendly game. When it comes to diet, these people thrive on structure and regular mealtimes and snacks. It's also better for them not to have their main meal at night as this will interfere with the quality of their sleep. They should therefore breakfast like a king, lunch like a prince and eat their evening meal like a pauper. Carrying a quartz crystal around with them will improve their chances of attracting happiness, as will wearing the color orange.

Career *Born executives*

The highly developed capacity of these people to verbally influence others augurs well for success in advertising, marketing, and sales and retail careers, as well as writing, politics and performing. Other careers that might appeal include management, working for themselves, business, education, research, journalism, the military, and promotion.

Destiny *To be agents of advancement and assistance*

The life path of people born on this day is to learn when to push forward and when to take a step back. Once they have developed a better sense of timing, their destiny is to act as agents of advancement and assistance.

Signs & symbols

Sun sign: Virgo

Ruling planet: Mercury, the communicator

Symbol: The Virgin

Birth date ruler: Sun, the individual

Tarot card: The Magician (will-power)

Favorable numbers: 1, 10

Lucky days: Wednesday and Sunday, especially when these days fall on 1 and 10 of the month

Lucky colors: Blue, orange, yellow

Birthstone: Sapphire

2 September

the birthday of
the egalitarian

Your greatest challenge is ...

putting yourself first

The way forward is ...

to understand that, just like everyone else, you have a right to be noticed for your accomplishments.

You're drawn to people born on ...

June 21 to July 22

This is a complementary and passionate match as long as you respect each other's need for freedom of emotional expression.

Luck maker

Get carried away

If you want to attract luck you need to ignore any advice you may have been given about not going overboard and allow yourself to get carried away with passion and excitement for what you want because this is what encourages others to want to help you.

People born on September 2 are idealistic and lively individuals with an egalitarian view of the world. They are usually the first to defend the rights of everyone, and when presenting their opinions they make sure they are understood by everyone, no matter what their background or level of education.

They cannot tolerate pretension or unnecessary complications of any kind, placing a high value on simplicity of language, behavior and action. Other people always know where they stand with them and they also know that, whatever the circumstances or situation, they will be given a fair hearing and a fair chance to prove themselves. In fact, these people place such a high value on egalitarianism and fair play that when in direct competition with others they will quite happily take a step back and allow others to race ahead, even if they are well qualified for the job or due for advancement. It is important for them to understand that pushing ahead when their talents merit it does not mean they are becoming pretentious or ego-centered; it simply means that they are placing a value on themselves.

After the age of twenty they will have an increased need for partnership and relating to others for the next thirty years, and again it is important for them not to undervalue themselves and realize that equal relationships with others can be indispensable to achieving their high ideals of fairness, honesty, inclusion, and respect. There are also opportunities during this time for them to develop their creativity; they should take advantage of these to inject some inspiration into their working life. After the age of fifty-one there is a turning point when they are more likely to get in touch with their personal power.

Whatever age they are, the sooner they realize that they don't live to work but work to live, the more fulfilling their lives will be, and the greater their chances of discovering their outstanding potential for exerting a beneficial and inspirational influence on others.

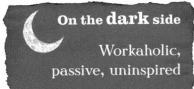

On the **dark** side

Workaholic,
passive, uninspired

At your **best**

Fair, direct,
vital

Love *Loyal and loving*

Whether they realize it or not, people born on September 2 can either sub-ordinate themselves completely to the needs of their partner or exercise a subtle control in their relationship. Both approaches are a direct contradiction to their egalitarian approach to life. At times hidden insecurities may indicate that instead of being their usual diplomatic self they can become argumentative and restless; but in general, when they learn to place a value on themselves they are loyal, loving and supportive partners.

Health *Weight training*

Although people born on this day are often bursting with vitality and energy, they need to make sure they don't push themselves too hard. They are particularly prone to stress-related digestive disorders, and a healthy, balanced diet along with stress-management techniques such as making sure they have plenty of time for rest and relaxation or simply laughing more often will help counteract these. They would benefit from learning the basics of good nutrition and cooking, not only because it will ensure they get all the nutrients they need, but also because it will also take their mind off work. Regular daily exercise that is moderate to vigorous is recommended, as are regular weight training or toning sessions. Wearing, meditating on and surrounding themselves with the color green will encourage them to find a better balance between their professional and emotional life.

Career *Born educators*

These people are great team players and enjoy work that has plenty of variety. They may be drawn to careers in the media, music, sport, social work, or public relations, or toward banking, the stock market and accountancy. Their analytical skills may suggest a career in education, writing or science, and their egalitarian spirit a career in health care.

Destiny *To exert a powerful and positive influence on others*

The life path of people born on this day is to learn to balance their own needs with those of others. Once they have understood that being fair does not have to mean being happy with second best, their destiny is to exert a powerful and positive influence on others.

Power Thought

❝I am not the person I was yesterday but a more enlightened being ❞

Signs & symbols

Sun sign: Virgo

Ruling planet: Mercury, the communicator

Symbol: The Virgin

Birth date ruler: Moon, the intuitive

Tarot card: The High Priestess (intuition)

Favorable numbers: 2, 9

Lucky days: Wednesday and Monday, especially when these days fall on 2 and 9 of the month

Lucky colors: Blue, silver, indigo

Birthstone: Sapphire

September 2

3 September

the birthday of the iron butterfly

Those born on September 3 are remarkably determined individuals, a quality that those who do not know them well may not appreciate until a situation arises to encourage them to be more confrontational. Generally, they prefer a gentler, conciliatory approach, believing that more can be achieved through communication than combat. This personal style can be highly effective but it can cause others to underestimate them or misjudge their iron will.

They are blessed with a sharp and independent mind, and a highly developed sense of justice and fair play, as well as great technical and organizational skills. Their desire for excellence will drive them to succeed personally and professionally and, although everything about them reflects this drive for perfection, their easy-going style and unassuming personality make it hard for others to resent them.

After the age of nineteen and for the next thirty years, they will become gradually more aware of the importance of relationships and partnerships. Their creative abilities will be enhanced too during this period, and some of these highly developed people may produce work that is way ahead of its time. Unfortunately, they are not always very good at demystifying their ideas and visions, sometimes taking it for granted that others are on the same wavelength when they clearly are not. Taking the time to simplify and explain their thoughts or methods to others will make all the difference. After the age of forty-nine there is a turning point which brings a strong emphasis on a deeper need for change, transformation and personal power.

Throughout their lives, however, if they can develop their self-confidence and overcome their fear of failure by understanding that no failure is a failure if you learn from it, they may just find that their novel ideas—combined with the iron will so artfully hidden behind their easy-going appeal—will not only help them outshine others, but make them influential agents of advancement and true progress.

Love *Deal with your self-doubts*

Just as people born on September 3 excel professionally, they also seek excellence in their personal life. This can make them set such high standards that it alienates them from others or makes them unwilling to compromise. Both approaches can give others the impression that affairs of the heart are not their first priority, which is just not the case. It is therefore important for them to be more open with others and to deal with their self-doubts.

Health *Too sedentary*

People born on this day like to lose themselves in work and if this work is sedentary or desk bound it can have a negative impact on their weight, mood and health in general. It is therefore important for them to make sure that they get plenty of fresh air and exercise every day, and to take regular breaks from work so that they return to it refreshed and energized. As far as diet is concerned, they should limit their intake of sugar, saturated fat and alcohol. Smoking will also have a damaging effect on them and interfere with their digestive health. Cultivating an interest or hobby outside work could be beneficial as it will help them put their own interests first; in fact, developing their self-esteem by learning to like themselves more will contribute much to their physical and emotional health. Wearing, meditating on and surrounding themselves with the color green will boost their self-confidence.

Career *Born judges*

These people are committed to finding practical or workable solutions that can benefit humanity, and may gravitate toward professions where they can make tangible progress such as sport, scientific research, engineering, or the arts. They also make great managers, organizers and executives, so careers in law, writing, education, or politics may appeal.

Destiny *To inspire others to make tangible progress*

The life path of people born on this day is to learn to take risks every now and again. Once they have the self-confidence to put themselves on the line and make their intentions clear, their destiny is to help and inspire others make tangible progress.

Signs & symbols

Sun sign: Virgo

Ruling planet: Mercury, the communicator

Symbol: The Virgin

Birth date ruler: Jupiter, the philosopher

Tarot card: The Empress (creativity)

Favorable number: 3

Lucky days: Wednesday and Thursday, especially when these days fall on 3 and 12 of the month

Lucky colors: Blue, jade green, silver

Birthstone: Sapphire

September 3

4 September

the birthday of
the master planner

Your greatest challenge is ...

valuing tradition

The way forward is ...

to understand that the past is not just something to be torn down; it is also there to be learned from and understood.

You're drawn to people born on ...

September 23 to October 22

You both have thoughtful and enquiring minds, and this can be an intense and rewarding union.

Luck maker

Count your blessings

What you pay attention to how much you have to be grateful for, the more good fortune you will attract. Gratitude will make you feel happier, and happy people are the luckiest people.

People born on September 4 are the master planners of the year. They bring process and precision to everything they do, and are forever planning, organizing, designing, and putting systems in place for a more productive future. Others will typically look to them not only for the last word on due process, but also for the first word on planning ahead.

With a natural understanding of how systems, procedures, buildings, establishments and just about everything else work, efficiency is very important to them and they are brilliant at finding short cuts or better ways of doing things. They can delight in exposing, criticizing or tearing down the Achilles' heel or fatal flaw in a project to make their point. Their knowledge is so great that they should ensure they put it to good use and do not divert their focus to unworthy causes. Unfortunately, the less highly developed and luckily very rare individuals born on this day can make formidable conmen or women.

After the age of eighteen there is an increased need for partnership and relating for these people; their sense of harmony and beauty is likely to be enhanced during this period. It is important during these years that their focus on planning for the future does not close their eyes to the possibility of happiness in the present. After the age of forty-nine there is a significant turning point which will highlight a growing emphasis on emotional and spiritual regeneration, as well as joint finances or corporate business activity.

Throughout their lives, the key to their success and happiness will not necessarily lie in material gain or career advancement, but in developing their spirituality, a goal that may confuse or frighten them. Once they understand, however, that spiritual growth—rather like material progress—is something that needs their concentration, dedication and passion, they will be able to realize their perceptive and inspirational hopes for the future in the most powerful way possible—in the present.

Love *Serious business*

People born on September 4 are often charming, with the ability to captivate others. They take their relationships seriously—a little too seriously at times—and are very committed. Their ideal partner will be someone intelligent and creative like themselves, who can help them loosen up and who is willing to appreciate, without taking for it granted, their willingness to commit.

Health *Fussy eaters*

There is a tendency for people born on this day to drive themselves into the ground with responsibilities and work. Unless they learn to take time out and pace themselves they could be heading for burnout. It is also important that they don't become so critical of what they see around them that they earn a reputation for grumpiness or cynicism. As far as diet is concerned, they may be extremely picky eaters with a small appetite, and they would benefit from experimenting more with their diet by eating more foods that are nutritious and wholesome such as fruits, vegetables, nuts, seeds, whole grains, and legumes, as well as oily fish to boost their brain function. Good quality sleep and plenty of mild to moderate exercise are also highly recommended to rejuvenate their bodies and minds. A warm bath with lavender essential oil is the ideal way for them to unwind, and wearing the color orange will induce feelings of warmth, security and enjoyment.

Career *Born property managers*

Being multi-talented, these people can achieve excellence in many careers but they are particularly well suited to the freedom offered by artistic and academic pursuits. Good at combining business with pleasure, they can be excellent diplomats but may also be drawn to careers such as teaching, counseling, sales, commerce, property management, manufacturing, engineering, and the medical profession.

Destiny *To realize their progressive and constructive aims*

The life path of people born on this day is to learn to value the past. Once they have found a way to balance work and relaxation, their destiny is to realize their constructive and progressive aims to benefit both themselves and others.

Power Thought

"I remind myself that there will never be another day like this one"

Signs & symbols

Sun sign: Virgo

Ruling planet: Mercury, the communicator

Symbol: The Virgin

Birth date ruler: Uranus, the visionary

Tarot card: The Emperor (authority)

Favorable number: 4

Lucky days: Wednesday and Sunday, especially when these days fall on 4 and 13 of the month

Lucky colors: Blue, white, green

Birthstone: Sapphire

5 September

the birthday of
the extraordinary mind

People born on September 5 are blessed with an extraordinary imagination, and the fantastic schemes and magical ideas they present to the world are always full of potential. Friends, family and co-workers are inspired by their innovative problem-solving skills, contagious wit, affectionate generosity, and infectious enthusiasm.

Magnetic, fast-moving and fast-thinking, these people are fueled by their desire to realize their own individual dreams, which are not just for their own benefit but for the benefit of humanity. However, despite their genuine desire to help others, their righteous energy may fail to realistically assess their chances of success and thereby unintentionally sabotage their best plans and efforts. It is important for them to learn how to improve their judgment so that they minimize the chances of failure, as well as actively taking steps to reduce the number of mistakes they make. One way they can do this is to learn to distinguish between what is realistically attainable and what is fantasy. If they stay with reality and strive to make things better, not perfect, they are likely to succeed in most of what they put their minds to.

From an early age they may have been rather reclusive and solitary figures, but around the age of seventeen, and for the next thirty years, there is a turning point when they grow more socially orientated with a strong need to be popular and appreciated. Professional and personal relationships will also start to play a more important part in their lives, and these are the years when their extraordinarily creative potential is likely to come to the fore. If they can learn to harness that creativity so that it is grounded in reality rather than in unattainable fantasy, their potential for success, fulfillment and recognition is outstanding. Whatever age they are, however, these people are blessed with positive, expansive energy and magical sparkle and—if a bit of good judgment is added to the mix—they are likely to get most, if not all, of what they most desire.

Power Thought

" I take full responsibility for my life "

Love *Party loving*

Because they have the ability to make friends effortlessly, people born on September 5 are often surrounded by admirers. It is important for them to employ discretion with this enviable capacity otherwise they could find themselves being too popular for their own good and unable to commit to anyone. It is important for them to slow down to ensure that they do not blindly speed past their ideal partner.

Health *Life in the fast lane*

Everything about people born on this day tends to be fast; they think fast, speak fast, move fast and live fast. Although this suits their personality it does not always suit their body, which occasionally needs a slower pace. They also need to make sure that they don't fall victim to self-destructive behavior. The loving support of a few close friends who can gently point out when they are heading off-track would be extremely helpful. As far as diet is concerned, they need to go easy on mood-boosting foods such as chocolate, cakes and sweets, as well as caffeine. Stocking their cupboards with healthy food will help them take control of their diet. Regular exercise is recommended, especially the kind they can perform alone such as walking or jogging; this will help them gather their thoughts and center themselves. Wearing, meditating on and surrounding themselves with the color blue will encourage them to feel calmer and more in control.

Career *Born fashion designers*

Their technical potential may draw these people to careers in science, engineering or computers, but their communication skills could help them in writing, promotion, sales, and law. They may also find success in gardening, property speculation and education. This birthday also indicates success for composers, songwriters, fashion designers, and performers.

Destiny *To formulate strategies for improvement*

The life path of people born on this day is to try to keep both their feet on the ground so their magical plans have a solid foundation. Once they have learned to improve their judgment, their destiny is to formulate innovative strategies for improvement.

Signs & symbols

Sun sign: Virgo

Ruling planet: Mercury, the communicator

Symbol: The Virgin

Birth date ruler: Mercury, the communicator

Tarot card: The Hierophant (guidance)

Favorable number: 5

Lucky days: Wednesday, especially when these days fall on 5 and 14 of the month

Lucky colors: Blue, chrome, pale green

Birthstone: Sapphire

499

6 September

the birthday of destiny

Despite their best efforts to plan and organize their lives, people born on September 6 seem destined to be confronted by the unexpected. Nothing ever seems to settle into a comfortable routine for them and, although they this can make them feel anxious and fill them with self-doubt, deep down they would have it no other way.

After the age of sixteen until the age of forty-six these people will feel a strong need for partnership; after the age of forty-seven there is a turning point when the evaluation of their own personal power comes to the fore, and these are the years when they are likely to feel less anxious and more confident. The older they get, the more they are likely to believe that destiny plays a hand in shaping their lives, the situations in which they find themselves and the people they meet.

The upside of their belief in destiny is that they soon develop the ability to focus their creativity and intensity on the details of the present moment, which is the recipe for a happy life. They can also be incredibly supportive and appreciative not just of the present moment but of all the people in their lives, making those around them feel good about themselves. The downside is that not enough thought or energy is put into planning or preparing for what might lie ahead; they can forget that their thoughts, actions and behavior today also create their future.

With their energy focused on the present moment and their belief that no person, word, action, or situation is trivial or unimportant, these people are both compassionate and fatalistic. As long as they make sure that their tendency to think negatively does not attract misfortune, that their belief in destiny does not make them over-cautious and that their giving nature does not prevent them taking from others as well, they have the potential to become highly developed, expressive, progressive, and truly inspirational souls.

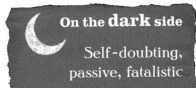
Power Thought
66 I always have a choice 99

Love *Assert your needs*

People born on September 6 are at their happiest and best when they are giving, but they also need to understand that a successful relationship is based on a balance between give and take. They have no problems falling in love, but accepting that someone else can fall in love with them as well may be more problematic. Their ideal partner is someone intelligent, entertaining and intuitive, just like themselves.

Health *Youthful energy*

People born on this day have a wonderful youthful quality, even in old age. However, their focus on present gratification, although endearing, may set them up for potential health problems. As far as diet and lifestyle are concerned, planning and delayed gratification are required. Good nutrition, regular exercise and plenty of quality sleep are the foundations of good health. They might have problems with their digestive system as well as catarrh and coughs; a multi-vitamin and mineral supplement might be a good insurance policy to boost their immune systems, and a glass of lemon juice with water first thing in the morning will boost their digestion. Vigorous exercise is recommended, preferably of the kind where they can record and monitor their progress, such as running, cycling and athletics. Wearing, meditating on and surrounding themselves with the color blue will help boost their self-confidence, encouraging them to enjoy today but also to plan for tomorrow.

Career *Born doctors*

These people may combine their talents to great effect as doctors, lawyers or social campaigners. Naturally analytical, they may also find fulfillment in science and psychology, as well as image making, advertising, the media, graphics, and photography. Careers involving sport, leisure, or the healing or caring professions may also appeal.

Destiny *To inspire others with their creativity and passion for life*

The life path of people born on this day is to conquer their self-doubt and occasional bouts of complacency, and take the initiative with their lives. Once they choose to be proactive their destiny is to inspire and invigorate others with their empathy, creativity and passion for life.

Power Thought
66 I always have a choice 99

Signs & symbols

Sun sign: Virgo

Ruling planet: Mercury, the communicator

Symbol: The Virgin

Birth date ruler: Venus, the lover

Tarot card: The Lovers (choices)

Favorable number: 6

Lucky days: Wednesday and Friday, especially when these days fall on 6 and 15 of the month

Lucky colors: Blue, pink, green

Birthstone: Sapphire

September 6

7 September

the birthday of tenacity

Your greatest challenge is …

showing yourself and others mercy

The way forward is …

to understand that until you can learn to ease up on yourself and others, your successes will feel hollow because you cannot fully enjoy them.

You're drawn to people born on …

October 23 to November 21

You both love knowledge and spontaneity, and this can be a passionate and intense union.

Luck maker

Don't make enemies

Lucky people try to avoid having enemies because they know that everyone in their lives could potentially be a source of good fortune for them.

People born on September 7 are blessed with remarkable tenacity. When they decide on a course of action, nothing can stand in their way. Their ambitious professional goals matter more than anything else; however many obstacles stand in their way they will not give up until they have achieved their objectives, even if this means making enemies along the way.

Although they can be ruthless in their determination to succeed they can also be fiercely loyal, protective and supportive to friends and family. Those close to them respect their determination to succeed, their passion for helping those less fortunate and their inner strength, but they may also be fearful of getting on the wrong side of them. Unfortunately, this means that friendships tend to linger at the first-base stage and they may find themselves with numerous acquaintances but few real friends.

Fortunately there are opportunities for them to rectify this situation, especially between the ages of fifteen and forty-five, when there is an emphasis on social life and relationships, both personal and professional, as well as a desire to develop their creative potential. They should take advantage of these opportunities by being a little more flexible in their relationships and approach to life, and by recognizing that professional success, however rewarding, will not give them the same fulfillment as positive relationships with others and themselves.

After the age of forty-six there is a turning point which encourages them to seek deeper meaning in their lives, placing the emphasis on personal transformation and finding inner harmony. If they can learn to work with this by looking within—rather than to work or other people—to find fulfillment, they will find the contentment for which they have always longed. They will also find that their tenacity, compassion for the underdog and courage in the face of adversity help them push the bounds of human knowledge and endeavor forward so that everyone, themselves included, can benefit.

At your **best**

Determined, courageous, ambitious

Love *Powerfully seductive*

Once people born on September 7 fall in love it is almost impossible for the object of their desire to resist, so powerful are their seductive powers. Once in a relationship, however, they can be prone to mood swings or to isolating themselves. It is important for their partner to give them plenty of freedom and, by the same token, for them to become more sensitive to their loved one's needs.

Health *The color purple*

Not surprisingly the health of people born on this day is often neglected in the pursuit of their professional goals. It is therefore crucial for them to understand that not only their performance but also their mood will improve dramatically if they take better care of themselves by eating a healthy, balanced diet and by exercising regularly. As far as diet is concerned, they should resist the temptation to buy pre-packaged meals because they are convenient and easy, and try to squeeze time into their busy lives for home-cooked meals. Regular exercise is a must because they are very physical people; if they don't get enough exercise they can become moody and cranky. Mind–body therapies such as yoga and meditation would be extremely beneficial as they would encourage them to look within. Wearing, meditating on and surrounding themselves with the color purple will encourage them to think of higher things.

Career *Born directors*

These people tend to be drawn to careers in which they can exert their progressive influence over others, such as business, management, teaching, writing, commerce, or industry, but since they identify so strongly with their work they may also be drawn to academic, artistic or musical careers where they can work unhindered.

Destiny *To exert a progressive influence over others*

The life path of people born on this day is to learn to look within for feelings of satisfaction. Once they have found a sense of balance between their personal and their professional goals, their destiny is to exert a progressive influence over others.

Power Thought

❝As I send out loving calmness, all those around me are inspired❞

Signs & symbols

Sun sign: Virgo

Ruling planet: Mercury, the communicator

Symbol: The Virgin

Birth date ruler: Neptune, the speculator

Tarot card: The Chariot (resilience)

Favorable number: 7

Lucky days: Wednesday and Monday, especially when these days fall on 7 and 16 of the month

Lucky colors: Sky blue, indigo, green

Birthstone: Sapphire

September 7

8 September

the birthday of complicated superiority

Most people born on September 8 have a very black-and-white view of the world. This makes it all the more surprising that, although others are quick to acknowledge their intellectual superiority, they often come across as complicated or enigmatic individuals. This is because instead of showing others their true selves, they will often take on the identity of the cause or group they're representing.

The fierce determination and conviction to set others on the right path, combined with their excellent communication skills, earns these people great respect from others, although this may not extend to affection. Problems—and occasionally bitter confrontation—can occur, however, when others do not agree with them. They are often so convinced of the superior merits of their position that they will often dismiss any conflicting viewpoint; this can not only gain them enemies but earn them a reputation for being narrow minded. It is crucial, therefore, for them to appreciate the negative effect their superior attitude can have on others, even those whose interests they are passionate about promoting.

Between the ages of fourteen and forty-five they will gradually become more aware of the importance of social relationships and their creative abilities will be enhanced. These years can be dynamic ones if they can learn to be a little less bossy and a little more sensitive toward others. After the age of forty-five there is a turning point when they are likely to become more self-aware; now the emphasis is on power, intensity and personal transformation. During these years, and indeed during any time in their lives, they are likely to have successfully assumed leadership positions or to have become an integral part of a leadership group.

Nothing is more important to their psychological growth during these years than their ability to show tolerance toward others, because although these advanced souls do often know what is best for others and for the world, other people and the world may not yet be ready to listen.

On the **dark** side
Difficult, unyielding, proud

At your **best**
Influential, progressive, committed

Power Thought

❝ One of the top priorities in my life is to be a source of love ❞

Love *Not black and white*

People born on September 8 may not always be easy to get close to and, because they don't tend to rely on the approval or opinions of other people, others may feel that they don't need anyone. This is of course untrue. People born on this day are at their happiest and best when in a loving and supportive relationship; they just need to relax a little and understand that when it comes to affairs of the heart, there are no rights or wrongs.

Health *Fixed ideas*

People born on this day can be very stubborn when it comes to their physical health and it is important that they don't neglect important advice from doctors and well-meaning advice from friends and loved ones. As far as diet is concerned, they need to steer clear of excess, especially when it comes to foods rich in sugar, salt, additives, preservatives, and added fat. The emphasis should always be on fresh and natural produce. Regular moderate exercise is also highly recommended as it will help them deal with stress, preventing the risk of cardiovascular disease or high blood pressure to which they are prone. They would also benefit from daily stretching exercises, such as those performed in yoga, as these would encourage them to be more flexible in both body and mind. Finally, wearing, meditating on, and surrounding themselves with the color yellow will encourage them to be more creative and optimistic.

Career *Born politicians*

These people tend to identify strongly with their careers and are well suited to careers in politics, the military, law, and education. Other careers that might appeal include commerce, research, science, writing, journalism, and the worlds of art or entertainment.

Destiny *To point others in the direction of progress*

The life path of people born on this day is to learn to let others make their own mistakes. Once they have found the courage to be themselves, their destiny is to point others in the direction of progress.

Signs & symbols

Sun sign: Virgo

Ruling planet: Mercury, the communicator

Symbol: The Virgin

Birth date ruler: Saturn, the teacher

Tarot card: Strength (passion)

Favorable number: 8

Lucky days: Wednesday and Saturday, especially when these days fall on 8 and 17 of the month

Lucky colors: Blue, brown, grey

Birthstone: Sapphire

9 September

the birthday of the missing link

Your greatest challenge is ...

to stop worrying

The way forward is ...

to understand that often your biggest worry is fear and the greatest antidote to fear is boldness. Whenever you act with boldness, you unlock your unused powers of creativity.

You're drawn to people born on ...

March 21 to April 19

A classic case of opposites attract; there is so much for you to learn from and love about each other.

Luck maker

Raise your vibrations

You can attract luck by using higher words and thoughts when you speak to yourself and others. So whenever you feel anxious or low, use positive, energetic words to raise your vibrations.

Although people born on September 9 have wonderfully inquisitive, original and sharp minds, they tend to come across as serious individuals with a strong sense of responsibility toward others. For reasons they themselves may not be able to understand, they often find themselves drawn to complicated and difficult situations. Part of the reason for this may be that they often feel as if something is missing from their lives, regardless of how successful, admired or settled they appear to be.

They may often have been searching for something to fulfill them—although they aren't sure exactly what—from an early age. As a result they are irresistibly drawn to people or situations that are challenging, complex or difficult. These people might not be the best for their personal development, and this incompatibility can cause them to become very anxious and insecure.

It is important for them to understand that the missing link they are seeking will never be found externally but by looking within and getting in touch with their spiritual needs. This may help them find a balance between their quest for excitement and the more meaningful aspects of life. Introspection may be a frightening prospect for them at first, and some may prefer to indulge in reckless or wild behavior rather than face it. But looking within is the only way for them to understand that the only person holding them back from their potential for success and fulfillment is themselves.

Between the ages of thirteen and forty-three there is an emphasis on socializing, partnership and relating to others, and these are the years when they are most likely to find themselves drawn toward complicated or destructive situations or relationships. After the age of forty-four there is a turning point that will highlight a growing emphasis on emotional and spiritual regeneration. This can spur them to new heights because, when driven by will, enthusiasm and self-belief, these people will not only find the missing link they have always been looking for, they will be able to achieve miracles.

At your **best**

Curious, responsible, committed

Love *Perceptive*

People born on September 9 have a highly developed sense of privacy but they are also extremely perceptive and receptive. They will often be surprised to find themselves in situations in which people reveal their innermost desires. Once in a secure relationship, however, they will slowly open up about themselves. They are drawn to complex, powerful individuals but need to make sure they keep their independence in a relationship.

Health *Sleep well*

People born on this day function best when they get plenty of good-quality sleep and they need to ensure that their bedroom is a comfortable and peaceful place where they can relax and unwind. Prone to worry and anxiety, they also need to make sure that they learn to recognize when worry is affecting their health and well-being. They should understand that worry achieves nothing and that the only way to change a situation is to take action. If no action can be taken, they should let go and move on. As far as diet is concerned, there could be anxiety-related problems causing digestion or food intolerances, so again it is important to recognize the warning signs. Stress-management techniques such as hypnotherapy, massage, meditation, and aromatherapy may all be beneficial, as would cognitive behavior therapy if negative thinking threatens to become overwhelming. Wearing, meditating on and surrounding themselves with the colors orange or yellow will encourage them to be more energetic and self-confident.

Career *Born writers*

These people are not just fascinated by other people; they often want to help or benefit them in some way, and so may be drawn to careers in education, social work, charity work, or politics. They may also be drawn toward public relations, negotiation, research, writing, art, drama, or music, as well as working for themselves.

Destiny *To inspire others with their compassion and originality*

The life path of people born on this day is to learn to believe in themselves. Once they have learned to send their inner critic on holiday, their destiny is to inspire others with their compassionate, tenacious and original approach.

Signs & symbols

Sun sign: Virgo

Ruling planet: Mercury, the communicator

Symbol: The Virgin

Birth date ruler: Mars, the warrior

Tarot card: The Hermit (inner strength)

Favorable number: 9

Lucky days: Wednesday and Tuesday, especially when these days fall on 9 and 18 of the month

Lucky colors: Blue, red, crimson

Birthstone: Sapphire

September 9

10 September

the birthday of inspired responsibility

Your greatest challenge is ...

following your heart

The way forward is ...

to understand that your needs and wants are just as important and as fascinating as those of others.

You're drawn to people born on ...

October 23 to November 22

You both have inquiring and thoughtful minds, and this can create a stimulating and loving relationship.

Luck maker

Use your imagination

Lucky people understand that imagination is the key that will unlock the door to their success. You can't accomplish anything without it first being pictured in your mind.

People born on September 10 tend to have strong wills and opinions. Focused, thoughtful and concerned about the welfare of others, their ability to categorize and notice every detail means that the aura surrounding them is one of concerned but resourceful responsibility.

Gifted with versatility and inner strength, they know how to survive and use their strengths to help others become more positive and independent. They take responsibility seriously but a part of them also longs to be free; the challenge they face throughout their lives is balancing these two drives. Between the ages of twelve and forty-two the emphasis tends to be on other people, particularly their strong need to be appreciated and relied upon. They are likely to learn early in life the importance of diplomacy and of accepting other people's weaknesses. As a result, other people tend to rely on them for a sense of stability but it is important that they don't allow others to take advantage of them while they wait patiently in the wings. Key to their psychological growth during this period will be their ability to develop their own creativity and individuality.

After the age of forty-two there is a turning point when their personal power is likely to become enhanced and there are opportunities for them to become more self-reliant. It is important that they take advantage of these opportunities, as they have a tendency to put the needs and talents of others before their own. They need to learn that their own needs and talents are just as valuable.

In fact, throughout their lives the sooner these multi-talented and innovative, occasionally revolutionary thinkers discover a sense of self-worth, the better. This is because when they start to listen to their hearts as well as their heads, an aura of glamour will be added to the aura of stability and responsibility they already exude. This will mean that when they walk into a room other people will look up, take notice and want to hear every inspired word they say.

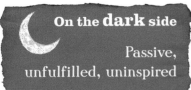
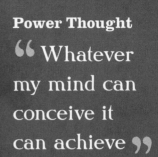

At your **best**

Capable, influential, responsible

Love *Let your hair down*

Romantic partners tend to rely on people born on September 10, and although they are more than happy to play the part of the sensible one they should also let their hair down from time to time and enjoy themselves. They are attracted to exciting and unusual partners but also need the freedom to be independent in their own right.

Health *All in the head?*

Many of the health complaints suffered by people born on this day are stress related. If things are going well for them, they tend to enjoy good health, but hidden anxieties emerge as soon as there are upsets, which can manifest in headaches, digestive troubles or fatigue. As far as diet is concerned, they should increase their intake of fiber, fresh fruits and vegetables. Snacking little and often rather than eating three big meals will also boost their mood and energy levels. Regular exercise, preferably outdoors, will be beneficial, as will getting to sleep before midnight. In fact, sports of all kinds will be an excellent outlet for their drive and enthusiasm. Wearing, meditating on and surrounding themselves with the color yellow will encourage them to feel more self-confident and creative.

Career *Born team captains*

These people are motivated by the urge to bring order and progress, making excellent managers, team captains, entrepreneurs, and leaders in whatever career they choose. They are also analytical, so may excel in research and technology as well as commerce and accountancy, but their communication skills and latent creativity may also lead them toward education, art, drama, and music.

Destiny *To benefit others*

The life path of people born on this day is to learn to balance responsibility to their own needs and to those of others. Once they are able to be both creative and compassionate, their destiny is to make changes or bring about direct progress that is of benefit to others.

Signs & symbols

Sun sign: Virgo

Ruling planet: Mercury, the communicator

Symbol: The Virgin

Birth date ruler: Sun, the individual

Tarot card: The Wheel of Fortune (change)

Favorable number: 1

Lucky days: Wednesday and Sunday, especially when these days fall on 1 and 10 of the month

Lucky colors: Indigo, yellow, orange

Birthstone: Sapphire

September 10

11 September

the birthday of the radical idealist

People born on September 11 think independently and clearly, and they will often shock or surprise others with their unconventional views. As well as being fiercely opinionated, they are also incredibly compassionate and their urge to help others may be so strong that it may take a radical form: either by passionately defending traditional views or by defiantly rebelling against them.

Whatever position they choose to defend, they will defend it passionately or take risks to prove their conviction. They can sometimes come across as extremely serious or critical, but behind this outward show of boldness and courage there is also a part of them that longs for stability or an authority figure to guide them. There may often be a silent battle or conflict going on within themselves that manifests itself in sudden mood swings of intense highs followed by intense lows.

Between the ages of eleven and forty-one there is an emphasis on relationships, and opportunities will be presented to explore their creativity. It is important that they take advantage of these because successful relationships will give them the sense of perspective they occasionally lack, and developing literary, artistic or creative interests will help them connect with their intuition, the key to their psychological growth. After the age of forty-two there is a turning point when they may undergo some kind of personal transformation, making them more self-reliant and in control.

If they can listen to their intuition rather than their conviction, become more tolerant and, most important of all, find a cause that is worthy of them, they will find that they no longer want to surprise or shock others with radical words and deeds. They want to realize their full potential and, by so doing, encourage others to do the same. In this way these determined and imaginative individuals will be making their own extraordinary mark on the world and fulfilling their destiny as the progressive revolutionaries or traditionalists of their age.

At your best

Idealistic, imaginative, passionate

Love *Intelligent and perceptive*

People born on September 11 have a tendency to live vicariously through their partners, but it is important for them to make sure that their own great deeds get the recognition they deserve. Intelligent and perceptive, they make loyal and passionate partners but can at times be inconsistent and careless when it comes to the feelings of others.

Health *Put good habits into place*

People born on this day need to make sure they understand the connection between healthy eating and exercise habits, and good health and feelings of well-being. This will help them pay more attention to their diet and lifestyle, which can get neglected for the demands of work or of others. They are particularly prone to food allergies and digestive upsets, and would benefit greatly by keeping a food diary to track down the culprits. Because their approach to life is often cerebral they can also become very sedentary and would benefit greatly from regular exercise, preferably in the fresh air so that they get all the mood-boosting benefits of fresh air and sunlight. It will be hard for them to stay on track with a healthy eating and exercise program, but they constantly need to remind themselves why it is important. They would also benefit from meditating and listening to their dreams, encouraging them to connect with their inner guidance or intuition. Wearing the color green stimulates feelings of balance and will help them inspire harmony in themselves and others.

Career *Born campaigners*

These people will often gravitate toward politics, social reform or law, but they may also choose to exert their influence through artistic means, as artists or writers. Other career choices that might appeal include administration, finance, statistics, economics, science, teaching, and therapy.

Destiny *To formulate practical strategies for improvement*

The life path of people born on this day is to learn to be more tolerant. Once they are able to take everything just a little less seriously, their destiny is to formulate clear-sighted and practical strategies for progressive change or improvement.

Signs & symbols

Sun sign: Virgo

Ruling planet: Mercury, the communicator

Symbol: The Virgin

Birth date ruler: Moon, the intuitive

Tarot card: Justice (discernment)

Favorable number: 2

Lucky days: Wednesday and Monday, especially when these days fall on 2 and 11 of the month

Lucky colors: Indigo, turquoise, sea green

Birthstone: Sapphire

12 September

the birthday of the motivator

People born on September 12 have bags of charisma, energy and strong ideals. They are also blessed with a strong desire to share their knowledge with the less fortunate and to encourage others to be the best that they can be. Excellent motivators, these are the people others tend to look up to and admire.

Driven by a desire to motivate, serve and educate others, they can fight hard and long for a cause they believe in. They rarely lack courage and are unfailingly responsive to the needs of friends, family and those less fortunate than themselves. Others tend to look to them for encouragement and support, and if their leadership skills are not advanced they will align themselves with someone powerful. At some point in their lives, however, they need to determine whether their desire to encourage and boost others is rooted in a deep-seated need to control rather than inspire. If it is the former, they run the risk of becoming a dictator or being ruled by one; but if it is the latter, their potential to positively shape the thoughts and behavior of others is extraordinary.

Until the age of forty they may find that their energies are directed toward chasing popularity; as a result they may overload themselves with work and commitments. During these years they will learn a lot about their motivations through close relationships with others. After the age of forty, however, there is a powerful turning point that will highlight the importance for them of evaluating what their unique contribution to the world will be. These are the years when they are likely to be more discerning.

Whatever age they are, however, they should realize that listening to their inner voice and picking and choosing to whom and what they want to devote their considerable talents and energies is the secret of their success. Time to reflect gives them the ability to make a real and positive difference, not just to the lives of others, but to the world around them.

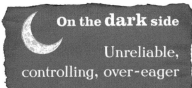

On the **dark** side
Unreliable, controlling, over-eager

At your **best**
Encouraging, optimistic, fearless

Love *Easily bored*

There is a tendency for people born on September 12 to be a little detached emotionally, but with the right partner they can learn to open up and share their private world. They are friendly and intelligent, and their witty personality ensures they are never short of admirers. They can, however, easily get bored if others don't offer them enough mental stimulation.

Health *Study*

People born on this day have a lively and sharp mind, and it is very important for their psychological well-being that they take courses of study where they can develop new skills or meet other people who are equally intelligent. As far as diet and lifestyle are concerned, they need to make sure they avoid or cut down on alcohol and smoking, as they may have an increased risk of heart disease. Digestive upsets are also an issue, so spicy, fatty and creamy foods should be treated with caution. Exercise is unlikely to be on the menu for them, so they need to make an extra special effort to incorporate at least 30 minutes of activity into their day. Gardening is a great form of exercise for them, as are walking, swimming and cycling. Lavender essential oil is an uplifting mood-boosting smell for them, and wearing the color yellow will help them feel more calm and in control during times of stress.

Career *Born trainers*

All careers involving education, teaching or training are well suited to these people, but they may also be drawn to careers in research, science and psychology. Their talent with words may lead them to the media and writing, as well as law and publishing. They also make excellent bankers and accountants, and their humanitarian side may draw them toward social work and politics. If they choose to develop their creativity, they may become designers, singers or musicians.

Destiny *To motivate and inspire others*

The life path of people born on this day is to learn to say "no" when they are feeling crowded or overloaded. Once they have learned to balance private time with responsibilities to others, their destiny is simple: to motivate and inspire others by their words or by their example.

Signs & symbols

Sun sign: Virgo

Ruling planet: Mercury, the communicator

Symbol: The Virgin

Birth date ruler: Jupiter, the speculator

Tarot card: The Hanged Man (reflection)

Favorable number: 3

Lucky days: Wednesday and Thursday, especially when these days fall on 3 and 12 of the month

Lucky colors: Blue, purple, violet

Birthstone: Sapphire

September 12

13 September

the birthday of ardent concentration

People born on September 13 tend to dedicate themselves passionately to their work or the task in hand. Their powers of concentration are unrivalled and their determination awesome. In fact, many born on this day have the ability to confront and rise successfully above any challenge that life throws at them.

One of the reasons they are such strong individuals is their powerful self-belief. They care greatly about being true to themselves regardless of what the current trends may be, and although their straightforward, uncomplicated but highly idiosyncratic approach can win them many admirers, it can also make them the butt of many jokes. This isn't likely to worry them, however, because they know that sooner or later others will see that their methods were right.

Although they are very advanced when it comes to will-power and concentration, in affairs of the heart they may not be able to demonstrate the same level of commitment or passion. It is important for them to make sure they don't suppress their emotions because it is only when they have learned to acknowledge, accept and manage their emotions that they will be able to grow psychologically. If they are unable to face their emotions, they run the risk of becoming uncompromising, controlling and ruthless. For those with such potential for creativity and sensitivity, this would be a tragedy.

Fortunately, until the age of thirty-nine there will be opportunities for them to develop and learn from close personal relationships. After the age of forty there is a turning point which puts the emphasis firmly on seeking a deeper meaning to their life and placing more emphasis on the power of personal transformation. Whatever age they are the sooner they learn to listen to their heart as passionately as they do to their heads, the sooner they will be able to devote their considerable talents to a cause that is worthy of them, lead by example and dedicate themselves to making the world a much better place.

At your **best**

Dedicated, intense, resilient

Love *More fun*

Although people born on this day can be sociable and charming, in personal relationships they can alternate between intense passion and intense detachment, even appearing secretive or aloof at times. It is important for them to inject more fun into their relationships, and to choose a partner who is as clever and hard working as they are.

Health *Face to face*

People born on this day often prefer to phone, text or email friends and colleagues rather than meet with them face to face, but they will find that weaning themselves off the mobile or computer will help their relationships blossom. They are also incredibly physical people and need to find an outlet for their energy. For them, team sports are ideal. Although these people are in general blessed with good health, they are at risk of stress-related illnesses and would benefit greatly from hobbies or outside interests that can take their mind off their worries. As far as diet is concerned, they need to make sure that they don't neglect the importance of good nutrition when their mind is focused on the task in hand. Wearing, meditating on and surrounding themselves with the color orange will help them get in touch with their own feelings and those of others.

Career *Born managers*

These people have fine problem-solving skills and may be drawn to scientific or business careers, although their original approach may also draw them to writing, art or research. They also make great team leaders and managers, particularly in sales, promotion, public relations, politics, accountancy, real estate, and the stock market. Their love of education may draw them toward teaching or law, and sport may be an excellent outlet for their energy.

Destiny *To achieve pioneering breakthroughs*

The life path of people born on this day is to get in touch with their feelings and those of others. Once their hearts are more open, their destiny is to fine-tune their skills and achieve pioneering breakthroughs.

Signs & symbols

Sun sign: Virgo

Ruling planet: Mercury, the communicator

Symbol: The Virgin

Birth date ruler: Uranus, the visionary

Tarot card: Death (change)

Favorable number: 4

Lucky days: Wednesday and Sunday, especially when these days fall on 4 and 13 of the month

Lucky colors: Blue, silver, turquoise

Birthstone: Sapphire

September 13

14 September

$$x / y + 2$$
$$(n \times 3.7777) - y$$
$$(xy - x + y + 9)$$
$$99.9 - y + z2$$
$$0.7 \times y \leq cc$$
$$+ 7. \quad 42x$$
$$=$$

the birthday of the problem solver

Your greatest challenge is …

to learn tact

The way forward is …

to put yourself in someone else's shoes and think how your opinions or behavior will impact them.

You're drawn to people born on …

August 23 to September 22

You have a lot in common, and as long as you don't chase unobtainable perfection this relationship has great potential.

Luck maker

Go with the flow

Lucky people understand that sometimes in life the best course of action is to go with the flow, let events unfold and trust that eventually the pieces of the puzzle will come together.

People born on September 14 are typically the first port of call when others want to find a solution or understand a situation better. Their critical abilities, creativity and problem-solving skills are exceptional and, because they are not afraid to rock the boat, uncover the underlying causes and tell it like it is, they have a reputation for being innovative and progressive thinkers.

Compromises or half-way solutions are not in their vocabulary and their goal is always to work for improvement. Although their ability to evaluate and suggest ways to improve can make them powerful agents of change and progress, it can also earn them a number of enemies because one skill they need to fine-tune is tact. They don't mean to offend other people; quite the opposite, as they often have the best interests of others at heart. It is just that they are so insightful, straightforward and direct that they don't understand that sometimes people aren't ready to hear the blunt, unadorned truth; they need it to be sugar coated or revealed subtly.

Until the age of thirty-eight there are numerous opportunities for them to become more diplomatic and tactful when relating to others, and to develop their creativity. They should take advantage of these opportunities because successful relationships with others and a flexible approach to situations and people will be the keys to their professional and personal success. After the age of thirty-nine there is a powerful turning point when they are likely to be more self-reliant. It is important at this stage that they understand the powerful influence their words and actions have on others. Listening to the silent voice of guidance in their head before they respond or react will help them interact productively and positively with others.

Whatever age they are, however, once these energetic and constructive individuals have found a cause that is worthy of them, they have the potential not just to turn things upside down but to make sure everyone—including themselves—flies high and lands the right side up.

On the **dark** side
Confrontational, tactless, controlling

At your **best**
Creative, influential, constructive

Love *Independent streak*

People born on September 14 are attracted to unusual people, like themselves, who are not afraid to challenge the status quo or stand up and be counted. With their charm and natural optimism they often attract people who believe in them, so it is important that they don't become too controlling in a relationship. They also have an independent streak and their relationship needs to allow them that freedom.

Health *A stress-free future*

People born on this day are generally careful about their health, paying attention to what they eat and how much they exercise. What they fail to understand, though, is the impact that stress can have on their health and well-being. Changing their attitude toward stress will change their life for the better and allow them to concentrate on their people skills and to develop their latent creativity. Plenty of good-quality sleep of around six to eight hours every night is highly recommended, as these people use up a lot of mental and physical energy in the day. Their need for life's sensual pleasures should also not be ignored, and being in a close, loving relationship will help them to thrive. Wearing, meditating on and surrounding themselves with the color indigo will encourage them to be calm and more sensitive to the effect they have on others.

Career *Born builders*

The scientific, legal and political professions are well suited to these people, but they may also be drawn to the building trade or planning. Other careers that might appeal include management, research, psychology, and education. Being multi-talented means that they need to feel genuinely enthusiastic about whatever career they choose, as they find it very hard to fake interest in something for which they don't have a passion.

Destiny *To make a substantial mark on the world*

The life path of people born on this day is to learn to be more sensitive to the needs or feelings of others. Once they have found a way of influencing others without giving offence, their destiny is to make a truly original and substantial mark on the world.

Power Thought
66 I look beyond the behavior of others to find the light within 99

Signs & symbols

Sun sign: Virgo

Ruling planet: Mercury, the communicator

Symbol: The Virgin

Birth date ruler: Mercury, the communicator

Tarot card: Temperance (moderation)

Favorable number: 5

Lucky days: Wednesday, especially when these days fall on 5 and 14 of the month

Lucky colors: Blue, navy, green

Birthstone: Sapphire

September 14

15 September

the birthday of the specialist

Your greatest challenge is ...

to transcend materialism

The way forward is ...

to understand that money is not necessarily a guarantee of happiness or success. However much you possess, without a spiritual or loving center you will feel unsatisfied.

You're drawn to people born on ...

September 23 to October 22

You both have enquiring and agile minds, and this relationship therefore has great potential.

Luck maker

Be patiently optimistic

Lucky people understand that when you feel angry, impatient or desperate you can't create luck. It also helps to believe that if things aren't going well now, something better may lie ahead.

People born on September 15 put a lot of effort into succeeding. Whatever line of work they choose to devote their considerable energies to, the chances are they will specialize in it, and their ability to master their chosen skill sets them apart.

Other people tend to admire these people for their technical skills and for their depth of knowledge about their chosen field of interest. Such is their devotion to their work that they can appear solitary figures; even though friends may not be high on their list of priorities, loved ones and family certainly are. The potential for people born on this day to excel professionally is outstanding, but the key to their success will lie not in their determination or technical skills but in their ability to wait for the right opportunity to present itself. If they jump before they have fine-tuned their skills or achieved mastery, they may find that their ambition has robbed them of success; but if they bide their time, slowly building up their store of experience and knowledge, they will reach the heights for which they seem destined.

There is no denying that these people like money, and lots of it. They also tend to equate status with financial reward, which can be damaging to their creativity and their integrity, so it is important for them to resist the urge to compromise or take short cuts to the top. Until the age of thirty-seven there are opportunities for them to develop the close personal relationships they need to give them a sense of perspective. After the age of thirty-eight there is a turning point which highlights a growing emphasis on emotional and spiritual regeneration, as well as joint finances or corporate business activity.

If they have learned by then to get a grip on their ambition and materialism, these are the years when they can really come into their own and step into the role for which they seem destined—that of the respected and, in some cases, world-renowned specialist.

518

Love *The things money can't buy*

Close relationships are important for people born on September 15 because without them they run the risk of losing themselves in their work. Potential partners will fall in love with their creative spirit but may find their inability to commit and absorption in work disappointing. Learning to value what money can't buy will help them succeed, not just in love but in life.

Health *Life is short*

People born on this day may suffer from symptoms of stress such as stiff shoulders, headaches, an inability to relax, and having difficulty making decisions. This is because their lifestyle is hectic and they are often able to buy what they want, whenever they want. They should schedule time for themselves when they are not working, traveling or shopping. They have a large appetite so they need to watch their weight, limiting their intake of rich, gourmet foods high in unhealthy fats and sugar, and increasing their intake of healthy whole grains, fruits, vegetables, nuts, seeds, oily fish, and legumes. Regular exercise would provide an outlet for their pent-up energy, and vigorous exercise such as jogging, hiking, dancing, and competitive sports is recommended. Wearing, meditating on and surrounding themselves with the color purple will encourage them to be less materialistic and think of higher things.

Career *Born researchers*

These people are both imaginative and organized, and this augurs well for success in a variety of professions from science to the arts. Careers they may be drawn to include medicine, education, the legal profession, and politics. Their latent creative and communication skills may also lead them to writing, business, architecture, design, psychology and finance, and their humanitarian spirit may inspire them to charity work.

Destiny *To increase awareness in their chosen field of knowledge*

The life path of people born on this day is to learn to balance their professional and their personal needs. Once they have got to grips with their materialism, their destiny is to increase awareness in their specialist field of knowledge.

Signs & symbols

Sun sign: Virgo

Ruling planet: Mercury, the communicator

Symbol: The Virgin

Birth date ruler: Venus, the lover

Tarot card: The Devil (instinct)

Favorable number: 6

Lucky days: Wednesday and Friday, especially when these days fall on 6 and 15 of the month

Lucky colors: Indigo, pink, green

Birthstone: Sapphire

September 15

16 September

the birthday of vitality

Your greatest challenge is ...

getting others on your side

The way forward is ...

to understand that the way to get others on your side is to emphasize what they can gain by offering their support.

You're drawn to people born on ...

February 19 to March 20

You are opposites and the outcome of this relationship is totally unpredictable, but that is the attraction for you both.

Luck maker

Know when to tone down

Lucky people understand that you can overdo enthusiasm. People are unlikely to want to help you or get involved if they feel backed into a corner.

People born on September 16 are passionate and enthusiastic individuals whose infectious joie de vivre enchants all those with whom they come into contact. Although they are lively and passionate, this does not mean they are also impulsive and impatient individuals; quite the opposite, they also have the discipline and patience to focus their outstanding energy on a particular skill or project.

These people are motivated by a desire to learn, master and then go beyond what has already been achieved. They are typically passionate about what they do and keen to recruit others to their cause. In addition, they can be courageous risk-takers not afraid to stand up for what they believe in or to fight their corner. Occasionally their passionate nature can lead to rebelliousness and they rarely respond well to any form of authority; a character trait which will have been noticed from childhood. Above all, though, they are bursting with vitality and energy, thriving on competition and challenge. Fiercely independent, they may find it hard to work with a group of people but in time they do learn the art of compromise and that giving their opinion gently yields far better results for them than their previous blunt, unsparing or attention-grabbing way.

Until the age of thirty-six they will find that relationships play an important part in their lives. They may also want to be popular and appreciated, but this may prove elusive until they learn to control their impulsive candor. From the age of thirty-seven there is an important turning point when their need for self-reliance is enhanced and the emphasis is on personal transformation.

It is extremely important for them to take advantage of any opportunities life offers them to become more in control of their energy, because once they learn to aim their passion in the right direction these big-hearted individuals will not only make a name for themselves, they will find true happiness by passing on their inspiration and happiness to others.

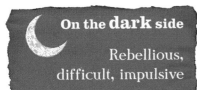

On the **dark** side
Rebellious, difficult, impulsive

At your **best**
Energetic, enthusiastic, warm hearted

Love *Passionate and generous*

People born on September 16 are not surprisingly passionate, generous and warm-hearted lovers, but they may become difficult or moody if their partner tries to restrict their freedom or change them in any way. Finding someone who is as intelligent as they are, and who can share a similar passion for life and love, is essential for them.

Health *Slow down*

People born on this day are so full of energy and excitement that the pace of their life often tends to be quite fast. This can lead to information overload and stress; learning to slow down every now again is therefore extremely important. It is also important for them to learn to eat more slowly, as fast eating and indigestion are associated with this birthday. Ridges on their fingers, a sore tongue and frequent stomach upsets could be signs of poor digestion. They need to take time over their meals, chew food slowly and not drink too much with their food, as this dilutes stomach acid and slows down digestion. They should also avoid drinking too much tea and coffee, and eating too much chocolate. A glass of lemon juice with water first thing in the morning may be beneficial. As far as exercise is concerned, they may be accident prone so should avoid extreme sports and concentrate on "safer," moderately intense activities like brisk walking and swimming. Mind–body therapies such as yoga and meditation will shift their focus to higher things, as will wearing the color purple.

Career *Born manufacturers*

These people love nothing better than to display the fruits of their labors and are well suited to careers in financial planning, science or the manufacturing trades. They may also be drawn toward business, mathematics, computers, education, law, medicine, education, acting, writing, or charity work.

Destiny *To make a positive contribution to humanity*

The life path of people born on this day is to learn to set clear goals and keep them in view. Once they have learned to work successfully with others to achieve a shared vision, their destiny is to inspire others with their infectious enthusiasm and, by so doing, make a positive contribution to humanity.

Power Thought

"Before I jump into my day, I will stop and connect with my spirit"

Signs & symbols

Sun sign: Virgo

Ruling planet: Mercury, the communicator

Symbol: The Virgin

Birth date ruler: Neptune, the speculator

Tarot card: The Tower (breakthrough)

Favorable number: 7

Lucky days: Wednesday and Monday, especially when these days fall on 7 and 16 of the month

Lucky colors: Indigo, blue, green

Birthstone: Sapphire

September 16

17 September

the birthday of honest determination

Your greatest challenge is …

being spontaneous

The way forward is …

to understand that sometimes thinking gets in the way of living.

You're drawn to people born on …

December 2 to January 19

You share a practical and realistic view of the world, and this can be a happy, stable relationship.

Luck maker

Show your eagerness

Lucky people understand that the more alive and energetic you are, the more people are likely to want to help you. Helping you makes them feel alive and energetic too.

People born on September 17 are strong, tough and determined individuals with a clear sense of right and wrong. They possess a heroic spirit, stamina, courage, and no fear of hard work. In fact they can easily take on tasks that make others cringe and perform them with little effort.

Control is important for people born on this day, and in anything they do their steady discipline and commitment to the smallest detail shine through. They can be imaginative but their preference is to organize their approach and their thinking logically; the facts, justice, fair play, tradition, and maintaining the status quo matter greatly to them. There is a fun side to them but it takes a lot to reveal it spontaneously; the downside of this is that they can come across as serious and heavy, but the upside is that when they do open up, others can be assured of their absolute sincerity.

Until the age of thirty-five there are opportunities for them to develop the more creative side of their personality, forging relationships with others both professionally and socially. They should take advantage of these opportunities to be less self-contained and more expressive, as they offer tremendous potential for happiness. After the age of thirty-six there is a turning point which stimulates them to seek a deeper meaning to their life and emphasizes the power of personal transformation.

Whatever age they are, they often do well financially in life, and enjoying a good standard of living is one of their first priorities. They will probably achieve their material goals, but to reach their full potential they should ensure they don't neglect their spiritual and emotional life; money alone will not completely satisfy them. Above all they are determined people, so when they do realize the true value of things money can't buy, their steady and resilient star won't just light their own path. It will inspire others to take a more disciplined, responsible, compassionate, and honest approach to work and to life.

On the **dark** side

Controlling, workaholic, heavy

At your **best**

Persistent, fair, resilient

Love *Passionate but reserved*

People born on September 17 are passionate but reserved individuals, and it will take a while for them to reveal their thoughts and feelings. They need a loving relationship built on trust and understanding before they feel they can open up. They can also be impatient and judgmental of others at times, and need to show themselves and others more patience and understanding.

Health *Sore eyes*

People born on this day can have workaholic tendencies and may be prone to stress, headaches, backache, and sore eyes, especially if they spend long hours at a desk or computer. They may also lead quite sedentary lives, making weight gain likely, so it is important for them not only to be more active but to make sure they cut down on the amount of saturated fat, sugary and salty food, animal products, and alcohol they eat and drink. If they suffer from concentration problems they would also benefit enormously from deep-breathing exercises as they tend to breathe quite shallowly, and this can deprive their brains of oxygen. Regular massage suits their sensual nature, and wearing, meditating on and surrounding themselves with the color purple will encourage them to focus on higher things.

Career *Born lawyers*

These people have a strong sense of fair play and are well suited to careers in law, accountancy and law enforcement. They can also excel in science, research, writing, economics, education, or in the news and media world. Computers and engineering may also appeal, as might the healing professions.

Destiny *To bring about concrete progress to inspire and benefit others*

The life path of people born on this day is to open up emotionally and spiritually. Once they are able to tap into their latent creativity, their destiny is to bring about concrete progress which inspires and benefits others.

Power Thought

"I am a being of color, light and creativity"

Signs & symbols

Sun sign: Virgo

Ruling planet: Mercury, the communicator

Symbol: The Virgin

Birth date ruler: Saturn, the teacher

Tarot card: The Star (hope)

Favorable number: 8

Lucky days: Wednesday and Saturday, especially when these days fall on 8 and 17 of the month

Lucky colors: Indigo, ocher, brown

Birthstone: Sapphire

18 September

the birthday of elusive devotion

There is something quite feline about people born on September 18; like a cat, they can be devoted and available one moment, independent and elusive the next. Although they can be sociable and are often extremely attractive individuals, few will get to know them very well; even getting to close to them is no guarantee that they will commit in any way.

So strong is their need for absolute freedom that these people will often change their minds or hearts at the last moment, leaving those around them feeling confused. Although this unpredictability adds to the attractive air of mystery they create around themselves, part of the reason they tend to vanish or isolate themselves from time to time is that they tend to have a low stress threshold, feeling that the best way for them to deal with conflict is to withdraw and reflect in private. Problems, however, arise when the need to withdraw and regroup becomes a need to hide or escape; they need to learn that conflict, although unpleasant, is essential for their psychological growth.

Until the age of thirty-four they will be presented with many opportunities to develop their friendly and sociable side, and they should take advantage of these, because left to their own devices they run the risk of being over-serious in their approach to life. After the age of thirty-five there is a turning point that brings an emphasis on their deep emotional need for change, intensity and personal power. During these years their powers of concentration are likely to be exceptional, and when they find a cause that is worthy of them their absolute devotion to it will attract incredible success and fulfillment their way.

Throughout their lives, however, as long as they make sure that they don't become so devoted or absorbed in their work or thoughts that they lose a sense of direction or their own identity, these highly advanced and unusual individuals will find their own unique way to contribute new knowledge and insight to the world.

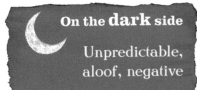

On the **dark** side

Unpredictable, aloof, negative

At your **best**

Disciplined, profound, devoted

Power Thought

66 Today I will face my fears, think and act boldly, and feel amazing 99

Signs & symbols

Sun sign: Virgo

Ruling planet: Mercury, the communicator

Symbol: The Virgin

Birth date ruler: Mars, the individual

Tarot card: Moon (intuition)

Favorable number: 9

Lucky days: Wednesday and Tuesday, especially when these days fall on 9 and 18 of the month

Lucky colors: Indigo, orange, crimson

Birthstone: Sapphire

Love *Your heart on the line*

People born on September 18 are highly sensitive and, when they are hurt, their natural reaction is to seek solace in books, ideas or their work. This stifles their emotional growth and they need to put their creative energy into reaching out and connecting with others instead. Sure, they may get hurt, but until they can take that risk and put their hearts on the line they will feel lonely and misunderstood.

Health *Perspective is everything*

People born on this day are prone to negativity and this can affect both their physical and emotional health. They may, for example, be prone to fatigue, headaches or sudden mood changes. They need to understand that although people and situations do not change, what can change is their outlook. Digestive disorders and minor ailments could also be a problem and, instead of soldiering on regardless, it is important for them to seek medical advice. As far as diet is concerned, they need to learn to recognize when they are hungry for food and when they are hungry for attention, affection or stimulation. Regular moderate to mild exercise such as brisk walking is recommended, as are relaxing therapies such as aromatherapy, yoga and acupuncture. Wearing the color yellow will encourage them to believe more in themselves, and wearing red will help them to feel more assertive.

Career *Born film-makers*

People born on this day have a natural affinity for writing, music and art, and they may be spectacular film-makers. They may also be attracted to scientific careers or to careers that benefit humanity as a whole. Other work choices may include research, statistics, accountancy, business, management, administration, law, law enforcement, psychology, publishing, and medicine.

Destiny *To contribute knowledge that benefits humanity*

The life path of people born on this day is to learn to deal with conflict in a positive way. Once they have learned to face rather than run away from challenges, their destiny is to contribute knowledge that benefits or inspires humanity.

19 September

the birthday of the immaculate presentation

People born on September 19 have their own unique style and a great awareness of the way they present themselves to the world. More often than not their appearance will be immaculate and elegant, but even if they appear casual or sloppy they will have spent time considering how their appearance will affect others. They believe that the world is a stage and that we are all players, but this doesn't make them cynical. Quite the opposite; they relish any opportunity to perform or play a role.

Spending an excessive amount of time worrying about their appearance, a running theme throughout their lives will be a wish to change something about their body or personal style. Other people may find this preoccupation with outward show frustrating and superficial, but many of these people do understand that inner beauty is just as important as outer beauty. They have the balanced perspective they need to attract success and find fulfillment. Unfortunately, there are a few people born on this day who run the risk of losing themselves in a world of superficiality.

Until the age of thirty-two there is an emphasis on relationships and socializing; during these years they need to make sure that they don't forget who and what really matters to them. After the age of thirty-three there is a significant turning point when issues concerning their sense of personal power become more prominent, and there may be an accent on transformation. During these years they will be presented with opportunities to give their lives more meaningful depth and, in addition to connecting with their intuition, the key to their psychological growth will be testing themselves out in a variety of different situations.

Overcoming personal and professional challenges will give them the confidence they need to step into the one role they have always been destined to play, but perhaps didn't realize it. This is the role of the profound, resilient and refined sage sought out by others for advice and inspiration.

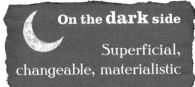
Love *Charming and friendly*

People born on September 19 know how to appear attractive to others and, because they are also charming and friendly, they are rarely short of admirers. There is a tendency for them to rush into relationships without thinking over compatibility issues, and even in a settled relationship they may be prone to bouts of restlessness and insecurity. They need a partner who will give them a sense of security, but also plenty of space to express themselves.

Health *Gardening*

People born on this day may find it hard to get going in the mornings as they enjoy staying up late into the night. If so, their health and concentration might benefit if they ensured that they were in bed by midnight. Exercising first thing in the morning instead of late at night is another good way of increasing their morning energy levels. As far as diet is concerned, making sure they eat most of their food before 7 p.m. will benefit their digestion, boosting their metabolism and energy levels during the day. As far as exercise is concerned, all forms are recommended including unlikely ones like gardening. In fact, gardening can be very therapeutic and comforting for people born on this day. Surrounding themselves with the scent of flowers or essential oils will lift their spirits, and wearing, meditating on and surrounding themselves with the color purple will encourage them to think of higher things.

Career *Born research writers*

These multi-talented people can thrive in any career that they choose, but they have the potential to make significant impact as scientists or artists. Other career choices that might interest them include those with plenty of variety, such as writing, law, teaching, and business. Their restless life could lead them to change professions many times, and this suits their inquisitive minds perfectly.

Destiny *To advise, help and inspire others*

The life path of people born on this day is to learn to look beyond the material to find something deeper and more meaningful. Once they are able to understand the importance of spiritual and emotional matters, their destiny is to draw on their rich experience of life to advise and help others.

Signs & symbols

Sun sign: Virgo

Ruling planet: Mercury, the communicator

Symbol: The Virgin

Birth date ruler: Sun, the individual

Tarot card: Sun (enthusiasm)

Favorable number: 1

Lucky days: Wednesday and Sunday, especially when these days fall on 1 and 19 of the month

Lucky colors: Indigo, orange, yellow

Birthstone: Sapphire

September 19

20 September

the birthday of the charming controller

Your greatest challenge is ...

learning to look before you leap

The way forward is ...

to understand that calculated, not impulsive, risk-taking is the key to success. You need to weigh up the pros and cons before you leap in.

You're drawn to people born on ...

June 21 to July 22

You are both passionate and intense individuals, and this can create an exciting and fulfilling union.

Luck maker

Find out what went wrong

Lucky people make mistakes just like everyone else, but the difference between them and other people is that they are able to learn from their mistakes so that they increase their chances of success next time.

People born on September 20 are often blessed with great charm, their outgoing personality tending to attract those in need of guidance. They are natural leaders and are at their happiest when guiding or controlling individuals or a group in a well-thought-out project.

The organizational skills of these people are often in great demand but because they can have problems saying "no" they may sometimes take on more than they can cope with. They are independent and resourceful, and like to pride themselves on being able to seek the best way to manage a situation. More often than not they are the most capable person on hand, but there will be times when even their best efforts don't succeed. How they cope with these setbacks or "failures" is the key to their psychological growth. If they can learn from their mistakes and move forward with increased awareness, their potential for success both personally and professionally is outstanding; but if they go on repeating the same mistakes or refuse to acknowledge where their words or actions may have been at fault, they will block their progress.

Until the age of thirty-one they will often feel a need to be popular and admired. They will stand a better chance of winning friends and allies if they don't overpower others with their opinions. After the age of thirty-two there is a turning point when their sense of personal power will increase and opportunities will be presented to them to become more self-reliant. During these years nothing will be more important for them than their ability to learn the art of caution and patience; this is because they have a tendency to leap before they look.

Although they should never lose their energetic and passionate spirit, their chances of happiness and fulfillment will increase once they have learned that the best way they can make their innovative and significant contribution to the world is to advise, organize and inspire not just others but themselves.

At your **best**
Organized, practical, intelligent

Love *Nurturing rather than controlling*

People born on September 20 need to make sure that they recognize when their affectionate and nurturing nature is starting to become too controlling or dictatorial. Friendly, sociable and always with something interesting to say, they rarely lack admirers but tend to be drawn to unconventional but intelligent individuals. Although passionate, they do not fall in love easily; if a relationship is going nowhere they will be quick to recognize it and leave.

Health *Keep your brain sharp*

People born on this day are often extremely intelligent and it is important for them to keep their brain active. If they don't they are likely to become despondent and forgetful. As well as mental activity, it is equally important for them to stay physically active as their love of delegation may mean that they spend a lot of time sitting rather than doing. Regular exercise is therefore essential; running, swimming and all kinds of aerobic activity are highly recommended. As far as diet is concerned, they need to avoid fad diets as they could be prone to weight problems, hormone imbalances and eating disorders which can all be triggered or made worse by erratic eating habits. Lavender essential oil will be an uplifting aroma for them when they are dealing with stress; wearing, meditating on and surrounding themselves with the color blue will encourage them to be more calm and logical in their response to situations and others.

Career *Born people planners*

These people have the potential to achieve success in a variety of careers but will often be drawn to the arts, music, writing, or the media. Other work choices that might appeal include people planning, sales, public relations, promotions, advertising, statistics, research, education, social reform, or psychology.

Destiny *To lead others to new and progressive areas of interest*

The life path of people born on this day is to learn to take a step back and weigh up the pros and cons before they make a decision. Once they have learned to take calculated risks, their destiny is to lead others to new situations and areas of interest.

Signs & symbols

Sun sign: Virgo

Ruling planet: Mercury, the communicator

Symbol: The Virgin

Birth date ruler: Moon, the intuitive

Tarot card: Judgment (responsibility)

Favorable number: 2

Lucky days: Wednesday and Monday, especially when these days fall on 2 and 20 of the month

Lucky colors: Blue, silver, white

Birthstone: Sapphire

21 September

the birthday of the sensation seeker

Your greatest challenge is ...

finding your own sense of direction

The way forward is ...

to understand that organizations or people can't give you a sense of purpose; the only way is to find out who you are.

You're drawn to people born on ...

November 22 to December 21

You both share a love of the unusual and this relationship has great creative potential.

Luck maker

Stop comparing yourself with others

Lucky people never compare themselves with other people because they know that jealousy blocks their luck. They also know that comparisons are futile because everyone is unique, with their own special gifts.

People born on September 21 are fascinated by all things unusual, unexpected, erratic, and, on occasion, dark. They have the wonderful ability to inject an air of mystery and suspense into even the most mundane of occasions.

Because they are hungry to learn or experience the unusual or complex, these people may be drawn to explore novel or bizarre subjects that those with less imagination would avoid. Highly sensual, they often feel compelled to seek out new sensations and to share their discoveries or viewpoints with others. Their messages are often profound but frequently misunderstood, and this can make them feel lonely and frustrated. Part of the reason others are sometimes unconvinced by their approach or theories is that they tend to lose themselves in their current obsession, leaving others with no sense of who they are and what they really believe in. It is therefore extremely important for them to try to stay true to their principles and keep a sense of personal identity.

Until the age of thirty-one they tend to gain much of their self-esteem and respect from their relationships with others, and they therefore need to learn to trust their own judgment. They also need to ensure that their sensation-seeking impulses do not lead them astray into a murky underworld of disreputable danger and strangeness. After the age of thirty-two there is an important turning point in their lives when there will be opportunities for them to feel more in control of their life. It is vital for their psychological growth that they take advantage of these opportunities to move from the passenger seat to the driving seat of their lives.

This is because once they are able to discover within themselves the mystery, wonder, sensation, and excitement that so enthralls them in the world around them, their attraction to the unconventional, new and different gives them the potential to become progressive and inspired instruments of human advancement.

Love *Erratic behavior*

People born on this day tend to be attracted to individuals who are difficult or different in some way. They are witty and fun to be around, and generally don't have problems making friends or attracting admirers. They can, however, suddenly run cold or become uncaring in relationships for no apparent reason. Only a partner as unpredictable as they are will be able to relate to and accept that.

Health *You can't do it alone*

Research has shown that the more people cut themselves off or alienate themselves from others, the unhappier they are likely to be. People born on this day therefore need to make sure that their love of the strange and unusual does not alienate friends and loved ones. If they find it hard to open up, they would also benefit enormously from therapy or counseling because getting in touch with their feelings, rather than trying to project their feelings onto others, is vital for their psychological growth. As far as diet is concerned, they need once more to steer clear of the bizarre and unusual as their health would benefit most from a diet that is simple, balanced and nutritious. Regular exercise, such as daily walking, is highly recommended for both physical and psychological reasons, as many people find walking conducive to constructive thinking. Wearing, meditating on and surrounding themselves with the color blue will give them the courage to express themselves freely and creatively.

Career *Born songwriters*

These people may be drawn to careers in music, art or the media, as well as more technical and administrative careers, such as computing, technology or accountancy. Other careers that might appeal include writing, sales, acting, politics, publishing, commerce, counseling, or teaching.

Destiny *To share and develop their original ideas with others*

The life path of people born on this day is to discover a sense of wonder and mystery from within, rather than seeking it outside themselves. Once they have a clearer sense of their identity, their destiny is to share and develop their original and progressive ideas with others.

Signs & symbols

Sun sign: Virgo

Ruling planet: Mercury, the communicator

Symbol: The Virgin

Birth date ruler: Jupiter, the philosopher

Tarot card: The World (fulfillment)

Favorable number: 3

Lucky days: Wednesday and Thursday, especially when these days fall on 3 or 12 of the month

Lucky colors: Blue, red, indigo

Birthstone: Sapphire

September 21

22 September

the birthday of the master builder

Your greatest challenge is ...

learning to relax

The way forward is ...

to understand that downtime is not time wasted but time gained because you give yourself an opportunity not just to rest but also to recharge.

You're drawn to people born on ...

August 23 to September 22

As long as you both learn to balance logic with intuition, this relationship has the potential to be intense and rewarding.

Luck maker

Don't have enemies

Lucky people try not to make enemies for one simple reason: enemies attract bad luck your way.

People born on September 22 tend to be multi-talented, hardworking and intelligent individuals with excellent communication skills and their own slightly eccentric but wonderfully endearing personal style. They are at their happiest and their best when they are creating or building, and such is their love of challenge that no sooner have they completed one project than they will jump to the next and then the next and so on, without a hint of a pause in between.

From an early age these people may have felt that they were here for a reason, and this explains their restless urge to constantly challenge themselves and make their mark on the world around them. Whatever it is that they feel called to do, they will follow their vision no matter how disruptive or difficult.

They may sometimes find that their ideals of fairness and equality and their superior intelligence clash with those in authority over them; this is potentially dangerous for them as enemies are not conducive to professional or personal success. Learning to compromise and play the game when necessary will be difficult for them but it will make their transition to success smoother.

Until they reach the age of thirty, relationships for these people are likely to be important, as will the need for harmonious surroundings in both private and professional spheres. Establishing a work–life balance so that they have enough time to spend on themselves and their friendships will be important during these years. After the age of thirty there is a turning point when they start to become more emotionally self-reliant and in control. If they can learn to be more flexible in their thinking, these are the years when they are likely to come into their own. This is because once they have learned to balance their restlessness with plenty of quality time out to recharge and connect with their intuition, amazing opportunities to build a career and a life of great and unique creativity will come their way.

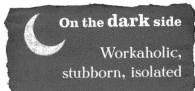

On the **dark** side

Workaholic, stubborn, isolated

At your **best**

Progressive, hard-working, individual

Love *Lasting unions*

People born on September 22 are outgoing and attractive, with plenty of acquaintances, but they can be slow to make close friends. Because they tend to avoid social situations, they may also find it hard to meet people they are attracted to outside of work. They believe in lasting unions and can be very affectionate and loyal in a relationship, but if they don't get the attention they feel they deserve, they can become insecure or anxious.

Health *Too busy*

Social isolation is the biggest health risk for people born on this day because it will make them prone to stress, anxiety and depression. Making an effort to stay in touch with friends is therefore recommended. It is important for them to make sure that they don't carry their work around with them at all times, having clear cut-off points when they leave work behind and get on with living. Drinking a cup of chamomile tea when they get home, chatting with friends, going to the movies, reading a book, relaxing in a aromatherapy bath are all great ways for them to switch off. As far as diet is concerned, they need to avoid food that is too spicy or rich as digestive problems may be an issue. A regular exercise program will encourage them to have a more balanced and focused approach to their lives. Carrying a citrine crystal around with them will help them deal with anger and stress, and wearing the color green will encourage them to find a balance between work, stress and play.

Career *Born architects*

These people are well suited to scientific, public service or humanitarian work, as well as the healing or caring professions, although they may also be drawn to writing or research. Other possible career choices include editing, teaching, sales, promotion, public relations, commerce, social reform, design, or architecture.

Destiny *To build progressive structures*

The life path of people born on this day is to find a balance between their need to push the boundaries and their need to be happy, fulfilled human beings. Once they have learned to be less self- or work-absorbed, their destiny is to build progressive structures from which others might learn.

Signs & symbols

Sun signs: Virgo/Libra

Ruling planets: Mercury, the communicator/Venus, the lover

Symbols: The Virgin/The Scales

Birth date ruler: Uranus, the visionary

Tarot card: The Fool (freedom)

Favorable number: 4

Lucky days: Wednesday and Sunday, especially when these days fall on 4 and 13 of the month

Lucky colors: Blue, pink, silver

Birthstone: Sapphire

September 22

23 September

the birthday of
the unassuming warrior

People born on September 23 tend to be charming but unassuming individuals with an appreciation of beauty, and a great deal of personal integrity and reliability. Behind all this, however, is a character of steely determination. They may appear gentle on the outside but from early in life they will have faced a series of challenges, setbacks and conflicts, most of which they have overcome and gained spiritual strength from.

Many of these people will be unaware of just how evolved, inspirational and creative they really are; as a result they may underplay their talents. For example, because they are often people of few words, others may step in to speak their part and take the credit; because they treat everyone with generosity and loyalty, they can become a target for those who are manipulative or simply lazy.

Most of the time, they approach daily life with pure, almost childlike pleasure, and if something or someone captivates their attention, their enthusiasm and zeal can become infectious. However, there will also be times when they don't feel that enthusiasm and run the risk of slipping into despondency or, in extreme cases, depression. This is because they are such honest people that they find it hard to pretend an interest. The key to their happiness, therefore, is to find a vocation, lifestyle or relationship that inspires and fulfills them.

Before the age of thirty they are likely to be concerned with relationship issues, but after the age of thirty there is a turning point that highlights a growing emphasis on deep emotional change. They may also be involved in joint finances or dealing with other people's money. After the age of sixty they may become more freedom loving and adventurous. Whatever age they are, however, once they figure out what works for them and what stops them moving forward, they have the inquisitive minds, the creativity and, above all, the fighting spirit to realize their cherished dreams and command not just the attention but the respect of all those with whom they come into contact.

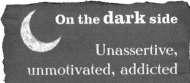
On the dark side

Unassertive, unmotivated, addicted

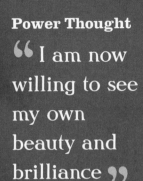
At your best

Charming, honest, passionate

Love *Indulgent mate*

People born on September 23 tend to be relaxed folk who are extremely loyal in a relationship, because the ideal of the perfect relationship appeals to them and they will work hard to resolve conflicts. Although they can be incredibly charming it is, not always easy to get close to them; many potential suitors will therefore have to settle with admiring them from a distance.

Health *Positive energy*

People born on this day tend to be athletic in build and will often excel in physical activities although their lack of competitive edge may prevent them from collecting all the trophies they deserve. As far as diet and lifestyle are concerned, they need to steer clear of excessive alcohol consumption, especially during times of low energy when they feel they need a boost. Other addictive substances such as nicotine, caffeine and—in particular—recreational drugs should also be limited or cut out altogether. They may have a sweet tooth and should steer clear of sugary foods low in nutrients and rich in additives and calories. They would benefit greatly from mind–body therapies such as meditation and yoga, and mind-control programs such as cognitive therapy or hypnotherapy which can help them reframe their perceptions about themselves in a more positive light. Wearing, meditating on and surrounding themselves with the color yellow will encourage them to be more expressive and assertive.

Career *Born musicians*

These people are often drawn to the arts and may share their talent with the world as an artist, musician, writer, or film-maker. Other career choices that might appeal include promotion, public relations, education, journalism, law, law enforcement, medicine, the healing professions, and charity work.

Destiny *To demonstrate their inspirational creative talents*

The life path of people born on this day is to stop underplaying their talents and stand up for what they believe in. Once they are able to find their voice, their destiny is to share with others their inspirational creative talent and empathy.

Signs & symbols

Sun signs: Libra/Virgo

Ruling planets: Venus, the lover/Mercury, the communicator

Symbols: The Scales/The Virgin

Birth date ruler: Mercury, the communicator

Tarot card: The Hierophant (guidance)

Favorable number: 5

Lucky days: Friday and Wednesday, especially when these days fall on 5 and 14 of the month

Lucky colors: Sky blue, lavender, orange

Birthstone: Opal

September 23

24 September

the birthday of
the restless humanitarian

Your greatest challenge is …

staying in one place for long enough

The way forward is …

to understand that however many times you move or change direction you take the same personality with you.

You're drawn to people born on …

September 23 to October 22

You are both charming and attractive, and this can be a passionate and intense relationship.

Luck maker

Stop trying and start doing

When you have chosen meaningful goals for yourself, go after them with all your heart. Lucky people don't just dream about their goals; they take active steps toward reaching them.

People born on September 24 tend to be hard to catch or pin down because they are nomads at heart. If their restlessness doesn't manifest externally in a love of travel or movement, they will be travelers in their minds, constantly reading, thinking and jumping to original conclusions.

Their desire to seek out the new will be a dominant theme in their lives, alongside their powerful desire to love and to be loved. Although they will naturally express themselves in different ways, they often tend to be orientated by an urge to discover and an urge to help others with their resourceful and creative efforts. Considerate and empathetic, they have the almost psychic ability to detect unhappiness in others, even if that unhappiness is unspoken, and this is followed up by a desire to relieve feelings of distress.

Despite their concern for the well-being of others, they also find it hard to commit to a settled existence. A part of them longs to feel secure but another part of them is always wondering whether the grass really is greener on the other side. As a result they vacillate a great deal. The key to their psychological growth will be when they are able not just to choose goals that inspire them, but to stick to them.

Before the age of twenty-eight they are likely to experiment in their social life, forming friendships and relationships with people from a wide variety of different backgrounds. There may also be numerous career changes or a spell of professional uncertainty. After the age of twenty-nine there is a turning point which highlights issues concerning emotional change, creating a desire to find deeper meaning to their lives. This is an extremely powerful and positive influence for them, because once they learn that discipline, perseverance and commitment can be liberating rather than restrictive, these versatile, progressive, humanitarian, and multi-talented people will discover within themselves the potential for tremendous power, which can both move and inspire others.

Love *Intimacy is a challenge*

Although people born on September 24 love to be admired, and their company is much sought after, few people get close enough to them to become really intimate. This is because they often have a fear of commitment and may find it hard to feel comfortable with intimacy. However, once they do find an intelligent partner who can teach them about intimacy, they blossom into passionate, supportive, generous, and loyal lovers.

Health *Comfort eating*

People born on this day need to be careful that their tendency to comfort eat when feeling low or bored does not lead to weight problems, especially as being overweight is linked to high blood pressure and other disorders. When they are feeling restless they need to find healthier ways to satisfy their "hunger," such as phoning a friend, writing in a journal, exercising, and so on. If emotional intimacy is a problem they may benefit from counseling or therapy to get to the root cause of their discomfort. If they are unable to open up they may be prone to stress, anxiety and depression, so taking this step could be very important. They also need to avoid any dependency on alcohol or recreational drugs, and should aim for a healthy, balanced diet with regular snacks and mealtimes, regular mild to moderate exercise, and plenty of quality sleep. Finding a creative outlet for their wonderful imagination, such as art, writing or design, will also be extremely therapeutic. Wearing, surrounding themselves with and meditating on the color gold will encourage them to commit to and persevere with their dreams.

Career *Born networkers*

These people will often be drawn to social, political or humanitarian causes but they may also excel in artistic endeavors. Career choices might include events organization, diplomacy, networking or fund raising, law, social reform, writing, drama, music, photography, or the arts.

Destiny *To take action to realize their progressive ideals*

The life path of people born on this day is to learn to focus their energies in one direction. Once they have learned to commit, their destiny is to realize their progressive ideals by means of direct action.

Signs & symbols

Sun signs: Libra/Virgo

Ruling planets: Venus, the lover/Mercury, the communicator

Symbols: The Scales/The Virgin

Birth date ruler: Venus, the lover

Tarot card: The Lovers (choices)

Favorable number: 6

Lucky days: Friday, especially when it falls on 6 and 15 of the month

Lucky colors: Pink, blue, lavender

Birthstone: Opal

September 24

25 September

the birthday of complexity

People born on September 25 are among the most complex individuals of the year. On the one hand they are extremely empathetic and can easily identify with others, but on the other they are fiercely independent and critical of what they see going on around them, being keen to set themselves apart from others.

One of the reasons they are often so complex is that they have a fairly black-and-white view of the world, but a part of them longs to live in a world of color. They tend to achieve great success in life, but more often than not this is because they work hard for it and they expect others to do the same. They can therefore become openly resentful of those who seem to attain success without putting in as much effort as they believe is necessary. It is important for them to learn to manage this tendency to criticize or judge because their words can wound others deeply.

Until the age of twenty-seven people born on this day are likely to be concerned with developing their social skills, creative talents and opportunities for material or financial success. After the age of twenty-eight there is a powerful turning point that emphasizes a growing need for personal transformation, change and power. After the age of fifty-eight there is another turning point, which indicates that they are likely to become more adventurous and freedom loving.

Whatever age they are, behind their soberness these people possess an amazing imagination, dynamic creativity and ability to shine or stand out in the crowd, because other people are always drawn toward complexity. The key to their psychological growth is to embrace and acknowledge their wonderful complexity. This is because when they learn to trust their intuition, think universally and acknowledge that life can never be explained in black and white, they have the potential to be not just the most complex but the most progressive, visionary and truly inspired individuals of the year.

At your **best**

Interesting, caring, progressive

Love *Power and determination*

People born on September 25 have a sharp tongue and, until they learn to be less judgmental and sarcastic, they will feel lonely and misunderstood. However, once they have learned to relax and be more forgiving, they can be a warm, loyal and loving partner. They are particularly drawn to people, like themselves, who project power and determination.

Health *Highly sensual*

People born on this day are often highly sensual and their appetite for physical pleasure is strong, sometimes so strong that it can cross over into addiction. However, getting them to exercise can be a tough assignment. A regular exercise program will not only help them lose weight, tone up and feel good, it can also help them manage their strong sexual energy positively. As far as diet is concerned, they need to make sure they avoid fad diets or any diet that excludes a certain food group, as balance is key. Alcohol should be avoided, as should foods high in saturated fat, sugar, salt, additives, and preservatives, and drinks high in caffeine that can lead to nutrient loss, and liver and kidney problems. Massage is definitely on the menu for people born on this day, especially those who regularly suffer from leg or back problems. Wearing, meditating on and surrounding themselves with the color green will encourage them to balance the conflicting aspects of their personality.

Career *Born journalists*

These people are not afraid to articulate the truth and can make excellent journalists and political and social campaigners, although they may also be drawn to the world of art or the media. Other career choices that might appeal include politics, advertising, publishing, museums, antiques, curating, the healing and caring professions, and lecturing in subjects such as literature, art, music, or theater.

Destiny *To become agents of progress*

The life path of people born on this day is to become more flexible in their thinking and their approach to life. When they can be as open and honest with themselves as they are with others, their destiny is to share their conclusions and by so doing become agents of progress.

Power Thought

" I improve the quality of my life and world with every positive word "

Signs & symbols

Sun sign: Libra

Ruling planet: Venus, the lover

Symbol: The Scales

Birth date ruler: Neptune, the speculator

Tarot card: The Chariot (resilience)

Favorable number: 7

Lucky days: Friday and Monday, especially when these days fall on 7 and 16 of the month

Lucky colors: Lavender, sea green, pink

Birthstone: Opal

September 25

26 September

the birthday of the perfection seeker

Your greatest challenge is …

coping when mistakes are made

The way forward is …

to understand that sometimes mistakes are important, even necessary, because they point you in a different, sometimes better direction.

You're drawn to people born on …

December 22 to January 19

If you can open up to each other emotionally, this can be an excellent and long-lasting partnership.

Luck maker

Relax your standards a little

Lucky people don't chase perfection because they know it is not human and is unattainable. Instead they work toward what they understand to be realistic and achievable.

Tenacity is the first name of people born on September 26 and discipline the second, but their last name is perfectionist. They demand nothing short of excellence from themselves and others, and simply cannot understand those with less drive.

The careers of these goal-orientated people are of supreme importance to them and, as a result, they often take on far too much. They possess, nevertheless, the ability to thrive under pressure and to inspire the admiration of others when they achieve what seemed to have been impossible. Not surprisingly, with such inspired ambition, determination, self-discipline, and focus, their career potential is of the highest order and more often than not they can and do rise to the very top. The downside is that their absorption in their work can become obsessive and compulsive; this is damaging to their psychological growth because it makes them ignore not only their own emotional needs, but those of their loved ones.

Before the age of twenty-six they are likely to be concerned with issues regarding money, but there will also be opportunities for them to develop strong relationships with others. They should take advantage of these opportunities because the support and company of others will help them keep a much-needed sense of perspective. After the age of twenty-seven the focus shifts to emotional change and intensity, and these are the years when they are most likely to become devoted or committed to their careers. During these years their potential for success is outstanding but for their psychological growth they need to make sure they take regular time out to ensure they nurture their relationships and find time for outside interests.

These people will always be driven, focused and occasionally bossy, but once they are able to moderate their obsession with work their tenacity and superior powers of concentration will yield results that can not only benefit others considerably but are also the subject of awed, if somewhat bemused, admiration.

Love *Struggle for power*

Although they are attractive and popular, people born on September 26 don't tend to fall in love easily, and anyone who tries to win them over quickly will be in for a struggle. This is because they like to be in charge of a situation. They need a partner who is as tough and uncompromising as they are, because the struggle for power that will result will keep them enthralled.

Health *Chill out more*

It's no surprise, given their perfectionist and workaholic tendencies, that people born on this day are prone to stress-related disorders such as aches and pains, headaches, fatigue, and anxiety. To counteract this they need to relax their expectations of perfection slightly and stop beating themselves up when they make mistakes. Taking time to relax a little more and ensuring that they have regular vacations are essential, as is spending time with loved ones and cultivating a hobby or interest outside work, however bizarre or unusual that interest might be. As far as diet is concerned, shopping for and cooking food from scratch will boost their nutrient intake, while chewing their food carefully before they swallow will boost their digestive health. Regular exercise is important, especially long walks in the fresh air where they can organize their thoughts and take their mind off work. Chamomile tea is extremely good for easing stress at the end of a busy day, as is relaxing in a rose oil aromatherapy bath. Wearing, meditating on and surrounding themselves with the color green will encourage them to relax.

Career *Born academics*

These people may be attracted to careers in science, research or academia, but the arts, in particular drama, literature, media, and music, may also appeal to their creativity. Other career options include sales, public relations, catering, education, and corporate business.

Destiny *To benefit others with the products of their efforts*

The life path of people born on this day is to learn that perfection is neither attainable nor desirable. Once they have learned to moderate their compulsion to work, their destiny is to benefit and inspire others with the products of their efforts.

Signs & symbols

Sun sign: Libra

Ruling planet: Venus, the lover

Symbol: The Scales

Birth date ruler: Saturn, the teacher

Tarot card: Strength (passion)

Favorable number: 8

Lucky days: Friday and Saturday, especially when these days fall on 8 and 17 of the month

Lucky colors: Lavender, burgundy, dark pink

Birthstone: Opal

September 26

27 September

the birthday of the paradox

Your greatest challenge is ...

being true to yourself

The way forward is ...

to understand that until you are true to who you are, life will forever feel confusing and overwhelming.

You're drawn to people born on ...

March 21 to April 19

You are very different characters but at the same time beautifully complementary.

Luck maker

Visualize what you desire

Visualize with positive expectation the way you want to be and your behavior will catch up with the mental image of yourself, attracting good luck in the process.

Although people born on September 27 often fail to recognize it, they have the ability to make a lasting and positive impression on all those they meet. This is because they are extremely versatile and sensitive to the feelings of others, and like nothing better than to bring harmony to any situation. Paradoxically, however, underneath their sociable and relatively normal persona they may often be riddled with doubts, insecurities, contradictions, and hidden fears. Learning to develop faith in their abilities, which are considerable, is crucial to their success and happiness in life.

These people are far deeper and complex than anyone, themselves included, realizes. This may be due to the fact that they set very high standards for themselves—failure simply isn't an option for them—but also because professional success tends to take priority in their lives over fulfillment. As a result they may find themselves mixing with groups of people or working in careers that are wholly unsuitable for them, although few would notice their discomfort. Until they get in touch with their feelings and find a path in life that is fulfilling, nagging feelings of depression and despondency will haunt them.

Before the age of twenty-six people born on this day are likely to be preoccupied with fine-tuning their people skills and carving themselves opportunities for career success. After the age of twenty-seven there is a shift in emphasis when issues concerning emotional change and transformation come to the fore; these are the years when they need to be alert to the way that their choice of career shapes their character.

As long as people born on this day believe that professional or material success is the only option, happiness and fulfillment will be elusive. However, once they understand that their hidden feelings and insecurities are not their enemies but their teachers trying to lead them to a fuller awareness of their potential, there is nothing these determined, driven, multi-talented, and vigorous individuals cannot achieve, if they set their inquisitive and highly creative minds to it.

On the **dark** side
Conflicted, insecure, frustrated

At your **best**
Charismatic, ambitious, successful

Love *Injection of self-confidence*

Although they are charismatic and attractive, when it comes to affairs of the heart people born on September 27 may lack confidence and self-belief. Until they gain self-confidence, their chances of success in relationships will be limited. They are attracted to powerful and determined individuals who know what they want and where they are going , and although they can learn much from them, they need to be careful not to become dependent.

Health *Pump iron*

It has been proved many times that exercise does not just boost immunity and manage weight, it also boosts confidence; more recent research has shown that lifting weights or muscle-toning exercises also has a positive effect on mood. Therefore, if they aren't already exercising their muscles, regular toning exercise or weight training—two or three sessions a week maximum—is highly recommended for people born on this day, as long as they don't take it to extremes. They also need to complement this toning work with plenty of aerobic exercise such as walking or running which can be performed every day. As far as their health goes, they need to take care of their liver, kidneys and reproductive organs, and a healthy, balanced diet rich in nutrients will help them do that. Learning the techniques taught by cognitive therapy and hypnotherapy will help them challenge negative thinking. Yellow is the color of optimism and self-confidence, and meditating on it will encourage them to have more faith in themselves.

Career *Born freelancers*

These people may be drawn toward politics or social and legal campaigning, or alternatively freelance artistic, technical or design projects. Other possible career choices include management, self-employment, entertainment, education, science, writing, music, and the caring professions.

Destiny *To point the way toward progress*

The life path of people born on this day is to learn to believe in themselves and their talents. Once they have accepted that to be human is to be complex, their destiny is to point the way toward progress through the most unlikely of approaches.

Signs & symbols

Sun sign: Libra

Ruling planet: Venus, the lover

Symbol: The Scales

Birth date ruler: Aries, the warrior

Tarot card: The Hermit (inner strength)

Favorable number: 9

Lucky days: Friday and Tuesday, especially when these days fall on 9 and 18 of the month

Lucky colors: Lavender, red, orange

Birthstone: Opal

September 27

28 September

the birthday of the seducer

Your greatest challenge is …

to tolerate boredom

The way forward is …

to understand that boredom is not necessarily something you should try to avoid; your need for constant stimulation may be holding back your personal development.

You're drawn to people born on …

July 23 to August 22

You are both charismatic and flirtatious and as long as you share the spotlight this can be a very passionate combination indeed.

Luck maker

Stop making excuses

Inaction and procrastination are the enemies of luck. Have you noticed how motivated people can become when told they may not have long to live? Start doing the things you have always wanted to, now.

Other people are often drawn to the magnetic and highly seductive people born on September 28. Whether they are attractive or not, they have the ability to wrap almost anyone they want around their little finger.

Many of them seek and find personal fulfillment through affairs of the heart, indulgence of the senses and the pursuit of beauty in all its forms. They are also highly imaginative and sensitive, with a strong desire to bring harmony and beauty to the world. However, they run the risk of believing that their ability to seduce others with their interesting and enlivening aura is enough to bring good fortune their way. They should understand that although charm will get them far, if they want to go all the way they need discipline, insight and hard work.

Until the age of twenty-four they are likely to be concerned with issues regarding relationships, but after the age of twenty-five there is an important turning point that emphasizes a need for emotional change, personal power and transformation in their lives. How they respond to the opportunities life presents them to back up their charm with substance will determine how successful they are personally and professionally. If they can move away from complacency, making practical decisions about how to realize their goals and backing these decisions up with hard work, they have the potential for success. If, however, the thrill of the chase becomes a dominant force, their potential creativity will be blocked by game playing, power struggles and procrastination.

These people will always have the ability to charm the birds off the trees but the key to their success and happiness, whatever age they are, will never be their seductive warmth but their will-power. This is because when they can take control of their passions and steer their energies in a clear direction, not only will they continue to seduce everyone who crosses their path, they will also be able to realize the ideals of beauty and harmony that are powerfully linked to their emotional fulfillment.

At your **best**

Charming, magnetic, exciting

Love *Master flirts*

People born on September 28 are masters at the art of flirtation and seduction and will often be surrounded by admirers. In a relationship they can also be masters of the art of manipulation, and are as capable of inflicting pain as they are of giving pleasure. Having said that, when they meet someone with whom they don't feel the need to play power games they can be loyal and dependable partners.

Health *Healthy libido*

People born on this day are often blessed with a sensual, passionate nature, but when life threatens to overwhelm them they may suffer from loss of libido. This can be extremely distressing for them but they should take it as a warning sign that something in their life isn't working. Talking to their doctor to rule out medical causes and possibly a therapist to highlight emotional burdens will all prove helpful, as will making sure they eat a healthy, balanced diet rich in libido-boosting fruits, vegetables, nuts, seeds, and oily fish. Regular mild to moderate exercise will also help balance their hormones and boost their libido. Looking good is important for people born on this day, and if they drink and smoke they need to question why they indulge in activities that will damage their looks as well as their health. Wearing, meditating on and surrounding themselves with cooling shades of blue will help them feel more in control of their emotions and their lives.

Career *Born opera singers*

These people generally flourish in careers in which they can indulge their passionate inclinations and inspire others at the same time, such as writing, art, acting, music, or even sport. Other work choices might include advertising, the media, publishing, the leisure and beauty industries, and public relations.

Destiny *To inspire others with their passionate inclinations*

The life path of people born on this day is to learn to manage their emotions instead of having their emotions control them. Once they are able to get into the driving seat of their lives, their destiny is to entertain and inspire others with their passionate and individualistic inclinations.

Power Thought

" I am powerful and inspired and enjoy getting my life in order "

Signs & symbols

Sun sign: Libra

Ruling planet: Venus, the lover

Symbol: The Scales

Birth date ruler: Sun, the individual

Tarot card: The Magician (will-power)

Favorable number: 1

Lucky days: Friday and Sunday, especially when these days fall on 1 and 10 of the month

Lucky colors: Pink, orange, yellow

Birthstone: Opal

September 28

29 September

the birthday of the maverick

Your greatest challenge is ...

coping with feeling like you don't fit in

The way forward is ...

to celebrate rather than feel ashamed of your uniqueness—going your own way is your destiny.

You're drawn to people born on ...

March 21 to April 19

You are both passionate and fiercely individualistic, and this can be a match made in heaven—or hell!

Luck maker

You're luckier than you think

If you start focusing more on the good than on the bad in your life, you will automatically feel happier. And whenever you feel happy, luck is never far behind.

People born on September 29 are mavericks at heart. At every possible opportunity they will question authority and convention, and if they find themselves disagreeing with rules and regulations they are not afraid to spark a rebellion.

Real livewires, life is never dull when these people are around. They are rebellious by nature, but this isn't because they lack discipline or self-control. Quite the opposite; they are capable individuals with the ability to startle others with their talents but, despite their intelligence and talents, they can also be rather unpredictable at times. They may, for example, suffer from bouts of low confidence because, however many followers they have, a part of them never really feels accepted. This sense of not belonging can make them swing between extroversion and introversion with confusing speed.

Until the age of twenty-three their emphasis will be on relationships, and during these years their incessant need to be on the cutting edge of things may earn them more enemies than friends. The friends they do have, however, will remain loyal for life. Their intense desire to be of service to others during these years, and indeed throughout their lives, may also make them subordinate their personal needs; but it is important for them to strike a more even balance between their different emotional drives because if they don't they may end up feeling unsatisfied, however great their success and popularity.

After the age of twenty-four there is a turning point which places the emphasis on emotional change. In the years that follow they will gradually begin to realize that, although they can compromise and work productively with others, they are not—and never will be—team players. The sooner they learn to listen to their intuition, go their own way and use their own methods, the sooner they will realize their outstanding potential for success and fulfillment. By the same token, others will celebrate rather than criticize the tenacity and originality of these inspirational leaders and talented organizers, together with the contributions they can make to society.

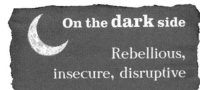
Love *Passionate and romantic*

The exciting and interesting people born on September 29 often attract many admirers, but their need to constantly challenge, question and shine can cause great tension in personal relationships. However, as they are also passionate and romantic, loving heartfelt gestures such as flowers, hearts and poems, partners tend to forgive them. Because their lives tend to be unpredictable, they thrive best with a partner who can offer them stability and security.

Health *Just say Om!*

People born on this day can be impulsive and prone to accidents and injuries, so it is important for them to exercise more caution when it comes to their physical well-being. As far as their emotional well-being is concerned, meditation or quiet time thinking will help them get in touch with their feelings and figure out where they want their life to be heading. Because they tend to be very opinionated, they may have certain theories about their diet and health which are worth getting checked out with a doctor to ensure that they are of maximum benefit to long-term health. Typically, people born on this day love exercise, especially running and swimming, and if they aren't already exercising regularly they are strongly advised to do so, as it will benefit them both physically and emotionally. Learning not to take things so personally will help them deal with rejection, and cultivating an attitude of positive expectancy will help them cope with bouts of negativity. Wearing, meditating on and surrounding themselves with the color purple will encourage them to celebrate their brilliant uniqueness.

Career *Born dramatists*

These people will be naturally attracted to all careers that are creative, dramatic or artistic, such as acting, writing, music, dance, and painting. Other choices include politics, social reform, the media, entertainment, business, self-employment, education, teaching, and lecturing.

Destiny *To inject excitement into the lives of others*

The life path of people born on this day is to learn not just to accept but to be proud of their uniqueness. Once they have gained self-confidence, their destiny is to inject a sense of excitement and possibility into the lives of others.

Power Thought

"I appreciate and place the highest value on all that I am "

Signs & symbols

Sun sign: Libra

Ruling planet: Venus, the lover

Symbol: The Scales

Birth date ruler: Moon, the intuitive

Tarot card: The High Priestess (intuition)

Favorable number: 2

Lucky days: Friday and Monday, especially when these days fall on 2 and 11 of the month

Lucky colors: Pink, silver, milky white

Birthstone: Opal

September 29

30 September

the birthday of revelation

Your greatest challenge is …

accepting that you might be wrong

The way forward is …

to understand that without an awareness of your own fallibility, you will never be able to uncover the truth in yourself or any situation.

You're drawn to people born on …

November 22 to December 21

You are both charming and insightful individuals, with enough differences and similarities to endlessly fascinate each other.

Luck maker

Believe the impossible

When you are able to open your mind to believe that what may appear impossible is really possible, you open the door to luck.

People born on September 30 tend to be focused and knowledgeable individuals with a strong desire to champion or reveal the truth. They have an uncanny ability for identifying intellectual or social rights and wrongs and suggesting progressive alternatives to bring about change or improvement.

These people are driven by the urge to expose injustice or unfairness in any form and, because they understand that revealing the truth as they see it can put them in the line of fire, they tend to create a tough and courageous exterior for themselves which inspires both respect and apprehension in those around them: respect, because others know that once these highly attractive and persuasive people are on the scene, they have the insight and star quality to attract support and success; apprehension, because their uncompromising sense of fairness and strong need to expose those who do not live up to their high moral standards can easily flip into judgmental or aggressive behavior. It is important, therefore, for them to understand that although pointing out the failings of those around them can clear the air, it can also have an uncomfortable effect on all concerned.

After the age of twenty-three there is a turning point that highlights issues of emotional intensity, change and transformation for these people; but whatever age they are, their challenge is not just to be more open and accepting in their beliefs, but to express as much interest in discovering the truth of their own lives as they do in uncovering the truth in others and in the world around them.

This is because once they are able to acknowledge their own vulnerabilities they can move beyond self-righteousness to greater tolerance of human weaknesses. When their tolerance is combined with their remarkable courage and impressive resourcefulness, not only can they ensure that justice is done and falsehood is exposed, they can also discover within themselves the ability to motivate and inspire others to work alongside them to create progressive and inspirational solutions for a fairer and better world.

At your **best**

Knowledgeable, fair, influential

Love *Fairness and openness*

Friends and loved ones of people born on September 30 will often find their words and actions put under the spotlight. Although September 30 people have the ability to make others laugh at their weaknesses, they need to be careful that they don't become overly critical. They demand absolute fairness and openness from their partners, and need to make sure they offer their partners the same in return.

Health *Love of food and drink*

People born on this day will often have excelled or been heavily involved in sporting activity when they were young; but once they leave school or college, there is a tendency for them to ease up on physical activity. Their love of food and drink may lead to a sedentary lifestyle and weight gain, especially around the middle. It is extremely important therefore for them to increase their activity levels and eat plenty of fresh, nutritious food to boost their metabolism. Fortunately, physical appearance matters greatly for them and the mirror is usually the only incentive they need to take control of their diet and exercise routine. Rose or jasmine are excellent essential oils for them if they feel lethargic and need a boost; wearing, meditating on and surrounding themselves with the color orange will encourage them to be more open, warm and accepting in their relationships with others.

Career *Born judges*

These people are clearly suited to careers in law, law enforcement, politics, social campaigning, and medicine, but they may also have a natural affinity for the arts and seek to help others by providing inspiration through writing, music, art, or song. Other careers that might appeal include publishing, journalism, education, and the catering industry.

Destiny *To be a dynamic force for progress, justice and reform*

The life path of people born on this day is to learn to be more tolerant of their own weaknesses and those of others. Once they understand that everyone has their own interpretation of the truth, their destiny is to be a dynamic force for progress, justice and reform.

Signs & symbols

Sun sign: Libra

Ruling planet: Venus, the lover

Symbol: The Scales

Birth date ruler: Jupiter, the speculator

Tarot card: The Empress (creativity)

Favorable number: 3

Lucky days: Friday and Thursday, especially when these days fall on 3 and 12 of the month

Lucky colors: Royal blue, purple, pink

Birthstone: Opal

September 30

1 October

the birthday of unusual capability

Although they are extraordinarily intelligent and capable individuals, people born on October 1 will often stand out in some way. Sometimes it will be the dignified way they carry themselves, or in their remarkable dedication and devotion to a cause they believe in, but whatever it is there is always something special and unique about them that makes others look or think twice.

On some occasions they can come across as stern, even proud, but to those who know them well they are incredibly warm and open-hearted. The cool front they present to the world is often a form of defense they have built up over the years as they learned how to overcome challenges and setbacks, but eventually their perseverance and dedication have earned them the just reward of rising to the top. Sadly, some of them may find that once they have reached the pinnacle of success they have aimed for all their lives, it isn't as rewarding as they hoped. The way for them to deal with this predicament is to worry less and live a little more; to feel truly successful and fulfilled they need to inject more laughter and fun into their lives.

Before the age of twenty-one they are likely to be concerned with developing their social and relationship skills, but after the age of twenty-two there is a turning point in which issues concerning personal power take center stage. It is absolutely crucial in the years that follow that they don't take themselves and their careers too seriously, and get a sense of perspective.

Above all, these people need to think big, aim high and set high standards for themselves. Their strength is the dedication they show to a purpose or goal, and as long as they don't isolate themselves from others with their perfectionist tendencies, they will not only be able to make a positive contribution to the world by transforming what is rough and ready into a smooth and progressive system, they will also discover within themselves an unusually large capacity for real happiness.

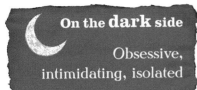
At your **best**

Dedicated, stylish, original

Love *Hidden passions*

People born on October 1 may take a while to open up to someone but when they do they can be incredibly loyal, supportive, patient, warm, and generous—and they expect the same in return. They may appear cool on the surface, but their partner will be delighted and surprised by their hidden sensuality and passion.

Health *Time out*

People born on this day are often extremely energetic and as a result they may take on too many responsibilities. Most of the time they are capable of multi-tasking and juggling home and work life, but sometimes they become stressed, anxious and fatigued. Regular vacations and downtime are therefore essential for their psychological and emotional health. As far as diet and exercise are concerned, they tend to have a sensible, balanced attitude but there will also be times when they overindulge. Alcohol could be their big weakness with potentially damaging impact on their liver and kidneys, as could recreational drugs, so they need to limit their exposure to both. Regular moderate to vigorous exercise is recommended to help boost their immune systems and channel pent-up anxiety and tension. Wearing, meditating on and surrounding themselves with the color orange will encourage them to be more spontaneous in their approach to life.

Career *Born supervisors*

These people have a strong affinity with the scientific and technical professions but they may also be drawn toward political and humanitarian pursuits or toward creative expression in art, music, drama, and dance. Other possible work choices include business, where they will excel in management or executive positions, or in law, financial advice, and education, where they may drift toward philosophy and psychology.

Destiny *To leave a lasting legacy behind*

The life path of people born on this day is to learn to balance their professional and personal life. Once they have understood the importance of nurturing themselves emotionally, their destiny is to effect social change, leaving a lasting legacy behind that will inspire and benefit their peers.

Signs & symbols

Sun sign: Libra

Ruling planet: Venus, the lover

Symbol: The Scales

Birth date ruler: Sun, the individual

Tarot card: The Magician (will-power)

Favorable numbers: 1, 2

Lucky days: Friday and Sunday, especially when these days fall on 1 and 2 of the month

Lucky colors: Purple, orange, yellow

Birthstone: Opal

October 1

2 October

the birthday of
the graceful conversationalist

In whatever situation they find themselves, the favored approach of people born on October 2 is a direct one. They like to talk, think and act quickly and decisively, and the graceful ease and certainty with which they go about their business endow them with tremendous potential.

These people will not hesitate to let others know exactly where they stand, but what impresses others most about them is that they are compelling conversationalists with considerable knowledge on a wide variety of subjects. It will not be unusual to find them deep in conversation with a sparkle in their eye because they love to stimulate their minds with intelligent talk. Although they enjoy talking, they also understand the importance of listening and are forever hungry for new information and ideas, eager to hear what others have to contribute. In fact, they tend to be more at home in the world of ideas and words than in the world of feelings and emotions.

Although the lively, inquisitive and candid approach of these people is refreshing and exciting for some people, for those more sensitive they can come across as unfeeling, ruthless and upsetting. It is therefore important for their psychological growth and their professional development that they learn to express their disagreement or disapproval in ways that are not overly negative or confrontational.

At the age of twenty they will reach a turning point that highlights a growing need for emotional change and personal transformation. In the years that follow they are likely to become more committed and decisive, and it is essential that they are more sensitive in their relationships with others and don't hide behind a mask of cynicism. This is because when they are able to lean toward the positive rather than the negative, and can encourage rather than discourage people with their intelligent insights, these charming conversationalists have the potential not just to entertain and enlighten, but to enlist and direct the support of others in the collective pursuit of their inspirational cause.

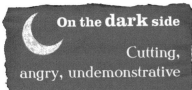
Love *Feelings run deep*

Even though they are gregarious and friendly enough to make friends and win admirers, it isn't always easy for people born on October 2 to open up to their partners about how they really feel. They need to feel secure in a relationship before they allow their true feelings to emerge; when this finally happens, their partner is very fortunate because he or she will have a generous, loving, loyal, and incredibly supportive lover.

Health *Mind and body, remember!*

People born on this day often have extremely active minds because they are constantly exercising it with study, reading, conversation, travel, and new experiences. When it comes to their bodies, however, they may not have such a proactive regime; it is important for them to make sure they incorporate activity into their daily lives. Because they are prone to sudden outbursts of anger they may be accident prone and, to avoid potential injury to themselves or others, stress- or anger-management therapies are recommended. As far as diet is concerned, because they tend to get absorbed in work they need to remind themselves to eat every few hours to keep their metabolism high. Wearing, meditating on and surrounding themselves with the color orange will encourage them to get in touch with their feelings, and the color blue will encourage them to be calmer and more in control when mood swings or sudden bursts of anger threaten to overwhelm them.

Career *Born mediators*

These people will often be drawn to careers in public relations or occupations dealing with the public in some way, such as the media, social work or negotiation. They may also excel as teachers, psychologists and counselors, or may choose to explore their creativity as artists or designers. Other possible career choices include sales, promotion, mediation, or arbitration.

Destiny *To express themselves and their beliefs honestly*

The life path of people born on this day is to learn to approach others with greater sensitivity. Once they have allowed others into their lives and their hearts, their destiny is, by example, to encourage others to express themselves and their beliefs honestly.

Power Thought

“ I listen with love to the messages my body and my heart send me ”

Signs & symbols

Sun sign: Libra

Ruling planet: Venus, the lover

Symbol: The Scales

Birth date ruler: Moon, the intuitive

Tarot card: The High Priestess (intuition)

Favorable numbers: 2, 3

Lucky days: Friday and Monday, especially when these days fall on 2 and 3 of the month

Lucky colors: Pink, white, silver

Birthstone: Opal

October 2

3 October

the birthday of the cutting edge

People born on October 3 love to be surrounded by all that is new and original. They are eager to explore the latest trends and technologies, and in some cases to set the trends as well. They are enthusiastic and up to date, so the place to find them is always right at the cutting edge.

These people hate to be out of fashion or not looking the part, and more often than not others will comment on how well presented they are. This doesn't mean, however, that they blindly follow the latest fashion or trend. Quite the opposite; they are highly original, hating to be categorized, and will usually add their own unique twist to new trends. There is a strong drive within them always to be one step ahead of everyone else, setting the pace so that others can follow. In fact, giving an example to others is what these gregarious people love to do more than anything else. They feel comfortable in the limelight and are good at playing their part to an adoring audience. Their greatest fear is to be ignored and, worse still, to be left out. Fortunately, with their talent and charisma this rarely occurs.

Although they can be the life and soul of their set, there is a part of these people that longs to hide or is reluctant to reveal their true feelings. It is important for them to listen carefully to what their feelings are telling them, because they have a tendency toward superficiality, and superficiality is no recipe for lasting happiness. After the age of twenty there will be opportunities for them to find deeper meaning to their lives and it is important for them to seize these opportunities.

This is because once they realize that the latest is not necessarily the best, and that their emotional development matters far more than being seen, their energy, dedication, style, and originality will take them to the only cutting edge that really matters—and the only place where true happiness and success can be found—that of personal fulfillment.

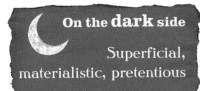
Love *Sense of adventure*

People born on October 3 are drawn to people with an adventurous streak and an inquisitive mind just like themselves; but they also want someone with whom they can build a secure and welcoming home. They can be extremely loving and giving as well as charming, and need to make sure they make strong rather than superficial connections with other people.

Health *Party animal*

People born on this day are always in demand and they may find themselves going from party to party or organizing social event after social event. Although this can be entertaining and rewarding, they need to focus more on quality rather than quantity when it comes to their social life. If they don't they will end up feeling exhausted and, ironically, lonely; it is impossible to connect properly with people on such a treadmill of engagements. Alcohol, cigarettes and coffee may be a weakness for them, but because they are intelligent they are probably very aware of the health risks already and don't need reminding that giving up or cutting down is strongly advised. As far as diet is concerned, cooking for one or two rather than for large numbers of people will encourage them to nurture themselves more, and regular exercise will also give them much-needed time to reflect and gather their thoughts. Wearing, meditating on and surrounding themselves with the color purple will encourage them to think of higher things.

Career *Born pioneers*

These people have the potential to be remarkable scientists or engineers, groundbreaking artists, or pioneering figures in politics, social reform, or indeed any sphere lucky enough to be blessed with their talents. Other work choices may include commerce, advertising, sales, law, education, and catering, as well as the performing arts, theater, fashion, or the film and music industries.

Destiny *To be groundbreaking pioneers*

The life path of people born on this day is to understand that the greatest treasure in their life can only be found within. Once they are able to be more self-contained, their destiny is to be groundbreaking pioneers.

Signs & symbols

Sun sign: Libra

Ruling planet: Venus, the lover

Symbol: The Scales

Birth date ruler: Jupiter, the philosopher

Tarot card: The Empress (creativity)

Favorable numbers: 3, 4

Lucky days: Friday and Monday, especially when these days fall on 3 and 4 of the month

Lucky colors: Pink, white, silver

Birthstone: Opal

October 3

4 October

the birthday of edgy congeniality

The desire for a harmonious environment that drives people born on October 4 makes them among the most agreeable and popular people of the year. They have sensual, esthetic tastes and love to surround themselves with pleasant people and beautiful things.

In whatever situation they are in, these people tend to come across as relaxed and at ease with themselves; this is in part due to their love of the good things in life, their naturally non-confrontational personality and their gift for getting along with just about anybody. This doesn't mean they don't have strong opinions; if pressed they can certainly be passionate and forthright in their beliefs. It's just that they like to present their case in a way that is not offensive to others and in a manner that is laced with humor, humility and tact, believing that this approach is more likely to get people on their side. They also have an astute way of looking at the world and a strong sense of realism about what is achievable and what is not.

After the age of nineteen, and lasting for the following thirty years, there is an important turning point for people born on this day that highlights a growing need for personal change, intensity and transformation. During these years they will feel a strong need to create a life of pleasure and harmony; with their congenial personality this is often just what they manage to create for themselves and others. However, they will also find that time and again life throws obstacles, challenges and conflicts in their path. The way they respond to these challenges will to some extent determine their success or failure personally and professionally.

If they can discover within themselves a fighting spirit and a determination to do their things their way, these remarkably gregarious, sensual but always level-headed and peace-loving people will find not only that they are extremely popular with others, but that others look to them for advice, guidance and inspiration about how to make the world a more beautiful place.

Love *Stand up for yourself*

People born on October 4 are charming, fun loving, and never short of friends and admirers. They are extremely tactile and affectionate. Their pleasure-loving and non-confrontational nature can, however, sometimes mean that they don't have their say in a relationship. They should understand that conflict need not destroy a relationship; sometimes it can keep it alive.

Health *Don't skip breakfast*

People born on this day tend to be pleasure-seeking individuals but they should ensure that they do not take their love of food, drink, spending, and sex to excess. It is also important for them not to lose themselves in a world of indulgence and superficiality; if they do, they will be prone to stress and depression. As far as diet is concerned, they need to make sure that they don't skip breakfast because this can cause a big drop in their blood sugar levels, affecting their mood and judgment, and rendering them prone to sugar cravings, which will just make the situation worse. Regular exercise, preferably on a daily basis, is highly recommended. Walking will be particularly beneficial as it will give them some time alone to think and reflect on where their life is heading. Wearing, meditating on and surrounding themselves with the color red will encourage them to be more confrontational, while the color purple will help them think of higher things.

Career *Born counselors*

Once these people understand that importance of setting tangible goals for themselves they may be drawn to careers in which they can benefit others, such as social work, medicine, law, engineering, education, counseling, or science. With their love of variety they need to choose careers that involve plenty of change, and their well-developed visual sense may draw them toward image making, photography, media, graphics, and design.

Destiny *To make the world a more harmonious place*

The life path of people born on this day is to take calculated risks and stand up for themselves when the situation demands it. Once they are able to be more assertive and to set themselves goals, their destiny is to make the world a more harmonious place.

Signs & symbols

Sun sign: Libra

Ruling planet: Venus, the lover

Symbol: The Scales

Birth date ruler: Uranus, the visionary

Tarot card: The Emperor (authority)

Favorable numbers: 4, 5

Lucky days: Friday and Sunday, especially when these days fall on 4 and 5 of the month

Lucky colors: Lavender, silver, electric blue

Birthstone: Opal

October 4

5 October

the birthday of dignified altruism

Your greatest challenge is ...

keeping a sense of perspective

The way forward is ...

to understand that getting carried away in your devotion to a cause is counterproductive; losing your perspective means losing your ability to make an effective contribution.

You're drawn to people born on ...

May 21 to June 20

You both love your freedom yet have a need for security; this can create a passionate and fulfilling union.

Luck maker

Keep your cool

If you keep your cool when things aren't going well you allow others to see that you are at ease with yourself and your limitations. This inspires others to believe in you and offer you opportunities.

People born on October 5 tend to put others or the cause they are promoting first and themselves second. They can't do enough to help, and so powerful is their conviction that others often find themselves persuaded to do good deeds as well. In addition, they also have a highly developed sense of fair play and are passionate in the defense of the rights of all, especially those who are less fortunate. As a result they often come across as unusually dignified as well as altruistic individuals.

In every situation in which they find themselves these people bring their concern for others and their strong sense of ethical responsibility. Their willingness to not just talk but take action earns them the respect and loyalty of those around them. Occasionally, however, they can lose their sense of perspective and get so wrapped up in their righteous propensity that they can become impatient and aggressive, failing to consider the consequences of their methods or the alternative viewpoints of others.

After the age of nineteen there is a turning point for people born on this day which emphasizes a growing need for emotional change and regeneration. This influence will continue for the next thirty years and during this time there will be opportunities for them to express their social instincts and make their mark. But if they are serious about being effective instruments of progress it is vital for them to learn to keep their cool, pay attention to the details and not get carried away with their own power. After the age of forty-nine there is another turning point which puts the spotlight on expanding their mind through study and travel.

Whatever age they are, these people will always be shining examples to others of joyful dedication to the ideals of justice and generosity of spirit. And once they learn to constructively direct rather than give free rein to their passion for altruism, they have the potential to become leading figures in humanitarian, spiritual or social reform.

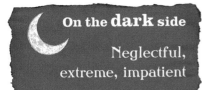
Love *Warm hearted*

People born on October 5 are warm-hearted, sensual and supportive partners, but their devotion to good deeds can make their partner feel neglected at times. They don't tend to have problems attracting friends and admirers. When they fall in love they fall in love deeply but may have to be careful of being involved in destructive power games.

Health *Emotional balance*

People born on this day have sharp minds and are capable and focused in their professional life. When it comes to matters concerning their own health and well-being, however, they can be surprisingly neglectful. They need to make sure that their emotional and physical health is not sacrificed for the sake of others because until they can look after themselves properly they will not be able to help others effectively. As far as diet is concerned, they need to make sure they eat regular meals and snacks to keep their energy levels consistent; increasing their intake of whole grains, fruits and vegetables will improve their digestive health. Hay fever or asthma could be a problem, especially during summer time, and they should avoid strenuous exercise during this season. Moderate to mild exercise is, however, highly recommended, particularly walking, swimming and cycling. Carrying a malachite crystal around with them will bring a sense of emotional calm and ease, and wearing the color green will encourage them to keep a sense of balance and perspective.

Career *Born humanitarians*

These people make successful social campaigners and charity workers and they may also excel in careers where they can give much of themselves to a vocation, such as acting, dance, art, music, or entertainment. They may also work for humanitarian causes or groups, or devote themselves to a career in politics or social reform.

Destiny *To devote themselves to a cause they believe in*

The life path of people born on this day is to learn to keep a sense of balance between their personal and their altruistic needs. Once they have set themselves clear boundaries and goals, their destiny is to redress perceived injustices and devote themselves to a cause they believe in.

Signs & symbols

Sun sign: Libra

Ruling planet: Venus, the lover

Symbol: The Scales

Birth date ruler: Mercury, the communicator

Tarot card: The Hierophant (guidance)

Favorable numbers: 5, 6

Lucky days: Friday and Wednesday, especially when these days fall on 5 and 6 of the month

Lucky colors: Lavender, green, cream

Birthstone: Opal

October 5

6 October

the birthday of
the romantic adventurer

Your greatest challenge is ...

being realistic

The way forward is ...

to understand that optimism can be as damaging as negativity, because there is good and bad in every situation and person.

You're drawn to people born on ...

March 21 to April 19

You both have in excess what the other lacks, and this can be a passionate and intense relationship.

Luck maker

Show others your fire

Don't be afraid to dig your heels in or fight for something if the situation demands it. Showing others that you are passionate about what you want can be a good-luck strategy.

People born on October 6 live each day as if it were the last. As a result they are one of the most alive and spontaneous individuals of the year. Every day for them is an adventure and an opportunity to fall in love with anyone or anything.

Romantic adventurers at heart, these people are driven by an irresistible urge to savor as many stimulations and sensations as life has to offer. They adore novelty and will waste no time in gathering as much information as possible before moving on to the next big adventure. Although their need to be stimulated is strong, they are not selfish people because their need to identify with and help others by means of their discoveries is equally strong.

After the age of seventeen they will reach a turning point in their lives, finding a growing need for emotional intensity, personal power and transformation. During this time there will be many opportunities for them to deepen their emotional commitment to others and they need to take advantage of these. This is because although they are often highly valued by their friends as a delight to have around, others may grow tired of their endless optimism and seeming inability to take into account the darker, more complex and deeper aspects of life. It is almost as if a part of them is like the romantic star of a story, with their character lacking depth and definition. However, once they start to understand that life cannot always be sunshine and roses and that suffering—however distressing—is essential to psychological growth, their life will become infinitely more exciting and rewarding.

After the age of forty-seven people born on this day are likely to become more freedom loving and willing to take risks emotionally and professionally; there may be opportunities for them to expand their minds and lives by traveling or studying. Whatever age they are, however, their versatile, energetic and inspirational contribution to the world draws luck and success to them, exerting a magnetic attraction on those around them.

On the **dark** side

Unreliable, superficial, sensationalist

At your **best**

Adventurous, energetic, spontaneous

Love *Unpredictable*

People born on October 6 can be wonderfully unpredictable when it comes to friends and relationships. For example, they may not turn up when they said they would but will then show up unexpectedly, much to the delight and surprise of others. Having said that, when they are in a close relationship they can be loving and loyal partners, as long as their partner understands that nothing will be predictable in their daily routine.

Health *Latent creativity*

People born on this day place a high priority on having fun, and although their refreshingly upbeat approach is commendable, they need to make sure their sensation-seeking nature does not become over-indulgent. As far as diet is concerned, they are often wonderful cooks and their love of variety will ensure that they get plenty of nutrients in their diet, but they need to steer clear of heavy and exotic foods, especially those rich in saturated fat. Surprisingly, for people who are so in love with life, there is a tendency to be prone to eating disorders or body-image problems. Counseling or therapy may help them deal with this, as will writing down and interpreting their dreams. Regular moderate exercise is recommended, as are mind–body therapies such as yoga or meditation. Wearing, meditating on and surrounding themselves with the color violet will encourage them to explore all aspects of their latent creativity.

Career *Born educators*

These people have pioneering potential and may be drawn toward the engineering, building or scientific realms, but the worlds of art, fashion, beauty, catering, cooking, and design also offer them wonderful opportunities to express themselves. Other career options include theater, writing, music, dance, promotion, production, education, and politics.

Destiny *To make an inspirational contribution to the world*

The life path of people born on this day is to understand that suffering is essential for psychological growth. Once they have been able to acknowledge the darker side of life, their destiny is to make an inspirational contribution to the world.

Signs & symbols

Sun sign: Libra

Ruling planet: Venus, the lover

Symbol: The Scales

Birth date ruler: Venus, the lover

Tarot card: The Lovers (choices)

Favorable numbers: 6, 7

Lucky day: Friday, especially when it falls on 6 and 7 of the month

Lucky colors: Lavender, pink, blue

Birthstone: Opal

7 October

the birthday of acquired taste

Your greatest challenge is ...

surrendering your stubbornness

The way forward is ...

to understand that stubbornness is very different from conviction; conviction is defending your principles, stubbornness is obstinately refusing to see another person's point of view.

You're drawn to people born on ...

September 23 to October 22

Although there is a tendency for you both to be indecisive, you have much to learn from each other.

Luck maker

Walk in someone else's shoes

Take a look at the world from the point of you of someone you think of as different. Lucky people understand that, however strong their convictions, there are always different viewpoints to consider.

October 7 people tend to be energetic and strong-minded individuals. They often have a reputation for speaking with deep-seated certainty and commitment to their set of beliefs. Indeed, reactions to them can be extreme—others either love them or hate them—but whether people agree or disagree with them they rarely fail to be impressed by their determination and strong will.

Although they could be described as an acquired taste, these people are rarely concerned about their impact on others since they believe that progress or improvements can't be made without someone rocking the boat or challenging the status quo. They would certainly prefer to win followers rather than enemies, but so strong is their belief in their ideals and their urge to pioneer progress that they have all the courage necessary to survive any opposition or criticism along the way.

From the age of sixteen there is a turning point for people born on this day that emphasizes for the next thirty years of their lives a growing need for emotional change, power and regeneration. During these years the key to their success is their ability to unite their ambition and drive with their awareness of the importance of diplomacy and cooperation. Another turning point occurs at the age of forty-six when they are likely to become more idealistic and optimistic, perhaps wishing to take more risks in their life or challenge their mind through study, travel or retraining. Whatever age they are, they need to keep their minds open, their rebelliousness under control and, most importantly, they need to understand that their way is not the only way.

Above all, people born on this day are strong-minded individuals. Once they are able to internalize their tremendous will-power so that it can improve their focus and effectiveness, rather than externalizing it in confrontational behavior, they have the potential to be among the world's truly brilliant innovators.

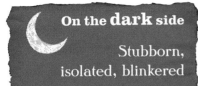

On the **dark** side

Stubborn, isolated, blinkered

At your **best**

Committed, resilient, fascinating

Love *Powerful and intelligent*

People born on October 7 are not people pleasers but they do have a lot of grace and charm. They may often feel that they want to be on their own but it is important for them to seek out the company of those who can offer a sense of security and acceptance. They are drawn to powerful, intelligent people like themselves, and can be a loyal and stimulating partner.

Health *Stable lifestyle recommended*

People born on this day may find it hard to stick to a stable diet or exercise routine if they don't see results immediately. It's important for them to understand that they need to keep trying. They can be prone to comfort eating, and regular meals and snacks will help them deal with food cravings, as will spending more time with friends and loved ones. As far as exercise is concerned, moderate to vigorous activities are recommended, such as jogging, dancing and team sports, because they can help them release pent-up tension and aggression. Back and kidney problems as well as bladder infections may be a chronic problem, while headaches and digestive problems could flare up during times of stress. The key to their health is to avoid isolation from friends and loved ones, and to establish stable dietary, exercise and sleep patterns. A relaxing rose or jasmine oil aromatherapy bath works well as an anti-depressant, and wearing, meditating on and surrounding themselves with the color blue will encourage them to be more open-minded.

Career *Born promoters*

People born on this day may choose to work independently or they may prefer to be of service to others as an agent, spokesperson or promoter. They also have a gift for music, art and writing; journalism might be a meaningful occupation for them, as might education, lecturing, publishing, advertising, counseling, negotiation, business, and financial advice.

Destiny *To set into motion the advances they believe in*

The life path of people born on this day is to open their minds to alternative viewpoints. Once they have rediscovered their curiosity, their destiny is to set into motion the advances they believe in and to move others with their strong sense of commitment.

Power Thought

❝ What I don't want to change is probably what I need to change the most ❞

Signs & symbols

Sun sign: Libra

Ruling planet: Venus, the lover

Symbol: The Scales

Birth date ruler: Neptune, the speculator

Tarot card: The Chariot (resilience)

Favorable numbers: 7, 8

Lucky days: Friday and Monday, especially when these days fall on 7 and 8 of the month

Lucky colors: Lavender, ocean blue, green

Birthstone: Opal

October 7

8 October

the birthday of the free spirit

Your greatest challenge is ...

keeping your feet on the ground

The way forward is ...

to understand that when your soaring visions don't take reality into account, they can isolate you from the very people you seek to inspire.

You're drawn to people born on ...

April 20 to May 20

You are both lovers of beauty with high ideals, and this can be a passionate and intense union.

Luck maker

Learn to focus

Research has shown that a tendency to be disciplined, committed and patient has a positive effect on happiness. Lucky people understand that the ability to concentrate has magical, luck-making powers.

From an early age, people born on October 8 may have felt a need to fly beyond the realms of existing knowledge. Their imagination is so creative that others may have regarded them as either highly original or slightly weird. But even those who find it hard to relate to or understand their wild creativity will be forced to admit that they are secretly envious of their ability to somehow disengage from the routine aspects of daily life.

These people may appear flighty and inconsistent because they are easily distracted and don't always show much common sense, but they have a powerful intellect and incredible insight into what motivates others. Unfortunately, that insight somehow doesn't always include an understanding of themselves and, because they have such an experimental approach to life, they can hop from one person or experience to another forever searching for excitement, freedom and inspiration. Although this makes them rather interesting and magnetic people, until they are able to understand why they find it hard to commit or face the realities of life they will feel restless and unsatisfied.

Before the age of forty-five these people will be presented with opportunities to discover more about themselves and what it is they actually want from life. Key to their personal and professional success during this period will be their ability to inject a heavy dose of discipline into their lives. After the age of forty-six there is a turning point which puts the emphasis on freedom and a desire to expand their horizons and take more risks. It is very important in the years that follow that they discover within themselves the adventure and excitement they crave, rather than relying on constant change to keep themselves from becoming bored.

With their active imagination, excellent communication skills and love of life they will often find themselves at the forefront of new ideas and trends. But only when they are able to unite their powerful emotions with a degree of will-power can they fulfill their destiny as a dynamic force for progress.

At your best

Imaginative, exciting, visionary

Love *Social butterflies*

People born on October 8 are often friendly, charming and gregarious individuals with an active social life. They tend to be drawn to unusual and creative people and should be careful that they don't attract needy, manipulative types. Commitment could be a big problem, especially before the age of forty, but when they do find someone special to join them on their journey through life they can be incredibly loyal and supportive.

Health *Keep your feet on the ground*

People born on this day generally tend to be blessed with good health and, because their minds are so creative, they tend to cope well with the minor stresses of daily life by escaping to an imaginary world. However, they are not so well equipped to cope with the major stresses of life—such as the death of a loved one. Because they tend to run away from rather than confront their feelings, counseling can be beneficial at any stage in their lives, as can a course in basic meditation techniques. As far as diet is concerned, they should remember to eat regularly, as they have a tendency to get so absorbed in an experience that they lose all sense of time. Regular exercise is also highly recommended to help them get in touch with their bodies. Wearing, meditating on and surrounding themselves with the color green will encourage them to keep both feet on the ground.

Career *Born novelists*

These people are highly creative and multi-talented, and could make their mark in many varied careers, such as business, science, sport, or technology. They may also want to put their creativity to good use in artistic careers or writing. Politics and social reform may also appeal, and a love of beauty could draw them to work in art galleries or antiques.

Destiny *To inspire others with their idealism*

The life path of people born on this day is to gain more insight into their own personality so that they can help themselves as well as others. Once they have learned to concentrate on and commit to a worthy cause, their destiny is to inspire others with their idealism and ability to transcend adverse circumstances.

9 October

the birthday of the psychologist

Very little escapes the attention of people born on October 9. Acutely observant, they are fascinated by all aspects of human behavior and interaction. In addition, they are extremely perceptive individuals with the ability to spot weaknesses or failings in others; but because they are also extremely sensitive, their insights and imaginative solutions will not offend but inspire others.

As natural psychologists, these people are extremely inquisitive individuals. They are fascinated by everyone they meet and every new situation they are in; when this open-mindedness is combined with their intelligence and energetic style, it is small wonder they are often very popular. They have many talents and will probably experiment with several different professions before they settle into the kind of work which can utilize them all. Although it may take a while—and there may be lots of stops and starts professionally—they do tend to find their feet eventually. Their personal life may be quite a different story. This is because the perception and insight that are the trademarks of these people somehow do not translate into self-awareness.

Until the age of forty-four there is an emphasis on issues concerning change and the transformation of their personal motivation. These are the years when they are most likely to look outside of themselves for a sense of purpose and identity, perhaps in their career or in their relationships with others. These are also the years when their eagerness to please can overshadow their will-power; it is vital for them to listen to and trust their intuition, which more often that not has been right all along. After the age of forty-five there is a turning point where they are likely to become more adventurous and freedom loving, and their genuine enjoyment of life will shine through clearly.

If they have learned to stand up for themselves and their dreams, this is the period during which these intelligent, intuitive and highly imaginative dreamers will finally be able to turn their visions of progress and improvement into a reality.

On the dark side

Passive, needy, jealous

At your best

Imaginative, insightful, popular

Love *An open book*

People born on October 9 tend to wear their heart on their sleeve when they fall in love and they will give their body and soul to their partner. Although this means they can be supportive, romantic and passionate, it can also mean that they become jealous and controlling, or that they become too accommodating. Developing their identity outside their relationship—and allowing their partner to do the same—are therefore crucial.

Health *Let go of grudges*

Being able to forgive and let go of angry or negative thoughts promotes not just emotional but physical health. It is important for these people to avoid holding grudges because they are prone to bouts of jealousy, anger and insecurity. Listening to their intuition when things don't go as planned will help them take the right action. It will also help them stand up for themselves when others try to take advantage of their giving nature. Positive thinking or assertiveness programs, such as cognitive behavioral therapy, will be extremely beneficial, as will yoga and meditation. As far as diet is concerned, they need to find out what kinds of food and drink suit them rather than allowing friends or partners to impose their diet regime. The same goes for exercise. Recreational drugs, alcohol and smoking should all be avoided, as there are addictive tendencies on this birthday. Wearing the color red will encourage them to be more assertive and have more self-belief.

Career *Born mentors*

These people may choose to direct their energy toward helping others in mentoring roles such as teaching, psychiatry, social work, or even religious work, but whatever career they choose they will feel an urge to inform and inspire others. Other careers that might appeal include research, medicine, writing, music, art, sport, design, theater, and the performing arts.

Destiny *To enlighten those around them*

The life path of people born on this day is to learn to examine themselves with the same accuracy and insight with which they examine others. Once they have greater self-awareness, their destiny is to help and enlighten those around them.

Power Thought

"I see myself as talented and unique. I am proud of me"

Signs & symbols

Sun sign: Libra

Ruling planet: Venus, the lover

Symbol: The Scales

Birth date ruler: Mars, the warrior

Tarot card: The Hermit (inner wisdom)

Favorable numbers: 1, 9

Lucky days: Friday and Tuesday, especially when these days fall on 1 and 9 of the month

Lucky colors: Lavender, scarlet, pink

Birthstone: Opal

1o October

the birthday of
the overseer

People born on October 10 despise chaos and disorder, and are at their happiest and their best when they can bring order and harmony to unproductive situations. In many respects they take more pleasure in their natural role of overseer, organizing and implementing improvements, than they do in seeing the rewards of their efforts.

Their career is extremely important to people born on this day and they want to find a vocation that is both fulfilling and meaningful. When it comes to their personal lives they will often display the same love of order at home as they do at work, running their houses or their families with smooth and effortless efficiency. Although they can sometimes come across as slightly serious and self-contained, they have an attractive sincerity that draws others to them. For example, they don't smile very much but when they do it can warm even the coldest heart with its sincerity. They are intelligent and articulate, but small talk is definitely not for them; as far as they are concerned, a conversation that is not meaningful in some way is a waste of time.

Until the age of forty-three there is an emphasis in their lives on issues concerning emotional sensitivity, personal power and transformation; in many ways the first part of their lives can be the most challenging for them. If, during these years, they allow their tendency to be logical and circumspect to overshadow their need to be emotionally spontaneous and creative, they run the risk of becoming overly serious and unfulfilled. If, however, they can open their minds, their hearts and their wallets, they can begin to lay the foundation stone for a life that is more balanced and fulfilling. After the age of forty-four there is a turning point which puts the spotlight on travel and new experiences.

Whatever age they are, however, the sooner they discover within themselves their adventurous spirit, the sooner they can become the inspired and progressive leaders they are destined to be.

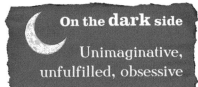
Love *Fear of love*

People born on October 10 pride themselves on their self-reliance, so intimacy may be something they avoid because they fear that they might be taken over by love, losing the self-control that is so dear to them. They need to understand that love is something that will keep them balanced. It is something they need in order to feel healthy, happy and fulfilled.

Health *Invest in your health*

People born on this day tend to place a high value on material wealth, and sometimes this means that their health comes second. It is important for them to understand that their health and well-being are the greatest treasure they will ever have; putting them at the very top of their priorities is essential. Investing in quality food and even supplements to ensure they get all the nutrients they need for optimum health is not a waste of their resources. Equally, taking time out each day to exercise and get fresh air is not a waste of their time, but an important investment for their short- and long-term emotional and physical well-being. Spending more time having fun with loved ones and friends is highly recommended, as it will help them loosen up and get in touch with the lighter side of life. Wearing, meditating on and surrounding themselves with the color orange will encourage feelings of warmth, enjoyment and security.

Career *Born team leaders*

These people are well suited to being supervisors, team leaders and business executives, but their talents suit them to a wide variety of careers including writing, law, education, administration, business, politics, and community work. On the other hand, their need for artistic expression may compel them to explore the world of art and entertainment through the medium of music, film or theater.

Destiny *To institute practical and innovative strategies*

The life path of people born on this day is to learn to be more spontaneous and imaginative. Once they have found a healthy balance between order and creativity, their destiny is to rectify disorder by instituting practical and innovative countermeasures.

Power Thought

❝I open the doors to the wonder and discovery of my imagination ❞

Signs & symbols

Sun sign: Libra

Ruling planet: Venus, the lover

Symbol: The Scales

Birth date ruler: Sun, the individual

Tarot card: The Wheel of Fortune (change)

Favorable numbers: 1, 2

Lucky days: Friday and Sunday, especially when these days fall on 1 and 2 of the month

Lucky colors: Purple, orange, pink

Birthstone: Opal

October 10

11 October

the birthday of social elegance

Your greatest challenge is ...

harnessing your ambition

The way forward is ...

to understand that popularity does not guarantee fulfillment; for a more rewarding life you need to set yourself personal goals.

You're drawn to people born on ...

June 21 to July 22

You are both sociable and sensitive individuals, and this can be a loving and rewarding relationship.

Luck maker

Stop procrastinating

Lucky people are not necessarily more talented than other people, but they set themselves goals and take proactive steps to see them realized.

People born on October 11 tend to be attractive and popular people. They are masters of the art of socializing, at their happiest and best when they are at the center of a group of colleagues or friends. Their style is easygoing and elegant, and their likable personality enables them to mix with people of all ages and all walks of life.

Others may envy the ease with which they merge into a group, strike up a conversation with a newcomer, advance up the career ladder, and ascend into the highest social circles. But underneath their graceful exterior, people born on this day may feel as if something important is missing. It's important for them to listen to this feeling because what's missing is personal ambition. Although their upbeat personality attracts popularity and position, they tend to drift into these positions rather than having clearly defined personal goals. As a result they may feel as if they have very little control over their lives; their aversion to conflict or challenge is even more damaging, because a little challenge and suffering in their lives will help them learn and grow emotionally.

Until the age of forty-two there is an emphasis in their lives on emotional change and a need for personal power. During these years they need to take advantage of opportunities to challenge themselves professionally and personally, because challenge is the key to their success. After the age of forty-three there is a turning point when they are likely to widen their interests, feel more free, and seek inspiration through study, relationships or travel. Again the key to their success and fulfillment will be their willingness to take calculated risks and embrace challenge.

This is because once they discover within themselves a drive to achieve and the courage to avoid the temptation of always taking the safest or most popular route, their outstanding grace, humanity and intellect will ensure that they don't just appear to be leading a charmed life—they will actually feel as if they are living it.

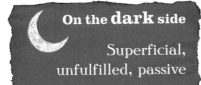

On the **dark** side

Superficial, unfulfilled, passive

At your **best**

Sociable, charming, popular

Love *Appealing style*

People born on October 11 rarely have problems attracting romantic admirers, although a tendency to alternate between being an intense and passionate lover and a need to feel like a free agent can cause problems in long-term relationships. It's important for them to be discriminating in their choice of partner, choosing someone for reasons other than looks and popularity.

Health *Delicate*

People born on this day need to take extra special care of their health because they can be delicate. They may, for example, need more sleep and rest than others and it may take them longer than normal to recover from an illness. Music can be extremely therapeutic for them, as can aromatherapy oils and dancing. There is a tendency for them to be sedentary so they need to make an effort to incorporate more activity into their daily lives, scheduling a regular program of exercise at least four or five times a week; walking is particularly recommended. They also need to avoid addictive substances like alcohol, tobacco and caffeine, and to satisfy their sweet tooth with fruit or seeds instead of chocolate. Meditation techniques will help them strengthen their will-power, and wearing, meditating on and surrounding themselves with the color blue will encourage them to imagine, plan and create clear goals for themselves.

Career *Born therapists*

These people may take some time to settle into a career and there may also be several career changes in their lifetime. They have the potential to flourish in many careers including writing, music, sport, social reform, sales, promotion, commerce, counseling, teaching, training, law, politics, advertising, art, design, and the media.

Destiny *To be an innovator in their chosen field*

The life path of people born on this day is to nurture personal ambitions. Once they have discovered what will give their life meaning, their destiny is to be a teacher or innovator in their chosen field.

Power Thought

" Every struggle is an opportunity for me to find myself "

Signs & symbols

Sun sign: Libra

Ruling planet: Venus, the lover

Symbol: The Scales

Birth date ruler: Moon, the intuitive

Tarot card: Justice (discernment)

Favorable numbers: 2, 3

Lucky days: Friday and Monday, especially when these days fall on 2 and 3 of the month

Lucky colors: Purple, silver, milky white

Birthstone: Opal

October 11

12 October

the birthday of effusive complexity

Heads turn when the larger-than-life personalities of people born on October 12 enter a room. They are determined to have their opinions heard and, if speaking loudly won't do the trick, they are not above resorting to outrageous tactics to get the attention they feel they deserve. Although they are attention seekers, they have a heart as expansive as their head, and their tantrums are just as likely to be on behalf of others as themselves. It is this curious mixture of wholehearted generosity and extreme self-indulgence that makes them such complex individuals.

This combination of characteristics can manifest itself in a number of different ways for people born on this day. Some may subordinate their pleasure-loving and sensation-seeking side in their dedication to serving others in an imaginative way, while others may be more non-conformist individuals with their own inimitable and expansive way of engaging with life. Common to them all, however, will be their infectious appetite for life, and their desire to inspire and invigorate others by their own passionate example.

Until the age of forty-one there will be an emphasis in their lives on emotional change, power and transformation. During these years their chances of success and happiness will improve significantly if they can learn to become less addicted to attention or the desire to seek a reaction from others, and become more focused on their personal ideals and goals in life. After the age of forty-two there is a significant turning point which will stimulate them to expand their perspective; they may, for example, have more contact with foreign people or places, or take up a new interest.

Whatever age they are, however, the key to their psychological growth and fulfillment will be their ability to take the feelings of others into account. Once they have found a balance between giving and taking, they will find that the reaction they provoke in others moves beyond surprise to respect, and in some cases awe.

On the **dark** side

Selfish, attention-seeking, outrageous

At your **best**

Dramatic, warm-hearted, exciting

Love *Expressive romantic*

People born on October 12 are passionate and expressive lovers capable of complete devotion to their partners. However, they expect the same if not more devotion and passion from their partners and, if they feel they aren't getting enough attention, they can become moody and aggressive. Indeed their tendency to be selfish when it comes to affairs of the heart can damage their chances of happiness, so they need to rein in their jealous and controlling nature, and learn to give and take more.

Health *Less is more*

People born on this day love life, and their appetite for the pleasures it can offer is huge. Therefore they need to beware of excess when it comes to food, drink and sex, because this can lead to weight problems and poor health. When it comes to their health their mantra should always be "less is more." As far as diet is concerned, they need to avoid rich and exotic food and focus more on simple foods. Taking time to chew their food and savor the taste will help them see that they don't really need to pour creamy, fatty sauces over their food to enhance its flavor. Regular exercise on a daily basis is an absolute essential, and if they aren't exercising already the sooner they start the better; leaving it too late could lead to weight and health problems, such as osteoporosis, later in life. Wearing, meditating on and surrounding themselves with the color purple will encourage them to be more disciplined, and to think less of themselves and more about higher things.

Career *Born performers*

Whatever career these people choose, they will want to make a contribution in some way to progress or advancement. They may excel as teachers, visionary researchers or academics. Other career choices include psychology, law, business, politics, journalism, architecture, design, media, entertainment, publishing, acting, music, opera, and songwriting.

Destiny *To be a pioneer in their chosen field*

The life path of people born on this day is to learn that they are not the only person that matters. Once they are more mindful of the feelings of others, their destiny is to be a pioneering and flamboyant innovator.

Signs & symbols

Sun sign: Libra

Ruling planet: Venus, the lover

Symbol: The Scales

Birth date ruler: Jupiter, the speculator

Tarot card: The Hanged Man (reflection)

Favorable numbers: 3, 4

Lucky days: Friday and Thursday, especially when these days fall on 3 and 4 of the month

Lucky colors: Pink, purple, silver

Birthstone: Opal

13 October

the birthday of
the polished diamond

As natural leaders, people born October 13 take their jobs and their lives very seriously indeed. Their total focus on their goals, their always polished performance and uncompromising strength inspire either devotion and awe, or hostility, sometimes fear, in others.

Those born on this day aren't people to fool around with, and their vigor and determination can shock almost everyone out of their lethargy. When they set their minds on something, nothing, including their own emotional and physical health, will stand in their way. Blessed with a sharp mind that cannot help but uncover and expose the weaknesses or failings of others, they are able to come up with ingenious solutions designed to inspire or benefit others. Not surprisingly, they are perfectionists; the tough and near-impossible expectations they place on themselves and others can make it very hard for them—and anyone who lives or works with them—to relax.

Until the age of forty, these people will experience a growing emphasis on issues concerning power, change and transformation of their personal motivation. These are the years when they are most likely to be harsh and unrelenting in the pursuit of their goals. Although this means they will succeed in whatever career they choose, personal happiness may be elusive unless they learn to ease up on themselves a little and open up to those they trust. They need to remind themselves that they are human and have emotions just like everyone else. After the age of forty-one there is a massive turning point, indicating a more optimistic and freedom-loving perspective. They may expand their mind through study, travel or new interests.

If they can learn to be less critical of themselves and others, allowing themselves to be directed by their inner voice rather than by pressure to perform, these are the years when they can really come into their own. Their driving urge to assist progress will not only bring about progressive and significant benefits to others, but also earn them their natural place in the spotlight.

At your **best**

Focused, courageous, powerful

Love *Don't take loved ones for granted*

It's all too easy for people born October 13 to neglect their family and loved ones in favor of their professional aspirations. They are romantic, passionate and, once committed, loyal and supportive; but they can also find it hard to express their feelings and their personal life would greatly improve if they could display their affection more openly.

Health *Don't cut back on quality sleep*

People born on this day have workaholic tendencies and may as a result turn to recreational drugs, alcohol or caffeine, or similar addictive substances to keep going. It is important for their physical and emotional health that they learn to relax and take time out. Regular vacations are essential, as is a good night's sleep. They may be tempted to cut back on sleep to increase their productivity, but lack of quality sleep will have the opposite effect, making them more prone to stress and loss of concentration. Turning the lights low in the evening and clearing out electrical appliances in their bedroom at night will help them if their minds are in overdrive and they find it hard to get to sleep. As far as diet and exercise are concerned, they need to avoid fad diets to lose weight fast and excessive amounts of exercise. Balance and moderation are crucial. Counseling and therapy, as well as mind–body techniques such as yoga and meditation, will help them become more self-aware. Wearing the color orange will encourage them to be warmer and more spontaneous.

Career *Born orators*

These people have the vision and the determination to excel in the political arena but they also make great lawyers, psychologists, social workers, orators, and teachers. Whatever career they choose, they will typically end up in leadership positions. Other work options that might appeal include advertising, marketing, business, journalism, and research.

Destiny *To inspire others with their clarity and determination*

The life path of people born on this day is to understand that mistakes are essential to learn and grow. Once they have become less critical of themselves and more tolerant of others, their destiny is to inspire with their courage, clarity and determination in pursuit of their convictions.

Signs & symbols

Sun sign: Libra

Ruling planet: Venus, the lover

Symbol: The Scales

Birth date ruler: Uranus, the visionary

Tarot card: Death (change)

Favorable numbers: 4, 5

Lucky days: Friday and Sunday, especially when these days fall on 4 and 5 of the month

Lucky colors: Pink, turquoise, yellow

Birthstone: Opal

October 13

14 October

the birthday of the middle path

People born on October 14 tend to be the steady rock to which friends and colleagues run for shelter when life gets stormy. They have a wonderfully calming influence and their ability to counter extreme situations with practicality and common sense often propels them into positions of authority.

Striving to achieve moderation and balance, doing the right thing in whatever situation they find themselves is the driving force of these people. They usually find the middle way, giving not just their own lives but the lives of those they live and work with great influence, stability and structure. Friends trust them to pull them back to reality when they are going to extremes, and colleagues trust them to be the voice of reason and common sense. Their greatest strength, however, can also become their greatest weakness if taken to extremes. This is because too much common sense and moderation can cause their behavior to become imbalanced with the result that they either don't take risks at all or they give themselves completely to self-indulgent behavior. Either way the results are a disaster for their psychological growth and well-being.

Until the age of thirty-nine there is a growing emphasis on personal power and transformation; during these years they need to listen as much to their intuition as they do to their common sense to decide what is appropriate to a situation. They also need to learn to let mistakes from the past go, as they have a tendency to blame themselves or other things and get stuck in the past, rather than looking ahead to the future. After the age of forty there is a significant turning point when they may wish to expand their mind through new experiences, the study of philosophy and spirituality, or traveling abroad.

Whatever age they are, if they can learn to look ahead with positive expectancy and find the middle way in all things, they have the potential to become imaginative and inspirational managers with a powerful and important message of moderation in all things.

On the **dark** side

Excessive, overly cautious, passive

At your **best**

Temperate, composed, reliable

Love *Don't settle down too soon*

People born on October 14 tend to look for partners who are as centered and composed as themselves but they really need someone who can keep them mentally and emotionally stimulated, even if that means a certain amount of conflict and tension. Once in a close relationship they can be warm, tender and loyal, although if things settle too much into a routine they can also become restless.

Health *So tired*

People born on this day are often regarded as the capable, dependable ones. For the great majority of times they are, but there will also be times when they feel drained and exhausted. When this is the case they need to pay special attention to the iron levels in their diet, as lack of iron can trigger fatigue. Poor diet and too much tea, coffee and alcohol can block the absorption of iron from their food. Egg yolks, spinach, sunflower seeds, and whole grains are all good sources. Whether or not iron is the trigger, eating a healthy, balanced diet, getting plenty of exercise and quality sleep, and taking regular breaks or time out from work will all help beat fatigue. Fatigue may also be caused by depression and weight problems, and all the possible causes should be checked out with a doctor. Wearing, meditating on and surrounding themselves with the colors orange or yellow will boost their energy levels, and carrying a carnelian crystal will help with feelings of lethargy and despondency.

Career *Born reporters*

These people may find themselves drawn to politics, law, education, art, and design. As inquisitive people with an interest in social and ethical issues, they may also make good reporters, journalists, photographers, and filmmakers; a deep desire to make a positive difference in the world may draw them toward medicine and the healing, caring professions.

Destiny *Gifted and original messengers of tolerance*

The life path of people born on this day is to find a way to satisfy their dual urge to promote their own interests as well as helping those around them. Once they have found this healthy balance, their destiny is to be gifted and original agents of progress and messengers of tolerance.

Power Thought

❝ I am excited about my future and the next step in my self-development ❞

Signs & symbols

Sun sign: Libra

Ruling planet: Venus, the lover

Symbol: The Scales

Birth date ruler: Mercury, the communicator

Tarot card: Temperance (moderation)

Favorable numbers: 5, 6

Lucky days: Friday and Wednesday, especially when these days fall on 5 and 6 of the month

Lucky colors: Pink, yellow, green

Birthstone: Opal

15 October

the birthday of
the provocative role model

People born on October 15 will often exert a hypnotic or seductive power over others and the key to their success will be the way in which they use this provocative influence. If they use it positively they can play a crucial role in the lives of others, helping them to develop a sense of their own individuality and power. If, however, they use it recklessly they can agitate others, exciting negativity with behavior that is sensationalist and attention-seeking.

Whether or not they are aware of their powerful influence over others, these people cannot bear to have their independent will constrained in any way; but this does not mean they are selfish. Quite the opposite. They often feel a strong connection to others, and friends treasure their thoughtfulness. It's just that their greatest wish is to make a positive contribution to the world. Being multi-talented, their potential for success is great and they will almost certainly make their mark; but even when they do earn the respect of others, they can become over-confident or attention-seeking in the process. It is therefore extremely important for them to appreciate how vulnerable others are to their charms, and to find ways to be a positive rather than a negative role model.

Until the age of thirty-eight there is a growing emphasis in their lives on issues regarding emotional change and personal power. During this period they would benefit greatly from the study of psychology. They already have a natural understanding of human nature, but investigating more deeply would provide them with the answers to many unanswered questions about themselves and others. After the age of thirty-nine a turning point occurs where they are likely to expand their mental perspective and become more adventurous in their approach.

During these years if they can learn to moderate their urge constantly to act as an independent agent and always remember that others look to them for guidance, insight and inspiration, they can become not only a positive role model but also a powerful agent of progress.

At your **best**
Charming, influential, intelligent

Love *The value of compromise*

People born on October 15 need a partner who can keep up with their dynamic mental energy. Naturally charming and seductive, they have no problems attracting partners, but once in a close relationship they may react badly with mood swings or tempestuous behavior if their freedom is restricted in any way. As a result, long-term commitment could be a problem until they have learned the value of compromise.

Health *You don't have to win every time*

People born on this day like to have things their own way, but their emotional health would benefit greatly if they were a little less competitive and self-promoting. This isn't to say these people should let others walk all over them; that would be just as disastrous an approach to life. But listening to what others say, allowing others to have their turn, and working cooperatively as part of a team will ease stress and boost their chances of happiness, while earning the loyalty and respect of others. As far as diet is concerned, if they are suffering from fatigue or low libido they may want to check that they are getting enough zinc-rich foods, such as nuts, seeds and seafood, in their diet. Regular exercise is highly recommended as there is a tendency for people born on this day to be more sedentary than is usual. Wearing the colors indigo or purple will encourage them to think about how their actions and behavior may be affecting others.

Career *Born philosophers*

Whatever they choose, because they are so intelligent and mentally restless these people will thrive best in careers that allow them a certain degree of autonomy and plenty of challenge. Possible career choices include publishing, education, promotion, philosophy, writing, music, law, sales, IT, engineering, social work, psychology, and the healing professions.

Destiny *To inform or educate others*

The life path of people born on this day is to learn to balance their needs with those of others. Once they have experienced the joys of synergy, their destiny is to inform or educate others.

Signs & symbols

Sun sign: Libra

Ruling planet: Venus, the lover

Symbol: The Scales

Birth date ruler: Venus, the lover

Tarot card: The Devil (instinct)

Favorable numbers: 6, 7

Lucky days: Friday, especially when it falls on 6 and 7 of the month

Lucky colors: Pink, lavender, blue

Birthstone: Opal

October 15

16 October

the birthday of the breakthrough

Your greatest challenge is ...

being consistent

The way forward is ...

to understand that, although your spontaneity is one of your greatest strengths, to earn the respect of others you have to prove that you are worthy.

You're drawn to people born on ...

June 21 to July 22

You are both difficult and unpredictable, but this can simply strengthen the bond of passion between you.

Luck maker

Press fast forward

Imagine you are ninety years old. Looking back, what do you wish you had taken advantage of in your life? By focusing on the joys rather than the stresses of your current situation, you increase your luck-making potential.

People born on October 16 are often blessed with a sharp mind and highly developed critical faculties. They love to observe and analyze everything and everyone they encounter, and human behavior provides them with an endless supply of material. Although they are perceptive and intelligent, their greatest talent is their ability to break through layers of confusion to expose failings and weaknesses with objective and brutal honesty.

They enjoy the company of others but their wit, independence and tendency to direct their criticism of others from a distance, for example in writing or in social campaigning, sets them apart from others. They are motivated by a desire to enlighten or inform, but the uncomfortable accuracy of their observations and the frank way in which they can express them may offend and alienate those they seek to educate. They place a high value on justice, striving for honesty and equality in all their dealings. When they get their own way—which they frequently do—they are models of charm, poise and magnanimity; but when their voice is ignored they can become defensive and moody, and will often refuse to accept failure or compromise.

Until the age of thirty-seven there will be an emphasis on issues concerning emotional sensitivity and power; these are the years when they are most likely to be stubborn and trying in the face of opposition. After the age of thirty-eight there is a significant turning point when they are likely to widen their perspective on life and may wish to expand their horizons through travel, study and finding adventure. They should take advantage of opportunities to work cooperatively with others and form partnerships during these years, as this will attract considerable success and good fortune their way, both personally and professionally.

Whatever age they are, however, their brilliant and unconventional minds and ability to cut to the core of any subject will eventually lead them toward self-analysis, and this is when they will make the most important and empowering breakthrough of all.

At your **best**

Intelligent, insightful, fair

Love *Stimulating company*

People born on October 16 can be a little demanding and trying in relationships. They can be unpredictable and impulsive one moment and silent and sulky the next, but their wit and intelligence make them fascinating people to spend time with. Although they can be trying, they possess a strong need for love and affection, and are willing to give much of themselves to those they love.

Health *Aches and pains*

Despite their considerable intelligence and insight, people born on this day don't always extend this common-sense awareness to their physical health. They can have addictive tendencies, and a love of alcohol is especially dangerous to their well-being. They can also push themselves too hard when it comes to work, and can be prone to stress-related disorders such as fatigue, insomnia, anxiety, and headaches. It is important for them to take time out to recharge their batteries. As far as diet is concerned, they need to go for structure and balance, aiming for regular meal and snack times. The same goes for their exercise routine—which should be at least 20 to 30 minutes daily, preferably in the outdoors—and their sleeping routine. They are advised to go to bed before midnight and wake up at approximately the same time each morning. If aches and pains are an issue, warm herb baths, in particular lavender and rosemary, may help. Wearing the shock-absorbing color orange will encourage them to be more sensitive to others.

Career *Born lecturers*

These people may be drawn to the academic world, in which they can be excellent teachers or lecturers. Other career choices that might appeal include writing, commerce, advertising, TV, publishing, community or charity work, as well as humanitarian or political reform.

Destiny *To expose the truth to others and instigate improvement*

The life path of people born on this day is to find ways to enlighten others without frightening or antagonizing them. Once they are able to speak their minds without breaking hearts, their destiny is to expose the truth to others and by so doing to instigate reform.

Signs & symbols

Sun sign: Libra

Ruling planet: Venus, the lover

Symbol: The Scales

Birth date ruler: Neptune, the visionary

Tarot card: The Tower (breakthrough)

Favorable numbers: 7, 8

Lucky days: Friday and Monday, especially when these days fall on 7 and 8 of the month

Lucky colors: Pink, lavender, sea green

Birthstone: Opal

17 October

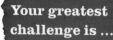

the birthday of the lucky escape

A central theme for people born on October 17 is the ability to pick themselves up when things don't work out and start again without complaint. Although they know how to be responsible, taking chances is a way of life to them and their life appears to others to be a delicate balancing act where lucky escapes, gambling or risk-taking are the order of the day.

The fearlessness of people born on this day inspires the respect and admiration of others, although their example may not perhaps be the best one to copy. This is because these people are perhaps the only individuals of the year with enough self-assurance, resilience and stamina to cope with the demands, disappointments, successes, and highs and lows of such a lifestyle. They are also not above embellishing the truth if they feel it will get them the attention they deserve. Although this never fails to entertain others, it can be dangerous for their emotional well-being, especially when they risk losing touch with what is fact and what is fantasy in their lives. Self-deception can be a big problem.

In their late twenties and early thirties they may experience an intense longing to find deeper meaning in their lives. This can send them either in the direction of greater risk-taking or more positively in the direction of greater self-awareness and a realization that what really needs to be balanced in their lives is their emotional life. Once they are able to step out from behind the image they have created for themselves to reveal their true self to others, they will find that their life takes on a whole new and positive meaning and direction.

Typically in their late thirties and forties they do finally find a balance between their impulsive and cautious natures, and as long as they stay positive, developing patience and tolerance, they will be able to combine their dynamic courage with the perseverance they need to achieve the clear potential for success and happiness associated with this birthday.

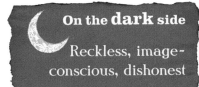

On the **dark** side

Reckless, image-conscious, dishonest

At your **best**

Adventurous, courageous, resilient

Love *Charming and stylish*

Ruled by their feelings but also in need of love and security, people born on October 17 thrive on change and variety. Things are no different when it comes to their personal life where they are likely to have many romantic opportunities; there is a real possibility that they may carry on several relationships at the same time. It is important that they are as honest as possible with others to avoid conflicts and tension later on.

Health *The great outdoors*

People born on this day don't tend to suffer from depression although they may be vulnerable to infections and stress-related fatigue. Fortunately, they are often body aware and tend to pay attention to their body's cries for help; if they don't it can lead to burnout. Taking time out to relax is therefore crucial and spending time in the countryside is the perfect way for them to do this. The greatest risk to their health is not surprisingly their attraction to risk-taking and apparent lack of fear. The wise counsel of friends and loved ones could be essential to making sure they don't head too far off track. As far as diet is concerned, moderation is the order of the day. When it comes to exercise, moderate to mild activity, in particular walking, is highly recommended. They would also benefit from cognitive behavioral therapy and meditation techniques, as these will help them feel more in control of their impulses. Wearing, meditating on and surrounding themselves with the color blue will encourage them to be more prudent, cautious and controlled.

Career *Born educators*

These people often feel compelled to further human knowledge in some way and may be drawn to careers in education, as well as scientific or technical research. Other choices might include translation, the media, writing, acting, publishing, lecturing, community work, psychology, and counseling.

Destiny *To further the advancement of humanity*

The life path of people born on this day is to be true and honest to themselves and others. Once they have learned that image isn't everything, their destiny is to anchor their adventurousness firmly within society and by so doing further the advancement of humanity.

Signs & symbols

Sun sign: Libra

Ruling planet: Venus, the lover

Symbol: The Scales

Birth date ruler: Saturn, the teacher

Tarot card: The Star (hope)

Favorable numbers: 8, 9

Lucky days: Friday and Saturday, especially when these days fall on 8 and 9 of the month

Lucky colors: Pink, lavender, burgundy

Birthstone: Opal

October 17

18 October

the birthday of vulnerable expectation

Your greatest challenge is …

believing in yourself

The way forward is …

to understand that from the moment of conception you were already a winner. Look at any baby; self-belief is your birth right.

You're drawn to people born on …

March 21 to April 19

You have much to learn and love from each other, and a great deal more in common than you think.

Luck maker

Balance yourself

Balance is crucial if you want to deal more effectively with life. So if you aren't feeling at your best, ask yourself whether you have taken care of yourself physically, mentally, emotionally, and spiritually.

People born on October 18 often have a regal, dignified air about them; from their early years expectations will have been high for them to achieve great success. As the years go by, more often than not they do fulfill those expectations by rising to the top; but although they long to make their mark on the world, another part of them longs to run away and hide.

With all the imagination, intellect and talent to blaze exciting trails in life, their need for the approval of others can crush their self-esteem and stop them developing to their full potential. Perhaps in childhood they were criticized or neglected too much; lasting feelings of inadequacy and insecurity continue to haunt them, however successful they are. It is therefore vital for their psychological growth that they work on rebuilding their vulnerable self-esteem. If they don't, they will be like reeds blown in the wind, flying high when others applaud them but falling down when the praise or support isn't there.

From the age of five until the age of thirty-five there is a growing emphasis for people born on this day on emotional change, power and transformation, and opportunities will be presented to them to take control of their lives. They must take advantage of these by becoming more proactive and saying "no" to others who seek to take advantage of them. Once they get a handle on their insecurities and realize their own worth, there is nothing they cannot achieve. When they approach their forties and beyond, there is another turning point when life will call upon them to be more adventurous, and it is more important than ever for them to leave self-doubt aside.

This is because once they see what everybody else sees and realize what creative, courageous and inspirational individuals they really are, they have the potential not just to promote the happiness of themselves and others but to be an inspirational force for the common good.

Love *Don't give too much*

There is a danger for people born on October 18 of giving more than they receive in relationships, and it is important for them to have the courage to stand up for themselves and to walk away from relationships that are damaging to their self-worth. Although charming and friendly, they may be reserved when it comes to attracting partners. But once they do find someone who can love and support them and make them feel good about themselves, they can be affectionate, loyal and expressive lovers.

Health *Tiger's eye*

Lots of physical activity is essential for people born on this day, not just because they have a lot of energy but also because it will help boost their self-esteem. All forms of exercise are recommended, in particular swimming and dancing. A regular stretching routine is also advised, especially if they are prone to aches and pains. As far as diet is concerned, portion control is advised as they tend to have a larger-than-life appetite, possibly setting themselves up for weight and health problems. It is important for them to avoid too much stress and not to overburden themselves with responsibilities and commitments to others; "no" is a word they need to practice saying more often. Meditation and visualization techniques will help build their self-confidence. Carrying a tiger's eye crystal will also help boost their confidence, as will wearing the color orange.

Career *Born translators*

These people will often be drawn to creative means of expression such as art, writing, acting, and music, but they may also put their imaginative talents to good use in education, sales, promotion, advertising, and social reform. A gift for communication and language may draw them to careers in translation or work in foreign countries.

Destiny *To inspire and benefit others with their discoveries*

The life path of people born on this day is to believe more in themselves, their creativity and their inner strength. Once they understand the importance of building their self-esteem, their destiny is to further their quest for knowledge, and inspire and benefit others with their discoveries.

Power Thought

" I am talented and creative; the only approval I really need is my own "

Signs & symbols

Sun sign: Libra

Ruling planet: Venus, the lover

Symbol: The Scales

Birth date ruler: Mars, the warrior

Tarot card: Moon (imagination)

Favorable numbers: 1, 9

Lucky days: Friday and Tuesday, especially when these days fall on 1 and 9 of the month

Lucky colors: Pink, lavender, red

Birthstone: Opal

October 18

19 October

the birthday of the peaceful activist

Your greatest challenge is …

allowing others to take the lead

The way forward is …

to understand that the mark of a truly evolved person is often their ability to feel comfortable in a supporting role.

You're drawn to people born on …

July 23 to August 22

You are both provocative and outspoken and are drawn to each other's power; a very passionate union indeed.

Luck maker

Sometimes say nothing at all

Lucky people understand how important listening is when dealing with people. This is because people who feel listened to are more likely to want to help you.

On the surface people born on October 19 appear peace loving and conventional, but underneath the surface—just waiting to appear at the first sign of conflict—is a great deal of independence and originality.

When things are going well for these lively people they can be wonderful team players, and their charm and optimism never fail to lift the spirits of all they are involved with. Rarely seen without a smile on their face, they will work long and hard to maintain the status quo. The moment that status quo is threatened or conflict arises, however, their toughness and independence as well as their explosive temper can surprise and shock even those who know them well. Indeed it is during difficult times that they tend to stand out, revealing their strength of character and both the best and the worst of themselves. Deep down, people born on this day are battlers and they just need a battle or a conflict to expose their crusading spirit. Once this is exposed, other people learn never to underestimate them again. Fortunately, their chosen weapon isn't intimidation but persuasion and logical presentation of their ideas; but if they are pushed in a corner they have it within themselves to lash out with wounding words and actions.

Until their mid thirties people born on this day are likely to be presented with opportunities for emotional growth, change and transformation. These are important character-building years where learning to control their temper and injecting enthusiasm into their life without conflict as a stimulus will be invaluable to their psychological growth. As they head toward forty there is another turning point where they may become more adventurous, possibly desiring to travel or seek more education.

Once again if they can learn to control their rebellious tendencies and direct their enormous vigor, optimism and courage toward a worthy cause, they have the potential to discover, shed light on and reverse injustices and by so doing bring the world closer to its natural peace-loving state.

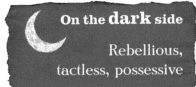
At your **best**

Independent, energetic, courageous

Love *Intimacy is good for you*

When people born on October 19 fall in love their passionate personality can shine through, delighting their partner with stimulating conversation and amazing lovemaking. Intimacy is very good for them but they do have a tendency to run hot and cold in relationships, and need to curb an extravagant or jealous streak.

Health *Highly sensitive*

There is a tendency for people born on this day to hold back or only reveal their passion during times of conflict, and this can damage their emotional health. As far as their physical health is concerned, they are accident prone when they act on impulse and are also highly sensitive to their environment. This sensitivity can cause them to feel inexplicably depressed or stressed at times. It can also make them prone to headaches and problem skin, as well as weight gain; comfort eating is often their way of coping during times of boredom or stress. Boredom is perhaps the greatest threat to their health, both emotional and physical, and they need to find ways to generate excitement and passion without waiting for external circumstances to force their hand. Wearing, meditating on and surrounding themselves with the color orange will energize them during times of peace, and wearing the color blue will help them be more tactful and objective during stressful times.

Career *Born crisis managers*

These people are natural innovators and may be drawn to careers in science, research, art, or technology. Other careers that might appeal include photography, writing, journalism, sales, promotion, fashion, education, the emergency services, the military, and counseling. Versatile and multi-talented, they need a career that offers them diversity, excitement and plenty of opportunities to reveal their talent for appearing strong during a crisis.

Destiny *To benefit others with their discoveries and actions*

The life path of people born on this day is to allow others to see their colorful personality during peacetime as well as during conflict. Once they have learned to be more tactful, their destiny is to benefit others by means of their original, independent and progressive discoveries or actions.

Signs & symbols

Sun sign: Libra

Ruling planet: Venus, the lover

Symbol: The Scales

Birth date ruler: Sun, the individual

Tarot card: The Sun (enthusiasm)

Favorable numbers: 1, 2

Lucky days: Friday and Sunday, especially when these days fall on 1 and 2 of the month

Lucky colors: Pink, orange, yellow

Birthstone: Opal

October 19

20 October

the birthday of the double life

Your greatest challenge is ...

admitting mistakes

The way forward is ...

to understand that the person who can admit they have made a mistake is not someone people disapprove of, but someone people can identify with and respect.

You're drawn to people born on ...

June 21 to July 22

You are both giving and creative individuals, with much to learn from each other about expressing and controlling yourselves.

Luck maker

Keep moving

When you hear the word "no," think of it as a temporary setback not a permanent problem. To get what you want in life you must keep moving, generating action and new opportunities.

People born on October 20 are something of a paradox, with two distinctively different sides to their personality. One side is the quintessential professional who spreads a message of harmony and collaboration. The other side is one of unpredictability, but also great artistry and an appreciation of sensuality, beauty and creativity.

Generally, people born on this day find a way to accommodate both sides of their personality, perhaps by pursuing conventional careers and indulging their artistic tastes as a hobby, or by placing an emphasis on matters of personal style. Indeed, their appearance is rarely a trivial concern for them and, however conventional their career choice, they will always find a way to express their individuality through their clothes, hairstyle or fashion sense.

The double life that they tend to lead also shows up in the way that they interact with others. They like to think they put the focus on others and are born democrats, but it is only a matter of time before they take center stage or a leadership role—this is the place they were born to be. This isn't to say they are scheming or insincere. Quite the opposite, they are extremely giving and caring individuals. It is just that their creativity and originality are so powerful it is impossible for them to contain or subordinate them for long.

In their twenties they may experience a growing emphasis on emotional change, personal power and regeneration, and they may struggle to find a way to express themselves creatively in their professional life. In their mid to late thirties there is, however, a turning point when they will become more adventurous. These are the years when it is absolutely crucial for them to find ways to reconcile their rational capacity with their creative, often artistic impulses. If they are able to find this delicate balance they will continue to lead a double life; the difference is that it will no longer feel conflicting and complicated, but completely natural and fulfilling.

Love *Never underestimate these people*

People born on October 20 are charming and stylish individuals who rarely lack admirers. They can come across as fun loving and occasionally lightweight on first acquaintance, but underneath they are forceful and independent. Anyone who enters into a relationship with them will underestimate them at their peril. Their ideal mate will be someone gentle enough to handle them during their sensitive moments, but strong enough to stand up to their forceful personality.

Health *Your health should always come first*

People born on this day may find that their desire to please or impress others sometimes takes a higher priority in their lives than their health and wellbeing. As a result they may push themselves too hard and increase the risk of stress, or focus too much on their appearance at the expense of emotional fulfillment. It is important for them to get their priorities right and to remember that their health should always come before anything. Allergies could be a problem for them, as they are often sensitive to their environment. As far as diet is concerned, certain foods may trigger digestive upsets, and an elimination diet will help them determine the cause. Regular exercise is highly recommended to boost their immune systems and also to help them feel more connected to their bodies. Wearing, meditating on and surrounding themselves with the color green will help them find greater balance in their lives and inspire harmony in others.

Career *Born publishers*

These people are multi-talented and suited to a variety of professions from science to politics, business, art and entertainment. Possible careers include writing, sales, public relations, education, publishing, journalism, counseling, therapy, medicine, commerce, and management.

Destiny *To produce independent, original and progressive results*

The life path of people born on this day is to find a balance between the opposing sides of their nature, so that both are fulfilled. Once they define a role for themselves in life or devote themselves to a worthwhile vocation, their destiny is to produce independent, original and progressive work.

Power Thought

" I am capable of more than I can possibly dream "

Signs & symbols

Sun sign: Libra

Ruling planet: Venus, the lover

Symbol: The Scales

Birth date ruler: Moon, the intuitive

Tarot card: Judgment (responsibility)

Favorable numbers: 2, 3

Lucky days: Friday and Monday, especially when these days fall on 2 and 3 of the month

Lucky colors: Pink, silver, white

Birthstone: Opal

589

21 October

the birthday of eloquent charm

As well as being charming, intelligent and multi-talented, people born on October 21 are also skilled communicators. Indeed their eloquence, whether verbal or written, is one of their greatest assets; used wisely it can help them win friends and influence the right people.

These people are very good at talking or writing down their thoughts, and although they may not be aware of it at the time their pronouncements will often make a lasting impact on those around them. As well as being articulate they are natural entertainers; people find themselves drawn not just to their stories but to their easygoing nature, emotional spontaneity and upbeat lightheartedness. Rarely unsettled by the attention they receive, they themselves would be the first to admit that they enjoy occupying center stage. Being accepted and well thought of by others means a great deal to them, but there is more to them than just being a social butterfly. They would like nothing more than to indulge their strong pleasure-seeking tendencies and share their enjoyment with a group of like-minded individuals. But they are also extremely perceptive, realistic and somewhat critical individuals who recognize the unfeasibility of such an agreeable lifestyle, and the importance of trying to improve the injustices and misfortunes of the world.

Despite their ability to subordinate their more selfish urges for the greater good, these people remain profoundly emotional creatures with a powerful desire to see their creative ideals realized. Before the age of thirty-two they are likely to lack in self-confidence and be conservative in their approach to life; but after the age of thirty-three there is a turning point which will stimulate them to be more adventurous, confident and freedom loving. It is important for them to realize during these years that although acting on impulse is exciting it can also be dangerous.

Whatever age they are, these outspoken, dynamic but eloquent and sensitive individuals will find fulfillment when they dedicate their gifts to healing, spirituality and an ideal of justice or beauty.

At your best

Charming, articulate, influential

Love *Love of adventure*

People born on October 21 need a partner who is as adventurous and communicative as they are, or someone who can spontaneously change plans and go on a journey at a moment's notice. Because they have so many interests and admirers, it may take a while for them to find a special someone, but they believe in the idea of a soul mate and can be extremely loyal to the person who finally captures their heart.

Health *Calm your mind*

People born on this day are impulsive by nature and this can make them accident or injury prone. They also love to travel but need to be especially careful when traveling that they safeguard their health as they are susceptible to digestive disorders and stomach complaints; exotic food does not always agree with them. Because they are so sensitive, they also need to make sure during times of loneliness, confusion or anxiety that they don't seek relief in comfort eating, alcohol or recreational drugs as they may have an addictive personality and dependency could soon develop. When it comes to diet they need to cut down on saturated fat and increase their intake of fruits, vegetables and whole grains. Regular moderate to mild exercise is also recommended, as is counseling to help them understand themselves better. Wearing, meditating on and surrounding themselves with the color blue will encourage them to calm down and take a step back whenever they want to rush forward. Meditation is also highly recommended.

Career *Born radio presenters*

These people will often become inspirational fiction writers, artists, musicians, and actors, but in addition to artistic pursuits they may also be drawn to teaching, training, the media, film, public relations, journalism, business, commerce, fashion, politics, advertising, and sales.

Destiny *To make a positive and creative contribution to society*

The life path of people born on this day is to learn to take control of their impulses without sublimating them completely. Once they find a balance between their need to express themselves and to help others, their destiny is to use their creativity to make a positive contribution to society.

Power Thought

"I express my creativity in ways that fulfill me and inspire others"

Signs & symbols

Sun signs: Libra/Scorpio

Ruling planets: Venus, the lover/Mars, the warrior

Symbols: The Scales/The Scorpion

Birth date ruler: Jupiter, the philosopher

Tarot card: The World (fulfillment)

Favorable numbers: 3, 4

Lucky days: Friday and Thursday, especially when these days fall on 3 and 4 of the month

Lucky colors: Pink, purple, blue

Birthstone: Opal

22 October

the birthday of the golden aura

Your greatest challenge is ...

not being in control

The way forward is ...

to understand that sometimes going with the flow or allowing events to unfold is the most empowering choice you can make.

You're drawn to people born on ...

January 20 to February 19

You are both highly individualistic and intelligent, and this can be an excellent relationship.

Luck maker

Don't feel guilty about receiving

Receiving does not make you vulnerable. When others give, it makes them feel good about themselves and, by extension, you. Luck is always knocking at your door; it won't come in unless you let it in.

Even if they wanted to, people born on October 22 could not fade into the background, so compelling is their presence and the seductive power they seem to have over others. In fact, throughout their lives all eyes seem to be drawn to their golden aura.

Although they do not object to being the focus of attention, a part of them longs to be recognized for their talents and capabilities rather than for their appearance or their ability to incite feelings of excitement or desire in others. Indeed these people have many hidden talents, including intelligence, intuition, discernment, and compassion for those less fortunate. Unfortunately, people don't often give them an opportunity to reveal or express these talents because it is enough for them to simply bask in their attractive and compelling presence. Not being taken seriously can therefore be a huge problem for people born on this day and they will often feel that they have to work twice as hard as anyone else to prove themselves.

Over the years they find ways to project the power of their intentions onto others but unfortunately they do not always do so in a constructive way. For example, they have a masterful control over their emotions and if they choose to they can also influence the way others feel. Their powers of projection are unsurpassed and it is therefore extremely important for them to use these powers wisely, making sure that their attempts to control situations do not end up hurting others and damaging themselves emotionally.

Before the age of thirty their tendency to manipulate others emotionally may come to the fore, but after this age there is a powerful turning point where they are likely to become less controlling and more optimistic, open-minded and adventurous. These are the years when they can really come into their own. When directed positively, their golden aura, or inner strength, can finally manifest itself as healing or creative ability, as well as the urge to help create a fairer world.

Love *At first sight*

People will often find themselves drawn to the magnetic, entertaining and warm presence of people born on October 22 and, with their powerful emotions, they will often experience intense attractions to others. Commitment could be a problem, but long-term happiness is likely with someone who is willing to give them plenty of freedom as well as plenty of support.

Health *Inside out*

Image matters a lot for people born on this day, and they may spend a great deal of time worrying about the way they look. They should really focus more on the way they feel because, as clichéd as it sounds, beauty and style really do start from the inside. Fortunately, weight issues do not tend to be a problem for them, but this does not mean they should skimp on healthy eating and exercise. Quite the opposite; to ensure that their skin glows and their hair is glossy and rich, they need to make sure that they cut down on saturated fat, alcohol and processed or refined foods, eating a healthy, balanced diet rich in nutrients. They should also get plenty of fresh air and exercise, preferably on a daily basis. Drinking a glass of lemon juice each morning will stimulate their digestion and encourage their bodies to expel toxins. Toning exercises will help give their body shape and definition, and stretching routines will help them become more flexible in both mind and body. Wearing, meditating on and surrounding themselves with the color purple will encourage them to think of higher things.

Career *Born actors*

With their powerful sense of justice, these people tend to thrive in careers in law, but being multi-talented and creative they can thrive in any career they choose, whether it be art, interior design, writing, music, acting, diplomacy, charity work, fundraising, engineering, politics, or humanitarian work.

Destiny *To defend and promote the interests of those less fortunate*

The life path of people born on this day is to use their seductive powers wisely and positively. Once they have understood that they do not always need to be in control of people or situations, their destiny is to defend and promote the interests of those less fortunate.

Signs & symbols

Sun signs: Libra/Scorpio

Ruling planets: Venus, the lover/Mars, the warrior

Symbols: The Scales/The Scorpion

Birth date ruler: Uranus, the visionary

Tarot card: The Fool (freedom)

Favorable numbers: 4, 5

Lucky days: Friday and Sunday, especially when these days fall on 4 or 5 of the month

Lucky colors: Lavender, silver, electric blue

Birthstone: Opal

October 22

23 October

the birthday of the maelstrom

Your greatest challenge is ...

loving unconditionally

The way forward is ...

to understand that there is no greater power on earth than the power of unconditional love.

You're drawn to people born on ...

August 23 to September 22

This is an extremely complementary match both intellectually and sexually.

Luck maker

Walk away from win-lose situations

Lucky people understand that life isn't about competitions or getting ahead at the expense of someone else's happiness. They never think win-lose but win-win, because win-win situations attract both luck and happiness.

People born on October 23 run on high-octane energy. Life is exciting when they are around because they seem to create a maelstrom around whatever situation they are in. Others admire their lively charm, intelligence and courage, but may sometimes wonder why they seem to want to make life so difficult for themselves.

These people have a low boredom threshold and they find themselves drawn to conflict, excitement and tension as ways to challenge themselves. Others may find this need to stir things up inexplicable but to these people it is simply the way they love to live. For them, life on the sidelines or life that has settled into an easy routine, no matter how successful or enjoyable, isn't a life worth living. Their compulsive zest for stimulation and ambition for improvement forces them to make groundbreaking advances or—if that's not possible—to experience or learn something new.

Above all, they need to be active, and even the calmer people born on this day will find that during times of crisis they really come into their own. Before the age of thirty they are likely to be concerned with issues of personal power; because there is a tendency for them to cling possessively to power when they feel they have earned it, they need to make sure power and control do not go to their head. After the age of thirty there is a turning point when they are likely to become even more adventurous, and they will have a strong desire to expand the horizons of their life. It is important in the years that follow that they find a balance between their need to test and challenge themselves, and their need to seek stability and harmony.

Whatever path in life they choose, change and instability will always be a feature. Once they understand, however, that they don't necessarily need a crisis to feel alive, their ability to respond instantly to stimulating opportunities for growth and improvement makes them among the most independent, progressive and compassionate individuals of the year.

At your **best**

Exciting, charismatic, inspiring

Love *A little less conversation*

When it comes to affairs of the heart, people born on October 23 surprisingly make love quite a low priority. This is perhaps because so much of their energy is taken up by other areas of their life and they tend to talk about rather than experience love. However, their seductive powers ensure they have plenty of admirers and, when they finally find someone they can open up to, they are loyal, passionate and exciting partners.

Health *Focus on what really matters*

People born on this day tend to lead very active lives both intellectually and physically and need to make sure they keep their energy levels high with regular meals and snacks. Unless they choose to become artists or athletes, they may find that a great part of their lives is taken up with conversations on their mobile phone and, although the health hazards have yet to be confirmed, they need to be aware that holding a handset to their head for long periods may have negative long-term effects on their health. Regular exercise, in particular jogging, dancing and gardening, is recommended, as are mind–body therapies such as yoga and meditation. Music may also have a therapeutic effect. Wearing, meditating on and surrounding themselves with the color blue or purple will encourage them to think more clearly, learn from their mistakes and focus more on what really matters.

Career *Born entrepreneurs*

These people have the energy and determination to excel in many careers and there may well be a lot of changes of direction in their lives. They may be draw to artistic or sporting careers, but they may also make excellent entrepreneurs and social campaigners. Other career choices that might appeal include law, education, business, IT, entertainment, medicine, healing, advertising, and film-making.

Destiny *To make groundbreaking advances*

The life path of people born on this day is to learn to seek excitement within themselves instead of outside themselves. Once they are able to relax their need to control every aspect of their lives, their destiny is to make groundbreaking advances that can assist or inspire others.

Signs & symbols

Sun signs: Scorpio/Libra

Ruling planets: Mars, the Warrior/Venus, the lover

Symbols: The Scorpion/The Scales

Birth date ruler: Mercury, the communicator

Tarot card: The Hierophant (guidance)

Favorable numbers: 5, 6

Lucky days: Tuesday and Wednesday, especially when these days fall on 5 and 6 of the month

Lucky colors: Red, maroon, green

Birthstone: Topaz

24 October

the birthday of irresistible intensity

People born on October 24 have an irresistible intensity about them that draws others to them. They are ruled by extreme emotions that they battle to control, but one of their greatest strengths—and the reason others tend to admire or aspire to be like them—is that they can play it cool, even when they feel totally insecure or out of control on the inside.

These people get absorbed in their work and feel compelled to present, often with dramatic flair, their discoveries or revelations to the world. This doesn't mean they are exhibitionists. It just means that they take their profession, craft or work extremely seriously and pride themselves on their accomplishments. Their intensity about what they do means that others can't help but be magnetically drawn into their world.

The upside of all this intensity is that they have enormous potential to shine in their careers, perhaps rising to the very top. In their personal life it means that they can fall passionately in love with someone to the exclusion of all else. The downside is that they can neglect their family and their emotional life in preference for their work. They can also become rather controlling, jealous and interfering, and this can alienate them from the support of those who can give them a much-needed sense of perspective.

Fortunately, around the age of twenty-nine there is a turning point which highlights a need for freedom and a more expansive outlook on life. They will be presented with opportunities to broaden their horizons through a quest for truth, education or travel. It is important for their psychological growth that they take advantage of these opportunities to diversity and explore, because it will help keep them in touch with the joy of life. Whatever age they are they should never lose their ability to devote themselves with enthusiasm to their work; when this is balanced with greater tolerance, flexibility and open-mindedness, they have outstanding potential not just to realize their ambitions but to enjoy the fruits of them as well.

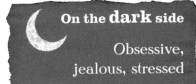

On the dark side

Obsessive, jealous, stressed

At your best

Hypnotic, dramatic, authoritative

Love *Scared of love*

People born on October 24 are extremely passionate and, once in a relationship, they will do all they can to keep the fires of love burning intensely. But committing to a relationship in the first place could be a big issue for them. Part of them is scared of love or being broken-hearted in a relationship, so the easiest solution is to avoid having one or to end a relationship before it starts getting serious. Trusting their instincts and allowing themselves to surrender is risky, but is the only way for them to find the fulfillment in love that they crave.

Health *Go green*

Prone to stress and tension, people born on this day need to get out into the countryside every now and again to relax and get as much fresh air and exercise as possible. Walking in green fields or among trees will be extremely beneficial because wearing, meditating on and surrounding themselves with the color green has a calming effect on their minds. Regular vacations and scheduled periods of relaxation in their busy day are also important to help them keep a sense of balance and perspective. As far as diet is concerned, they need to increase their intake of fruits, vegetables and whole grains and they should not neglect the importance of regular exercise, again preferably in the fresh air. Starting a hobby and spending more time with friends and loved ones are also highly recommended.

Career *Born researchers*

Whatever career they choose, these people are likely to thrive because of the strength of their dedication and focus. They may find themselves drawn to careers in public relations, sales, publishing, promotion, agency work, show business, education, research, the music industry, counseling, the healing and caring professions, and the sport and leisure industries.

Destiny *To lead by example*

The life path of people born on this day is to do less and be more. Once they have understood the importance of a balanced lifestyle for success and happiness, their destiny is to lead by their dedicated and focused example.

Power Thought

"I constantly find new ways to love the world around me"

Signs & symbols

Sun signs: Scorpio/Libra

Ruling planets: Mars, the warrior/Venus, the lover

Symbols: The Scorpion/The Scales

Birth date ruler: Venus, the lover

Tarot card: The Lovers (choices)

Favorable numbers: 6, 7

Lucky days: Tuesday and Friday, especially when these days fall on 6 and 7 of the month

Lucky colors: Red, pink, lavender

Birthstone: Topaz

25 October

the birthday of tangible results

Your greatest challenge is ...

putting the needs of others above your own

The way forward is ...

to understand that helping and supporting others earns you their lasting loyalty and respect.

You're drawn to people born on ...

February 19 to March 20

This is a happy, passionate and sensitive pairing where you both provide the magic your partner is longing for.

Luck maker

Don't burn your bridges

Lucky people don't have enemies because enemies bring ill feeling and bad luck their way.

People born on October 25 are forceful and tenacious, and their actions and behavior are driven by the urge to give concrete expression or provide tangible results for the original visions that inspire them. In other words, the driving force of people born on this day is their desire to translate their progressive dreams into reality.

Although they are articulate and intelligent, these people don't have much time for small talk. Results are what matter to them and, "Actions speak louder than words" is their motto. Others may accuse them of not being visionary enough, but this is not the case. They have dreams and visions, and respect the dreams of others, but ideas mean nothing to them unless they can somehow be substantiated in the real world.

Quiet and straightforward with a result-based, no-nonsense approach to life, they can often be a comforting presence in the lives of those around them. This doesn't mean they are necessarily compassionate and supportive; indeed they are not the most caring and sharing individuals of the year. It means that for most of the time they are a steadying and reassuring presence and a role model of self-belief, determination, focus, and organization. Unfortunately, though, there are also times when they can be critical and intolerant, and this can earn them potentially dangerous enemies.

When these people enter their late twenties there is a turning point where they are likely to become more expansive in their outlook. This may involve taking more risks or expanding their horizons through philosophy, study or travel. While they should never lose sight of their goals, they need to take advantage of the opportunities life offers them to open their heart and spread their wings. This is because by actively involving themselves in new experiences and relationships, they can keep their spirit of adventure and romance alive. In this way they can achieve their goal of bringing about tangible progress, not just on their own path to happiness and fulfillment, but also in the lives of others.

Love *Give and take*

With their ability to make people feel secure, people born on October 25 will not be short of admirers. They can, however, have problems opening up in a close relationship, preferring to hide or ignore their true feelings. They are often drawn to individuals who are giving and affectionate, and it is important for them not to take this affection for granted, making sure that they are not the ones doing all the taking in the relationship.

Health *Regular check-ups*

People born on this day have perfectionist and workaholic tendencies and they need to be alert to the warning signs of stress and work overload. If they don't, they could easily slump into periods of despondency and depression. They also need to make sure that they schedule regular health check-ups with their doctor because they are likely to ignore warning signs of poor health and need an expert to underline for them the importance of preventative medicine. As far as diet is concerned, they don't tend to have problems, but unless they take regular exercise they could be prone to weight gain, especially around the waist. Regular, quality sleep is essential and they will also function at their best when they are in a loving, affectionate and intimate relationship with a partner who understands them. Wearing, meditating on and surrounding themselves with the color orange will encourage them to be more loving, open and giving.

Career *Born manufacturers*

Whatever career these people choose they will bring along their perfectionist, result-orientated approach and, as a result, they are capable of outstanding achievement. Possible work options include science, education, art, drama, music, management, law, business, manufacturing, or invention, or they may decide to work for themselves.

Destiny *To give concrete expression to their original ideas*

The life path of people born on this day is to learn to give and receive in equal measure. Once they are able to decide on a goal that is worthy of them and keep it in sight without losing focus, their destiny is to give concrete expression to their original ideas.

Signs & symbols

Sun sign: Scorpio

Ruling planet: Mars, the warrior

Symbol: The Scorpion

Birth date ruler: Neptune, the speculator

Tarot card: The Chariot (resilience)

Favorable numbers: 7, 8

Lucky days: Tuesday and Monday, especially when these days fall on 7 and 8 of the month

Lucky colors: Blood red, maroon, sea green

Birthstone: Topaz

26 October

the birthday of
the powerful planner

The goal-orientated individuals born on October 26 are perhaps the most hardworking individuals of the entire year. They are ambitious and conscientious but their motivation isn't money or success but power, and they are at their best when they are organizing and managing others.

Although these people are hungry for power, this is not to say that they are lonely, power-crazed egomaniacs. Quite the opposite; they simply believe that organizing people to work collectively is the most effective way to achieve progress. And with their ability to focus on the distant goal, while at the same time orchestrating the collective effort of others, they are gifted and inspired leaders whose dedication and authority inspire respect. More often than not, they will be found planning events, serving on committees or putting structures in place for community reform. Their desire to manage people, to plan and put systems in place extends as much to their personal life as it does to their professional life, and they will expend a lot of energy trying to get others to think along the same lines as them. If others agree with them then their loving, affectionate qualities surface; the opposite is true if others disagree with them, and they can be extremely cold and disinterested to the unconverted.

Before the age of twenty-six people born on this day may find that their progress is blocked by crippling shyness, but after the age of twenty-six there is a turning point that offers them opportunities to grow in confidence and self-belief. They may become more optimistic and may wish to expand their mental outlook, perhaps through learning or through contact with foreign places or people. Whatever career path they eventually choose, they will often find themselves coordinating and directing others.

Outstanding professional success is strongly associated with this birthday. However, to ensure that this magic extends to their personal life as well, they need to trust their intuition more and remember that the greater good is not always served by suppression of originality, and that includes their own.

On the **dark** side

Obsessive, rigid, dull

At your **best**

Cooperative, organized, perceptive

Love *Loyalty and trust*

One thing people born on October 26 can't plan or organize is love. As a result they have a tendency to repress their need for emotional intimacy even though intimacy is good for them as it can help them release tension and stress. Once in a close relationship, however, they will be willing to show their profound depths; but this can only occur in an atmosphere of trust.

Health *Weighty issues*

People born on this day may struggle with weight issues during certain periods of their life, particularly when they are stressed or are starting a new routine. They should ensure that the number they read on the scales does not dictate the mood they are in for the rest of the day; tossing away the scales and relying on their common sense and clothes size as a weight guide would be far more beneficial. Paying attention to their digestive health, as well as the nutrients they eat, will help boost their metabolism; so too will a regular exercise routine involving around 30 minutes of aerobic activity a day, and three to five toning sessions a week to give their body definition. Fad diets and extreme exercise routines are not recommended as these can slow their metabolism right down. Drinking plenty of water, avoiding saturated fat, alcohol and caffeine and increasing their intake of fruits, vegetables and whole grains are recommended. Wearing, meditating on and surrounding themselves with the color yellow will encourage them to be more spontaneous and self-confident.

Career *Born conductors*

These people are well suited to careers in politics, community work, business, accountancy, banking, and social events organization. They may also be drawn to law, science, medicine, social reform, the caring professions, administration, and the world of music and theater.

Destiny *To demonstrate the value of synergy to the world*

The life path of people born on this day is to learn to leave enough flexibility in their plans for the unexpected. Once they are able to go with the flow a little more, their destiny is to organize, coordinate and motivate others to reach a collective goal.

Power Thought

66 Trusting my intuition is like taking in a deep cleansing breath of clarity 99

Signs & symbols

Sun sign: Scorpio

Ruling planet: Mars, the warrior

Symbol: The Scorpion

Birth date ruler: Saturn, the teacher

Tarot card: Strength (passion)

Favorable numbers: 8, 9

Lucky days: Tuesday and Saturday, especially when these days fall on 8 and 9 of the month

Lucky colors: Red, brown, black

Birthstone: Topaz

October 26

27 October

the birthday of the galvanizer

People born on October 27 are emotional individuals. They tend to react instantly and spontaneously to anyone or anything they encounter. Acting on their impulses comes as second nature to them, and their ability to excite and galvanize others with the intensity of their emotions gives them outstanding potential to lead and motivate others.

Impossible to ignore, these people are at their happiest and their best when they are expressing their thoughts and feelings, and influencing or directing those around them. Their decisions and opinions are undoubtedly driven by emotion, but they also have the intellect, communication and practical skills they need to see their goals realized. Once their imagination or heart has been touched they are, quite literally, unstoppable.

Given their impulsive nature, it is not surprising that they are also prone to mood swings, and a recurring theme in their life will be intense highs followed by intense lows. One of the reasons for this unpredictability is that beneath their outspoken, expressive exterior there is often a fragile and vulnerable side that simply isn't getting the nurturing or respect it needs. This is especially the case if getting the approval of others matters more to these people than anything else. It is therefore extremely important that they work on building their self-esteem, learning to listen more to their intuition as their inner wisdom will be able to gently warn them when their emotions are blocking their potential for luck and happiness.

Before the age of twenty-five the emotional impulsiveness of people born on this day will be heightened, but after the age of twenty-six they are likely to become less sensitive, and more independent and adventurous. Whatever age they are, however, they will always follow their heart rather than their head, and they will feel things more deeply than other people. The key to their success will be to direct their emotional intensity and energy positively so that they don't just galvanize but light up both their own lives and the lives of others.

Love *Don't hide*

Although they are intensely emotional individuals, when it comes to affairs of the heart people born on October 27 can be surprisingly hesitant. They may for example try to hide their feelings behind a mask of small talk, bravado or in some cases jealousy and controlling behavior. Love can be scary for them, but throwing themselves in its path will be easier for them than the anxiety that avoiding it causes.

Health *Don't put all your eggs in one basket*

People born on this day can take longer to recover from disappointments and setbacks than others. They need to make sure, therefore, that they take every opportunity they can to rest and recharge. It's also a good idea that they don't put all their eggs in one basket so that if one area of their life isn't going well they can draw strength from another area that is. Overwork is a big threat to their health and, because they are so impulsive, accidents and injuries can also be a common problem. It really is important for them to stop pushing themselves so hard. As far as diet is concerned, they need to pay attention to their digestive health and eat a diet rich in fruits, vegetables and whole grains. Exercise such as walking is also recommended for its mood-boosting benefits, as well as its ability to calm and quiet the mind. Wearing, meditating on and surrounding themselves with the color blue will have a cooling, calming effect.

Career *Born musicians*

These people will flourish in careers in which they can impart their knowledge or ideals to others such as teaching or journalism, but they may also thrive as musicians, actors and writers. Other career options include promotion, sales, media, advertising, and the caring and healing professions.

Destiny *To play a directional role in life*

The life path of people born on this day is to find balance and harmony within themselves. Once they are able to think before they speak or act, their destiny is to play an educational, inspirational or directional role in life.

Power Thought

66 No matter what anyone thinks, I will listen to my gut feelings 99

Signs & symbols

Sun sign: Scorpio

Ruling planet: Mars, the warrior

Symbol: The Scorpion

Birth date ruler: Mars, the individual

Tarot card: The Hermit (inner strength)

Favorable numbers: 1, 9

Lucky day: Tuesday, especially when it falls on 1 or 9 of the month

Lucky colors: Scarlet, orange, red

Birthstone: Topaz

October 27

28 October

the birthday of preparation

Your greatest challenge is …

taking a risk

The way forward is …

to understand that when a risk is calculated, it is not reckless but a way to move forward with your life.

You're drawn to people born on …

July 23 to August 22

You have much to learn from each other, and this can be a fiery, intense and passionate relationship.

Luck maker

Break rules now and again

Lucky people understand that rules are made to be broken. This isn't to say they break the law but they don't blindly follow the rules; they use their creativity and originality to work their way around them.

People born on October 28 tend to be very committed to their career and therefore the choice of career is of utmost importance to them. They may take a while to find their vocation, but once they do they nearly always reach the top of the field. This is in part due to the incredible effort they are willing to put in and their eye for detail. One of their biggest fears is being caught unprepared but this is largely unfounded as they are among the most organized and well-prepared individuals of the year.

They will often be completely absorbed in their work to the extent that they don't have much of a life outside. Although this means that they nearly always reach the very top of their field, which more often than not is dedicated to improving or educating others, there is a heavy price to pay. They may come across as overly serious or preoccupied and, if they haven't got friends and family to give them a sense of perspective, they are in danger of becoming emotionally isolated, completely losing their spontaneity and ability to have fun.

Until the age of twenty-five they are likely to be at their most serious and intense but after this age there is a turning point that highlights a need for freedom. Opportunities will be presented to them to expand their horizons, whether through travel, further education or study, and it is important that they take advantage of these because they offer them the chance to become a more fully rounded and fulfilled human being, rather than a human working.

Above all, these people are inquisitive individuals with an insatiable desire to explore. Fascinated with the tiny details that can make all the difference, their logical mind gives them the potential to make pioneering contributions to the world. And if they can learn to expend as much energy discovering and preparing themselves for the wonderful adventures life has to offer outside work, they will also be able to create lasting connections with the world.

On the **dark** side

Workaholic, detached, confused

At your **best**

Dedicated, detailed, inquisitive

Love *Late bloomers*

People born on October 28 may start their love life later than is usual, and it may be a while before they gain confidence in the love stakes. At the beginning of a relationship they may come across as reserved and uncertain, but when they finally do open up they can surprise both themselves and their partner with the strength of their passion and emotional confidence.

Health *Natural grazers*

People born on this day are natural grazers when it comes to eating. They may have been criticized for this tendency early in life, but they were in fact right all along. Eating little and often is far healthier than eating three large square meals; it may explain why people born on this day don't tend to have too many problems with their weight because snacking regularly keeps their metabolism high. As far as exercise is concerned, they may be rather sedentary, and long hours hunched over a book, desk or computer may have given them eye or back problems. Regular moderate to intense exercise, in particular team sports, is highly recommended, as are dance or yoga classes that can teach them about the importance of correct breathing and posture. Wearing, meditating on and surrounding themselves with the color orange will encourage feelings of warmth and security.

Career *Born scientists*

These people may find themselves drawn to the world of science and technology, but their desire to benefit others may also draw them to social and humanitarian reform, and community or charity work. Other possible career choices include philosophy, psychology, writing, and education.

Destiny *To ensure that progress is made*

The life path of people born on this day is to learn not to neglect the areas of their lives that aren't devoted to work. Once they are able to lead a more balanced life, their destiny is to prepare for and ensure that progress is made.

Power Thought

"I am a human being not a human, doing "

Signs & symbols

Sun sign: Scorpio

Ruling planet: Mars, the warrior

Symbol: The Scorpion

Birth date ruler: Sun, the individual

Tarot card: The Magician (will-power)

Favorable numbers: 1, 2

Lucky days: Tuesday and Monday, especially when these days fall on 1 and 2 of the month

Lucky colors: Red, orange, yellow

Birthstone: Topaz

29 October

the birthday of the chess master

People born on October 29 are highly accomplished tacticians and strategists prepared for any scenario, but this is not to say they are predictable in any way. They are in fact extremely independent and innovative individuals, bursting with new ideas and energy. It's just that one of the reasons they invest so much energy in preparing and planning for potential outcomes is that, like a chess master, they appreciate the element of surprise and the benefits of keeping others in the dark about their true intentions.

Secrecy and surprise are recurring themes in the lives of these people. They are secretive in both their professional and personal lives, so others never really understand what makes them tick, and are surprised by their sudden changes of direction. For example, they can be caring and considerate one moment, then cold and self-absorbed the next; or needy and insecure in one situation, and confident and dynamic in another.

All of this only makes sense when the bigger picture of their lives is taken into account, and in this bigger picture is a pronounced desire to organize and direct others toward their personal goals or ideals. To some this may appear manipulative but to people born on this day unpredictability is an empowering tactic to strengthen their personal and strategic position; when applied to their professional life it can be extremely useful. Problems arise, however, when they use the same tactic in their personal life as it can make others feel excluded or mistrusted.

Before the age of twenty-three, people born on this day may be shy or reserved and it may take a lot to draw them out of themselves. After the age of twenty-four, however, there is a turning point when they become more optimistic and adventurous, and this may lead them to open up and take more chances emotionally. Whatever age they are, they should make a huge effort to reveal more to others because, although outstanding professional success is assured, personal success is more elusive until they can connect more honestly and openly.

Love *Checkmate*

Although highly attractive and charismatic, when it comes to affairs of the heart people born on October 29 are not as well prepared as they are in other areas of their lives. It may take them a while to be emotionally mature enough to connect fully with a partner. After the age of thirty, however, they will begin to understand that finding a loving, supportive partner is the checkmate they need to win in the game of life, and with their charisma and magnetic charm they should have no problem finding this mate.

Health *Home is your castle*

Home is very important to the emotional health of people born on this day. They thrive in environments that are tidy and orderly, and if their homes are disorderly they feel stressed. Clearing away clutter will help clear their mind. Plants in their home or office can also lift their mood, as can playing uplifting music as they work or do their chores. As far as diet is concerned, they are advised to stay away from any fad dieting regime, as it is important for their body to find its natural weight. Sticking to a healthy, balanced diet, drinking lots of water and getting plenty of non-competitive exercise are the best ways for them to manage their weight, and boost their mood and concentration. Wearing the color orange will encourage them to be more open and spontaneous, as will carrying a turquoise crystal.

Career *Born criminologists*

These people are multi-talented and are likely to thrive in whatever career they choose, although they may find themselves drawn to military, political, legal, or commercial careers. Other work options include psychology, publishing, writing, science, music, healing, social reform, and charity work.

Destiny *To formulate visionary and innovative plans of action*

The life path of people born on this day is to be more open and honest with themselves and others. Once they are able to let go and trust their intuition more, their destiny is to formulate visionary and innovative plans of action.

Signs & symbols

Sun sign: Scorpio

Ruling planet: Mars, the warrior

Symbol: The Scorpion

Birth date ruler: Moon, the intuitive

Tarot card: The High Priestess (intuition)

Favorable numbers: 2, 3

Lucky days: Tuesday and Thursday, especially when these days fall on 2 and 3 of the month

Lucky colors: Red, silver, pure white

Birthstone: Topaz

October 29

30 October

the birthday of the deep-sea diver

People born on October 30 like to immerse themselves fully in whatever project, situation or relationship captures their vivid imagination. Like deep-sea divers, they throw themselves in at the deep end and their whole world is taken over by their current interest or concern.

Whatever it is that engages the interest of these people, it will often monopolize all their attention. The upside of this is that their energy, absorption and one hundred per cent dedication give them great potential for success in whatever field they have chosen to plunge into. Their infectious enthusiasm and charismatic charm encourage others to take the plunge with them. They are also not afraid to deal with the mundane aspects of the goal to which they have committed, and this practicality—combined with their logical and progressive intellect and excellent communication skills—makes them natural organizers and motivators of others. The downside, however, is that, as well as neglecting other important areas of their lives, when a particular challenge has been overcome or their current passion has settled into a routine they tend to lose interest. This can leave their disillusioned followers without a motivated leader.

Before the age of twenty-three they are largely concerned with the development of their personal power and how to handle their strong feelings. They may come across during this period as rather intense and serious individuals. However, after the age of twenty-four there is a turning point which emphasizes a growing need for more optimism and expansion in their lives. They need to take full advantage of opportunities to study, travel and expand their horizons.

Whatever age they are, these fascinating and sincere individuals will always have a strong spirit of enterprise. When they are able to expand and diversify their life from a one-dimensional to a multi-dimensional focus, not only will they fulfill their potential as inspirational teachers, managers and leaders, they will finally be able to come out of the water and breathe.

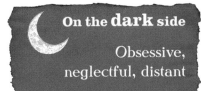
At your **best**

Fascinating, charismatic, passionate

Love *Head over heels*

Although they can initially come across as reserved, when people born on October 30 fall in love it is head over heels and they expect the same passion and intensity in return. The challenge for them is keeping this passion and intensity alive as they may decide to end a relationship prematurely instead of investing energy into reigniting it.

Health *Stand tall*

People born on this day can get so absorbed in their work or interests that they forget to pay attention to what they are putting into their mouths. It is extremely important for them to make sure they get enough nutrients by eating a diet rich in fruits, vegetables, whole grains, oily fish, and nuts and seeds. They would also benefit from drinking six to eight glasses of water a day, and weaning themselves off alcohol and processed and refined foods. Exercise is just as crucial for their well-being, and walking a mile or two daily or investing in a treadmill is strongly advised. As they may spend long hours at their desk, they also need to pay attention to their posture to avoid backache. Carrying a quartz crystal will encourage them to feel happier in all situations, and wearing or meditating on the color green will encourage them to have a more balanced perspective on life.

Career *Born playwrights*

Given their ability to devote themselves passionately to a chosen vocation and their need for challenge, these people will often thrive in careers that offer them plenty of variety within a specific field, such as teaching, publishing, medicine, and the healing professions. Their magnetism will help them in careers that involve dealing with people, such as public relations, advertising or retail work, and their talent for words may draw them to writing, the media, politics, film and theater.

Destiny *To help others grow, learn and develop*

The life path of people born on this day is to learn to diversify. Once they realize the importance of finding a healthy balance in life between their personal and professional life, their destiny is to devote their energy to the growth, education and development of others.

Signs & symbols

Sun sign: Scorpio

Ruling planet: Mars, the warrior

Symbol: The Scorpion

Birth date ruler: Jupiter, the philosopher

Tarot card: The Empress (creativity)

Favorable numbers: 3, 4

Lucky days: Tuesday and Thursday, especially when these days fall on 3 and 4 of the month

Lucky colors: Red, amethyst, royal blue

Birthstone: Topaz

October 30

31 October

the birthday of the indomitable cooperator

People born on October 31 have all the talent, originality, intellect, and creativity they need to excel in whatever field they choose, but their natural modesty often prevents them from stepping forward to take the credit. They much prefer to guide and praise others; as a result, people tend to rely on them for support, comfort and inspiration.

Although people born on this day are accommodating by nature, they are not so self-effacing that they don't know how to accept praise when they feel that they have genuinely earned it. In fact, when they sense that injustice has been done, toward themselves or others, their indomitable fighting spirit will emerge, and they can display remarkable courage and resilience. Their outspokenness and willingness to take risks will indeed surprise those who may have wrongly pigeonholed them as gentle, unassuming souls.

These people will give their all to a cause or ideal in which they believe, and when their indomitable will is combined with their logical turn of mind, excellent communication skills and superior organizational skills, they are a force to be reckoned with. The only chink in their armor is that they can get bogged down with details, and this can lead to confusion and despondency. It's important for them to always keep their ultimate goal or the bigger picture in mind, and not to get sidetracked along the way.

After the age of twenty-two there will be a growing need for people born on this day to expand their horizons, whether through further education or contact with foreign people and places. It's important for them to take advantage of opportunities for new sights and experiences, as these will energize them. However, they need to bear in mind that they work better when they have a plan for what they want to achieve, and if they can stick to it—and move from the passenger seat to the driving seat of their life—they will be able to satisfy their strong desire to contribute something of lasting value to the world.

On the dark side

Passive, self-effacing, confused

At your best

Sympathetic, supportive, indomitable

Love *Real harmony*

In love, people born on October 31 are openly affectionate and non-competitive. Their greatest desire is harmony and, with their attractive personality and caring ways, the chances are they will achieve just that. Most of the time they stand up for themselves, but some born on this day may become overly dependent and this needs to be avoided for long-term happiness.

Health *Discover the warrior within*

People born on this day are highly sensual individuals and are at their happiest and best when in an intimate long-term relationship, although some may prefer to play the field. Taking care of their health needs to be a top priority in their lives; if they feel physically and mentally fit they are more likely to feel confident and willing to grab the steering wheel of their lives rather than passively watching others take the lead. As far as diet is concerned, they need to make sure they increase their intake of whole grains, fruits and vegetables and limit their intake of saturated fat and animal products, because this will benefit their digestion and boost their energy levels. Regular exercise is also highly recommended, in particular martial arts such as karate, which can help them discover the warrior within. Cognitive behavioral therapy will also help them be more assertive, as will wearing the color red.

Career *Born constructors*

These people are best suited to careers in which they can contribute toward the common good, such as social work, the caring professions, law enforcement, and community work. Other careers that might appeal include education, counseling, medicine, psychology, writing, literature, and performing, and their desire to build something of lasting value may draw them toward architecture or construction.

Destiny *To contribute to the greater good*

The life path of people born on this day is to learn to be more proactive. Once they have decided to take control of their lives and stand up and be counted, their destiny is to making a lasting contribution to the greater good.

Signs & symbols

Sun sign: Scorpio

Ruling planet: Mars, the warrior

Symbol: The Scorpion

Birth date ruler: Uranus, the visionary

Tarot card: The Emperor (authority)

Favorable numbers: 4, 5

Lucky days: Tuesday and Thursday, especially when these days fall on 4 and 5 of the month

Lucky colors: Red, silver, light blue

Birthstone: Topaz

1 November

the birthday of the quarterback

The greatest fear for people born on November 1 is a life without variety and challenge. They despise inaction and lack of progress, being stimulated by progressive, even radical concepts. Doers, rather than thinkers, offense rather than defense, as soon as they have completed one challenge they throw themselves wholeheartedly into the next.

These people are up for any challenge life can throw at them because the excitement and uncertainty taxing situations offer them make them feel alive. If they find a way to satisfy their hunger for adventure and stimulation, their boundless energy and vital spark give them the power and potential to make things happen. If, however, they find themselves in an environment where they do not need to be in battle mode, they can sink into despondency, even depression.

They tend to be honest and outspoken individuals, willing to offer their opinion on anything. Although their self-confidence is admirable, it does not always help them achieve their goals because one thing they can lack is good judgment. They may, for example, take dangerous risks or underestimate or misinterpret people and situations, and their inability to listen to the sound advice of others, even those who are experts in their field, can work against them. In other words, they make excellent quarterbacks, but very poor defenders, and in tough situations their lack of defensive strategy can leave them wide open to attack.

Until the age of twenty-one they may come across as intense and serious, but after the age of twenty-two they break out of their shell and their adventurous nature shines through. They want to take more chances and challenge themselves in new areas to build up their sense of purpose. Whatever age they are, their courageous spirit and expansive outlook give them remarkable potential to extend the bounds of human knowledge. But to become the inspirational and influential force they are destined to be, self-knowledge and a powerful dose of common sense are crucial.

At your best

Inventive, exciting, energetic

Love *Exciting*

People born on November 1 are magnetic and exciting, and can make friends easily. Although they are in great demand, they can have difficulty in choosing a partner because they have incredibly high expectations. They want someone who is passionate and supportive, but need to watch out for jealousy and controlling behavior. Once they do find someone who is their physical and intellectual equal, the effect on them is grounding and positive.

Health *Going for touchdown*

People born on this day are injury and accident prone and, as in all aspects of their lives, better judgment and common sense are required. Not surprisingly, vigorous exercise is highly recommended for them as it provides an outlet for their astonishing energy. They will naturally drift toward activities that are competitive, in particular football, soccer, baseball, and basketball. Other activities that might appeal include martial arts, boxing and mountain climbing, but they need to make sure they take proper precautions and exercise caution. As far as diet is concerned, moderation is key as they tend to eat whatever is available to them, rather than thinking or planning their diet to maximize their chances of good health. Carrying a malachite crystal will bring calmness into their lives, and wearing, meditating on and surrounding themselves with the color blue will encourage them to think before they act and speak.

Career *Born healers*

These people must have careers that offer them plenty of variety, challenge and, if possible, excitement. They make excellent business entrepreneurs but may also excel in artistic, inventive or legal and scientific fields. Their constant need for challenge may lead them to the world of sport. Other career options include sales, banking, the stock market, tourism, writing, acting, music, education, medicine, and social work.

Destiny *To explore and develop new ideas*

The life path of people born on this day is to acquire greater self-knowledge. Once they have learned to exercise better judgment, their destiny is to explore and develop new ideas and to inspire others to do the same.

Power Thought

❝ I can be responsible, and when I relax my inner wisdom is clear and available ❞

Signs & symbols

Sun sign: Scorpio

Ruling planet: Mars, the warrior

Symbol: The Scorpion

Birth date ruler: Sun, the individual

Tarot card: The magician (will-power)

Favorable numbers: 1, 3

Lucky days: Tuesday and Sunday, especially when these days fall on 1 and 3 of the month

Lucky colors: Red, orange, hunter green

Birthstone: Topaz

November 1

2 November

the birthday of regeneration

Your greatest challenge is …

resisting the temptation to interfere

The way forward is …

to understand that change for the sake of change serves no purpose but unsettles and confuses both yourself and others.

You're drawn to people born on …

June 21 to July 22

You are both spontaneous and impulsive individuals, and this can be a creative and rewarding union.

Luck maker

Pick your moment

Good judgment increases your chances of good luck, but good judgment isn't just about saying and doing the right thing; it's about tuning into your environment so that you say and do the right thing—at the right time.

Like a serpent that sheds its skin, people born on November 2 often appear to be in the process of change, rebirth or renewal. Nothing gets them more excited in life than a new start.

But it isn't only their own lives that are constantly changing and evolving; they can also play an integral part in changing the lives of others in some way or in altering the course of events. For example, they may play a significant role in changing the structure of a business or they may encourage others to change the direction of their lives in some way, perhaps by leaving a relationship or by expanding their horizons with travel. As self-awareness doesn't tend to be strong in these people, many of them will not realize just how influential they can be. It is important therefore for them to guard against advising change for the sake of change.

Ironically, despite their love of change and regeneration, the one area of life they may be surprisingly resistant to change is themselves. Many of them simply aren't aware of their real needs and, instead of focusing on their inner life, they will direct their energy outwards with constant fresh starts or changes of direction. It's only when they can learn to listen to the quiet still voice within them that they will begin to realize that too much change is counterproductive.

After the age of twenty, they enter a thirty-year period when there is an emphasis on expansion and adventure in their lives. This may come through study, education or travel. After the age of fifty there is a turning point which highlights the need for greater order, structure and realism in achieving their goals. Whatever their age or stage in life it will be an exciting one, but for the lasting success and outstanding creative potential associated with this birthday to be unlocked they need to understand that, although regeneration is a necessary process for psychological growth, it is not a goal in itself.

At your best

Energizing, influential, flexible

Power Thought

66 I am in a good place at a good time. It is safe to stay here 99

Love *Taste for the new*

People born on November 2 are imaginative, clever and rarely short of admirers but their taste for new experiences may lead them into short-lived relationships rather than lasting, meaningful ones. For a while this can be exciting and fun, but over the years a part of them will begin to long for something more enduring. When that longing emerges they will attract the right person into their lives.

Health *Intellectual and physical challenge*

People born on this day don't tend to have addictive personalities but alcohol and smoking could become a health problem, so it would be wise for them to limit or cut down on these. Nose, ear and throat problems, as well as problems with the digestive and reproductive organs, could also give problems so it is important for them to take special care of their health, with plenty of healthy, nutritious high-fiber food and plenty of exercise, preferably in the fresh air so they get all the mood-boosting effects of sunshine. Because they have an active and inquisitive mind, they are strongly advised to keep agile and not rely on work as a way of doing this; all forms of study, reading and intellectual challenge are therefore recommended, as is learning a new language. Meditation techniques will help them search within rather than without for answers, as will counseling and therapy, and wearing the color purple will encourage them to look beyond the material and focus on higher things.

Career *Born arbitrators*

These people need careers that offer them constant variety and they are well suited to careers in tourism, aviation, finance, sales, law, public relations, psychology, education, charity work, and the media. Alternatively, they may express their creativity in music, drama or photography, and careers involving sport and leisure can be good outlets for their energy and ambition.

Destiny *To make a positive contribution to the welfare of others*

The life path of people born on this day is to learn that the most important changes in their life are those that take place within. Once they are more in touch with their feelings and motivations, their destiny is to make a positive contribution to the welfare of others.

Signs & symbols

Sun sign: Scorpio

Ruling planet: Mars, the warrior

Symbol: The Scorpion

Birth date ruler: Moon, the intuitive

Tarot card: The High Priestess (intuition)

Favorable numbers: 2, 4

Lucky days: Tuesday and Monday, especially when these days fall on 2 and 4 of the month

Lucky colors: Red, silver, white

Birthstone: Topaz

3 November

the birthday of the marathon runner

People born on November 3 have all the strength and staying power of a long-distance runner. They are ambitious and energetic but know how to bide their time and go the distance to achieve their goals.

With the ability to keep calm under the most intense pressure, they can earn the reputation for being extremely cool, sometimes ruthless, customers. At times they may appear to be hesitant or passive, but all the while they are simply waiting for the right moment to strike out and achieve their goals. If there is one thing, however, that can unsettle the masterful self-control of these people it is defeat or failure. They are terrible losers and, instead of trying to find alternative solutions, they may waste tremendous energy on self-recrimination and in some cases this can lead to depression.

Although they can be overwhelmingly negative at times, the upside is that when things are going well they can be energetic, charismatic, pleasure loving, and stimulating. Those lucky enough to catch them in one of these moods will be enchanted and uplifted. They can also be compassionate and supportive during these moments, with a deep understanding of the feelings of others. Unfortunately, when it comes to understanding themselves they lack similar insight, so they should look deep within to understand why the need to win can sometimes overpower their need to feel happy.

Despite being moody and intense as a teenager, after the age of twenty they will acquire a more optimistic and expansive outlook; this may lead them to broaden their horizons to seek truth, travel or study. After the age of forty-nine there is another turning point when financial and emotional stability is likely to take center stage. Throughout their lives they will always be highly competitive warriors, but once they understand that the only battle really worth winning is the one within themselves they can apply their progressive intellect, superb communication skills and almost superhuman endurance to the only cause that's always a winner—one that furthers the common good.

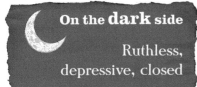

On the dark side

Ruthless, depressive, closed

At your best

Persistent, focused, progressive

Love *All or nothing*

Idealistic and romantic, people born on November 3 can't see the point of half-hearted relationships. They want to be involved with someone they can share their heart and their life with; anything less is simply a waste of their energy. They long to find their soul mate and, like most things in their lives, what these people long for they tend to get.

Health *Pleasure loving*

People born on this day tend to hide their emotions and true intentions both professionally and personally, and as a result they can be prone to stress and depression. Cognitive behavioral techniques to help them reprogram their thoughts from negative to positive can be extremely beneficial, as can counseling or psychotherapy. As far as diet and lifestyle are concerned, pleasure seeking is the order of the day and they need to go easy on saturated fat and rich, exotic food because digestive problems and weight gain can be a problem. Spending more time cooking and eating at home rather than dining out or doing the party rounds is recommended, as is a healthy, nutritious and balanced diet along with plenty of vigorous exercise, such as running, cycling and team sports. Carrying a malachite crystal will help bring a sense of calmness and ease, boosting their mood during times of depression, as will wearing the color orange.

Career *Born stockbrokers*

These people are often drawn to professions where they can exert an influence over others, such as education, management or entertainment. Other career options include business, negotiation, financial advice, writing, and the healing or caring professions.

Destiny *To transform the ambitions that drive them into reality*

The life path of people born on this day is to learn to be more spontaneous and forgiving in their approach to life. Once they are able to be more tolerant, their destiny is to transform the progressive ambitions that drive them into a reality that benefits not just themselves but others.

Signs & symbols

Sun sign: Scorpio

Ruling planet: Mars, the warrior

Symbol: The Scorpion

Birth date ruler: Jupiter, the philosopher

Tarot card: The Empress (creativity)

Favorable numbers: 3, 5

Lucky days: Tuesday and Thursday, especially when these days fall on 3 and 5 of the month

Lucky colors: Red, green, purple

Birthstone: Topaz

4 November

the birthday of the ice breaker

Your greatest challenge is ...

being less provocative

The way forward is ...

to understand that being controversial is not the only way to make people notice or remember you.

You're drawn to people born on ...

August 23 to September 23

This is a brilliantly complementary match as you are sexually and intellectually compatible.

Luck maker

Look better and act dumber

When you are self-deprecating you bring people closer to you and make them more likely to want to help you, because you are admitting you have the same fears as everyone else.

Although they can sometimes come across as conformist and sincere, as soon as people born on November 4 start interacting with others their provocative nature shines through. They have a talent for uncovering hidden weaknesses and insecurities in people and situations, and for luring everyone they meet into their tangled web of controversy and excitement.

They are extremely persuasive individuals, and in their minds they know that they have the ability to win over almost anyone to their point of view. This is not to say they are manipulative. Quite the opposite; they are principled and honest. It is just that it is almost impossible for them to believe there are any alternatives to the truth as they see it.

Above all, these people are ice breakers wherever they find themselves. They make full use of the element of surprise and are somehow able to articulate what is unspoken or unacceptable in the most humorous or convincing way, so that others are lured into either agreeing with them or at least reviewing their own position. Unfortunately, however, their shock tactics can work against them. They may, for example, find that the situations they have stirred up have got out of hand or the views they are expressing have truly overwhelmed or offended.

Until the age of eighteen, they may have come across as shy or intense. After the age of nineteen, however, that slowly recedes and is replaced by a growing need for freedom and the desire to expand their horizons through study, education or travel. After the age of forty-eight there is another turning point when the emphasis is on financial and emotional security. Whatever age they are, the key to success is to use their common sense and become more aware of the way their stance toward life is affecting others and, ultimately, themselves. When greater self-awareness and self-discipline are combined with their intuitive perception and natural leadership qualities, they are capable of achieving not controversial or shocking but truly spectacular results in life.

Love *Inventive and intelligent*

People born on November 4 are quick to throw themselves into social situations that can maximize their chances of attracting admirers and potential partners. Once they learn to love themselves for who they are and overcome hurts from their past, they have the potential to attract and hold on to their ideal partner—someone inventive and intelligent like themselves.

Health *The mind–body link*

People born on this day need to be aware of the powerful link between their physical and emotional or mental health. When they are feeling run down or have succumbed to a bout of illness, the chances are a period of stress, uncertainty or unhappiness was the trigger. Although a certain amount of illness keeps their immune system in working order, if they find they are lurching from one infection or virus to another they need to take a long hard look at their life and relationships to see where the weakness might lie. It is important to ensure they schedule into their busy diary plenty of time for rest and relaxation. As far as diet is concerned, the fresher and more natural their food the better; they could have digestive upsets if they eat food too rich in additives and preservatives. Regular exercise, in particular long walks in the park or countryside, is highly recommended to help them gain a sense of balance and perspective. Wearing, meditating on and surrounding themselves with the color green will help bring greater harmony and hope.

Career *Born social reformers*

These people need to be in careers where they can reach the widest possible audience, so they may be drawn to acting, writing, journalism, and performing, or even politics and social reform. Other career options that might appeal include business, commerce, medicine, psychology, education, and the worlds of religion or philosophy.

Destiny *To instigate reform*

The life path of people born on this day is to learn to take a more neutral, balanced perspective. Once they are able to tone down their enthusiasm to a level that supports but does not offend, their destiny is to effectively present their viewpoints to instigate reform.

Power Thought

" The greatest excitement and adventure is found within "

Signs & symbols

Sun sign: Scorpio

Ruling planet: Mars, the warrior

Symbol: The Scorpion

Birth date ruler: Uranus, the visionary

Tarot card: The Emperor (authority)

Favorable numbers: 4, 6

Lucky days: Tuesday and Sunday, especially when these days fall on 4 or 6 of the month

Lucky colors: Red, silver, electric blue

Birthstone: Topaz

5 November

the birthday of the representative

People born on November 5 like to be at the center of things; this is often where you will find them. They are the ones others tend to turn to if they want to be in the know, not just because they can be assured of an honest and informed response but because consciously or unconsciously they are representatives of the social group, family or occupation they belong to.

As information gatherers, these people keep up to date with what is current, not because they are gossips or busy bodies, but because their forte is spotting cutting-edge trends before anyone else. Sometimes their mind seems to be focused in another dimension because it is suffering from information overload, but despite their occasional absent-mindedness they are determined individuals and real powerhouses who get things accomplished. Their realism means that they refuse to let their idealism get in the way of practical considerations.

Until the age of seventeen they may have presented a somewhat withdrawn or intense persona, but after the age of eighteen there is a dramatic change which sees them becoming more confident and outgoing. This may lead them to expand their mental outlook and to develop their characteristic fascination with what's going on around them. After the age of forty-eight they become more organized and industrious, with a greater understanding of their goals in life. The key to their success, whatever their age or stage in life, will not be their ability to adapt to what is going on around them, but their ability to control and direct it.

The lesson in life they need to learn is that until they are as fascinated in their own self-development as they are in keeping up with what other people are doing, the outstanding potential for personal achievement associated with this birthday will remain elusive. However, once they start to become more self-aware, not only will they find greater happiness, they will also be able to use their incredible insight and knowledge to represent and to benefit others.

Love *Sensitive and powerful*

People born on November 5 have sensitive and powerful emotions, and a part of them fears that they will disappear in a close relationship. But when they find the right partner, giving love and sharing space with another human being is a liberating and empowering experience for them. They are drawn to intelligent, honest and independent people, like themselves.

Health *Steer clear of the latest fads*

People born on this day have a tendency to be reactive in their dealings with other people, and this can trigger anxiety and uncertainty. Self-knowledge and the ability to control their responses to people and situations are therefore crucial for their emotional health. To achieve these they may need plenty of time alone, perhaps even therapy or counseling, to discover who they are and what they want out of life. When it comes to their physical health, they are likely to be very up to date with the latest trends, but they should steer clear of fad diets and exercise routines. Instead they should stick with a healthy, balanced diet that includes all food groups and a moderate exercise program that includes aerobic activity for 30 to 40 minutes at least five times a week, toning exercises every other day and gentle stretching daily. Carrying a carnelian crystal around with them will help promote balance, courage, compassion, vitality, and personal power.

Career *Born advertisers*

Scientific, technology and business careers as well as writing and acting could be ideal careers for these people, but they may also be drawn to negotiation, arbitration, public relations, sales, or advertising. They may have a gift for selling or promoting ideas or products, but their excellent organizational skills and inquisitive mind will help them succeed in any career that they choose.

Destiny *To enlighten others*

The life path of people born on this day is to take charge of their lives rather than allowing circumstances or other people to set the tone. Once they are able to establish a sense of their own identity, their destiny is to reveal information and help enlighten others in the process.

Power Thought

"I am at the center of my world. What I think and feel matters"

Signs & symbols

Sun sign: Scorpio

Ruling planet: Mars, the warrior

Symbol: The Scorpion

Birth date ruler: Mercury, the communicator

Tarot card: The Hierophant (guidance)

Favorable numbers: 5, 7

Lucky days: Tuesday and Wednesday, especially when these days fall on 5 and 7 of the month

Lucky colors: Red, green, orange

Birthstone: Topaz

6 November

the birthday of the energetic over-achiever

Vibrant and stimulating, people born on November 6 have boundless energy and the ability to create an enthusiastic environment wherever they go, stimulating and motivating others with their infectious, limitless and honest enthusiasm.

Driven and ambitious, with a can-do attitude, these people typically refuse to be sidetracked or blocked from the goals that excite them by limitations or obstacles. Although this gives them incredible potential for success there is a danger, however, that they can get ahead of themselves with their enthusiasm and become too confident of success without the necessary plans or back-up. Sometimes their aims can appear so far reaching that others simply brand them as unfeasible; although they will often shake off criticism with humor, a part of them feels deeply hurt that others don't believe in them enough.

Surrounding themselves with people who are as optimistic and upbeat as themselves will lift their spirits, but it is also important for them to make sure that they inject a heavy dose of realism into their lives. A realistic outlook is not a negative one but one that takes into account both the upsides and the downsides of a situation.

After the age of sixteen, people born on this day start to develop their characteristic enthusiasm, energy and drive, and they are likely to be positive and expansive in their outlook. This may lead them to further education or travel, or stimulate them to be adventurous and take chances. This influence continues until the age of forty-six, when they become more realistic, practical and organized in their approach to life, with a strong need for order in their lives. Given the fact that realism is an important ingredient for their psychological growth, these are the years when they will finally be able to come to terms with the fact that there will always be positive and negative outcomes to consider. This rational outlook will empower them on their dedicated quest to enlighten others and realize their innovative visions.

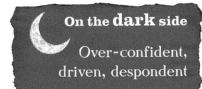

On the **dark** side
Over-confident, driven, despondent

At your **best**
Optimistic, energetic, uplifting

Love *Take your pick*

People born on November 6 tend to be attracted to people who are unobtainable and aloof. This is their way of protecting themselves, but as an approach to love it is damaging. They need to take a good long look at what they can have; and with their charming and attractive personality, when it comes to affairs of the heart they can have a lot.

Health *Pace yourself*

People born on this day are blessed with limitless supplies of energy, but even they can overreach themselves. If they don't take care of themselves with regular health check-ups, a healthy diet and plenty of moderate exercise, they could find that their energy suddenly slumps. Fatigue and burnout are a real concern, and it is important for them to learn to pace themselves. Regular vacations and plenty of time to relax and unwind, as well as quality sleep most nights, are essential. They may also benefit from mind–body techniques such as yoga and meditation that can encourage them to slow down both mentally and physically. As far as diet is concerned, drinking a glass of lemon with water as soon as they get up in the morning will help boost their digestive system, and increasing their intake of fiber is beneficial too. Carrying a malachite crystal with them can help balance their emotions, bringing a sense of calmness and ease.

Career *Born entertainers*

These people need to find a career that puts their incredible energy to good use and they may find themselves drawn to the world of entertainment, international business, tourism, the leisure and sports industries, and education. With their talent for troubleshooting and need for action, they may also thrive in technology, science, politics, and the emergency services. Music, dance or writing may also be attractive options for them.

Destiny *To pursue the common good*

The life path of people born on this day is to learn to temper their enthusiasm with realism. Once they have learned how to handle setbacks, their destiny is to be inspired leaders and to follow their instincts to pursue the common good.

Signs & symbols

Sun sign: Scorpio

Ruling planet: Mars, the warrior

Symbol: The Scorpion

Birth date ruler: Venus, the lover

Tarot card: The Lovers (choices)

Favorable numbers: 6, 8

Lucky days: Tuesday and Friday, especially when these days fall on 6 and 8 of the month

Lucky colors: Red, lavender, pink

Birthstone: Topaz

November 6

7 November

the birthday of the curious adventurer

Your greatest challenge is …

to be decisive

The way forward is …

to understand that your mind will present you with all sorts of excuses not to move forward with your life, but inaction will keep you stuck.

You're drawn to people born on …

February 19 to March 20

You are both sensual and emotionally aware individuals, and this can be a magical union.

Luck maker

Write down what you want

If you want to make good luck happen, you have to write down what you want. You can't create luck unless you know what you want to achieve.

People born on November 7 tend to be inquisitive and progressive types with an adventurous, pioneering spirit. They relish any opportunity to learn and discover something new, and to test their skills in demanding challenges.

There is very little that they don't want to learn about or understand better. Their curiosity is limitless and nothing gives them more satisfaction than being able to figure out what makes a person tick or how something works. In addition they are extremely ambitious and driven individuals who thrive on variety and change; being caught in a mundane, routine existence is their personal nightmare. Although the potential for remarkable success in exploring the outermost parameters of human knowledge is great for these people, the biggest threat to their potential is their lack of focus. In some ways their greatest strength—their inquisitive spirit—is also their greatest weakness, because their constant need to struggle, learn and challenge can stop them setting achievable goals for themselves.

Until the age of forty-five they are likely to be at their most restless and may have a burning urge to study, travel and expand their horizons in as many new directions as possible. After the age of forty-five, however, there is an important turning point when—with a strong need for order and structure—they are likely to become more realistic, practical and organized in order to achieve their goals in life.

This is not to say that the first part of their lives is chaotic, because if they set themselves personal goals and pursue them actively they can achieve great success. It is just that for many of these people the second part of their lives tends to be the most fulfilling and rewarding. This is because they can build on the incredible knowledge and experience they have gained in their youth and use it as a launching pad to work toward realizing their goals—those that they believe will be of great benefit not just to themselves and those they live and work with, but to the wider world.

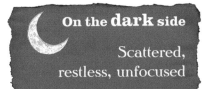

At your **best**

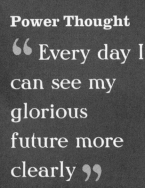

Inquisitive, pioneering, refreshing

Love *Intelligent lovers*

People born on November 7 are thoughtful, affectionate, supportive, and intelligent lovers, but they need to be given the freedom to explore and investigate outside a relationship—not physically but intellectually. There is a tendency for them to be controlling and jealous; for their long-term happiness they need to give their lover the same freedom and trust that they expect for themselves.

Health *Check your iron levels*

Fatigue, both intellectual and physical, can be a big problem for people born on this day, and to make sure they don't suffer from energy slumps they need plenty of good quality sleep and sufficient iron in their diet. If they have been on and off diets for years, drink lots of tea and coffee and are vegetarian, low iron levels could be a problem, so a vitamin and mineral supplement which includes iron is advised. Problems with their digestive and reproductive systems could also occur so they should ensure they have regular check-ups with their doctor and eat a diet rich in hormone-balancing and digestion-boosting nutrients. Regular exercise is important, whether they have weight problems or not. Fortunately, most people born on this day love to move, so this should not be an issue. Wearing or meditating on the color blue will encourage them to be more goal-orientated.

Career *Born discoverers*

These multi-talented people have the potential to thrive in any career and to pioneer progress. Possible work options include social reform, sporting or artistic careers and scientific innovation, but they may also be drawn toward writing, education, research, politics, and the world of entertainment. Alternatively, they may prefer to work on a self-employed basis.

Destiny *To inspire and educate others with their positive attitude*

The life path of people born on this day is not to let their love of knowledge interfere with their potential to make a mark on the world. Once they have learned to focus, their destiny is to inspire and educate others with their positive and enthusiastic attitude.

Signs & symbols

Sun sign: Scorpio

Ruling planet: Mars, the warrior

Symbol: The Scorpion

Birth date ruler: Neptune, the speculator

Tarot card: The Chariot (resilience)

Favorable numbers: 7, 9

Lucky days: Tuesday and Monday, especially when these days fall on 7 and 9 of the month

Lucky colors: Red, sapphire blue, sea green

Birthstone: Topaz

November 7

8 November

the birthday of
dark fascination

Your greatest challenge is …

developing a sense of humor

The way forward is …

to understand that if you take yourself too seriously you will lose the sense of perspective and objectivity you need to make good judgments.

You're drawn to people born on …

December 22 to January 19

This is an excellent match in which you find the intensity and security you both crave in a relationship.

Luck maker

Honor your inner child

Children are a never-ending source of amazement and insight. They can teach you a lot about yourself, what's important in life and how to be happy.

Although they are blessed with imaginative and progressive minds, people born on November 8 can come across as serious or intense. They tend to be attracted to unusual subjects that others would consider borderline, shadowy or dark. In some cases their interests may even be considered peculiar or, at the very least, out of the ordinary.

They are brilliant at concentrating their energy on achieving their goals, and this, combined with their courage and ambition, augurs well for professional success. Many will attract money their way, rise to the top of their career or make a comfortable standard of living an important goal in their lives. Sometimes the desire to achieve materially can be so strong that it becomes overpowering in its intensity; it is important for these people to remember what is truly important in life.

It is their curiosity which draws these people to the shadowy aspects of life, and a part of them longs to push the boundaries of knowledge and experience to their limits. If they are able to maintain objectivity they have the potential to be innovating pioneers; but if they can't keep their distance, there is a real risk of their becoming too closely identified with the darker aspects of the world and the shadow side of themselves.

Until the age of thirty-three, the urge for these people to explore the unconventional is at its strongest; during these years they need to remember that, as fascinating as the unconventional is, there is also much to be learned from what is routine. After the age of thirty-four there is a turning point when they start to become more practical, disciplined and goal-orientated in the realization of their objectives. Whatever age they are, however, the key to their success is their ability to confront their inner fears rather than seeking it outside. When they can do this, their hunger to explore the meaning of life will inevitably draw them away from the darkness within to the light of understanding, compassion, love, and what is truly important in life.

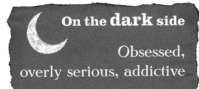

On the **dark** side

Obsessed, overly serious, addictive

At your **best**

Deep, driven, inquisitive

Love *Strong and passionate desires*

Although they may come across as somewhat reserved or serious, people born on November 8 have strong and passionate desires. They may be tempted to date people who are unusual or dangerous in some way, but their chances of happiness will increase significantly if they date someone clever and interesting, but also grounded and secure.

Health *Overspending*

People born on this day like to spend, and it is important for them to make sure that this doesn't get out of hand, as being in debt will make them feel anxious and unsettled. As for alcohol, gambling and recreational drugs, they need to avoid them too as they will lead them down a dangerous path. Because they find it hard to open up to others they may bottle up their emotions; this can have a damaging effect, so counseling or therapy might prove beneficial. As far as diet is concerned, the emphasis needs to be on fresh, natural or organic, and the more colorful fruits and vegetables they have on their plate the better. Regular moderate exercise is recommended, in particular yoga and tai chi which can encourage their minds and their bodies to become more flexible. Above all, spending more time relaxing and having fun is highly recommended to help them keep a sense of perspective and be a little less intense. Wearing the color orange will help them feel more spontaneous and encourage them to reach out to others.

Career *Born criminologists*

These people are well suited to careers in which they can express their creativity and indulge their curiosity; they may make superb criminologists, psychologists, writers, musicians, or pioneering scientists and engineers. Other careers that might appeal include administration, education, counseling and law, or occupations of a philosophical or religious nature.

Destiny *To expand the frontiers of human knowledge*

The life path of people born on this day is to balance the shadowy and the lighter sides of their personality. Once they have developed a healthy sense of balance and perspective, their destiny is to explore the unconventional and expand the frontiers of human knowledge.

Signs & symbols

Sun sign: Scorpio

Ruling planet: Mars, the warrior

Symbol: The Scorpion

Birth date ruler: Saturn, the teacher

Tarot card: Strength (passion)

Favorable numbers: 1, 8

Lucky days: Tuesday and Saturday, especially when these days fall on 1 and 8 of the month

Lucky colors: Red, burgundy, indigo

Birthstone: Topaz

November 8

9 November

the birthday of temptation

Many times during their lives people born on November 9 will find themselves in situations that test and challenge their resolve. Temptation and the moral issues it uncovers for them are a constant factor in their lives.

The pursuit of physical and material pleasure is a powerful drive for these people. The great majority of the time they do find a balance between satisfying their urges and doing the right thing, but occasionally they can dip into behavior that is morally questionable. This isn't to say that they are amoral. Quite the opposite; they are honest and well-intentioned individuals. It's just that sometimes they can get so caught up in the enticement of the moment that they lose a sense of perspective and of right and wrong.

Not surprisingly, these people are risk-takers, and this gives them the potential to go all the way to the top. Unfortunately, they aren't always good at dealing with rejection and, instead of treating it as a learning experience, they are likely to isolate themselves with resentment and self-pity. Learning to become more resilient or to roll with the blows by tapping into their inner strength is therefore essential for their psychological growth.

Until the age of forty-two, they are most likely to feel a need to expand their horizons, take risks and seek out new challenges. Developing a more positive attitude will encourage them to seek out opportunities that can enlighten rather than confuse or disorientate them. After the age of forty-three there is a turning point when they are likely to become more industrious and practical, needing a strong sense of order and structure in their lives. Making sure that the spiritual side of their life is not neglected is absolutely crucial during these years, because when they are able to connect with their inner wisdom they will not only be able to resist the temptations that block their chances of good fortune, they will be able to rise above these and achieve remarkable success both professionally and personally.

Love *Strong yearnings*

People born on November 9 love deeply and intensely, and, because they are extraordinarily seductive, they rarely lack admirers. Surprisingly, given their energetic and sexual nature, some born on this day may choose to be celibate. In the right mood they can be spontaneous and passionate, but they can also be moody and distant, which may confuse their partner.

Health *Strong reactions*

People born on this day may be prone to allergies of all kinds, in particular hay fever, but they may also find it hard to deal with cigarette smoke and dust. Keeping away from smoky environments and heavy traffic, and making sure their house is regularly cleaned and bed linen is washed at least once a week, will help. As far as diet is concerned, they could suffer from food allergies and intolerances; if this is the case, checking with a nutritionist to determine the cause is advisable. Because their lives tend to be stressful, making sure they eat a balanced diet, get plenty of exercise and a good night's sleep will all help keep them grounded. Meditation and yoga are also recommended to help them get in touch with their thoughts and feelings. Wearing, meditating on and surrounding themselves with the colors white or silver will encourage them to examine situations carefully, and make the right choices for themselves and for others.

Career *Born forensic officers*

The limitless possibilities of art and design have obvious appeal for these people but they may also be drawn toward law, psychology, research, or medicine. They have a natural talent for writing and lecturing, and may also excel in business, commerce, sales, promotion or negotiation, as well as show business and politics.

Destiny *To uncover the truth*

The life path of people born on this day is to learn to look beyond the present moment. Once they have an awareness of the future consequences of their actions, their destiny is to inspire others to uncover the truth about themselves and their lives.

Power Thought

" The path I choose is one of wisdom, light and joy "

Signs & symbols

Sun sign: Scorpio

Ruling planet: Mars, the warrior

Symbol: The Scorpion

Birth date ruler: Mars, the warrior

Tarot card: The Hermit (inner strength)

Favorable numbers: 2, 9

Lucky day: Tuesday, especially when it falls on 2 and 9 of the month

Lucky colors: Red, white, maroon

Birthstone: Topaz

1O November

the birthday of awareness

Your greatest challenge is ...

developing self-confidence

The way forward is ...

to understand that you are as confident as you believe yourself to be; change your thoughts about yourself and you can change your world.

You're drawn to people born on ...

July 23 to August 22

You both have what the other lacks, and this can create an intense and passionate bond.

Luck maker

Express your emotions

You won't attract luck if you are reserved. You need to be excited about everything, so people think of you as inspiring; the more appealing you are, the more likely you are to attract good fortune your way.

People born on November 10 are among the most self-aware of the year. From an early age they will have got to know their strengths and weaknesses very well, and as a result they have a realistic idea of what is or is not achievable for them. This self-knowledge gives them a huge advantage in the game of life and, when combined with their curiosity, intelligence and originality of thought, their potential for success is considerable.

These people don't simply have a unique understanding of themselves; they also have a natural understanding of how objects, strategies or methods work. For example, they are the first person to whom others will turn when things break down, because to others they are the fixers and menders in life.

There is, however, one subject of which people born on this day have very little understanding and awareness, and that is other people. Individual and group dynamics are a mystery to them, so when it comes to socializing and networking they may feel out of their depth. They need to learn that, however good they are at their job, if they don't have the right connections or social skills to promote themselves there is a strong likelihood that they will not get the recognition or success they deserve. Working on their self-confidence and social skills is therefore a top priority.

Fortunately, until the age of forty-two there are opportunities for them to step outside themselves and reach out to others; they should take these opportunities, however hard or frightening they may appear, because becoming unhealthily self-absorbed is a real risk to their chances of happiness and fulfillment. After the age of forty-three there is another turning point when they are likely to become more practical, disciplined and goal orientated; again, if they can learn to overcome their shyness, put the spotlight on others instead of themselves and resist the temptation to hold back when they should be pushing forward, they will be able to make the most of their remarkable creative potential and achieve almost anything.

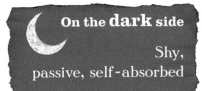

On the **dark** side

Shy, passive, self-absorbed

At your **best**

Self-aware, creative, practical

Love *Emotional damage*

People born on November 10 can come across as reserved, but once they have learned to be more confident in social settings they will have no problems attracting admirers. In relationships they can be intense and passionate, but there is a tendency for them to draw outwardly confident but inwardly emotionally damaged individuals to them. This will continue until they allow themselves to be more assertive.

Health *Confidence boost*

People born on this day tend to bottle up their emotions, and this can lead to stress and poor health. It is important for them to learn to open up and to be more trusting because when they do, all aspects of their life—emotional, physical and spiritual—will improve. Counseling and therapy could be beneficial. They also tend to have long-term health problems that they learn to live with, but instead of learning to live with these it would be far better if they took a proactive approach and constantly challenged their doctor for new treatments or new advice to ease their conditions. As far as diet is concerned, they love to eat a wide variety of different foods and, as long as they avoid excess, this is extremely positive for their health. Regular exercise, in particular dancing which can encourage them to be more expressive, is also highly recommended. Wearing the color orange will increase feelings of warmth, physical enjoyment, security, and sexuality, and wearing the color yellow will give them a confidence boost.

Career *Born academics*

Careers that offer them intermittent solitude appeal to these people and they may be drawn to academia, the arts and science. Other career choices include psychology, investigative work, education, philosophy, medicine, tourism, and the world of entertainment.

Destiny *To inspire others with their progressive concepts*

The life path of people born on this day is to learn to reach out to others with confidence. Once they have fine-tuned their people skills, their destiny is to enlighten, inspire or help others with their progressive concepts.

Signs & symbols

Sun sign: Scorpio

Ruling planet: Mars, the warrior

Symbol: The Scorpion

Birth date ruler: Sun, the individual

Tarot card: The Wheel of Fortune (change)

Favorable numbers: 1, 3

Lucky days: Tuesday and Sunday, especially when these days fall on 1 and 3 of the month

Lucky colors: Red, orange, yellow

Birthstone: Topaz

November 10

631

11 November

the birthday of the painted veil

Your greatest challenge is …

overcoming inertia

The way forward is …

to understand that you are letting fear or laziness take control of your actions. Change this by regaining control of your life.

You're drawn to people born on …

June 21 to July 22

You are both intense individuals and, if you can learn to give and take, this can be a fulfilling union.

Luck maker

Let others in

Locking everyone out never helps you get in touch with what you want. The more you share your ideas with others, the more others are likely to offer you opportunities.

People born on November 11 will often present an energetic, bright and cheerful face to the world, but to those who know them better this is more often than not a veil masking an intense and original but sometimes troubled personality.

These charismatic individuals know how to appear attractive to others and as a result they tend to get their own way, often without others realizing it because veiling their powerful ambition is, they believe, the best way to win others to their point of view. Above all, they are complex characters with the ability to surprise others with their hidden talents and unexpected sides to their character. Unfortunately, they are often extremely confused about what their motivations are, what they want out of life and in which direction they should be heading. This can obviously have a confusing effect on others, presenting a straightforward, energetic persona and clear-cut goals on the one hand, but manifesting a propensity for anxiety and uncertainty on the other. It is only when they are able to reconcile these two sides of their personality that their potential for success and happiness can finally be unveiled.

Until the age of forty there is a growing need for optimism and expansion through study, travel or a personal quest for meaning in life. If they can find a way to be more assertive in stating what their needs are, and be more flexible and creative when setbacks occur, the promise they may have showed from an early age will manifest. After the age of forty there is a turning point when they are likely to become more pragmatic and realistic in their approach to life.

It is more important than ever during these years that they don't allow hidden fears and insecurities to plunge them into procrastination, resentment and obscurity. This would be a tragedy because, if they can summon the courage to lift their veils, they are destined to shine, contributing their talents and energies to the greater good.

On the **dark** side

Insecure, dependent, unaware

At your **best**

Enthusiastic, inspiring, generous

Love *In need of guidance*

People born on November 11 are sociable and attractive, and their generous nature ensures they will have plenty of friends and admirers. When it comes to close relationships, however, they may find that they are drawn to older or parental figures who can take care of them and offer them support and guidance. As long as they understand this dynamic and don't abuse it, their potential for success and happiness in love is strong.

Health *Boost self-esteem*

People born on this day will often be extremely concerned about their appearance and physical health. Although this is a positive thing, they should not go to extremes because this will have the opposite effect from that which was intended, making them feel anxious, tired and unattractive. For example, they should not over-exercise, or go overboard with health and beauty treatments. Reminding themselves of the clichéd but true fact that beauty comes from within is important. They would benefit greatly from counseling and therapy to gain a better understanding of themselves; meditation and yoga are also recommended. There is a danger, however, of becoming over-dependent on doctors, gurus or health advisors. As far as diet is concerned, they could have addictive personalities and need to limit their intake of alcohol, caffeine, foods high in fat and sugar, and all kinds of recreational drugs. Wearing, meditating on and surrounding themselves with the color yellow will help them feel more confident and in control.

Career *Born builders*

These people may lean toward careers that involve writing, performing or research, those in which they can demonstrate hands-on skills such as building, repair or technical work. They may also become good psychologists, advisors, lecturers, and teachers. Occupations connected to the public or tourism might appeal, as might community or charity work.

Destiny *To assist, direct and inspire others by their example*

The life path of people born on this day is to learn to set themselves goals. Once they have found a sense of direction, their destiny is to assist, direct or inspire others with their positive example.

Power Thought

❝I am a rich treasure ready to be found ❞

Signs & symbols

Sun sign: Scorpio

Ruling planet: Mars, the warrior

Symbol: The Scorpion

Birth date ruler: Moon, the intuitive

Tarot card: Justice (discernment)

Favorable numbers: 2, 4

Lucky days: Tuesday and Monday, especially when these days fall on 2 and 4 of the month

Lucky colors: Red, silver, milky white

Birthstone: Topaz

November 11

12 November

the birthday of mesmerizing prerogative

Your greatest challenge is …

taking responsibility

The way forward is …

to understand that until you can own up to the part you play in shaping your destiny, life will feel confusing and out of control.

You're drawn to people born on …

October 23 to November 21

You are both sensual and uninhibited; if you can learn to be more tolerant, this can be an electrifying union.

Luck maker

Be a role model

Think of yourself as an inspiring role model for the next generation. When you think about what others can admire about you, your behavior will soon catch up and attract luck your way.

People born on November 12 feel it is their right to attract attention or get whatever they want from others and from life. With such powerful expectations, the chances should be good for their success and happiness. Unfortunately, in some cases the opposite is true.

These people have the potential to be the most mesmerizing and seductive individuals of the year. In some cases others don't just listen to or even follow them, but worship the fact that they can bring excitement and beauty into their lives. Their boldness and imagination are outstanding, but unfortunately they aren't always the positive force they seem to have been destined to be from an early age. This is because they have a tendency to flout not just convention but moral and ethical codes to get what they want. In some cases the ends may justify the means, but there will also be times when they do not; their success may depend on how subtle they are in bending the rules, and how considerate and kind they are toward others.

Despite their golden aura, in many ways they are complex individuals able to bring beauty and harmony to the world, but possessing deep internal conflicts between their strong, sometimes dark and always confusing emotions. These conflicts may prevent them from realizing their goals and it is only after great personal struggle that they are finally in a position to claim their victory.

Until the age of thirty-nine there is an emphasis in their lives on adventure and freedom, and they may wish to explore and expand their mental outlook through study or travel. After the age of forty there is a turning point when they are likely to take a more disciplined and practical approach. Whatever age they are, the key to their success will be their ability to remember the importance of the emotional well-being that is vital to their happiness. When they are able to do that, happiness and success won't just be their prerogative—they will be their reality.

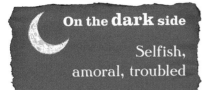

On the dark side

Selfish, amoral, troubled

At your best

Illuminating, magnetic, generous

Love *Lucky in love*

People born on November 12 are charming, seductive and sensual, and attracting partners comes easily to them. Once in a relationship they can be loyal and passionate, as well as tender. They can, however, sometimes have problems accepting that they are loved and may try to provoke tension or conflict, where there is none, to elicit a response.

Health *You are what you think*

People born on this day need to remember that what they think about tends to manifest in their lives, so if their thoughts are negative they will attract people who are negative. This is especially the case for them as they are so mesmerizing that others tend to gravitate toward them. Learning to concentrate and retrain their thoughts is therefore essential for their success, as well as their physical and emotional health. As far as diet is concerned, they may be prone to comfort eating, and again will-power is called for. Regular exercise, in particular running, may also help take their mind off food, as can chatting with friends, taking up a hobby or treating themselves to a massage or a good book. Meditation, yoga and the study of spirituality may also be beneficial, and wearing and meditating on the color purple will encourage them to think less of themselves and more of higher things.

Career *Born gurus*

Although a lot of these people's energy will be taken up by their internal conflict they have a great deal of energy left over for others, and this may lead to an interest in careers in which they can offer their support, advice and assistance. They may be drawn to teaching, the healing or caring professions, medicine, law, the emergency services, social and charity work. In addition, they possess a good aptitude for business, promotion and sales, or may choose to become actors, directors, writers, and musicians.

Destiny *To give an illuminating gift to humanity*

The life path of people born on this day is to learn that it is not just their right to be happy and fulfilled, but everyone's right. Once they have learned to confront their inner demons, their destiny is to make an illuminating gift to humanity.

Signs & symbols

Sun sign: Scorpio

Ruling planet: Mars, the warrior

Symbol: The Scorpion

Birth date ruler: Jupiter, the speculator

Tarot card: The Hanged Man (reflection)

Favorable numbers: 3, 5

Lucky days: Tuesday and Thursday, especially when these days fall on 3 and 5 of the month

Lucky colors: Red, purple, royal blue

Birthstone: Topaz

November 12

13 November

the birthday of conversion

Your greatest challenge is …

changing your mind

The way forward is …

to understand that refusing to acknowledge alternative viewpoints or possibilities blocks the possibility of change and progress.

You're drawn to people born on …

April 20 to May 19

You are passionate and sensual; if you both guard against stubbornness this can be a rewarding and fulfilling union.

Luck maker

Open your mind

An open and curious mind is an essential luck-making tool. Narrow-minded people miss opportunities because when something better comes along they are so wrapped up in their familiar beliefs that they can't see it.

People born on November 13 are highly observant, with strong and passionate convictions. They can absorb all kinds of data, subject it to rigorous analysis and then pronounce their strong opinions. At some point they may have undergone a powerful conversion of some kind which now influences all their beliefs and opinions.

The views that these people present to the world tend to be well informed but their personal conviction will always shine through. The conversion that they may have undergone will not necessarily have been religious, it could simply be a specific way of looking at the world; but whatever it was, there is a tendency for them to gather information to support their beliefs rather than the other way around. This is not to say that they are not logical or reasonable. Quite the opposite; their opinions will always be well presented and clearly thought out. It's just that they are so optimistic and passionate in their beliefs that they find it impossible to acknowledge that there can be any other truth than their own.

Until the age of thirty-eight they tend to be at their most zealous, with a strong emphasis on idealism and optimism. It is extremely important during these years that they don't become inflexible and authoritarian, and make a real effort to take on board what other people are saying to them. After the age of thirty-nine there is a turning point when they start to have a more determined and disciplined approach to life. During these years it's crucial that they don't allow their idealism to slip into dogmatism. If they can learn to be more flexible in their beliefs, they are less likely to alienate or offend others and attract misfortune.

Whatever age they are, getting to know themselves better will help them see that having strong opinions is not the same as having a sense of self. With a more flexible and open mind they will discover within themselves the potential to promote their cause or their opinions in a remarkable way.

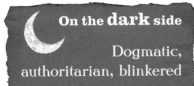

At your **best**
Passionate, determined, spiritual

Love *Determined and inspiring individuals*

People born on November 13 are often attracted to hardworking, determined and inspiring individuals like themselves who share similar beliefs. It would be healthier for them, however, if they chose a partner with a different set of beliefs or way of approaching life, as this would encourage them to be open-minded. Once in a relationship they can be devoted and affectionate, but they have a tendency to be insecure.

Health *The healing powers of music*

People born on this day tend to lead fast-paced lives and, if they don't give themselves enough time to relax and unwind, they can become very unhappy and exhausted. Music can be a great healer for them, in particular classical music. Many born on this day could also benefit from more time spent in the countryside observing the natural rhythms of nature and the seasons. Yoga and meditation are also highly recommended, as well as karate or other disciplines which involve some kind of mental training. Regular moderate to mild exercise is recommended, as is a healthy balanced diet low in salt and sugar, because high blood pressure and weight gain could be a health risk for them. Wearing, meditating on and surrounding themselves with the color green will encourage them to have a sense of balance and perspective; the color blue will encourage them to be more objective.

Career *Born politicians*

These people may find themselves drawn to scientific or technical careers, but they may also be interested in professions that enable them to instruct or inspire others such as teaching, journalism, politics, or religion. Other work options include writing, law, psychology, research, lecturing, and the medical and healing professions. Whatever career they choose, it is important for them to have a passionate belief in it.

Destiny *To inform or enlighten others*

The life path of people born on this day is to learn to open their mind to let other viewpoints in. Once they have greater objectivity, their destiny is to inform or enlighten others.

Signs & symbols

Sun sign: Scorpio

Ruling planet: Mars, the warrior

Symbol: The Scorpion

Birth date ruler: Uranus, the visionary

Tarot card: Death (change)

Favorable numbers: 4, 6

Lucky days: Tuesday and Sunday, especially when these days fall on 4 and 6 of the month

Lucky colors: Red, silver, electric blue

Birthstone: Topaz

14 November

the birthday of the guide

Your greatest challenge is …

being sensitive to the feelings of others

The way forward is …

to understand that the truth presented tactfully can be motivational but the truth presented harshly can make others defensive.

You're drawn to people born on …

June 21 to July 22

You both have a lot to learn and love about each other, and this can be a passionate and creative union.

Luck maker

Thrust and squeeze

The bonding power of a firm handshake signifies energy, trust and strength and is more likely to impress people and make them want to offer their support than a limp wrist. Most lucky people have firm handshakes.

People born on November 14 have an intense and earnest air about them, others immediately sensing their conviction and self-reliance. They are driven by their desire to fully understand what life presents them with but most of all by their urge to guide others toward improvement.

Tending to observe others with a degree of affectionate distance, this gives these people the detachment and objectivity they need to guide and improve the lives of others. More often than not the insights and advice they offer are embraced wholeheartedly by colleagues, friends and loved ones, but sometimes they can be too meddling. It is important for them to understand that there are situations in which their advice will not necessarily be welcome and occasions where their judgments will not be appreciated.

Until the age of thirty-seven there will be opportunities for people born on this day to become more expansive in their outlook and, because of their tendency to connect with others on an intellectual rather than an emotional level, they should try to integrate more with others and with society as a whole. It is also important during this time that they evaluate their choice of career intensely and if need be make changes, because it might significantly impact their psychological growth. After the age of thirty-eight there is a turning point when they may become more realistic, persevering and security conscious, seeking more structure and order.

Whatever career they choose, they tend to see themselves as teachers or guides and have all the passion, integrity and intellect they need to be a positive force in the lives of others. However, it is not until they are able to turn the spotlight on their own needs, in particular their own need for guidance and support, that they will be able to balance their orientation toward others with their own needs. Ironically, it is only when they can find what gives their own life meaning and fulfillment that they can truly assist others, becoming the inspirational guide and role model they were destined to be.

On the **dark** side
Interfering, controlling, frustrated

At your **best**
Intelligent, observant, helpful

Love *Trust is everything*

Relationships are deep and intense for people born on November 14, and trust means everything to them. It may take them a while to give that trust, but once they do they love forever, sometimes even when that trust is betrayed. They are attracted to dramatic and intelligent people like themselves, who can inspire them to be more expressive and original than they already are.

Health *Naturopathy*

People born on this day may suffer from mild rashes and bouts of insomnia. These could be food intolerances but could also be a result of unnecessary stress and anxiety about their health. They may visit their doctor once too often for minor ailments; although it is important to take precautions, they should have more faith in their body's ability to heal itself; perhaps studying the principles of naturopathy will be beneficial. As far as diet is concerned, they tend to be very good cooks and, as long as they don't go overboard on sugar, salt and rich sauces and spices, their diet is often healthy. If weight is a problem they need to make sure that they don't get obsessed with exercise, reminding themselves that although regular exercise is beneficial for health and will help them lose weight, the key to weight control often lies in the head; they may need to stop thinking of themselves as overweight. Carrying a quartz crystal will help boost their mood and reenergize their zest and vitality in all situations.

Career *Born advisors*

These people have a natural affinity with careers in which they can help, guide or assist others, such as social work, therapy, the medical professions, counseling, and teaching. They may also be drawn toward writing, research and psychology, as well as the theater, music and the arts.

Destiny *To guide, assist and inspire others*

The life path of people born on this day is to learn to maintain a healthy intellectual and emotional equilibrium. Once they have learned to balance their own needs with those of others, their destiny is to offer practical and emotional support, guidance and assistance to others.

Signs & symbols

Sun sign: Scorpio

Ruling planet: Mars, the warrior

Symbol: The Scorpion

Birth date ruler: Mercury, the communicator

Tarot card: Temperance (moderation)

Favorable numbers: 5, 7

Lucky days: Tuesday and Wednesday, especially when these days fall on 5 and 7 of the month

Lucky colors: Dark blue, deep red, green

Birthstone: Topaz

November 14

15 November

the birthday of the cobra

Your greatest challenge is …

really trusting other people

The way forward is …

to appreciate that people tend to respond to your expectations of them; approach them in the spirit of trust and they are likely to return the favor.

You're drawn to people born on …

April 20 to May 20

You have much to learn from each other about passion, emotions, spontaneity, and purpose.

Luck maker

Emit a new signal

What you are suspicious of, you tend to attract because you are powerfully focused on it. To change your fortunes for the better, go within and emit a new signal with your thoughts and feelings.

People born on November 15 have an air of the unexpected about them. Smooth and slick but with the deadly accuracy of a cobra, they can strike out suddenly and unexpectedly in defense or attack.

These people never have a straightforward existence and their life appears to be a series of unforeseen encounters, challenges or confrontations; but instead of crumbling under this kind of intensity, they thrive on it. In fact, these people are unlikely to avoid any kind of conflict or challenge, and once engaged in an argument they will never be the first to back down. They are brilliant at defending themselves and finding the weak spot in their opponent's arguments or situation—they are enemies to be truly feared. They also know how to wait until the moment is right to strike; when they do, their timing is typically perfect.

What these people often fail to appreciate is that not every situation in their lives is a battle. They can be suspicious or covert when they don't need to be and this can alienate others or create negativity when there is no cause for it. Sometimes, too, their love of challenge and change can make them create conflict just for the sake of it to enjoy the "excitement" it generates.

Until the age of thirty-six their risk-taking tendencies will be at their most intense and there will be many opportunities for them to take chances, some of which will pay off, some of which won't. After the age of thirty-seven, however, there is a significant turning point when they may start to become more disciplined and realistic. This is a positive development but, whatever age they are, injecting a healthy dose of optimism and self-belief into their lives to balance out their undercover tendencies will give them the courage to keep their spirit of adventure alive. It might also give them sufficient confidence and trust to put down their sword so that their heart of gold, and clear potential for happiness, success and fulfillment, can come out into the open.

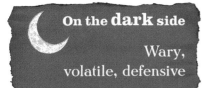
Love *Fascinating attraction*

When it comes to affairs of the heart, people born on November 15 can be highly skeptical and noncommittal, preferring to keep their feelings to themselves, but they can also be extremely affectionate and seductive. Although this can send out very mixed signals to potential partners, it can also add to their fascination and attraction. The right partner, however, will be able to teach them that love is about letting go and being free to trust.

Health *Your own worst enemy*

People born on this day may expend a lot of energy on resisting the "attacks" of others, but their greatest enemy is themselves. They create an incredible amount of stress and tension for themselves and, if they could learn to be more trusting and open, they would find that their emotional well-being changed for the better. As far as their physical health is concerned, they tend to be fighting fit but can be accident prone. When it comes to diet, they should cut down on saturated fats, animal products, sugar, additives, and preservatives, increasing their intake of whole grains, fruits and vegetables. Vigorous exercise is highly recommended, in particular martial arts—as long as they exercise caution—as they will safely release pent-up energy. Wearing, meditating on and surrounding themselves with the color orange will encourage them to be more spontaneous, trusting and open.

Career *Born secret agents*

These people will tend to gravitate toward roles where they can be constantly challenged, and to careers that involve plenty of travel and change. The secret service and military careers may appeal, as might the work of a bodyguard. Business, politics and law are other options, and they may also have a gift for writing, acting and music.

Destiny *To prepare others for the unexpected*

The life path of people born on this day is to learn to trust and let go more. Once they have become less suspicious of everyone and everything, their destiny is to keep the spirit of adventure alive and help others prepare for the unexpected.

Signs & symbols

Sun sign: Scorpio

Ruling planet: Mars, the warrior

Symbol: The Scorpion

Birth date ruler: Venus, the lover

Tarot card: The Devil (choices)

Favorable numbers: 6, 8

Lucky days: Tuesday and Friday, especially when these days fall on 6 and 8 of the month

Lucky colors: Deep red, lavender, pink

Birthstone: Topaz

November 15

16 November

the birthday of the authority

Your greatest challenge is …

resisting the urge to control everything

The way forward is …

to understand that true leaders or directors empower others to make their own decisions.

You're drawn to people born on …

February 19 to March 20

This is a sensual and passionate pairing where you can give each other the magic you have been longing for.

Luck maker

Let go of anger

Forgiveness is tough but it is also a powerful luck magnet. This is because when you are weighed down with anger or guilt you can't move forward, and the energy you need to create luck is blocked.

People born on November 16 have a naturally authoritative manner and, because they are also intelligent, perceptive and display a remarkable strength of purpose, their command is rarely questioned. In addition, they usually have the best interests of everyone at heart. As a result, people learn to listen to what they have to say and more often than not follow their advice or instructions.

Fiercely individualistic and independent, these people may have challenged the status quo as children or teenagers. As they grow older, however, they often reach the conclusion that they can be more effective agents for change if they work within the system to try and change it for the better, rather than being a lone voice on the outside. They are particularly well suited to leadership roles where they can exert a powerful or informative influence over others.

Those around them generally respect their conviction and genuine desire to promote the common good, as well as the tact they display when enlisting support for their aims. There will be times, however, when their urge to enlighten and inspire others is so strong that their behavior becomes controlling, manipulative or intolerant, and they stubbornly refuse to acknowledge any other way forward but their way.

Until the age of thirty-five they are likely to want to expand their horizons though study or travel. After the age of thirty-six they reach a turning point where they start to take a more practical, ordered and realistic approach to life. Whatever age they are, it is important for them to make sure that they use their natural authority wisely and don't abuse the position of trust they tend to earn for themselves. If they can remember always to keep the interests of others in their mind and to respect others' right to hold different opinions to their own, not only will they become a voice of unquestionable authority, they also have the creativity and imagination to become a voice of insight, inspiration and wisdom.

On the **dark** side
Self-involved, controlling, judgmental

At your **best**
Authoritative, influential, understanding

Love *Learn to take as well as give*

Despite being incredibly generous and supportive themselves, people born on this day can have big problems accepting the help, support or even love of others. It is crucial for their emotional well-being that they learn to trust more and open their heart, because the loyalty and support of a loving partner are of vital importance to them. Sometimes a sense of true happiness and fulfillment will be delayed until that partner takes center stage.

Health *By the seaside*

People born on this day often feel attuned to the sea or ocean, and spending time by the coast can help relax and calm them. Swimming is a fantastic way for them to exercise. If they have a sedentary lifestyle they are strongly advised to get up and move more, because exercise has wonderful mood-boosting powers, not to mention the fact that it will also speed up their metabolism and help them lose weight if they have weight to lose. As far as diet and lifestyle are concerned, overeating could be a problem, as could heavy alcohol consumption. As these could both lead to weight and liver problems, they are strongly advised to eat a healthy, balanced diet and to cut down on alcohol. Relaxing herbal teas and foot massages are music to their souls, carrying the crystal citrine in their purse or wallet can help them deal with anger and frustration in any situation, and the crystal turquoise will encourage them to reach out to others.

Career *Born managers*

These people will often be drawn to politics and teaching, as well as more artistic activities where they can inspire a broader audience. Possible work options include self-employment, research, education, law, philosophy, psychology, sales, water sports, diving, writing, and acting. In the world of business they are likely to assume management or directorship roles.

Destiny *To further the boundaries of human endeavor*

The life path of people born on this day is to learn to use their authority wisely. Once they have the best interests of both themselves and others at heart, their destiny is to further the boundaries of human knowledge and endeavor.

Signs & symbols

Sun sign: Scorpio

Ruling planet: Mars, the warrior

Symbol: The Scorpion

Birth date ruler: Neptune, the visionary

Tarot card: The Tower (breakthrough)

Favorable numbers: 7, 9

Lucky days: Tuesday and Monday, especially when these days fall on 7 and 9 of the month

Lucky colors: Deep red, sea green, sky blue

Birthstone: Topaz

17 November

the birthday of the facilitator

Your greatest challenge is …

setting yourself clear goals

The way forward is …

to remember that going with the flow or following the herd can sometimes lead you over the cliff.

You're drawn to people born on …

December 22 to January 19

You are both adventurous and sensual, with much to learn about balancing spontaneity with a clear sense of direction.

Luck maker

Find your purpose

Don't just think about what you want, think about why you want it. You need to know why you want something before you can start to make it happen.

People born on November 17 are extremely intuitive and sensitive, with a powerful orientation toward others. Many times in their lives they will find themselves in the important role of integrator or facilitator.

One of the reasons these people are so good at encouraging others to work better together or ensuring that everyone gets on and things run smoothly is that they have a real understanding of the importance of compromise. Perhaps in their own lives they have had to learn the hard way that in the real world everyone can't get exactly what they want and that there is always a certain amount of trade-off. For example, they may have given up their dreams of performing to teach instead, or have scaled down their career to devote more time to their family. Whatever the nature of the compromise, they have convinced themselves that greater satisfaction can be found by placing the interests of others above their own.

This rightfully earns them great respect from others, but the downside is that they can become overly dependent on the satisfaction they get from helping others. They may also have a tendency to over-identify with the concerns of others, neglecting their own interests and psychological growth in the process. Until the age of thirty-four these people are more likely to take chances but after the age of thirty-five they reach a turning point when they start to become more progressive, determined and serious in their approach to life. After the age of sixty-five they begin to place more emphasis on friendship and independence.

Whatever age they are, it is crucial that they don't shut down emotionally and over-identify with the role of facilitator. As valuable and important as that role is, nothing is more valuable and important for their psychological growth—and for their ability to unlock the outstanding potential for success and happiness associated with this birthday—than their acknowledgment of and willingness to express their own dynamic creativity, independence and sense of purpose.

On the **dark** side

Unfocused, self-sacrificing, aloof

At your **best**

Helpful, inspiring, charming

Power Thought

" Today I will express my creativity in ways that fulfill me "

Love *Don't be a pushover*

People born on November 17 are charming, romantic, intelligent, and compassionate, and it is no surprise that they will often be surrounded by admirers. They are strongly advised to take their time and exercise their good judgment rather than being a pushover or giving more than they take in a relationship. The right partner for them will be someone who has a big heart but who is detached enough to give them the freedom they need to be themselves.

Health *Me time*

People born on this day tend to be so involved in the lives of others and so needed by them that they don't have a lot of time for themselves. Their spirits will suffer, however, if they don't give themselves plenty of time to pursue their own interests and indulge their latent creativity. If they don't allow themselves this space and freedom they will be prone to unexplained bouts of depression and insomnia. As far as their physical health is concerned, they need to pay attention to their posture as back pain could be an issue. They also need to make sure they don't ignore warning signs of poor health and schedule regular check-ups with their doctor. When it comes to food, digestive disorders may occur, and increasing their intake of fiber and drinking plenty of water as well as a glass of lemon juice first thing every morning are advised, as is regular mild exercise. Carrying a tiger's eye crystal will promote confidence and courage.

Career *Born interviewers*

These people tend to do well in careers that involve plenty of teamwork and cooperation, but they can also do well in media, sales, business, journalism, or lecturing. The dramatic side of their multi-talented character may find fulfillment in politics, design, fashion, retail, theater, or show business.

Destiny *To follow their hearts and to inspire others to do the same*

The life path of people born on this day is to learn that it is okay to be themselves and to express their creativity and originality. Once they have found a healthy balance between their own needs and those of others, their destiny is to progress in a positive direction and empower others to do the same.

Signs & symbols

Sun sign: Scorpio

Ruling planet: Mars, the warrior

Symbol: The Scorpion

Birth date ruler: Saturn, the teacher

Tarot card: The Star (hope)

Favorable numbers: 1, 8

Lucky days: Tuesday and Saturday, especially when these days fall on 1 and 8 of the month

Lucky colors: Deep red, burgundy, brown

Birthstone: Topaz

645

18 November

the birthday of sensitive exuberance

Like a ray of warm sunshine, the exuberant, energetic individuals born on November 18 have the ability to enliven any situation with their good cheer, optimism and humor. They are refreshingly upbeat in their approach to everyone and everything, and not surprisingly their company is much sought after.

Not only do they enjoy being the center of attention, they are also fiercely ambitious, making them natural candidates for leadership. Those who do not know them well, however, would be surprised to discover that underneath the happy face they present to the world there can be a lot of uncertainty and conflict. This is because they are unusually sensitive to the feelings of others, sometimes to the extent that they don't know where their feelings end and another person's begin. As a result, despite their clear potential and suitability to be winners or innovators in life, they often end up feeling confused, purposeless and directionless.

If they can find a way to balance their sensitivity toward others with their ambitious urge to realize their own life goals, their success is assured. If, however, the balance tilts in either direction they can lose a sense of direction; the indecisiveness that results can stunt their psychological growth, blocking their chances of professional and personal success.

Until the age of thirty-three there is an emphasis in their lives on issues relating to freedom, adventure and expansion. They may want to study, travel or experiment with their choice of career in these years. After the age of thirty-four there is an important turning point when they are likely to become more responsible, precise and practical in their approach to life, seeking structure and order. Whatever age they are, however, they need to use their sharp and probing mind to investigate their own power and potential. This is because with greater self-awareness and greater belief in their star potential—and a lot of dedication and hard work—these vivacious individuals can achieve almost anything they set their mind to.

On the **dark** side

Needy, moody, confused

At your **best**

Innovative, entertaining, vivacious

Love *Exceptionally responsive*

People born on November 18 can be fun, sexy, entertaining, responsive, and romantic as long as their partner gives them plenty of attention and affection. But if the reassurance they need isn't given, they can lapse into attention-seeking behavior and temperamental mood swings. It is important for them to make sure they are with a partner who is as giving and energetic as they are.

Health *Boosting self-esteem*

People born on this day tend to have a rather negative image of themselves, and this can make them prone to stress and depression. Boosting their self-esteem is therefore absolutely crucial to both their physical and emotional health. The place to start is in their heads, and cognitive behavioral therapy techniques may be able to help them reprogram their thoughts from negative to positive. Spending more time with people who are upbeat and optimistic, and avoiding those who are glum and self-involved, will also help, as will a diet rich in fresh, natural produce and low in refined or processed foods. Regular moderate to vigorous exercise is also highly recommended for its mood-boosting and health-boosting effects, as well as for building up discipline and will-power. Carrying a tiger's eye crystal or placing it next to their bed at night will have a balancing and calming effect, promoting greater confidence and courage.

Career *Born innovators*

People born on this day may be drawn to careers in science, research or technology where they can be potential innovators, as well as the world of art, music and literature, where they can excel as writers. Once they believe more in themselves, other career options might include business, teaching, lecturing, politics, and the world of entertainment.

Destiny *To point others in the direction of progress*

The life path of people born on this day is to learn to believe in themselves and their creativity more. Once they are able to discover their sense of purpose, their destiny is to achieve or point the way to tangible progress on behalf of themselves and others.

Signs & symbols

Sun sign: Scorpio

Ruling planet: Mars, the warrior

Symbol: The Scorpion

Birth date ruler: Mars, the warrior

Tarot card: The Moon (imagination)

Favorable numbers: 2, 9

Lucky days: Tuesday, especially when these days fall on 2 and 9 of the month

Lucky colors: All shades of red

Birthstone: Topaz

November 18

19 November

the birthday of the crusader

Your greatest challenge is …

to think before you act

The way forward is …

to understand that sometimes the best way to resolve a situation is by biding your time. Let some time pass and it may maximize your chances of success.

You're drawn to people born on …

July 23 to August 22

Although you will have your fair share of conflict, this is a fiery, intense and passionate relationship between equals.

Luck maker

Believe something better will happen

When things don't go according to plan, concentrate on positive expectations for the future and believe there must be something better in store.

People born on November 19 tend to focus their energies outward onto their progressive goals. Born reformers, they are at their happiest and best when they can take on the role of crusader or of the representative of a revolutionary cause that aims to replace the old and the outdated with the new and innovative.

These people may have felt from an early age that they were destined to make a significant contribution to the world, and there is something about them which makes people stop and stare. Whatever life path they choose, their ultimate purpose is to play a part in changing the lives of others for the better. They will often do this by directing or organizing other people according to principles which they believe will benefit the greater good.

The confidence and crusading sense of purpose with which they are blessed will often propel them into the limelight as natural leaders; people tend to look to them for motivation and guidance. Their confidence, however, can also work against them because their self-belief can be so powerful at times that they close their ears and minds to alternative viewpoints, as well as to common sense. It is important for them to resist the urge to act on impulse. They should weigh up the pros and cons and listen to the advice of others before making decisions because, although they come close, they are not and never will be superhuman.

Until the age of thirty-two they may want to extend their mental horizons through study and travel, but after the age of thirty-three there is a turning point when they are likely to become more responsible, precise and hard-working in their approach to life. Whatever age they are, once they learn to pace themselves, take on board the advice of others and never allow pride to get in the way of progress, they will not only realize their dream of making a significant contribution to the world, they will play a vital part in changing it for the better.

On the **dark** side

Blinkered, over-confident, proud

At your **best**

Progressive, energetic, ambitious

Love *Dynamic and idealistic*

Although they are never short of admirers, people born on November 19 would rather be alone than invest their energy in a relationship that isn't going anywhere. They are attracted to people who are as dynamic, loyal and idealistic as themselves, but to ensure long-term success when it comes to affairs of the heart they need to make sure that they don't slip into selfish, moody or controlling behavior.

Health *You are what you eat*

Fatigue or low energy could be a problem for people born on this day. This could be due to dieting and low nutrient intake or simply to careless fast-food eating. It is extremely important that they make sure they get enough essential fats and vitamins in their diet, especially vitamin B12 if they are vegetarians. Taking a multi-vitamin and mineral supplement is advised, but the best investment in their health is to make sure they eat a healthy, balanced diet. Regular exercise, in particular jogging or vigorous sports like squash, is also beneficial for them as it will help release pent-up tension and improve their powers of concentration. They would also benefit from meditation, yoga or any discipline which encourages them to take a step back and be more objective in their thinking and reacting. Wearing, meditating on and surrounding themselves with the color blue will help them stay cool emotionally and mentally, as will carrying a titanium quartz crystal.

Career *Born high flyers*

Whatever career they choose, these people have the conviction and energy to take them all the way to the top. Work options that might appeal include business, where they are likely to assume management roles, social reform, promotion, charity work, politics, media, law, sales, public relations, lecturing, acting, counseling, and the media.

Destiny *To champion their progressive convictions*

The life path of people born on this day is to learn to look before they leap. Once they have learned the value of good judgment and patience, their destiny is to champion and encourage others to embrace their progressive convictions.

Power Thought

" My choices are based on thoughtfulness, humility, love and compassion "

Signs & symbols

Sun sign: Scorpio

Ruling planet: Mars, the warrior

Symbol: The Scorpion

Birth date ruler: Sun, the individual

Tarot card: The Sun (enthusiasm)

Favorable numbers: 1, 3

Lucky days: Tuesday and Monday, especially when these days fall on 1 and 3 of the month

Lucky colors: Red, orange, gold

Birthstone: Topaz

November 19

20 November

the birthday of the wrestler

Your greatest challenge is …

not to take yourself too seriously

The way forward is …

to understand that a lighthearted, subtle approach can often have just as much impact and power as a forceful, direct one.

You're drawn to people born on …

June 21 to July 22

You are both spontaneous and instinctual in your approach to life, and this can be a loving and passionate union.

Luck maker

Treat everyone as potential helpers

Lucky people treat everyone with respect, no matter what their qualifications, background or status are. Who knows who could eventually be of help to you?

Struggle is a major theme for people born on November 20. This can express itself in a struggle for recognition in the outside world or an inner conflict where the impulsive and impatient aspects of their personality wrestle for dominance with the more self-controlled and disciplined urges.

From an early age, these people will never have been afraid of standing up for what is right, even if that means standing alone. They are capable of incredible fixity of purpose and energy; more often than not they will blaze a pioneering trail though life, inspiring many others along the way to follow their lead. If a cause or an authority figure does not have their respect, however, they will strongly and openly criticize or reject it, sometimes making enemies they don't need along the way. This impulsive response, although honest and direct, is not surprising given that they have an emotional response to life. In fact, much of their life is ruled by their never-changing emotions; one moment they are optimistic and enthusiastic, the next they are bitterly disillusioned and in the depths of despair. Although their intensity and seriousness of purpose will attract considerable success and respect, they would feel far happier and more fulfilled if they could find it within their hearts to take themselves just a little less seriously.

Before the age of thirty-one they are most likely to move forward with their lives in a spirit of optimism; these are the years when they are most likely to take risks. After the age of thirty-two, however, there is a turning point when they are likely gradually and over a period of years to become more practical, ambitious and realistic in their approach to life, desiring order and structure.

The key to their success—whatever their age and stage in life—will be their ability to acknowledge and accept their emotions, in particular their anger, successfully. This will give them the mental advantage they need to triumph over almost any obstacle, challenge or opponent that stands in their way.

Power Thought

"I am calm and in control"

Love *Love sick*

People born on this day are kind-hearted, generous and sincere, but they can be possessive and selfish at times, and are also prone to mood swings. They have deep and powerful emotions but will sometimes try to chase people who they know will turn them down simply because they love the thrill of the chase and, for reasons even they could not explain, the melancholy of lovesickness.

Health *Anger management*

People born on this day have a rash and impulsive side and this can make them accident and injury prone. If anyone was prone to road rage, bank rage, supermarket rage, or any kind of rage it would be them, and they may benefit from anger-management techniques. Regular moderate to vigorous exercise is strongly advised for its health-boosting and calming effects, and learning how to relax and not to take things so personally is also helpful. As far as exercise is concerned, they need to increase their intake of whole grains, fruits and vegetables, and to eat less red meat and rich food. One of the best ways to boost their health, however, will be for them to find the stability they need in a long-term loving relationship. Wearing, meditating on and surrounding themselves with the color blue will help them keep calm during times of crisis and uncertainty.

Career *Born business leaders*

These people tend to excel in business-related careers, but their dramatic sense can also help them succeed in politics, the entertainment world or the arts. Other work options include education, writing, sales, city planning, environmental issues, and charity work.

Destiny *To lead so others can follow*

The life path of people born on this day is to learn to understand and manage their emotions. Once they understand that emotions have important messages to deliver, their destiny is to blaze a pioneering trail through life for others to follow.

Signs & symbols

Sun sign: Scorpio

Ruling planet: Mars, the warrior

Symbol: The Scorpion

Birth date ruler: Moon, the intuitive

Tarot card: Judgment (responsibility)

Favorable numbers: 2, 4

Lucky days: Tuesday and Monday, especially when these days fall on 2 and 4 of the month

Lucky colors: Red, silver, white

Birthstone: Topaz

21 November

the birthday of finesse

Your greatest challenge is …

intimacy

The way forward is …

to understand that opening yourself up to someone else is not a sign of weakness, but a sign that you are human.

You're drawn to people born on …

November 22 to December 21

As long as there is no secrecy or pretense, this can be an intense and passionate union.

Luck maker

Luck loves openness

Expressive and open people are appealing and more likely to get offers of help than people who are self-contained and closed. Because they are alive and energetic, helping them makes us feel alive and energetic.

People born on November 21 love freedom and live by their own rules, but they also have a strong sense of justice, their mission being nothing less than to change the world. Regal and refined by nature, they are natural leaders who have no trouble working with the best, and more often than not being the best.

Those born on this day bring a quality touch to everything they do, and a major theme in their lives is refinement, and an insistence on creating and surrounding themselves with excellence. This finesse can manifest itself in their bewitchingly stylish appearance or approach, and it can manifest itself internally in the fine-tuning of their ideas. However it manifests itself over the years, they will be constantly improving and refining themselves in some way and, in the process, attracting considerable success and respect from others. This will not just be for their ability to learn from their mistakes, but also for their ability to make the impossible seem possible. The only downside with this careful, detailed approach is that it can make them a little too self-reliant, smooth and serious; they run the risk of losing their sense of humor and spontaneity along the way.

Until the age of thirty these people may find that they want to experiment and broaden their horizons; these are the years when they are most likely to make mistakes professionally or choose professions to which they are unsuited. After the age of thirty, however, there is a turning point when they are likely to take a more disciplined, determined and serious approach to life, ensuring that they make fewer and fewer mistakes professionally.

They need to beware of making the biggest mistake of all: denying themselves the happiness and fulfillment of close relationships with their fellow human beings. But once they have got in touch with their own feelings and the feelings of others, they have the ability to rise above any difficult situation and solve problems—perhaps even change the world for the better—with their inspired thinking.

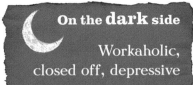
Love *Keeping a distance*

People born on November 21 like to be their own boss, and their self-reliant search for perfection can make them loners. Intimacy can be a problem, and they may use their ironic sense of humor to keep everyone smile, but at arm's length. For the sake of their happiness it is important for them to reconnect with their childlike vulnerability, not allowing their intense focus on achieving their goals to alienate them from the love of the people they seek to inspire and impress.

Health *Crank your energy levels up*

People born on this day are prone to moods swings, depression and bouts of self-pity when life doesn't go as planned or people don't respond to them in the way that they had hoped. They need to understand that feeling sorry for themselves is a waste of their energy because it is likely to push people away rather than make them gather round to offer support. When it comes to diet, they need to eat little and often throughout the day to keep their energy levels up, and to spend more time cooking and less time shopping. Regular moderate exercise is extremely beneficial, especially team sports or social forms of exercise such as aerobics or dance classes which can crank their energy levels up and encourage them to interact more socially. Wearing, meditating on and surrounding themselves with the color orange will encourage them to be more spontaneous and open, as will carrying a turquoise crystal.

Career *Born editors*

These people are hardworking and adaptable, tending to rise to positions of power and prominence. They may be drawn to the world of business, to advertising, publishing and the media, or they could find themselves excelling in politics, charity work and the healing professions. They may also express their creativity in teaching, writing or the arts.

Destiny *To inspire others to make positive changes*

The life path of people born on this day is to get in touch with their own feelings and those of others. Once they are able to reveal their vulnerable side and express their fun and creative side, their destiny is to inspire others to make positive changes in their lives.

Power Thought

66 My progress as a loving and spontaneous person is my gift to the world 99

Signs & symbols

Sun signs:
Scorpio/Sagittarius

Ruling planets: Mars, the warrior/Jupiter, the philosopher

Symbols: The Scorpion/The Archer

Birth date ruler: Jupiter, the philosopher

Tarot card: The World (fulfillment)

Favorable numbers: 3, 5

Lucky days: Tuesday and Thursday, especially when these days fall on 3 and 5 of the month

Lucky colors: Red, purple, blue

Birthstone: Topaz

November 21

22 November

the birthday of provocative aspiration

Even as a child, people born on November 22 will often have felt that they thought differently from other people. They are always slightly ahead, with a desire to free themselves from authority or conventional thinking.

These people like to make their own rules and they aren't that bothered about what other people think of them. Although these liberated people are like a breath of fresh air when it comes to challenging restrictive or unimaginative thinking, wherever they encounter it, their rebellious, provocative nature can get them into a lot of trouble. It is important for their psychological growth and professional success that they learn to be more tactful, reading their audience better for clues as to the appropriate level of intensity. If they don't, they will be branded as troublemakers.

Not surprisingly, given their free-thinking nature, these people work best independently in situations that give them lots of room for creative choice. In the right kind of environment they can be a powerful force for good, coming up with creative and innovative solutions to improve the welfare of those around them. In the wrong kind of environment—and this tends to be one that is structured or unchallenging—their provocative approach can, however, create tension and unrest.

Until they reach the age of twenty-nine they will want to expand their horizons and seek out opportunities through new ventures, study or travel. After the age of thirty, however, there is a turning point when they are likely to become more practical and realistic; these are the years when they are most likely to realize their professional goals. Ironically, because they love challenge so much, they may find in the thirties and beyond that despite achieving great success they pine for the time when anything in life seemed possible. The key to their success will be their ability to set themselves new goals and dream up new ideas to challenge and reinvent themselves. If they can do this, they will unlock the outstanding potential for personal fulfillment and happiness associated with this birthday.

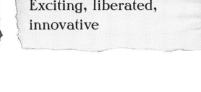

On the dark side

Rebellious, provocative, frustrated

At your best

Exciting, liberated, innovative

Love *Exciting and romantic*

People born on November 22 are exciting and romantic partners, and life with them is never boring. They are attracted to free-thinking, intelligent, emotional, and adventurous individuals like themselves, but they should guard against becoming too wild. In a secure relationship they can be generous and compassionate, as long as they dictate the terms.

Health *Grow old gracefully*

People born on this day need to be careful that their wild nature does not make it impossible for them to enjoy the quieter side of life. They may also find it extremely hard to accept that they are getting older. They need increasingly to reinvent themselves naturally so that they don't put their physical health at risk with unnecessary medical procedures. Sex is extremely important to them and they could have addictive tendencies which counseling or therapy would address. As far as diet is concerned, they would benefit from increasing their intake of whole grains, legumes, fruit, vegetables, oily fish, and nuts and seeds. Moderate to mild exercise is highly recommended, as is daily stretching and regular toning. They might also benefit from daily meditation or yoga. Wearing, meditating on and surrounding themselves with the color blue will help them keep their cool, and carrying a rose quartz crystal will inspire their creative confidence.

Career *Born freelancers*

These people are not generally suited to careers in a highly structured or disciplined environment. They need to feel free to express their creativity and may be drawn to the world of media, show business, music, publishing, advertising, the leisure and beauty industries, and politics. Alternatively they may be drawn to teaching or the arts, or they may find themselves in the role of counselor in the caring or healing professions.

Destiny *To inspire and excite others*

The life path of people born on this day is to learn to read people better and to constantly pay attention to their personal growth. Once they are able to find a vocation where they can set themselves new goals, their destiny is to inspire others with their creativity and originality.

Signs & symbols

Sun signs:
Sagittarius/Scorpio

Ruling planets: Jupiter, the philosopher/Mars, the warrior

Symbols: The Archer/The Scorpion

Birth date ruler: Uranus, the visionary

Tarot card: The Fool (freedom)

Favorable numbers: 4, 6

Lucky days: Thursday and Sunday, especially when these days fall on 4 and 6 of the month

Lucky colors: Blue, purple, silver

Birthstone: Turquoise

23 November

the birthday of sweet confrontation

People born on November 23 know how to think on their feet and their wit and grace make them much sought after, both at home and at work. They have a way with words and seem to know exactly the right thing to say at exactly the right time, whether they are comforting a friend, presenting at work or talking sweetly to their lover. When their communication skills are combined with their intelligence and originality, these people have the ability to make a significant and benevolent contribution to society.

There is a side to them, however, that seems to draw them irresistibly to confrontational people or situations. This often happens when their inspirational aims are challenged in any way; they may even go so far as to provoke unnecessary arguments to make their position clear. If they are not careful tension can become a constant theme in their lives, starting early in their childhood—they may have been in conflict with parents or teachers—and continuing right through their lives with colleagues, partners, friends, and loved ones. This can be an extremely negative and difficult pattern to break, especially as they aren't that good at handling conflict despite their attraction to it. They can suffer greatly when others launch a counterattack on them and target their hidden insecurities.

Until the age of twenty-eight they are likely to be concerned with issues of freedom and expanding their horizons through education, study or travel, but after the age of twenty-nine they are likely to develop a more pragmatic, orderly and structured approach to life, with a powerful emphasis on achieving their professional goals.

If they want to avoid road blocks to their success, and spending a great deal of time alone, it is crucial for them to learn to avoid engaging in conflict for the sake of it. This is because once they have learned to choose their battles wisely, they can save their energy for what really matters: developing their outstanding potential for becoming authoritative, innovative, expressive, and above all, truly motivational role models.

Love *Sweet talk*

People born on November 23 are drawn to strong-willed individuals who show a lot of purpose and determination, like themselves. They are extremely seductive and charming, and can sweet talk even the most unlikely of people into a relationship. However, to keep that relationship going in the long term they have to learn to be less provocative and argumentative, making sure that they don't confuse conflict with passion.

Health *Just breathe*

People born on this day may suffer from sensitive skin and allergies, particularly during the winter months when central heating takes over. They would benefit from more time spent outside in the fresh air, and gentle breathing exercises would help bring greater balance and calmness into their lives. Because they can be easily hurt, they may also be prone to bouts of reactive depression and feelings of being alone. Learning not to take everything so personally will help them develop a thicker and more resilient skin. As far as diet is concerned, they need to take simple steps each day to ensure that what they are putting into their mouth is as fresh and healthy as possible. Mild to moderate exercise, preferably outdoors, will also help balance their moods and keep their weight down. Spiritual disciplines such as meditation and yoga, or studying religion, will help them stay calm in the face of adversity, while meditating on the color purple will encourage them to think of higher things.

Career *Born politicians*

These people have leadership potential but they need work that gives them as much freedom as possible. They may decide to go into business for themselves rather than working for a company. Other work choices include education, law, science, writing, politics, and the world of entertainment, in particular acting and music.

Destiny *To point the way forward to innovative change*

The life path of people born on this day is to learn to be more objective. Once they are able to take control of their emotions and exercise good judgment, their destiny is to devise or point the way to innovative options for change and progress.

Signs & symbols

Sun signs:
Sagittarius/Scorpio

Ruling planets: Jupiter, the philosopher/Mars, the warrior

Symbols: The Archer/The Scorpion

Birth date ruler: Mercury, the communicator

Tarot card: The Hierophant (guidance)

Favorable numbers: 5, 7

Lucky days: Thursday and Wednesday, especially when these days fall on 5 and 7 of the month

Lucky colors: Purple, blue, grey

Birthstone: Turquoise

November 23

24 November

the birthday of intrigue

Your greatest challenge is ...

overcoming the feeling that you don't fit in

The way forward is ...

to understand that everyone feels out of place at times; they just learn to hide it. You can do the same.

You're drawn to people born on ...

September 23 to October 22

This is a very natural and spontaneous pairing, and you can bring out the best in each other.

Luck maker

Practice that winning feeling

When you vividly imagine yourself winning or succeeding it becomes a reality in your unconscious mind. As you change your expectation of yourself, both you and your luck will improve.

People born on November 24 tend to be energetic, outgoing and spirited individuals with the ability to strongly influence the opinions of others. They will never avoid problems or challenges, and are at their happiest and best when debating issues or troubleshooting for a solution. People are irresistibly drawn to their courageous spirit and exciting ideas, and the air of mystery that hangs around them only adds to their attraction.

It doesn't matter how settled or secure the life of these people is, intrigue will never be far behind. Whether this manifests in situations or relationships that are complicated, or internal conflicts that are all-absorbing, there is always some kind of question mark in their lives and the outcome never appears certain. Although this means that their lives are never boring and are an endless topic of conversation for others, there will be times when they feel overwhelmed by feelings of uncertainty and confusion and unsure what their motivations are. They may aim for the top in their professional life only to find that the sacrifices they need to make are ones they are unwilling to make; or they may create an active social life, only to find that they long to be left alone.

Until the age of twenty-seven they are likely to be adventurous and will seek to expand their horizons through enterprising ventures, study and travel. After the age of twenty-eight they may start to settle down and become more practical, goal orientated and realistic in their approach. Another turning point occurs at the age of fifty-eight when they have a growing need for freedom, new ideas and expressing their individuality.

At every age and stage in their life there are opportunities for them to develop their original notions and big plans, but the key to their success — and indeed to solving the mystery of their lives—is to simply accept themselves for who and what they are: highly unusual, creative and courageous individuals who can never fit into the mold because their destiny is to break it.

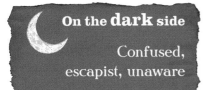
Love *Mysterious encounters*

People born on November 24 may find themselves drawn into complicated relationships or love triangles, and it is important for them to seek balance, greater simplicity and honesty in this area of their lives. Sensitive and restless, they need to be in a relationship that is not stuck or has become uneventful, and thrive best with a partner who is as interesting and as intelligent as themselves.

Health *Routine gets you down*

People born on this day may find that when their life gets into too much of a routine they suffer from fatigue and mood swings. They need to understand, however, that the answer does not necessarily lie in changing their job, partner or lifestyle, but within themselves. Cognitive behavioral therapy techniques are particularly recommended, as they can help them make these internal changes by changing the way they think about themselves. As far as diet is concerned, they tend to have a hearty appetite for a wide variety of foods but they need to make sure they don't overindulge in alcohol, fattening foods and red meat. Vigorous exercise is highly recommended, as it will help them release some of that pent-up energy. Wearing, surrounding themselves with and meditating on the color purple will encourage them to look within rather than without for inspiration.

Career *Born psychiatrists*

These people have the communication and people skills to succeed in any line of work, but they may be drawn to the caring professions, counseling, psychiatry, social reform, teaching, writing, philosophy, research, music, and the world of entertainment, as well as the study of metaphysics and spirituality.

Destiny *To help others unravel the mysteries of their lives*

The life path of people born on this day is to learn to accept themselves for who they are. Once they have found a sense of self-worth, their destiny is to help others unravel or uncover the mysteries of their lives.

Power Thought

" A new attitude can change a stifling situation into one of joy "

Signs & symbols

Sun signs: Sagittarius/Scorpio

Ruling planets: Jupiter, the philosopher/Mars, the warrior

Symbols: The Archer/The Scorpion

Birth date ruler: Venus, the lover

Tarot card: The Lovers (choices)

Favorable numbers: 6, 8

Lucky days: Thursday and Friday, especially when these days fall on 6 and 8 of the month

Lucky colors: Purple, lavender, pink

Birthstone: Turquoise

November 24

25 November

the birthday of social responsibility

Your greatest challenge is ...

establishing your independence

The way forward is ...

to understand that until you are able to strike out on your own, the contribution you make to a team will not be as effective or valuable.

You're drawn to people born on ...

October 23 to November 21

This relationship is so exciting because when directness and optimism meet subtlety and intensity, anything can happen.

Luck maker

Let yourself off the hook

Rigid expectations of success and relentlessly beating yourself up for some perceived or real weakness will do nothing to improve your self-esteem, drive, motivation, or luck-making potential.

People born on November 25 are rational, capable and quietly progressive individuals who are willing to take all the time needed to complete a project perfectly. Their motivation is a benevolent urge to achieve excellence and make a difference, rather than gain power and money, and this gives them the staying power to make things happen and the humility to be the essential means of support for a powerful individual or social group.

Social responsibility is an important theme in their lives. This isn't to say that they are not independently minded; indeed their desire for personal fulfillment is strong. It's just that they are ultimately concerned with inspiring, enlightening or otherwise acting on behalf of others or society as a whole. Their fixity of purpose, self-discipline and high expectations of themselves and others can, however, make them become overly fixated on their goals and too judgmental of others. Learning to establish an identity for themselves outside of their work or the social group with which they identify, and learning to accept and work with those who have alternative views, are essential requirements for their psychological growth and fulfillment.

Until the age of twenty-six they may find that they are concerned with issues of freedom, and they should take advantage of opportunities to expand their horizons through study or travel. After the age of twenty-seven there is a turning point that is likely to focus their minds on a more pragmatic, ordered and structured approach to life. There is another turning point at the age of fifty-seven when there is a growing need for original and progressive ideas and, at long last, independence. Whatever age or stage they are at, they should try to find the courage to strike out on their own, directing their creative intellect toward finding a path in life that combines their need for personal fulfillment with their socially orientated concerns. Having done this, they will gain an enriching dimension to their lives by unlocking their potential for making a real and important difference in the world around them.

At your best

Steady, accomplished, supportive

Love *As good as it gets*

People born on November 25 have very high expectations and ideals when it comes to affairs of the heart. Sometimes these can be so high that they are impossible to attain. They need to learn that simply feeling and being happy with someone really is good enough and quite sufficient reason to build a life with them.

Health *The joy of healthy living*

People born on this day have workaholic, perfectionist tendencies and when it comes to their health they will often be just as thorough and demanding of themselves. They therefore need to make sure that their concern to eat only the very best does not rob them of the joy of eating, and that their desire for fitness does not take away the joy of movement; and these people love to eat and move. Moderation, as far as exercise and diet are concerned, is therefore strongly recommended. A routine of regular meals and snacks is highly advised, as is regular exercise to boost their circulation, reduce the risk of heart disease and enhance their mood. Their natural optimism tends to make them underrate illness until it becomes serious, so regular check-ups with their doctor are advised. Wearing, meditating on and surrounding themselves with the color green will encourage them to be more tolerant and accepting of others, and the colors yellow or red will encourage them to stand up for themselves.

Career *Born teachers*

These people may work as teachers, scientists, politicians, or in any career that allows them to combine their personal ambitions with their urge to be socially responsible. They may also be drawn to social and charity work, the caring and healing professions, law and law enforcement. Their need for self-expression may express itself in writing, music, art, or the entertainment world.

Destiny *To assist, educate and inspire others*

The life path of people born on this day is to balance their own needs with those of others. Once they have learned to stand up for what they want and say "no" if they have to, their destiny is to assist, educate and inspire others.

Signs & symbols

Sun sign: Sagittarius

Ruling planet: Jupiter, the philosopher

Symbol: The Archer

Birth date ruler: Neptune, the speculator

Tarot card: The Chariot (resilience)

Favorable numbers: 7, 9

Lucky days: Thursday and Monday, especially when these days fall on 7 and 9 of the month

Lucky colors: Purple, sea green, light blue

Birthstone: Turquoise

26 November

the birthday of multi-talented uniqueness

Your greatest challenge is …

forming close relationships with others

The way forward is …

to understand that the more comfortable you are with yourself, the more comfortable you will be with other people.

You're drawn to people born on …

December 22 to January 19

You both admire qualities in the other that you lack, and have much to learn and love about each other.

Luck maker

Set the tone

People decide how to treat you and whether or not they want to help you based on their observations of you. So to boost your chances of luck, be the one who sets the tone in your life.

The free-thinking individuals born on November 26 would appear to have the world at their feet. Not only are they charismatic and intelligent, they are also creative, multi-talented and capable of excelling in just about any profession they choose.

Despite their incredible versatility, they may have felt from an early age that they were somehow different or removed from their fellow human begins. Part of the problem is that because they have so many talents and such an inquisitive mind, too many paths are open to them so choosing one becomes a daunting task. They may also struggle to reconcile their practical, logical orientation with the part of them that is highly creative and imaginative. At various points in their life they will lurch between these two extremes, but happiness and fulfillment can only be found when they are able to balance the two.

As success-orientated people, when they are not working toward a goal they can feel restless and unsatisfied, so the sooner they decide on a path in life and set themselves targets to achieve the better. If they don't do this, indecision, anxiety and uncertainty will submerge their huge potential.

Up to the age of twenty-five there may be a lot of experimentation regarding their career, as they focus on adventure, creativity and opportunity; but after the age of twenty-six they start to become more practical, goal orientated and realistic in their aims. This is a positive development, as long as they make sure they don't lose touch with their imagination and creative fire. Another turning point occurs at the age of fifty-six when expressing their individuality takes center stage. Hopefully, however, they will have realized far earlier in life that the key to their success is to celebrate and make full use of their uniqueness rather than try to hide it. They have been right all along; there is and never will be anybody quite like them with their unique talents, original perspective, and courage and determination to prove everyone wrong by achieving their fantastic aims.

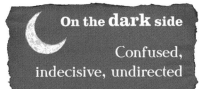
Love *Born free*

When it comes to affairs of the heart, people born on November 26 can have problems because they like their own company and are unwilling to sacrifice their freedom. They are capable of forming close relationships but these tend to be with their friends rather than lovers. But when they do find someone who captures their heart, they have it within them to make dutiful and devoted partners.

Health *Keep in touch*

People born on this day tend to be vigorous and athletic, and they rarely suffer long from illnesses. They can, however, over-indulge in food and drink from time to time, and they may also be prone to accidents and injuries resulting from sports or risky activities. From a psychological perspective, the biggest risk to their emotional health is their tendency to withdraw or to isolate themselves from others, and making an effort to stay in touch with friends and family will benefit them enormously. As far as diet is concerned, they need to increase their intake of vegetables and fruit to boost their digestion. Moderate to vigorous exercise is recommended to help keep their weight down and their immune system strong. Wearing, meditating on or surrounding themselves with the color orange will encourage them to be warmer and more spontaneous when in the company of others.

Career *Born video game creators*

People born on this day have a meticulous approach to their work and will excel in careers that are research-based. Possible work options include education, philosophy, writing, engineering, IT, and the world of video game creation and toy manufacturing or design.

Destiny *To make original contributions to society*

The life path of people born on this day is to find a way to reconcile the disparate parts of their personality by looking within themselves. Once they are more balanced in their outlook and approach, their destiny is to make an outstanding contribution to humanity.

Power Thought

❝ The sense of direction, harmony and fulfillment I seek already lie within me **❞**

Signs & symbols

Sun sign: Sagittarius

Ruling planet: Jupiter, the philosopher

Symbol: The Archer

Birth date ruler: Saturn, the teacher

Tarot card: Strength (passion)

Favorable numbers: 1, 8

Lucky days: Thursday and Saturday, especially when these days fall on 1 and 8 of the month

Lucky colors: Purple, maroon, brown

Birthstone: Turquoise

November 26

27 November

the birthday of the vortex

Your greatest challenge is ...

asking for help

The way forward is ...

to understand that asking for help is not a sign of weakness but a sign of self-knowledge, honesty and inner strength.

You're drawn to people born on ...

March 21 to April 19

This is a tremendously energetic and passionate combination, with great potential for long-term happiness.

Luck maker

Don't be a self-sufficient hero

If you continue to insist on doing everything yourself you will cause people to fear or exclude you, and this will block your chances of luck.

People born on November 27 are vortexes of energy, enthusiasm, and excitement. Fiercely individualistic, they go where their imagination leads them, preferring to seek out knowledge and truth for themselves and then formulating their own opinions and plans. The only trouble with this wildly spontaneous approach is that they often have no idea in which direction they are heading, and their enthusiasm tends to overwhelm their common sense.

They are not afraid to listen to their instincts, and although this intuitive approach can bring them spectacular success it can also lead to disappointments and rejection. It is important for them to learn to distinguish between intuition and wishful thinking, and the only way to do that is to try to understand themselves better and to take a more realistic view of situations before they decide to throw themselves in at the deep end. Although they will encounter setbacks along the way, they are remarkably resilient, possessing a buoyant spirit in the face of adversity. However, their self-reliance can also work against them; they are extremely proud and don't like to ask for help. This significantly decreases their chances of success.

Until the age of twenty-four they will probably keep their career options open, preferring to experiment, travel or study to broaden their horizons. However, around the age of twenty-five there is a turning point when they are likely to become more pragmatic, focused and orderly in order to realize their goals. Another turning point occurs around the age of fifty-five when they may feel a growing urge to be more adventurous and independent.

Whatever age they are, however, the secret to unlocking their potential for success and happiness will be their ability to control the powerful energy within them and direct it to a worthy cause. Once they are able to do that—and to ask for help and advice along the way—they will still be vortexes of dynamic energy and originality but this time they will be vortexes who know where they are heading, and that is usually to the very top.

Love *More haste, less speed*

People born on November 27 tend to rush into relationships very quickly and to idealize potential partners rather than look at them in the cold light of day. Although they tend to jump from relationship to relationship, they rarely fall completely in love because their freedom is so important to them. They are drawn to creative and hardworking individuals, but need to find someone who is solid and dependable enough to give them the support they need in good times as well as bad.

Health *Slow down*

People born on this day are fast eaters and this can cause trouble with their digestion, because digestion starts in the mouth. Taking time to chew their food thoroughly and put their knife and fork down between mouthfuls is therefore recommended, as is dining at the table rather than eating on the go. When it comes to their physical health, they also need to slow down, allowing plenty of time for rest and relaxation. If they don't they could be in danger of burnout because even their incredible energy reserves can run low from time to time. As far as diet is concerned, spending more time cooking is highly recommended as it will encourage them to think about the quality of their diet. Moderate exercise on a daily basis is advised as it will help calm their minds and boost their immune system. Carrying a malachite crystal around with them will bring calmness and a sense of ease into their lives.

Career *Born rock stars*

These people will thrive in any career in which they can pursue their quest for knowledge unhindered. They may therefore be drawn to the worlds of sport, art and entertainment. Their desire to benefit others may incline them toward politics, education and social reform. Other career choices may include writing, tourism, advertising, and working for themselves.

Destiny *To enlighten, inspire and invigorate others*

The life path of people born on this day is to understand that they are in charge of their emotions, not the other way round. As they develop greater self-awareness and control, their destiny is to enlighten, inspire and invigorate others with their positive energy.

Signs & symbols

Sun sign: Sagittarius

Ruling planet: Jupiter, the philosopher

Symbol: The Archer

Birth date ruler: Mars, the warrior

Tarot card: The Hermit (inner strength)

Favorable numbers: 2, 9

Lucky days: Thursday and Tuesday, especially when these days fall on 2 and 9 of the month

Lucky colors: Purple, orange, red

Birthstone: Turquoise

November 27

28 November

the birthday of impulse

Your greatest challenge is ...

making realistic plans

The way forward is ...

to set short-term goals that you can reach, then set more. In this way you'll be able to move ahead.

You're drawn to people born on ...

July 23 to August 22

You both have huge hearts and the spirit of adventurers, and this can create a stimulating and passionate union.

Luck maker

Finish what you start

Lucky people have discipline and are willing to do things that they don't always like to do because they know it will lead them to their goals.

Those born on November 28 are free spirits with a thirst for knowledge. They are natural philosophers and their aim is to broaden their vision and sense of possibility. They are the scientists who never leave the lab, the composers and writers who labor late into the night, and the workers who stay late at the office—and forget to clean up their mess when they leave.

Filled with natural curiosity and eagerness for the future, there is a tendency for these people to overextend themselves with too many activities. Not surprisingly, they can be flirtatious—with ideas as well as people—tending to show their enthusiasm at the start of new endeavors or relationships but then withdrawing it as the project progresses into details, or the relationship settles into a routine. They need to learn that commitment and freedom are two separate entities that don't have to be mutually exclusive.

Despite the sparkling wit and apparent flightiness of these people, they have a deeper and more complex side to them. As they tend to feel their way through life, their emotions can go up and down, so it is important for them to find a trusted friend who can gently warn them when they are heading off track. When hurt, they withdraw into a cloud of silence, eventually emerging from their reticence with sarcastic comments that can be blunt, insensitive and tactless. Too emotionally honest to hide their feelings, whether disillusionment, frustration or boredom, they can't help but "say it like it is."

Others may criticize them for their moodiness and messiness, but they don't hold grudges for long and it's always a creative and innovative mess. But if they want to achieve the success and recognition their talents deserve, they need to combine this with dedication and discipline. Fortunately after the age of twenty-four there is a powerful and significant turning point when there will be greater emphasis on responsibility and the work they need to do to achieve their imaginative and progressive goals.

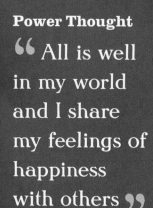
Love *Shared dreams*

People born on November 28 try to do whatever they can to make their partner happy, although they may struggle with some indecisiveness, as well as insecurity and jealousy. The imprisoning world of dull routine and dreary responsibility is poison for them. What they really want is a lover who can give them freedom, share their dreams and be there when they land with a bump. To attract and keep this kind of lover they need to believe in themselves more.

Health *Self-discipline required*

People born on this day often enjoy rich living and may have problems managing their weight, particularly around the hips and thighs. Regular massage and a strenuous exercise regime emphasizing flexibility, together with a nutritious diet with plenty of fresh water to flush away toxins, can help with this. To keep energy levels consistent they should aim to eat five mini-meals a day, instead of three big ones, and go easy on fatty foods and alcohol. The more time these people spend outdoors in natural surroundings the better, because this will have a calming and balancing influence on them. They would also benefit from yoga and meditation; wearing or meditating on the color blue will encourage them to be more consistent and disciplined in their approach.

Career *Born journalists*

These people are drawn to careers that involve travel, communication and creativity. They prefer intellectually demanding work which benefits others. Possible careers are in publishing, law, medicine, social reform, politics, writing, journalism, or the arts. Once they get serious about their responsibilities, they could do well in business pursuits or humanitarian group projects.

Destiny *To be an inspirational force in the world*

The life task of people born on this day is to learn to find their focus, trust their instincts and develop their talent for self-expression. When used positively, this can be an inspirational force in the world and their destiny therefore is to uplift others.

Signs & symbols

Sun sign: Sagittarius

Ruling planet: Jupiter, the philosopher

Symbol: The Archer

Birth date ruler: Sun, the individual

Tarot card: The Magician (will-power)

Favorable numbers: 1, 3

Lucky days: Thursday and Sunday, especially when these days fall on 1 and 3 of the month

Lucky colors: Blue, purple, orange

29 November

the birthday of controversy

Your greatest challenge is …

learning to listen

The way forward is …

to think like a mirror. A mirror doesn't judge or give advice. It reflects back what the person is saying.

You're drawn to people born on …

July 23 to August 22

You are both passionate and spontaneous, and there will be plenty of love and laughter in this relationship.

Luck maker

Do as you say

Research has shown that commitment to following through on agreed changes makes all the difference to your credibility and happiness. If people can't trust you, opportunities won't come your way.

When November 29 people walk into a room the atmosphere instantly changes, and everyone feels a sense of excitement and possibility. This is because they are energetic and dynamic individuals who are stimulated by challenge and the desire to move forward with their personal goals, career goals and, if possible, the greater good.

Although they are innovative, exciting and optimistic and can encourage others to be more courageous in their thinking, these people have a habit of stirring up controversy because they like to think outside the box. Challenging the status quo, whether necessary or not, is a way of life for them, and they are hopeless at keeping their unconventional ideas to themselves. In fact they love to express their opinions, and it doesn't matter to them if they get a negative response—what they really want from others is a reaction, and a negative one is better than none. Sometimes, however, their provocative manner does step over the mark and they need to ensure that they don't highlight emotional vulnerabilities in others for no reason but to demonstrate their own power over them.

Up to the age of twenty-one they may want to expand their opportunities through enterprising ventures, study or travel, but after the age of twenty-three they start to become more realistic and goal-orientated in their approach to their achievements. During this period, there will be a need for more order and structure in their lives. Another turning point occurs around the age of fifty-three when expressing their individuality comes into the spotlight.

Whatever age they are they will always be a catalyst for change. If they can make sure that this is not change for the sake of excitement but positive change that can encourage progress—on their own behalf as well as those of others—these invigorating people have the potential to become inspired thinkers with a gift not just for keeping everyone on their toes but with a gift to offer the world through their work or creative expression.

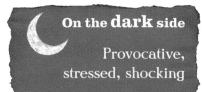

On the dark side

Provocative, stressed, shocking

At your best

Invigorating, dramatic, daring

Love *Time alone*

People born on November 29 thrive on interacting with others, and because they are so fascinating and energetic they rarely lack admirers or friends. They may struggle, however, if they have to spend long periods of time alone. It is important that they become more content in their own company because, if they don't, they run the risk of becoming manipulative or over-dependent on others.

Health *In your own company*

People born on this day need to make sure that they find ways to amuse or occupy themselves rather than always relying on the company of others to feel alive. Once they are able to be more self-sufficient and to feel happy in their own company, they will discover that stress, nervousness and depression become moods of the past and that life is so much more fulfilling. As far as diet is concerned, the emphasis needs to be on fresh and natural; going through their kitchen and fridge and throwing out ready meals and everything loaded with additives and preservatives, sugar, saturated fat, and salt is highly recommended. Recommended too is regular vigorous exercise to release pent-up energy. Daily walks may also be beneficial because they will give them time to be alone with their thoughts. Wearing, meditating on and surrounding themselves with the color purple will encourage them to search for excitement within as well as in the world around them.

Career *Born commentators*

These people may gravitate toward careers in science, teaching or the arts, but they also make excellent debaters, media correspondents, film directors, journalists, and literary critics or commentators. Other work options include law, politics, social reform, business, medicine, administration, charity and community work.

Destiny *To enliven others and point the way toward progress*

The life path of people born on this day is to learn to step down from their pedestal every now and again to mingle with the crowd. Once they are able to listen and take on board the opinions of others, their destiny is to enliven others and make progress in everything they undertake.

Power Thought

" The adventure I seek is already within me "

Signs & symbols

Sun sign: Sagittarius

Ruling planet: Jupiter, the philosopher

Symbol: The Archer

Birth date ruler: Mars, the warrior

Tarot card: The High Priestess (intuition)

Favorable numbers: 2, 4

Lucky days: Thursday and Monday, especially when these days fall on 2 and 4 of the month

Lucky colors: Blue, silver, white

Birthstone: Turquoise

30 November

the birthday of
incisive thoroughness

People born on November 30 often feel that there simply aren't enough hours in their day or years in their life to accomplish all their ambitions. They have so many talents and abilities that it can be hard for them to know where to invest their energies. Once they settle on a chosen course, their strong sense of responsibility and incisive mind ensure that they give it their complete concentration.

They are extremely thorough in their approach and their attention to detail is second to none. As a result they are always well prepared for virtually any situation in which they might find themselves and, because they never leave anything to the last minute, they are always composed, calm and convincing. Others will usually be influenced by what they have to say, but on the odd occasion that their preparation fails to pay off they can find it hard to accept that anyone could say no to them or not be impressed by them. If anyone tries to criticize them, they can become extremely defensive and at times hurtful themselves. They should therefore learn to handle criticism with as much grace and control as they demonstrate in other areas of their lives.

After the age of twenty-two they are likely to feel a need to be pragmatic, orderly and structured in their approach to life. Given the fact that they already have a tendency to be highly controlled and lacking in spontaneity, it is vital during the next thirty years that they get in touch with their intuition, take themselves and others less seriously, and incorporate more fun and laugher into their lives. After the age of fifty-two there is a turning point which highlights issues regarding friendships and personal identity.

Whatever age they are, the sooner they can loosen up and trust their heart and powerful intuition as much as they trust their rational side, the sooner they can maximize their potential for success, making their unique and valuable contribution to the world.

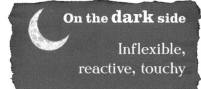
At your **best**

Thorough, multi-talented, convincing

Love *Knowledgeable and educated*

People born on November 30 make generous and supportive friends, although they have a fragile ego that friends need to learn to tiptoe around. Their long list of accomplishments, qualifications and ambitious plans for the future will impress, but if they want to find true love they need to put their lists and plans aside, and devote their energy to making another person feel loved and happy.

Health *Comfort and calm in nature*

People born on this day should aim to travel more because traveling will open their mind to new possibilities and ways of looking at the world. They would also benefit from time spent in the countryside, particularly long walks in the beauty of nature. Depression is a real threat, and they are most at risk when their plans go wrong. This is hard for them to understand but they should realize that attracting success isn't just about doing or saying the right thing but about feeling and thinking the right thing and following their instincts. They have workaholic tendencies, so they need to make sure they pace themselves, eat a healthy diet and follow a regular exercise routine. Wearing, meditating on and surrounding themselves with the color orange will encourage them to be more spontaneous in their approach to life, and a calming cup of chamomile tea will relax them at the day's end.

Career *Born editors*

These people have excellent communication skills and may excel in writing, publishing, sales, politics, music, acting, or entertainment. Other career choices include teaching, law, business, and administration, but whatever career they choose their disciplined and thorough approach will help them thrive from promotion to promotion.

Destiny *To help others advance with carefully thought-out strategies*

The life path of people born on this day is to learn to be more instinctive in their approach to people and to life. Once they understand that some situations simply cannot be controlled or predicted, their destiny is to help themselves and others advance with carefully thought-out strategies.

Power Thought

66 My intuition allows me to blend and connect with everyone and everything **99**

Signs & symbols

Sun sign: Sagittarius

Ruling planet: Jupiter, the philosopher

Symbol: The Archer

Birth date ruler: Jupiter, the philosopher

Tarot card: The Empress (creativity)

Favorable numbers: 3, 5

Lucky day: Thursday, especially when it falls on 3 and 5 of the month

Lucky colors: Purple, blue, white

Birthstone: Turquoise

November 30

1 December

the birthday of outrageous charm

Your greatest challenge is ...

knowing what you want

The way forward is ...

to appreciate that acquiring self-knowledge is not only the beginning of wisdom; it is also a lifelong task.

You're drawn to people born on ...

July 23 to August 22

You are both courageous and outspoken individuals, and there will be plenty of love and laughter in this relationship.

Luck maker

Give to the appreciative

Generosity guarantees you a place at the top of people's list, which is often all you need to improve your luck.

People born on December 1 are extremely energetic. Unhindered by convention, they express themselves freely and delight in surprising others with their outrageous wit and seducing them with their charm. Any attempts to restrict their freedom will simply have the effect of spurring them along their idiosyncratic path with renewed enthusiasm and determination.

Although these people will defend or promote their ideas fiercely, they are not necessarily combative or confrontational; they prefer to influence or win others over with the sheer force of their personalities. They may at times lack tact or diplomacy but they also radiate self-confidence, and this draws others to them. Underneath their entertaining, occasionally superficial but always eyebrow-raising mask, however, they are far more deep and complex than others realize. In fact sometimes they feel so complex that even they aren't sure what their motivations are; the vibrant, funny personality they present to the outside world is simply their way of coping with the confusion.

After a rebellious childhood, at around the age of twenty there is an important turning point for these people lasting about thirty years. During this period there are opportunities for them to become more pragmatic, orderly and structured in their approach to life. As long as they don't neglect friends and loved ones they should take advantage of these opportunities to focus on their career; the sooner they find a professional sense of direction and purpose the better, as work can be an important outlet for their energy and talents. After the age of fifty-one there is an another important turning point which highlights a growing need for independence and for sharing some of their progressive ideas with others.

Throughout their lives they should never forget that they are free spirits, but if they can learn to be a little more diplomatic, cautious and self-aware they will find that they will not only be able to bring pleasure, love and enlightenment to the lives of others; they will also be able to blaze their own, highly original, trail through life.

Power Thought

❝ Balancing my priorities helps me rediscover my happiness ❞

Love *Uninhibited and fun loving*

In their teens and twenties, people born on December 1 may feel a bit shy when it comes to affairs of the heart. But when they hit their thirties and beyond they come into their physical prime as charismatic, fun-loving and uninhibited lovers. When in a close relationship they can be generous and supportive, but they need to be careful that they aren't too busy to give those they love the time they deserve.

Health *Regular check-ups*

People born on this day are often vigorous and athletic children, but as they get older they can be prone to weight gain, especially around the middle. Over-indulgence in food or drink can be their downfall, as can accidents and injuries caused by sport or risk-taking. Exercising caution with their physical health is advised, as is scheduling regular health check-ups with their doctor, as they tend to ignore niggling health complaints until they get serious. As far as diet is concerned, fad diets should be avoided because they will make it harder for them to lose weight in the long term; a healthy, balanced diet rich in nutrients from all the food groups and plenty of moderate to vigorous exercise at least five times a week is advised instead. Cognitive behavioral therapy is advised to help them become more aware of how their thoughts are influencing their moods, and carrying a titanium quartz crystal with them will help them find their true path in life.

Career *Born comedians*

These people work well in any career in which they can act independently and make their individual contribution. Although they can function well in a team, they may prefer to be self-employed. They are well suited to the sporting or artistic fields, as well as the world of acting, music, film, media, advertising, comedy, and entertainment.

Destiny *To entertain and enlighten others*

The life path of people born on this day is to learn to be a bit more diplomatic. Once they have found a cause that is worthy of them and improved their self-knowledge, their destiny is to bring pleasure and enlightenment to others.

Signs & symbols

Sun sign: Sagittarius

Ruling planet: Jupiter, the philosopher

Symbol: The Archer

Birth date ruler: Sun, the individual

Tarot card: The Magician (will-power)

Favorable numbers: 1, 4

Lucky days: Thursday and Sunday, especially when these days fall on 1 and 4 of the month

Lucky colors: Purple, blue, orange

Birthstone: Turquoise

December 1

673

2 December

the birthday of
the kaleidoscope

Your greatest challenge is ...

outgrowing your constant need for recognition

The way forward is ...

to realize that no matter how much recognition and applause others give you, it will never be enough until you can grow in self-esteem.

You're drawn to people born on ...

October 23 to November 21

You have so much to love and learn from each other; anything could happen in this exciting relationship.

Luck maker

Sometimes put yourself second

There is nothing more powerful than asking people what they think and quietly listening to their responses. This makes them feel important, special and far more likely to want to help you.

People born on December 2 are dynamic and colorful characters who tend to command attention wherever they go. They wear their heart on their sleeve and are so spontaneous that the whole kaleidoscope of their constantly changing emotions will be on display for all to see.

Their emotional honesty and energy can be refreshing, and their drive and determination make them excellent leaders and an inspiration to friends and co-workers. The effect they can have on others is dramatic, but it could be life changing for both themselves and others if they learned to balance their directness with a little tact, occasionally stepping back to examine what their emotions are telling them. With a little more self-understanding they might see that some kind of pattern is emerging.

Until the age of nineteen they may be something of a wild child, exploring and expanding their horizons in as many different directions as possible. After the age of twenty there is a turning point when there are opportunities for them to become more practical, goal-orientated and realistic in their approach to life. They should take advantage of these opportunities to establish order and structure in their life, because if they don't too many changes of direction can lead to confusion and uncertainty. After the age of fifty there is another turning point that highlights a growing need for more independence, but also a need to become more humanitarian in their approach.

Above all, these people are charismatic individuals, but they are also problem solvers looking for a deeper meaning or pattern to their life. Their inner sensitivity, however, may not always be visible from their colorful, confident front. Once they find a way to connect and work with it, not only will they be able to intuitively know the answer to other people's dilemmas; they will be able to take charge of their constantly changing and confusing emotions, find a cause in life that is worthy of their creative talents, and create the magical pattern of peace and happiness they so richly deserve.

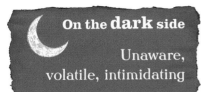

On the dark side

Unaware, volatile, intimidating

At your best

Inspirational, creative, demonstrative

Love *Incorrigible flirts*

People born on December 1 don't mean to but simply can't help being terrible flirts. They will often be surrounded by admirers even when they are in a committed relationship. There are many sides to their personality, and potential partners will need to adjust to their shifting moods. But once they find someone they can connect with on a deep level, they make loyal and loving partners.

Health *Let the music play*

Music is a great therapy for people born on this day. It can help clear their mind and encourage them to see patterns and connections instead of confusion or fantasy. They should therefore try to listen to music as much as they can to enhance their creativity and language skills, as well as the logical, analytical side of their brain. As far as diet is concerned, they would benefit from spending more time carefully planning their menus and meal plans; they might also benefit from going on a cookery course. Regular moderate exercise is absolutely essential, preferably on a daily basis to keep their weight under control and boost their circulation, as they are prone to circulation problems and varicose veins. Time spent reading and studying spiritual disciplines or mastering the techniques of meditation will not be wasted, and wearing, meditating on and surrounding themselves with the color blue will help bring order and clarity when there is confusion.

Career *Born opera singers*

These people have the potential not only to achieve personal happiness but also to make significant contributions to society, perhaps as pioneering scientists, or as inspirational artists and performers. There may be a number of career changes, but work opportunities that might also appeal to them include education, sales, publishing, media, writing, charity work, and the tourist and leisure industries.

Destiny *To make an inspirational mark on the world*

The life path of people born on this day is to take charge of their emotions so that they feel more in control of their lives. Once they are more self-aware, their destiny is to make an inspirational or pioneering mark on the world.

Signs & symbols

Sun sign: Sagittarius

Ruling planet: Jupiter, the philosopher

Symbol: The Archer

Birth date ruler: Moon, the intuitive

Tarot card: The High Priestess (intuition)

Favorable numbers: 2, 5

Lucky days: Thursday and Monday, especially when these days fall on 2 and 5 of the month

Lucky colors: Purple, silver, milky white

Birthstone: Turquoise

December 2

3 December

the birthday of progressive expertise

People born on December 3 are blessed with inquisitive and progressive minds and are at their happiest and best when formulating original strategies to bring about improvements. Although their ideas are highly original, unorthodox even, they are also thorough and rational types. When these qualities are added to their formidable organizational and technical skills, the result is a person with stunning expertise in their chosen field.

Not surprisingly, given their perfectionist nature, work plays a huge part in their lives and they will often dedicate themselves wholeheartedly to their career. They will also tend to seek out others with similar mind sets to their own and, while others respect their energy, ambition and focus and admire their well-deserved professional success, they can feel as if these individuals are hard to get to know. This is to some extent true, as they don't really have much time for socializing and often feel a need to simply be alone. This isn't for religious or spiritual reasons, but simply to help renew their focus and concentration, and fine-tune their skills. When they are ready they will emerge from their silence to astonish all those around them with their accomplishments.

The dedicated and ambitious aspects of their personality don't tend to emerge until they are at least in their twenties, but when they do they give them a focus and determination that is second to none. After the age of fifty, however, there is a significant turning point when there will be opportunities for them to focus on friendship and group awareness.

Whatever their age, they need to take advantage of any opportunity they can to participate more fully and freely with others because this will help them understand that their ambition is not only driven by a desire to achieve professional excellence but also by a desire to assist others and play an inspirational role in their lives. As long as they make sure their emotional needs do not take second place to their work, they have the innovative potential to become dynamic instruments of progress.

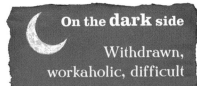

At your **best**

Innovative, meticulous, ambitious

Power Thought

❝I work to live, I don't live to work❞

Love *When you are ready*

People born on December 3 are intense and independent individuals. They may spend long periods of time alone, unaware that they actually have an army of admirers silently waiting in the wings; but when they finally feel ready to open up emotionally they will not be short of admirers. They need to find a partner who respects their independence and need for freedom, but who will also give them plenty of love and support.

Health *Pleasure in simple things*

People born on this day run the risk of losing themselves in work, so they need to constantly remind themselves of the importance of taking pleasure in simple things. Activities like gardening, cooking, flower arranging, walks in the countryside, talking to friends, and holding hands with a loved one should never be dismissed as a waste of time; for their emotional and physical well-being they need to make a real effort to stay in touch with those they love. As far as diet is concerned, they should experiment with a wide variety of foods and, although their interest in nutrition is admirable, they should never forget that food is also meant to be enjoyed. Regular moderate exercise, in particular social forms of exercise such as dancing, is recommended, and wearing, meditating on and surrounding themselves with the color orange will encourage them to be more spontaneous and expressive.

Career *Born engineers*

These people can combine their innovative potential with their technical skills to excel in careers such as science, psychology and engineering, as well as in the world of sport. Other possible work options include sales, advertising, public relations, promotion, education and charity work, as well as art, music, writing, and drama.

Destiny *To influence and inspire others with their expertise*

The life path of people born on this day is to learn to balance their professional and personal needs. Once they feel ready to participate more fully in society, their destiny is to influence and inspire others with their expertise and progressive ideas.

Signs & symbols

Sun sign: Sagittarius

Ruling planet: Jupiter, the philosopher

Symbol: The Archer

Birth date ruler: Jupiter, the philosopher

Tarot card: The Empress (creativity)

Favorable numbers: 3, 6

Lucky day: Thursday, especially when it falls on 3 and 6 of the month

Lucky colors: All shade of purple and blue

Birthstone: Turquoise

December 3

4 December

the birthday of the captain

Your greatest challenge is …

coping with not being listened to

The way forward is …

to understand that authority is something that has to be earned; balance your leadership skills with a concern for the welfare of others.

You're drawn to people born on …

January 20 to February 18

Although you are different in many ways, there is much you can learn to love about each other.

Luck maker

Be an energy source

When you invite other people into your limelight or offer them recognition, you become an energy source and others will want to keep you center stage. The outcome of your generosity will be new opportunities for you.

People born on December 4 are ambitious, hardworking and resilient individuals who can display remarkable self-control in both their professional and personal lives. They have the rare ability to take charge of their emotions without losing their creativity, and this gives them tremendous self-confidence, power over themselves and authority over others. They are like flamboyant and daring but highly skilled and well-prepared captains with a thirst for adventure and all the courage and ingenuity they need to successfully steer through uncharted waters to undiscovered lands.

Although they cherish their own individuality and are unwilling to submit themselves to the ideas or authority of others, they may feel compelled to impose their ideas on those around them, sometimes forcefully. Unaware of this contradiction between their directional urges and their own right to autonomy, they can come across as dictatorial or egotistical; but this is rarely the case. For the great majority of the time they are genuinely concerned for the greater good, rather than any selfish ambitions. Like a brave captain who will not leave their ship until everyone is safe, their natural sense of justice and honor will propel them toward activities that are intended to bring about a more enlightened or better-regulated society.

At the age of eighteen, people born on this day may start to manifest their natural leadership skills and over the next thirty years they will gradually become more practical, goal-orientated and realistic in their approach to achievement. They may also have a strong desire for order and structure in their lives. After the age of forty-eight there is another significant turning point which highlights a growing need for freedom, new ideas and expressing their individuality within a group setting.

Whatever age they are, if they can find a middle way between nobility and ambition, love and success, compassion and power, independence and the need to compromise, they will not only be capable of inspired leadership, they will also be capable of becoming the visionaries of their generation.

Love *Give and take*

People born on December 4 rarely have problems attracting potential partners, but long-term relationships may prove elusive. It is important for them to learn the importance of give and take in a relationship, and to find a balance between their idyllic romantic optimism and practical reality. Once they do decide to commit, they need to find a partner who can give them the freedom they need to feel alive.

Health *Healthy balance*

People born on this day tend to have an optimistic approach to life and are not prone to depression. There will be times, however, when they feel tired or run down, and they should learn to pace themselves and take regular vacations. They also need to master the art of delegation. Allowing others to help them will not only ease their workload, it will give them time to find a healthy balance of interests outside of work. Meditation techniques are highly recommended because they will enjoy the sense of calm, peace and balance they can bring. As far as diet is concerned, they need to cut down on sugar and processed and refined foods, and to increase their intake of whole grains, fruits and vegetables. Moderate to vigorous exercise is recommended, particularly team sports and outdoor activities where they can work off their aggressive tendencies. Wearing, meditating on and surrounding themselves with the color purple will encourage them to think about higher things, and bring a true sense of harmony, peace and balance into their lives.

Career *Born conservationists*

These people may be drawn toward careers in politics or they may choose to promote their ideological beliefs through the arts. Other possible career choices include business, commerce, advertising, sport, agriculture, conservation, management, and the world of entertainment.

Destiny *To advance the greater good*

The life path of people born on this day is to learn to listen to others' views and find a balance between their idealism and ambition. Once they can achieve their goals while retaining the affection and respect of those with whom they live and work, their destiny is to advance the greater good.

Signs & symbols

Sun sign: Sagittarius

Ruling planet: Jupiter, the philosopher

Symbol: The Archer

Birth date ruler: Uranus, the visionary

Tarot card: The Emperor (authority)

Favorable numbers: 4, 7

Lucky days: Thursday and Sunday, especially when these days fall on 4 and 7 of the month

Lucky colors: Blue, silver, light yellow

Birthstone: Turquoise

5 December

the birthday of the self-assured adventurer

Your greatest challenge is ...

taking the advice of others

The way forward is ...

to understand that other people always bring different perspectives; these are always worth listening to as you may have overlooked them.

You're drawn to people born on ...

May 21 to June 20

You are both inquisitive and adventurous spirits, and you can make a great couple.

Luck maker

Don't get over-confident

Although positive thinking will get you far, being over-confident will not; humility is an important part of the luck equation.

People born on December 5 reach for the skies both personally and professionally and, although others may think they are overreaching themselves, somehow or other they manage to get to where they want—or at the very least, close to it.

From an early age they may have displayed unusual self-confidence and willingness to go it alone. If this isn't the case, life may have given them a series of knocks to dent their confidence; sooner or late their characteristic optimism will emerge. They truly believe that anything is possible, and throughout their lives they will be a shining example of what confidence and self-belief in the face of adversity can achieve. Sometimes they can be over-confident and unwilling to listen to the cautionary advice of others; although this may result in remarkable innovations, it can also lead to serious errors of judgment.

Around the age of seventeen they will start to think seriously about their life goals and the mark they want to leave on the world. Although they should never lose their idealism and optimism, it is important for them to make sure that the goals they set are realistic and achievable; otherwise they are setting themselves up for disappointment. Listening to the advice of others could be the key to unlocking their potential. After the age of forty-seven they may become even more progressive and original in their ideas and, if they have managed to learn from past experience and improve their judgment by taking a careful look at themselves and their situation, these are the years when they can really come into their own.

December 5 people are hard to ignore or dislike, and even though their ambitions may at times be over the top, colleagues and friends will often regard them with affection and tolerance. They have a real desire to make a positive contribution to society and, once they can direct their determination, focus and will-power to a worthy cause, they can and do find ways to benefit the greater good.

At your best

Self-assured, daring, energetic

Love *Love–hate*

People born on December 5 long for a settled and secure relationship, but as soon as they are in one they may start to pick arguments or stir up trouble simply to keep the intensity alive. Partners may find this particularly difficult to deal with, and for long-term happiness in a relationship people born on this day need to find someone who is emotionally confident and direct.

Health *Conserve your energy*

People born on this day need to conserve their energy and watch out for problems with their bones and joints. Making sure they have enough calcium and magnesium in their diet is important, as is eating a healthy balanced diet rich in whole grains, fruits, vegetables, legumes, nuts, seeds, and oily fish. It would be wise for them to cut down on the amount of coffee they drink, as this can lead to insomnia; they need to be equally careful about excess sugar, salt, additives, and preservatives. Regular exercise will keep their bones and joints flexible, boosting all aspects of their health, while lots of different activities are recommended to keep them interested and motivated. Spending more time with loved ones is advised and, for those times when they feel alone, a few drops of rose, clary sage or frankincense essential oil on a handkerchief to breathe in will help produce feelings of inner security and self-acceptance; for relaxation and a good night's sleep—which are both particularly important for them—they should try lavender.

Career *Born fashion designers*

These people will thrive in any career in which they can be constantly stimulated. They may find themselves drawn to art, writing, music, fashion, film-making, and the world of entertainment. They may also excel in careers such as education, research, social reform, politics, and charity work.

Destiny *To introduce innovative concepts to the world*

The life path of people born on this day is to learn to be more realistic in their assessment of people and situations. Once they are able to examine themselves honestly, their destiny is to introduce and promote innovative concepts.

Signs & symbols

Sun sign: Sagittarius

Ruling planet: Jupiter, the philosopher

Symbol: The Archer

Birth date ruler: Mercury, the communicator

Tarot card: The Hierophant (guidance)

Favorable numbers: 5, 8

Lucky days: Thursday and Wednesday, especially when these days fall on 5 and 8 of the month

Lucky colors: Blue, turquoise, orange

Birthstone: Turquoise

6 December

the birthday of the developer

Practical and clear sighted, people born on December 6 have a real talent for management. They will often be found organizing teams of people and trying to improve or develop situations or ideas so that they produce better results. They are the people to whom everyone turns first when things aren't working, and others value them for their consistently rational and perceptive way of looking at the world, as well as the tactful way they present their conclusions so that others feel motivated to make positive changes rather than feeling vulnerable and disappointed.

Lacking any hidden agenda, these people are direct, honest and to the point in both their professional and personal life. They can see immediately the weaknesses or flaws in a situation, and how these can be replaced, removed or improved so that the best possible result can be achieved. Although friends and co-workers are often extremely grateful for their sage advice, occasionally their desire to interfere and control can come across as meddling. As illogical as it may seem to them, they need to respect the fact that some people are stuck in their ways and don't actually want someone wading in with advice on how their situation can change or improve.

Until the age of forty-five they will feel a growing need for order and structure in their lives, and there is a big emphasis on practical issues. During these years, evaluating concepts and systems, and devising strategies to improve them, are likely to be top of their agenda. After the age of forty-six there is a turning point that highlights a growing need for more independence but also for group awareness. They will feel more experimental, but these are also the years when they are likely to enlist the support of others and be the spearhead for highly motivated and smoothly operating teams.

Although creativity isn't the strong point for these people, their highly developed qualities of clear thinking, objectivity and progressiveness make them natural leaders with the potential to achieve results that enhance their own lives and everyone else's they come into contact with.

Love *Interesting conversation*

The bright and articulate people born on December 6 are attracted to intelligent and hardworking people, and nothing is more enjoyable to them—or sensual, if it is the right person—than an interesting conversation. Others will be drawn to them in time of need for guidance and support, and it is important for them to pick and choose who they help, making sure their energy isn't dimmed by clingy or needy people.

Health *The scent of ginger*

People born on this day have workaholic tendencies and may rely on stimulants such as caffeine and smoking to keep them alert. This is bad for their health and they should ensure that they find healthier ways to stay alert, such as eating little and often to keep their blood sugar balanced and their brains alert, and eating foods rich in concentrated nutrients, such as oily fish, nuts and seeds. Regular exercise, if possible on a daily basis for around 30 minutes, will also boost their energy levels, and they need to get lots of good-quality sleep. Burning candles with ginger scent may help clear their head and improve their memory when they work or study; to combat stress they should try burning a chamomile, lavender or sandalwood candle. Wearing, meditating on or surrounding themselves with the color purple, and taking up drawing or writing as a hobby, will all encourage them to connect with their intuition and latent creativity.

Career *Born managers*

These people will thrive in any career in which they are given the freedom to organize and implement improvements. Possible career options include management, publishing, advertising, sales, business, administration, law, social reform, and education, and a deeper need for harmony may also draw them to an interest in music and the arts.

Destiny *To be at the forefront of progress*

The life path of people born on this day is to understand that not everything in life needs to be organized and managed. Once they learn to leave others alone when their advice isn't required, their destiny is to be at the forefront of progress.

Signs & symbols

Sun sign: Sagittarius

Ruling planet: Jupiter, the philosopher

Symbol: The Archer

Birth date ruler: Venus, the lover

Tarot card: The Lovers (choices)

Favorable numbers: 6, 9

Lucky days: Thursday and Friday, especially when these days fall on 6 and 9 of the month

Lucky colors: Blue, lavender, pink

Birthstone: Turquoise

7 December

the birthday of the dreamer

Your greatest challenge is ...

finding the right career

The way forward is ...

to keep experimenting and gather as much information and advice as possible. Try also to develop outside interests; one of those may develop into a career.

You're drawn to people born on ...

October 23 to November 21

You are both dreamers but one is more practical than the other, keeping your intense relationship on track.

Luck maker

Stay focused but flexible

Successful people know that success often results from something they least expect, so stay focused but flexible in your goal setting.

People born on December 7 often feel as if there is a special purpose to their life. They dare to be different, and as highly original and creative thinkers they do indeed stand apart from the crowd. Although they have a thirst for adventure, they are first and foremost dreamers and their minds are capable of taking them to places others simply haven't the imagination to go.

They are often trendsetters who make up their own rules as they go along and their free-thinking, pioneering style will often startle others. Tending to be loners, they also know how to blend in when they want to, and their conversation is always colorful and interesting. The big problem, however, is that they tend to talk more than they act; if there is no follow-through people may dismiss them as dreamers not doers. To a certain extent this is true, as they are so creative and original they tend to get lost in their ideas.

Until the age of forty-four they will often feel a need to be more practical and realistic in their approach to their goals. They should pay attention to this because their tendency to flit from job to job or to stick with a job to which they are clearly unsuited can cause them great unhappiness. After the age of forty-five there is a turning point when their desire to express their individuality will be stronger than ever. If they haven't found their vocation by then, they are strongly advised to seek advice from experts about retraining for a new career. Alternatively, they may decide to seek satisfaction and fulfillment outside of work; if this is the case they need to make sure that they do not compromise too much of their spirit for the sake of financial security.

Conformity will never be for them, but these people need to find what makes their heart sing. It would truly be a tragedy if the world did not benefit from their unique but truly magical creativity.

On the **dark** side

Detached, stressed, muddled

At your **best**

Creative, individual, original

Love *Meaningful relationships*

People born on December 7 have highly romantic expectations when it comes to affairs of the heart, and the quest for a soul mate will have begun from an early age. Relationships have to be meaningful for them and as long as they find an intelligent, idealistic partner who can keep up with their quick mind and ever-expanding search for knowledge, they can be spontaneous, passionate and loyal partners.

Health *Don't skip breakfast*

The more people born on this day can escape into the countryside the better, because nature has a calming and uplifting effect on them. If they live in the city they should seek out local parks, and make sure there are plenty of plants in their living and working area. Classical music is also highly therapeutic when they are suffering from the bouts of stress and anxiety to which they are prone. Mixing with people who are upbeat, positive and focused will encourage them to find a sense of purpose and direction for themselves, and they should stay away from people who are negative or cynical in their approach to life. As far as diet is concerned, they should make sure they always eat breakfast because missing it can unsettle their metabolism, leading to weight gain, especially around the waist and thighs. Regular moderate to mild exercise, in particular walking, is also recommended. Placing a titanium quartz crystal near them at home or at work, or carrying a small crystal when they meditate, will help them find their true path in life.

Career *Born teachers*

These people are well suited to careers in which they can act independently. Possible career options include teaching, writing, law, politics, commerce, sales, promotion, or negotiation. Alternatively their need for creative self-expression may lead them to music, art or drama.

Destiny *To educate, inform and inspire others*

The life path of people born on this day is to balance their imaginative, creative side with their need to find a meaning and purpose in life. Once they find ways to put everything into place, their destiny is to use their imagination and creativity to educate, inform and inspire others.

Power Thought

"Today I will be part of the solution not the problem"

Signs & symbols

Sun sign: Sagittarius

Ruling planet: Jupiter, the philosopher

Symbol: The Archer

Birth date ruler: Neptune, the speculator

Tarot card: The Chariot (resilience)

Favorable numbers: 1, 7

Lucky days: Thursday and Monday, especially when these days fall on 1 or 7 of the month

Lucky colors: Blue, azure, sea green

Birthstone: Turquoise

8 December

the birthday of passion

Your greatest challenge is ...

being responsible

The way forward is ...

to understand that being responsible and passionate are not mutually exclusive, and working together they can put you on the winning team.

You're drawn to people born on ...

December 22 to January 19

You have much to argue about, but the attraction between you is such that making up afterwards will be wonderful.

Luck maker

Think before you act

Lucky people actively take steps to reduce the number of mistakes they make by learning about the issues involved and listening to knowledgeable people before acting.

People born on December 8 tend to sparkle with energy and enthusiasm and their lively personality will attract attention wherever they go. Their passionate approach to life is their defining feature, and they display intense emotional and sensual responses. When an opportunity presents itself in either their personal or professional life, they rarely hesitate and jump in head first.

Whether it is committing to an individual, a team, a project, or an idea, they can't see the point of being half-hearted; their nature is to give one hundred per cent. True idealists, people born on this day are constantly engaged in a quest to find fulfillment, emotional, intellectual or spiritual, and their infectious optimism may inspire others to seek their own personal nirvana. The trouble is that the perfect fulfillment they seek is unobtainable, and this can cause them to become manic or confused in their search for stimulation. Relaxing their expectations of perfection and understanding that imperfection is the natural human state is essential for their psychological growth.

Until the age of forty-three there is an emphasis in their lives on the need for order or structure; they should take advantage of opportunities presented to them to be more practical in their approach. This is because they don't always tend to direct their energy well, and their lack of good judgment can cause them to get involved in relationships or situations that are destructive or obsessive. After the age of forty-four there is another turning point, and this time they may feel a growing need to develop their individuality.

Whatever age they are, the key to their potential for happiness and success is to be more cautious and aware in their approach to people and situations so that their passionate intensity does not overpower their common sense. With a little more realism added to their stunning repertoire of creativity and idealism, they will find the fulfilling passion they have been searching for all their lives, in the process bringing great happiness to others.

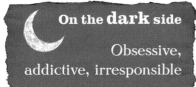
Love *Tempestuous*

People born on December 8 tend to be attracted to people with opposing views to their own and therefore to tempestuous relationships. It is important for them not to confuse tension with passion. Once in a long-term relationship they can be incredibly romantic and spontaneous, but their partner needs to be aware that their resolve may not always hold firm when they are tempted to stray.

Health *Don't burn the midnight oil*

People born on this day tend to go to bed in the small hours of the morning and if possible to get up as late as they can. Although everyone has natural sleep preferences, they should try to make sure they are in bed by midnight as studies show that people who do this tend to get better-quality sleep, which is essential for the physical and emotional health and well-being of these people. They should also beware of recreational drugs and alcohol because they have addictive tendencies that need to be managed and minimized. As far as diet is concerned, moderation is the key; the same goes for exercise, which is extremely important for them for its mood-boosting powers. Wearing, meditating on and surrounding themselves with the color blue will encourage them to be more objective and responsible, and carrying a titanium quartz crystal can help them think before they act.

Career *Born dancers*

These people tend to go where their heart leads them, and as long as they can sustain their passionate intensity their potential for success is strong whatever career they choose. They also have a great desire to inspire others, so they may excel as writers, dancers, actors, singers, artists, and performers. Self-employment will be an appealing option for them, as might working for large enterprises with plenty of opportunities for career advancement, change and travel.

Destiny *To bring happiness to others*

The life path of people born on this day is to balance their passion with their need to be more responsible. Once they are able to direct their instincts, their destiny is to bring happiness to others.

Signs & symbols

Sun sign: Sagittarius

Ruling planet: Jupiter, the philosopher

Symbol: The Archer

Birth date ruler: Saturn, the teacher

Tarot card: Strength (passion)

Favorable numbers: 2, 8

Lucky days: Thursday and Saturday, especially when these days fall on 2 and 8 of the month

Lucky colors: Purple, brown, maroon

Birthstone: Turquoise

December 8

9 December

the birthday of the dashing hero

People born on December 9 are blessed with a fertile imagination. From childhood they will have cast themselves in the role of the dashing hero or heroine swooping in to save the day and astonishing everyone with acts of daring and courage. In adulthood they often become highly energetic individuals who love to be the center of attention.

They have a powerful urge to make important and inspirational contributions to the world and, with their imaginative mind, fixity of purpose and adventurous spirit they do possess outstanding pioneering potential. Born leaders, their biggest challenge is patience. Their patience can easily snap when things aren't going exactly the way they want them to or when people aren't listening to their suggestions. They need to learn when to promote their progressive ideals and when to step back and let things unfold. Calming their emotional intensity in response to any challenge they meet is crucial for their psychological growth, as well as for their chances of both professional and personal success.

Although they may have been shy as children, by the time they reach their twenties they will start to come out of their shells; if they can't manage this, developing their self-confidence is crucial because these people were born to be in the limelight. Until the age of forty-two there will be opportunities for them to find realistic ways to achieve their goals in life. They need to take advantage of these; if they don't, their dreams of progress and adventure will never move beyond the planning stage. After the age of forty-three there is a turning point when they may feel a desire to be more independent and to express their individuality.

At whatever age or stage in life they are, they have an all-encompassing, albeit occasionally self-centered urge to play a leading role in the lives of those around them. If they can implement their original and progressive visions it will give them the potential to make not just an imaginative but a real and significant contribution to the world.

On the **dark** side
Selfish, controlling, unrealistic

At your **best**
Progressive, romantic, dynamic

Love *Emotional intensity*

People born on December 9 are romantic, ardent and passionate lovers, but for long-term success in relationships they need to find someone who can also show them the joys of the simpler, quieter things in life. Although routine and responsibilities are not for them and they need the freedom to travel and explore different experiences, when they do find a partner who is romantic and adventurous, but also solid and dependable, they can be surprisingly loyal and supportive.

Health *Pent-up energy*

People born on this day tend to be high-energy individuals who live fast and eat fast. This can cause digestion problems so it is important for them to learn to slow down, sit down and chew their food carefully. Eating on the go is bad news for their digestive health and their waistline because they are more likely to eat foods that are high in calories, fat, and additives and preservatives. For their psychological and physical health they also need to control their temper; when blinded by anger they can become accident prone. If they cannot find ways to deal with their anger it can lead to stress and frustration, both potentially dangerous to themselves and others. Anger-management techniques are recommended if the problem is severe; for milder cases, meditation and breathing techniques, or cognitive behavioral therapy, will help. Regular vigorous exercise, running in particular, is recommended as it can release pent-up tension. Wearing, meditating on and surrounding themselves with the color blue will help them to be more in control of their emotions.

Career *Born lawyers*

These people may find themselves drawn to the political or scientific spheres, or to artistic media such as music, writing, literature, or drama. They love to express their ideas, so they may also be drawn to education, law, business, journalism, social reform, and the world of entertainment.

Destiny *To lead others toward progress*

The life path of people born on this day is to learn to be calmer and more realistic in their approach. Once they have taken charge of their emotions, their destiny is to lead others to implement original and progressive changes.

Signs & symbols

Sun sign: Sagittarius

Ruling planet: Jupiter, the philosopher

Symbol: The Archer

Birth date ruler: Mars, the warrior

Tarot card: The Hermit (inner strength)

Favorable numbers: 3, 9

Lucky day: Thursday, especially when it falls on 3 and 9 of the month

Lucky colors: Blue, red, purple

Birthstone: Turquoise

December 9

10 December

the birthday of calm intensity

A defining characteristic of people born on December 10 is their remarkable strength of spirit and steady determination to achieve their goals. Deep and intense thinkers, they are often driven by an urge to further human knowledge or instigate reform. Blessed with an inner calm that can help them stand back and make decisions objectively, their organizational skills are outstanding.

These people have leadership potential and, when they find a cause they believe in, they will wholly devote themselves to it. The key word here is "belief," because if they don't believe in what they are doing they simply won't be able to go through the motions. As a result their choice of career will often have a vocational element; they need to feel they are serving some kind of higher cause, be it in education or in spiritual matters. They will devote a great deal of time to examining the meaning of not just their own life, but the lives of everyone and even the universe. For this reason they can sometimes come across as slightly removed from the world they live in. This isn't to say they aren't sociable; they are. It's just that the sensitive part of them always seems to live in a world where injustice and suffering do not exist; not the real world, then.

Until the age of forty-one they will be presented with opportunities to be more practical and to put more order and structure into their lives. They should take advantage of these opportunities to develop a thicker skin and be more resilient in the face of adversity, as they don't tend to cope well during times of stress and conflict. After the age of forty-two there is a turning point that highlights a growing need for independence.

Whatever age they are, when they do finally find an ideal or cause about which they are passionate they will discover within themselves all the self-discipline, responsibility and passion they need to live up to their exceptional potential to become gifted, inspired and progressive leaders.

On the **dark** side

Elusive, isolated, overly sensitive

At your **best**

Determined, spiritual, devoted

Power Thought

❝ My life is a celebration to be shared with everyone I know ❞

Love *Love freely*

People born on December 10 are charming and attractive individuals who rarely have problems attracting friends and admirers. They may, however, make things harder for themselves by falling in love with someone who lives far away or who is from a completely different background or even culture. They should always follow their heart but should not let their romantic idealism destroy their chances of finding real happiness in love.

Health *Don't retreat*

People born on this day have a tendency to isolate themselves during times of stress, and it's important for them to keep in touch with friends and loved ones. They need to ensure that they don't become too detached because reaching out to others will not just boost their emotional health, it will boost their physical health too. They also need to ensure that they don't put all their emotional eggs in one basket, relying solely on one person to support and uplift them. As far as diet is concerned, they could be prone to eating disorders and so need to make sure that food or denying themselves food does not become a way of avoiding uncomfortable feelings. Regular moderate exercise is highly recommended, especially in the outside so they get all the mood-boosting properties of sunshine. Wearing, meditating on and surrounding themselves with the color orange will increase feelings of warmth, physical enjoyment and security; it may lift their love life too.

Career *Born event managers*

These people may find fulfillment in careers in people or event management, in politics or in other forms of community service. They may also be drawn to the academic world. Other possible work options include writing, promotion, sales and therapy, and they may also wish to explore their creativity in art, film, drama or architecture.

Destiny *To formulate effective strategies*

The life path of people born on this day is to get in touch with their own feelings and those of others. Once they can keep alive strong bonds with others and become more resilient in the face of conflict, their destiny is to formulate effective plans or strategies for the benefit of themselves and others.

Signs & symbols

Sun sign: Sagittarius

Ruling planet: Jupiter, the philosopher

Symbol: The Archer

Birth date ruler: Sun, the individual

Tarot card: The Wheel of Fortune (change)

Favorable numbers: 1, 4

Lucky days: Thursday and Sunday, especially when these days fall on 1 and 4 of the month

Lucky colors: Blue, yellow, orange

Birthstone: Turquoise

11 December

the birthday of intense purpose

Your greatest challenge is ...

having fun

The way forward is ...

to understand that the ability to take things less seriously is one of the most powerful and influential ways to influence people or get your point across.

You're drawn to people born on ...

September 23 to October 22

You have so much to learn from and love about each other, making this a natural and easygoing combination.

Luck maker

Have faith

Studies show that people who believe there is plenty of luck to go around tend to have a higher level of life satisfaction than those who do not. Believe in luck and it will change your life.

People born on December 11 may have felt from an early age that there was a serious purpose to their lives. Whatever profession they choose, they are notable for the driving energy and determination they bring to their causes and visions.

As perfectionists they will demand as high a level of commitment and dedication from others as they demand from themselves. This will mean that they often excel professionally, but it can also work against them and exhaust everyone involved, including themselves. As far as their personal and social life is concerned, there is no let-up in their intensity; they are influential and persuasive individuals with the ability to win over—or in some cases wear down—others with their charming persistence. In fact, when it comes to advancing their cause or agenda, one of their favorite approaches is to cultivate influential contacts, because they know that with powerful backing almost anything is possible.

Until the age of forty a running theme will be the need for a more practical and realistic approach to achieving their goals in life. During these years they are likely to assume positions of responsibility or authority but they should ensure that the single-minded pursuit of their goals does not make them manipulative or overly materialistic. It is particularly important that their networking strategy does not slump into ambitious social climbing. After the age of forty-one there is a turning point, highlighting a desire to express their individuality and independence. They may become more involved with social issues and establishing a life outside work.

It would benefit these people always to consider the way others perceive them or the image they present to the world. Once they discover the lighter side of life, together with the spiritual ideals to balance their materialistic inclinations, they will find that their serious purpose is to become an outstanding human being capable of improving the lives of all around them—and in some cases humanity as a whole.

Love *Inveterate charmer*

People born on December 11 are charming and seductive, and few can resist their spell. However, they need to ensure that they don't abuse their magnetic power to get who they want. They are drawn to ambitious, hardworking individuals like themselves, but may feel happier with someone who has a more spontaneous, relaxed approach to life.

Health *Take care of your soul*

People born on this day pay great attention both to their appearance by making sure they are always well presented, and to their minds by making sure they are stimulated. But unless they learn to nurture their soul as well they are likely to feel unfulfilled and unhappy. They would benefit greatly from a more spiritual outlook on life and more quiet time spent alone reflecting on their real priorities in life. As far as diet is concerned, they need to cut down on red meat and dairy products, while increasing their intake of fresh fruits, vegetables, whole grains, legumes, oily fish, nuts, and seeds. They should throw away any ready meals or similar foods high in additives and preservatives. Regular exercise is essential for them, and to keep their weight down and their mood up they should aim for at least 30 minutes of aerobic activity a day, with three to four sessions of body toning a week. Wearing, meditating on and surrounding themselves with the color purple will encourage them to think of higher things, as will regular meditation and yoga sessions.

Career *Born executives*

These people may be drawn to careers in engineering, technology or mechanics, but they may also excel in business, debating, law, and research. With their fine mind they could also be gifted teachers, artists and writers, and their natural executive skills might place them in senior management positions.

Destiny *To achieve their progressive aims*

The life path of people born on this day is to learn that their need for a serious sense of purpose is in fact their need to find a higher purpose. Once they have rediscovered their spiritual dimension and their sense of humor, their destiny is to work with energy and determination toward the achievement of their progressive aims.

Signs & symbols

Sun sign: Sagittarius

Ruling planet: Jupiter, the philosopher

Symbol: The Archer

Birth date ruler: Moon, the intuitive

Tarot card: Justice (discernment)

Favorable numbers: 2, 5

Lucky days: Thursday and Monday, especially when these days fall on 2 and 5 of the month

Lucky colors: Blue, silver, white

Birthstone: Turquoise

December 11

12 December

the birthday of
the outspoken teacher

People born on December 12 often feel that they have an important message to deliver to the world—one that they believe will help others progress and learn. They also long to broaden their mind through study and travel, and as well as being mentally agile they also tend to be physically agile, enjoying traveling about from place to place or experience to experience.

These people's insatiable appetite for knowledge and experience is heavily influenced by their powerful desire to make a tangible, beneficial and enlightening contribution to the lives of others. Colleagues and friends will often admire their mental dexterity and their ability to identify areas in need of improvement and communicate their remedial visions to those around them in ways that are truly memorable.

Until the age of thirty-nine there is an emphasis in their lives on the need for order and structure. These are the years when they are most likely to feel boxed in or tied down, and the struggle between their desire to establish themselves and their thirst for adventure can be complicating and confusing for them. After the age of forty there is an important turning point when they are likely to become even more experimental in their approach to life and when the drive toward freedom will be particularly strong. The term mid-life crisis would not be inappropriate here, and these people may suddenly feel the need to make dramatic changes in their personal and professional life.

These people must never forget that they possess a tremendous amount of will-power and, when they finally devote themselves to a worthy career and set themselves clear goals and objectives, they have all the ambition and talent they need to be a success. When it comes to their personal life, if they can channel some of their energy inward to develop their intuition and spirituality, they will be able to draw on their extensive knowledge and life experience to realize their ambition of delivering an empowering message of hope, love and positive expectation to the world.

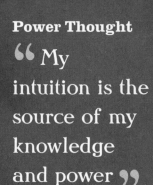

Love *Let's get physical*

People born on December 12, whether they are conventionally attractive or not, often have a seductive voice and a powerful and dramatic physical presence. They can use these to their advantage when it comes to attracting potential partners. They will probably have many relationships, but once they finally find a partner they want to commit to they are likely to fully commit to the relationship to make it work.

Health *Preventative health*

People born on this day can sometimes think that they have inherited poor health and that they are likely to succumb to the same illnesses or conditions as their parents. In the great majority of cases their fears are unfounded, and if they take good care of themselves by practicing preventative medicine they can reduce or completely eliminate their risk of dementia, osteoporosis and high blood pressure. Once they understand the connection between their current eating, sleeping and lifestyle habits and the long-term health risks involved, it is often enough for them to make positive changes. These will include making sure their diet is fresh, nutritious and healthy, and that their exercise routine becomes a part of their life. They would benefit greatly from grounding and calming activities such as tai chi and yoga, and mental disciplines such as meditation. Wearing, meditating on and surrounding themselves with the color purple will encourage them to look within for a sense of excitement.

Career *Born advisors*

These people have a message for the world, and careers that allow them to impart knowledge such as lecturing, teaching, writing, counseling, advising, politics, coaching, and training will therefore all appeal. They may also be drawn toward advertising, sales—especially the promoting of innovative new products—media, publishing, the theater, or the arts.

Destiny *To educate, advise and inspire others*

The life path of people born on this day is to balance their need for freedom with their need to establish themselves. Once they have added a spiritual dimension to their lives, their destiny is to educate, advise and inspire others.

Signs & symbols

Sun sign: Sagittarius

Ruling planet: Jupiter, the philosopher

Symbol: The Archer

Birth date ruler: Jupiter, the philosopher

Tarot card: The Hanged Man (reflection)

Favorable numbers: 3, 6

Lucky day: Thursday, especially when this day falls on 3 and 6 of the month

Lucky colors: Blue, lilac, purple

Birthstone: Turquoise

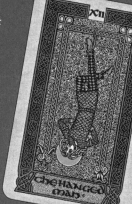

13 December

the birthday of erratic precision

People born on December 13 bring confidence, resourcefulness and tenacity to everything they do, plus a precise and occasionally painstaking attention to the smallest detail. Although their potential for professional and personal success in the long term is great, their careful and time-consuming approach can become over-cautious and hesitant. This, unfortunately, can lead to disillusionment.

These people with an eye for detail can be incredibly observant and perceptive when it comes to their fellow human beings. Regrettably, when it comes to themselves they can lack awareness and may not realize that they have erratic habits that not only irritate others, but also stop them working as efficiently as they might like. For example, they don't seem to know when to back off when an argument is going nowhere or when their point has been made, and will unnecessarily and hurtfully restate their case over and over again. In addition, they may have a habit of procrastinating when something important needs to be done, making life much harder for themselves than it need be.

Until the age of thirty-eight these people may feel a need for a practical and realistic approach to achieving their goals; these are the years when they need to be especially careful not to focus so much on the details that they lose sight of the bigger picture. After the age of thirty-nine there is a turning point and they are likely to want to express their individuality more. This can be an incredibly liberating time for them; they can start to put their personal mark on the success they have already built up for themselves.

Regardless of their age and stage in life, these people need to guard against becoming too exacting and finicky. This is because when they are able to step back and look at the impressive picture they are painting with their lives they will realize that they have both a lot to be grateful for and a lot to look forward to.

Love *Don't put your lover on a pedestal*

People born on December 13 have a passionate side to them and when it is first unleashed in a relationship they will feel liberated and their partner will feel cherished. However, they need to resist the tendency to put their partner on a pedestal and then wear them down with constant criticism and nit-picking. Once they understand that no one is perfect, they will get their priorities right and place love at the very top.

Health *Balance your blood sugar*

Work is extremely important for people born on this day, but for their health and happiness they need to cultivate things that make them happy. They may also have a tendency only to socialize with people from work; they might feel far happier if they looked to the outside world for companionship. They should try to cut down the amount of caffeine and sugar that they ingest, because these can cause anxiety and extreme blood sugar fluctuations respectively. Instead, they should reach for fruit, vegetables or a wholegrain cracker. Regular moderate-intensity exercise will also help ease anxiety attacks and boost their feeling of well-being. Regular check-ups with their doctor should be scheduled but they should also make sure they don't get obsessive about their health because this is counterproductive. Wearing, meditating on and surrounding themselves with the color orange will encourage them to be more creative and spontaneous.

Career *Born computer programmers*

These people will thrive in careers where patience and attention to detail are essential and they may be drawn toward editing, restorative or museum work, art, writing, decorating, and archaeology, as well as computer programming. Occupations that involve travel and plenty of variety will be beneficial, as will any kind of work that keeps them mentally challenged.

Destiny *To suggest ingenious and effective technical advances*

The life path of people born on this day is to learn to move on when situations can't be mended or their point has been made. Once they have learned to look at themselves as objectively as they like to look at others, their destiny is to suggest ingenious and effective technical advances.

Power Thought

" Every day I am more and more at ease with myself and with life "

Signs & symbols

Sun sign: Sagittarius

Ruling planet: Jupiter, the philosopher

Symbol: The Archer

Birth date ruler: Uranus, the visionary

Tarot card: Death (choices)

Favorable numbers: 4, 7

Lucky days: Thursday and Sunday, especially when these days fall on 4 and 7 of the month

Lucky colors: Purple, silver, electric blue

Birthstone: Turquoise

December 13

14 December

the birthday of the flamboyant philosopher

People born on December 14 rarely merge into the crowd. This doesn't mean they are attention seekers. Quite the opposite; they can be deeply private individuals. It's just that their flamboyant tastes and unique ideas set them apart as much as their controlled energy, capability and efficiency. As natural philosophers, finding their own truth rather than conforming to the rules of others will always be important to them.

Although their provocative nature can outrage, it can also surprise and stimulate others, encouraging them to think outside the box. Nothing gives them greater satisfaction than the knowledge that they have fired someone's creativity or imagination. This is because activity and progress are their driving forces, and they cannot bear complacency when there are issues to explore and progress to be made. Blessed with strong organizational skills as well as considerable energy, they approach everything they do with enthusiasm, determination and insatiable curiosity.

These people are sociable and generous to others but in many respects they are also extremely self-contained and self-reliant. Their potential for fulfillment lies in the quest for discovery and progress, and although they will never turn away those who come to them for guidance, a part of them longs to shut out all outside distraction so they can pursue their personal goals undisturbed. They prefer to step into the limelight only when the time is right for them to reveal the fruits of their labor.

Until the age of thirty-eight there is an emphasis on practical order and structure in their lives, making them more goal-orientated and responsible; but after the age of thirty-nine there is a turning point when they will become more concerned with expressing their individuality and making contribution to the world. The keys to their success will be their ability to find a work–life balance and their willingness to develop their diplomatic skills so that they motivate others to follow their example and become potent, productive and truth-seeking forces for positive change and progress.

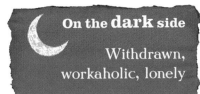
Love *Unique and intelligent*

People born on this day like to mix with people who are as intellectually quick and inquisitive as themselves. Although they are idealistic, they may not always be good at opening up emotionally and, if they have been hurt by someone they cared for deeply, work may take center stage in their lives. When they do find someone who loves them for their uniqueness, they will really come into their own.

Health *Get your life in balance*

People born on this day can suffer from low self-esteem, and this can have a negative effect on their emotional and physical health. Burying themselves in work or withdrawing from others is not the answer, but taking care of their mind, body, heart, and soul is. Only when all these four aspects of their life are being nurtured daily will their life feel balanced and their self-esteem soar. They should avoid recreational drugs at all costs and limit their alcohol consumption because they may have addictive tendencies. When it comes to diet, the secret is to keep everything as balanced and structured as possible. Moderation in all things is the key, not just for diet but for all aspects of their life. Mild to moderate exercise is recommended for its health-boosting qualities and calming effect, and wearing or meditating on the color blue will encourage them to be more objective and diplomatic in their approach to life.

Career *Born philosophers*

Their decisiveness and perceptiveness make these people natural leaders, but they tend to thrive in careers where they can operate independently, and where research or development plays a key role. Possible career choices include sales, business, education, acting, philosophy, writing, advertising, publishing, and sport.

Destiny *To inspire others to discover and progress*

The life path of people born on this day is to learn to balance their emotional with their professional needs. Once they can take the time to consider the impact of their words or actions, their destiny is to inspire others to look in the direction of discovery and progress.

Signs & symbols

Sun sign: Sagittarius

Ruling planet: Jupiter, the philosopher

Symbol: The Archer

Birth date ruler: Mercury, the communicator

Tarot card: Temperance (moderation)

Favorable numbers: 5, 8

Lucky days: Thursday and Wednesday, especially when these days fall on 5 and 8 of the month

Lucky colors: Purple, orange, green

Birthstone: Turquoise

December 14

15 December

the birthday of the optimist

Your greatest challenge is ...

accepting your limitations

The way forward is ...

to understand that an overly optimistic evaluation of a situation is just as unhelpful as one that is overly pessimistic. Strike a balance between the two.

You're drawn to people born on ...

September 23 to October 22

You are both charming and easygoing, and this relationship has great potential for happiness.

Luck maker

Be bold, yet realistic

Unlucky people set unattainable goals for themselves, preparing themselves to fail. The more realistic and obtainable your goals, the more likely you are to achieve them.

People born on December 15 are among the most upbeat individuals of the year. Once they set their sights on something, however unattainable, they truly believe that they can attain it. This positive, can-do and can-have attitude tends to attract most, if not all, of the professional and personal success their many talents deserve.

As well as being expansive and optimistic in their outlook, they are also blessed with an insatiable curiosity. They delight in discovering new information and in sharing what they have learned with colleagues and friends. Although their curiosity is infectious and their optimism energizing, it is important for people born on this day to consider whether or not the information they are revealing and the sense of possibility they are encouraging are in the best interests of themselves and others. This is because they see the world through the eyes of an optimist, and an optimist doesn't take into account or protect themselves against the negative potential of a situation. In other words, their plans can sometimes be unrealistic or—worse still—foolish, and their influence on others can be condescending or irresponsible.

Until the age of thirty-five people born on this day will have many opportunities to develop a more practical and realistic approach to life and they need to take advantage of these because optimism can only take them so far. After the age of thirty-six, however, there is a turning point which highlights a growing need for independence, progressive ideas and expressing their individuality. During these years it is vital for them to learn to listen to the advice of others, weighing up the pros and cons of a situation before jumping in over their heads.

Throughout their lives the key to their success will be their ability to recognize and leave behind situations that are unproductive, so that they can invest their outstanding potential in doing what they do best: moving in the direction of progress, while motivating and inspiring others with their invigorating enthusiasm, stunning creativity and can-do attitude.

At your best
Energizing, inspirational, popular

Love *Spoiled for choice*

People born on December 15 are passionate and sensual individuals who rarely lack admirers. They also have an insatiable appetite for new experiences and, although lovers will be plentiful, a quality relationship will prove elusive until they learn greater self-control. Once in a relationship with someone special they are capable of great devotion, but they can suffer from fluctuating moods to which their partner needs to be sensitive.

Health *Breakfast like a king*

The optimism that is characteristic of people born on this day tends to carry through into their attitude toward their health. They tend to take their health for granted and to overlook problems for which they should seek their doctor's advice. As far as diet is concerned, they are advised to breakfast like a king, lunch like a prince and supper like a pauper, because stacking their food intake in this way can give their digestive system a rest while they sleep. It will also help them sleep better, as they can be prone to insomnia and night waking. When it comes to exercise, the best advice for these people is to take up an activity that they enjoy, whether it be dancing, tennis, swimming, or any other sport, because studies show that when people enjoy exercise they tend to stick to it. Wearing, meditating on and surrounding themselves with the colors blue or indigo will encourage them to be more realistic in their approach to life, as will carrying a malachite crystal.

Career *Born advertisers*

These people have the ability to excel in business, new technology and management, but they may also be drawn to sales, writing, teaching, music, the media, advertising, and performing. Whatever career they choose, variety and plenty of travel will help keep them motivated.

Destiny *To enlighten, inspire and educate others*

The life path of people born on this day is to learn to see all aspects of a situation, not just the ones they want to see. Once they have improved their judgment and learned to be more realistic, their destiny is to enlighten, educate and inspire others and, by so doing, make their mark on society.

Signs & symbols

Sun sign: Sagittarius

Ruling planet: Jupiter, the philosopher

Symbol: The Archer

Birth date ruler: Venus, the lover

Tarot card: The Devil (choices)

Favorable numbers: 6, 9

Lucky days: Thursday and Friday, especially when these days fall on 6 and 9 of the month

Lucky colors: Purple, pink, lavender

Birthstone: Turquoise

16 December

the birthday of
the creative anthropologist

Your greatest challenge is ...

resisting the impulse to criticize

The way forward is ...

to understand that sometimes the best approach to a situation is to focus on the solution not the problem.

You're drawn to people born on ...

November 22 to December 21

You are both imaginative and adventurous, and this can be an exciting and fulfilling relationship.

Luck maker

Don't isolate yourself

If you isolate yourself to satisfy your career aspirations or personal interests, you isolate yourself from the biggest source of luck in life—other people.

People born on December 16 are blessed with a soaring imagination but their logical and objective approach to situations and people ensures that they never succumb to flights of fancy. In fact they have the ability to view everyone and everything in their life with the inquisitive detachment of an anthropologist.

Nothing escapes the scrutiny of these intelligent and sharp-witted people, and when their analytical, logical and determined mind is combined with their imaginative intellectual qualities, they have the potential to engineer far-reaching innovations. Once they have settled on their objectives, they will pursue them with remarkable determination, and although this dramatically enhances their potential for professional success—they often rise to management level or the very top of their careers—their single-minded focus on their career goals can isolate them emotionally from others.

Until the age of thirty-five they will lean toward a more practical and realistic approach to their goals, and these are the years when they are most likely to lose themselves in their career. During these years establishing a work–life balance and becoming more sensitive to the feelings of others are important. After the age of thirty-six, however, there is a significant turning point which highlights a need to be free from responsibilities, to be more independent and to express their individuality. They may become involved with humanitarian ideals or issues of universal spirituality. At first this shift in focus may feel confusing and disorientating for them, but as the years go by they start to understand themselves better and experience life less as a research lab and more on a deeper, intuitive level where certain things are simply to be experienced rather than examined.

They also begin to realize that the key to unlocking their potential for outstanding achievement is to keep their lives as real and as grounded as possible, so that they are relaxed and receptive enough to tune into their powerful intuition and make the right choices for themselves and others.

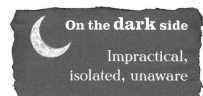

On the dark side

Impractical, isolated, unaware

At your best

Innovative, thorough, visionary

Love *Poetic spirit*

People born on December 16 are loving and supportive mates who pride themselves on being a good judge of character, and understand the importance of give and take in a relationship. Sometimes, however, their pragmatic approach can be interpreted as passionless, so it is important for them to be more spontaneous to keep the romantic sparkle in their relationships. They tend to be attracted to those who are artistic or creative in some way, because deep down inside them is a poet's spirit longing to express itself.

Health *The color violet*

People born on this day can be prone to fatigue and digestive disorders with an unexplained origin, and they might find that there is more stress in their lives than they think. They may also find that their diet isn't quite as healthy or nutritious as it could be, and that their exercise routine needs updating. They would benefit from increasing the amount of fruit, vegetables, whole grains, and legumes in their diet to boost their digestive health; moderate exercise, preferably outdoors so they get all the mood-boosting benefits of sunshine, will help improve their mood and increase their chances of a good night's sleep. Wearing, meditating on and surrounding themselves with the color violet will help them get in touch with their intuition. Carrying a quartz crystal with them will also improve the quality of their life, re-energizing their zest and vitality in all situations.

Career *Born psychologists*

People born on this day will probably feel stifled within corporate structures and may prefer to work for themselves. They are also well suited to careers in research, science, production management, and software development. Other careers that might interest them include education, writing, politics, strategic planning, music, art, acting, and psychology.

Destiny *To pioneer far-reaching innovations and ideals*

The life path of people born on this day is to get in touch with their own feelings and those of others. Once they have developed an intuitive sense of what is right and wrong for them, their destiny is to pioneer far-reaching innovations and ideals.

Signs & symbols

Sun sign: Sagittarius

Ruling planet: Jupiter, the philosopher

Symbol: The Archer

Birth date ruler: Neptune, the speculator

Tarot card: The Tower (breakthrough)

Favorable numbers: 1, 7

Lucky days: Thursday and Monday, especially when these days fall on 1 and 7 of the month

Lucky colors: All shades of blue

Birthstone: Turquoise

December 16

17 December

the birthday of the practical realist

Your greatest challenge is ...

seeing the funny side

The way forward is ...

to understand that one of the quickest ways to improve life satisfaction is to take everything and everyone, including yourself, a little less seriously.

You're drawn to people born on ...

August 23 to September 22

You are both sensual and practical people, and this can be a passionate and fulfilling relationship.

Luck maker

Carry a good-luck charm

What matters here is not whether the charm works but the luck-attracting sense of wonder and positive expectation of good fortune it can inspire in you.

People born on December 17 tend to say exactly what they mean, and they expect others to do the same. Success to them is something that can be measured in concrete terms and, as a practical realist, they garner a good deal of responsibility and a reputation for honesty and hard work.

With the courage and vitality to achieve almost any goal they set for themselves, these people are doers rather than thinkers. What interests them is facts, results and actions, not dreams, debates or theories. Everything is focused on what can be achieved or produced right now; this ability to concentrate only on what is before their eyes means they can achieve spectacular results.

Although the friends and family of these people value their sincerity and steady temperament, social involvement with others can be an area of confusion and difficulty for them. Their organizational skills mean that they are excellent at keeping in touch with old friends, but somehow true intimacy may prove elusive. This is largely because they simply don't understand how important small talk and a sense of humor are for breaking down barriers between people. It's important for them to learn to be a little less serious and to recognize that emotions sometimes can't be explained or categorized.

Until the age of thirty-four there is an emphasis on practical issues, and a need for order and structure in their lives. Since they already have a tendency to be pragmatic and realistic, it is important during these years that they don't become too materialistic. After the age of thirty-five there is a turning point when they may want freedom or to be more experimental in their approach to life. Although this is disorientating at first, they will ultimately find this change of emphasis liberating. Above all the key to their success and happiness will be their ability to introduce a spiritual dimension into their lives, because this will give them the sense of certainty, truth, order, and wonder that they have always been seeking.

On the **dark** side
Prosaic, tactless, uninvolved

At your **best**
Honest, structured, steady

Love *For keeps*

People born on December 17 are sensual individuals who thrive in the company of intelligent, enterprising people like themselves, and they will not be short of friends . They believe in long-term relationships and seek someone whom they can trust and settle down with. To ensure success in their relationships, as in life, they need to inject some spontaneity and romance.

Health *Stand tall*

People born on this day tend to have a sedentary lifestyle and this could have a negative impact on their physical and emotional health, triggering weight problems and bouts of fatigue or despondency. Bloating could also be an issue, and to avoid that they need to cut down on salt, alcohol and caffeine, drink lots of water and get plenty of fresh air and vigorous exercise. Cutting down on meat, saturated fats, and processed and refined foods, and eating fresh, wholesome food such as fruits, vegetables and whole grains will also help keep bloating and weight gain at bay. Paying attention to their posture and gently pulling in their stomach with their back straight and their head held high will not only help them feel slimmer, but make them feel more upbeat in their approach. They also need plenty of quality sleep but should aim for no more than eight hours a night; long hours in bed will simply make them feel more tired. Wearing, meditating on and surrounding themselves with the color orange will encourage them to be more spontaneous, and carrying a turquoise crystal will help them be more expressive and communicative.

Career *Born managers*

These people may be attracted to careers that offer management opportunities. They may be drawn to business, retail, commerce, administration, and sales, but may also excel in education, writing, science, or research. The artistic side of their personality may eventually pull them toward music or other creative pursuits.

Destiny *To pioneer creative plans of action*

The life path of people born on this day is to learn to be more creative in their approach to life. Once they are more in touch with their emotions and those of others, their destiny is to devise pioneering and creative plans of action.

Signs & symbols

Sun sign: Sagittarius

Ruling planet: Jupiter, the philosopher

Symbol: The Archer

Birth date ruler: Saturn, the teacher

Tarot card: The Star (hope)

Favorable numbers: 2, 8

Lucky days: Thursday and Saturday, especially when these days fall on 2 and 8 of the month

Lucky colors: Brown, maroon, blue

Birthstone: Turquoise

December 17

18 December

the birthday of possibility

People born on December 18 are blessed with a soaring imagination and a sense of possibility that those who are less imaginative would dismiss or even ridicule. Their determination to translate their dreams into reality is, however, so powerful that they can withstand almost any criticism.

From an early age people born on this day are likely to have been quick learners, soaking up information and mastering skills long before others; when all this knowledge is added to their incredible creativity, anything is quite literally possible. They may develop a game plan for life in their teens or twenties that includes far-reaching plans and then, as the years pass, they will devote themselves fully to achieving their goals and realizing their dreams. These people think in the long term and not in the short term, and although progress may appear slow to others, they are slowly, carefully and steadily climbing their way to the very top.

Until the age of thirty-three they may find that life offers them opportunities to develop a more practical and realistic approach to achieving their goals. They should take advantage of these opportunities by accepting assistance when it is offered, involving others in their plans, and simplifying their workload and their long-term goals. They run a real danger otherwise of becoming exhausted, disappointed and alienated. After the age of thirty-four there is a turning point when they may wish to become more independent and to express their individuality.

These years are filled with potential for people born on this day, but whatever age they are the key to their success is their ability to set themselves realistic goals and their willingness to slow down the pace of their lives so they can get in touch with their intuition or the silence within. Connecting with their feelings will help them see that the sense of wonder, discovery and possibility they long to—and are destined to—create in the world around them already exists within them; all they need to do is find it.

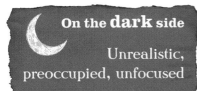
Love *No time for us*

The sense of possibility possessed by people born on December 18 inspires respect and admiration in others but it can also cause feelings of frustration because they can appear to be taking on too much. Although they are sensual, charismatic and like to take the lead in relationships, they will often bury themselves in work, only emerging when they want support or attention. Others may wish that they could simplify their lives so that they have more time not just for friends and loved ones, but for themselves.

Health *Learn to pace yourself*

People born on this day tend to fill their lives with constant activity. Although this means they are extremely productive, it can also mean that they rarely take time out to relax. It is therefore important for them to know what their limits are and not to bite off more than they can chew because otherwise they are prone to stress and even burnout. As far as diet is concerned, they also need to slow down and should resist the tendency to eat food as quickly as possible. They should also cut down on sugar, caffeine and other stimulants used to keep their energy levels high, and replace these with fruit, nuts and seeds. Mild exercise is highly recommended, as are meditation and breathing activities to help them find the space and stillness within. Wearing, meditating on and surrounding themselves with the color green will encourage natural healing and balance.

Career *Born directors*

People born on this day will thrive in careers that allow them to think and act independently in the pursuit of their visions; they may therefore be drawn to science, technology, art, or sport. Other possible work options include business, writing, sales, publishing, teaching, charity work, fundraising, politics, social reform, and the worlds of film-making, entertainment and the media.

Destiny *To inspire others to follow their dreams*

The life path of people born on this day is to get in touch with their own feelings and those of others. Once they have made contact with the power of their intuition and set themselves attainable goals, their destiny is, by example, to inspire others to follow their dreams.

Signs & symbols

Sun sign: Sagittarius

Ruling planet: Jupiter, the philosopher

Symbol: The Archer

Birth date ruler: Mars, the warrior

Tarot card: The Moon (imagination)

Favorable numbers: 3, 9

Lucky day: Thursday, especially when it falls on 3 and 9 of the month

Lucky colors: Purple, red, orange

Birthstone: Turquoise

December 18

707

19 December

the birthday of revealing honesty

People born on December 19 come across as sensitive individuals, but this conceals their remarkable hidden strength and courage. They are not afraid to express themselves freely, and when people cross or upset them they are honest enough to reveal their true feelings. Others may mistake their sensitivity and outspokenness as weaknesses, but releasing their emotions in this way actually makes them feel stronger.

They are uncompromisingly individualistic in their approach and are unlikely to thrive in environments where they need to conform. They have a strong need to challenge convention, question norms and generate original alternatives. Although their revealing honesty can work against them, others tend to respect them for their integrity and individuality. Their greatest desires are to educate or enlighten others and to further human progress.

When faced with challenges or setbacks they will reveal their fighting spirit and steady determination to succeed. This gives them endless potential for professional success, but unfortunately they sometimes seem unable to show a similar resilience in their personal life. In fact they are prone to bouts of negativity and self-pity that can manifest in flashes of anger or outrageous behavior, perplexing and confusing themselves and others. If they can learn to get a grip on their negativity by turning inward the same spirit of daring and courage that they display in the outside world, there are no mountains too high for them to climb.

Until the age of thirty-two they are likely to focus on practical issues and there will be a need for order and focus in their lives. A turning point occurs around the age of thirty-three where there is a growing desire for more personal freedom and experimentation. If they can learn to think before they act and to positively redirect their thoughts when they start to spiral into negativity, these are the years when they can really come into their own, finally revealing to the world just how committed they are to making a valuable contribution to the greater good.

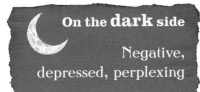

On the **dark** side

Negative, depressed, perplexing

At your **best**

Courageous, honest, expressive

Love *Expressive and open*

People born on December 19 love to flirt, and others are instantly drawn to their expressive and open personality. They attract lovers easily but need to be careful about their choice of partner because they are prone to bouts of anxiety and negativity. They need a partner who is both sensitive and supportive to help them work through these bad patches.

Health *Calm and in control*

The biggest threat to the health and well-being of people born on this day is their tendency to indulge in negative feelings. Depression is a real possibility if they do not learn to accept and manage their emotional intensity. They should remind themselves that they are in charge of their feelings and not the other way round. If they are unable to attain this level of objectivity, cognitive behavioral therapy techniques will certainly help them reprogram their thoughts. They should steer clear of drugs of all kinds, and also limit their consumption of alcohol because when under the influence their lack of control can have potentially dangerous, even violent, consequences for both themselves and others. The best way for them to keep their thoughts and mood positive is to eat a healthy, balanced diet, get between six and eight hours of quality sleep every night, and take plenty of vigorous exercise. Staying in touch with friends and loved ones, keeping a diary and developing interests and hobbies outside work are also recommended. Wearing, meditating on and surrounding themselves with the color blue will encourage them to be calmer and more in control of their emotions and lives.

Career *Born performers*

These people will often choose to share their knowledge with others through writing and teaching, but they may also be drawn to music, acting, the media world, publishing, advertising, the healing professions, and art.

Destiny *To enlighten and enchant others*

The life path of people born on this day is to learn to accept and manage their emotions, even the negative ones. Once they are able to loosen up and enjoy their life a little more, their destiny is to enlighten, influence, educate, and enchant others with their emotional honesty.

Signs & symbols

Sun sign: Sagittarius

Ruling planet: Jupiter, the philosopher

Symbol: The Archer

Birth date ruler: Sun, the individual

Tarot card: The Sun (enthusiasm)

Favorable numbers: 1, 4

Lucky days: Thursday and Sunday, especially when these days fall on 1 and 4 of the month

Lucky colors: Purple, orange, gold

Birthstone: Turquoise

December 19

20 December

the birthday of the producer

People born on December 20 are energetic and gifted problem solvers and decision makers with a marked talent for motivating and organizing others. Born leaders, they are motivated by a desire to help society progress and are at their happiest and best when generating ideas and initiating projects. Once a project has got off the ground, however, they prefer to move on to the next project and put others at the helm, content in their self-appointed role of producer and creator.

There simply aren't enough hours in the day for people born on December 20. Their impulse to keep moving forward is strong, and because they are also efficient their output and achievements are often remarkable. Their instinct is always to understand the bigger picture, and when they are heading toward their goals criticism will not deter them. Hardworking and committed, they can, however, make the mistake of assuming that others are as tireless and determined as they are, becoming frustrated and impatient with those who simply can't keep up or match their output. Despite their vital concern for the welfare of others and their intense desire to make the world a better place, their interpersonal skills often need attention.

Until they reach the age of thirty-one they are likely to be more practical and realistic in their approach to achieving their goals, and their results-orientated approach will draw as much praise as it does criticism from those who feel that they are too superficial or paying insufficient attention to details. After the age of thirty-two there is a turning point when they will start to feel the need to be more independent and put their individual stamp on things. These are the years when both professional and personal success is most likely.

Whatever age they are, however, developing their latent imaginative and creative powers and rediscovering their joyful childlike spirit will give them the ability not only to generate innovative ideas—and to motivate and inspire others to develop them—but to lift people's spirits and really enjoy life.

On the dark side

Superficial, hasty, stubborn

At your best

Productive, energetic, fast

Power Thought

❝I am grateful for the precious breath of life❞

Love *Short fuse*

People born on December 20 are energetic and vital, and potential partners will be drawn to their directness and can-do attitude. Their short fuse and tendency to be impatient when things aren't going their way can, however, threaten long-term relationships. Restless and sensitive, they may try many different relationships before finally settling on a partner who can bring out the youthful and fun-loving aspects of their personality.

Health *Boosting immunity*

People born on this day may suffer from endless coughs and colds, especially during the summer months, so building up their immune systems and strengthening their delicate constitution has to be a priority. Eating a healthy, nutritious diet rich in fruits and vegetables and getting plenty of moderate non-competitive exercise, preferably on a daily basis, are the foundation stones, but they should also make sure that they don't run themselves down with too many activities and too much pressure. They would benefit from regular check-ups with their doctor. Burning essential oil of frankincense in an oil burner while working or relaxing is particularly beneficial for respiratory infections and mild depression caused by lack of natural sunlight. Wearing, meditating on and surrounding themselves with the color green will help them seek balance in their lives, and carrying a malachite crystal around with them will bring calmness and a sense of ease.

Career *Born agents*

People born on this day are well suited to careers where they can play the role of agent, leader, or guide, and they may excel in fields as diverse as politics, teaching, the arts, or science. Other possible work choices include business, public relations, promotions, sales, writing, music, the entertainment business, alternative healing, and the world of sport.

Destiny *To play a tutelary or guiding role*

The life path of people born on this day is to learn from their mistakes and to slow down every now and again to assess their progress. Once they are able to take on board the advice of others, their destiny is to play a tutelary or guiding role in life.

Signs & symbols

Sun sign: Sagittarius

Ruling planet: Jupiter, the philosopher

Symbol: The Archer

Birth date ruler: Moon or intuition

Tarot card: Judgment (responsibility)

Favorable numbers: 2, 5

Lucky days: Thursday and Monday, especially when these days fall on 2 and 5 of the month

Lucky colors: Purple, silver, white

Birthstone: Turquoise

21 December

the birthday of the secret

Although they are energetic and strong willed, it's very hard to know what people born on December 21 are really thinking and feeling as they are by nature secretive. They prefer to express themselves with actions rather than words, and their powerful, silent presence can be inscrutable even to those closest to them.

Even though they might be a mystery to others, this does not mean they are reserved or passive. Quite the opposite; they are determined to achieve their goals and get their point across. It is just that instead of an exchange of opinions they usually prefer to push ahead regardless of what others are saying or thinking. If this means there will be battles along the way, so be it. In fact, their presence can be intimidating not just because others never know what to expect from them but because when they do lash out their few carefully chosen words can be harsh and cutting. Others may therefore feel that they can never relax around them because they are like a dormant volcano, quiet on the outside but with a burning intensity on the inside.

Despite sometimes appearing menacing or brooding, they are surprisingly insecure, although they would never allow others to know this. It's this insecurity, however, which forces them to be defensive, to nurture hidden resentments against those that cross them and, above all, to crave the admiration and respect of others. They should understand that they already have the admiration of others, but what they really need is their affection; this can only be earned when they learn to trust and share their feelings.

Around the age of thirty-two there will be a turning point when there are opportunities for them to focus less on proving themselves and more on finding their place within society. If they can take advantage of these opportunities and learn to open their minds to alternative viewpoints and their hearts to the magical potential within them and others, they will not only discover the secret of their happiness but the secret of everyone else's too.

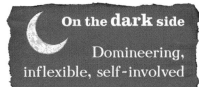
Power Thought

66 Whatever the question, I know that love is the answer 99

Love *A feisty partner*

People born on December 21 are attractive but also slightly unsettling for potential partners. This is because they like to do their own thing but won't allow others to do theirs. If things aren't perfect for them they will withdraw or move on without explanation or discussion. A feisty partner who isn't intimidated by them would help them find happiness.

Health *Open up and share*

People born on this day can suffer from tension and mental overload, so solitude is vital for them to quiet and calm their mind. They need to be careful, though, not to go overboard in their need for space and quiet, because too much time spent alone is not good for them. They may find that the best way to deal with tension is to spend more time with friends and loved ones. Counseling or therapy is advised if they find it very hard to open up and share. As far as diet is concerned, they need to watch their intake of sweet and fatty foods because weight gain, particularly around the middle, can be a problem. Caffeine and alcohol should also be limited and, if they smoke, they are advised to quit immediately to reduce the risk of heart disease. Vigorous exercise, preferably of the social kind such as dancing, aerobics or team sports, is recommended. Wearing, meditating on and surrounding themselves with the color orange will encourage them to be more spontaneous and expressive, as will carrying a turquoise crystal.

Career *Born entrepreneurs*

These people may often be found dominating in a variety of careers in the fields of science, business, sports, arts, and the world of entertainment. They typically rise to management level, but may also work for themselves and become high-flying entrepreneurs.

Destiny *To become the pioneers and leaders in their chosen field*

The life path of people born on this day is to recognize the power of positive thinking. Once they have understood that they are in charge of who or what they attract into their lives, their destiny is to combine their authority and decisiveness with compassion and flexibility, becoming outstanding leaders in their chosen field.

Signs & symbols

Sun signs: Sagittarius/ Capricorn

Ruling planets: Jupiter, the philosopher/Saturn, the teacher

Symbols: The Archer/The Goat

Birth date ruler: Jupiter, the philosopher

Tarot card: The World (fulfillment)

Favorable numbers: 3, 6

Lucky day: Thursday, especially when it falls on 3 and 6 of the month

Lucky colors: Purple, blue, white

Birthstone: Turquoise

December 21

22 December

the birthday of enduring poise

Your greatest challenge is …

broadening your outlook

The way forward is …

to understand that there is a difference between being focused and being one-track in your approach to achieving success. The former is called determination, the latter is called stupidity.

You're drawn to people born on …

June 21 to July 22

You share an appreciation of family and tradition, and can give each other the unconditional love you crave.

Luck maker

Have more fun

The more relaxed you are and the more fun you have with your life, the more likely you are to feel good about yourself and attract good luck your way.

People born on December 22 may have formulated a long-term plan for their lives as early as childhood. At various stages in their lives they will review their goals, setting themselves new ones to achieve in the next five or ten years ahead. These people know what they want out of life and how they are going to go about achieving it; this augurs well for both professional and personal success.

Understanding the importance of preparation, they are willing to bide their time and work steadily toward their goals in a self-assured and dignified way. Their remarkable poise is the result of an absolute belief that winning in the end is their absolute birthright; because they are so comfortable in their self-belief they can be a great role model for others. The danger, however, is that they can sometimes become a little too complacent, remaining for years in a position that doesn't challenge them. When a difficult challenge finally does emerge, they may fail to live up to their own and everybody's high expectations. The secret of their success is to keep learning, fine-tuning their skills and testing themselves; that way they can live up to the hype that they have created.

Until the age of twenty-nine they are likely to be goal-orientated and to have a practical approach to their achievements. But at the age of thirty they reach a turning point that highlights a growing need for freedom, new ideas and expressing their creativity. After the age of sixty there is another turning point when there is likely to be more emphasis on their emotional receptivity, imagination and intuitive awareness.

Whatever their age or stage in life, they need to find a balance between self-belief and humility, between long-term planning and spontaneity, and between seriousness and having more fun. As soon as they do strike this balance they will maintain it with their characteristic poise, finding themselves at last in exactly the right position to develop the unusual potential for happiness, success and fulfillment associated with this birthday.

Love *Accomplished*

People born on December 22 tend to be attracted to people as accomplished and as intelligent as themselves, but they may actually feel happier with those who are more rough and ready in their approach to life. It may take a while for them to let down their guard and show their partner that they are human, but when they do they can be passionate and loyal lovers.

Health *Flexibility and variety*

The sooner people born on this day learn to play as hard as they work the better. This is because unwinding, having fun and spending more time with loved ones will give them the sense of balance and perspective they need to be more productive at work and find the sense of fulfillment they long for. They also have a tendency to repress feelings that are difficult for them to understand, and the more they can open up and trust the better. Friends and family may help them do this but they may find counseling or therapy beneficial. As far as diet is concerned, they should aim for as much variety as possible, and when it comes to exercise they would benefit most from activities that encourage them to reach, jump, bend, and stretch, encouraging them to be equally flexible in their approach to life. Wearing, meditating on and surrounding themselves with the color orange will encourage them to be more open and fun-loving.

Career *Born architects*

People born on this day will flourish in careers that offer them clear signs of progression. Possible work options include finance, stockbroking, accountancy, administration, politics, management, research, science, and community work. Alternatively they may wish to explore their latent creativity in acting, design, architecture, or music.

Destiny *To put their innovative plans into action*

The life path of people born on this day is to find a balance between their professional and personal needs. Once they understand that life is a series of challenges and that there will never be a time when they stop learning about themselves and about life, their destiny is to put their plans or innovative concepts into action so that they benefit society.

Power Thought

" Problems are unique opportunities for me to learn and to grow "

Signs & symbols

Sun signs: Sagittarius/ Capricorn

Ruling planets: Jupiter, the philosopher/Saturn, the teacher

Symbols: The Archer/The Goat

Birth date ruler: Uranus, the visionary

Tarot card: The Fool (freedom)

Favorable numbers: 4, 7

Lucky days: Thursday and Sunday, especially when these days fall on 4 and 7 of the month

Lucky colors: Indigo, electric blue, light yellow

Birthstone: Turquoise

December 22

23 December

the birthday of the cautious revolutionary

People born on December 23 are hardworking, quietly ambitious individuals who are at their happiest and their best when they can identify areas of improvement and then formulate original, sometimes radical but always practical solutions. Gifted organizers, they prefer to plan and work toward and then carefully prepare for improvement.

Those born on this day distrust sudden change and feel uncomfortable when it is thrust upon them as it upsets their steady and determined plans for progressive change and progress. In fact, when they assume positions of power—which more often than not they do, given their authoritative presence and excellent communication skills—they can be resistant to change. They can also become controlling and authoritarian when challenged, and when alternative viewpoints to their own are given they can become hostile and defensive. It is therefore extremely important for their psychological growth and their professional success that they learn to be more flexible and open-minded in their approach to people and situations.

Before the age of twenty-eight, they may have shown a responsibility beyond their years, perhaps getting their foot on the property ladder long before their peers, taking on the responsibilities of a partner and family, or firmly establishing themselves in their career. After the age of twenty-nine, however, there is a gradual shift of emphasis which highlights a growing need to be more carefree and independent and to express their individuality. Another turning point occurs when they are sixty: they are likely to become more sensitive and responsive to their creative urges.

Whatever their age or stage in life, they need to resist the urge to withdraw into stubbornness, inflexibility and complacency. This is because when they start to be more spontaneous and to share their compassion, generosity, creativity and curiosity with others, they will discover that they have the ability to lead and inspire others to follow them along the optimum path to progress, in whatever direction, or directions, it takes everyone.

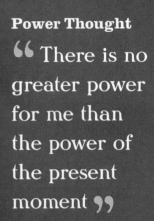

On the **dark** side
Complacent, authoritarian, inflexible

At your **best**
Responsible, innovative, steady

Love *Dynamic but cold*

People born on December 23 are dynamic, charming and rarely short of admirers, but they can be quite cold and withdrawn when it comes to affairs of the heart. It's crucially importance that they get in touch with their own feelings and those of others because their strong emotions need to express themselves positively in a loving, supportive relationship.

Health *Cautious*

People born on this day tend to have a conservative, cautious but stable approach to their health. Although this can sometimes block their progress in life, their chances of living to a ripe and healthy old age are high. On the down side, however, are their tendencies to worry and overwork, which can lower their immunity and make them prone to stress and mood swings. Rheumatism could be a problem with advancing age and they need to make sure they keep as active and flexible as possible in their daily lives. A regular program of moderate activity is highly recommended, as are daily stretching exercises. They also need to keep as mentally flexible as possible; whatever their age, learning a new skill or language is highly recommended, as is further education. As far as diet is concerned, these people need to cut down on salt and sugar, and increase their intake of whole grains, fruits, vegetables, oily fish, nuts, and seeds to keep their skin and hair glowing and their libido healthy. Wearing, meditating on and surrounding themselves with the color red will encourage them to be more passionate and impulsive.

Career *Born judges*

These people are well suited to careers in politics, law enforcement or commerce, although those who wish to use their creativity may be attracted to science, art or spirituality. Possible work options include management, administration, promotion, photography, art, writing, music, and drama.

Destiny *To advance the greater good*

The life path of people born on this day is to learn to be more tolerant, accepting and flexible. Once they are able to go more with the flow of life, their destiny is to direct others along lines that can advance the greater good.

Power Thought

" There is no greater power for me than the power of the present moment "

Signs & symbols

Sun signs: Capricorn/ Sagittarius

Ruling planets: Saturn, the teacher/Jupiter, the philosopher

Symbols: The Goat

Birth date ruler: Mercury, the communicator

Tarot card: The Hierophant (guidance)

Favorable numbers: 5, 8

Lucky day: Thursday, especially when it falls on 5 or 8 of the month

Lucky colors: Purple, dark green, gray

Birthstone: Garnet

December 23

24 December

the birthday of complicated far sight

Your greatest challenge is ...

learning from your mistakes

The way forward is ...

to understand that if an approach doesn't work the first time around, unless changes are made it won't work the second time either.

You're drawn to people born on ...

April 20 to May 20

You are both sensual and dramatic individuals; if you remain loyal, this can be a fulfilling and intense union.

Luck maker

Show people how help helps

When you ask people for advice or input, keep them updated on your progress; it's amazing how something as simple as an update can keep them motivated to continue sending opportunities your way.

People born on December 24 seem destined to live complicated, uncertain but exciting and fast-moving lives. Life is never straightforward or stress-free for them, but they have a knack of rising above challenges and achieving great success.

There are many reasons why life can appear unnecessarily stressful for people born on this day. They can find it hard to react with tact and diplomacy to people and situations, and they aren't very good at learning from their mistakes. They also have a gift for seeing into the future, or for knowing which methods will or won't work. In this respect they could be described as visionary, but unfortunately for them it takes a while for others—and themselves—to recognize and appreciate their gift of far-sightedness. Until that recognition is forthcoming others will wonder why they insist on making life so difficult, and they themselves will wonder why life always feels so complicated.

Until the age of twenty-seven they tend to place practical considerations and a desire for order and security first, but after the age of twenty-eight things start to change and they will often feel a growing need for independence and a desire to express their individuality. After the age of fifty-eight there is more emphasis on emotional receptivity, and these are the years when their intuitive potential may develop into psychic ability. Whatever their age or stage in life, the key to their success will be their ability to learn from their mistakes and be more sensitive and tactful with others, especially those who recognize their potential and want to help them. If a dose of self-confidence is thrown into the mix, not only will they will start to understand themselves and the people around them better, but life will start to feel and become much easier and more rewarding for them. When all this comes together, they will finally be able to see their potential clearly and to attract considerable success and happiness into their lives.

At your best

Innovative, visionary, exciting

Love *Magnetic*

People born on December 24 can be extremely attractive to others in a sexual way, and potential partners will find them honest, romantic and exciting. As they are so sensitive, demonstrations of love and affection are especially important to them, and can help them feel calmer and less confused about themselves and their action-packed lives. Although they may have many partners, their need for security will help them settle down and commit when they find the right person.

Health *Building self-confidence*

The lives of people born on this day can be very complicated emotionally and as a result they are likely to suffer from stress, anxiety and occasionally depression. Learning to accept and manage their emotions is crucial because, once they understand that they are in control of the way they feel and that their emotions do not control them, their lives will improve immeasurably. They need to be careful that they don't attract people or experiences into their lives that are damaging for them, and should stay away from recreational drugs of all kinds. Building their self-confidence and sense of self-worth is central here. As far as diet is concerned, they should aim for variety, and when it comes to exercise, vigorous exercise at least four or five times a week will help them deal with pent-up emotions. Wearing, meditating on and surrounding themselves with the color blue will help give them the objectivity they need to make better decisions.

Career *Born innovators*

They may choose to work as technical, commercial, political, or educational innovators, or they may become pioneers in the arts. Possible work options include writing, teaching, acting, politics, or the world of entertainment. They may also be attracted to the study of philosophy, metaphysics or mysticism.

Destiny *To point the way toward progress*

The life path of people born on this day is to learn from the past, not repeat it. Once they have started to build their self-esteem, their destiny is to better themselves and, by so doing, to better society and point the way toward progress.

Signs & symbols

Sun sign: Capricorn

Ruling planet: Saturn, the teacher

Symbol: The Goat

Birth date ruler: Venus, the lover

Tarot card: The Lovers (choices)

Favorable numbers: 6, 9

Lucky days: Saturday and Friday, especially when these days fall on 6 and 9 of the month

Lucky colors: Indigo, pink, lavender

Birthstone: Garnet

25 December

the birthday of the peak experience

People born on December 25 can struggle with the more mundane aspects of life, and the main theme in their lives is their search for a state of heightened awareness where they can transcend the everyday. Others may dismiss them as unrealistic dreamers but may secretly admire the sense of awe and wonder they bring to everything they say and do.

In both their professional and their personal lives, they bring energy, strength of purpose and a gift for organization. Above all, they bring a willingness to push things just that little bit further than others would dare in search of the peak experience they long to experience. One of the reasons people born on this day may feel the need to make their experience of life extraordinary is because they generally receive less attention on their birthday than anyone else in the year. They may therefore feel they are missing out on life in some way. These feelings persist throughout their lives, giving them the drive and the determination to stand out and achieve their ambitious aspirations.

Before the age of twenty-six they are likely to have a goal-orientated, straightforward approach to their achievements, but after the age of twenty-seven and for the next thirty years they are likely to feel a growing need to experiment with different concepts and express their individuality. Another turning point comes at the age of fifty-seven when they are likely to place more emphasis on their already enhanced sensitivity and feelings.

Whatever their age or stage in life, however, they will always place spiritual aspirations above material ones; this doesn't just set them apart, it puts them way ahead of the rest. As long as these goals are not used as a means of escaping from the complications of life, and as long as they can find ways to increase their chances of success by injecting realism into their idealistic visions, these people are capable not only of great happiness and fulfillment, but of making lasting contributions to the greater good.

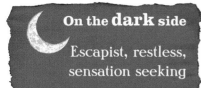

On the **dark** side

Escapist, restless, sensation seeking

At your **best**

Visionary, courageous, spiritual

Love *Higher love*

People born on December 25 have a strong need for love and affection and this may cause them to search for an idealized romance. They are happiest with someone who shares their spiritual aspirations. Although their gentle, uplifting charm can attract admirers, they should not flit from one relationship to another; once in a relationship they need to make sure they don't put their lover on a pedestal and become overly dependent.

Health *Keep your feet on the ground*

When it comes to their health, people born on this day can be extremely sensitive to allergies of all kinds and they need to steer clear completely of recreational drugs because there is an addictive side to their personality. As far as diet is concerned, cutting down on caffeine, sugar, salt, saturated fat, and food additives, drinking plenty of water, and increasing their intake of food that is as fresh and as natural as possible are highly recommended. Regular rather than sporadic exercise will not only help boost their self-esteem but help them feel more connected to their bodies, as they have a tendency to detach at times and live in their dreams. Wearing, meditating on and surrounding themselves with the color green will help keep them grounded, and carrying a tiger's eye crystal will help promote feelings of confidence and courage.

Career *Born philanthropists*

These people have the ability to combine their practical skills with intellectual insight and they may be drawn to science, business, politics, or the arts, where they will demonstrate humanitarian or philanthropic inclinations. Possible career choices might include social reform, charity work, the healing professions, teaching, writing, music, astronomy, chemistry, and biology. Their love of metaphysics may also inspire them to study or teach philosophy, astrology, religion, and spirituality.

Destiny *To inspire others with their idealism*

The life path of people born on this day is to retain their sense of awe and wonder but keep their feet firmly on the ground. Once they are able to discover the intensity and joy of living in the here and now, their destiny is to inspire others with their progressive and idealistic outlook.

Signs & symbols

Sun sign: Capricorn

Ruling planet: Saturn, the teacher

Symbol: The Goat

Birth date ruler: Neptune, the speculator

Tarot card: The Chariot (resilience)

Favorable numbers: 1, 7

Lucky days: Saturday and Monday, especially when these days fall on 1 and 7 of the month

Lucky colors: Indigo, sea green, pale blue

Birthstone: Garnet

26 December

the birthday of the vantage point

People born on December 26 are never afraid to push themselves and their ideas forward, and with their non-stop energy and determination it is not surprising that they often achieve what they strive for in life. Once they reach the top, however, they often refuse to move anywhere else and their energy is no longer devoted to moving forward but to sustaining their vantage point.

They are therefore a curious mixture of ambition, single-minded perseverance and a desire for security and stability. The danger with this combination, even though it does attract considerable professional success their way, is that they run the risk of becoming too mechanical or unfeeling, not just toward themselves but toward others. It is vital for their psychological growth that they get in touch with their feelings and those of others, as they can come across at times as intense, serious and "hard" individuals.

Until the age of twenty-five they will often feel a need for order and structure in their lives, and practical considerations are important. During these years—and indeed at any stage in their lives—the key to their success will be to practice the art of compromise, remembering that the feelings of other people should always be taken into consideration. After the age of twenty-six there is a significant turning point, giving them opportunities to express their individuality. After the age of fifty-six there is likely to be an increased emphasis on emotional receptivity, imagination, or psychic and spiritual awareness, and these are the years when they are likely to feel at their most content and fulfilled.

Whatever stage or age they are at, they must avoid the tendency to cling to what they know, or to become complacent or overly security conscious. Once they understand that often the greatest forward progress requires taking risks, giving up some ground, and exploring unfamiliar territory, they have the potential not only to make things happen on a grand scale, but also to inspire others.

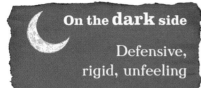

On the **dark** side

Defensive,
rigid, unfeeling

At your **best**

Energetic, methodical,
inspirational

Love *Dynamic*

People born on December 26 are dynamic, attractive individuals, and once they set their sights on someone they tend to get them. They have a tendency to be controlling in close relationships and should learn to give others the freedom and autonomy they expect for themselves. Loyalty is extremely important for them, and any kind of indiscretion on the part of their partner is particularly hard for them to deal with.

Health *A big shrug*

People born on this day can suffer from tension in their bodies, triggering aches, pains, headaches, and fatigue. They should perform exercises—particularly shrugging around the shoulder area—to release some of this pent-up energy, otherwise their health will suffer. As far as diet is concerned, they may suffer from digestive problems and should therefore increase the amount of fiber, fruits and vegetables in their diet and cut down the amount of sugar, salt, caffeine, saturated fat, and processed or refined food they eat. Moderate exercise is essential, especially activities such as dance, swimming or aerobics which encourage them to be more flexible; yoga is also highly recommended. Wearing, meditating on and surrounding themselves with the color orange will encourage them to be more spontaneous and warm in their approach to life.

Career *Born publishers*

These people may find themselves drawn to technology, politics, social services, or the media. Possible work choices might include big business, publishing, advertising, promotion, writing, acting, and the film world. Whatever career they choose, they need to one that offers them plenty of diversity and challenge.

Destiny *To make radical changes*

The life path of people born on this day is to get in touch with their emotions and the feelings of others. With an open mind and an open heart, their destiny is to promote ideals that can make wide-ranging and concrete improvements in the lives of both themselves and others.

Power Thought

" My loving heart knows no bounds and my flexible mind knows no boundaries "

Signs & symbols

Sun sign: Capricorn

Ruling planet: Saturn, the teacher

Symbol: The Goat

Birth date ruler: Saturn, the teacher

Tarot card: Strength (passion)

Favorable numbers: 2, 8

Lucky day: Saturday, especially when this day falls on 2 and 8 of the month

Lucky colors: Indigo, gray, burgundy

Birthstone: Garnet

December 26

723

27 December

the birthday of the golden heart

Your greatest challenge is …

saying "no"

The way forward is …

to understand that saying "no" when you are not in a position to give is saying "yes" to yourself.

You're drawn to people born on …

October 23 to November 22

You have so much to learn from and love about each other, making this a passionate and powerful combination.

Luck maker

Receive without guilt

To receive makes you vulnerable but to create luck you must be fluid, spontaneous, vulnerable and, above all, willing to gratefully accept help when it is offered to you.

People born on December 27 may give the impression of being sturdy and strong on the outside, but on the inside they have a heart of pure gold. Although they can be stubborn at times, they are life's givers, not takers. They also have a heroic side to them and will be the first to rush to offer their support or help when someone is in trouble.

These people set incredibly noble standards for themselves and are giving to the point of self-sacrifice. They pride themselves on being kind, thoughtful and compassionate human beings who will always do the right thing or offer their support if it is needed. However, because their goodwill makes it hard for them to refuse any request, they may become overburdened with problems that aren't their own. Their generosity and good-natured charm may win them many admirers, but underneath they can often be plagued by self-doubts and silent frustration. Part of the reason for their insecurity is that they can feel torn between their strong feelings of personal responsibility and the need for time and space to pursue their own interests.

Until the age of twenty-four they will often have a very goal-orientated, practical approach to life; but after the age of twenty-five there is a shift in emphasis, and opportunities will be presented to them to develop their individuality. It is important that they take advantage of these because only when they are able to reconcile their desire to help others with their desire to find personal fulfillment can they unlock their remarkable potential.

At first those who live and work with these people may find it unsettling to see them becoming more independent, but it is absolutely crucial that they don't allow this to unsettle them. They only have to make the effort to strike out on their own and pay attention to what they want to achieve in life to perform miracles, rise to the top of their career, and achieve long-lasting success while maintaining the respect and affection of those around them.

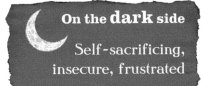

On the dark side

Self-sacrificing, insecure, frustrated

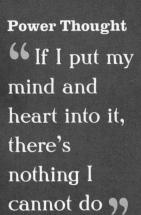

At your best

Generous, charming, noble

Power Thought

❝ If I put my mind and heart into it, there's nothing I cannot do ❞

Signs & symbols

Sun sign: Capricorn

Ruling planet: Saturn, the teacher

Symbol: The Goat

Birth date ruler: Mars, the warrior

Tarot card: The Hermit (inner strength)

Favorable numbers: 3, 9

Lucky days: Saturday and Tuesday, especially when these days fall on 3 and 9 of the month

Lucky colors: Dark green, red, indigo

Birthstone: Garnet

Love *Give and receive in equal measure*

When it comes to affairs of the heart, people born on December 27 may be drawn to wild, unconventional and sometimes selfish characters, but they are happiest with a partner who can offer them security, affection and support. They need to be careful that they don't become too dependent in their romantic affairs, and to take as much as they give.

Health *Learn to accept praise graciously*

People born on this day may be prone to anxiety, worry and depression. This is in part due to their giving nature and the fact that others may take advantage of them; it is also due to the fact that they can suffer from low self-esteem. They need to learn to accept praise and to place their own happiness at the top of their list of priorities. When it comes to diet, they need to eat a diet low in salt and sugar, and ensure they eat plenty of whole grains, fruits and vegetables. As far as exercise is concerned, the more they do the better; as well as keeping their weight down and keeping their bones and joints flexible, exercise will boost their self-esteem. Wearing, meditating on and surrounding themselves with the color red will boost their confidence, and carrying a tiger's eye crystal or placing it next to their bed at night will promote their self-esteem, giving them the courage to put themselves first.

Career *Born counselors*

These people are multi-talented, so whatever career they choose they are likely to make extremely valuable contributions. They may be drawn toward teaching, nursing, medicine, the caring professions, public relations, human resources, counseling, charity work, emergency services, the leisure and beauty industries, sport, and social reform. Alternatively their desire to express themselves creativity may lead them to writing or the performing arts.

Destiny *To be a role model for others*

The life path of people born on this day is to learn to balance their own needs with those of others. Once they are able to take as well as give, their destiny is to show others, by example, that there is always a place in this world for compassion, kindness and understanding.

28 December

the birthday of
the shining example

Your greatest challenge is ...

coping with disappointment

The way forward is ...

to remember that everyone, however successful, makes mistakes and you are no exception. Start to view setbacks not as failures but as stepping stones on the road to success.

You're drawn to people born on ...

July 23 to August 22

You are both self-assured and sophisticated individuals, and this can be a passionate and fulfilling relationship.

Luck maker

Focus on the positive

You tend to get what you focus on, so focus on the positive and leave negativity behind. You can put a positive spin on everything, even rejection, by acknowledging that it will help you learn and grow.

People born on December 28 tend to impress others greatly with their energy and clear sense of direction. They are a shining example of calmness, self-assurance and dependability to whom people often turn for support or advice during a crisis; and that support is typically given without hesitation.

The image that they tend to present to the world is one of capability and sophistication, but their competent exterior can often mask their intense search for a deeper and more fulfilling meaning to their lives. Their charismatic presence can have both a positive and a negative effect for them: positive, in that they gain enormous satisfaction from helping or motivating others; negative, in that their concern for the well-being of others may often cause them to neglect their own needs. Their careers, or having a family, will often give them a way of uniting these external and internal orientations with outstanding results, so they don't constantly feel torn between the two.

As self-assured individuals, they have the ability to inspire confidence and even awe in those around them by means of their incredible perception, compassion and real desire to help others progress. They would be almost perfect if it were not for the fact that they find it incredibly hard to deal with rejection and, instead of fighting back, will often slump into depression, bouts of uncertainty or confusion. They can also give the impression that they have all the answers, which is of course not the case. This over-confidence can alienate even those who previously championed them.

After the age of twenty-four there are opportunities for them to become less concerned about the image they are presenting to the world and more concerned about expressing their individuality. They should take advantage of these opportunities because, once they have recognized that personal fulfillment and being of service to others are not incompatible but highly compatible human needs, they can unlock their potential to be shining and inspirational examples to others.

On the dark side

Over-confident, fragile, serious

At your best

Inspiring, sophisticated, confident

Love *Cool head but a warm heart*

The cool-headed but warm-hearted people born on December 28 are too serious to be flirts, but all the same they will often find themselves surrounded by admirers. They tend to be attracted to sophisticated and intelligent individuals like themselves, but might actually fare better with someone who can introduce some excitement and adventure into their lives.

Health *Don't get stuck in the mud*

People born on this day are often passionate about music, and listening to music can be a great morale booster when life knocks them back. Owning a pet, in particular a dog, may also be helpful for them as it will encourage them to express their playful, spontaneous side. As far as their diet is concerned, they should aim for as much variety as possible and not stick to the same meal plans and menus time and time again. Variety is also the key when it comes to exercise; if they have been doing the same kind of exercise routine for years they are strongly advised to cross-train and find another way to challenge themselves physically. Not only will this boost efforts at weight loss if they have weight to lose, but it will also encourage them to take on new and different challenges in other areas of their lives. Wearing, meditating on and surrounding themselves with the color orange will encourage them to be more spontaneous, and a few drops of jasmine oil on a handkerchief to breathe in will lift their spirits when life seems to be working against them.

Career *Born models*

These people are often attracted to fields where they can help, guide, enlighten, or delight others, and they may choose careers in the arts, the media, fashion, communications, or spiritual studies. Possible work options include teaching, writing, acting, singing, journalism, charity work, social reform, and the healing and caring professions.

Destiny *To inform, guide and enlighten others*

The life path of people born on this day is to learn from their mistakes instead of repeating them. Once they have found a balance between their own needs and those of others, their destiny is to guide, enlighten and delight others.

Signs & symbols

Sun sign: Capricorn

Ruling planet: Saturn, the teacher

Symbol: The Goat

Birth date ruler: Sun, the individual

Tarot card: The Magician (will-power)

Favorable numbers: 1, 4

Lucky days: Saturday and Sunday, especially when these days fall on 1 and 4 of the month

Lucky colors: Dark green, orange, yellow

Birthstone: Garnet

December 28

29 December

the birthday of
the laid-back commander

People born on December 29 are often in great demand because they are extremely confident, responsible and adaptable, and also because they relish opportunities to assist or enlighten others. They are not overly ambitious, but because they have a great sense of timing they will often find themselves in positions of responsibility.

Although people born on this day can be quite laid back, they are willing to work hard for what they want. They are also willing to work hard to help others get what they want, and while this may endear them to others they need to be careful not to take on too much. Their greatest strength is their facility for commanding or controlling people and situations without appearing domineering. Part of the reason they can do this so successfully is that they have excellent communication skills.

They can come across as serious or deadpan at times, but the more time people spend with them, the more they begin to appreciate their wonderful sense of irony and dry humor. Given the chance they can hypnotize audiences with their intelligent choice of words and wickedly perceptive observations, realizing that humor can get their message across strongly and effectively without others feeling offended or criticized.

After the age of twenty-three they become less influenced by rules and traditions and more willing to develop their own unique perspective. Another turning point arrives at the age of fifty-three when there is an emphasis on their emotional life, reflected in dreams and an intuitive understanding of others. Whatever age they are, the key to their success is to stop living in the past and stop doubting themselves, because they are bursting with creativity and have all the talent they need to make pioneering innovations that can advance knowledge or prosperity in some way. In short, they have the potential; all they need to do is to step into their own shoes, shake off any pessimism and negativity, and become the great leader or pioneer they are destined to be.

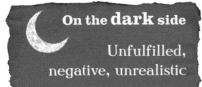

On the dark side

Unfulfilled, negative, unrealistic

At your best

Supportive, entertaining, commanding

Love *Strong need for companionship*

People born on December 29 have a strong need for companionship, and their ideal partner will be someone who is successful and creative, like themselves. Once committed to a relationship, they understand the importance of keeping a work–life balance, but they need to make sure they keep the spirit of passion and romance alive by staying as spontaneous as they can.

Health *Bring more color into your life*

People born on this day may go through phases in their life when they are more sedentary than they should be. It is important for them to treat exercise not as something they do occasionally but as something that is as much a part of their daily routine as brushing their teeth or combing their hair. They are advised to stay away from recreational drugs of all kinds, and to make sure they have regular check-ups with their doctor because they may be prone to rheumatism, bone disease and circulatory disorders. When it comes to diet, they should remember first and foremost that food is something to be enjoyed, and making sure there is always plenty of color—in the form of fruit and vegetables—on their plate will boost their nutrient intake and their mood. Wearing, meditating on and surrounding themselves with the color yellow will encourage them to believe in themselves more, as will carrying a tiger's eye crystal around with them.

Career *Born interpreters*

These people are especially suited to realms where they can offer guidance and support to others, such as teaching or politics, or to fields where they can advance knowledge in some way, such as science or engineering. Other possible career choices might include lecturing, research, communication technology, interpreting, translation, music, acting, and poetry.

Destiny *To advance human knowledge*

The life path of people born on this day is to learn to trust themselves more. Once they have started to think more positively about their potential for success, their destiny is lead others toward advancement in human knowledge.

Signs & symbols

Sun sign: Capricorn

Ruling planet: Saturn the teacher

Symbol: The Goat

Birth date ruler: Moon, the intuitive

Tarot card: The High Priestess (intuition)

Favorable numbers: 2, 5

Lucky days: Saturday and Monday, especially when these days fall on 2 and 5 of the month

Lucky colors: Indigo, silver, white

Birthstone: Garnet

3O December

the birthday of the choreographer

Your greatest challenge is ...

expressing yourself

The way forward is ...

to understand that explaining yourself or your methods to others builds bridges of understanding.

You're drawn to people born on ...

November 22 to December 21

You both have personality traits that can balance each other's, giving this relationship great potential for long-term happiness.

Luck maker

Change your talk about luck

If you think that luck always slips through your fingers, that's exactly what will happen. Tell yourself instead that luck does come your way and, with this attitude of positive expectancy, the chances are it will.

People born on December 30 are at their happiest and their best when they are bringing order to confused situations. They are not only gifted in being able to identify what doesn't work or is in need of improvement; they also have the creativity and vision to make effective changes.

In many ways these people are like choreographers who can direct and coordinate the details with the bigger picture in mind. At times it may seem unclear what their intentions are, but in the end everything always seems to come together. Their ability to motivate and inspire those around them to perform at their best makes them successful leaders. They can occasionally be prone to a glass-half-empty approach to life but this doesn't mean they don't know how to have fun. Quite the opposite; they can appreciate humor and the lighter side of life, and love relaxing and having fun with friends. It is just that they are practical realists and will always consider worst-case scenarios in their game plan.

Their decisive tendency to take immediate charge of others to coordinate collective efforts can have excellent results, and they are often on the cutting edge when it comes to their professional life. One personality trait that can block their progress, however, is that they can at times come across to others as disinterested because they are a person of few words. When they do speak, however, others will often be stunned by their perceptiveness; but working on their communication skills will benefit them considerably in both their personal and their professional lives.

Before the age of twenty-one they are likely to have been cautious in their approach to life, but after the age of twenty-two there are opportunities for them to be more adventurous, more independent and less influenced by the opinions of others. They should take advantage of these opportunities to express their individuality because, once they come to realize how creative and capable they can be, their self-confidence will flower and they will attract all the success and happiness they deserve.

At your best

Perceptive, capable, authoritative

Love *Don't get complacent*

Although people born on December 30 can attract attention, they don't tend to be demonstrative when it comes to affairs of the heart. They need to be careful that complacency or fear of putting themselves on the line does not mean that they miss out on opportunities for love. They may find themselves attracted to gregarious and dramatic individuals who can encourage them to be more outgoing.

Health *Quartz crystal*

Unless people born on this day see instant results, they may find it hard to stick with a regular exercise and healthy eating program. But if they just stick with these for at least three to four months they will notice significant improvements. Regular check-ups with their doctor should also be scheduled, as they have a tendency to ignore the warning signs of poor health. They are prone to bouts of negativity and depression, and they are sensitive to stress, but again healthy eating and a regular program of exercise, as well as plenty of sleep, will help them conquer these. Cognitive behavioral therapy techniques can help them to reprogram their thoughts in a more positive direction. Wearing, meditating on and surrounding themselves with the color orange will encourage them to be more positive, and placing a cluster of quartz crystals in their living room, workplace or anywhere they spend a lot of time will help them feel happier and will re-energize their zest and vitality in all situations.

Career *Born commanding officers*

These people work well in business or commercial ventures, but they may also be drawn to politics, teaching, coaching, training, the military, diplomacy, and other positions which require them to coordinate large numbers of people. Other work options include management, art, music, or writing.

Destiny *To bring harmony, cohesion and cooperation*

The life path of people born on this day is to reprogram their thoughts so that both negative and possible outcomes are taken into account. When they have learned to be more flexible and more forgiving, their destiny is to bring harmony, cohesion and cooperation.

Power Thought

"I am rich in inner wisdom and can express my inspirations clearly and eloquently"

Signs & symbols

Sun sign: Capricorn

Ruling planet: Saturn, the teacher

Symbol: The Goat

Birth date ruler: Jupiter, the philosopher

Tarot card: The Empress (creativity)

Favorable numbers: 3, 6

Lucky days: Saturday and Thursday, especially when these days fall on 3 and 6 of the month

Lucky colors: Dark green, purple, royal blue

Birthstone: Garnet

December 30

31 December

the birthday of
the connoisseur

Your greatest challenge is ...

accepting that you are not always right

The way forward is ...

to understand that what is right for you may not necessarily be right for someone else. We are all unique individuals and diversity makes life wonderful.

You're drawn to people born on ...

September 23 to October 22

You both have excellent taste and refined manners, and this can be a loving and beautiful union.

Luck maker

Say, I didn't know that!

Demonstrating a willingness to learn will draw others to you because people like to help those who try to help themselves.

People born on 31 December pride themselves on their immaculate taste, and their confidence and charisma draw admirers to them wherever they go. They are esthetes and idealists at heart, aiming for perfection; but being realists they have the common sense to accept that there is a lot of ugliness in the world.

These people are on a mission to make the world a more beautiful place and they will try to add a touch of refinement or style to the environments they live and work in. They may also pay great attention to their own appearance, cultivating an attractive presence that is always well groomed and presented. They set high standards for themselves and others, but what makes them such gifted and fair leaders is that they will never expect more from others than they themselves can deliver.

The one big problem for them is that they are sometimes guilty of imposing their own standards of what is or is not beautiful or correct in a situation, the opinions or visions of others being dismissed out of hand. If this tendency isn't checked it can make them somewhat narrow-minded and intolerant of the opinions, taste and individuality of others. They need to remind themselves over and over again that beauty lies in the eye of the beholder.

Before the age of twenty they may come across as artistic but disciplined and sensible young adults, but after the age of twenty-one there is a dramatic turning point when they become less influenced by tradition and more independent. New opportunities to present their unique perspective will emerge and they will start to play a key role in making the world a more beautiful place. After the age of fifty-one there is another turning point which puts the emphasis on sensitivity and a strong inner life. But whatever age they are, getting in touch with their intuition will show them that beauty isn't just something that can be created in the outside world—first and foremost it must be created within.

At your **best**

Tasteful, well groomed, charismatic

Love *Free spirit*

People born on December 31 easily attract admirers with their flair and natural dramatic sense. They can give the impression of being a free spirit but those who know them well will soon realize that they have a deep need for security and affection in a close relationship. They may suffer from low moods from time to time, but can also be a loyal, passionate and supportive partner.

Health *Moonstone*

Worry, pessimism and overwork tend to be the downfall of people born on this day, so it is important for them to look within for self-confidence and fulfillment. Until they can do so they will not be able to find these qualities in the outside world. Social occasions may be a bit of a strain for them as they don't like the false façades people put on, but spending more time with close friends and loved ones is highly recommended. As far as their diet is concerned, they could be prone to food allergies and may need to check with their doctor or nutritionist so that the culprit can be eliminated from their diet. Appearance matters greatly for them, so they are likely to eat well and get plenty of exercise. These are the foundations of true beauty for them, and cosmetic surgery is not advised. Holding a moonstone and meditating on it will help strengthen their intuition, their capacity to understand what they want out of life and their ability to recognize the beauty that lies within.

Career *Born team builders*

These people are suited to careers where they can create harmony, and may be drawn to business management, events organization, education, lecturing, and interior design, or they may choose to develop their creativity and work in the theater, opera or art studio.

Destiny *To bring harmony and beauty to the world*

The life path of people born on this day is to remember that everyone has their own idea of taste and beauty. Once they are willing to compromise, their destiny is to construct organized methods for advancement and to make the world a more harmonious and beautiful place.

Signs & symbols

Sun sign: Capricorn

Ruling planet: Saturn, the teacher

Symbol: The Goat

Birth date ruler: Uranus, the visionary

Tarot card: The Emperor (authority)

Favorable numbers: 4, 7

Lucky days: Saturday and Sunday, especially when these days fall on 4 and 7 of the month

Lucky colors: Dark green, silver, light yellow

Birthstone: Garnet

December 31